CRYSTALLINE BASEMENT OF THE ANTARCTIC PLATFORM

M. G. Ravich and E. N. Kamenev

CRYSTALLINE BASEMENT OF THE ANTARCTIC PLATFORM

Translated from Russian by N. Kaner
Translation edited by R. Bogoch

A HALSTED PRESS BOOK

JOHN WILEY & SONS
New York · Toronto

ISRAEL PROGRAM FOR SCIENTIFIC TRANSLATIONS
Jerusalem · London

© 1975 Keter Publishing House Jerusalem Ltd.

Sole distributors for the Western Hemisphere
HALSTED PRESS, a division of
JOHN WILEY & SONS, INC., NEW YORK

Library of Congress Cataloging in Publication Data

Ravich, Mikhail Grigor'evich.
   Crystalline basement of the Antarctic platform.

   Translation of *Kristallicheskiĭ fundament Antarkti-*
cheskoĭ platformy.
   "A Halsted Press book."
   Bibliography: p.
     1. Rocks, Crystalline. 2. Gondwana (Geology).
3. Petrology – Antarctic regions. I. Kamenev, Evgeniĭ
Nikolaevich, joint author. II. Title.
QE475.A2R3813   552'.4   74-13646
ISBN 0-470-70990-1

Distributors for the U.K., Europe, Africa and the Middle East
JOHN WILEY & SONS, LTD., CHICHESTER

Distributors for Japan, Southeast Asia, and India
TOPPAN COMPANY, LTD., TOKYO AND SINGAPORE

Distributed in the rest of the world by
KETER PUBLISHING HOUSE JERUSALEM LTD.
ISBN 0 7065 1401 7
IPST cat. no. 22101

This book is a translation from Russian of
KRISTALLICHESKII FUNDAMENT ANTARKTICHESKOI
PLATFORMY
Gidrometeoizdat
Leningrad, 1972

Printed and bound by Keterpress Enterprises, Jerusalem
Printed in Israel

CONTENTS

PREFACE

This monograph summarizes twelve years' study by Soviet geologists of the Antarctic crystalline basement which is intermittently exposed over more than 8,000 km along the eastern Antarctic coast. Block tectonics have resulted in the uplift and exposure of the oldest sediments of the Gondwanian Antarctic Platform. These are represented by granulitic and amphibolitic facies rocks, formed under ultrametamorphic conditions and intruded by a large number of gabbro-anorthosite and charnockite bodies.

Beginning in the Upper Archean, the crystalline basement underwent repeated tectonic-magmatic events resulting in polymetamorphic complexes in which ortho-schists and apointrusive rocks of metasomatic origin are present.

The metamorphic strata were examined in terms of paragenesis, and certain geological-tectonic data suggest a two-stage structural history. A possible geochronological history of the basement was also constructed.

Polymetamorphic and intrusive rocks from superimposed metamorphic and ultrametamorphic stages related to basement reactivation processes are noted for the first time. A map of the Precambrian in the eastern Antarctic at a scale 1 : 10,000,000 is presented together with various maps of other parts of the continent.

This monograph is the first geological and petrographic summary of the Antarctic crystalline basement. A comparison is made with the basements of other Gondwanian platforms in the southern hemisphere.

INTRODUCTION

The Antarctic Platform covers an area of some 10,000,000 km², the principal exposures of which consist of rocks from the Precambrian basement. Practical studies of these rocks began in 1956 during preparations for the International Geophysical Year, and have continued to the present day. During this period, Soviet geologists have investigated more than half of the exposed* crystalline basement, centered in the coastal regions of East Antarctica (250,000 to 300,000 km²). An area of 80,000 km² was examined in Enderby Land and in the central part of Queen Maud Land (1:100,000); some 2,500 km² were surveyed in the Humboldt Mountains, Petermann Range, Bunger Oasis, the area of the Mirny Observatory, etc. (medium to large scale); other territories in the Sør Rondane Mountains, Prince Charles Mountains, Mac-Robertson Land and Queen Mary Land were covered by reconnaissance mapping at a scale 1:2,500,000. Some exposures of the crystalline basement were studied by geologists from the South African Republic in the area west of Queen Maud Land /58/, by Belgians in the Sør Rondane Mountains /80/, by Japanese in the Yamato Mountains /110/, by Australians on Mac-Robertson Land /132/, and by the French on Adelie Land /84/.

The main emphasis of these studies was on the processes of formation of the crystalline basement. An attempt was made to divide the rocks into metamorphic facies and subfacies based on paragenetic and chemical studies of their minerals and to define stable and unstable assemblages. Thus, certain consistencies were found with regard to the metamorphism and ultrametamorphism and to the structure of the crystalline basement and its deep-seated features, thereby outlining the problems for further study.

Special attention is given in this report to charnockite formations, which are unusually widespread in the Antarctic basement. The diverse modes of origin, covering the entire range of ultrametamorphic processes, from metasomatic recrystallization of solid (and partially plastic) material to the formation and crystallization of anatectic and complete melts are described. A comprehensive description is given of metamorphic rocks, many of which were noted for the first time in Antarctica. The authors have endeavored to avoid a repetition of the routine data reported in earlier papers /57, 58/. New findings, mostly unpublished, are presented in detail, primarily those related to the geology of Enderby Land, Humboldt Mountains, and the Petermann Range (on Queen Maud Land), and areas in the upper reaches of the Lambert Glacier.

---

* These exposures include mountain ranges, rock oases, rock islands, isolated nunataks (together with the intervening glaciers, where rock outcrops amount to 10—30% of the area glaciated).

Acknowledgements: D. S. Solov'ev played an important role in the field work and wrote the section on the quartzite-jaspilite formation which he discovered. In processing the field data, the authors were ably assisted by Z. P. Golubeva, A. G. Markovich, and L. A. Chaika (the latter wrote the section on the physical properties of charnockites). The more than 250 chemical analyses of minerals were carried out in the chemical and spectroscopic laboratory of the Research Institute of Arctic Geology, headed by R. S. Rubinovich. The authors would like to express their heartfelt thanks to all these and to others who made this study possible.

Chapters I, II, and IV of this monograph were written by E. N. Kamenev, and Chapters III, V, VI, and VII by M. G. Ravich, who was also responsible for the scientific supervision of the Antarctic studies and for editing the entire monograph.

ABBREVIATIONS OF THE NAMES OF MINERALS USED IN THIS MONOGRAPH

alb	— albite	Kfs	— potash-feldspar
act	— actinolite		
alm	— almandine	magn	— magnetite
amph	— amphibole	musc	— muscovite
andr	— andradite	oliv	— olivine
apat	— apatite	orem	— ore minerals
biot	— biotite	orth	— orthite
		orpy	— orthopyroxene
calc	— calcite	orcl	— orthoclase
carb	— carbonate		
clpy	— clinopyroxene	phl	— phlogopite
coru	— corundum	plag	— plagioclase
cord	— cordierite	pyr	— pyrope
cumm	— cummingtonite	qz	— quartz
diop	— diopside	rut	— rutile
dol	— dolomite		
		spph	— sapphirine
ep	— epidote	scap	— scapolite
		sill	— sillimanite
fay	— fayalite	spes	— spessartite
fors	— forsterite	spin	— spinel
gar	— garnet		
grph	— graphite	woll	— wollastonite
gros	— grossular	zirc	— zircon
hem	— hematite		
horn	— hornblende		
hum	— humite		
hyp	— hypersthene		

PUBLISHER'S NOTE

Certain terms, symbols and conventions used in this translation require some explanation.

1) The term "shadow granite" appearing throughout the text is a rendering of the Russian "tenevoi granit" denoting a mixed rock with more than 65% granite. According to the same classification, a migmatite is a rock containing 35–65% granite, and an injection gneiss is a rock with less than 35% granite.

2) For want of a better term, the word "ferruginosity" is used to convey the meaning of the Russian "zhelezistost'" (literally ironiness). This is expressed by the symbol $f = \dfrac{Fe}{Fe + Mg} \times 100$ at. %.

3) Azimuths of dips and strikes have been converted from the Russian to the American system, i.e., they are measured clockwise, from south.

4) The tables listing the chemical compositions of rocks also feature norms, coordinates of the ACF diagrams and Zavaritskii's numerical characteristics. As the latter are not familiar to the Western reader, their derivation and conversion to Niggli values are explained in the Appendix.

5) Refractive indices of biaxial minerals are given as $n_x\,(= n_\alpha)$, $n_y\,(= n_\beta)$, and $n_z\,(= n_\gamma)$.

Chapter I

BRIEF GEOLOGICAL DESCRIPTION OF
THE CRYSTALLINE BASEMENT

The crystalline basement of the Antarctic Platform emerges from under the ice along a comparatively narrow coastal zone of East Antarctica. It is over 8,000 km long, extending from 12°W long. to 145°E long. (Greenwich). In places it reaches up to 260 km in width, but is usually not over 100 km across. Seven types of exposures are known: rock oases on islands and coasts, isolated rock outcrops in the coastal scarp, groups of nunataks and cliffs, isolated nunataks and cliffs, bedrock outcrops at margins of glacial valleys, block mountain massifs, and mountain ranges. Most bedrock outcrops of the crystalline basement are concentrated in the sector between the Lambert and Penck (Jutulstraumen) meridional glaciers (1°W long. − 70°E long.).

Stable and mobile types of the crystalline basement regions were defined /59/. Enderby Land is a typically stable and Queen Maud a typically mobile region.

Enderby Land (45−56°E long., 66−69°S lat.) is built of sedimentary and volcanic strata together with igneous intrusions, mostly metamorphosed in the granulite facies. The following three series occur on Enderby Land (Appendix 2): 1) the Raggatt Series, mainly represented by intermediate to basic volcanics metamorphosed to pyroxene-plagioclase schists, enderbites, and charnockites. The series contains occasional lenses and intercalations of diopsidic rocks formed from calciphyres, as well as garnet-bearing granites and quartzites;

2) the Condon Series, including terrigenous sedimentary rocks metamorphosed to various high-alumina schists, gneisses, and quartzites. These are strongly migmatized and granitized. These rocks are intimately interlayered with one another and with lesser pyroxene-plagioclase schists, enderbites, and charnockites;

3) the Nye Series, originally mainly igneous and similar to the Raggatt Series, It differs from the latter by the presence of thick sheets and lenses of marbles, calciphyres, diopsidic rocks, and high-alumina schists among migmatized pyroxene-plagioclase schists (which are the most prominent rocks in this series), enderbites and charnockites. These sheets and lenses may have formed during the metamorphism of the initial carbonate and terrigenous sedimentary rocks. If it is assumed that rocks of the same series identified in separated areas correspond to the same portion of its stratigraphic section, then the relationships in large-scale fold structures suggest that the Condon Series occupies a higher stratigraphic position than the Raggat Series, but is below the Nye Series.

1

Two regional structural-facies zones (Napier and Rayner) can be differentiated on Enderby Land, based on the nature and sequence of metamorphism. The Napier zone includes the Enderby Land peninsula and Scott Mountains. Its northern boundary is a deep fault along the margin of hypersthene granosyenite massifs, while its eastern, western, and southern boundaries are marked by fault systems (represented by the valleys of the Rayner, Thyer, Wilma, and Beaver outlet glaciers and by the subglacial sea channel /27/ which separates the Enderby Land peninsula from the mainland). The metamorphic rocks of this zone are distinguished by the highest temperature and most deep-seated parageneses of the granulite facies and are the oldest in the crystalline basement. The magmatic and metamorphic events following the granulitic metamorphism in the Napier zone are only expressed locally. The Rayner zone surrounds the Napier zone and can be traced in a strip up to 50 km wide along the Enderby Land coast from Molodezhnaya Station to Øygarden Islands. It comprises the Nye Mountains, the Sandercock, McLeod, and Doggers nunataks, Knuckey Peaks and Dismal Mountains.

The Rayner zone is characterized by a comparatively low-temperature subfacies of the granulite facies, occasionally developing into the amphibolite facies. Rocks of this zone were ultimately transformed into the hornblende-granulite facies of Turner /71/. Repeated metamorphism was accompanied by higher unilateral pressure. In the upper reaches of the Wilma and Robert glaciers and on Øygarden Islands the metamorphism occurred under conditions of stress and resulted in a superposition of high-pressure paragenesis on the high-temperature granulitic paragenesis. As a result "eclogite" schists /42/ and "Saxon" granulites /137/ were formed. Amphibolite metamorphism in these areas is poorly developed (largely retrogressive). Magmatic and metamorphic events in the Rayner zone which followed the repeated metamorphism are expressed only locally.

Ultrametamorphic phenomena (granitization and migmatization) are characteristic of both metamorphic zones. Granitization is more common in the Napier zone, and migmatization in the Rayner zone. The principal ultrametamorphic products in the Napier zone are enderbites (first stage) and perthitic charnockites (second stage), and their garnetiferous analogs, with or without hypersthene. In the Rayner zone, enderbites and especially perthitic charnockites are regarded as relict formations, while the principal ultrametamorphic products are charnockites proper and their analogs (partly formed as products of repeated metamorphism and partly at the expense of perthitic charnockites). Selective melting phenomena are more characteristic of the Rayner zone in which the repeated metamorphism occurred in previously granitized rocks. Therefore, bodies of porphyroblastic hypersthene granosyenites which occur along the boundary between the Napier and Rayner zones are classified together with the ultrametamorphic products.

Various igneous rocks were undoubtedly the basic material for the metamorphic series of Enderby Land. However, most of their characteristic features were lost due to the metamorphism. Thus, only dolerite dikes which clearly cut the metamorphites are regarded as magmatic. Especially prominent among these are dikes metamorphosed under epidote-amphibolite facies conditions, and obviously younger dikes which are arbitrarily classified with the Mesozoic trap formation. However, the distribution of both types has not yet been studied in detail. Some 60 dolerite dikes were found on Enderby Land and are apparently irregularly distributed. Most of these are located in the Scott, Tula, and Napier mountains. None were encountered west of the Rayner Glacier.

Rocks of the metamorphic series form a complex system of folds with E-W and NE-SW axial planes. The Raggatt and Condon Series form a giant anticlinorium /27, 28/, the outlines of which correspond to those of the Napier metamorphic zone. The anticlinorium contains widespread diapiric folds and domes separated by narrow compressed linear fold zones. Shadow granitoids emerge in the cores of the diapiric folds and domes. The dips near the arches of the folds are very small, becoming steeper in the limbs. The linear fold zones are composed of less granitized rocks, usually mottled, high-alumina quartzites of the Condon Series. The latter feature synclinal folds, which are more or less distinctly preserved even where completely granitized. The linear folds are essentially vertical.

In the south, and possibly also in the north, the anticlinorium is apparently adjoined to a synclinorium the boundaries of which coincide with those of the Rayner metamorphic zone. The Nye and Condon Series are linearly folded with alternating large anticlinal and synclinal brachy-folds of relatively simple structure with northward dipping axial planes. The fold arches are usually gently undulating. These large structures are in places complicated by small, partly isoclinal folds and sporadic domes which may be analogous to Wegmann's granitic diapirs /139/. They are composed of porphyroblastic hypersthene granosyenites. In areas of superimposed amphibolite facies metamorphism, the brachyfolds are obscured by smaller isoclinal shear folds, e.g., in the area of Molodezh-naya Station. Still smaller folds and plications are common in the mig-matite complexes of the Rayner zone. They also occur to a lesser extent in migmatites of the Condon Series in the Napier zone and are very rare in homogeneous shadow granitoids of the Napier zone. Together with the folds, different degrees of lenticular and boudinage structures, which are characteristic of highly metamorphosed rocks of varying plasticity, also occur. The boudinaged layers or bodies consist of granitized pyroxene-plagioclase schists, quartzites, calciphyres, and less commonly, enderbites.

These structural features of metamorphism place the Napier zone of Enderby Land in a similar category with certain of the older regions of the Earth /46/, including many Canadian and Ukrainian areas /49/. It should be noted that the same features are found in crystalline basements of other Gondwanian platforms, in particular those of south and east Africa. The Rayner zone compares well with the protogeosynclinal forma-tions typical of the Aldan complex of the Siberian Platform, the White Sea complex of the Baltic Shield, etc. /46, 49/. The various features of the Rayner zone on Enderby Land are also characteristic of other regions with granulite facies rocks east of Enderby Land and up to Oates Coast. They include the coast of Mac-Robertson Land /132/, most of Prince

Charles Mountains /131/, Bunger Oasis /57/, and possibly Adélie Land. The extensive occurrence of these formations merely emphasizes their protogeosynclinal nature. These differ from typical geosynclinal troughs in their greater width and more gentle downwarp /46/.

Faults resulting in a separation of the metamorphic rocks on Enderby Land vary in their nature, orientation, and age. Among the oldest are the deep-seated faults with E-W strikes which occur at boundaries of polymetamorphic zones along which are intruded porphyroblastic hypersthene grano-syenites and biotite granites. Younger faults trending nearly N-S occur along local zones of retrograde metamorphism (epidote-amphibolite facies). Still younger faults are accompanied by mylonite zones. The youngest faults, which resulted in the block structures, are located along large outlet glaciers. The tectonic nature of the glacier valleys is expressed by their morphology. These faults are related to Meso-Cenozoic block movements /57/. They include faults which formed the scarp relief of Enderby Land and its coast. Blocks of crystalline rocks on Enderby Land are very large. One single block consists of the Raggatt and Scott mountains and another, which contains the Lamykin and Enderby Land peninsulas, exceeds 35,000 km².

Studies of the geological structure of Enderby Land /28/ have suggested the following sequence of metamorphic and magmatic events: 1) metamorphism to high-grade granulite facies; 2) intrusion of gabbroic rocks; 3) repeated metamorphism of medium-grade granulite facies (and regressive amphibolite facies); 4) formation of porphyroblastic granitoid massifs, including intrusives; 5) intrusion of gabbroic dikes; 6) local retrograde metamorphism in the epidote-amphibolite facies. The last expression of metamorphism was probably the formation of pegmatites from aplitic veins; these cut all rocks in the region, including the retrograde epidote-amphibolite facies. The formation of mylonitic zones and their transverse dolerites and dolerite porphyry dikes occurred after the consolidation of the shield.

The Enderby Land crystalline rocks have not yet been reliably dated. The tectonic similarity between Enderby Land and proto-platform regions as well as the high-grade metamorphism suggests an Early Archean age for the Napier zone, and a Late Archean age for the Rayner zone (by analogy with the dating of protogeosynclines on other continents). The available isotopic dates of seven specimens from Enderby Land and three specimens from Øygarden Islands off the eastern coast of Enderby Land do not confirm these assumptions. The oldest date was obtained by the lead method (2120 million years). Potassium-argon dates range from 460 to 620 million years. However, the method was only applied to pegmatite minerals and spatially associated rocks. The dating of pegmatites appears to be reliable since it was confirmed by the lead method. The formation of pegmatites requires a temperature of about 500°C /24/. Loss of argon begins at 300°C, resulting in younger dates /47/. Thus, metamorphic rocks close to pegmatites would be expected to yield younger ages as well. The age of the metamorphic rocks appears to be more than 2120 million years, since that date was determined from chevkinite formed along cracks in the perthite charnockites. These would also be younger than the charnockitization. Preliminary geological data suggest that older isotopic dates for Enderby Land will be obtained in the future.

Queen Maud Land appears to belong to a different crystalline basement region. Even the morphology of its mountains differs from those in other regions. They form in narrow discontinuous ranges 40—120 km wide over a distance of more than 2,500 km parallel to the East Antarctica coast, usually at a distance of more than 100 km from the shore. The mountainous ridges, transected by N-S flowing glaciers, extend in a few places up to 700 km in central Queen Maud Land. Isolated nunataks and small mountain massifs locally emerge from under the ice. The mountains in central Queen Maud Land, the Sør Rondane and Yamato mountains have been studied more thoroughly than other regions. They all have a similar geological structure /58/. However, a more detailed study of other areas in Queen Maud Land indicates a somewhat different structure. A detailed structural description of Queen Maud Land is not presented herein, since this was included in an earlier work /58/ and is also given in the description of the Humboldt Mountains and the Petermann Range (see chapter on polymetamorphic formations and Appendix 3). However, its major regional features are described.

The mountains on Queen Maud Land are block structures. Certain blocks consist only of amphibolite facies rocks, whereas others are composed of polymetamorphic formations. It was also established that granulite facies schists were highly altered during retrograde amphibolite facies metamorphism. Other blocks consist of intrusive apomagmatic and rheomorphic bodies. A general metamorphic pattern emerges from an examination of these blocks: there are two types of structural-facies zones on Queen Maud Land, differing sharply in their geological setting, nature of metamorphism, composition of original rocks, and types of intrusions. Contacts between the two are faults. No specific rock type dominates either of these zones. For the sake of descriptive convenience, the two zones are termed the polymetamorphic zone and the amphibolite facies zone.

The polymetamorphic zone differs little from the Rayner zone on Enderby Land and other protogeosynclinal regions in Antarctica with regard to the composition of the original rocks. The lower part of the section is composed of terrigenous sedimentary rocks transformed into high-alumina schists and migmatites with intercalations of quartzites, calciphyres, and metabasites. The upper portions are composed of volcanic rocks (with lenses of carbonates) converted to bipyroxene schists, migmatites, shadow granites, marbles, and calciphyres. However, the metamorphic parageneses of the granulite facies have largely been replaced by minerals of the superimposed amphibolite facies. The repeated metamorphism was preceded and also accompanied by high lateral pressures, resulting in the replacement of shadow granites and schists by widespread Saxon-type granulites /58/. Marbles, capable of translation gliding, sometimes "intruded" along fractures, and in places developed a good cleavage, generally parallel to the bedding. The metamorphic rocks are cut by a fairly dense network of fine- and medium-grained biotite-microcline granite veins which are products of the amphibolite facies of metamorphism. Pegmatite veins also occur.

Within the polymetamorphic zones, there are a few dikes of ultrabasites which have been partially metamorphosed in the amphibolite facies. In most cases, gabbroic rocks together with diorite-syenites, syenites, and granosyenites, as well as anorthosites, make up isolated blocks of the crystalline basement. An anorthosite massif, the largest in Antarctica, is exposed in the Wohlthat Mountains over an area of about 900 km². The anorthosites underwent fairly intensive metamorphic transformations (amphibolite facies — unilateral pressure). Apparently, the anorthosite blocks are associated with polymetamorphic rocks.

Massifs of charnockites (described in a separate chapter) occur along the contacts of the polymetamorphic and amphibolite facies zones. They exhibit both intrusive and tectonic relationships with rocks of the polymeta-morphic zone but only tectonic relationships with rocks of the amphibolite zone. Charnockite intrusions are controlled by nearly E-W deep-seated faults. Folded structures in the polymetamorphic zone are similar to the linear brachy-folded complexes of the Rayner zone on Enderby Land. This type of structure is well illustrated by the Humboldt syncline, described later in this volume.

Polymetamorphic zones are widespread in central Queen Maud Land (Petermann Range, Humboldt, Payer, Shcherbakov, Conrad, and Filchner mountains and other minor mountain ranges). They also build isolated nunataks on the margins of the Sør Rondane, Yamato and Tottan Fjella mountains, and rock oases on the coast of Lützow-Holm Bay.

Two types of metamorphics are found in the amphibolite facies zone. One is represented by biotite-amphibole plagiogneisses, their migmatites and, in part, shadow granites with intercalations of marbles, calciphyres, quartzites and amphibolites. The second type consists of biotite and biotite-garnet plagiogneiss together with thick layers of sillimanite-garnet, sillimanite-biotite, and other high-alumina plagiogneisses, schists, and quartzites.

In some regions of Queen Maud Land only one of these types is encoun-tered. For example, the second type is missing in the Petermann Range, Humboldt, Sør Rondane and Yamato mountains. On the other hand, both types are present in western Queen Maud Land and on the Prince Olav Coast. Based on structural relationships, the "biotite-amphibolite" type is older than the "biotite-garnet" type. A complex of basic magmatic rocks, intensely metamorphosed in the amphibolite facies, is associated with the biotite-amphibole plagiogneiss, and is especially widespread in the central part of the Sør Rondane Mountains. Such rocks are also en-countered in amphibolite facies zones on the Prince Olav Coast, in the Yamato Mountains, Petermann Range, and western Queen Maud Land. Granitization is less important than injection migmatization in the amphi-bolite facies zone. Intrusive granitic rocks are represented in the amphibolite facies zones by small (up to tens of km²) complex massifs of clino-pyroxene syenites, hornblende granosyenites and biotite granites. Based on a study of the clinopyroxene syenites in the Sør Rondane and Yamato mountains, these rocks are considered to have resulted from the syenitiza-tion of gabbros. This process is possible under highly alkaline conditions at deep-seated levels during amphibolite facies metamorphism.

The most typical magmatic units are hornblende granosyenites and biotite granites; their intrusion resulted in distinct contact metamorphic phenomena: skarnitization and marbles, quartzitization, ferruginization, garnetization (andratite), and muscovitization of the biotite-amphibole and biotite-sillimanite gneisses; formation of fluorite-celestite and magnetite veinlets. Aplitic pegmatite veins with tourmaline, beryl and muscovite mineralization (greisenization) are fairly common in the gneiss-ic units of the amphibolite facies zone.

The tectonic structures in the amphibolite facies are consistent in most areas. Commonly observed structures are large-scale open linear folds with an apex to apex span of 10—15 km. A characteristic feature of these folds is an undulation of axial trends. The axial planes are inclined. Folded structures of higher orders are also linear and strike in the same manner as the limbs of the larger folds. Strongly migmatized areas display even smaller folds. These are isoclinal with limb spreads of 3—5 m. Within amphibolite facies zones, in contrast to polymetamorphic zones (where processes of granitization and migmatization are extensive), these folds are largely confined to migmatite areas of hundreds or, more rarely, of thousands of square kilometers. The general structure of the amphibolite facies zone in the Sør Rondane Mountains, the Humboldt Mountains and the Petermann Range is synclinorial. Granitic magmatism is poorly expressed. A correlation between granitic intrusions and folds has not yet been reliably established. Only in isolated cases are intrusions located in the near-axial part of second-order synclines. The margins of syenites and grano-syenites are often gneissified and therefore appear to have formed before completion of folding in the metamorphic strata.

Aside from the amphibolite facies metamorphism, Queen Maud Land also contains epidote-amphibolite and greenschist facies zones (retrograde) which are the largest in Antarctica. These occur along fault lines, generally within areas of amphibolite facies zones. However, they often include polymetamorphic zone rocks as well. The latter are especially well expressed in the Penck Trough /58/ and along the southern margin of the Sør Rondane Mountains.

According to these data, Queen Maud Land (including Prince Olav Coast) may be compared with Early Proterozoic geosynclinal systems, in particular with the Kola and Karelia systems of the Baltic Shield /49/, and with certain Indian and African systems /46/. In fact, Queen Maud Land contains a series of geosynclinal troughs (amphibolite facies zones) bounded by deep-seated faults along which were intruded porphyroblastic granosyenites. These troughs are separated by polymetamorphic zones. Folding and other deformations transformed the troughs into synclinoria which are only partly preserved. The lowermost rocks of the synclinoria are volcanics, terrigenous sediments, and limestones. The terrigenous sediments are represented by various banded plagiogneisses which are predominant. The polymetamorphic zones form anticlinoria. The characteristic features of Queen Maud Land are the Early Proterozoic system, its unusually large areal extent and its curvilinear nature /46/.

As in Enderby Land, isotope dates do not confirm the ancient origin of Queen Maud Land or the relative sequence of metamorphic and magmatic processes. These dates generally lie between 450 and 550 million years. It should be noted, however, that the metamorphic rocks of Queen Maud Land are overlain by a thin sedimentary-igneous platform; the oldest date (K-Ar) of these sedimentary rocks (argillites) is about 1050 million years.

The Antarctic crystalline basement also includes a third type of metamorphosed sequence. This consists of amphibolite and greenschist facies strata (e.g., the mountains surrounding the Lambert Glacier). This region has a two-stage structure. The lowermost stage is represented by rocks metamorphosed in the lower amphibolite facies with a well-marked superimposed greenschist metamorphism. The upper stage is composed of two greenschist facies series: the first, typified by the exposures at Sodruzhestvo, consist of phyllites, marble, and jaspilites; the second is composed of quartzites and chlorite-mica-quartz schists and is found at Menzies. The Menzies Series is considered to be the older. The metamorphic rocks underwent complex isoclinal folding. In general, however, the area has not been examined in detail. The mica schists of the Menzies Series were dated (K-Ar) at about 500 million years, but relict microfossils suggest a Middle Proterozoic age.

Rocks of the amphibolite facies were also discovered in the Vestfold and Grearson oases in eastern Antarctica, their grade of metamorphism being the same as that on Queen Maud Land. The fold systems in these areas may be similar to those in Queen Maud Land.

The metamorphic and ultrametamorphic formations of the crystalline basement are intruded by rocks of various ages and compositions. These formed during the three epochs of the tectonic-magmatic rejuvenation of the platform.

The gabbro-dolerite complex (absolute age 1800—2000 million years) comprises a fairly uniform group of basic rocks. These crystallized as dikes which vary in thickness from a few meters to 200 meters. They are most common in the central sector of East Antarctica, especially in the Bunger and Vestfold oases, where hundreds of dikes occur in intrusions of charnockitized gabbroics and rheomorphic charnockites as well as in migmatites. The dikes may be spatially related to NW-SE faults in the Bunger Oasis and to E-W faults in the Vestfold Oasis. The gabbro-diabases are strongly autometamorphosed and cataclastized. Their mineral and chemical compositions resemble intermediate tholeitic dolerites of Mesozoic trap formations, differing from them only by their somewhat more basic composition and a nearly complete absence of magmatic differentiation.

The nepheline-syenite complex (absolute age 330—340 million years) occurs in western Queen Maud Land (Gburek Mountains), but has not yet been identified in other regions of East Antarctica. It consists of a single intrusion of nepheline syenite over an area of about 30 km^2 together with numerous veins of alkali rocks genetically related to syenite. These include sölvsbergite, grorudite, tinguaite, syenite-pegmatite, albitite, limburgite and small bodies of melteigite. The geological setting of this group is controlled by the intrusions which are confined to a major fault zone which forms a tectonic contact between crystalline basement and the younger platform rocks.

The trap complex (absolute age 165—170 million years) is represented in the crystalline basement by dolerite dikes 0.5—30 m thick, which
cut through all other crystalline rocks (including the gabbro-diabase and
syenite groups, as well as the greenschist facies series). The trap rocks
are typical derivatives of a theoleitic basalt magma and are analogous to
Early Mesozoic traps on other Gondwanian continents (both in respect to
their petrological features and age).

Chapter II

GRANULITE FACIES

Rocks of the granulite facies in the crystalline basement of the Antarctic Platform are varied in their mineralogical and structural properties. Many of them, having undergone regional metamorphism, inherited their composition from the original sedimentary, volcanic, and intrusive rocks. Most underwent ultrametamorphism, especially granitization, in granulite and high-grade amphibolite facies. The granitization considerably altered the composition of the regionally metamorphosed rocks. Successive manifestations of granitization resulted in a wide range of composition and structure of these rocks. Considerable alteration also resulted from repeated metamorphic events (amphibolite facies) under thermodynamic conditions differing from those of the regional metamorphism (granulite facies).

Granulite facies rocks are particularly common in the crystalline basement of the Antarctic Platform. The following locations exhibit the granulite facies predominantly: Enderby Land /28/, Mac-Robertson Land, Prince Charles Mountains /132/, Ingrid Christensen Coast (Vestfold and Larsemann oases), Pravda Coast (Mirny Station area), Bunger Oases /57/, and Adélie Land /84/, as well as certain areas of Queen Maud Land /58/ (Appendix 1). The best studied and best exposed crystalline basement regions are Enderby Land, Bunger Oasis, and Queen Maud Land, and, therefore, the description of the granulite facies is based on geological data from these particular regions.

In Queen Maud Land, it is sometimes difficult to distinguish between rocks of the granulite facies proper and the predominant polymetamorphic zones. Nevertheless, for purposes of comparison, a description of the Queen Maud Land metamorphic suites, with special emphasis on the granulite facies, is presented in this chapter.

The following products of granulite facies metamorphism were identified within the various groups of regionally metamorphosed rocks. I) marbles and calciphyres; II) magnesian schists; III) calcareous-magnesian schists and their ultrametamorphic products — migmatites and shadow granitic rocks (enderbites and charnockites); IV) alumina schists and their ultra-metamorphic products — migmatites, and shadow granitoids; V) quartzites; VI) metasomatic high-alumina rocks. These are rare bimetasomatic rocks which occupy a special position at the contact between pyroxene-plagioclase schists and shadow granitoids oversaturated in alumina.

MARBLES AND CALCIPHYRES

Marbles and calciphyres are found throughout the crystalline basement of the Antarctic Platform. They generally form boudinaged, lenticular and concordant beds within schists and migmatites. The thickness of the boudinaged calciphyres ranges from 0.4 to 50 m, and rarely up to 100 m. The boudins and lenses are 1—100 m long. Boudinaged beds can be traced over distances of hundreds of meters and up to 1 km along strike.

The carbonate rock sheets and lenses are interbedded with pyroxene-plagioclase schists on Enderby Land, and with migmatites and schists in the Bunger Oasis and on Queen Maud Land, and exhibit heterogeneous compositions. They include relatively pure dolomitic marbles, and calciphyres which are generally diopsidic and forsteritic, but occasionally contain humite and spinel (Table 1). The marbles and calciphyres are intimately interbedded within the strata, where they form continuous or discontinuous layers of about 1 cm in thickness. However, thick sheets and lenses of calcitic marbles, containing only sporadic dolomite grains, were found on Queen Maud Land and in the Bunger Oasis /57, 58/. The diopsidic calciphyres occur near the margins and spinel calciphyres occur near the center of the thick layers. The spinel-forsterite calciphyres contain a few thin boudinaged intercalations of corundum-bearing spinel-forsterite rocks. The enclosing calciphyres contain very sparse disseminations of similar corundum (bluish). Diopside rocks, sometimes containing spinel, consistent-ly occur at the contacts of the calciphyre beds. They contain streaks and pockets of coarse-grained plagioclase pegmatoid. The calciphyres enclos-ing the pegmatoids are highly amphibolized. Phlogopite pockets often develop in these diopsidic rocks. The phlogopite also forms scattered veinlets in lenticular inclusions of the diopsidic rocks, but the mica in this case is not directly related to the calciphyre.

The marbles and calciphyres have a hetero-granoblastic texture. Small (0.3—1.5 mm), often oval-shaped grains of olivine and spinel, and somewhat larger, irregular-shaped diopside grains are incorporated within a relatively coarser-grained (up to 1—4 mm) aggregate of rounded to irregular-shaped carbonate grains. Phlogopite flakes are often present, forming poikiliticlike metablasts with small rounded carbonate inclusions. Late-formed diopside rims around forsterite grains are locally observed. The transition to marginal diopsidic rocks is characterized by the appear-ance in the calciphyres of larger (3.5—4 mm) diopside porphyroblasts. These increase in content with continued metamorphism, until the rock becomes nearly monomineralic diopside and the carbonate aggregates gradually disappear. Amphibole, scapolite, and phlogopite developed in diopside rocks, clearly replace diopside along grain contacts and cracks.

The carbonates which constitute the bulk of the marbles and calciphyres contain both dolomite and calcite. The former is present mainly as small rounded, generally untwinned grains. Calcite forms coarser, irregular grains that are partly xenoblastic with respect to the dolomite. They ex-hibit polysynthetic twins, oriented diagonally relative to the rhombohedral cleavage. Refractive indices of the carbonates indicate that they are essentially free of isomorphic impurities (Kennedy's diagram of 1947)

TABLE 1. Mineral compositions of marble, calciphyre, and diopsidic rocks of the granulite facies and the characteristics of their minerals

Specimen No.	Mineral composition, vol.%												An content in plagioclase	Characteristics of the minerals					
	carb	fors	spin	diop	plag	scap	amph	phl	qz	sphene	gar	orem		carb		fors			
														n_o	n_e	n_z	n_x	$2V°$	f at.%
167 a	100	—	—	—	—	—	—	—	—	—	—	—	—	1.654	1.553	—	—	—	—
566 d	100	—	—	—	—	—	—	—	—	—	—	—	—	1.658	1.556	—	—	—	—
159 a	60	32	2	6	—	—	—	—	—	—	—	—	—	1.680	1.580	1.682	1.653	+84	5
159 b	64	23	1	10	—	—	—	1	—	—	1	—	—	1.680	1.580	—	—	+88	—
271 g	74	20	1	1	—	—	—	2	—	—	2	—	—	1.680	1.580	1.674	1.643	—	2
566 g	77	3	1	10	3	2	1	1	—	2	—	—	—	1.658	1.556	—	—	+88	10
613	60	37	—	—	—	—	—	3	—	—	—	—	—	—	—	1.676	1.648	—	3
629 a	77	21	1	1	—	—	—	—	—	—	—	—	—	—	—	—	—	+85	5
692 a	52	24	1	22	—	—	—	1	—	—	—	—	—	—	—	—	—	+85	5
22 v	82	17	1	—	—	—	—	—	—	—	—	—	—	—	—	1.670	1.640	+83	0
799 r	80	—	—	—	—	—	—	—	—	2	—	—	—	—	—	—	—	—	—
820 zh	83	—	—	8	7	—	—	—	—	2	—	—	80	—	—	—	—	—	—

Sample																			
135 v	—	—	—	—	—	—	—	—	—	—	1	—	4	94	1	—	—
435	—	—	—	—	—	—	—	o.s.*	—	—	—	2	1	—	3	92	1	—	1
543 m	—	—	78	—	—	—	—	1	—	1	—	3	3	95	—	—	1
152 b	—	—	90	—	—	—	—	—	1	—	2	96	—	—	1
579 g	—	—	83	—	—	1	o.s.	3	—	—	2	93	—	—	1
820 z	—	—	92	—	—	2	—	—	—	5	25	60	—	—	8
858 zh	—	—	75	—	—	3	10	—	2	—	41	43	—	—	1
1140 v	—	—	92	—	—	1	—	12	—	—	12	75	—	—	—
1074 b	—	—	70	—	—	—	—	22	—	—	20	50	—	—	8
199 a	—	—	69	1	—	2	—	35	—	—	27	35	—	—	—
234 b	—	—	54	2	—	6	11	—	—	—	70	10	—	—	—
538 e	—	—	—	—	—	3	54	—	—	16	—	25	—	—	1
543 e	—	—	—	—	—	—	2	—	—	8	—	80	—	—	10
543 zh	—	—	—	—	·	—	—	—	—	5	—	90	—	—	5
543 k	—	—	—	—	—	—	64	—	—	30	—	5	—	—	1
800 k	—	—	—	—	—	1	—	—	1	49	—	50	—	—	—
855 d	—	—	—	—	—	1	—	1	—	40	—	53	—	—	5
853 zh	—	—	—	—	—	—	2	—	—	48	—	50	—	—	—

* [o.s. = optic sign.]

TABLE 1 (continued)

Characteristics of the minerals

Specimen No.	spin n	spin f at.%	diop n_z	diop n_x	diop cn_z	diop $2V_u$	diop f at.%	scap n_o	scap n_e	scap % meionite	phl n_z	phl f at.%	Location
167 a	—	—	—	—	—	—	—	—	—	—	—	—	Bunger Oasis
566 d	—	—	—	—	—	—	—	—	—	—	—	—	"
159 a	1.720	1—2	1.700	1.670	—	—	9	—	—	—	—	—	"
159 b	—	—	1.704	1.676	—	—	15	—	—	—	—	—	"
271 g	1.720	1—2	—	—	—	—	—	—	—	—	1.570	3	"
566 g	1.724	3	—	—	—	—	—	—	—	—	1.573	4	"
613	—	—	—	—	—	—	—	—	—	—	1.573	4	"
629 a	1.726	3—4											"
692 a	1.726	3—4											"
22 v	1.718	0											Queen Maud Land, central
799 r	1.718	0											As above; 19% humite
820zh	—	—	1.710	1.682	38	+59	25						"
135 v	—	—	1.696	1.667			3				1.582	7	Bunger Oasis
435	—	—	1.702	1.675			12				1.578	6	"
543m	—	—	1.702	1.675			12						"

Sample													Locality
152b	—	—	1.708	1.679	38	+58	21	—	—	—	—	—	Queen Maud Land, central
579g	—	—	1.708	1.679	39	+58	21	—	—	—	—	—	As above
820z	—	—	—	—	—	—	—	—	—	—	—	—	
858zh	—	—	1.715	1.688	44	+58	33	—	—	—	—	—	
1140v	—	—	1.720	1.693	39	+58	40	—	—	—	1.588	10	
1074b	—	—	1.711	1.685	40	+59	26	—	—	—	1.588	10	
199a	—	—	—	—	—	—	—	—	—	—	—	—	Bunger Oasis
234b	—	—	1.706	1.680	—	—	14	—	—	—	—	—	
538e	—	—	1.716	1.693	—	—	34	1.585	1.554	68	—	—	
543e	—	—	1.698	1.670	—	—	5	—	—	—	—	—	
543zh	—	—	1.707	1.677	—	—	20	—	—	—	—	—	
543k	—	—	—	—	—	—	—	1.583	1.554	66	—	—	Queen Maud Land, central
800k	—	—	—	—	—	—	—	1.591	1.557	79	—	—	As above
855d	—	—	1.713	1.686	39	+59	30	—	—	—	—	—	
853zh	—	—	1.711	1.683	37	+58	26	1.587	1.564	81	—	—	

Notes. 1. The iron content of the olivine, spinel, and diopside were determined from the diagram proposed by Deer et al. /6, 19/. 2. The iron content of the phlogopite was determined from Treger's /72/ diagram. 3. The meionite content in scapolite was determined from the diagram proposed by Deer et al. /19/. 4. The An content in plagioclase was determined according to Fedorov's method.

/108/. Only one specimen (566 g), in which dolomite constituted a small fraction of the carbonate mass (5%), contained a 3 to 4% admixture of ankerite (n_o = 1.684).

Forsterite occurring in rounded colorless grains may account for as much as 20 vol.% of the calciphyre; however, it generally forms less than 10% of the rock. The fayalite component in forsterite does not exceed 10% (usually 3–5%). Only in one sample (271 g, from the Bunger Oasis), was a more ferruginous olivine (pinkish color) observed in thin section. It contains 23% fayalite (n_z= 1.720, n_x = 1.689). This type of olivine developed at the expense of nearly pure forsterite which is common in this rock. It is of interest to note that this sample contains red garnet, which is extremely rare in these rocks. The garnet has the following composition: 60% almandine, 25% grossular and 15% pyrope (a= 4.06 Å; n = 1.780; the determination was made from Winchell's diagram of 1958). Garnet occurs as rare, small (1–1.5 mm) fractured crystals. It is closely associated with glomeroblastic accumulations of olivine. The forsterite is largely serpentinized, resulting in fibrous pseudomorphs of serpentine containing small relicts of incompletely replaced forsterite. Fibrous greenish biotite is occasionally developed along fractures in the forsterite.

The presence of chondrodite and clinohumite in the calciphyres of Queen Maud Land is the most important distinguishing feature relative to the calciphyres of Enderby Land and the Bunger Oasis. Chondrodite occurs as irregular grains interstitial to the carbonate and olivine. It replaces the latter along crystal boundaries and fractures. The same calciphyres contain clinohumite, which forms complex intergrowths with the olivine. Clinohumite occurs as an independent mineral in calciphyres of the Humboldt Mountains, where it almost completely replaces forsterite. In these rocks, two generations of the clinohumite were distinguished /58/. The refractive indices of the clinohumite are n_z= 1.656; n_x=1.622; $2V$ = +69° (specimen 799r).

Spinel generally occurs as sporadic, small rounded grains, making up less than 3–5% (vol.) of these rocks. It is usually colorless or slightly bluish, and is distinguished by a very low iron content (0–4 at.%). However, calciphyres in the Bunger Oasis (specimen 613) also contain another, more ferruginous spinel (green color, n= 1.736, f= 15 at.%). The spinel is replaced by phlogopite along the crystal boundaries. It is less commonly surrounded by fine fibrous aggregates of hydrotalcite.

Diopside, which occurs as fine grains, porphyroblasts, and rims around forsterite or clinohumite, is represented by a variety which is colorless in thin section, and which often exhibits distinct diallage joints. Its optical properties indicate a very low iron content (f= 9–15 at.%). Similar diopside is common at the edges of the calciphyre beds. However, the same edges contain a different clinopyroxene, which is associated with scapolite. It is characterized by a green color and weak pleochroism, ranging from dark green (n_z) to yellowish green (n_x). It forms diablastic intergrowths with the scapolite. The optical properties of this clinopyroxene (specimen 820zh) indicate the presence of large amounts of the iron component.

Amphibole occurs almost exclusively in association with diopside. It frequently clearly replaces the latter along crystal boundaries and fractures.

The amphibole has a pale green color and possesses weak pleochroism ranging from bluish greenish (n_z) to slightly yellowish greenish (n_x). Its optical properties are $2V = +88°$; $cn_z = 18°$ (specimen 642b), which indicate a low-iron pargasite.

Phlogopite forms fine flakes or sporadic larger "dropletlike" metablasts (up to $10-15$ cm) containing rounded inclusions of carbonate. It is also developed along cracks or on the crystal boundaries of olivine, spinel, and diopside. The color is generally yellowish; it is weakly pleochroic in comparison to common phlogopite (nearly colorless for n_x). The refractive indices indicate a nearly pure magnesian variety $(f = 3-4$ at.%).

The accessory minerals of the marbles and calciphyres include apatite, which forms small prismatic grains, and sphene, occurring mainly in small aggregates of cuneiform grains.

The calciphyre group also includes the so-called diopside rocks, which are directly related to calciphyre lenses. These are generally in contact with silica-rich rocks, or form lenses and intercalations in the calcareous ultrametamorphic series. The diopsidic rocks may be divided into the following three varieties (in terms of their mineral composition, apparently differing by a deficit of Al + Na + K with respect to Ca): 1) diopside rocks; 2) diopside-plagioclase rocks; 3) diopside-scapolite rocks.

The diopside variety has the simplest composition. The rock is crystalline, inequigranular, often monomineralic, massive and green to dark green in color. It also contains small amounts $(1-5\%)$ of plagioclase, scapolite, phlogopite, sphene, spinel, quartz, and ore minerals. The rocks are heterogranoblastic. Certain occurrences are entirely composed of isometric, $0.5-1$-mm grains forming mosaic aggregates. Other occurrences exhibit large individual diopside crystals reaching $1-2$ cm in length. These crystals are elongated but with irregular boundaries. In places, they contain inclusions of smaller early-generation grains. Many of the diopside grains are twinned. Aggregates of tremolite or pargasite are developed along the network of microcracks.

Fine-grained diopside is represented by the most magnesian variety $(f = 3$ at.%); coarse-grained diopside is more ferruginous $(f = 12$ at.%). An analysis of fine-grained diopside (specimen 435b) from the Bunger Oasis yielded the following results (wt.%); 54.12% SiO_2; traces of TiO_2; 1.28% Al_2O_3; 0.18% Fe_2O_3; 1.07% FeO; 0.09% MnO; 17.81% MgO; 24.20% CaO; 0.08% Na_2O; 0.05% K_2O; 0.02% P_2O_5; 0.85% loss on ignition: total = 99.75%. The crystallochemical formula of the diopside is $(Na_{0.01}Ca_{0.95}Mg_{0.97}Fe_{0.04}Al_{0.03})_2[Si_{1.93}Al_{0.02}]_2O_6$; $f = 3.7$ at.%.

Diopside is even more ferruginous $(f = 21$ at.%) when it occurs at contacts with migmatites and granitic rocks.

Plagioclase first appears as sporadic irregular segregations filling small interstices between diopside grains and occasionally within microcracks. As the plagioclase content increases $(20-30\%)$, plagioclase-diopside rocks are formed in which the feldspar usually occurs in aggregates of well-developed crystals. Areas intersected by leucocratic granitic veins may develop large plagioclase porphyroblasts together with abundant diopside and some carbonate. Fine-grained plagioclase aggregates often have quartz segregations (2—3%) and locally, sporadic grains of K-feldspar occur. Veinletlike accumulations of coarse quartz grains may also form. The development of quartz is generally accompanied by the amphiboliza-tion of diopside where the latter is replaced by light green and green hornblende along crystal boundaries and cleavage cracks. Amphibole aggregates occur in segregations together with deformed diopside. Phlogopite is fairly common, almost always forming ingrowths in the diopside and, less commonly, independent aggregates of randomly oriented flakes.

The diopside content is nearly always higher than that of plagioclase. The iron content of diopside in plagioclase-diopside rocks is considerably higher than in the relatively pure diopside rocks ($f = 14$—33 at.%). The most iron-rich diopside was found in specimens taken from ores close to contacts with granitic rocks ($f = 40$ at.%). The anorthite content in plagioclase varies from 69 to 92%. In the rare cases when plagioclase is the predominant rock constituent, it becomes more acid (up to 54% An). Such rocks are richer in sphene and also contain biotite, considerable amounts of apatite, as well as orthoclase and quartz. These phenomena are related to granitization of the plagioclase-diopside rocks.

The green scapolite-diopside rocks are massive with an heteroblastic texture. Fine diopside grains are stubby whereas coarse second-generation grains are elongated with irregular crystal boundaries and poikilitic, due to the presence of fine relict grains of first-generation diopside. Scapolite usually forms grain clusters. The scapolite may partially or completely replace the diopside. Some occurrences of scapolite-diopside rocks are enriched with fine-grained quartz aggregates. Silicification of scapolite-diopside rocks is typical of boudinaged areas or areas cut by numerous leucogranite veins. The rock structure is complicated by the secondary development of amphibole, phlogopite and garnet. The average mineral composition of the quartz-scapolite-diopside rocks is as follows: 60% diopside, 17% scapolite, 23% quartz; some specimens also contain a total of up to 1—2% calcite, spinel, sphene, plagioclase, phlogopite, amphibole and grossular-almandine garnet. Fine-grained diopside is nearly pure ($f = 5$ at.%). Coarse-grained, second-generation diopside is richer in iron ($f = 20$ at.%). Unusually iron-rich second-generation diopside occurs in rocks intersected by veins of leucogranite ($f = 34$ at.%). Coarse diopside locally exhibits polysynthetic twinning.

Scapolite is represented by meionite containing up to 32% marialite. It has a grayish shade in thin sections due to the presence of finely dis-persed carbonaceous material. Amphibole is represented by tremolite which forms aggregates of thin colorless prisms (rarely cruciform). Tremolite grains locally form intergrowths with irregular segregations of carbonate. Some tremolite prisms contain profuse relicts of diopside, resulting in a skeletal appearance.

Marbles and calciphyres remained relatively stable during granitization. Although often occurring among shadow granites, they are virtually not granitized. Nevertheless, the marbles and calciphyres were definitely

altered during ultrametamorphism. A prominent alteration is the replacement of the forsterite (or clinohumite)-spinel paragenesis by that of
diopside and phlogopite. Thin sections contain associations of all four
minerals, although the diopside and phlogopite are distinctly superimposed.
Other changes in calciphyres occur mainly at their contacts with shadow
granites or migmatitic vein material. This consists in the development
of bimetasomatic diopside, diopside-plagioclase, and diopside-scapolite
rocks. Thin layers of calciphyres are frequently completely replaced by
diopside rocks. The diopside-plagioclase and diopside-scapolite rocks were,
in turn, slightly granitized during a later stage of ultrametamorphism.
Expressions of repeated ultrametamorphism include the agmatization of
diopside rocks (less commonly calciphyres) and the appearance of a more
ferruginous second-generation diopside, phlogopite and a small amount
of orthoclase.

MAGNESIAN SCHISTS

Magnesian schists were probably formed by the metamorphism of the
oldest ultrabasic magmatic rocks (ultrabasites). These are not abundant
and were encountered only in a few exposures in the central part of
Enderby Land and in Queen Maud Land. The magnesian schists generally
form sheets and lenses which are concordant with the gneissic and banded
structures of the enclosing metamorphic rocks. The thickness of these
bodies varies from 1 to 10 m and they can be traced over tens and hundreds
of meters along strike. Extended sheets are usually boudinaged, where the
predominant boudinage type is lenticular. The size of the boudins ranges
from several centimeters to a few meters. Bodies of magnesian schists
which are discordant with respect to the surrounding rocks are much less
common. Only two such bodies were discovered in the granulite facies
regions in Antarctica, one on Mount Smethurst, Enderby Land, within shadow
mesoperthitic charnockites and the other close to the cliffs of the Arctic
Institute on Queen Maud Land.

A conformable series of subparallel schists of peridotite composition
were observed on one of the "hydrographers' islands" in the Khmara inlet
(exposure 58, Enderby Land). Their average thickness is 10 m and they
lie within shadow enderbites. At the contact with the enderbites coarse-
grained pyroxene rocks, with ortho- and clinopyroxene, occur. The enderbites near the contact are intersected by fine veins of coarse-grained
pyroxene rocks.

Thinner, conformable bodies (2–5 m thick) of magnesian schists were
observed within pyroxene-plagioclase schists (exposure 485) and shadow
enderbites (exposures 356, 453) on Enderby Land. These rocks form sheets
which are traceable over more than 50 m along strike. Sometimes the
sheets are locally boudinaged.

The composition of the magnesian schists in exposure 485 is similar
to peridotite. In exposures 356 and 453, the central portions of the sheets

are composed of peridotite, while the near-contact zones consist of a bipyroxene coarse-grained rock. The composition of the relatively thinner, (up to 1—2 m) conformable sheets, of magnesian schists occurring in shadow garnet granites (exposures 155, 60, Enderby Land), is limited to bipyroxene rocks.

The largest body of magnesian schists on Enderby Land is dike-shaped with an apparent thickness of 80 m. It lies within the shadow perthite charnockites on Mount Smethurst (exposure 798). The contact of the schists and charnockites is very irregular, although it generally appears to be cross-cutting. "Tongues" of charnockites penetrate deep within the schists. Branches of syenite veins, consisting of coarse-grained perthite, which cut the magnesian schists emerge from the shadow charnockites. These veins contain sporadic quartz and hypersthene grains together with the dominant perthite.

On the whole, the schist body has the appearance of a ramified migmatite, transitional to agmatitic. Its composition is similar to peridotite, except for the monomineralic hypersthene rocks which occur at the contact with syenite veins. The hypersthene rocks also form chains of boudinaged lenses within the syenite veins and at contacts with perthite charnockites. "Chains" of boudinaged lenses emerge from the schist body into the shadow charnockites. The near-contact portion of the meta-ultrabasites which consist of hypersthene rocks is about 5 m wide. The nature of the contact of the schists and shadow charnockites suggests an intrusion of the original ultrabasites prior to charnockitization.

Olivine-pyroxene schists are fine- to medium-grained, nearly massive rocks of dark gray or black color, with a faint schistosity. Olivine and titanomagnetite grains may be distinguished by the naked eye. The titano-magnetite is rather nonuniformly distributed within the rock, its content reaching 10% in some areas. The texture is controlled by the euhedral development of all the rock-forming minerals and may be defined as grano-blastic. The average grain size diameter is 1.0—1.5 mm, but certain ortho-pyroxene grains reach 3 mm. The distribution of olivine grains in the rock is characteristically nonuniform. This mineral often forms monomineralic equigranular segregations. Olivine may fill intergranular space between orthopyroxene grains and the contact between the two is irregular. Poikilitic inclusions of pyroxene in the olivine are fairly common, but the reverse relationship is rare. These rocks are always biotitized and amphibolized to a certain extent. Amphibole usually occurs in large (up to 2 mm) xenomorphic grains with inclusions of pyroxene. The interstices are filled with biotite flakes which are frequently intergrown with the olivine and pyroxene.

The quantitative mineral composition and data on the properties of rock-forming minerals in the magnesian schists with a peridotite composition are presented in Table 2. Olivine predominates in rocks occurring within layers of pyroxene-plagioclase schists. The rocks in contact with ender-bites contain approximately equal amounts of olivine and orthopyroxene. The latter is heavily predominant in the dikelike body occurring within the shadow perthite charnockites. The amount of clinopyroxene is always

TABLE 2. Mineral composition and characteristics of minerals in magnesian schists

Specimen No.	Mineral composition, vol.%									An content of plagioclase	Characteristics of the minerals							
											olivine				orthopyroxene			
	oliv	orpy	clpy	amph	biot	plag	gar	orem	apat		n_z	n_x	$2V°$	f at.%	n_z	n_x	$2V°$	f at.%
58—1	41	35	14	9	—	—	—	o.s.*	—	—	1.727	1.690	−88	28	1.697	1.685	−76	20
58—2	—	74	25	—	o.s.	o.s.	—	1	—	—	—	—	—	—	—	—	—	16
485b	62	18	7	7	3	"	—	3	—	—	1.712	1.676	+87	20	1.690	1.679	−83	18
453a	29	56	5	3	3	—	—	4	—	—	1.708	1.672	+88	18	1.693	1.682	−83	18
356a	32	40	8	20	—	—	—	2	—	—	—	—	—	—	—	—	—	—
155b	—	61	25	2	12	—	—	+	+	—	—	—	—	—	1.710	1.697	−70	32
60—2	—	38	55	—	—	5	3	2	—	38	—	—	—	—	—	—	—	—
60—1	—	15	70	1	1	—	5	3	—	—	—	—	—	—	—	—	—	—
798b	24	71	2	o.s.	o.s.	—	—	3	—	—	1.702	1.666	+88	14	1.687	1.677	−88	15
798d	—	96	o.s.	—	"	—	—	4	—	33	—	—	—	—	1.687	1.677	−88	15
798g	—	94	—	—	5	1	—	o.s.	—	51	—	—	—	—	—	—	−78	—
869b	—	40	30	10	—	5	—	15	—	—	—	—	—	—	1.718	1.700	—	41
54b	—	80	—	8	—	—	—	12	—	—	—	—	—	—	1.707	1.695	—	28
803	—	67	—	10	5	8	—	10	—	—	—	—	—	—	1.730	1.714	—	54
817d	—	87	—	—	2	5	5	1	—	—	—	—	—	—	1.706	1.693	—	27
60b	38.2	39.2	0.7	12.5	4.2	0.1	—	0.9	0.3	—	1.706	1.670	−87	16	1.684	1.674	−83	13
208a	—	84	—	—	2	10	—	o.s.	—	—	—	—	—	—	—	—	—	—

* [o.s. = optic sign.]

TABLE 2 (continued)

Specimen No.	clinopyroxene						amphibole					biotite	
	n_z	n_y	n_x	$2V°$	cn_z	f at.%	n_z	n_x	$2V°$	cn_z	f at.%	$n_y = n_z$	f at.%
58—1	1.711	1.692	1.686	+54	40	25	1.684	1.659	−88	15	59	—	—
58—2	—	—	—	—	—	—	—	—	—	—	—	—	—
485b	1.714	1.697	1.690	+58	43	29	1.692	1.665	−82	15	67	1.647	41
453a	1.710	1.692	1.685	+59	43	24	—	—	—	—	—	1.608	23
356a	—	—	—	—	—	—	—	—	−86	19	—	—	—
155b	1.720	1.701	1.694	+54	42	37	1.691	1.668	—	16	66	1.609	24
60—2	—	—	—	—	41	—	—	—	—	—	—	—	—
60—1	—	—	—	—	38	—	—	—	—	—	—	—	—
798b	1.714	1.696	1.690	+58	43	29	1.687	1.661	—	—	61	1.636	36
798d	1.710	1.692	1.685	+58	43	24	—	—	—	—	—	1.618	28
798g	—	—	—	—	—	—	—	—	—	—	—	—	—
869b	—	—	—	—	—	—	—	—	—	—	—	—	—
54b	—	—	—	—	—	—	—	—	—	—	—	—	—
803	—	—	—	—	—	—	—	—	—	—	—	—	—
817d	—	—	—	—	—	—	—	—	—	—	—	—	—
60b	—	—	—	—	—	—	1.678	1.658	—	—	53	1.612	25
208a	—	—	—	—	—	—	—	—	—	—	—	—	—

Characteristics of the minerals

TABLE 2 (continued)

Specimen No.	Geological setting
58—1	Enderby Land, concordant body within enderbites.
58—2	As above.
485b	Enderby Land, concordant body within pyroxene-plagioclase schists.
453a	Enderby Land, concordant body within enderbites.
356a	Enderby Land, boudinaged intercalation in shadow enderbites.
155b	Enderby Land, subconcordant body within shadow garnet granites.
60—2	As above.
60—1	As above, near border of body.
798b	Enderby Land, dikelike body in shadow mesoperthite charnockites (central part of body).
798d	As above, near border of body.
798g	Enderby Land, lens within a mesoperthite vein cross-cutting the body of magnesian schists.
869b	Queen Maud Land.
54b	" " " "
803	" " " "
817d	" " " "
60b	Queen Maud Land, Arctic Institute cliffs, dike with subconcordant contacts in migmatized garnet-sillimanite gneisses.
208a	Enderby Land, central portion of agmatite block in shadow charnockites. + 4% quartz.

N o t e s : 1. The iron component in the orthopyroxene (here and elsewhere in text) was determined from Kamenev's diagram presented herein (Figure 19). 2. Iron contents of clinopyroxene (here and elsewhere in text) were determined from the diagrams of Hess and Muir /101, 115/. 3. The iron content of the amphibole, represented by cummingtonite (here and elsewhere in text) was calculated from Deer's diagram /16/. 4. The iron content of biotite (here and elsewhere in text) was determined from the Drugova and Glebovitskii diagram /22/.

considerably less than that of olivine and orthopyroxene (2—14%). Its minimal content was found in magnesian schists occurring in perthite charnockites. The amphibole and biotite contents are independent of the nature of the enclosing rocks and seem to be controlled by their location in a particular metamorphic zone. These minerals do not exceed 20% of the rock. Ore minerals are always present in quantities of 1—4%.

Olivine in the magnesian schists is colorless and the fresh grains are highly cracked. These cracks are commonly filled with ore minerals and serpentine-iddingsite aggregates. The olivine belongs to chrysolites in its optical properties. The orthopyroxene replacing olivine has the highest ferruginosity and is the bronzite variety; it is colorless and rarely pleochroic, following the usual pattern. It may contain fine striated ingrowths of clinopyroxene as a result of exsolution. Banded structures are fairly common in the bronzite, and may be accounted for by stress at high temperatures and pressures. The only chemical analysis of bronzite (specimen 798b) revealed a high alumina content, 3.44% by weight, which suggests a metamorphic nature for the bronzite, since aluminous orthopyroxenes are typical minerals of the granulite facies /68/. The clinopyroxene is a colorless variety. Its grains are impregnated with fine-grained ore. A precise identification of the clinopyroxene is difficult since chemical analyses were not carried out and a correlation between optical properties and composition is approximate. The optical data plotted on the Ca — Mg — Fe diagram indicate a composition between diopside-hedenbergite and augite. However, this is essentially due to the $2V$ parameter which was measured at a low accuracy (wide variations even in a single grain) and the determined composition must be taken as very approximate.

Secondary amphibole develops mainly at the expense of clinopyroxene, forming rims around the latter. The amphibole is colorless to dull brown. Colored amphibole is pleochroic (n_z = light brown and n_x = pale yellow). Its optical properties are those of cummingtonite. Biotite generally replaces bronzite and is pleochroic (brown to light yellow). Low-iron biotites are only slightly colored.

Iron and magnesium contents in the principal rock-forming minerals vary only slightly. The iron content of olivine varies from 14 to 20 at.%, that of bronzite from 15 to 20 at.% and that of clinopyroxene from 24 to 29 at.%. The ferruginosity of bronzite is less than or equal to that in coexisting olivine whereas, except in rare cases, the ferruginosity of clinopyroxene was found to be higher than that in coexisting bronzites and olivines. This is unexpected since both olivine and bronzite are generally more ferrophile than clinopyroxene. However, the high iron content of the clinopyroxene was determined from optical data and is probably too high for a mineral which is a solid solution between clinohypersthene and diopside-hedenbergite. Variations in the ferruginosity of cummingtonite are 8 at.% (59 to 67 at.%). Its absolute value is much larger than the iron content in the coexistent minerals. The variation of ferruginosity in cummingtonite is directly related to the variation in the ferruginosity of clinopyroxene. The iron content of the biotite has a high range from 23 to 41 at.%.

Olivine-free magnesian schists occur at the contact with granitized calcareous-magnesian schists, or form thin intercalations in granitized alumina schists and calcareous-magnesian schists. Biopyroxene varieties of schist occur in contact with enderbites or with garnet granites. Ortho-pyroxene schists occur at the contact with charnockites. The schists occurring in garnet granite contain garnet. The pyroxene schists may be termed pyroxenolites, by analogy with amphibolites.

Pyroxenolites differ very little from olivine-pyroxene schists, except possibly in their coarser grain size (2—2.5 mm). They are dark greenish gray in color, massive, and occasionally weakly foliated, the latter feature being more common in bipyroxene varieties. The texture is characterized by a polygonal development of pyroxene grains and is mosaic granoblastic. Certain specimens contain coarse hypersthene porphyroblasts, subprismatic in form and up to 8 mm in diameter. Blastocataclastic textures have also been observed. Pyroxene is replaced by biotite and amphibole, and segregations of fine-grained ore minerals (Figure 1).

FIGURE 1. Photomicrograph of magnesian schist (pyroxenolite) with mosaic texture (× 10, regular light — thin section 798d).*

The quantitative ratios of pyroxene types in pyroxenolites vary, with different minerals dominating in different cases. This clearly depends on the composition of the substrate from which the pyroxenolites formed. The content of secondary minerals does not exceed 15% and ore minerals are always present. Orthopyroxene is represented either by bronzite or low-

* The mineral compositions are given in the various tables.

iron hypersthene. Exsolutions of thin lamellar clinopyroxene are much more common in orthopyroxenes from pyroxenolites than in olivine-bearing schists. Foliation is also more common. Orthopyroxene is generally colorless in thin section; however, it is rarely weakly pleochroic with the normal shades. Clinopyroxene is similar to the analogous mineral in olivine-bearing schists. In places it exhibits lamellar exsolutions of orthopyroxene and diallage joints. Amphibole and biotite are the same as those in the olivine-bearing schists. Pyroxenolites may contain small amounts of plagioclase of clearly metasomatic origin. It occurs in fine xenoblastic grains, is intergranular and partly replaces the minerals with which it lies in contact. The composition is oligoclase-andesine (An = 33—38%). Pyrope-almandine garnet is rare in the pyroxenolites. It forms fine xenoblastic grains, 0.1 to 0.3 mm in diameter. The garnet forms rims around pyroxene grains at their boundary with ore minerals. Skeletal garnet grains contain inclusions of ore and pyroxene. Anomalous birefringence "spots" indicate the presence of relatively large amounts of the grossular component.

The ferruginosity of the rock-forming minerals in the pyroxenolites varies to a greater degree than that in the olivine-bearing schists. The iron content of orthopyroxene varies from 15 to 32 at.% and that of clinopyroxene from 24 to 37 at.%. The orthopyroxene in the olivine-bearing schists and in the "near-contact" pyroxenolites, contain similar amounts of the iron component. The ferruginosity of clinopyroxene is lower in the "near-contact" pyroxenolites. The iron content of pyroxenes is much higher in thin intercalations of pyroxenolites than in the "near-contact" pyroxenolites.

The chemical composition of the magnesian schists is given in Table 3. The composition of the olivine-pyroxene schists differs from that of igneous peridotites of similar mineral compositions /75/ in that the former has 1) a somewhat higher silica content (Q varies from −19.1 to −22.8); 2) a higher titanium content (0.2—0.4 at.%); 3) a high stable alumina content (3.4—3.5 at.%); 4) a low ferric iron content (0.3—1.1 at.%); 5) a very high ferrous iron content ($f' = 19$—22); 6) a low, generally stable magnesia content ($\sim$42 at.%); and 7) a low phosphorus content.

The pyroxenolites under consideration differ from igneous pyroxenites with a corresponding mineral composition in their higher alumina (3.6 at.%), calcium (3.2 at.%), and ferrous iron (6.4 at.%) contents. According to criteria given by Zavaritskii, c, f' and c' have larger values than in typical bronzitites described by Daly /65/; the differences are apparently unrelated to biotitization and amphibolization of the rock but are due to the unusual composition of the orthopyroxene. This is also confirmed by a comparison of the norm and modal compositions of rocks.

Bipyroxene schists differ markedly in their chemical composition from websterites of a similar mineralogical composition. The differences are as follows: The bipyroxene schists have 1) a lower silica content (40.6—45.6 at.%); 2) a higher alumina content (6.1—6.3 at.%, $\sim$ 1.5 times higher); 3) a high ferrous iron content (nearly double); 4) a lower magnesia content (12.6—27.2 at.%); 5) a lower ($\sim^2/_3$) calcium oxide content (6.1—7.6 at.%);

and 6) a fairly high K_2O content, due to biotitization. The pyroxenolites contain a large amount of normative olivine. The values of Zavaritskii's characteristics, a and c, are larger in pyroxenolites than in websterites, indicating a higher alkalinity of the pyroxenolites and the presence of alumina in the pyroxenes. The internal chemical distribution differs in the pyroxenes of the websterites relative to that in the pyroxenolites (as indicated by the b characteristic). In the case of websterites, $f' = 12.3$, and $c' = 18.5$, as compared to $f' = 28.4$ and $c' = 9.1$ (specimen 155b) in the bipyroxene pyroxenolites.

Interesting data are gleaned by a comparison of the rock compositions from the contact portion (pyroxenolites) and central portion (olivine-pyroxene schists) of the same body (specimens 798b and 798d, respectively). Both rocks are characterized by virtually very similar alumina, alkalis, and titanium contents; they differ in their silica and femic contents. The ferrous iron and magnesia contents are lower, while the ferric iron and calcium oxide contents are higher in the pyroxenolites. These differences are indicated in the f', c' and m' values. The iron content of bronzite is the same in both rock types, but it is lower in the clinopyroxene (determined from optical data) of the pyroxenolite. The content of normative clino-pyroxene in pyroxenolite is three times that for schists with the composition of peridotite; the relationship of the modal clinopyroxene in these rocks is reversed.

Magnesian schists of Queen Maud Land differ only slightly, in terms of petrography and petrochemistry, from the olivine-pyroxene schists of Enderby Land. The former are distinguished by a higher content of ore minerals, and a greater degree of amphibolization and feldspathization. Olivine-bearing schists and bipyroxene pyroxenolites are rarely found in the magnesian schists of Queen Maud Land. The ferruginosity of pyroxenes is usually high. As a rule, the orthopyroxenes are represented by hyper-sthenes, with iron components up to 54 at.%. In all other respects, the magnesian schists of the granulite facies of Queen Maud Land are similar to those of Enderby Land.

Like the calciphyres, the magnesian schists are relatively stable during granitization. Ultrametamorphic alterations are similar for both rock types and include the development of bipyroxene or bronzite rocks contain-ing "alumina" bronzite in border portions of olivine-pyroxene bodies. Where the magnesian schists occur within enderbites, bipyroxene schist border zones are formed; bronzitite border zones form where the magnesian schists occur within charnockites. Thin bodies of magnesian schists may be entirely converted to pyroxenolites. The alteration process is probably bimetasomatic, similar to that resulting in the development of diopside rocks within calciphyre beds. A later stage of ultrametamorphism, with a higher alkali potential, also modified the pyroxenolites, resulting in the appearance of biotite, amphibole, and, in rare cases, sporadic grains of K-feldspar and quartz.

TABLE 3. Chemical composition of magnesian schists in Enderby Land

Component	Specimen No.																	
	485b			155b			798b			798d			803			208a		
	wt%	at.%	R/Al	wt%	at.%	R/Al	wt%	at.%	R/Al	wt%	at.%	R/Al	wt%	at.%	R/Al	wt%	at.%	R/Al
SiO_2	43.15	38.4	10.67	49.14	45.6	7.48	45.15	39.8	11.58	53.01	47.3	13.15	39.94	40.6	6.45	57.71	51.9	9.43
TiO_2	0.54	0.4	0.11	0.88	0.6	0.10	0.24	0.2	0.06	0.17	0.1	0.03	10.00	7.6	1.26	0.32	0.2	0.04
Al_2O_3	3.36	3.5	1.00	5.55	6.1	1.00	3.34	3.4	1.00	3.44	3.6	1.00	5.28	6.3	1.00	5.21	5.5	1.00
Fe_2O_3	1.66	1.1	0.31	0.91	0.7	0.11	0.38	0.3	0.09	1.26	0.8	0.22	6.36	4.8	0.76	0.88	0.7	0.13
Cr_2O_3	0.50	0.3	—	—	—	—	0.92	—	—	1.25	0.8	—	—	—	—	—	—	—
FeO	12.65	9.4	2.63	14.83	11.5	1.89	15.58	11.5	3.38	8.56	6.4	1.78	19.37	16.5	2.62	8.19	6.2	1.13
MnO	0.21	0.2	—	0.26	0.2	—	0.21	0.2	—	0.20	0.2	—	0.36	0.3	—	0.27	0.2	—
MgO	31.85	42.2	12.06	19.66	27.2	4.45	31.71	41.7	12.27	27.71	36.9	10.25	8.30	12.6	2.00	23.07	30.9	5.62
NiO	0.22	—	—	—	—	—	0.19	—	—	0.07	—	—	—	—	—	—	—	—
CaO	3.35	3.2	0.91	6.10	6.1	1.00	2.32	2.2	0.65	3.37	3.2	0.89	7.01	7.6	1.26	3.34	3.2	0.58
Na_2O	0.50	0.9	0.26	0.22	0.4	0.06	0.28	0.5	0.15	0.27	0.4	0.11	1.07	2.2	0.35	0.50	0.9	0.16
K_2O	0.33	0.4	0.11	1.18	1.5	0.24	0.25	0.3	0.09	0.25	0.3	0.08	0.63	0.8	0.13	0.15	0.2	0.04
P_2O_5	0.03	—	—	0.10	0.1	—	0.02	—	—	0.01	—	—	0.80	0.7	—	0.11	0.1	—
Loss on ignition	2.07	—	—	—	—	—	0.06	—	—	0.80	—	—	1.20	—	—	0.44	—	—
Σ	100.42	100.0	—	100.11	100.0	—	100.65	100.0	—	100.37	100.0	—	100.32	100.0	—	100.19	100.0	—

TABLE 3 (continued)

	Specimen No.					
	485 b	155 b	798 b	798 d	803	208a
Numerical characteristics (after A. N. Zavaritskii)						
a	1.2	1.8	0.8	0.7	3.0	1.1
b	57.2	46.2	55.9	48.1	43.1	41.4
c	1.2	2.4	1.4	1.5	1.9	2.3
s	40.4	49.6	41.9	49.7	52.0	55.2
Q	−22.8	−6.8	−19.1	−3.5	−3.9	+5.9
f'	19.0	28.4	22.0	16.0	60.2	18.0
m'	77.0	62.5	76.5	80.0	35.0	79.4
c'	4.0	9.1	1.5	4.0	4.8	2.6
Coordinates of ACF diagram (after P. Eskola and D. S. Korzhinskii)						
A	3.9	8.6	4.6	5.9	8.3	10.0
C	5.6	12.4	3.7	6.5	18.9	7.2
F	90.5	79.0	91.7	87.6	72.8	82.8
Norm, % (after T. Barth)						
Albite	4.3	2.0	2.4	2.1	11.1	4.3
Anorthite	5.6	10.6	6.7	7.2	8.4	11.4
Orthoclase	1.9	7.3	1.3	1.3	4.1	0.8
Olivine	61.0	17.5	56.8	5.7	—	—
Orthopyroxene	16.1	44.9	28.6	73.9	30.8	71.8
Clinopyroxene	8.3	15.2	3.4	9.9	19.3	3.2
Magnetite	1.6	1.0	0.5	1.2	6.1	1.0
Chromite	0.5	—	—	1.3	—	—
Ilmenite	0.7	1.2	0.3	1.3	15.2	0.4
Apatite	—	0.3	—	0.2	1.8	0.3

N o t e s. 1. The mineral composition of the analyzed rocks is given in Table 2.   2. $\frac{R}{Al}$: ratio between atomic weight % of an element to that of alumina.

CALCAREOUS-MAGNESIAN SCHISTS

Calcareous-magnesian schists predominate in the granulite facies of the metamorphic strata in the Antarctic basement. This group of rocks has been subdivided /21, 41/ into quartz-free pyroxene-plagioclase schists and quartz-bearing pyroxene plagiogneisses. It should be noted, however, that plagiogneisses proper are generally not found in ultrametamorphic complexes.

Plagiogneisses are readily converted to shadow granitoids during granitization, whereas the basic composition of the pyroxene-plagioclase schists ensures their relative preservation under the same conditions. Granitization products of plagiogneiss, such as shadow enderbites and charnockites, occur in the granulite facies. Smaller bodies of similar rock types may also result from the granitization of pyroxene-plagioclase schists. The most important granulite facies metamorphic products from the schists are coarse foliated migmatites with a composition between schists and shadow granitoids.

Four main rock groups may be defined among the calcareous-magnesian schists of the granulite facies: 1) pyroxene-plagioclase schists and their garnetiferous varieties; 2) migmatized pyroxene-plagioclase schists and their varieties transitional to enderbites; 3) shadow enderbites; 4) shadow charnockites. Intermediate types between charnockites and other calcareous-magnesian rocks also occur. These intermediate types are usually termed "feldspathized," although this is not quite accurate. Feldspathized rocks occur in several units in a manner similar to amphibolized and biotitized rocks. The presence of such rocks suggests separate ultrametamorphism stages accompanying "enderbitization" and "charnockitization." Other geological data supporting this concept are presented later in the text.

Pyroxene-plagioclase schists and their garnetiferous varieties

Pyroxene-plagioclase schists are widespread among metamorphic rocks of the Antarctic crystalline basement. They form thick, fairly homogeneous units varying from tens to hundreds of meters in thickness (up to 2 km in the Bunger Oasis), as well as numerous intercalations and lenses 0.5—20 m thick within metamorphic rocks of various compositions. Individual intercalations are often boudinaged, the boudins being generally lenticular. Certain of the schist bodies form cross-cutting relationships with the host rocks, suggesting their possible origin as dikes. Due to their relatively unique textures, physical properties and composition, these schists are often only slightly altered even within highly granitized rocks.

On a macro-scale, the pyroxene-plagioclase schists appear uniform; weakly coarse-banded and gneissic, mainly fine-grained and dark gray with a brownish green tinge. Schistosity is well pronounced in amphibolized and biotitized varieties. These schists are distinguished by approximately equal amounts of plagioclase and dark-colored minerals. The relative quantities of the latter vary widely (Tables 4, 5 and 6), but hypersthene is more abundant than clinopyroxene in most cases. Clinipyroxene predominates over hypersthene in schists from carbonate-bearing metamorphic strata; however, the ratio of pyroxenes is reversed in strata rich in alumina schists. Thus, although the composition of the original rocks (apparently largely volcanogenic) has a decisive influence on the quantitative ratios of pyroxenes (and other minerals), the composition of the host strata also controls, to a certain extent, the ratios of minerals in the pyroxene-plagioclase schists. Enderbitized varieties contain small amounts of quartz (up to 8%) and sporadic interstitial orthoclase. A few samples contain up to 6%, and rarely 10 to 20% orthoclase or microcline. Such schists display a greater development of orthoclase relative to plagioclase, which is a sign of charnockitization. The content of ore minerals varies from 1 to 10%. Apatite is the only other accessory. Amphibolization and biotitization of pyroxene-plagioclase schists can be regarded as a superimposed process related to ultrametamorphism or to amphibolite facies polymetamorphism. Based on this possibility, several other phenomena observed in these rocks may be better understood. Several units of migmatized amphibolized hypersthene-plagioclase schists in the Tula Mountains of Enderby Land show a secondary schistosity (S_2) exhibited by amphiboles oriented at an angle to the banding. This schistosity is apparently related to amphibolization of the rocks. Several of the exposures are irregularly amphibolized and biotitized (more and less intensive alterations within the same exposure). The development of biotite and amphibole, whether separately or together, is largely dependent on the chemical composition of the original rocks.

Granoblastic textures with stubby crystal forms and a common development of polygonal plagioclase are characteristic of the pyroxene-plagioclase schists in most exposures. Blastocataclastic and granulitic textures occur in enderbitized schists, and they may also be granoblastic; however, in the latter case, the crystal boundaries are serrate rather than rounded and polygonal. The rock-forming minerals vary in grain size, and glomeroblastic textures or a "clustered" arrangement of the mafic minerals and plagioclases may occur. Metablastic textures are also observed. The porphyroblasts are not always easily distinguished in the matrix, although some plagioclase and hypersthene metablasts stand out (reaching a size of 3— 4 mm). They are usually subhedral and generally contain inclusions of other minerals. Quartz develops interstitially (Figures 2 and 3). Feldspathized pyroxene-plagioclase schists are texturally similar to enderbitized schists: porphyroblastic textures are widespread, and frequently exhibit orthoclase replacing plagioclase. Resorbed inclusions of plagioclase and hypersthene occur in marginal portions of the orthoclase.

Amphibolized and biotitized schists have metablastic textures. The amphibole and biotite metablasts develop at the expense of pyroxenes. Large amphibole and biotite grains occasionally contain small ingrowths of quartz along their margins. Rocks unusually rich in amphibole are

TABLE 4. Mineral composition and characteristics of the pyroxene–plagioclase schists on Enderby Land

Specimen No.	Mineral composition, vol. %										An content of plagioclase		Characteristics of the minerals — hypersthene			
	qz	plag	Kfs	hyp	clpy	horn	biot	apat	zirc	orem	central	marginal	n_z	n_x	$2V°$	f, at.%
774b	o.s.*	45	—	42	10	—	—	o.s.	—	3	60	60	1.726	1.712	−54	50
802b	—	57	—	5	37	—	o.s.	r	—	1	52	54	1.715	1.701	−59	37
472a	—	60	—	15	20	—	—	r	—	5	56	58	1.724	1.709	−47	48
153b	—	45	—	48	5	1	—	r	—	1	63	80	1.714	1.700	−60	36
203g	—	25	—	32	25	o.s.	15	r	—	3	50	50	1.708	1.696	−62	30
27	—	28	—	40	20	5	o.s.	r	—	7	70	57	1.729	1.713	−52	52
777v	—	20	—	32	19	17	12	r	—	—	61	57	1.703	1.691	−71	25
63—1	—	40	—	25	15	—	20	r	—	—	80	59	1.710	1.696	−62	32
800-b	o.s.	45	—	50	3	—	o.s.	o.s.	—	2	37	37	1.708	1.694	−59	30
760g	1	65	—	30	4	—	+	r	—	o.s.	39	37	1.713	1.699	−68	35
812a	o.s.	53	—	20	27	—	o.s.	r	—	·	45	40	1.715	1.701	−53	37
156a	·	43	—	30	25	—	—	r	—	2	46	42	1.709	1.695	−58	31
472b	1.5	92	—	3	2	—	o.s.	o.s.	—	1.5	40	39	1.724	1.709	−47	48
807b	—	48	—	27	23	—	r	r	—	2	48	48	1.722	1.708	−54	46
754a	—	74	—	20	5	—	—	r	—	1	53	53	1.730	1.715	−56	54
176a	—	50	—	24	23	1	—	r	—	3	44	44	1.721	1.706	−50	45
177	—	60	—	5	30	—	—	r	—	4	50	50	1.726	1.711	−57	50
458	—	35	—	8	56	—	+	r	—	1	50	50	1.723	1.709	−51	47
26	5	49	—	15	29	—	—	r	—	2	45	40	1.726	1.711	−55	50
32	—	65	—	19	10	2	1	o.s.	—	3	37	31	—	—	—	—
167a	—	36	36	23	1	—	—	r	—	4	82	69	1.718	1.703	−59	41
663a	2	52	—	43	—	—	—	r	—	3	82	82	1.715	1.701	−53	37

Sample																
191a	54	—70	1.715	1.730	42	42	2	—	o.s.	—	—	—	36	o.s.*	57	5
201a	46	—52	1.708	1.722	38	46	3	—	▪	2	25	—	20	—	50	o.s.
45—1	52	—53	1.714	1.728	58	52	5	—	o.s.	—	1	28	8	—	56	2
343b	52	—59	1.714	1.728	54	46	5	—	▪	—	1	24	19	—	49	2
171	41	—50	1.703	1.718	80	72	3	—	▪	—	—	7	30	—	59	1
192	49	—50	1.711	1.725	77	59	3	—	▪	—	—	20	25	—	52	—
766a	47	—48	1.709	1.723	44	44	2	—	▪	—	22	27	22	—	27	—
383a	38	—54	1.702	1.716	90	60	2	—	▪	—	27	26	17	—	28	—
638v	50	—52	1.711	1.726	87	52	2	—	▪	5	20	10	18	—	50	—
305a	59	—52	1.721	1.737	46	46	5	—	▪	7	25	12	10	—	43	2
625a	—	—	—	—	46	46	4	—	▪	3	25	5	—	1	56	—
637	52	—49	1.714	1.729	65	53	3	—	▪	17	25	15	6	—	48	—
51	42	—50	1.705	1.719	45	45	4	—	▪	18	—	5	23	—	51	2
609	47	—48	1.708	1.723	44	44	o.s.	—	▪	1	—	18	9	—	53	—
87g	41	—55	1.704	1.718	42	42	2	—	▪	2	17	7	8	—	65	5
87v	41	—57	1.704	1.718	40	39	7	—	▪	o.s.	18	2	9	—	57	—
234	41 / 46	—56 / —56	1.704 / 1.707	1.718 / 1.722	67	48	3	—	▪	▪	1	10	26	—	60	3
53a	—	—	—	—	75	48	5	—	—	2	2	18	27	—	45	1
79a	—	—	—	—	38	37	4	—	—	4	9	12	5	—	67	7
79b	—	—50	—	—	37	37	2	—	—	20	18	3	—	—	66	2
836e	—	—	—	—	83	45	1	—	o.s.	—	2	10	13	—	53	—
49g	48	—58	1.709	1.724	66	65	—	—	▪	10	9	30	8	—	52	—
238g	41	—56	1.704	1.718	67	48	—	—	▪	o.s.	15	40	25	—	10	—
646	46 / 24	—57	1.707 / 1.689	1.722 / 1.702	62	62	—	o.s.	▪	20	—	—	25	—	75	—
70—2	41	—	1.703	1.718	43	40	—	—	▪	—	—	—	25	20	35	—

* [o.s. = optic sign.]

TABLE 4 (continued)

Specimen No.	clinopyroxene				hornblende				biotite		Geological setting of the specimen
	n_z	n_x	$2V°$	f at.%	n_z	n_x	$2V°$	f at.%	n_z	f at.%	
774b	1.722	1.697	+48	40	—	—	—	—	—	—	Intercalations in granitized sillimanite–garnet quartzites
802b	1.717	1.693	+60	32	—	—	—	—	—	—	Lenses in shadow enderbites
472a	1.722	1.696	+52	41	—	—	—	—	—	—	Intercalations in enderbites
153b	1.723	1.698	—	42	—	—	—	—	—	—	" "
203g	1.719	1.694	+53	36	—	—	—	—	1.636	37	Intercalation within enderbitized schists
27	1.724	1.699	+50	44	1.697	1.673	−82	51	—	—	Schist unit
777v	1.717	1.692	+55	33	1.681	1.662	−87	38	1.618	28	Boudin in shadow charnockites
63—1	1.718	1.694	+51	35	—	—	—	—	1.605	24	Intercalation in garnet gneisses
800b	1.716	1.690	+53	32	—	—	—	—	—	—	Lens in shadow mesoperthite granites
760g	—	—	—	—	—	—	—	—	—	—	Intercalations and lenses in mesoperthite garnet-bearing granites
812a	1.718	1.694	+50	34	—	—	—	—	—	—	Intercalations in shadow mesoperthite granites
156a	1.719	1.695	+50	36	—	—	—	—	—	—	Inclusions in shadow perthite charnockites
472b	1.721	—	+57	—	—	—	—	—	—	—	Intercalations in shadow enderbites
807b	1.724	1.696	+45	38	—	—	—	—	—	—	Intercalations in shadow mesoperthite granites
754a	1.719	1.699	+53	44	—	—	—	—	—	—	Thick schist unit
176a	1.719	1.695	+53	36	—	—	—	—	—	—	" "
177	1.720	1.696	+51	37	—	—	—	—	—	—	Schist unit with intercalations of shadow enderbites
458	1.719	1.694	+52	36	—	—	—	—	—	—	Schist unit with intercalations of shadow enderbites and shadow charnockites
26	1.722	1.697	+55	40	—	—	—	—	—	—	Thick schist unit
32	1.725	1.699	+54	46	—	—	—	—	—	—	Intercalations within shadow perthite charnockites, (without distinct contacts)
167a	—	—	—	—	—	—	—	—	—	—	
663a	—	—	—	—	—	—	—	—	—	—	Intercalations in garnet gneisses

Characteristics of the minerals

Sample											Description
191a	—	—	—	—	—	—	—	—	—	—	Intercalations in shadow mesoperthite garnet granites
201a	—	—	—	—	1.689	1.665	—85	44	—	—	Lenticular inclusions in shadow perthite charnockites
45—1	1.724	1.698	+53	44	—	—	—	—	—	—	Inclusions in plagioclasites
343b	1.726	1.701	+56	47	—	—	—	—	—	—	Schist unit with amphibolized intercalations
171	1.716	1.691	+53	32	—	—	—	—	—	—	Interbedded with garnet gneisses in the cataclastic zone
192	1.719	1.695	+53	36	1.706	1.678	—	58	—	—	Intercalations in shadow ganet granitoids
766a	1.721	1.699	+55	38	—	—	—	—	—	—	Schist unit in contact with garnet gneisses
383a	1.722	1.697	+55	40	1.688	1.667	—	43	—	—	Schist unit
638v	1.725	1.700	+53	46	1.712	1.686	—	65	—	—	Boudin in garnet gneisses
305a	1.727	1.708	+53	48	1.702	1.679	—	56	1.673	52	Intercalations in garnet gneisses
625a	1.720	1.695	+56	37	1.693	1.671	—	48	1.656	44	Thick schist unit
637	1.723	1.699	+51	42	1.695	1.672	—	49	1.651	43	Interbedded with biotitized schists
51	1.718	1.694	+58	34	—	—	—	—	1.653	43	Thick schist unit
609	1.723	1.694	+54	43	—	—	—	—	1.659	47	Interbedded with garnet gneisses
87g	1.721	1.696	+53	38	1.698	1.674	—69	52	1.658	46	Intercalations in a granitized and amphibolized shadow enderbite unit
87v	1.721	1.696	+54	38	1.698	1.674	—73	52	1.658	46	As above
234	1.721	1.695	+55	38	1.708	1.683	—87	61	—	—	Interbedded with shadow enderbites
53a	—	—	—	—	—	—	—	—	—	—	Six-meter bed within enderbites
79a	—	—	+54	—	—	—	—68	—	—	—	Schist unit
79b	—	—	+57	—	—	—	—71	—	—	—	"
836e	—	—	—	—	—	—	—	—	—	—	Intercalation in shadow garnet granites
49g	1.721	1.695	+58	38	1.706	1.682	—80	59	—	—	Schist unit
238g	1.721	1.695	+56	38	1.708	1.683	—87	61	1.662	48	Boudins in schists
646	—	—	—	—	—	—	—	—	—	—	Heterogeneously migmatized schists
70—2	—	—	—	—	—	—	—	—	1.634	36	Lenses within interbedded enderbites and garnet gneisses

Note: The ferruginosity of hornblende (here and later in text) was determined from the diagram proposed by G.M. Drugova and A.Glebovitskii /22/.

TABLE 5. Mineral composition and characteristics of pyroxene-plagioclase schists in Bunger Oasis

| | Mineral composition, vol.% | | | | | | | | | An content of plagioclase | Characteristics of the minerals | | | | | | | | | | | |
| Specimen No. | qz | plag | Kfs | hyp | clpy | horn | biot | apat | orem | | hypersthene | | | clinopyroxene | | | hornblende | | | biotite | | Remarks |
											n_z	n_x	f at.%	n_z	n_x	f at.%	n_z	n_x	f at.%	n_z	f at.%	
106	—	56	—	18	22	—	—	o.s.*	4	73	1.709	1.695	31	1.715	1.689	30	—	—	—	—	—	Bipyroxene-plagioclase schists
152	—	56	—	8	32	—	—	"	4	48	1.712	1.701	33	1.712	1.684	25	—	—	—	—	—	
823	—	59	—	16	19	—	—	"	6	56	1.720	1.704	43	1.722	1.696	40	—	—	—	—	—	
590a	—	50	—	40	2	—	—	"	8	77	1.718	1.703	41	—	—	—	—	—	—	—	—	
62k	1	46	—	50	3	—	—	"	1	70	1.718	1.704	41	—	—	—	—	—	—	—	—	
139b	2	61	—	19	15	—	—	"	4	42	1.730	1.716	54	1.723	1.698	42	—	—	—	—	—	
609b	—	58	—	14	16	—	—	"	10	41	1.727	1.712	51	—	—	—	—	—	—	—	—	
155b	2	62	—	20	11	—	1	o.s.	6	68	1.709	1.695	31	1.715	1.689	30	—	—	—	1.623	30	Biotitized bipyroxene-plagioclase schists
264	—	63	—	18	15	—	4	"	1	63	1.707	1.689	28	—	—	—	—	—	—	—	—	
178b	2	49	—	28	16	—	1	"	2	63	1.702	1.690	24	1.711	1.686	24	—	—	—	—	—	
94zh	—	60	—	16	22	—	2	"	1	55	1.720	1.703	43	1.721	1.693	38	—	—	—	—	—	
164	2	65	—	15	12	—	1	"	4	56	1.723	1.709	47	1.720	1.690	37	—	—	—	—	—	
126	—	53	—	7	34	—	18	"	5	45	1.709	1.696	31	1.717	1.687	32	—	—	—	1.623	30	
445v	—	10	—	50	18	—	3	"	4	79	1.712	1.696	33	1.710	1.685	21	—	—	—	—	—	
60g	1	50	—	25	16	—	3	"	5	68	1.713	1.700	35	1.713	1.688	27	—	—	—	—	—	
420	1	42	—	45	8	—	2	"	1	63	1.702	1.690	24	1.711	1.686	24	—	—	—	—	—	
421	—	56	—	35	5	—	1	"	2	75	1.719	1.704	42	1.721	1.697	38	—	—	—	—	—	
904b	—	64	—	18	10	—	22	2	5	48	1.724	1.706	48	1.713	1.688	29	—	—	—	1.640	38	
619b	—	17	—	23	35	—	25	2	1	49	1.709	1.695	31	1.716	1.690	32	—	—	—	1.630	33	
847a	—	36	—	16	30	—	30	1	2	45	1.714	1.698	36	1.719	1.688	36	—	—	—	1.636	36	
97	8	51	—	5	9	—	11	o.s.	2	50	1.721	1.706	44	—	—	—	—	—	—	1.648	42	
429	7	53	1	5	8	—	30	"	2	50	1.720	1.703	43	1.716	1.690	32	—	—	—	—	—	
94k	8	46	—	8	9	—	10	"	2	47	1.722	1.706	46	1.722	1.696	40	—	—	—	1.648	42	
190	5	57	—	20	6	—	—	o.s.	7	41	1.726	1.710	50	—	—	—	—	—	—	—	—	
552b	—	50	—	14	13	16	—	"	4	69	1.712	1.695	33	1.714	1.689	28	1.686	1.669	41	—	—	Amphibolized bipyroxene-plagioclase schists
443a	—	55	—	13	20	8	—	"	5	75	1.714	1.698	36	—	—	—	1.678	1.656	34	—	—	
59g	4	52	—	22	1	16	—	"	5	73	1.703	1.690	25	1.714	1.688	29	—	—	—	—	—	
771b	—	50	—	15	20	10	—	"	5	53	1.714	1.700	36	1.714	1.688	29	1.685	1.665	40	—	—	

Group labels (spanning the right side of the table):

- Biotitized and amphibolized bipyroxene-plagioclase schists
- Hypersthene-plagioclase schists, mostly biotitized

Sample	C1	C2	C3	C4	C5	C6	C7	C8	C9	C10	C11	C12	C13	o.s.	C15	C16	C17	C18	C19	C20	C21
636b	—	—	40	1.662	1.685	30	1.690	1.715	35	1.700	1.713	53	6	•	—	18	14	12	—	50	—
248a	—	—	35	1.656	1.679	35	1.692	1.718	36	1.698	1.714	50	1	•	—	30	11	9	—	49	—
386	—	—	48	1.680	1.693	30	1.683	1.715	28	1.694	1.707	56	3	•	—	22	10	20	1	45	5
329	—	—	59	1.683	1.704	29	1.689	1.714	53	1.712	1.729	47	3	•	—	16	5	18	2	52	8
463	—	—	58	1.679	1.703	45	1.700	1.724	55	1.715	1.731	46	3	•	—	13	2	11	—	61	2
291	—	—	61	1.689	1.707	44	1.703	1.724	55	1.714	1.732	41	5	•	—	8	10	19	—	56	—
714b	—	—	56	1.661	1.702	37	1.694	1.720	51	1.710	1.727	50	5	•	—	25	10	10	—	50	—
663	—	—	38	1.658	1.681	30	1.690	1.715	32	1.698	1.711	50	4	•	—	32	20	7	—	48	2
160a	—	—	48	1.680	1.693	42	1.697	1.723	31	1.696	1.709	70	5	—	1	—	8	17	—	55	—
149a	—	—	40	1.602	1.685	28	1.688	1.713	50	1.711	1.726	65	4	o.s.	1	21	9	33	6	33	4
434b	—	—	38	1.662	1.681	30	1.686	1.715	40	1.700	1.717	69	4	•	4	22	14	16	2	48	3
340	—	—	52	1.674	1.698	30	1.690	1.715	38	1.702	1.716	53	7	•	2	9	13	25	1	54	2
380	—	—	50	1.670	1.694	30	1.690	1.715	33	1.696	1.712	56	3	•	1	18	11	17	—	53	1
593	—	—	58	1.679	1.703	40	1.697	1.722	36	1.699	1.714	56	6	•	6	8	4	9	—	55	3
121	—	—	58	1.627	1.703	30	1.690	1.715	38	1.701	1.716	48	3	•	3	17	7	11	—	60	8
389a	47	1.644	55	1.686	1.700	32	1.687	1.717	52	1.712	1.728	43	1	—	10	17	5	20	—	50	5
628	—	—	40	1.663	1.684	—	—	—	47	1.703	1.723	47	4	—	12	5	17	6	—	53	6
951a	—	—	47	1.665	1.691	—	—	—	55	1.714	1.732	47	5	o.s.	15	29	1	8	—	55	5
176	43	1.650	36	1.660	1.680	—	—	—	33	1.694	1.712	41	2	•	6	20	10	15	—	50	3
64	45	1.656	—	—	—	—	—	—	44	1.707	1.721	41	6	•	3	38	8	8	—	38	1
281	—	—	—	—	—	—	—	—	43	1.695	1.709	47	1	•	1	10	10	1	—	41	—
482	53	1.650	—	—	—	—	—	—	42	1.707	1.720	72	3	•	5	56	—	28	—	58	—
606	61	1.659	—	—	—	—	—	—	29	1.702	1.719	79	6	o.s.	13	—	—	2	—	19	—
246g	—	—	—	—	—	—	—	—	43	1.695	1.708	78	2	o.s.	—	—	—	5	—	52	—
334a	47	1.660	—	—	—	—	—	—	46	1.706	1.720	80	5	•	1	—	—	18	—	57	—
246v	—	—	—	—	—	—	—	—	38	1.708	1.722	68	7	•	1	—	—	34	—	49	—
301b	—	—	—	—	—	—	—	—	42	1.703	1.716	52	2	•	3	—	—	40	—	60	—
605b	—	—	—	—	—	—	—	—	52	1.702	1.719	43	6	•	1	—	—	45	6	63	—
437a	—	—	—	—	—	—	—	—	41	1.713	1.728	50	3	•	20	—	—	25	2	49	—
773b	—	—	—	—	—	—	—	—	—	1.704	1.718	41	2	•	10	—	—	27	—	48	—
522d	38	1.640	—	—	—	—	—	—	—	—	—	49	1	•	18	—	—	38	—	63	—
597	—	—	—	—	—	—	—	—	—	—	—	—	—	•	—	—	—	24	—	50	—
112	38	1.640	—	—	—	—	—	—	—	—	—	—	—	—	—	—	—	20	—	—	—

* [o.s. = optic sign.]

TABLE 6. Mineral composition and characteristics of pyroxene-plagioclase schists in certain regions of Antarctica

Specimen No.	qz	plag	Kfs	hyp	clpy	hom	biot	apat	orem	An content of plagioclase	hypersthene n_z	hypersthene n_x	hypersthene f at.%	clinopyroxene n_z	clinopyroxene n_x	clinopyroxene f at.%	hornblende n_z	hornblende n_x	hornblende f at.%	biotite n_z	biotite f at.%	Remarks
Queen Maud Land																						
835 g	—	65	—	5	5	—	8	o.s.*	2	40	1.730	1.714	54	1.720	1.694	37	—	—	—	1.650	42	Biotitized schists
831	—	45	—	5	20	—	9	.	1	41	1.716	1.701	38	1.718	1.694	34	—	—	—	1.660	47	
852 v	5	60	—	15	7	—	10	.	3	51	1.728	1.712	52	—	—	—	—	—	—	1.660	47	
883	—	45	—	20	25	5	—	o.s.	5	54	—	—	—	—	—	—	1.694	1.663	40	—	—	Amphibolized schists
882	—	40	—	10	15	30	—	.	—	56	1.728	1.708	52	—	—	—	1.702	1.665	56	—	—	
866 v	—	30	—	15	15	30	—	.	10	43	1.735	1.725	57	1.728	1.704	51	1.683	1.656	39	—	—	
840 a	—	35	—	10	10	35	—	.	—	79	1.714	1.700	36	1.709	1.678	23	1.672	1.651	29	—	—	
875	—	45	—	15	15	25	—	.	5	76	1.721	1.704	44	—	—	—	1.682	1.660	38	—	—	
835 d	—	45	—	15	25	12	—	.	3	52	1.721	1.705	44	1.714	1.690	29	—	—	—	—	—	
829 g	—	35	—	25	15	45	—	.	—	49	1.714	1.700	36	1.716	1.692	32	1.688	1.667	43	—	—	
Mirny area																						
862	2	35	—	25	10	15	5	o.s.	8	50	—	—	—	—	—	—	1.676	1.653	33	1.643	39	Amphibolized and biotitized schists
857 d	—	39	—	7	8	40	5	.	1	76	1.730	1.714	54	—	—	—	1.687	1.661	42	1.638	37	
756 d	—	30	—	8	5	50	5	.	2	53	1.716	1.703	38	—	—	—	1.672	1.652	28	—	—	
794 z	—	24	—	8	5	60	1	.	2	40	1.718	1.699	41	—	—	—	1.668	1.643	25	—	—	
857 g	2	46	—	8	14	15	10	.	5	40	—	—	—	—	—	—	—	—	—	—	—	
1140 b	—	59.1	1.1	15	20.6	—	0.3	0.5	3.3	—	1.728	1.708	52	1.724	1.705	43	—	—	—	1.660	47	Biotitized schists

Sample																						Notes
1123a	—	46.4	—	25.2	20.2	2.0	4.6	0.4	1.2	—	—	1.731	1.715	55	1.728	1.704	51	1.703	1.679	58	1.666	49	Amphibolized and biotitized schists

Vestfold Oasis

Sample																						
55	1	68	—	11	10	2	2	1	5	40	—	—	—	—	—	—	—	—	—	—	—	—

Mountain fringe of Lambert Glacier

Sample							o.s.	2V											Notes
302	—	52	—	30	15	2	1	72	1.723	1.708	47	1.717	1.692	34	—	—	—	1.638	37	Biotitized schists
3021	3	60	—	30	—	5	2	72	1.727	1.712	51	—	—	—	—	—	—	1.641	38	
315b	3	50	—	27	—	20	o.s.	46	1.720	1.705	43	—	—	—	—	—	—	—	41	
302a	—	40	—	—	35	25	″	42	—	—	—	1.716	1.690	33	—	—	—	1.647	41	
314	—	60	—	25	5	9	1	o.s.	46	1.730	1.715	54	1.727	1.701	48	1.699	1.672	53	—	Amphibolized and biotitized schists
11	1	58	—	15	2	15	9	″	44	1.743	1.727	62	—	—	—	1.684	1.660	40	1.670	51
2b	—	50	—	3	15	15	15	2	42	1.740	1.724	60	1.728	1.701	51	1.690	1.668	45	1.668	50

Yamato Mountains *

Sample																			Notes
4659	—	45.2	—	10.1	23.9	—	20.2	0.4	0.2	—	1.710	—	1.704	32	—	15	—	1.624	31	Biotitized schists

* [o.s. = optic sign.]

FIGURE 2. Photomicrograph of pyroxene-plagioclase schist with granoblastic texture (x 10, crossed nicols, thin section 802b).

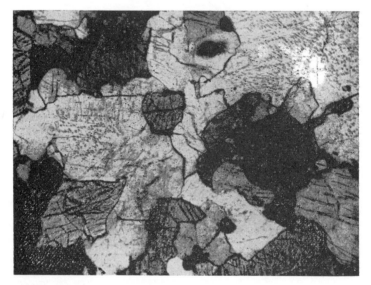

FIGURE 3. Photomicrograph of enderbitized pyroxene-plagioclase schist with anti-perthite plagioclase (x 30, crossed nicols, thin section 760g).

nematogranoblastic, the amphibole having a linear orientation. Lepido-granoblastic textures are extensively developed in rocks which have been strongly biotitized (Figure 4). Typical granulitic textures are extensively developed in amphibolized and biotitized schists of Enderby Land, especially in the Rayner metamorphic zone, as well as on Queen Maud Land. Mafic minerals are segregated in "fusiform" aggregates resulting in a fine banding. In the same rocks, plagioclase replaces pyroxene and complex symplectites of hypersthene and plagioclase are formed. Pyroxene inclusions in plagioclase appear to be relicts. Polysynthetic twins of clino-pyroxene are overgrown on hypersthene. The same specimens exhibit a reversed plagioclase zonality; the pyroxene ingrowths are concentrated in the anorthite marginal zone.

FIGURE 4. Photomicrograph of amphibolized and biotitized pyroxene-plagioclase schist with lepido-nematogranoblastic texture (× 10, regular light, thin section 777v).

Amphibolized, biotitized and feldspathized pyroxene-plagioclase schists are fairly extensive in the Bunger Oasis and in western Enderby Land (Molodezhnaya Station area). These rocks are distinguished by complex blastoclastic textures: they contain, in part, relatively coarse-grained zones (up to 5—6 mm) with relict granoblastic and newly formed metablastic textures (metablasts of amphibole, biotite, and orthoclase); they also include fine-grained homogeneous quartz-feldspar aggregates. These are separated by hornblende and biotite grains in a "sievelike" texture. These rocks, in both their coarse-grained and fine-grained portions, show evidence of a late development of amphibole and biotite. Samples exhibiting pyroxene replaced by hornblende and by younger biotite are widespread in the relatively coarse-grained areas; in the fine-grained aggregates, the hornblende first develops along a network of fine cracks, then forms large poikilitic xenoblasts with inclusions of relict pyroxene, lesser plagioclase and numerous rounded grains of "newly formed" quartz. Quartz locally forms aggregates with biotite and amphibole. Indications of a hornblende younger than orthoclase are not definitive, although amphibole often occurs in fine cracks within the orthoclase.

Variations in the composition and texture of plagioclase are indicative of different groups of pyroxene-plagioclase schists. These variations are dependent on the initial composition of the rocks and on the type of metamorphism: enderbitization, charnockitization, amphibolization, biotitization, etc. Thus the schists may be divided into the following varieties: 1) those containing essentially calcic plagioclase (> 50% anorthite); 2) intermediate plagioclase (32—50% anorthite); 3) plagioclase with reversed zoning.

The first variety is characterized by a maculose structure and normal zoning (the narrow margin is the best expressed zone). The composition of the plagioclase ranges from labradorite and bytownite in the center to andesine and acid labradorite in the margins of the grains. The zoning is continuous. The composition of the central zone and particularly of the marginal zones varies in different grains, even in a single thin section. Plagioclase compositions in these rocks vary within ± 10% of the An content; this variation rarely reaches ±20—25%. These features suggest that the "decalcification" processes in plagioclase were heterogeneous and did not proceed to completion. In general, biopyroxene-plagioclase schists are characterized by a more basic plagioclase than the hypersthene-plagioclase schists; compositional fluctuations are less pronounced in the latter (± 5—6% of the An content).

Andesine-bearing schists are enderbitized. The basicity of the plagioclase fluctuates as much as 5—6% within a single specimen. The characteristic structure is maculose and zoning is normal. The general increase of the An content in the plagioclase of the andesine schists relative to that in the bipyroxene-plagioclase schists, is accompanied by up to 25% antiperthite exsolution ingrowths in the plagioclase. In these rocks there is a resorption of both pyroxenes. The hypersthene is poikilitic, with plagioclase ingrowths. Antiperthite plagioclase always replaces a more basic nonantiperthite plagioclase and forms fairly large metablasts.

Reverse zoning in plagioclase is commonly observed in amphibolized and biotitized schists in the Rayner zone of Enderby Land. The plagioclase varies from andesine in the center to bytownite in the margins of the grains. There is also a reverse zoning around inclusions in the plagioclase. In general, the plagioclase in these rocks is highly basic, ranging from An 40 to An 95. Zoning is usually diffuse, although some grains display a fairly distinct narrow marginal zone of basic composition. The composition of the plagioclase varies even within a single thin section, suggesting nonequilibrium conditions during the development of the reverse zoning. Remarkably, these plagioclases scarcely contain antiperthite ingrowths.

Most orthopyroxenes in the schists are hypersthenes with a ferruginosity of 30—50 at.%. Ferrohyperstenes with a ferruginosity of 51—59 at.% are less common. Bronzites are even rarer. The ferruginosity of the bronzite is never less than 24 at.%, and usually ranges from 25 to 28 at.%. According to most authors who discuss pyroxenes from metamorphic rocks, the ferruginosity of orthopyroxene seldom falls below 38—40 at.% /16, 74/. The content of the iron component in orthopyroxenes from norites and gabbros usually varies from 23 to 40 at.% /94, 95/. On the other hand, the ferruginosity of pyroxenes in rocks of the granulite facies is known to increase during granitization /34, 57/. These data suggest that the pyroxene-plagioclase schists containing hypersthene with a ferruginosity of less than 30 at.%, are incompletely metamorphosed intrusives.

A statistical evaluation of data on orthopyroxenes in Antarctic schists indicates a decrease in ferruginosity from west to east: Queen Maud Land — Enderby Land — Bunger Oasis (Table 7).

TABLE 7. Average ferruginosity of orthopyroxenes in Ca-Mg schists by regions

Region	Average ferruginosity, at.%	Number of measurements
Queen Maud Land	45.50	12
Rayner zone of Enderby Land	45.05	21
Napier zone of Enderby Land	41.48	25
Bunger Oasis	40.00	63

Orthopyroxenes in nonamphibolized and nonbiotitized schists possess two additional characteristics: 1) They display zonal extinction. This phenomenon is tentatively assumed to indicate a variation in the hypersthene composition during a nonequilibrium process (most probably enderbitization). 2) Internal banding in the hypersthene, perpendicular to the cleavage and the long axes of the grains. The bands suggest twins with very sharp contacts. Extinction is not simultaneous, due perhaps to stress under high pressures /61/. The pleochroism of orthopyroxene in the group of rocks under discussion is not intense, thus confirming the comparatively low ferruginosity and medium alumina content.

The clinopyroxenes in schists are either salites, containing a small amount of jadeite and hypersthene molecules, or augites, also containing some jadeite. A characteristic feature of the clinopyroxenes is polysynthetic twinning along (001) and thin exsolution lamellae along (001) and (100). The latter are more characteristic of ferruginous clinopyroxenes. In places, the orthopyroxene lamellae become larger, and acquire an irregular shape. It is clear that the high content of alumina and ferromagnesian components may be accounted for by the presence of a solid solution of hypersthene or pigeonite in augite. However, the thinness of the lamellae prevents an accurate optical determination of their composition (orthopyroxene or pigeonite).

Unfortunately, optical methods are not diagnostic of the ferruginosity of the clinopyroxenes, since the refractive index and the $2V$ are affected both by accessories and by exsolution effects. The true Ca, Mg, and Fe contents may differ from those determined optically by at least 5—6% /105/. However, given the maximum error, the ferruginosity of clinopyroxenes is equal to or greater than that of co-existing bronzite or low-iron hypersthene.

Similar relationships between the iron components of these minerals occur in meta-ultrabasites, which are clearly intrusive. In these rocks, the ferruginosity of orthopyroxene is generally 8—10 at.% higher than that of the clinopyroxene /100/. Deviations from the usual relationships may either denote the lack of equilibrium between the two pyroxenes /116/ or may be due to a different metamorphic history /141/. In this particular case, both factors are in evidence, since, as indicated above, the schists with low-iron pyroxenes have certain characteristics of intrusive rocks. The retention of these features testifies to an incomplete metamorphism of the meta-ultrabasites, in comparison with the host rock. The clinopyroxene ferruginosity of Enderby Land schists varies from 29 to 48 at.%, of Bunger Oasis schists from 21 to 45 at.%, and of Queen Maud Land schists from 23 to 51 at.%. The regional variation of average ferruginosity in clino-pyroxenes is the same as that in the orthopyroxenes.

Amphibole develops along pyroxene crystal boundaries, and replaces both clinopyroxene and orthopyroxene (mainly the former). The amphibole is represented by common hornblende, the color of which may vary from brown to greenish brown to brown-green in the same thin section. The edges of the grains are darker green. The ferruginosity of amphiboles is regularly higher than that of pyroxenes and is generally proportionally related to it. The ferruginosity of Enderby Land hornblende is 38—65 at.% (mainly 48—61 at.%), that of the Bunger Oasis hornblende is 34—61 at.%, and that of Queen Maud Land hornblende is 25—56 at.%.

Biotite is another mineral exhibiting reactive relationships with the pyroxenes. Its later development with respect to the hornblende can be established in many cases. Biotite mainly replaces hypersthene, over-growing the latter along the crystal boundaries and penetrating into it along micro-cracks. Replacement of hypersthene by biotite is accompanied by a separation of small amounts of ore. The very fine ore grains fill cleavage cracks in biotite or are concentrated on the periphery of the grains. The color of the biotite is most frequently reddish brown, but common cinnamon-brown biotite with the usual pleochroism is also encountered. The ferruginosity of the mica in biotitized schists is slightly lower than that of hypersthene. Biotite ferruginosity in schists that have been both biotitized and amphibolized is always higher than that of hypersthene, but lower than or equal to that of amphibole. The ferruginosity of biotite is 24—52 at.% in Enderby Land rocks, 30—51 at.% in Bunger Oasis rocks and 37—47 at.% in Queen Maud Land rocks. The regional trend of biotite ferruginosity is the same as that of hypersthene.

The variable properties of orthoclase in feldspathized schists from different regions of Antarctica should be mentioned. Orthoclase from the feldspathized schists in the Napier zone of Enderby Land is perthitic

($2V = 50-51°$; containing 5—10% perthite). The orthoclase of feldspathized, biotitized, and amphibolized schists from the Rayner zone of Enderby Land is highly variable. In relatively orthoclase-poor schists, where it develops along contacts with, and partly replaces, plagioclase, it is anhedral and exhibits a nonuniform distribution of perthitic ingrowths ($2V = -55$ to $-56°$). In large segregations (up to 7 or 8 mm) that are characteristic of the highly feldspathized rocks, microcline, of varying grain size and sharpness of crystal boundaries, is irregularly distributed, mainly on the periphery of anhedral orthoclase. The development of microcline nuclei first occurs along fine cracks in the orthoclase, which resulted from cataclasis. Near the area of microcline euhedra, the anhedral orthoclase develops a significant increase in the optical axes angle (e. g., from 55—56° to 60—64° and even 75—80°). Most of the late-formed orthoclase in partially feldspathized schists of the Bunger Oasis possess a distinct twinning lattice and may be classified as microcline ($\perp(001)n_y = 13-15°$).

The chemical composition of pyroxene-plagioclase schists is given in Tables 8 and 9. There is no significant difference in the chemical composition of these rocks from different regions of Antarctica. The variation in chemical compositions of the schists is very wide due to the unequal degrees of alteration (enderbitization, charnockitization, biotitization, and amphibolization). The ranges in Zavaritskii's principal characteristics are: $a = 2.2-11.9$; $b = 18.2-43.8$; $c = 2.6-11.5$; $s = 50.3-64.6$; $Q = -17.0$ to $+3.6$. These values indicate that the schists occupy three classes (4, 5, and 6) of Zavaritskii's chemical classification (identical positions in each class), i. e., melanocratic rocks, low in alkalis.

A comparison was made between the chemical compositions of pyroxene-plagioclase schists and chemical compositions of igneous rocks (according to Daly /83/). Of the 26 pyroxene-plagioclase schists analyzed, three (53a, 149a, 238g) have no analogous compositions among the igneous rocks (intermediate between basic and ultrabasic). Three samples (79a, 79b, and 55kh) have mafic mineral and plagioclase compositions similar to those in quartz gabbro and quartz basalt; however, they are richer in alkalis and have a slightly higher calcic content in the mafic minerals. Two samples (167a and 94k) have higher alkali contents and fewer mafic minerals than in average basalts. They are also unique among other pyroxene-plagioclase schists and basic igneous rocks in their significant predominance of potassium over sodium. Furthermore, sample 94k has a relatively low anorthite content, similar to that in samples 149a and 238g. Sample 951a has an unusual composition, approaching that of average bekinkinite and leucitic absarokite (alkaline gabbroids); however, it differs somewhat from the latter mineralogically by a predominance of potassium over sodium and by a somewhat smaller content of dark silicates. It contains 2.2% normative nepheline.

Amphibolization had no apparent effect on the chemical composition of pyroxene-plagioclase schists. However, a comparison with nonamphibolized rocks (Si : Al ratios) reveals an increase in alumina and, consequently, a difference in the content of other oxides. Thus, amphibolization

TABLE 8. Chemical composition of pyroxene-plagioclase schists from Enderby Land

Component	Specimen No.														
	26			802b			32			238 g			53a		
	wt%	at.%	$\frac{R}{Al}$	wt%	at.%	$\frac{R}{Al}$	wt%	at.%	$\frac{R}{Al}$	wt%	at.%	$\frac{R}{Al}$	wt%	at.%	$\frac{R}{Al}$
SiO_2	49.40	46.4	2.71	53.04	48.9	2.88	52.70	49.0	3.45	48.19	45.5	5.84	47.74	47.3	4.78
TiO_2	1.25	0.9	0.05	0.40	0.3	0.02	0.40	0.3	0.02	1.12	0.8	0.12	2.45	1.8	0.18
Al_2O_3	15.59	17.1	1.00	15.65	17.0	1.00	13.06	14.2	1.00	6.95	7.8	1.00	8.56	9.9	1.00
Fe_2O_3	1.34	1.0	0.06	1.19	0.8	0.05	0.92	0.7	0.05	2.82	2.0	0.26	4.76	3.5	0.35
FeO	9.94	7.8	0.46	7.62	5.9	0.35	8.54	6.6	0.46	12.82	10.1	1.29	16.98	14.2	1.44
MnO	0.22	0.2	—	0.18	0.2	—	0.17	0.2	—	0.27	0.2	—	0.31	0.2	—
MgO	8.18	11.4	0.67	8.25	11.3	0.66	9.68	13.4	0.94	13.27	18.6	2.38	7.12	10.5	1.06
CaO	11.55	11.6	0.68	10.47	10.3	0.61	10.85	10.8	0.76	11.67	11.8	1.51	9.83	10.5	1.06
NaO	1.73	3.1	0.18	2.68	4.8	0.28	2.30	4.1	0.29	1.04	2.0	0.26	0.95	1.8	0.18
K_2O	0.25	0.3	0.02	0.40	0.4	0.02	0.50	0.6	0.04	0.86	1.1	0.14	0.12	0.1	0.01
P_2O_5	0.29	0.2	—	0.07	0.1	—	0.11	0.1	—	0.18	0.1	—	0.28	0.2	—
Loss on ignition	0.34	—	—	0.41	—	—	0.45	—	—	0.99	—	—	0.70	—	—
Σ	100.08	100.0	—	100.36	100.0	—	99.68	100.0	—	100.18	100.0	—	99.80	100.0	—

TABLE 8 (continued)

Specimen No.

Component	836e wt%	836e at.%	836e R/Al	79b wt%	79b at.%	79b R/Al	79a wt%	79a at.%	79a R/Al	634a wt%	634a at.%	634a R/Al	634 wt%	634 at.%	634 R/Al	167a wt%	167a at.%	167a R/Al
SiO_2	50.41	47.1	2.74	54.63	51.4	2.68	53.24	49.9	2.61	55.15	51.7	3.13	56.04	52.2	3.14	51.56	48.7	2.75
TiO_2	1.12	0.8	0.05	0.91	0.6	0.03	0.94	0.7	0.04	0.64	0.4	0.02	0.60	0.4	0.02	1.14	0.8	0.05
Al_2O_3	15.63	17.2	1.00	17.31	19.2	1.00	17.28	19.1	1.00	15.01	16.5	1.00	15.07	16.6	1.00	15.93	17.7	1.00
Fe_2O_3	1.67	1.2	0.07	3.73	2.7	0.14	3.18	2.3	0.12	3.69	2.6	0.16	3.81	2.7	0.16	3.59	2.6	0.15
FeO	9.02	7.0	0.41	5.18	4.1	0.21	6.62	5.1	0.27	5.66	4.4	0.27	4.38	3.4	0.20	6.43	5.0	0.28
MnO	0.15	0.1	—	0.18	0.2	—	0.21	0.2	—	0.13	—	—	0.13	—	—	0.29	0.2	—
MgO	8.23	11.4	0.66	3.97	5.5	0.29	4.13	5.8	0.30	5.06	7.1	0.43	5.05	7.0	0.4	5.83	8.2	0.46
CaO	7.98	8.0	0.47	7.56	7.6	0.40	8.12	8.1	0.42	5.90	5.9	0.36	5.96	5.9	0.36	8.69	8.8	0.50
Na_2O	2.56	4.6	0.27	3.84	7.0	0.36	3.93	7.2	0.38	3.94	7.2	0.44	3.98	7.2	0.43	0.84	1.6	0.09
K_2O	2.12	2.5	0.15	1.21	1.5	0.08	1.09	1.4	0.07	3.14	3.8	0.23	3.54	4.2	0.25	5.28	6.3	0.36
P_2O_5	0.16	0.1	—	0.25	0.2	—	0.36	0.2	—	0.61	0.4	—	0.61	0.4	—	0.16	0.1	—
Loss on ignition	0.86	—	—	1.25	—	—	1.04	—	—	0.75	—	—	0.63	—	—	0.53	—	—
Σ	99.91	100.0	—	100.02	100.0	—	100.08	100.0	—	99.68	100.0	—	99.80	100.0	—	100.27	100.0	—

TABLE 8 (continued)

	Specimen No.										
	26	802b	32	238 g	53a	83be	79b	59a	634a	634	167a
Numerical characteristics (after Zavaritskii)											
a	4.1	6.3	5.5	3.3	2.2	8.6	10.5	10.6	13.3	13.8	9.7
b	30.4	27.0	31.5	43.8	39.8	27.4	18.2	20.1	19.6	19.7	24.0
c	8.3	7.2	5.5	2.6	4.4	6.1	6.7	6.6	3.5	3.1	6.0
s	57.2	59.5	57.5	50.3	54.6	57.9	64.6	62.7	63.6	63.4	60.3
Q	−2.1	−0.8	−1.5	−8.6	−0.6	−7.5	+1.5	−2.4	−2.9	−3.9	−4.8
f'	35.6	30.1	27.7	30.4	51.2	36.6	46.8	46.8	40.9	37.2	39.5
m'	45.6	50.1	49.8	46.3	30.2	50.4	37.8	35.8	40.9	42.2	40.9
c'	18.7	19.8	22.5	23.3	18.6	13.0	15.4	17.4	18.2	20.6	19.6
Coordinates on the ACF diagram (after Eskola and Korzhinskii)											
A	30.8	29.7	23.5	10.4	18.4	27.5	38.2	35.6	24.2	23.7	30.5
C	25.9	26.2	26.7	25.8	24.2	21.9	27.1	27.1	25.6	27.6	27.5
F	43.3	44.1	49.8	63.8	57.4	50.6	34.7	37.3	50.2	48.7	42.0
Norm, % (after Barth)											
Albite	15.5	24.1	20.6	9.6	9.2	23.0	35.1	35.7	36.0	36.0	7.9
Anorthite	34.3	29.1	23.7	11.9	19.9	25.3	26.9	26.5	13.9	12.7	24.4
Orthoclase	1.4	2.2	2.8	5.4	0.6	12.3	7.3	6.8	18.8	21.0	31.8
Olivine	—	—	—	15.5	—	12.8	—	—	—	—	—
Orthopyroxene	27.3	24.8	27.4	16.2	30.5	11.8	11.6	13.7	14.7	11.9	15.1
Clinopyroxene	17.6	17.3	23.6	37.0	24.5	11.2	7.9	9.9	9.9	11.0	15.0
Magnetite	1.4	1.2	1.0	2.9	5.2	1.7	4.0	3.4	3.9	4.0	3.9
Ilmenite	1.8	0.6	0.6	1.2	3.6	1.6	1.2	1.4	0.9	0.9	1.6
Apatite	0.6	0.3	0.3	0.3	0.6	0.3	0.5	0.6	1.1	1.1	0.3
Quartz	0.1	0.4	—	—	5.9	—	5.5	2.0	0.8	1.4	—
Nepheline	—	—	—	—	—	—	—	—	—	—	—

Note. The mineral compositions of specimens are listed in Table 4.

TABLE 9. Chemical composition of pyroxene-plagioclase schists from various regions in Antarctica

Component	Specimen No.																	
	160a			264			321			340			904b			94zh		
	wt%	at.%	$\frac{R}{Al}$	wt%	at.%	$\frac{R}{Al}$	wt%	at.%	$\frac{R}{Al}$	wt%	at.%	$\frac{R}{Al}$	wt%	at.%	$\frac{R}{Al}$	wt%	at.%	$\frac{R}{Al}$
SiO_2	45.29	42.9	2.04	53.00	49.3	2.82	53.26	50.5	2.76	51.99	49.4	2.99	44.13	42.9	2.45	52.16	48.8	3.00
TiO_2	1.58	1.1	0.05	0.57	0.4	0.02	0.69	0.5	0.03	2.12	1.5	0.09	4.07	3.0	0.17	1.68	1.2	0.07
Al_2O_3	18.88	21.0	1.00	15.95	17.5	1.00	16.82	18.3	1.00	14.83	16.6	1.00	15.23	17.5	1.00	14.82	16.3	1.00
Fe_2O_3	4.17	3.0	0.14	1.55	1.1	0.06	1.03	0.7	0.04	1.36	1.0	0.06	5.51	4.9	0.28	2.15	1.5	0.09
FeO	7.59	6.0	0.29	7.19	5.6	0.32	9.58	7.6	0.42	10.84	8.6	0.52	10.30	8.4	0.48	9.59	7.5	0.46
MnO	0.21	0.2	0.01	0.26	0.2	0.01	0.20	0.2	0.01	0.23	0.2	0.01	0.25	0.2	0.01	0.17	0.1	—
MgO	6.54	9.2	0.44	7.52	10.4	0.59	5.70	8.0	0.44	6.24	8.9	0.54	4.10	5.9	0.34	6.84	9.5	0.58
CaO	13.0	13.2	0.63	11.10	11.0	0.63	9.21	9.4	0.51	8.64	8.8	0.53	9.70	10.0	0.57	8.74	8.7	0.53
Na_2O	1.39	2.6	0.12	1.91	3.5	0.20	2.01	3.7	0.20	2.36	4.3	0.26	3.03	5.7	0.33	3.23	5.9	0.36
K_2O	0.29	0.3	0.01	0.79	1.0	0.06	0.80	1.0	0.06	0.48	0.6	0.04	0.82	1.1	0.06	0.44	0.5	0.03
P_2O_5	0.51	0.5	0.02	0.02	—	—	0.11	0.1	—	0.17	0.1	—	1.64	1.3	0.07	0.02	—	—
Loss on ignition	0.98	—	—	0.66	—	—	0.92	—	—	0.77	—	—	1.07	—	—	0.63	—	—
Σ	100.43	100.0	—	100.52	100,0	—	100.33	100.0	—	100.07	100.0	—	99.85	100.0	—	100.47	100.0	—

TABLE 9 (continued)

Component	149a			663			121			281			482			951a		
	wt%	at.%	R/Al	wt%	at.%	R/Al	wt%	at.%	R/Al	wt%	at.%	R/Al	wt%	at.%	R/Al	wt%	at.%	R/Al
SiO_2	47.77	44.8	3.56	46.44	44.9	2.66	50.91	47.8	2.90	50.37	48.1	2.99	48.45	45.7	3.07	47.05	44.6	3.43
TiO_2	0.78	0.6	0.05	2.16	1.6	0.09	1.25	0.8	0.05	2.62	1.9	0.12	1.30	0.9	0.06	1.06	0.8	0.06
Al_2O_3	11.40	12.6	1.00	14.93	16.9	1.00	15.02	16.5	1.00	14.42	16.1	1.00	13.35	14.9	1.00	11.66	13.0	1.00
Fe_2O_3	2.76	1.9	0.15	3.05	2.3	0.14	3.60	2.6	0.16	2.37	1.7	0.11	5.00	3.5	0.23	2.16	1.5	0.12
FeO	11.21	8.8	0.70	10.88	8.7	0.51	9.00	7.0	0.42	12.47	9.9	0.61	7.24	5.7	0.38	6.58	5.2	0.40
MnO	0.52	0.4	0.03	0.25	0.2	0.01	0.24	0.2	0.01	0.20	0.2	0.01	0.11	—	—	0.20	0.2	0.02
MgO	13.14	18.3	1.45	6.43	9.2	0.54	7.65	10.7	0.65	5.70	8.1	0.50	7.46	10.4	0.68	12.74	17.9	1.38
CaO	10.03	10.1	0.80	9.94	10.2	0.60	8.94	9.0	0.61	6.52	6.6	0.41	11.99	12.1	0.81	8.34	8.4	0.65
Na_2O	1.00	1.8	0.14	3.25	4.2	0.25	2.56	4.6	0.28	2.98	5.5	0.34	3.04	5.5	0.37	1.73	3.1	0.24
K_2O	0.60	0.7	0.06	1.08	1.5	0.09	0.65	0.7	0.04	1.28	1.6	0.10	1.02	1.2	0.08	3.75	4.5	0.35
P_2O_5	—	—	—	0.35	0.3	—	0.10	0.1	—	0.35	0.3	0.02	0.14	0.1	—	1.05	0.8	0.06
Loss on ignition	1.22	—	—	1.43	—	—	0.44	—	—	0.75	—	—	0.94	—	—	3.32	—	—
Σ	100.43	100.0	—	100.19	100.0	—	100.36	—	—	100.03	100.0	—	100.04	100.0	—	99.63	100.0	—

TABLE 9 (continued)

Component	94k wt%	94k at.%	94k R/Al	756d wt%	756d at.%	756d R/Al	1140b wt%	1140b at.%	1140b R/Al	1123a wt%	1123a at.%	1123a R/Al	55 wt%	55 at.%
SiO_2	53.00	50.1	3.23	45.54	42.6	2.24	50.71	47.6	2.78	48.94	46.5	3.08	52.25	48.7
TiO_2	1.04	0.7	0.05	1.65	1.2	0.06	1.92	1.3	0.08	1.46	1.1	0.07	1.23	0.8
Al_2O_3	13.99	15.5	1.00	17.13	19.0	1.00	15.44	17.1	1.00	13.55	15.1	1.00	17.01	18.7
Fe_2O_3	2.32	1.6	0.10	2.06	1.4	0.07	1.41	1.0	0.06	2.78	1.9	0.13	3.67	2.6
FeO	5.48	4.4	0.28	10.50	8.2	0.43	9.34	7.3	0.43	14.13	11.3	0.75	6.36	5.0
MnO	0.21	0.2	0.01	0.17	0.1	—	0.24	0.2	0.01	0.36	0.3	0.02	0.15	0.1
MgO	7.37	10.3	0.66	8.50	11.9	0.63	7.03	9.9	0.58	7.20	10.2	0.68	4.58	6.4
CaO	7.10	7.2	0.46	10.06	10.1	0.53	9.84	10.0	0.58	7.36	7.5	0.50	7.72	7.7
Na_2O	1.40	2.6	0.17	2.26	4.1	0.22	2.57	4.6	0.27	2.55	4.7	0.31	4.69	8.5
K_2O	5.42	6.5	0.42	1.11	1.3	0.07	0.60	0.7	0.04	1.04	1.3	0.09	0.90	1.1
P_2O_5	1.15	0.9	0.06	0.09	0.1	—	0.41	0.3	0.02	0.12	0.1	—	0.48	0.4
Loss on ignition	2.06	—	—	1.45	—	—	0.80	—	—	1.01	—	—	1.00	—
Σ	100.54	100.0	—	100.52	100.0	—	100.31	100.0	—	100.50	100.0	—	100.04	100.0

Specimen No.

TABLE 9 (continued)

	Specimen No.																
	160a	264	321	340	904b	94zh	149a	663	121	281	482	951a	94k	756d	1140b	1123a	55
Numerical characteristics (after Zavaritskii)																	
a	3.8	5.4	5.7	5.9	8.3	7.6	2.8	8.9	6.4	8.5	8.0	8.8	10.8	6.7	6.4	7.1	11.9
b	28.6	26.5	23.4	25.9	28.6	26.9	39.5	30.8	28.7	26.4	32.6	35.6	24.4	30.6	27.1	31.4	21.3
c	11.5	7.8	8.4	7.0	6.6	5.9	5.8	5.5	6.7	5.4	4.8	3.1	3.9	8.4	7.2	5.4	5.6
s	56.1	60.3	62.5	61.2	56.5	59.6	51.9	54.8	58.2	59.7	54.6	52.5	60.9	54.3	59.3	56.1	61.2
Q	−6.9	+2.0	+5.2	+3.6	−10.2	−1.9	−7.6	−13.7	−3.1	−3.0	−11.2	−15.7	−3.7	−13.2	−1.4	−7.4	−17.0
f'	40.6	31.4	44.4	45.2	53.9	40.6	32.2	44.7	41.0	53.8	33.4	22.6	30.0	23.2	38.0	50.6	44.6
m'	40.9	47.7	42.2	41.0	25.7	42.5	53.3	37.0	44.6	36.6	37.7	58.7	50.6	63.5	44.1	38.5	37.2
c'	18.5	20.9	13.4	13.8	20.4	16.9	14.5	18.3	14.4	9.6	28.9	18.7	19.4	13.3	17.9	10.9	18.2
Coordinates on the ACF diagram (after Eskola and Korzhinskii)																	
A	38.7	32.3	35.0	30.7	30.4	27.6	21.2	28.6	29.4	26.7	22.4	14.5	22.7	31.0	30.2	23.8	32.1
C	28.3	27.4	24.1	23.1	28.6	24.4	21.1	26.7	23.6	19.6	33.2	22.8	25.2	23.0	25.4	19.5	27.2
F	33.0	40.3	40.9	46.2	41.0	48.0	57.7	45.8	47.0	53.7	44.4	62.7	52.1	46.0	44.4	56.7	40.7
Norm (after Barth)																	
Albite	13.1	17.3	18.2	21.7	28.3	29.4	9.0	20.9	23.0	27.5	24.2	11.9	13.0	18.0	23.5	23.3	42.6
Anorthite	45.2	32.4	34.1	29.4	26.9	24.8	25.4	28.4	27.8	22.6	20.3	13.6	16.1	33.8	28.9	22.8	22.7
Orthoclase	1.7	5.0	5.1	2.9	5.2	2.5	3.4	7.0	3.7	8.0	6.3	22.4	32.4	6.8	3.5	6.6	5.6
Olivine	1.0	—	—	—	0.5	—	11.5	8.7	—	—	8.5	26.0	—	22.7	—	9.1	3.2
Orthopyroxene	17.3	21.3	25.2	25.7	13.0	22.8	26.7	11.5	25.0	27.6	31.4	17.9	21.5	—	24.0	21.8	9.5
Clinopyroxene	13.9	18.3	9.6	11.0	10.7	15.3	20.0	16.3	13.0	6.6	5.2	2.3	10.4	12.6	14.0	11.0	9.8
Magnetite	4.4	1.6	1.0	1.4	6.0	2.2	2.9	3.3	3.9	2.6	1.8	1.6	2.4	2.1	1.5	2.9	3.9
Ilmenite	2.3	0.9	1.0	3.0	6.0	2.4	1.1	3.1	1.7	3.8	0.3	2.1	1.5	2.4	2.8	2.2	1.6
Apatite	1.1	—	0.3	0.3	3.4	0.6	—	0.8	0.3	0.7	—	—	2.3	0.3	1.0	0.3	1.1
Quartz	—	3.2	5.5	4.4	—	—	—	—	1.6	0.6	—	—	0.4	—	0.8	—	—
Nepheline	—	—	—	—	—	—	—	—	—	—	2.0	2.2	—	1.3	—	—	—

Note. The mineral compositions of specimens are listed in Tables 5 and 6.

results in an increase in the potassium, sodium, titanium, ferric and ferrous iron oxide content, and a decrease in the magnesium and calcium oxides content. Where feldspathization is not accompanied by either amphibolization or biotitization, alterations in the chemical compositions of pyroxene and plagioclase are clearly discerned. Feldspathized specimens have a lower content of ferrous iron, magnesium, and calcium and higher content of potassium and ferric iron. A comparison of samples with similar Si : Al ratios also reveals a decrease in the sodium content in the feldspathized rocks. However, both the sodium and potassium contents are considerably higher in specimens retaining signs of intensive enderbitization in comparison to weakly enderbitized specimens. The content of other elements follows the same pattern as in feldspathization. A comparison between only biotitized and unaltered samples reveals that the biotitization is accompanied by an increase in potassium, and a small decrease in ferrous iron, calcium, and sodium contents. Rocks which underwent more than one alteration process present considerably more complicated patterns.

It is evident, however, that enderbitization, amphibolization, biotitization, and feldspathization (charnockitization) all result in similar changes in the calcium and potassium contents of the rocks. Enderbitization and feldspathization also have the same effect on the ferrous iron, ferric iron and magnesium contents; however, they exert opposing effects on the sodium content. Biotitization and feldspathization have the same effect on the contents of ferrous iron and sodium. Thus, combinations of these alteration processes control the degree and trend of chemical alterations in a rock, a fact borne out by a comparison of the more and less altered schists.

Although the degree of alteration depends on the alkalinity of ultrametagenic solutions and the permeability of strata during ultrametamorphism, it is also, to a certain extent, controlled by the content of certain low-mobility elements in the rock (e. g., silicon, titanium, and aluminum) /32/. The metamorphic minerals formed by the reaction of alkalic solutions with the rocks are aluminosilicates; consequently, the quantity and quality of the alkalis precipitated from the solution depends on the Si : Al ratio in the rock. Therefore, in any group of rocks with different silica saturations, comparisons are best made between rocks with similar Si : Al ratios.

Even in a single outcrop in ultrametamorphic terrain, closely bedded schists exhibit different degrees of alteration. Although certain of these contain larger or smaller amounts of silica and aluminum, this does not necessarily indicate that some layers were silicified during granitization while others were not. The silica content in a rock is probably controlled by its initial silica content; the appearance of free quartz in the rock can only be due to the formation of biotite during granitization (the biotite is low in silica compared to the hypersthene which it replaces). The fact that the strongly feldspathized rocks are also the most highly silicified rocks, is not due, in the authors' opinion, to a simultaneous influx of silica and alkalis into the rock; it is due to the fact that, other conditions being equal, acid rocks are more rapidly and intensively feldspathized.

Thus, the chemical composition of pyroxene-plagioclase schists reflects the chemical properties of the original rock (which is mainly controlled by the Si : Al ratio), the nature of alkalinity of the ultrametamorphic solutions (controlled by the ratio of alkalis), and the nature of the mineralogical alterations during ultrametamorphism (controlled by the ratio of the alkali content to that of Fe, Mg, and Ca). In turn, the nature of mineralogical alterations is controlled by the activity of alkalis and water as well as by the original composition of rocks.

Garnetiferous varieties of pyroxene-plagioclase schists are characterized by an association of clinopyroxene and plagioclase with garnet. Nearly all samples of these rocks contain amphibole and ore minerals. More than half of the investigated specimens contain hypersthene and biotite. Apatite is present as an accessory mineral. The schists often contain quartz, in some cases up to 50–60%. The quartz-rich varieties also contain orthoclase.

These specific rocks are confined to certain zones. Quartz-free varieties occur in the southeastern part of the Rayner zone on Enderby Land, in the Øygarden Islands, and in the central part of Queen Maud Land; they were very rarely encountered in the Bunger Oasis and are equally uncommon in other areas of Enderby Land. Associated rocks are granulites. These garnetiferous schists form fairly thick (up to 70 m) units in isolated outcrops, or occur as intercalations, lenses, and boudins, as well as fully or partially transecting dikes in granulitic strata. Apparently, formation of the garnet + clinopyroxene + plagioclase in Ca-Mg rocks was accompanied by granulitization of the enclosing series.

In hand specimen, the garnet-pyroxene-plagioclase schists are gray to dark gray in color, fine grained and massive to banded. The most coarse-grained varieties are also the most melanocratic. A coarse grain size is especially characteristic of rocks with high hypersthene contents. The following varieties may be differentiated according to their mineral composition: garnet-clinopyroxene-plagioclase schist, garnet-bipyroxene-plagioclase schist, garnet-clinopyroxene schist and garnet-bipyroxene schist (the latter two varieties contain plagioclase, though in insignificant amounts).

The mineral composition of the garnet-clinopyroxene-plagioclase schists is given in Table 10. Their texture is typically granoblastic. Intergrowths of colored minerals are uniformly distributed throughout the rock. The garnet, clinopyroxene, and plagioclase grains are all roughly equidimensional with irregular crystal boundaries. The clinopyroxene and plagioclase are replaced by garnet-containing clinopyroxene relicts. This relationship between plagioclase and garnet is reversed in weakly feldspathized varieties, i. e., the plagioclase forms rims around the garnet. Amphibole and magnetite are secondary in origin, developing along crystal boundaries and in cracks in the clinopyroxene. Granitized varieties also contain intergranular quartz and orthoclase, both of which corrode the plagioclase. Biotite develops on magnetite and partially replaces garnet.

Plagioclase has wavy block extinction, kinked twin planes and contains sparse (up to 5%) laminated and maculose antiperthite ingrowths, apparently the result of feldspathization. The plagioclase varies from An 36 to 57. The nonfeldspathized specimens contain two types of plagioclase grains: larger grains of andesine (An 38—40) and finer grains with An 47—50.

The ferruginosity of clinopyroxene is 29—49 at.%. The iron-rich varieties are slightly pleochroic. The ferruginosity of garnet is 67—80 at.%. It displays anomalous birefringence along its margins. The hornblende has an iron content of 45—63 at.% and is brown-green in color. These mafic minerals have interdependent ferruginosities, emphasizing the dependence of the mineral composition on that of the rock. Accessory minerals include biotite, apatite, sphene and orthite.

The principal feature of the mineral composition of the garnet-bipyroxene-plagioclase schists (Table 10) is the direct relationship between the hypersthene and plagioclase contents on the one hand, and the clinopyroxene and garnet contents on the other. The lower the hypersthene and plagioclase contents, the higher the contents of garnet and clinopyroxene. The granoblastic texture of the rocks is complicated by reactive interrelations between minerals and the partial blastocataclasis (Figures 5 and 6). The average grain size of garnet, pyroxene, and plagioclase is 0.3— 0.8 mm. In leucocratic blastocataclastic varieties, some plagioclase grains appear as metablasts and are surrounded by smaller grains. The pyroxene and plagioclase grains are anhedral while the garnet grains are nearly euhedral. The clinopyroxene is surrounded by rims of hypersthene (monograins), while garnet is surrounded by rims of symplekite (hypersthene and plagioclase) or by plagioclase. In general, plagioclase corrodes both clinopyroxene and garnet, while magnetite is developed on all the mafic minerals in the rock. In the amphibolized varieties, both pyroxenes are replaced by metablastic amphibole.

Plagioclase is generally represented by andesine (An 30 − 45) and rarely by labradorite (An 51). It is maculose, exhibits reverse zoning (only a small variation in An content − 5%) and has a wavy and block extinction. Clinopyroxene has wavy and block extinction, and occasionally exhibits polysynthetic twinning. Its ferruginosity varies from 32 to 48 at.%. Hypersthene is slightly pleochroic; its ferruginosity is 42—59 at.%. The ferruginosity of the brown-green hornblende is 50—73 at.%. It is similar to hastingsite with regard to the alkali, alumina, and titanium contents, and to the crystal coordination. As in hastingsite, Al replaces Si. An outstanding feature of the hornblende is the high potassium content (isomorphous with sodium and calcium). Such hornblendes are usually classified in the granulite facies /43/. The ferruginosities of clinopyroxene, hypersthene, and amphibole vary in a similar manner. The least ferruginous varieties of these minerals occur together with the most basic plagioclase. The garnet ferruginosity also follows a similar pattern, although to a lesser extent (varying within 66—79 at.%). The ferruginosity of the rarely encountered biotite is 47—49 at.%. The most ferruginous colored minerals occur in rocks with the highest magnetite contents. The ferruginosity of colored minerals apparently depends on the composition of the rock.

TABLE 10. Mineral composition and characteristics of the garnet-pyroxene-plagioclase schists

Specimen No.	qz	plag	Kfs	hyp	clpy	amph	gar	biot	apat	orem	other accessory minerals	An content center	An content margin	hypersthene n_z	hypersthene n_x	hypersthene $-2V°$	hypersthene f at. %	clinopyroxene n_z	clinopyroxene n_x
58	o.s.*	68	o.s.	—	25	o.s.	5	—	o.s.	2	sphene	36	34	—	—	—	—	1.727	1.700
58a	—	53	—	—	33	1	8	o.s.	1	4	sphene, orthite	47	38	—	—	—	—	1.727	1.700
41b	—	30	—	5	48	o.s.	15	—	o.s.	2	—	45	42	1.719	1.704	51	42	1.716	1.690
42	—	29	—	5	33	18	12	—	٭	3	zircon	48	43	1.728	1.714	57	52	1.724	1.697
41v	—	45	—	5	25	7	13	—	٭	5	—	33	30	1.733	1.718	55	56	1.727	1.700
41d	—	10	—	o.s.	35	5	45	—	٭	5	—	38	33	—	—	—	—	1.725	1.698
58d	—	25	—	5	25	5	30	o.s.	٭	10	—	32	30	1.732–1.736	1.716–1.719	—	55, 58	1.727	1.700
41e	—	4	—	47	15	+	23	11	—	o.s.	—	47	46	1.710	1.695	58	32	1.710	1.684
640v	—	52	—	15	o.s.	17	16	o.s.	o.s.	٭	—	80	58	1.722	1.707	54	46	—	—
304	20	36	15	—	٭	10	15	12	—	—	zircon	45	37	1.733	1.717	55	56	1.722	1.698
58b	56	4	15	3	6	6	7	2	—	1	—	27	26	—	—	—	—	1.728	1.701
41	73	5	10	—	2	4	3	o.s.	o.s.	3	—	30	30	—	—	—	—	1.724	1.697

Enderby Land

* [o.s. = optic sign.]

TABLE 10 (continued)

Specimen No.	Characteristics of the minerals									Geological setting
	clinopyroxene		amphibole				garnet		biotite	
	$+2\,V°$	f at.%	n_z	n_x	$-2\,V°$	f at.%	n	f at.%	n_z	f at.%	

Enderby Land

Specimen No.	$+2\,V°$	f at.%	n_z	n_x	$-2\,V°$	f at.%	n	f at.%	n_z	f at.%	Geological setting
58	57—58	49	1.709	1.684	82	63	1.798	80*	—	—	Interbedded with the rocks represented by specimen 58a
58a	56—58	49	—	—	—	—	1.798	79	—	—	As above, specimen 58
41b	33—55	32	—	—	—	—	1.789—1.790	68*	—	—	An 8.0 m intercalation in rocks represented by specimen 41v
42	53—55	44	1.710	1.685	82—83	64	1.790	70*	—	—	70-m thick unit
41v	52	48	1.719	1.692	79—80	73	1.797—1.799	78—79	—	—	40-m thick unit
41d	53	46	1.718	1.690	87	72	1.796	78*	—	—	Boudin in the rock represented by specimen 41v
58d	—	49	1.710	1.685	—	64	1.797—1.798	78—79	1.655	49	Discordant metabasite dike
41e	55	24	—	—	—	—	1.775	62	1.650—1.655	43	Lens in the rock represented by specimen 41 (0.3 × 1.0 m²)
640 v	—	—	1.695	1.670	74	50	—	—	—	—	Intercalations (0.2 m) in Pyroxene-plagioclase schists
304	55	40	1.704	1.680	61	60	1.791	74	1.677	54	Represents the outcrop
58b	55	51	1.701	1.675	—	56	—	—	1.667	50	Thin intercalations in granulites
41	56—58	45	1.700	1.675	80	55	1.797	78	—	—	70-m thick unit

TABLE 10 (continued)

Specimen No.	Mineral composition											An content of plagioclase		hypersthene				clinopyroxene	
	qz	plag	Kfs	hyp	clpy	amph	gar	biot	apat	orem	other accesory minerals	margin	center	n_z	n_x	$-2V°$	f at. %	n_z	n_x
Bunger Oasis																			
139a	2	58	—	18	7	7	1	3	—	4	—	—	40	1.730	1.714	—	54	1.714	1.689
243	23	25	30	1	8	3	1	5	—	4	—	—	36	—	—	—	—		
Queen Maud Land																			
879	—	25	—	—	30	15	25	—	—	5	—	—	57	—	—	—	—	1.718	1.691
867	—	35	—	8	12	22	10	5	—	8	—	—	43	1.730	1.714	—	54	1.723	1.698
830	5	30	—	15	10	15	15	—	—	10	—	—	36	1.719	1.702	—	42	1.720	1.696
843b	5	35	—	—	2	23	10	15	—	3	—	—	39	—	—	—	—	—	1.691
856b	8	40	—	6	17	20	10	—	—	6	—	—	51	1.724	1.709	—	48	1.717	1.688
817a	8	30	—	—	13	—	40	3	—	2	—	—	40	—	—	—	—	1.714	1.690
816	10	25	—	5	10	35	15	10	—	3	—	—	40	—	—	—	—	1.714	—
866	10	49	—	—	3	3	10	11	—	3	—	—	34	1.738	1.720	—	59	—	1.696
814d	15	16	—	8	12	20	25	1	—	10	—	—	40	1.728	1.713	—	52	1.720	1.696
794d	21	35	3	10	5	10	10	1	—	3	—	—	30	1.721	1.704	—	44	1.720	1.701
830b	2	35	3	10	10	23	12	7	—	9	—	—	35	1.736	1.720	—	58	1.725	1.697
864v	8	37	5	15	10	5	5	7	—	10	—	—	46	—	—	—	—	1.722	1.702
843k	10	25	10	—	10	30	10	2	—	3	—	—	40	—	—	—	—	1.728	—
798	15	37	5	—	8	10	15	3	—	3	—	—	34	—	—	—	—	1.730	1.702
863b	20	35	5	10	15	2	5		—	5	—	—	35	1.746	1.728	—	64		

TABLE 10 (continued)

Speci-men No.	clinopyroxene		amphibole				garnet		biotite		Geological setting
	$+2\,V°$	f at.%	n_z	n_x	$-2\,V°$	f at.%	n	f at. %	n_z	f at.%	
Bunger Oasis											
139a	—	—	—	—	—	—	—	—	—	—	
243	—	29	—	—	—	—	—	—	—	—	
Queen Maud Land											
879	—	34	1.691	1.666	—	46	1.782	67	1.662	48	
867	—	42	1.698	1.672	—	53	—	—	—	—	
830	—	37	1.697	1.672	—	52	1.786	70	—	—	
843b	—	—	1.698	1.674	—	53	1.797	78	—	—	
856b	—	33	1.695	1.669	—	50	1.780	66	—	—	
817a	—	29	—	—	—	—	—	—	—	—	
816	—	29	1.690	1.667	—	45	—	—	1.665	49	
866	—	—	—	—	—	—	1.798	79	1.665	49	
814d	—	37	1.700	1.674	—	55	1.787	71	1.666	50	
794d	—	37	1.697	1.672	—	52	1.790	73	—	—	
830v	—	46	1.702	1.677	—	57	1.786	70	—	—	
864b	—	40	1.702	1.680	—	57	1.795	76	1.660	47	
843k	—	—	1.700	1.675	—	55	1.798	79	1.675	53	
798	—	51	1.708	1.686	—	62	1.8 5	84	—	—	
863b	—	52	1.708	1.687	—	62	1.795	76	1.685	58	

Note. The ferruginosity of garnets (here and later in text) was determined from E. N. Kamenev's diagram (Figure 23).

FIGURE 5. Garnet-bipyroxene-plagioclase schist of granoblastic texture (× 12, regular light — thin section 58d).

FIGURE 6. Leucocratic garnet-bipyroxene-plagioclase schist with blastocataclastic texture (× 10, regular light — thin section 61).

Metagabbroids which developed from dikes are similar to the garnet-bipyroxene-plagioclase schists with regard to composition, texture, and minerals, although they contain more garnet due to a somewhat lower content of plagioclase and clinopyroxene, and the magnetite content is higher (10%). The ferruginosity of colored minerals is high in relation to the relatively low An content of the plagioclase (Table 10, specimen 58d). The hornblende has a somewhat lower ferruginosity than it has in the schists (64 at.%), possibly due to its replacement by biotite. The ferruginosity of the latter in the metabasite is 48 at.%. The manifestation of blastocataclasis is somewhat more intense in the metagabbroids, evidently due to their greater rigidity during differential movements.

The garnet-pyroxene schist is close to eclogite in composition (specimen 41d). The texture of these rocks is granoblastic, almost mosaic, with polygonal grains of clinopyroxene and garnet surrounded by rims of hypersthene-plagioclase symplektite and replaced by amphibole. The plagioclase (An 33—34) is intergranular, with a reverse zoning and antiperthite ingrowths. The ferruginosity of colored minerals is high. According to spectroscopic analysis of the silicates, clinopyroxene and garnet are generally similar in composition to the minerals from the garnet-clinopyroxene-plagioclase schists, but differ somewhat from the latter in their lower contents of the jadeite, grossular, and spessartite components. The hornblende is very high in alkalis and contains more titanium and aluminum than the amphibole from the garnet-bipyroxene-plagioclase schists.

Garnet-bipyroxene schist (specimen 41e) is distinguished by the high An content in the plagioclase (46—47) and the low ferruginosity of the colored minerals. Its texture is very coarse grained and poikiloporphyroblastic. The hypersthene metablasts replacing garnets and especially clinopyroxene include relics of the minerals they replace. The garnet is rimmed by plagioclase and hypersthene-plagioclase symplektite. The rock contains scattered grains of brown amphibole. The pyroxene is also replaced by biotite with an iron content of 43 at.%.

Three available analyses of garnetiferous quartz-free rocks having a clinopyroxene + garnet + hypersthene association (from Enderby Land — Table 11) are not significantly different from the data for the pyroxene-plagioclase schists. When comparing rocks having similar Si : Al ratios, from both types, the only difference is a somewhat higher calcium and iron content in the pyroxene-plagioclase schists. The mineral compositions of the rocks with identical Si : Al ratios are as follows: 1) amphibole-free, garnet-clinopyroxene-plagioclase schists and amphibolized-biotitized pyroxene-plagioclase schists; 2) garnet-clinopyroxene schists and pyroxene-plagioclase schists. These differences in mineral compositions between garnetiferous pyroxene-plagioclase schists and pyroxene-plagioclase schists of similar chemical composition, is indicative of different metamorphic conditions. This case provides a clear example of Eskola's facies principle, i.e., a given facies comprises all the rocks that have originated under temperature and pressure conditions so similar that a definite chemical composition has resulted in the same set of minerals, quite regardless of the mode of crystallization /68/.

TABLE 11. Chemical composition of garnet-pyroxene and garnet-pyroxene-plagioclase schists from Enderby Land

Component	Specimen No.								
	58			41b			41a		
	wt%	at.%	$\frac{R}{Al}$	wt%	at.%	$\frac{R}{Al}$	wt%	at.%	$\frac{R}{Al}$
SiO_2	53.15	49.6	2.57	52.15	49.1	3.23	42.29	41.6	2.87
TiO_2	0.79	0.6	0.03	0.61	0.4	0.03	2.77	2.1	0.14
Al_2O_3	17.53	19.3	1.00	13.82	15.2	1.00	12.45	14.5	1.00
Fe_2O_3	2.14	1.5	0.08	1.30	0.9	0.06	3.65	2.7	0,19
FeO	6.61	5.2	0.27	9.88	7.8	0.51	18.59	15.3	1.05
MnO	0.23	0.2	—	0.23	0.2	—	0.36	0.3	—
MgO	3.42	4.8	0.25	7.50	10.5	0.69	6.53	9.6	0.66
CaO	10.86	10.9	0.56	11.43	11.5	0.76	11.37	11.9	0.82
Na_2O	3.88	7.0	0.36	2.22	4.0	0.26	0.57	1.1	0.08
K_2O	0.66	0.7	0.04	0.32	0.3	0.02	0.39	0.5	0.03
P_2O_5	0.30	0.2	—	0.09	0.1	—	0.46	0.4	—
Loss on ignition	0.57	—	—	0.50	—	—	0.84	—	—
Σ	100.14	100.0	—	100.05	100.0	—	100.27	100.0	—

Component	Specimen No.		
	58	41b	41a
Numerical characteristics (after Zavaritskii)			
a	9.6	5.0	1.8
b	20.7	30.0	39.5
c	7.3	6.5	7.3
s	62.4	58.5	51.4
Q	−1.7	+0.5	−8.1
f'	41.1	34.9	54.5
m'	28.6	41.3	17.1
c'	30.3	23.8	28.4
Coordinates of ACF diagram (after Eskola and Korzhinskii)			
A	35.6	26.8	25.8
C	33.4	28.2	23.8
F	31.0	45.0	50.4
Norm, % (after Barth)			
Albite	35.1	19.8	5.3
Anorthite	29.1	27.3	32.3
Orthoclase	3.6	1.7	2.4
Olivine	—	—	7.8
Orthopyroxene	8.1	23.4	23.3
Clinopyroxene	18.8	23.4	19.7
Magnetite	2.3	1.4	4.1
Ilmenite	1.1	0.9	4.1
Apatite	0.6	0.3	1.0
Quartz	1.3	1.8	—

Note. Modal compositions of analyzed rocks are given in Table 10.

Migmatites from pyroxene-plagioclase schists and their varieties transitional to enderbite

Migmatites from Ca-Mg schists occur in the Bunger Oasis and on Queen Maud Land. They are less common on Enderby Land, occurring mainly in the Rayner metamorphic zone.

The following morphological varieties of the migmatites can be distinguished according to the distribution of the paleosome: 1) coarsely layered migmatites, with paleosome layers of constant thickness (varying from 10 cm to 2 m); 2) finely layered migmatites, with paleosome layers varying in thickness (1—6 cm); 3) "maculose" lenticular migmatites, in which the paleosome occurs as lenticular blocks, with the veins penetrating in intricate patterns. The outlines of these blocks are often indistinct; 4) agmatites, in which irregularly shaped paleosome blocks, ranging from a few decimeters to several meters in diameter, are separated from one another by veined material; 5) ptygmatites /57/. All these varieties of migmatites may make up a single outcrop. In most varieties (with the exception of ptygmatite), the relative amounts of vein material (metasome) and paleosome are nearly equal; however, matrix material tends to predominate (60—70%).

In mineral composition and nature of minerals (Table 12), the matrix paleosome differs little from the corresponding varieties of pyroxene-plagioclase schists, the latter being somewhat more melanocratic. The paleosome plagioclase is generally andesine and rarely labradorite. The paleosome has undergone low-grade granitization, which is reflected in its recrystallization, in some alteration in the composition of the major minerals, in the development of reactive relationships between minerals, and lastly, in the sporadic appearance of small amounts of new-formed quartz, biotite, amphibole, and orthoclase. The various metamorphic alterations in the paleosome are thus not dealt with in any detail, and the following discussion is largely concerned with the characteristics of the vein material.

The vein material (metasome) of these migmatites may be divided into the following two types: 1) essentially plagioclase and 2) essentially orthoclase; the former is much less common than the latter. The plagioclase-rich vein material is close to enderbite in its composition and is characteristic only of the coarsely layered migmatites. The orthoclase-rich vein material occurs in the majority of migmatites. Its composition is close to that of shadow charnockites or leucogranites.

Enderbite vein material is especially common in the Enderby Land migmatites. It also occurs in migmatites of the Bunger Oasis, but is nearly absent from those in Queen Maud Land. This vein material differs little from the corresponding enderbite, belonging to the leucocratic variety, often containing only scattered grains of hypersthene.

The charnockitic vein material is predominant in Bunger Oasis migmatites and is common in the Rayner zone of Enderby Land, but is rare in other regions of Antarctica. It is generally fine-grained and less commonly medium-grained. Xenoblastic mineral forms are predominant, because of the intensive processes of replacement and corrosion. The charnockite vein material consists of orthoclase (35—60%), plagioclase An 30 (10—25%), quartz (25—40%), biotite (2—10%), orthopyroxene relicts (0—4%), and sporadic garnet (0—10%). The most euhedral forms are plagioclase lathes reaching the size of 3—5 mm, but smaller (1 mm) plagioclase grains have been preserved as relicts within larger segregations of orthoclase. The plagioclase lathes are riddled with antiperthite ingrowths together with irregular metasomatic inclusions of orthoclase. The plagioclase crystal boundaries are strongly corroded by quartz, and relict grains often develop myrmekite rims at thier contact with orthoclase. Wavy extinction and bending of twin planes are common.

K-feldspar segregations do not form crystalloblasts, although large segregations resemble porphyroblasts. It ranges in grain size from small xenoblastic grains (0.5—1 mm) to irregular segregations (up to 5—6 mm). The latter may penetrate and replace plagioclase laths; microperthite ingrowths are common. Microcline crosshatching occurs only in the largest segregations, but even there it is uncommon. The more common microperthites, in which numerous optic angle measurements $(\perp(001)n_y)$ indicate different values even within a single thin section (from 5 to 9° with $2V$ ranging from −50° to −60°), most likely correspond to orthoclase with an admixture of sodium. Cataclastic quartz is irregular, sinuous, lenticular, or even vein-like, and varies in size from 1 to 5 mm. These quartz segregations are so strongly shattered that they locally form aggregates of mosaic granules (0.2—0.3 mm). Quartz penetrates along cracks in all other minerals and is universally present as poikiloblastic inclusions.

The vein material of migmatites from the pyroxene-plagioclase schists of Queen Maud Land has a fairly uniform mineral composition, close to that of shadow biotite and less commonly to amphibole-biotite granites, with a distinct gneissic texture. Granites proper predominate, although plagiogranites or alaskites occur in places. The vein material is mainly granoblastic, with porphyroblastic and poikiloblastic elements of typical corrosion-metasomatic character. This uniform composition indicates the deviation of the vein material from a single source: selective fusion, close to the quartz-feldspar eutectic. The vein material contains varying amounts of colored minerals (2—15%), depending on the migmatitic grade. Thus, the migmatites with a large metasome content contain a relatively smaller amount of colored minerals. The most widespread vein material consists of 30—35% plagioclase, 30—40% orthoclase, 25—30% quartz, 10% biotite, and 0—8% amphibole. The metasome from granulite and amphibolite facies migmatites of Queen Maud Land is of a fairly constant mineral composition. This, together with the nature of the mineral composition, suggests an overall amphibolite facies origin of the metasome in the migmatites of Queen Maud Land.

The plagioclase in the vein material has a consistent anorthite content: acid andesine. Elongated, prismatic laths predominate, but stubby laths 0.2—2 mm in diameter with irregular boundaries and indistinct polysynthetic

twins also occur. Recrystallization produced larger porphyroblastic, untwinned plagioclase lathes up to 5—6 mm. These porphyroblasts contain
an abundance of antiperthite ingrowths and poikiloblastic quartz. A weak
maculose sericitization of plagioclase is found throughout the rock.
Corrosion of the plagioclase by orthoclase produces myrmekite zones in
some cases and albite rims in others, mainly at plagioclase porphyroblast
and K-feldspar contacts. The K-feldspar generally shows microcline crossed
twinning. The microcline forms irregular grains 0.3—1 mm in size, which
are often concentrated in lenticular and vein-like aggregates cross-cutting
other minerals. Its individual grains are interstitial to plagioclase laths.
Larger porphyroblastic K-feldspar also occurs. The microcline may
contain inclusions of relict sericitized plagioclase laths; microperthitic
ingrowths are rare. The shape and size of quartz grains is similar to
that of microcline grains. Large quartz grains, up to 3—4 mm, are
apparently porphyroblastic. They contain profuse inclusions of all other
minerals in the rock, and especially plagioclase. In places, quartz forms
lenticular segregations oriented parallel to the gneissosity, resulting in a
granulite texture. Unlike the microcline, minute poikilitic quartz grains
incorporated in other minerals appear to have been formed as excess
components during recrystallization. The quartz grains are unaltered, but
exhibit wavy extinction throughout. Biotite forms thin platelets, aligned
parallel to the gneissosity, and aggregates of small flakes. It differs little
from paleosome biotite, although its ferruginosity is often higher. The same
applies to the amphibole which occurs as irregular grains clustered in
aggregates together with the biotite.

The vein material of migmatites from pyroxene-plagioclase schists has
the following genetic characteristics: 1) metablastic textures, due to
the metasomatic recrystallization; 2) it is similar to certain near-leucocratic
granites, i. e., hypersthene-bearing metasome in migmatites from the
Bunger Oasis and Enderby Land and biotite-bearing metasome in migmatites from Queen Maud Land; 3) widespread replacement of plagioclase
by K-feldspar resulting in alaskitic granite; 4) constant composition of
plagioclase irrespective of the composition of the coexisting K-feldspar.
This indicates a stable potassium and sodium content in the partial melt,
closely approaching the content of these elements in the granite magma.

These features suggest that the metasome crystallized from a partial
melt under conditions of alkaline metasomatism in the paleosome.

Certain characteristics in the composition of the metasome suggest
different metamorphic levels in its formation. Thus, the Enderby Land
migmatites are typical of deep levels of the granulite facies, the Bunger
Oasis migmatites were apparently formed under conditions transitional
between the granulite and amphibolite facies, while crystallization from
the metasome partial melt on Queen Maud Land occurred under amphibolite
facies conditions. A comparison of the mineral compositions in the vein
material and paleosome of the migmatites (Table 12) generally reveals a
more sodic plagioclase and a higher ferruginosity of colored minerals in
vein material, which is in accordance with its higher alkalinity.

The available data on the chemical composition of the paleosome and
the vein material permit a comparison of their chemical properties

TABLE 12. Mineral composition and characteristics of migmatites derived from pyroxene-plagioclase schists in Antarctica

Speci-men No.	qz	plag	Kfs	hyp	clpy	amph	biot	orem	An content of plagioclase	hypersthene n_z	hypersthene n_x	hypersthene f at.%	clinopyroxene n_z	clinopyroxene n_x	clinopyroxene f at.%	amphibole n_z	amphibole n_x	amphibole f at.%	garnet n	garnet f at.%	biotite n_z	biotite f at.%	Note
													Bunger Oasis										
21	—	45	—	18	7	20	3	7	53	1.717	1.702	40	—	—	—	—	—	—	—	—	—	—	Paleosome
21a	17	38	42	1	—	—	1	1	28	—	—	—	—	—	—	—	—	—	—	—	—	—	Vein material (Metasome)
86a	4	55	—	30	—	—	8	3	47	1.720	1.705	43	—	—	—	—	—	—	—	—	1.635	35	Paleosome
86	35	25	35	—	—	—	3	2	30	—	—	—	—	—	—	—	—	—	—	—	—	—	Vein material (Metasome)
383b	1	57	6	3	10	1	20	2	33	—	—	—	1.718	1.690	34	—	—	—	—	—	1.632	34	Paleosome
383a	23	70	—	4	—	—	2	1	—	—	—	—	—	—	—	—	—	—	—	—	—	—	Vein material (Metasome)
129	—	56	—	14	26	—	—	4	33	1.717	1.703	40	1.721	1.695	38	—	—	—	—	—	—	—	Paleosome
129a	27	68	—	4	—	—	—	1	33	1.721	1.706	44	—	—	—	—	—	—	—	—	—	—	Vein material (Metasome)
198	—	58	—	6	26	—	8	2	32	1.720	1.707	43	1.722	1.695	40	—	—	—	—	—	1.632	34	Paleosome
198a	27	25	44	2	—	—	1	1	32	1.724	1.707	48	—	—	—	—	—	—	—	—	—	—	Vein material (Metasome)
													Enderby Land										
488	4	53	—	41	—	—	o.s.	2	46	1.727	1.711	51	—	—	—	—	—	—	—	—	—	—	Paleosome
488	33	64	—	6	—	—	—	1	46	1.727	1.711	51	—	—	—	—	—	—	—	—	—	—	Vein material (Metasome)
238	—	54	o.s.*	5	30	4	—	7	38—49	1.724	1.709	48	1.721	1.695	38	1.707	1.682	60	—	—	—	—	Paleosome
238a	35	64	—	o.s.	—	—	1	+	36—37	1.718	1.704	41	—	—	—	—	—	—	—	—	1.657	47	Vein material (Metasome)
238v	35	65	—	•	—	—	—	+	32—33	—	—	—	—	—	—	—	—	—	—	—	—	—	As above
													Queen Maud Land										
829	8	45	—	5	15	15	10	2	33	—	—	—	—	—	—	1.687	1.665	42	—	—	1.658	45	Paleosome
829v	40	19	39	—	—	1	1	1	27	—	—	—	—	—	—	1.703	1.681	58	—	—	—	—	Vein material (Metasome)
721	25	47	—	—	12	—	16	—	33	—	—	—	1.722	1.697	40	—	—	—	—	—	1.665	49	Paleosome
721a	30	28	40	—	—	—	1	1	25	—	—	—	—	—	—	—	—	—	—	—	—	—	Vein material (Metasome)

* [o.s. = optic sign.]

with those of the corresponding nonmigmatized schists and shadow granitoids (Table 13). The chemical composition of the paleosome is similar to
the pyroxene-plagioclase schists occurring outside the migmatite fields.
On the other hand, the paleosome does not contain any unaltered schists;
they are all enderbitized, amphibolized or biotitized and feldspathized to
varying degrees. The nature of the alteration in the paleosome is dependent
on the composition of the vein material. Where the vein material is normal
granite, the paleosome is biotitized. In a few cases, biotite also appears in
the paleosome where enderbite is the metasome; however, in such cases,
biotite is also found in the metasome. This post-migmatite biotitization is
apparently related to potassium metasomatism following the formation of
migmatites.

The metasome in various migmatites hardly differs from the corresponding shadow granites. Nevertheless, some of its distinctive features should
be mentioned. Enderbite vein material belongs to enderbites that are the
highest in silica and lowest in alumina, and therefore with the highest
Si : Al ratio. The contents of other components vary fairly widely. However, there is a trend toward a reduction in the amount of mafic minerals.
Similar conclusions can also be drawn from a comparison of the enderbites
and enderbitic metasome from the Bunger Oasis. The metasome has a
higher content of alkalis, especially potassium, which places it closer to
charnockites. However, in contrast to charnockite, the granitic metasome
has a low Si : Al ratio. Furthermore, it has a much higher sodium content
(nearly double) and a somewhat lower potassium content than shadow
charnockites, although its total alkali content is high. Where the iron
content of the metasome is close to that of leucocratic charnockites, its
calcium content corresponds to that of melanocratic charnockites. Thus
the metasome of enderbitic composition formed closer to the granite
eutectic than did the enderbite. In contrast, the charnockite metasome
differs from shadow charnockites in that it formed at higher temperatures
than the granite eutectic. This may indirectly indicate that the migmatites
with an enderbitic metasome (vein material) were formed after the development of shadow enderbites, while the migmatites with a charnockitic
metasome formed prior to the development of shadow charnockites. This
conforms with the common zoning of migmatite fields /57/ in which migmatites with a charnockitic metasome and shadow charnockites are widespread (e. g., Bunger Oasis migmatites).

The chemical composition of the metasome of Queen Maud Land migmatites is close to that of charnockite (Table 13) but differs from the
shadow charnockites in its higher Si : Al ratio. It was thus apparently
formed after the shadow charnockites. In Queen Maud Land, the relationships between these rocks are more distinct than those in the "enderbite"
region; the mineral composition of Queen Maud Land shadow charnockite
and migmatite metasomes reflects their formation under different physicochemical conditions.

A comparison of migmatite paleosome and metasome reveals the
following variations in their compositions (for all types of migmatite):
the metasome contains more silica and potassium and less iron, magnesium

TABLE 13. Chemical composition of the matrix and vein material of migmatites derived from pyroxene-plagioclase schists

Specimen No.

Component	21 (paleosome)			21a (metasome)			383v (paleosome)			383a (metasome)			129 (paleosome)			129a (metasome)		
	wt%	at.%	$\frac{R}{Al}$	wt%	at.%	$\frac{R}{Al}$	wt%	at.%	$\frac{R}{Al}$	wt%	at.%	$\frac{R}{Al}$	wt%	at.%	$\frac{R}{Al}$	wt%	at.%	$\frac{R}{Al}$
SiO_2	45.11	42.5	2.48	65.60	60.3	3.12	48.83	45.7	2.61	70.11	66.1	4.21	50.48	47.8	3.21	69.29	64.9	3.80
TiO_2	1.28	0.9	0.05	0.32	0.2	0.01	1.23	0.8	0.05	0.57	0.4	0.03	2.11	1.5	0.10	0.42	0.3	0.02
Al_2O_3	15.39	17.1	1.00	17.77	19.3	1.00	15.83	17.5	1.00	14.13	15.7	1.00	13.40	14.9	1.00	15.56	17.1	1.00
Fe_2O_3	7.44	5.3	0.31	0.95	0.7	0.04	5.32	3.7	0.21	0.86	0.6	0.04	5.04	3.6	0.24	0.99	0.7	0.04
FeO	7.32	5.8	0.34	1.57	1.2	0.06	5.31	4.2	0.24	2.96	2.3	0.15	10.53	8.4	0.56	2.47	1.9	0.11
MnO	0.26	0.2	0.01	0.06	—	—	0.11	—	—	0.06	—	—	0.24	0.2	0.01	0.09	—	—
MgO	7.43	10.4	0.61	1.01	1.4	0.07	6.40	8.9	0.51	1.47	2.0	0.13	5.96	8.4	0.56	1.44	2.0	0.12
CaO	11.69	11.8	0.69	4.05	4.0	0.21	7.36	7.4	0.42	0.95	1.0	0.06	7.84	8.0	0.54	3.33	3.3	0.19
Na_2O	2.50	4.5	0.26	4.40	7.8	0.40	2.61	4.7	0.27	2.85	5.2	0.33	3.41	6.3	0.42	4.38	7.9	0.46
K_2O	1.01	1.2	0.07	4.22	5.0	0.26	5.25	6.2	0.35	5.57	6.6	0.42	0.60	0.7	0.05	1.60	1.9	0.11
P_2O_5	0.40	0.3	0.02	0.08	0.1	—	1.08	0.9	0.05	0.09	0.1	—	0.24	0.2	0.01	0.03	—	—
Loss on ignition	0.72	—	—	0.33	—	—	0.43	—	—	0.22	—	—	0.52	—	—	0.68	—	—
Σ	100.55	100.0	—	100.36	100.0	—	99.76	100.0	—	99.84	100.0	—	100.37	100.0	—	100.28	100.0	—

TABLE 13 (continued)

Specimen No.

Component	238 (paleosome)			238a (metasome)			238v (metasome)			721 (paleosome)			721a (metasome)		
	wt%	at.%	$\frac{R}{Al}$	wt%	at.%	$\frac{R}{Al}$	wt%	at.%	$\frac{R}{Al}$	wt%	at.%	$\frac{R}{Al}$	wt%	at.%	$\frac{R}{Al}$
SiO_2	49.30	47.6	3.39	68.71	65.1	4.86	71.39	67.5	3.97	58.84	55.4	3.30	75.53	70.7	4.84
TiO_2	2.08	1.5	0.11	0.33	0.3	0.02	0.10	—	—	1.47	1.1	0.07	0.10	—	—
Al_2O_3	12.35	14.1	1.00	11.95	13.4	1.00	15.32	17.0	1.00	15.21	16.8	1.00	13.30	14.6	1.00
Fe_2O_3	7.12	5.1	0.36	1.43	1.0	0.07	0.58	0.4	0.02	2.10	1.5	0.09	0.42	0.3	0.02
FeO	9.57	7.7	0.55	4.42	3.5	0.26	2.53	2.0	0.12	5.28	4.2	0.25	0.76	0.6	0.04
MnO	0.25	0.1	—	0.09	—	—	—	—	—	0.09	—	—	0.02	—	—
MgO	5.99	8.1	0.57	4.31	6.1	0.46	0.44	0.6	0.04	3.73	5.3	0.32	0.42	0.6	0.04
CaO	9.94	10.3	0.73	3.75	3.8	0.28	4.42	4.5	0.26	4.86	4.9	0.29	1.60	1.6	0.11
Na_2O	2.55	4.8	0.34	2.45	4.5	0.34	3.77	6.9	0.41	3.83	7.0	0.42	3.29	5.9	0.40
K_2O	0.41	0.4	0.03	1.78	2.2	0.16	0.87	1.1	0.06	2.78	3.4	0.20	4.80	5.7	0.39
P_2O_5	0.36	0.3	—	0.13	0.1	—	0.07	—	—	0.49	0.4	0.02	0.02	—	—
Loss on ignition	0.31	—	—	0.31	—	—	0.26	—	—	1.12	—	—	0.23	—	—
Σ	100.23	100.0	—	99.71	100.0	—	99.75	100.0	—	99.80	100.0	—	100.49	100.0	—

TABLE 13 (continued)

	Specimen No.										
	21 (paleo-some)	21a (meta-some)	383v (paleo-some)	383a (meta-some)	129 (paleo-some)	129a (meta-some)	238 (paleo-some)	238a (meta-some)	238v (meta-some)	721 (paleo-some)	721a (meta-some)
Numerical characteristics (after Zavaritskii)											
a	7.0	15.9	13.5	13.7	8.2	11.8	6.1	7.7	9.6	12.5	13.7
b	33.7	5.0	25.6	8.2	28.9	6.4	31.4	12.8	3.8	15.2	2.0
c	6.8	4.0	4.0	1.1	4.7	4.0	5.1	3.9	5.4	4.0	1.7
s	52.5	75.1	56.9	77.0	58.2	77.8	57.4	75.6	81.2	68.3	82.6
Q	−15.8	+14.4	−17.2	+25.5	−4.7	+28.0	−2.5	+31.9	+37.8	+7.6	+36.1
f'	40.4	46.5	37.8	42.6	49.4	49.5	48.3	41.0	76.8	45.5	56.6
m'	37.4	34.3	42.6	29.5	34.4	37.9	29.9	54.9	19.6	41.9	33.4
c'	22.2	19.2	19.6	—	16.2	—	21.8	4.1	—	12.6	10.0
a'	—	—	—	27.9	—	12.6	—	—	3.6	—	—
Coordinates on the ACF diagram (after Eskola and Korzhinskii)											
A	28.6	49.6	24.2	42.0	24.2	50.0	25.3	33.4	56.2	31.2	51.0
C	29.9	30.5	27.2	10.5	24.2	22.7	29.3	18.9	27.7	23.3	28.4
F	41.5	19.9	48.6	47.5	51.6	27.3	45.4	47.7	16.1	45.5	20.6
Norm (after Barth)											
Albite	20.1	29.2	16.0	26.0	31.4	39.6	23.8	22.5	34.8	34.8	29.6
Anorthite	28.4	16.0	16.3	4.0	19.9	16.6	22.1	16.8	21.8	16.4	7.3
Orthoclase	6.2	24.8	31.2	33.1	3.4	9.5	2.3	10.8	5.4	17.0	28.6
Olivine	10.7	—	11.5	—	—	—	—	—	4.6	—	—
Orthopyroxene	—	2.9	—	7.4	20.0	6.7	14.4	17.1	—	13.6	1.6
Clinopyroxene	22.6	—	11.0	—	14.8	—	21.8	1.2	0.7	3.6	0.7
Magnetite	7.9	1.0	5.6	0.9	5.4	1.0	7.6	1.5	0.1	2.2	0.5
Ilmenite	1.8	0.4	1.7	0.8	3.0	0.6	2.3	0.6	0.2	2.1	0.1
Apatite	0.8	0.3	2.2	0.3	0.4	—	0.7	0.3	0.3	1.1	—
Quartz	—	12.9	—	25.2	1.7	25.3	5.0	29.2	32.5	9.2	31.6
Corundum	—	—	—	2.3	—	0.7	—	—	—	—	—
Nepheline	1.5	—	4.5	—	—	—	—	—	—	—	—

Note. Modal compositions of analyzed samples are given in Table 12.

manganese, calcium and phosphorus than the paleosome; there is a difference in the relative contents of aluminum and sodium. The former compositional variations emphasize a granitization trend in the formation of the metasome; the latter variation indicates the different original compositions of the paleosome and metasome (considering the inert behavior of aluminum), and the different roles played by sodium in different migmatite types.

Quartz-rich pyroxene-plagioclase migmatized schists are fairly widespread in the migmatization and granitization zones of the Bunger Oasis and apparently occur also in other regions of East Antarctica, where they are spatially associated with migmatites. Their mineral composition (Table 14) approaches that of melanocratic enderbites. However, they differ from these enderbites in the frequent presence of clinopyroxene, the high An content of the plagioclase, a lower quartz content and a somewhat higher content of colored minerals, among which biotite commonly plays an important role. These rocks differ from the normal pyroxene-plagioclase schists in their high quartz and plagioclase contents, the lower content of colored minerals, and the high ferruginosity of the hypersthene. In some areas, these rocks possess features similar to charnockites; thus they may contain appreciable amounts of free K-feldspar and highly ferruginous hypersthene of the type ordinarily found only in charnockites. These and other features of the migmatized quartz-rich plagioclase-pyroxene schists suggest a high degree of nonequilibrium in their mineral associations resulting from reactions with partial melts, which apparently played an important role during the ultrametamorphism of the rocks in the Bunger Oasis.

These rocks are characterized by the three following mineral paragenetic sequences: 1) quartz (12—23%), plagioclase (48—61%), hypersthene (15—26%), clinopyroxene (3—7%), ore minerals (3—5%); 2) quartz (9—32%), plagioclase (35—60%), hypersthene (10—22%), clinopyroxene (0—6%), biotite (5—20%) and ore minerals (1—5%); 3) quartz (8—25%), plagioclase (33—65%), K-feldspar (3—16%), hypersthene (11—35%), clinopyroxene (0—3%), biotite (0—10%) and ore minerals (1—5%).

Hornblende occurs sporadically in the first and second types. Their textures are distinguished by xenoblastic minerals; the form of certain of the minerals is controlled by other recrystallized minerals. The rocks are distinctly gneissic. Hetero-porphyroblastic, poikiloblastic and lepidoblastic textures with replacement features are widespread. The order of replacement of minerals is the same as in the pyroxene-plagioclase schists.

A characteristic feature of the first paragenetic type is the combination of "acid" labradorite with ferrohypersthene. The plagioclase porphyroblasts are prismatic and contain profuse poikiloblastic inclusions of quartz and, in places, antiperthite ingrowths. Smaller plagioclase grains form idioblastic laths. On the other hand, as pyroxene grains become coarser (up to 2 mm), they acquire xenoblastic skeletal-diablastic forms and are riddled with small inclusions of quartz and ore minerals. Thus, it appears that the recrystallization of plagioclase in these rocks was incomplete, whereas hypersthene was almost completely recrystallized. Apparently, the recrystallization of clinopyroxene was also incomplete, inasmuch as

TABLE 14. Mineral composition of Bunger Oasis schists transitional to enderbites

Speci-men No.	Mineral composition, vol. %									Characteristics of the minerals										
	qz	plag	Kfs	hyp	clpy	apat	biot	orem	An content of plagio-clase	hypersthene			clinopyroxene			amphibole			biotite	
										n_z	n_x	f at.%	n_z	n_x	f at.%	n_z	n_x	f at.%	n_z	f at.%
321	15	60	—	18	3	—	—	4	56	1.726	1.720	50	1.718	1.694	35	—	—	—	—	—
162	20	48	—	26	3	—	—	3	55	1.740	1.723	60	—	—	—	—	—	—	—	—
62 v	23	50	—	20	3	2	—	4	51	1.756	1.740	74	1.718	1.692	35	—	—	—	—	—
89	15	56	—	20	3	—	—	4	51	1.740	1.724	60	1.724	1.699	44	—	—	—	—	—
90	12	61	—	20	7	—	7	5	51	1.743	1.724	62	1.730	1.705	50	—	—	—	1.637	37
85	18	60	—	15	—	—	8	2	50	1.716	1.702	38	—	—	—	—	—	—	—	—
186	30	46	—	13	5	—	5	4	50	1.716	1.702	38	—	—	—	—	—	—	—	—
433 b	25	44	2	12	6	—	16	3	50	1.717	1.704	40	1.716	1.690	32	—	—	—	1.640	38
114	10	54	—	18	—	—	20	2	50	1.719	1.704	42	1.719	1.690	36	—	—	—	1.654	44
422 a	17	40	—	10	—	—	18	1	50	1.719	1.704	42	—	—	—	—	—	—	1.640	38
400 a	9	57	—	22	—	—	14	3	50	1.719	1.704	42	—	—	—	—	—	—	—	—
434 a	10	60	—	13	5	—	12	3	45	1.723	1.708	47	—	—	—	—	—	—	1.648	42
234 zh	10	58	—	13	—	—	10	3	43	1.727	1.712	51	—	—	—	—	—	—	1.664	49
424 g	32	35	—	15	—	—	5	5	39	1.728	1.713	52	—	—	—	—	—	—	1.668	51
470	15	50	5	15	2	4	10	2	72	1.741	1.723	61	1.722	1.697	40	—	—	—	1.659	47
325	8	60	5	20	1	—	—	1	67	1.732	1.719	55	—	—	—	—	—	—	1.657	46
66	8	58	3	15	7	—	2	3	65	1.728	1.713	52	1.719	1.689	36	—	—	—	—	—
295	10	50	3	15	—	—	3	3	65	1.727	1.712	51	—	—	—	—	—	—	—	—
263	15	59	5	23	5	—	1	3	64	1.741	1.724	61	—	—	—	—	—	—	—	—
422	15	65	6	14	2	—	6	2	61	1.740	1.722	60	—	—	—	—	—	—	—	—
307	12	47	5	11	8	—	3	4	57	1.729	1.712	53	—	—	—	—	—	—	—	—
165	6	66	5	28	—	—	—	4	54	1.728	1.713	52	1.721	1.692	38	—	—	—	1.655	45
330	8	54	4	11	5	—	—	5	54	1.729	1.712	53	1.722	1.697	40	—	—	—	—	—
270 b	10	46	4	19	2	—	1	3	54	1.729	1.714	53	—	—	—	—	—	—	—	—
207	15	52	10	35	8	1	6	2	50	1.733	1.714	56	—	—	—	—	—	—	—	—
62 a	14	55	8	20	—	—	2	4	48	1.733	1.717	56	1.727	1.696	48	—	—	—	—	—
430	12	48	16	15	—	3	—	3	48	1.736	1.720	58	—	—	—	—	—	—	—	—
462	12	55	9	14	5	—	—	4	47	1.740	1.723	60	—	—	—	—	—	—	—	—
269	14	52	16	10	5	—	6	3	42	1.741	1.724	61	—	—	—	1.704	1.680	59	—	—
94 d	12	65	12	8	—	—	2	4	39	1.740	1.722	60	—	—	—	—	—	—	—	—
400	25	33	12	20	—	—	7	3	35	1.746	1.729	64	—	—	—	—	—	—	—	—

TABLE 15. Chemical composition of migmatitic quartz-bearing pyroxene-plagioclase schists, transitional to enderbites

Component	Specimen No.								
	263			62a			430		
	wt%	at.%	$\frac{R}{Al}$	wt%	at.%	$\frac{R}{Al}$	wt%	at.%	$\frac{R}{Al}$
SiO_2	57.38	55.4	3.40	56.14	53.9	3.31	58.37	55.9	3.54
TiO_2	2.01	1.4	0.09	1.38	1.0	0.06	2.04	1.4	0.08
Al_2O_3	14.43	16.3	1.00	14.35	16.2	1.00	13.99	15.8	1.00
Fe_2O_3	2.61	1.9	0.12	2.24	1.6	0.10	2.27	1.6	0.09
FeO	9.24	7.4	0.45	9.44	7.5	0.46	8.15	6.5	0.41
MnO	0.28	0.2	0.01	0.25	0.2	0.01	0.22	0.2	0.01
MgO	2.63	3.8	0.23	4.02	5.8	0.36	3.23	4.6	0.26
CaO	6.38	6.6	0.40	7.31	7.5	0.46	5.89	6.0	0.34
Ng_2O	1.86	3.5	0.21	2.07	3.9	0.24	2.19	4.0	0.23
K_2O	2.68	3.4	0.21	1.85	2.2	0.13	3.07	3.7	0.21
P_2O_5	0.23	0.1	—	0.25	0.2	0.01	0.42	0.3	0.02
Loss on ignition	0.61	—	—	0.99	—	—	0.35	—	—
Σ	100.34	100.0	—	100.29	100.0	—	100.19	100.0	—

	Specimen No.		
	263	62a	430
Numerical characteristics (after Zavaritskii)			
a	8.2	7.3	9.3
b	18.1	21.0	17.8
c	5.7	6.1	4.7
s	68.0	65.6	68.2
Q	+13.9	+10.5	+13.1
f'	62.6	53.5	55.4
m'	25.2	32.8	30.8
c'	12.2	13.7	13.8
Coordinates on ACF diagram (after Eskola and Korzhinskii)			
A	34.4	30.0	31.6
C	24.0	22.3	23.8
F	41.6	47.7	44.6
Norm (after Barth)			
Albite	17.4	19.3	20.1
Anorthite	23.7	25.4	19.8
Orthoclase	16.8	11.2	18.7
Olivine	—	—	—
Orthopyroxene	14.8	19.2	14.9
Clinopyroxene	6.7	8.5	6.2
Magnetite	2.8	2.4	2.4
Ilmenite	2.9	2.1	2.9
Apatite	0.3	0.4	0.9
Quartz	14.6	11.5	14.1

Note. Modal compositions of the analyzed rocks are given in Table 14.

its iron content is compatible with the An content of the plagioclase but is incompatible with the iron content of the hypersthene. A similar combination of high-iron hypersthene with basic plagioclase, and with clinopyroxene having a medium ferruginosity, is observed in rocks of the third paragenetic type. In this type, the plagioclase is highly antiperthitic; pyroxene grains are skeletal-diablastic.

The mineral associations nearest to equilibrium occur in the second paragenetic type. These are distinguished by a combination of andesine-labradorite with pyroxenes and biotite of medium ferruginosity. These rocks are the closest to enderbite, although they contain a considerable amount of biotite. They often occur at contacts between pyroxene-plagioclase schists and enderbites, and are a typical transitional variety from the former to the latter.

A comparison of the chemical composition of these rocks (Table 15) with that of pyroxene-plagioclase schists and enderbites reveals a high silica content in the former (corresponding to the Si content in melano-cratic enderbites), whereas the alumina content is somewhat low, approaching that in amphibolized schists. The Si : Al ratio in type 3 rocks is similar to the strongly biotitized or feldspathized pyroxene-plagioclase schists, but the former are higher in silica and alumina. Type 3 rocks differ from unaltered schists in their higher potassium and silica contents and their lower calcium, magnesium, and alumina contents; the sodium, iron, and titanium contents are relatively similar. They differ from melanocratic enderbites in their lower alumina and sodium contents and higher calcium, potassium, and titanium contents; the silica, iron, magnesium, and sodium contents are relatively similar.

The chemical composition of the migmatized quartz-rich pyroxene-plagioclase schists is unique and cannot be explained only by an enderbitization of pyroxene-plagioclase schists, nor can they be considered as feldspathized enderbites. They probably formed from reactions between pyroxene-plagioclase schists and a partial melt. As a result of this reaction, the schists would probably become enriched in silica and potassium accompanied by the removal of calcium and magnesium. The normally inert alumina may have undergone a partial redistribution in the minerals during this process. Hence, it may be assumed that a reaction between pyroxene-plagioclase schists and selective melts resulted in the formation of migmatites as well as rocks with a composition transitional between the parent schists and shadow granitoids. The geological setting of these transitional rocks in contact zones of schists with shadow granitoids resulted in intensive tectonic reworking. This induced conditions favorable for chemically active interactions between the solid paleosome and partial melts formed during ultrametamorphism.

The term shadow granitoids is used herein to describe ultra-metamorphic rocks possessing certain specific features which place them apart from other metamorphic rocks. Both large-scale exposures and hand specimens of these rocks exhibit a nearly massive texture, but traces of the original structures or heavily altered relics of initially granitized rocks may also be observed. Such relics are remnants of the original rocks preserved from complete granitization. Relict structural elements are manifested as finely banded, linear and slightly maculose segregations of a more melanocratic composition (remnant of the altered paleosome) which impart gneissosity to the rocks. Such textural features in shadow pyroxene granitoids, together with their mineral composition, suggest that they were predominantly formed by metasomatic substitutions in regionally metamorphosed rocks during regional granitization. The nature of the granitization products are affected by the composition of the original rock, the chemical properties of the granitizing melts and solutions and the thermodynamic conditions of granitization. This apparently explains the diversity of shadow granitoids. Among those formed from Ca-Mg crystalline rocks, two types may be distinguished: largely sodium alkalinity and largely potassium alkalinity. The largely Na and largely K granitoids bear the general terms of enderbites and charnockites, respectively.

Enderbites

Enderbites (shadow hypersthene plagiogranites) are predominantly metasomatic granitoids formed by unusual granitization at deep levels of the granulite facies. They formed from Ca-Mg crystalline rocks and have been variously described in the literature on Antarctica and other regions of the world /27, 130/.

Enderbites are uniformly grayish brown with a greenish shading. The fine-grained enderbites exhibit a weak gneissosity which is essentially expressed as thin lenticular inclusions of pyroxene-plagioclase schists (about 5 vol.% of the rock) and strongly linear hypersthene. Macroscopic grains of bluish quartz which are heterogeneously distributed, form linear elongations parallel to the gneissosity. Quartz grain aggregates locally form small lenses or veinlets also parallel to the gneissosity, and thus impart a granulitic texture to the rock. Certain varieties of enderbites are massive; the strongly banded types are generally charnockitized.

Enderbites are most common on Enderby Land, their classic location, where they spread over thousands of square kilometers. In places, they form the metasome of coarsely layered migmatized pyroxene-plagioclase schists or form the paleosome in shadow charnockites. Enderbites also occur in other regions of Antarctica. They were encountered in the mountains around the Lambert Glacier, in the Mirny Station area, and on Queen Maud Land. In the Bunger Oasis, enderbites are closely interbedded with shadow charnockites where they apparently form the paleosome. Enderbites in the Mirny Station area occur as intercalations and lenses in the paleosome of complex migmatites. In this area, they exhibit a distinct banding manifested as alternating brownish nearly quartz-free layers and somewhat lighter brownish gray quartz-bearing layers, up to 2—3 m thick. In other regions, enderbites are less common, and charnockites take their place.

The mineral composition of enderbites varies considerably (Tables 16 and 17). This is mainly due to the composition of the original rocks. Melanocratic enderbites with a relatively low quartz content (10—15%), and a high hypersthene content (10—20%) are apparently formed from rocks compositionally similar to pyroxene-plagioclase schists. Enderbites with high quartz contents (15—50%), and a low hypersthene content (1—10%) probably formed from plagiogneisses, which are unstable in the granulite facies conditions. Aside from the major, rock-forming minerals (quartz, hypersthene, and plagioclase), enderbites may contain up to 1% clino-pyroxene and/or amphibole. There are also small amounts of perthitic orthoclase (1—5%). The content of ore minerals varies from 1 to 5%. Biotite (1—5%) is common in enderbites of the Bunger Oasis and other Antarctic regions. In the enderbites from their classic location, biotite is usually an accessory mineral, with a content reaching 2% only in the Rayner zone. Apatite is the most common accessory; zircon and monazite are of lesser importance.

FIGURE 7. Shadow enderbite (x 12, crossed nicols, thin section 29).

Shadow enderbites have a hetero-granoblastic texture. Metablasts of antiperthitic plagioclase and quartz, with complex relationships, develop from fine-grained recrystallized plagioclase-hypersthene aggregates. Blastocataclastic to granulitic textures, with lenticular quartz and hypersthene, are also common. Hypersthene metablasts occur in places. In massive rocks, the plagioclase is characterized by a tabular habit; it is locally prismatic-granular (Figure 7). Plagioclase in relicts with a grano-

TABLE 16. Mineral composition and characteristics of minerals in enderbites from Enderby Land

Specimen No.	qz	plag	Kfs	hyp	clpy	amph	biot	orem	An content of plagioclase	hyp n_z	hyp n_x	hyp $-2V°$	hyp f at.%	cpx n_z	cpx n_x	cpx $+2V°$	cpx f at.%	amph n_z	amph n_x	amph f at.%	biot n_z	biot f at.%	Geological setting
755a	13	65	—	19	—	—	o.s.*	3	34–38	1.715	1.701	59	37	—	—	—	—	—	—	—	—	—	Interbedded with garnetiferous gneisses
791a	30	55	—	15	—	—	—	o.s.	39–40	1.728	1.714	51	52	—	—	—	—	—	—	—	—	—	Exposure with small lenses of pyroxene-plagioclase schists
177b	45	25	1	30	—	—	—	4	44–46	1.727	1.711	55	51	—	—	—	—	—	—	—	—	—	Intercalation in pyroxene-plagioclase schists
459b	13	66	—	17	—	—	—	4	43–44	1.727	1.711	54	51	—	—	—	—	—	—	—	—	—	Intercalations in sillimanitic quartzites
492	18	62	1	17	—	—	o.s.	2	30–31	1.730	1.714	68	54	—	—	—	—	—	—	—	—	—	Interbedded with garnetiferous gneisses
636	10	65	—	20	—	—	—	2	33	1.727	1.711	50	51	—	—	—	—	—	—	—	—	—	Isolated nunatak
767v	10	70	—	15	—	—	2	3	40	1.714	1.700	58	36	—	—	—	—	—	—	—	—	—	Small lenses in mesoperthitic charnockites
750v	12	65	—	20	—	—	—	3	47	1.714	1.700	53	36	—	—	—	—	—	—	—	—	—	Contact of metasome from layered migmatites with pyroxene-plagioclase schists
307b	15	53	—	26	—	—	o.s.	6	33	1.727	1.711	50	51	—	—	—	—	—	—	—	—	—	As above
238b	17	62	—	16	1	1	"	3	31–32	1.722	1.708	50	46	—	—	—	—	1.708	1.683	63	—	—	Exposure with small lenses of pyroxene-plagioclase schists
764v	41	55	—	4	1	—	—	o.s.	32–37	1.729	1.713	71	53	—	—	—	—	—	—	—	—	—	As above
802a	42	54	—	4	—	—	—	•	32–37	1.726	1.712	52	50	1.724	1.698	54	44	—	—	—	—	—	Isolated nunatak
803a	24	65	—	8	1	—	—	2	37–40	1.729	1.713	51	53	—	—	—	—	—	—	—	—	—	As above
153a	16	78	o.s.	5	o.s.	—	—	1	31–33	1.734	1.718	55	57	—	—	—	—	—	—	—	—	—	As above
25	11	86	—	1.5	0.5	—	—	—	35	—	1.709	51	48	—	—	—	—	—	—	—	—	—	A 2-m intercalation in mesoperthitic granites
472	14	79	—	5	4	—	•	2	34–37	1.724	1.713	58	51	1.723	1.698	55	43	—	—	—	—	—	A 1-m intercalation in pyroxene-plagioclase schist
815a	10	63	—	7	—	—	—	16	48–51	1.727	1.713	—	—	—	—	—	—	—	—	—	—	—	A 1-m intercalation in pyroxene-plagioclase schist
174a	6	90	—	4	—	—	—	o.s.	38	1.719	1.704	52	42	1.717	1.692	54	33	—	—	—	—	—	Interbedded with pyroxene-plagioclase schists
232a	30	68	1	o.s	o.s.	—	o.s.	1	36	1.718	1.704	62	41	—	—	—	—	—	—	—	1.657	47	Isolated nunatak
53	30	69	1	2.5	—	5	"	o.s.	30	1.722	1.708	—	—	—	—	—	—	1.708	1.583	63	—	—	Paleosome of layered migmatites, with charnockitic metasome
233a	27	61	3		0.5	5	•	•	32	—	—	—	46	—	—	—	—	—	—	—	—	—	Isolated nunatak
778a	34	49	9	7	—	—	—	1	29–33	1.735	1.720	63	57	—	—	—	—	—	—	—	1.640	37	Paleosome of layered migmatites, with charnockitic metasome

Note. Variations of the plagioclase composition in a single thin section are indicated.

* [o.s. = optic sign.]

TABLE 17. Mineral composition and characteristics of minerals in enderbites from various regions in Antarctica

Specimen No.	Mineral composition, vol.%								An content of plagioclase	Characteristics of minerals										
										hypersthene			clinopyroxene			amphibole			biotite	
	qz	plag	Kfs	hyp	clpy	amph	biot	orem		n_z	n_x	f at.%	n_z	n_x	f at.%	n_z	n_x	f at.%	n_z	f at.%
Quartzitic rocks from Bunger Oasis																				
270	20	64	—	10	—	—	5	1	40	1.727	1.709	51	—	—	—	—	—	—	—	—
133	15	59	5	12	6	—	—	3	40	1.727	1.712	51	1.721	1.690	38	—	—	—	—	—
98	15	65	5	12	—	—	1	3	42	1.728	1.713	52	—	—	—	—	—	—	—	—
113	27	60	—	10	2	—	1	2	40	1.724	1.709	48	—	—	—	—	—	—	1.650	42
116v	46	36	3	11	—	—	1	1	42	1.725	1.711	49	—	—	—	—	—	—	1.655	44
148	24	63	—	11	—	—	1	1	40	1.730	1.714	54	—	—	—	—	—	—	—	—
Leucocratic enderbites from Bunger Oasis																				
240a	18	70	—	8	—	—	2	2	40	1.727	1.712	51	—	—	—	—	—	—	1.650	42
408	9	80	—	6	—	—	5	1	40	1.727	1.712	51	—	—	—	—	—	—	—	—
197	20	64	4	6	—	—	5	1	40	1.729	1.712	53	—	—	—	—	—	—	—	—
58	19	77	—	2	—	—	o.s.*	1	28	1.722	1.707	46	—	—	—	—	—	—	—	—
383	11	74	6	7	4	—	∗	5	27	1.713	1.699	35	—	—	—	—	—	—	—	—
128	11	74	—	6	3	—	—	2	27	1.716	1.700	38	—	—	—	—	—	—	—	—
137	29	60	—	6	—	—	—	2	30	1.717	1.704	40	—	—	—	—	—	—	—	—
433a	15	76	3	4	—	—	o.s.	4	30	1.723	1.708	47	—	—	—	—	—	—	—	—
444	9	79	—	7	—	—	—	3	31	1.715	1.701	37	—	—	—	—	—	—	—	—
478	10	78	—	9	—	—	o.s.	1	30	1.716	1.700	38	—	—	—	—	—	—	—	—
491b	35	55	—	6	2	—	—	1	28	1.722	1.707	46	—	—	—	—	—	—	—	—
492	36	55	3	3	—	—	∗	2	25	1.719	1.710	42	—	—	—	—	—	—	—	—
495	29	55	3	8	—	—	—	5	30	1.716	1.700	38	—	—	—	—	—	—	1.638	37

Mountains around the Lambert Glacier

Sample	1	2	3	4	5	6	7	8	9	ng–np	2V	ng–np	2V	ng–np	2V	n	2V
314b	12	72	—	4	8	2	—	2	38	1.732–1.717	55	1.726–1.700	48	1.701–1.675	55	—	—
11b	7	76	—	5	2	3	6	1	38	1.743–1.727	62	1.729–1.703	50	—	—	1.668	50

Yamato Mountains

Sample	1	2	3	4	5	6	7	8	9	ng–np	2V	ng–np	2V	ng–np	2V	n	2V
UA-85	19	48.4	11.4	2.7	8.3	+	9.1	o.s.	25	1.733–1.716	57	1.723–	43	—	—	1.667	49

Queen Maud Land

Sample	1	2	3	4	5	6	7	8	9	ng–np	2V	ng–np	2V	ng–np	2V	n	2V
830a	27	35	4	10	14	1	1	8	28	1.719–1.702	42	1.720–1.696	37	—–1.698	—	1.650	42
766a	21	50	—	1	2	15	10	1	28	1.726–	—	1.726–1.700	47	1.698–1.672	52	1.655	44
721	25	47	—	—	12	—	16	—	33	1.722–	—	1.722–1.697	40	—	—	1.665	49

Mirny area

Sample	1	2	3	4	5	6	7	8	9	ng–np	2V	ng–np	2V	ng–np	2V	n	2V
1128	7	67.5	0.6	19.4	—	—	o.s.	5.5	40	1.738–1.721	60	—	—	—	—	1.678	54
1131v	18.1	62.6	0.6	16.4	—	—	0.8	1.5	41	1.731–1.713	55	—	—	—	—	1.666	49
1131a	34.0	54.2	2.1	7.6	—	—	1.6	0.5	41	—	—	—	—	—	—	—	—
1147a	47.1	30.0	0.5	21.6	—	—	o.s.	0.8	43	1.735–1.717	58	—	—	—	—	1.677	54
1135v	51.0	21.1	—	18.8	—	—	0.1	9.0	42	1.735–1.717	58	—	—	—	—	—	—

* [o.s. = optic sign.]

blastic texture exhibits a diffuse zoning (normal), and is maculose in large segregations. Its composition may vary, even within individual grains, from oligoclase (An 26-28) to andesine (An 40-45). Universal stage measurements (Fedorov stage) indicate a relatively higher An content of plagioclase from melanocratic enderbites as compared to those from leuco-cratic enderbites. In general, the plagioclase on Enderby Land is more basic than that in the Bunger Oasis. On the average, melanocratic enderbites from Enderby Land are characterized by plagioclase with An 44-45, whereas leucocratic enderbites contain plagioclase of An 32-33. Melanocratic and leucocratic enderbites in the Bunger Oasis generally contain plagioclase with An 40 and An 29-30, respectively.

In many cases, hypersthene from enderbites exhibits deformed structures, transverse bands, and thin laths of clinopyroxene inclusions formed by exsolution from solid solutions. According to optical data, the ferruginosity of hypersthene is 36-57 at.%, i. e., on the average somewhat higher than in the pyroxene-plagioclase schists. Melanocratic enderbites from Enderby Land generally contain a less ferruginous hypersthene than do the leuco-cratic enderbites, but this relationship is reversed in the Bunger Oasis. The ferruginosity of the clinopyroxene which occurs in certain enderbites is 8-9 at.% lower than that in the coexisting hypersthene. The iron content of hornblende in enderbites is much higher than that in the coexisting pyroxenes, while the iron content in biotite from Enderby Land enderbites is higher than that in the coexistent hypersthene; this relationship is reversed in Bunger Oasis enderbites.

The chemical compositions (Tables 18 and 19) of the various rocks classified as enderbites have a number of features in common; however, they differ appreciably in the contents of the major rock-forming minerals. All enderbites are distinguished by considerable predominance of sodium over potassium (factor of 3 to 4). In most rocks, the iron content of the colored minerals is higher than that of the magnesium. The computed norm in a majority of enderbites includes corundum, indicating a certain degree of oversaturation in alumina. An important parameter for the classification of enderbites is the Ca : Al ratio, which is relatively stable (0.21-0.28 for Enderby Land enderbites). The Ca : Al ratio in melanocratic enderbites of the Bunger Oasis is 0.27-0.39; in leucocratic enderbites of the same area, Ca : Al = 0.19-0.20. These three enderbites with different Ca : Al ratios also differ in other chemical properties. This is evident from a comparison of specimens with identical or similar Si : Al ratios. Thus, the leucocratic enderbites of the Bunger Oasis differ from Enderby Land enderbites in their lower content of titanium and calcium, and their higher content of potassium. Melanocratic enderbites from the Bunger Oasis differ from the Enderby Land enderbites in their higher content of iron, magnesium, calcium and potassium and their lower content of sodium. The potassium contents in both varieties of enderbites in the Bunger Oasis are similar, but they differ in contents of iron, magnesium, calcium and sodium. These differences between Enderby Land and Bunger Oasis enderbites suggest different conditions of formation. The potassium activity

TABLE 18. Chemical composition of Enderby Land enderbites

Specimen No.

Compo-nent	63b			755a			25			238b			791a			764v			53		
	wt%	at.%	R/Al	wt%	at.%	R/Al	wt%	at.%	R/Al	wt%	at.%	R/Al	wt%	at.%	R/Al	wt%	at.%	R/Al	wt%	at.%	R/Al
SiO_2	62.06	57.6	3.22	66.26	61.7	3.53	66.95	62.3	3.19	66.01	62.4	3.56	68.16	64.3	3.80	68.53	64.2	3.92	73.81	69.5	4.70
TiO_2	0.72	0.5	0.03	0.68	0.5	0.03	0.55	0.4	0.02	0.68	0.5	0.03	0.46	0.3	0.02	0.38	0.3	0.02	0.07	—	—
Al_2O_3	16.34	17.9	1.00	15.96	17.5	1.00	17.70	19.5	1.00	15.74	17.5	1.00	15.15	16.9	1.00	14.89	16.4	1.00	13.01	14.5	1.00
Fe_2O_3	0.73	0.4	0.02	1.38	1.0	0.06	1.01	0.7	0.04	1.46	1.0	0.06	2.13	1.5	0.09	0.58	0.5	0.03	0.58	0.5	0.03
FeO	6.93	5.4	0.30	3.52	2.7	0.15	1.43	1.1	0.06	3.27	2.5	0.14	3.65	2.8	0.17	4.60	3.7	0.23	1.75	1.4	0.10
MnO	0.10	—	—	0.05	—	—	0.03	—	—	0.05	—	—	0.07	—	—	0.07	—	—	0.07	—	—
MgO	3.32	4.6	0.26	2.70	3.7	0.21	0.88	1.2	0.06	1.90	2.6	0.15	1.44	2.0	0.12	2.40	3.3	0.20	1.55	2.1	0.14
CaO	3.94	3.9	0.22	4.64	4.6	0.26	4.93	4.9	0.25	4.37	4.4	0.25	4.45	4.5	0.27	3.33	3.4	0.21	3.32	3.3	0.23
Na_2O	4.52	8.2	0.46	3.84	6.9	0.39	5.00	9.1	0.47	3.55	6.5	0.37	3.56	6.4	0.38	3.60	6.5	0.40	3.89	7.1	0.49
K_2O	1.10	1.4	0.08	1.00	1.2	0.07	0.65	0.7	0.04	2.04	2.4	0.14	0.94	1.2	0.07	1.40	1.7	0.10	1.32	1.6	0.11
P_2O_5	0.23	0.1	—	0.25	0.2	—	0.12	0.1	—	0.31	0.2	—	0.13	0.1	—	0.04	—	—	0.05	—	—
Loss on ignition	0.29	—	—	0.17	—	—	0.44	—	—	0.34	—	—	0.24	—	—	0.16	—	—	0.35	—	—
Σ	100.28	100.0	—	100.42	100.0	—	99.69	100.0	—	99.72	100.0	—	100.38	100.0	—	99.98	100.0	—	99.77	100.0	—

TABLE 18 (continued)

	Specimen No.						
	636	755a	25	238b	791a	764v	53
Numerical characteristics (after Zavaritskii)							
a	11.5	9.9	12.2	10.9	9.2	9.7	10.2
b	13.4	9.1	3.9	7.8	7.8	9.1	5.4
c	4.7	5.6	6.0	5.3	5.4	4.0	3.3
s	70.4	75.4	77.9	77.0	77.6	77.2	81.1
Q	+13.1	+35.3	+25.4	+25.9	+31.8	+31.0	+38.5
f'	53.0	49.6	57.2	56.2	67.0	46.8	42.0
m'	41.4	49.6	39.2	42.0	31.3	37.8	46.9
c'	—	—	3.6	1.8	—	—	11.1
a'	5.6	0.8	—	—	1.7	15.4	—
Coordinates of ACF diagram (after Eskola and Korzhinskii)							
A	37.8	45.6	57.1	47.4	49.2	44.2	44.8
C	17.5	22.7	29.1	24.1	24.3	18.2	26.5
F	44.7	31.7	13.8	28.5	26.5	37.6	28.7
Norm % (after Barth)							
Albite	40.7	34.6	45.2	32.3	32.1	32.6	35.6
Anorthite	18.7	21.8	23.8	20.4	21.8	16.3	14.1
Orthoclase	6.7	6.1	3.6	11.9	5.9	8.5	7.9
Orthopyroxene	18.6	11.0	3.3	8.4	7.7	12.8	5.8
Clinopyroxene	—	—	—	—	—	—	1.6
Magnetite	0.7	1.5	1.0	1.5	2.2	0.7	0.7
Ilmenite	1.0	1.0	0.8	1.0	0.7	0.6	0.1
Apatite	0.3	0.4	0.3	0.6	0.3	0.2	0.2
Quartz	12.4	23.0	21.8	23.4	28.8	26.6	34.0
Corundum	0.9	0.6	0.2	0.5	0.5	1.7	—

Note. Modal composition of analyzed rocks is given in Table 16.

TABLE 19. Chemical composition of Bunger Oasis enderbites

Component	270			133			148			383			58		
	wt%	at.%	R/Al	wt%	at.%	R/Al	wt%	at.%	R/Al	wt%	at.%	R/Al	wt%	at.%	R/Al
SiO_2	58.19	54.9	3.10	62.20	58.7	3.72	62.53	58.7	3.14	65.58	61.0	3.57	67.70	62.6	3.18
TiO_2	1.10	0.8	0.05	0.94	0.7	0.04	0.74	0.5	0.03	0.57	0.4	0.02	0.11	—	—
Al_2O_3	15.92	17.7	1.00	14.18	15.8	1.00	16.88	18.7	1.00	15.55	17.1	1.00	18.14	19.7	1.10
Fe_2O_3	1.20	0.8	0.05	2.58	1.8	0.11	0.78	0.6	0.03	1.53	1.1	0.06	0.78	0.6	0.03
FeO	9.38	7.4	0.42	6.07	4.8	0.30	5.52	4.3	0.23	3.25	2.5	0.15	1.36	1.1	0.06
MnO	0.19	0.2	0.01	0.20	0.2	0.01	0.15	0.1	—	0.07	—	—	0.07	—	—
MgO	4.74	6.7	0.38	3.84	5.4	0.34	2.90	4.1	0.22	2.60	3.6	0.21	0.82	1.1	0.06
CaO	5.24	5.3	0.30	5.98	6.1	0.39	5.47	5.5	0.29	3.28	3.3	0.19	3.90	3.9	0.20
Na_2O	2.78	5.0	0.28	2.62	4.8	0.30	3.38	6.1	0.33	4.66	8.4	0.49	5.33	9.5	0.48
K_2O	0.94	1.2	0.27	1.35	1.6	0.10	1.12	1.3	0.07	2.11	2.5	0.15	1.25	1.5	0.08
P_2O_5	0.03	—	—	0.08	0.1	—	0.11	0.1	—	0.14	0.1	—	—	—	—
Loss on ignition	0.49	—	—	0.30	—	—	0.50	—	—	0.46	—	—	0.60	—	—
Σ	100.20	100.0	—	100.34	100.0	—	100.08	100.0	—	99.80	100.0	—	100.06	100.0	—

Specimen No.

TABLE 19 (continued)

	Specimen No.				
	270	133	148	333	58
Numerical characteristics (after Zavaritskii)					
a	7.5	7.6	9.2	13.1	13.5
b	19.1	16.1	11.5	9.0	4.7
c	6.4	5.6	6.7	3.8	4.8
s	67.0	70.7	72.6	74.1	77.0
Q	+12.6	+20.6	+20.1	+18.2	+22.2
f'	52.9	50.0	53.6	48.9	44.1
m'	42.1	39.9	43.4	48.9	29.4
c'	—	10.1	—	2.2	—
a'	5.0	—	3.0	—	26.5
Coordinates of ACF diagram (after Eskola and Korzhinskii)					
A	36.8	36.4	44.5	39.5	59.0
C	17.2	23.6	21.7	21.0	26.1
F	46.0	40.0	33.8	39.5	14.9
Norm, % (after Barth)					
Albite	25.2	23.8	30.8	41.9	47.5
Anorthite	26.6	23.6	26.4	15.6	19.4
Orthoclase	5.9	8.2	6.8	12.3	7.5
Orthopyroxene	26.2	15.1	15.4	10.7	3.8
Clinopyroxene	—	4.8	—	—	—
Magnetite	1.2	2.7	0.8	1.6	0.8
Ilmenite	1.6	1.4	1.0	0.8	0.1
Apatite	—	0.3	0.3	0.3	—
Quartz	12.5	20.1	17.9	16.8	19.9
Corundum	0.8	—	0.6	—	1.0

Note. Modal composition of analyzed rocks is given in Table 17.

must have been considerably higher during the formation of Bunger Oasis enderbites than during the formation of Enderby Land enderbites. It is also probable that Bunger Oasis enderbites were formed at lower temperatures.

The high content of colored minerals in the melanocratic enderbites suggests that their formation was due to an enderbitization of rocks with the composition of pyroxene-plagioclase schists. However, the bulk of enderbites seems to have been formed from other, more acid, rocks, corresponding in composition to pyroxene plagiogneisses, which may have originated as andesitic-basaltic rocks. In fact, andesite and possibly quartz diorite may be regarded as the igneous equivalents of enderbite. As a rule, enderbites differ from these rocks in their somewhat higher silica and sodium contents and lower contents of ferric iron, manganese, calcium, and potassium (also ferrous iron and magnesium in leucocratic varieties). A comparison of Zavaritskii's numerical characteristics for andesites and enderbites reveals a relative enrichment in andesites of alkalis, anorthite and colored minerals, whereas the enderbites are richer in silica. Further- more, enderbites are often oversaturated in alumina, which is a less com- mon phenomenon in andesites. Indeed, progressive metamorphism of andesites should result in their enrichment in silica in the greenschist stage, their depletion in potassium in the amphibolite stage /68/, while their enderbitization in the granulite stage should involve an enrichment in sodium and a depletion in calcium (corresponding to a removal of alumina from plagioclase and its inclusion in the colored minerals). The balance of the mafic components can also be explained in a like manner.

A comparison of the norm and mode of enderbites confirms the charac- teristics of their mineral composition. Normative corundum is evidently a component of the modal hypersthene. The presence of normative ortho- clase, in contrast to its total absence in the modal composition, indicates its presence in solid solution with plagioclase.

Charnockites

Charnockites (shadow hypersthene granites) are metasomatic granitoids formed by potassium metasomatism of Ca-Mg crystalline rocks. Charno- kites are, to a certain extent, potassium equivalents of enderbites. They may have formed as a result of a continued metasomatic alteration of enderbites under certain physicochemical conditions. Unlike enderbitization, which can be traced in one form or another throughout the granulite facies (evidently due to large reserves of sodium in the granulitic rocks), charnockitization is, in fact, a retrogressive process. This is also evident from the geological relationship of enderbites and charnockites which occur in certain tectonic zones.

In general, charnockites built various outcrops and nunataks, with visible thicknesses reaching hundreds of meters, and rarely up to 2 km. The charnockites are especially abundant on Enderby Land, where they crop out over thousands of square kilometers. Shadow granitoids on

Queen Maud Land generally form concordant bodies within migmatites, with thicknesses ranging from a few to several hundred meters (rarely up to 1 km). They occur as layers extending over hundreds of meters and up to several kilometers, which wedge out locally. Shadow granites frequently partially replace and are interbedded with layered mig- matites, thus forming a part of the migmatite fields. In places, the shadow granites exhibit small-angle cross-cutting contacts which indicate the start of rheomorphic processes.

Charnockites in layered migmatitic pyroxene-plagioclase schists are fairly common in the Bunger Oasis. Large areas composed only of charnockites occur in the southern part of the oasis. Granulite facies charnockites are also common in other regions of Antarctica, including the Yamato Mountains, MacRobertson Land, Vestfold Oasis, etc. However, the geological setting of charnockites in these regions has not yet been determined. Pyroxene-plagioclase schists, which consistently form intercalations with enderbites, occur to a lesser extent in charnockites as wedged-out intercalations and boudinaged lenses. Charnockites may form thick units interbedded with shadow garnetiferous granites. This apparent inter- bedding seems to have resulted from the granitization of laminated rocks of various compositions (aluminous and calcareous). Charnockites fre- quently contain well-defined small lenses and concordant veinlets of metasomatic pyroxene rocks. Aside from lenses of feldspathized pyroxene- plagioclase schists, charnockites in places contain small diffuse inclusions of enderbite. Furthermore, charnockites and enderbites may occur in the same exposure as concordant members, layers with transitional contacts. The macroscopic differences between them are very slight, even within the same outcrop; thus the enderbites contain slightly more mafic minerals and are darker brown in color.

Fresh specimens of charnockite appear leucocratic and are gray with yellowish and pinkish tinges. Weathered surfaces of these rocks are nearly always light brown. They are generally medium grained. Thick zones of charnockites are very homogeneous. In general, they contain up to 5% colored minerals (almost exclusively ferrohypersthene) uniformly distributed in the form of thin veinlets or streaks, imparting a weak gneissosity to the rock. Superimposed granulitization in charnockites is manifested as ubiquitous fine-grained bluish quartz. This feature is better expressed and occurs over larger areas than in enderbites. Charnockites exhibit a variety of textures, the most common of which is hetero-granoblastic where the predominant K-feldspar grains are relatively coarse (1.5—2 mm) in comparison to the other minerals (0.3—1.5 mm). Where large segregations of K-feldspar occur (up to 4—6 mm), the texture is metablastic, and normally shaped K-feldspar results in a porphyro- blastic texture, i.e., similar to intrusive charnockites.

The large K-feldspar segregations contain numerous generally round inclusions of quartz, plagioclase, and less frequently hypersthene. Inter- stitial myrmekites are common. In most cases, the mineral grains have irregular boundaries. Corrosion structures are very common, where plagioclase is replaced by quartz and K-feldspar, and quartz is replaced by

K-feldspar. In granulitized varieties, all minerals tend to be replaced by quartz which frequently contains relicts of plagioclase and hypersthene. In places, the texture is blastocataclastic, and fine biotite plates replace hypersthene. The latter is accompanied by a segregation of ore minerals.

The charnockites are divided into the following two subgroups with respect to the mineral composition and nature of the feldspar: a) perthitic charnockites and b) normal charnockites (bifeldspar charnockites); to date, perthitic charnockites have been discovered only on Enderby Land, where they make up most of the large exposures in the Napier zone. Normal charnockites occur in many parts of Antarctica, but have been best studied in the Bunger Oasis. The normal charnockites are characteristically related to layered migmatites, which is not true for perthitic charnockites.

The mineral composition of perthitic charnockites (Figure 8) are as follows (Table 20): quartz (5—50%), perthite (27—28%), plagioclase (0—8%), ore minerals (0—3%); the hypersthene content ranges from near zero (sporadic grains) to 24%. Clinopyroxene and secondary biotite (replacing hypersthene) occur sporadically. Accessory minerals are represented by zircon, monazite and, to a lesser extent, apatite. The plagioclase in most charnockites contains 20—35% anorthite. Maculose and antiperthitic plagioclases are extremely rare, generally An 35—39. According to optical data, the perthite in charnockites contains 40—60% perthitic plagioclase ingrowths (lenticular to rodlike shapes). The thin marginal fringe of the K-feldspar grains is usually free from ingrowths and consists of orthoclase or, less commonly, oligoclase. The $2V$ measurement, which ranges between 50 and 70°, suggests that the K-feldspar is a slightly microcline-bearing orthoclase. A diffuse microcline crosshatching is commonly observed in the marginal portions of the K-feldspar grains. In some samples, the K-feldspar consists mainly of microcline ($2V = 70—80°$). Measurements of the refractive indices of perthites ($n_z = 1.528—1.532$) indicate the presence of the plagioclase component (44—64%) which conforms to the data presented above. Determinations of the composition of the perthitic plagioclase ingrowths by Fedorov's method yields values ranging from An 23 to An 36, which approximately corresponds to the plagioclase composition in separate grains.

Hypersthene in perthitic charnockites does not exhibit exsolution phenomena. It is distinctly pleochroic and is represented by highly ferruginous varieties, $f = 47—76$ at.% (average, 57 at.%). More magnesian varieties are locally encountered. Orthopyroxene in the charnockites is commonly replaced by iddingsite and fine plates of biotite. The clinopyroxene which is present in some charnockite specimens belongs to the more ferruginous varieties ($f = 52$ at.%, based on optical data).

Normal charnockites (Figure 9) differ from the perthitic charnockites by the presence of considerable amounts of plagioclase along with orthoclase and the absence of perthitic alkali feldspar. Their textures are similar to those of perthitic charnockites; however, some leucocratic specimens contain elements of a prismatic-granular texture. The mineralogical composition of charnockites is quite variable, particularly with regard to

FIGURE 8. Shadow perthitic charnockite (× 30, crossed nicols, thin section 822a).

FIGURE 9. Shadow bi-feldspar charnockites (× 12, crossed nicols, thin section 52).

TABLE 20. Mineral composition and characteristics of perthitic charnockites of Enderby Land

Specimen No.	Mineral composition, vol.%							An content of plagioclase		Characteristics of minerals								Geological setting
	qz	plag	perthite	hyp	clpy	biot	orem	mar-gin	cen-ter	hypersthene				clinopyroxene				
										n_z	n_x	$-2V°$	f at.%	n_z	n_x	$+2V°$	f at.%	
798a	21	3	71	5	—	—	o.s.*	24	32	1.734	1.719	56	57	—	—	—	—	Nunatak
800a	51	5	44	o.s.	—	—	—	23	34	1.746	1.728	53	64	—	—	—	—	Nunatak—contains lenses and intercalations of pyroxene-plagioclase schists
801a	26	—	70	4	—	—	o.s.	27	—	1.748	1.731	64	64	—	—	—	—	Nunatak
806a	19	o.s.	78	4	—	—	″	31	31	1.748	1.731	64	64	—	—	—	—	Nunatak—contains sparse intercalations of garnet gneisses
810a	28	″	70	1	—	—	1	29	28	—	—	—	—	—	—	—	—	Nunatak—contains lenses of pyroxene rocks
811a	34	″	58	6	2	o.s.	—	20	20	1.742	1.725	—	62	1.729	1.704	58	52	Nunatak—contains rare lenses of pyroxene-plagioclase schists
759a	27	4	62	7	—	—	o.s.	36	36	1.727	1.713	63	51	—	—	—	—	Outcrop
764a	28	—	67	5	—	o.s.	″	22	—	1.724	1.710	73	48	—	—	—	—	Nunatak—contains lenses of pyroxene rocks and shadow enderbites
767a	51	—	47	2	—	″	″	33	—	1.726	1.710	67	50	—	—	—	—	Outcrop—contains shadow enderbites
156	4	—	67	24	—	—	3	29	—	1.737	1.721	55	59	—	—	—	—	Outcrop—contains rare lenses of pyroxene rocks
160a	14	4	77	3	o.s.	o.s.	2	29	29	1.734	1.720	53	57	—	—	—	—	Outcrop
163	14	1	78	4	o.s.	—	2	—	32	1.754	1.737	72	72	—	—	52	—	Outcrop—contains rare lenses of pyroxene rocks
488a	60	o.s.	27	11	—	—	2	—	39	1.740	1.724	64	61	—	—	—	—	Outcrop
489	25	7	60	6	—	—	2	—	33	1.723	1.710	60	47	—	—	—	—	″
208	25	3	72	o.s.	—	o.s.	1	28	35	1.713	1.698	—	37	—	—	—	—	″
166e	22	4	69	4	—	o.s.	1	—	—	—	—	—	—	—	—	—	—	Metasome of agmatites of bronzitic metasomatic rocks
54	30	5	61	1	—	o.s.	3	—	—	—	—	—	—	—	—	—	—	Outcrop ″

* [o.s. = optic sign.]

the relative contents of feldspars (Table 21); the content of plagioclase varies from 10 to 55%, and that of K-feldspar from 10 to 70%. These charnockites often contain biotite (after hypersthene) which varies from sporadic plates to 5—6% in content. In the Queen Maud Land charnockites, biotite reaches 16%, and hornblende is present in considerable amounts (8—13%). Hypersthene (1—13%), and ore minerals (up to 5%) occur in all charnockites.

Oligoclase-andesine (An 26—36) is a typical plagioclase in the charnockites. Enderby Land charnockites contain oligoclase-andesine with An 22—23; Bunger Oasis charnockites contain basic andesines, An 44—50 and even labradorites, An 52. Signs of replacement by K-feldspar are apparent only in comparatively basic plagioclase, rather than in more acid plagioclase with which perthite may have been associated. The latter also occurs in microperthitic ingrowths in alkaline feldspars. Some plagioclases contain small amounts of antiperthitic ingrowths. K-feldspar in charnockites from Enderby Land, Bunger Oasis, and Prince Charles Mountains is represented by microperthitic orthoclase (Enderby Land: $\perp (001) n_y = 4-7°$, $2V = -50$ to $67°$; Bunger Oasis: $\perp (001) n_y = 6-12°$; $2V = -50$ to $-60°$). Microperthitic ingrowths usually form 15—20% of the volume of an orthoclase grain. K-feldspar, which replaces and contains relicts of plagioclase, often contains the greatest amount of microperthitic ingrowths, thus approaching perthite. The Enderby Land and Bunger Oasis charnockites also locally contain microcline-orthoclase with a $2V$ ranging from −80 to −82°; these are more abundant in Queen Maud Land charnockites, where microcline occurs (in varying degrees), in nearly all K-feldspar: $\perp (010) n_y = 81-85°$; $\perp (1502)$ [sic] = 77—81°; $2V = -67$ to $-81°$.

In most of the examined charnockites, orthopyroxene has a high iron content (57—75 at.%) and may be considered a ferrohypersthene. However, the Bunger Oasis charnockites also contain less ferruginous hypersthenes ($f = 51-52$ at.%) which places them closer to the hypersthene in enderbites. Rocks with low-iron hypersthenes (apparently relicts) occur most frequently near contacts with lenses of pyroxene-plagioclase schists or pyroxene rocks. In places, clinopyroxene occurs together with ferro-hypersthene, where it is represented by highly ferruginous varieties ($f = 73$ at.%). The iron contents of biotite and hornblende in Bunger Oasis charnockites containing low-iron hypersthene are 43 at.% and 57 at.%, respectively. These minerals are considerably more iron-rich in the charnockites of Queen Maud Land; biotite, $f = 51-86$ at.%, hornblende, $f = 61-94$ at.%.

The chemical composition of charnockites is given in Tables 22 and 23. The principal variations within perthitic charnockites are in the silica (range of 9 wt%) and alumina (range of 5 wt%) contents. Other components range only within 1 to 1.5 wt%. The perthitic charnockites have similar sodium and potassium contents, with a slight predominance of potassium over sodium. The potassium content in rocks with compositions intermediate between enderbites and perthitic charnockites is somewhat lower than the sodium content; however, in rocks transitional between normal charnockites and enderbites, the potassium content is several times that of sodium. The most stable chemical parameter of perthitic charnockites

TABLE 21. Mineral composition and characteristics of normal charnockites in Antarctica

Specimen No.	Mineral composition, vol.%								Characteristics of minerals											
	qz	plag	Kfs	hyp	clpy	amph	biot	orem	An content of plagioclase	hypersthene n_z	hypersthene n_x	hypersthene f at.%	clinopyroxene n_z	clinopyroxene n_x	clinopyroxene f at.%	amphibole n_z	amphibole n_x	amphibole f at.%	biotite n_z	biotite f at.%
Enderby Land																				
777 a	40	21	32	5	—	—	—	2	25—26	1.748	1.731	64	—	—	—	—	—	—	—	—
776 a	14	46	34	5	—	—	o.s.*	o.s.	32—36	1.741	1.726	61	—	—	—	—	—	—	—	—
173	20	10	65	2	—	—	—	3	35	1.745	1.728	63	—	—	—	—	—	—	—	—
190	20	8	65	4	1	o.s.	2	—	22	1.759	1.743	76	1.743	1.716	73	—	—	—	—	—
Bunger Oasis																				
115	22	30	34	4	5	—	4	1	52	1.728	1.713	52	—	—	—	—	—	—	—	—
446 v	19	30	36	11	—	—	4	—	50	1.729	1.714	53	—	—	—	—	—	—	1.652	43
326	15	50	19	10	2	—	—	4	48	1.742	1.728	62	—	—	—	—	—	—	—	—
187	29	28	32	4	—	—	4	3	48	1.747	1.733	64	—	—	—	—	—	—	—	—
458	18	50	12	13	—	4	—	3	48	1.735	1.719	57	—	—	—	—	—	—	—	—
44	20	35	25	10	—	5	—	5	44	1.748	1.732	65	—	—	—	1.702	1.678	57	—	—
248	23	11	61	3	—	—	1	1	32	1.727	1.707	51	—	—	—	—	—	—	—	—
121 a	32	27	34	4	—	—	1	2	32	1.727	1.708	51	—	—	—	—	—	—	—	—
66 zh	28	15	55	2	—	—	—	—	—	—	—	—	—	—	—	—	—	—	—	—
21 a	17	38	42	1	—	—	1	1	28	—	—	—	—	—	—	—	—	—	—	—
Mountains around the Lambert Glacier																				
2	10	40	42	2	—	—	5	1	35	1.744	1.722	63	—	—	—	—	—	—	—	—
306 e	30	28	37	4	—	—	—	1	37	1.756	1.740	74	—	—	—	—	—	—	—	—
313 a	10	45	42	2	—	—	1	o.s.	35	—	—	—	—	—	—	—	—	—	—	—
315	38	10	50	1	—	—	1	•	—	1.745	1.728	63	—	—	—	—	—	—	—	—
Yamato Mountains																				
504 b	28	13	51	2	—	o.s.	4	2	26—32	1.745	1.728	63	—	—	—	—	—	—	1.679	55
Queen Maud Land																				
827 e	25	10	50	1	—	8	6	—	26	—	—	—	—	—	—	1.724	1.698	94	1.686	86
806 g	10	30	35	1	2	10	11	3	32	—	—	—	—	—	—	1.708	1.685	61	1.670	51
806 v	15	32	18	4	2	13	10	6	32	1.754	1.736	73	—	—	—	1.706	1.682	59	1.678	54

* [o.s. = optic sign.]

TABLE 22. Chemical composition of shadow perthitic charnockites from Enderby Land

Specimen No.

Compo-nent	798a			801a			160a			208			166e			54		
	wt%	at.%	R/Al	wt%	at.%	R/Al	wt%	at.%	R/Al	wt%	at.%	R/Al	wt%	at.%	R/Al	wt%	at.%	R/Al
SiO_2	70.39	66.0	3.86	74.49	70.7	4.71	69.01	65.4	4.01	75.57	72.0	5.81	71.9	67.5	4.27	78.05	75.0	6.36
TiO_2	0.28	0.2	0.01	0.24	0.2	0.01	0.31	0.2	0.01	0.38	0.3	0.02	0.19	0.2	0.01	0.35	0.3	0.03
Al_2O_3	15.28	17.1	1.00	13.46	15.0	1.00	14.61	16.3	1.00	11.00	12.4	1.00	14.31	15.8	1.00	10.39	11.8	1.00
Fe_2O_3	0.86	0.6	0.04	0.67	0.4	0.03	2.46	1.8	0.11	0.80	0.5	0.04	0.52	0.3	0.02	0.92	0.7	0.06
FeO	1.90	1.5	0.09	1.26	1.0	0.07	1.95	1.5	0.09	2.60	2.1	0.17	2.87	2.3	0.15	0.86	0.7	0.06
MnO	0.06	–	–	–	–	–	0.07	0.05	–	–	–	–	0.03	–	–	0.03	–	–
MgO	0.80	1.1	0.06	0.40	0.5	0.03	0.65	0.9	0.06	2.54	3.6	0.29	0.91	1.2	0.08	0.36	0.5	0.04
CaO	3.17	3.0	0.18	1.79	1.8	0.12	2.26	2.25	0.14	1.34	1.4	0.11	2.18	2.2	0.14	1.29	1.3	0.11
Na_2O	3.87	7.0	0.41	3.34	6.1	0.41	3.70	6.80	0.42	1.95	3.6	0.29	3.39	6.2	0.39	1.84	3.5	0.30
K_2O	2.87	3.4	0.20	3.45	4.2	0.28	3.96	4.7	0.29	3.27	4.0	0.32	3.52	4.2	0.27	5.00	6.1	0.55
P_2O_5	0.08	0.1	–	0.08	0.1	–	0.10	0.1	–	0.09	0.1	–	0.08	0.1	–	0.09	0.1	–
Loss on ignition	0.42	–	–	0.47	–	–	0.75	–	–	0.29	–	–	0.01	–	–	0.49	–	–
Σ	99.98	100.0	–	99.65	100.0	–	99.83	100.0	–	99.83	100.0	–	99.91	100.0	–	99.67	100.0	–

TABLE 22 (continued)

	Specimen No.					
	798a	801a	160a	208	166e	54
Numerical characteristics (after Zavaritskii)						
a	12.7	11.9	14.1	8.4	12.4	10.9
b	3.7	3.6	3.3	9.3	4.1	2.4
c	3.7	2.1	2.6	1.5	2.6	1.2
s	79.9	82.4	80.0	80.8	80.9	85.5
Q	+28.7	+38.9	+29.2	+43.3	+34.4	+48.0
f'	58.0	48.1	71.0	31.7	53.0	66.7
m'	32.0	18.5	20.0	43.5	26.0	22.2
c'	—	—	—	—	—	11.1
a'	10.0	33.4	9.0	24.8	21.0	—
Coordinates of the ACF diagrams (after Eskola and Korzhinskii)						
A	52.8	57.8	49.7	40.6	48.7	46.9
C	25.5	22.5	23.3	11.6	19.8	28.4
F	21.7	19.7	27.0	47.8	31.5	24.7
Norm, % (after Barth)						
Albite	35.1	30.8	34.1	18.0	31.0	17.3
Anorthite	14.7	8.3	10.3	6.0	10.1	4.3
Orthoclase	17.2	20.9	23.6	19.9	20.9	30.6
Olivine	—	—	—	—	—	—
Orthopyroxene	4.0	2.3	2.6	10.2	6.3	1.6
Clinopyroxene	—	—	—	—	—	—
Magnetite	1.0	0.6	2.7	0.8	0.5	1.0
Ilmenite	0.5	0.3	0.5	0.5	0.3	—
Apatite	0.3	0.3	0.3	0.3	0.3	0.3
Quartz	26.6	35.2	25.3	41.9	29.2	43.5
Corundum	0.6	1.3	0.6	2.4	1.4	0.5
Sphene	—	—	—	—	—	0.9

Note. Modal compositions of analyzed rocks are given in Table 20.

TABLE 23.   Mineral composition and characteristics of garnet-hypersthene shadow granitoids from Enderby Land

Speci-men No.	Mineral composition, vol.% qz	plag	Kfs	orpy	gar	biot	orem	accessory minerals	An content of plagioclase	hypersthene n_z	n_x	$-2V°$	f at.%	garnet n	f at.%	biotite n_z	f at.%	Geological setting
179 v	4	64	–	28	3	o.s.	1	Apatite, zircon	48	1.722	1.707	59	46	1.800	77	–	–	Interbedded with garnet gneisses
836 b	28	61	–	9	o.s.	2	o.s.	Amphibole	–	–	–	–	–	–	–	–	–	Interbedded with biotite-garnet gneisses
215 v	63	20	o.s.	4	4	5	"	Apatite, zircon, graphite—4%	23	1.729	1.715	75	53	1.795	72	1,620	28	Schlieren at contact with shad-ow granite granites containing lenses of spinel quartzites
213b	17	63	2	10	5	o.s.	2	Apatite—1%, zircon	28	1.749	1.732	61	65	1.809*	80*	–	–	Diffuse bands with shadow mesoperthitic charnockites
179 a	15	35	4	3	10	30	–	Xenotime—3%	33	–	–	–	–	1.782	63*	–	–	Interbedded with garnet gneisses
765b	61	22	12	4	o.s.	o.s.	1	Zircon	34—29	–	–	–	–	1.803	83*	–	–	'Blobs' and lenticular bodies with indistinct outlines (represented by specimen 756a)
40	21	39	13	6	17	2	o.s.	Zircon, rutile—1%, graphite — 1%	39	1.715	1.702	70	57	1.775	57	–	–	Interbedded with enderbites
215	50	6	30	3	6	1	2	Zircon	29	1.738	1.722	82	59	1.799	76	–	–	Intercalations within shadow mesoperthite granite granites
478 b	3	20	40	1	26	7	1	Zircon, spinel	28	1.720	1.705	64	44	1.790*	70*	1.633	37	Three-meter thick intercala-tions within garnet shadow gran-ites and magnetite-bearing charnockites
836zh	10	27	50	1	o.s.	9	3	Zircon	41	1.724	1.709	69	48	–	–	–	–	Interbedded with biotite-garnet gneisses
467	14	12	58	4	10	1	1	Zircon	28	1.720	1.705	64	44	–	–	–	–	Outcrop
162	19	3н.	60	3	10	1	1	Rutile, zircon	–	–	–	–	–	1.783	62*	1.654	44	.
765a	25	8	63	o.s.	o.s.	8	1	Zircon, apatite	37—32	–	–	–	–	1.796	78*	–	–	.
756 b	20	–	80	+	.	–	–	Zircon	–	–	–	–	–	–	–	–	–	

Note. These values are based on spectroscopic silicate analyses.

* [o.s. = optic sign.]

is the Ca : Al atomic ratio (0.12—0.14, exclusive of extreme values).
Furthermore, all perthitic charnockites are characterized by an oversaturation in alumina (normative corundum and high values of the a
characteristic). A comparison of the perthitic charnockites with Enderby
Land enderbites reveals the following data: 1) the Si : Al atomic ratio is
smaller in most enderbites than in normal charnockites, due to the higher
alumina and lower silica contents in the enderbites; consequently, considering the low mobility of silicon and aluminum under the high temperature conditions of the granulite facies, it may be assumed that most of
these charnockites formed from rocks of somewhat different composition
than that of typical enderbites; 2) some enderbite specimens are comparable to perthitic charnockites with regard to the Si : Al ratio. Apparently
rocks with this Si : Al ratio were the original rocks for most perthitic
charnockites and were preserved within the enderbites. A comparison
between enderbites and perthitic charnockites with identical or similar
Si : Al ratios reveals lower contents of ferrous iron, magnesium, calcium,
and sodium and higher contents of potassium and silica in perthitic
charnockites. In general, perthitic charnockites differ from the enderbites in their higher alkalinity, lower amounts of colored minerals and
lower An content in plagioclase. Perthitic charnockites are frequently
similar to enderbites with regard to supersaturation in silica and alumina.

These differences between perthitic charnockites and Enderby Land
enderbites suggest a transformation of certain enderbites into charnockites
by metasomatic granitization accompanied by an introduction of potassium
and the removal of iron, magnesium, calcium, and sodium.

Normal charnockites differ from the perthitic variety primarily by a
twofold predominance of potassium over sodium (total alkali contents are
similar), and by their higher content of colored minerals. A comparison of
both types of charnockite having similar Si : Al ratios indicates additional
differences: higher contents of ferrous iron and magnesium in the normal
charnockites. These differences are reflected in the presence of biotite in
normal charnockite and its absence from perthitic varieties. Thus, normal
charnockites are more melanocratic rocks and formed under conditions of
higher water activity and higher mobility and activity of potassium;
perthitic charnockites formed under lower water and potassium activities.
Lower temperatures and pressures during normal charnockite formation
are also indicated. This is confirmed by paleotemperature measurements.
Transitions between perthitic and normal charnockites on Enderby Land
may indicate potassium metasomatism of perthitic charnockites in different
thermodynamic conditions (resulting in decomposition). A comparison of
normal charnockites with Bunger Oasis enderbites is also of interest,
although similar Si : Al ratios do not occur. All the normal charnockites
have lower alumina contents while their silica content is somewhat higher.
The alkali contents of enderbites and normal charnockites are virtually the
same, although the Na : K ratios are reversed. Enderbites are richer in
calcium and magnesium, although the iron content is nearly the same in
both rocks. When comparing Zavaritskii's characteristics for these rocks,
it is apparent that normal charnockites differ from enderbites in lower

An contents in plagioclase and higher silica contents as well as by a more marked prevalence of iron over magnesium in the dark-colored part of the rock.

If normal charnockites are assumed to have been formed from ender-bites, then the enderbites must have been enriched in potassium and silica and depleted in sodium, calcium, magnesium and aluminum. This mode of granitization seems possible, except for loss of aluminum. It has also been noted that enderbites and normal charnockites in the Bunger Oasis are often interlayered. In this case it is difficult to assume that enderbites were not charnockitized only because they contained more aluminum and less silicon. Such selective metamorphism would have been possible in the case of highly alkaline charnockites, as is the case in the perthitic charnockites of Enderby Land. However, in the Bunger Oasis, normal charnockites are not granitized enderbites, but were apparently formed from a melt derived from perthitic charnockites. In view of the abundance of hydrous minerals in the rocks of the Bunger Oasis, selective crystalliza-tion is more probable than on Enderby Land. On the other hand, alaskitelike varieties occur extensively among the Bunger Oasis charnockites. Granitoids of this composition must have been crystallized initially.

Thus, two modes of genesis are suggested for normal charnockites: potassium metasomatism and selective melting and recrystallization of perthitic charnockites. Both processes occur under conditions different from the conditions of formation of perthitic charnockites, i. e., higher water saturation activity with a greater mobility and activity of potassium, and apparently lower temperatures. These conditions occurred in the upper amphibolite facies rather than in the granulite facies. The similar composition of normal charnockites and igneous granitoids (ranging from granodiorite to alaskite) is an expression of their genetic relationship, currently recognized by most researchers. However, some geologists differ in their views on the relative role played by metamorphic and magmatic processes in the formation of shadow granites, and in particular, charnockites.

Certain geological features of shadow pyroxene granitoids of the crystal-line basement of the Antarctic Platform suggest that they may have been source rocks for magmatic granites. If, however, further studies may indicate that magmatic granites were the source rocks for granulite facies charnockites, then the process would have been a closed cycle. Therefore, the authors prefer to retain their original assumption, as stated above, that shadow granitoids did not originate from granites, but rather from basic and intermediate igneous rocks. This would correspond to a spiral process of development.

A group of more melanocratic rocks containing garnet, and approaching enderbites and charnockites in composition, stands out among the shadow hypersthene granitoids. On Enderby Land, they form fusiform to lenticular bodies with diffuse contacts (skialiths) within shadow garnet granites and less commonly within enderbites and charnockites. They make up entire exposures in the southeastern part of the Napier zone. Hypersthene-plagioclase schists and enderbitized plagioclase quartzites are fairly often associated with garnet-hypersthene shadow granitoids. In the Bunger Oasis, melanocratic garnet-hypersthene enderbites and their charnockitized varieties are present in the paleosome of migmatites. Leucocratic ender-bites and charnockites constitute the metasome in these migmatites and are present in regions of shadow hypersthene granitoids where they occur as separate forms having diffuse contacts. Only shadow garnet-hypersthene charnockites were encountered on Queen Maud Land.

The mineral composition of garnet-hypersthene enderbites and charnock-ites is extremely variable, depending on the different degrees and nature of granitization and on the initial composition of the rocks. The composi-tional ranges of the rock-forming minerals are as follows: quartz (3—63%), plagioclase (6—75%), perthitic K-feldspar (0—80%), hypersthene (1—28%), biotite (0—30%), ore minerals (1—12%), garnet (scattered grains to 26%). Accessory minerals include apatite, zircon, graphite, xenotime, rutile, and spinel (hercynite). The graphite content locally reaches 1—4% (Tables 24 and 25). The texture of rocks resembles that of shadow enderbites and charnockites. One common feature is the granulitic, lenticular-banded, and fusiform distribution of colored minerals and quartz. Furthermore, nearly all investigated specimens exhibit development of garnet at the contact between hypersthene and plagioclase or ore minerals and plagioclase. In places, garnet, and garnet-quartz symplektites form with hypersthene and/or ore mineral. Thus a "reaction" origin of the garnet is certain in approximately half of its occurrences. In other cases, the relationship between hypersthene and garnet is obscure or weakly indicated. Therefore, the possibility that the hypersthene-garnet association originated as an equilibrium pair during regional metamorphism cannot be ruled out (Figure 10).

The An content in the plagioclase (28—48) is generally somewhat lower than in plagioclase of the corresponding hypersthene varieties. The plagioclase is nearly always antiperthitic. Its characteristic features are a maculose structure, bent twin planes and a wavy extinction. K-feldspar in rocks from the Napier zone of Enderby Land is most often represented by perthite. The $2V$ (-60 to $-64°$) and refractive indexes ($n_x = 1.522, n_z = 1.528$ — specimen 467) suggest that the K-feldspar is soda orthoclase. However, in other specimens (765a, 765b), the $2V$ varies from -79 to $-83°$, which is characteristic of microcline. Microcline cross-hatching is often very indistinct. The composition of the plagioclase in perthitic ingrowths corresponds to its composition in charnockites. The K-feldspar in garnet-hypersthene shadow granitoids of the Bunger Oasis and Queen Maud Land is similar to K-feldspar from the charnockite in the same regions.

The hypersthene is generally distinctly pleochroic, even in varieties with low iron contents. Some hypersthene grains from rocks with an enderbitic composition exhibit a transverse banding. The ferruginosity of the hypersthene is 36—65 at.%, which approximately corresponds to that of hypersthenes from garnet-free shadow charnockitoids of similar compo-sition found in corresponding regions. Only on Enderby Land is the iron content of hypersthene slightly lower in the perthitic garnet-hypersthene

TABLE 24. Chemical composition of normal shadow charnockites from the Bunger Oasis and Enderby Land

Component	Specimen No.																	
	187			115			248			121a			66zh			776a		
	wt%	at.%	$\frac{R}{Al}$	wt%	at.%	$\frac{R}{Al}$	wt%	at.%	$\frac{R}{Al}$	wt%	at.%	$\frac{R}{Al}$	wt%	at.%	$\frac{R}{Al}$	wt%	at.%	$\frac{R}{Al}$
SiO_2	63.65	62.0	4.00	69.30	66.2	4.04	71.45	67.7	4.84	72.74	68.2	4.64	72.77	68.8	4.71	72.11	68.5	4.48
TiO_2	1.30	0.9	0.06	0.42	0.3	0.02	0.51	0.3	0.02	0.38	0.3	0.02	0.05	—	—	0.23	0.2	0.01
Al_2O_3	13.67	15.5	1.00	14.40	16.2	1.00	12.48	14.0	1.00	13.23	14.7	1.00	13.18	14.6	1.00	13.73	15.3	1.00
Fe_2O_3	4.42	3.3	0.21	0.81	0.6	0.04	0.47	0.3	0.02	1.72	1.2	0.08	0.66	0.5	0.03	0.84	0.6	0.04
FeO	5.24	4.3	0.28	2.82	2.2	0.14	4.32	3.4	0.24	2.01	1.6	0.11	1.61	1.2	0.08	1.88	1.5	0.10
MnO	0.22	0.2	0.01	0.09	—	—	0.08	—	—	0.11	—	—	0.04	—	—	0.05	—	—
MgO	0.90	1.3	0.08	1.50	2.1	0.13	1.62	2.3	0.16	0.74	1.0	0.07	1.09	1.5	0.10	0.85	1.2	0.08
CaO	3.99	4.2	0.27	2.96	3.0	0.19	1.33	1.4	0.10	1.85	1.9	0.13	1.28	1.3	0.09	1.84	1.6	0.11
Na_2O	2.00	3.7	0.24	1.66	3.0	0.19	1.94	3.6	0.26	2.61	4.8	0.33	2.20	4.0	0.27	2.77	5.1	0.34
K_2O	3.42	4.3	0.28	5.21	6.3	0.39	5.77	7.0	0.50	5.31	6.3	0.43	6.74	8.1	0.55	4.85	5.9	0.39
P_2O_5	0.40	0.3	0.02	0.13	0.1	—	0.02	—	—	0.01	—	—	—	—	—	0.08	0.1	—
Loss on ignition	0.54	—	—	0.42	—	—	0.16	—	—	0.57	—	—	0.42	—	—	0.52	—	—
Σ	99.75	100.0	—	99.72	100.0	—	100.15	100.0	—	100.28	100.0	—	100.04	100.0	—	99.75	100.0	—

TABLE 24 (continued)

	Specimen No.					
	187	115	248	121a	66zh	776a
Numerical characteristics (after Zavaritskii)						
a	9.4	11.1	12.2	13.0	14.3	12.8
b	11.1	6.8	7.8	4.7	3.8	4.9
c	4.5	3.6	1.6	2.1	1.5	1.9
s	75.0	78.5	78.4	80.2	80.4	80.4
Q	+26.7	+31.2	+30.8	+32.3	+30.7	+36.3
f'	85.2	50.0	56.3	72.9	52.6	50.6
m'	13.8	37.0	33.6	25.7	47.4	28.8
c'	3.7	—	—	1.4	—	—
a'	—	13.0	10.1	—	—	20.6
Coordinates of the ACF diagram (after Eskola and Korzhinskii)						
A	43.6	47.8	32.4	42.6	38.2	49.7
C	23.7	21.3	13.0	22.2	19.5	19.2
F	32.7	30.9	54.6	35.2	42.3	31.1
Norm, % (after Barth)						
Albite	18.7	15.2	17.9	23.8	19.9	25.4
Anorthite	18.4	14.3	6.8	9.1	6.5	7.7
Orthoclase	21.1	31.4	34.9	31.6	40.6	29.4
Orthopyroxene	6.3	7.6	10.5	3.4	5.1	4.3
Clinopyroxene	—	—	—	0.2	—	—
Magnetite	4.9	0.9	0.5	1.9	0.7	0.9
Ilmenite	1.9	0.6	0.7	0.6	—	0.3
Apatite	0.8	0.3	—	—	—	0.3
Quartz	27.6	28.6	28.0	29.4	27.2	30.4
Corundum	—	1.1	0.7	—	—	1.3

N o t e . Modes of analyzed rock are given in Table 21.

TABLE 25. Mineral composition and characteristics of garnet-hypersthene shadow granitoids

Specimen No.	Mineral composition, vol.%							An content of plagioclase	Characteristics of minerals						
									hypersthene			garnet		biotite	
	qz	plag	Kfs	hyp	gar	biot	orem		n_z	n_x	f at.%	n	f at.%	n_z	f at.%
Bunger Oasis															
161b	15	50	—	26	3	1	5	40	1.729	1.712	51	1.785	65	—	—
155	7	68	—	17	3	3	2	40	1.722	1.708	46	1.778	60	—	—
127	45	20	—	9	22	—	4	35	1.716	1.703	38	1.780	61	—	—
161zh	25	63	5	7	2	1	2	40	1.731	1.715	55	—	—	—	—
177	20	44	5	8	2	16	5	40	1.727	1.712	51	1.778	60	—	—
85b	12	64	2	11	5	1	2	35	1.720	1.706	44	1.780	61	—	—
127a	6	45	5	24	11	—	12	35	1.714	1.699	36	1.785	65	—	—
445b	25	48	2	6	10	7	2	35	—	—	—	1.780	61	—	—
84	33	30	5	4	18	9	2	32	1.731	1.715	55	—	—	—	—
412	12	70	3	10	2	2	1	42	1.734	1.716	57	—	—	—	—
401	10	75	3	10	1	—	1	43	1.729	1.714	53	1.790	69	1.654	44
201	12	21	46	8	3	6	4	35	1.733	1.716	56	—	—	—	—
254a	15	38	32	10	1	3	1	34	—	—	—	—	—	1.654	44
346	18	22	53	1	1	4	1	32	—	—	—	—	—	—	—
714	15	27	50	5	1	1	1	31	1.728	1.710	52	—	—	—	—
Queen Maud Land															
873	20	35	15	6	15	4	5	36	1.746	1.728	64	1.798	75	1.665	48
867v	25	18	35	2	15	4	1	32	1.738	1.720	59	1.800	77	—	—
827	30	20	24	4	7	15	—	28	1.755	1.738	73	1.805	81	1.677	54

charnockites than in garnet-free charnockites. According to optical data,
the ferruginosity of garnet in garnet-hypersthene shadow granites is
57—83 at.% on Enderby Land, 60—69 at.% in the Bunger Oasis and 75—81 at.%
on Queen Maud Land. The ferruginosities of hypersthene and garnet
increase in a parallel manner, but the ferruginosity of garnet is always
greater than that of hypersthene. In general, garnets that are the lowest
in calcium (3—5% grossular or andradite) are found in rocks with distinct
"reaction" garnet, whereas garnets of higher calcium content (8—14%
grossular) are usually found in rocks in which the reaction origin is
obscure. These two rock groups may have different parageneses which
are intertransitional but which originated under different physicochemical
conditions. Biotite, a usual component of these rocks, generally has a lower
iron content (28.51 at.%) than the coexisting garnet and hypersthene. Biotites
with the lowest iron contents are found in rocks free of K-feldspar.

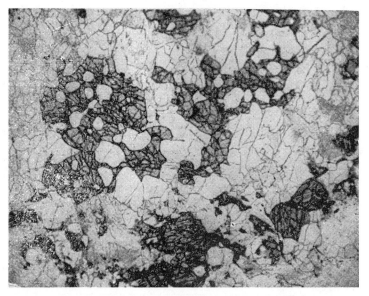

FIGURE 10. Garnet-hypersthene shadow granitoid (x 10, regular light, thin section
768a).

The chemical composition of garnet-hypersthene enderbites and
charnockites is presented in Table 26. The most important feature of
these rocks is their saturation in alumina. Among the corresponding
garnet-free varieties, there are also certain rocks which are saturated
in alumina, but they are generally also most saturated in quartz. In
garnet-bearing rocks, alumina saturation is encountered in all specimens. The garnet-bearing enderbites differ from the Enderby Land
enderbites in their higher contents of iron, magnesium, and calcium and

TABLE 26.   Chemical composition of garnet-hypersthene shadow granitoids

Component	179v			836b			765b			836d			765a		
	wt%	at.%	R/Al	wt%	at.%	R/Al	wt%	at.%	R/Al	wt%	at.%	R/Al	wt%	at.%	R/Al
SiO_2	59.52	55.9	3.36	66.34	61.3	3.92	74.35	70.5	4.98	69.53	66.1	4.12	71.16	67.6	4.39
TiO_2	0.66	0.5	0.03	0.24	0.2	0.01	0.22	0.2	0.01	0.45	0.3	0.02	0.26	0.2	0.01
Al_2O_3	15.00	16.6	1.00	14.40	16.1	1.00	12.79	14.3	1.00	14.15	15.8	1.00	13.71	15.4	1.00
Fe_2O_3	0.77	0.4	0.02	1.10	0.8	0.05	0.61	0.4	0.03	1.40	1.0	0.06	0.96	0.7	0.05
FeO	9.79	7.6	0.46	5.47	4.3	0.26	1.87	1.5	0.10	2.75	2.2	0.14	3.41	2.7	0.18
MnO	0.14	0.1	—	0.12	—	—	0.05	—	—	0.04	—	—	0.08	—	—
MgO	5.64	7.9	0.48	3.74	5.3	0.32	0.43	0.6	0.04	1.42	2.0	0.13	0.38	0.5	0.03
CaO	4.80	4.8	0.29	5.32	5.4	0.33	1.11	1.1	0.08	2.40	2.5	0.16	1.11	1.1	0.07
Na_2O	3.06	5.5	0.33	2.24	4.1	0.25	2.65	4.9	0.34	2.24	4.1	0.26	2.58	4.7	0.31
K_2O	0.55	0.6	0.04	0.62	0.6	0.04	5.45	6.5	0.45	4.92	5.9	0.37	5.70	7.0	0.45
P_2O_5	0.16	0.1	—	0.09	0.1	—	0.03	—	—	0.16	0.1	—	0.09	0.1	—
Loss on ignition	0.28	—	—	0.51	—	—	0.47	—	—	0.35	—	—	0.42	—	—
Σ	100.37	100.0	—	100.19	100.0	—	100.03	100.0	—	99.81	100.0	—	99.86	100.0	—

Specimen No.

TABLE 26 (continued)

	Specimen No.														
	756b			179a			412			201			346		
Component	wt%	at.%	R/Al	wt%	at.%	R/Al	wt%	at.%	R/Al	wt%	at.%	R/Al	wt%	at.%	R/Al
SiO$_2$	74.35	70.6	4.98	69.35	66.3	4.64	62.54	59.0	3.22	63.94	62.0	4.59	67.70	63.5	3.80
TiO$_2$	0.22	0.2	0.01	0.88	0.6	0.04	0.84	0.6	0.03	1.70	1.2	0.09	0.55	0.4	0.02
Al$_2$O$_3$	12.79	14.2	1.00	12.73	14.3	1.00	16.45	18.3	1.00	11.82	13.5	1.00	15.14	16.7	1.00
Fe$_2$O$_3$	0.61	0.4	0.03	0.63	0.5	0.03	1.10	0.8	0.04	3.86	2.8	0.21	0.45	0.3	0.01
FeO	1.87	1.5	0.11	5.64	4.5	0.31	5.98	4.7	0.26	8.36	6.8	0.50	4.71	3.7	0.22
MnO	0.05	—	—	0.04	—	—	0.10	—	—	0.12	—	—	0.08	—	—
MgO	0.43	0.6	0.04	3.09	4.5	0.31	2.78	3.9	0.21	2.58	3.7	0.27	1.86	2.6	0.16
CaO	1.11	1.1	0.08	2.51	2.6	0.18	4.72	4.8	0.26	0.86	0.9	0.07	1.71	1.7	0.10
Na$_2$O	2.65	4.9	0.35	1.68	3.1	0.22	2.75	5.0	0.27	1.80	3.4	0.25	2.67	4.9	0.29
K$_2$O	5.45	6.5	0.46	2.85	3.5	0.24	2.39	2.8	0.15	4.58	5.7	0.42	5.09	6.1	0.37
P$_2$O$_5$	0.03	—	—	0.12	0.1	—	0.11	0.1	—	0.02	—	—	0.09	0.1	—
Loss on ignition	0.47	—	—	0.49	—	—	0.27	—	—	0.47	—	—	0.08	—	—
Σ	100.03	100.0	—	100.01	100.0	—	100.03	100.0	—	100.11	100.0	—	100.13	100.0	—

TABLE 26 (continued)

	Specimen No.									
	179v	836b	765b	836d	765a	756b	179a	412	201	346
Numerical characteristics (after Zavaritskii)										
a	7.5	5.7	13.3	11.9	13.7	13.3	7.6	9.5	10.2	12.8
b	18.7	13.0	3.6	6.9	5.0	3.4	12.0	12.5	18.0	10.9
c	5.9	6.4	1.3	2.9	1.3	1.3	3.0	5.8	0.9	2.0
s	67.9	74.9	81.8	78.3	80.0	82.0	77.4	72.2	70.9	74.3
Q	+14.9	+32.0	+35.7	+29.9	+28.7	+36.1	+36.6	+19.6	+20.5	+21.0
f'	48.8	47.4	63.0	53.0	65.0	63.0	41.0	53.6	60.0	43.4
m'	46.8	48.4	20.3	33.0	10.0	20.0	37.0	37.7	23.3	27.7
c'	—	—	—	—	—	—	—	—	—	—
a'	4.4	4.2	16.7	14.0	25.0	17.0	22.0	8.7	16.7	28.9
Coordinates of the ACF diagram (after Eskola and Korzhinskii)										
A	41.2	42.8	46.2	46.4	45.0	46.2	40.3	43.7	28.0	41.8
C	19.1	20.5	18.9	19.7	14.3	18.9	13.4	19.9	5.5	12.3
F	39.7	36.7	34.9	33.9	40.7	34.9	46.3	36.4	66.5	45.9
Norm, % (after Barth)										
Albite	27.5	20.5	24.5	20.5	23.7	24.4	15.5	25.3	16.9	24.5
Anorthite	23.3	26.2	5.7	11.4	4.8	5.6	12.1	23.0	4.3	7.6
Orthoclase	3.1	3.4	32.7	29.7	34.9	32.6	17.5	14.1	28.5	30.3
Orthopyroxene	29.9	18.1	3.4	6.8	5.2	3.4	16.0	15.4	15.9	11.5
Clinopyroxene	—	—	—	—	—	—	—	—	—	—
Magnetite	0.7	1.2	0.7	1.5	1.0	0.6	0.7	1.2	4.2	0.5
Ilmenite	1.0	0.3	0.3	0.6	0.5	0.3	1.3	1.1	2.4	0.8
Apatite	0.3	0.3	—	0.3	0.3	—	0.4	0.3	—	0.3
Quartz	13.1	29.2	32.2	28.0	28.0	32.1	33.6	18.5	25.1	21.8
Corundum	1.1	0.8	0.5	1.2	1.6	1.0	2.9	1.2	2.7	2.7

Note. Modal compositions of analyzed samples are given in Tables 24 and 25.

lower alkalis. These differences are particularly emphasized when specimens with identical Si : Al ratios are compared. There are comparable differences between enderbites and garnet-hypersthene enderbites of the Bunger Oasis. The garnet-hypersthene perthitic charnockites of Enderby Land differ from the corresponding garnet-free varieties mainly in their higher iron and potassium contents and lower sodium and calcium contents; their alkali contents are closely similar The garnet-bearing charnockites from the Bunger Oasis differ from analogous garnet-free charnockites in their higher magnesium (and sometimes iron) contents, and their lower silica saturation. The differences between garnet-bearing enderbites and charnockites are the same as between their garnet-free varieties.

The chemical relationships between the garnet-hypersthene shadow granitoids and their garnet-free varieties suggest a specific composition for the parent rock of the garnet-hypersthene enderbites. However, the origin of garnet and its distinct reaction relationships with plagioclase and hypersthene (or ore minerals) in charnockites and charnockitized enderbites may also have come about during granitization accompanied by loss of calcium and a release of the excessive alumina. This could take place only at relatively low alkali activity since the excessive alumina (in view of the saturation of the rock in quartz) would be consumed in the formation of alkaline feldspar, which is not the case. The problem of the removal of the Fe-Mg components from these rocks is also related to a low alkali activity. On the other hand, garnet-hypersthene charnockites could also be formed by granitization of garnet-hypersthene enderbites.

A third possible mode of origin for the garnet-hypersthene association is bimetasomatism at the contact between aluminous and calcareous-magnesian rocks.

ALUMINOUS SCHISTS

Aluminous schists together with gneisses of acid composition are essential components of the ancient highly metamorphosed series. They were encountered in nearly all parts of the crystalline basement of the Antarctic Platform and often combine with other rocks to form metamorphic groups. However, the proportion of these rocks in the total metamorphites is significantly smaller than that of Ca-Mg rocks, and they play only a subordinate role in the sections across high-grade metamorphic regions. Inasmuch as these gneisses and schists are saturated in alumina and silica, they are easily subject to migmatization and granitization, and hence the nearly complete absence of nongranitized rocks among them. Most aluminous schists are strongly migmatized, mostly to layered varieties. Two types of migmatites can be distinguished according to the relationships between the paleosome and the metasome:

1) Finely layered migmatites, in which intercalations of paleosome and metasome (of various shapes) range from one to several centimeters in thickness, are the most widespread. Their structure is often complicated

by microfolding and plication. In most varieties, the metasome predominates significantly over the paleosome. They are thus close to shadow
granites and are only arbitrarily termed migmatites. Therefore, in the
present consideration of these rocks, they are not distinguished from the
corresponding shadow granites.

2) Coarsely layered migmatites, which occur to a much lesser extent
than the finely layered varieties. The bands of paleosome and metasome
vary in thickness from 5 to 40 cm. Interlayer contacts are sinuous
and sometimes discontinuous. Coarsely layered migmatites are often
accompanied by the finely layered varieties.

Shadow granites formed from aluminous schists are transitional to finely
layered migmatites and are conformable with them, forming separate
layers (up to 1 m thick) or comparatively thin (5—30 cm) layers within
migmatites. They differ from the latter only in the homogeneity of their
texture. These shadow granites contain one, or more commonly, two
feldspars (plagioclase or plagioclase plus K-feldspar). A third variety of
shadow granite contains predominant amounts of alkali feldspars (perthitic
granites). Thick perthitic granites covering large regions are uniformly
homogeneous. To date, these perthitic granites have been encountered only
in the Napier zone of Enderby Land, where they are accompanied by a small
quantity of coarsely banded migmatites. The latter contain only perthitic
feldspar in the metasome.

Finely layered migmatites with a plagiogranite metasome together with
shadow plagioclase granites are widespread in the Bunger Oasis and in
the Rayner zone of Enderby Land. They are less common on Queen Maud
Land and in the Denman Glacier area, where they often appear as the
paleosome in finely banded migmatites and as shadow granites, containing
K-feldspar in addition to the plagioclase. Bifeldspar finely layered migmatites and shadow granites (which are absent from the Napier zone of
Enderby Land) are widespread.

The mineral composition and structure of rocks of the following five
groups of migmatized and granitized aluminous schists are considered
below: 1) shadow plagioclase granites and finely layered migmatites with
a plagiogranite metasome; 2) coarsely layered migmatites with a perthitic
metasome; 3) shadow perthitic granites; 4) coarsely layered migmatites
with a granitic metasome; 5) shadow granites and finely layered migmatites.

Shadow plagioclase granites and finely layered mig-
matites differ from the other granitized aluminous schists in that their
important high-alumina colored mineral is garnet, with only subordinate
biotite. In their geological and structural features, the garnet plagiogranites
resemble enderbites of Enderby Land. In that location, the garnet plagiogranites are either interbedded with enderbites and enderbitized pyroxene-
plagioclase schists or are remnants of paleosome in shadow garnet granites.
Their most massive varieties build nunataks in zones of intensive enderbitization of Ca-Mg schists. Other varieties form finely layered migmatites (with plagiogranite metasome). Shadow plagiogranites also occur
in the Bunger Oasis, where they usually form strata within migmatized
pyroxene-plagioclase schists having an enderbitic metasome. Shadow

garnet plagiogranites of more uniform structure occur within uniform groups of pyroxene-plagioclase schist beds. In the Denman Glacier area, shadow garnet plagiogranites form a fixed group of rock strata, containing sillimanite quartzites as paleosome remnants. Similar isolated units of shadow garnet plagiogranites have been encountered on Queen Maud Land in the Schirmacher Oasis and on western slopes of the Humboldt Mountains, where they are interbedded with pyroxene-plagioclase schists, marbles, calciphyres and quartzites. Less commonly, they form the paleosome of layered migmatites, in which shadow garnet granite is the metasome.

Garnet shadow plagiogranites are distinguished by a brownish gray or yellowish gray color and an indistinct gneissosity, not infrequently complicated by the presence of large garnet porphyroblasts, and by augen in varieties affected by cataclasis followed by recrystallization. Their composition is highly variable (Table 27), primarily with respect to the quartz content which varies from 15 to 50%. In general, varieties with high quartz contents have lower contents of colored minerals. The plagioclase content usually nearly doubles that of quartz, the ratio of these minerals approaching unity only in rare cases (in varieties with a high quartz content). In addition to the plagioclase, approximately one-half of the investigated specimens also contain insignificant amounts of K-feldspar. The colored minerals in these rocks are always represented by garnet and biotite, in highly variable amounts. The content of these minerals exceeds 20% in melanocratic varieties. Magnetite and other ore minerals occur in small amounts (1–2% and rarely reaching 4%). Accessory minerals consist of zoned zircon and rarely apatite or rutile.

The granites under consideration have metablastic and less commonly granoblastic textures. The metablasts are near-isometric or elongated garnet grains up to 3–4 mm across, with complex outlines. They contain inclusions of plagioclase, biotite and quartz and are thus nearly diablastic. The matrix is lepidogranoblastic inequigranular. The texture is determined by a subparallel distribution of biotite (up to 1 mm long) embedded in a blasto-mesostasis consisting of ragged plagioclase grains and more or less lenticular quartz grains with serrated and irregular crystal boundaries. In places, quartz grains are granulated and include sporadic biotite and zircon. This texture is often complicated by corrosion and replacement of plagioclase and garnet by quartz and biotite. K-feldspar is intergranular, and also develops in cracks within the rock and in individual plagioclase grains. Myrmekite fringes are formed in places at the boundary of plagioclase with K-feldspar. The rocks display fairly distinct signs of cataclasis followed by recrystallization — large quartz grains exhibit a marked "blocky" extinction, plagioclase has a wavy extinction and bent twin boundaries. Locally, there is a mosaic aggregate of quartz interstitial to plagioclase grains. Garnet grains are roughly lenticular and mostly cracked. Biotite and K-feldspar are only slightly affected or unaffected by cataclasis or recrystallization, indicating their later origin in comparison with the other minerals.

TABLE 27. Mineral composition and characteristics in shadow garnet plagiogranites of Antarctica

Specimen No.	Mineral composition, vol.%						Characteristics of minerals					Geological setting
	qz	plag	clpy	gar	biot	ore and accessory minerals	An content of plagioclase	garnet n	garnet f at.%	biotite n_z	biotite f at.%	
Enderby Land												
836a	23	60	—	7	10	—	—	—	—	—	—	Interbedded with enderbites
312	20	40	—	25	15	o.s.*	32	1.791	68	—	—	Intercalations in enderbites
179g	17	36	2	30	15	.	30	1.783	59	—	—	Intercalations within garnet-hypersthene and garnet shadow granitoids
631b	25	60	1	2	10	2	37	1.811	83	—	—	Augen garnet plagiogneiss within shadow garnet granitoids
644a	18	40	—	22	20	—	37	—	—	—	—	Interbedded with plagioclase quartzites
638	37	53	5	+	4	1	37	—	—	—	—	Outcrop containing lenses of pyroxene-plagioclase schists
481	50	47	3	+	+	—	—	—	—	—	—	As above
44—1	29	60	—	3	7	1	43–50	1.785	64	—	—	Interbedded with pyroxene-plagioclase schists and enderbites
Bunger Oasis												
93b	30	35	5	25	3	2	39	1.788	66	1.650	43	Plagiogneiss
470a	25	45	10	15	4	1	38	—	—	1.668	51	Plagiogneiss
143a	30	56	—	6	6	2	30	1.780	60	1.623	30	Finely layered migmatites with plagiogranite metasome
144	29	59	—	6	4	2	27	—	—	—	—	
205	20	60	—	12	7	1	30	1.784	63	—	—	
277a	30	57	—	8	4	1	29	1.780	60	1.625	31	
438	35	42	2	10	10	1	31	1.785	64	—	—	
665	30	50	—	10	7	2	30	1.785	64	—	—	
Denman Glacier area												
1176	22	60	—	5	12	1	41	—	—	1.664	48	Mt. Bortsov
1170b	20	61	—	7	11	1	43	—	—	—	—	Mt. Gist
Queen Maud Land												
852	30	35	10	20	4	1	35	1.776	58	1.641	38	Plagiogneiss
802	20	45	5	18	10	2	30	1.780	60	1.634	35	
734	15	58	—	15	10	2	29	1.780	60	1.670	52	Migmatite paleosome

* [o.s. = optic sign.]

Plagioclase in garnet plagiogranite differs little from that in enderbites. It ranges from An 27 to 43, generally corresponding to andesine (An 34). Both antiperthitic and pure plagioclase occur within single samples. There are also plagioclase inclusions (An rises to 43–50) in antiperthitic plagioclase. The average ferruginosity of garnet is 64 at.%, only rarely rising to 83 at.%. The ferruginosity of biotite is 30–52 at.%. K-feldspar, locally occurring in shadow plagiogranites, has a low $2V$ (from –50 to –60°) and is thus an orthoclase. However, it exhibits a fine microcline crosshatching in its margins in rocks from the Bunger Oasis and Queen Maud Land.

The chemical composition of shadow plagiogranites is given in Table 28. Based on Zavaritskii's classification, they may belong to rocks oversaturated in SiO_2 and Al_2O_3 but low in alkalis. Although the contents (by weight) of aluminum in enderbites and plagiogranites are practically the same, the plagiogranites are richer in silica and lower in calcium, thus permitting the release of an additional quantity of aluminum for the formation of high-alumina minerals. The iron content in plagiogranites is the same as that in enderbites. Therefore, the formation of garnet instead of hypersthene + sillimanite is due to the $P-T$ conditions during formation of the plagiogranites, and not to the chemical composition of the rocks /26/. The Ca : Al ratio in the garnet plagiogranites is 0.15–0.24 which is comparable to its value in the leucocratic enderbites of the Bunger Oasis. The sodium content is 3–4 times that of potassium, also similar to the enderbites. Potassium may be more abundant than sodium, by approximately 1%, only in specimens containing free K-feldspar. This is another factor indicating that free K-feldspar appears in the rock due to feldspathization and not to a segregation of exsolved antiperthite. The plagiogranites of Queen Maud Land are more enriched in alkalis (mostly sodium) and therefore less saturated in aluminum. They differ in this respect from the garnet plagiogranites of Enderby Land and Bunger Oasis. Possibly, their higher sodium content is due to the lower temperature of formation and higher alkalinity of the metasomatizing solutions.

Shadow garnet plagiogranites have no analogies among igneous rocks with respect to chemical composition. They are the most closely approached, in that respect, by various quartz-feldspar sandstones /67/ which contain less alkalis and more calcium than the plagiogranites. In view of the fact that the influx of alkalis into a rock in the course of granitization is accompanied, in the first place, by a loss of calcium, it may be assumed that the garnet plagiogranites originated by the metamorphism of quartz-feldspar sandstones. Apparently, the different initial composition is also responsible for the occasionally considerable fluctuations in the contents of silica, alumina and other oxides (iron, magnesium, calcium) in the plagiogranites. These fluctuations, however, also depend, to a lesser extent, on the grade of granitization.

Coarsely layered migmatites have a perthitic-granitic metasome similar to that of shadow garnet perthitic granites and apparently formed in situ by partial fusion. As a rule, the high-alumina paleosome also contains aluminous quartzites (described in the next chapter). The high alumina and quartz contents in the paleosome of these migmatites result

TABLE 28. Chemical composition of shadow garnet plagiogranites of Antarctica

Specimen No.

Component	179g			179a			836a			143a			734		
	wt%	at.%	$\frac{R}{Al}$	wt%	at.%	$\frac{R}{Al}$	wt%	at.%	$\frac{R}{Al}$	wt%	at.%	$\frac{R}{Al}$	wt%	at.%	$\frac{R}{Al}$
SiO_2	57.11	53.5	2.66	69.69	66.1	3.80	71.32	68.2	4.40	70.59	66.7	4.00	65.15	61.0	3.37
TiO_2	0.78	0.6	0.03	0.28	0.2	0.01	0.56	0.4	0.03	0.30	0.2	0.01	0.72	0.5	0.03
Al_2O_3	18.27	20.1	1.00	15.36	17.4	1.00	13.78	15.5	1.00	15.05	16.7	1.00	16.35	18.1	1.00
Fe_2O_3	0.99	0.7	0.03	0.60	0.5	0.03	0.73	0.5	0.03	0.83	0.6	0.04	0.88	0.7	0.04
FeO	9.05	7.1	0.35	3.41	2.7	0.16	4.81	3.8	0.24	3.55	2.8	0.17	5.85	4.6	0.25
MnO	0.15	0.1	—	0.08	—	—	0.20	0.2	0.01	0.16	0.1	—	0.09	—	—
MgO	4.97	6.9	0.34	1.68	2.4	0.14	1.86	2.6	0.17	1.10	1.5	0.09	1.42	2.0	0.11
CaO	3.07	3.1	0.15	4.13	4.2	0.24	2.68	2.8	0.18	3.00	3.1	0.19	3.75	3.8	0.21
Na_2O	3.00	5.4	0.27	2.84	5.2	0.30	2.51	4.6	0.30	3.79	6.9	0.41	4.01	7.3	0.40
K_2O	2.20	2.6	0.13	1.12	1.3	0.07	1.10	1.4	0.09	1.10	1.4	0.08	1.58	1.9	0.10
P_2O_5	0.03	—	—	0.06	—	—	—	—	—	—	—	—	0.12	0.1	0.01
Loss on ignition	0.39	—	—	0.39	—	—	0.59	—	—	0.53	—	—	traces	—	—
Σ	100.01	100.0	—	99.91	100.0	—	100.14	100.0	—	100.00	100.0	—	99.92	100.00	—

TABLE 28 (continued)

	Specimen No.				
	179g	179a	836a	143a	734
Numerical characteristics (after Zavaritskii)					
a	9.3	7.6	6.7	9.7	11.1
b	24.1	8.8	12.6	8.5	10.7
c	3.6	6.4	3.1	3.6	4.5
s	63.0	77.2	77.6	78.2	73.7
Q	+3.8	+32.8	+36.7	+33.4	+20.7
f'	38.0	40.0	40.5	47.4	59.7
m'	33.4	30.0	23.6	20.8	22.0
c'	—	—	—	—	—
a'	28.6	30.0	35.9	31.8	18.3
Coordinates of the ACF diagram (after Eskola and Korzhinskii)					
A	41.3	53.6	50.3	53.0	45.9
C	10.5	21.0	14.5	19.2	19.6
F	48.2	25.4	35.2	27.8	34.5
Norm, % (after Barth)					
Albite	27.1	26.2	23.0	34.6	36.6
Anorthite	15.5	20.5	13.8	15.3	18.0
Orthoclase	12.9	6.8	6.9	6.8	9.6
Orthopyroxene	26.4	9.2	12.1	7.9	11.5
Magnetite	1.0	0.7	0.7	0.8	1.0
Ilmenite	1.1	0.5	0.8	0.5	1.0
Apatite	—	0.2	—	—	0.3
Quartz	10.1	33.3	38.7	31.8	20.4
Corundum	5.9	2.6	4.0	2.3	1.6

Note. Mineral compositions of analyzed rocks are given in Table 27.

in a high melting point. Consequently, if the rocks saturated in quartz and alumina had been interbedded with feldspathic rocks having lower melting points (e. g., shadow granites), the latter would have been converted to the metasome and the former would have remained as the paleosome. This was probably the formation mechanism of these migmatites. The composition of some xenoliths in intrusive charnockites is analogous to that of the paleosome of the migmatites under consideration.

The mineral composition of the migmatite paleosome is given in Table 29. The following varieties can be differentiated with respect to the content of aluminous minerals: 1) spinel-sillimanite-cordierite; 2) spinel-sillimanite-garnet; 3) spinel-sillimanite-garnet-cordierite. The third variety locally contains sapphirine or hypersthene, and rarely corundum. The majority of specimens contain perthite, biotite (up to 7—9%) and plagioclase grains (up to 3—11%). Quartz is an essential component of these rocks, ranging from 5—30%. The quantitative ratios of the rock-forming minerals are variable; nevertheless cordierite and/or garnet are the predominant minerals. Their contents appear to be mutually related; a low cordierite content corresponding to high garnet content, and vice versa. Of other high-alumina minerals, sillimanite makes up 2—8% of the rock. The spinel content does not exceed 5%. A noteworthy feature is the ubiquitous presence of the following minerals: quartz, spinel and sillimanite. This is evidently the primary association whereas the others originated during the course of various transformations during granitization and selective fusion. Bimetasomatic exchange reactions between the paleosome and metasome of migmatites probably played an important role.

The textural relationships between minerals are rather complicated. The spinel-sillimanite-quartz-cordierite paleosome has a granoblastic texture combining certain poikiloblastic features. The rock consists of irregular, slightly flattened grains of cordierite and quartz, containing rutile needles and uniformly oriented columnar crystals of sillimanite. The cordierite also contains spinel and is highly corroded by quartz which forms rounded ingrowths. The feldspathized variety contains intergranular perthite, which intensively replaces cordierite, and biotite which result in a lepidogranoblastic texture. The replacement of sillimanite and spinel by cordierite is clear. There are also small aggregates of spinel and corundum. Feldspathized spinel-sillimanite-quartz-garnet paleosome has a metablastic texture, due to large irregular garnet metablasts (up to 4 mm) in a fine-grained mesastasis (0.5—1 mm) consisting of the other minerals. Spinel is overgrown by sillimanite and its relicts are included in the garnet. The latter replaces quartz and spinel and contains sillimanite inclusions only in marginal portions of its grains. There is obviously a replacement of the spinel-quartz association by the garnet-sillimanite association. K-feldspar, represented by perthite, occurs in grain aggregates with inclusions of relict plagioclase granules. In turn, quartz contains idiomorphic granules of garnet, sillimanite and rutile needles. Flattened quartz grains and sillimanite prisms are similarly oriented.

TABLE 29. Mineral composition and characteristics in Enderby Land granitoids

Speci-men No.	Mineral composition						An content of plagioclase	Garnet		Geological setting
	qz	plag	perth-ite	gar	biot	ore and accessory minerals		n	f at.%	
179b	3	2	83	10	o.s.**	2	34	1.780	65*	Shadow granitoid layers
479	38	5	48	6	2	1	35	1.780	60	A 20-m intercalation in shadow charnockites
486a	13	—	85	2	o.s.	o.s.	—	1.810	82	Outcrop
813d	27	—	66	7	"	"	—	1.791	68	Unit of various high-alumina gneisses and quartzites
179	30	1	68	1	—	"	30	1.791	62*	Shadow granitoid layers
21	27	6	58	8	6	"	25	—	62*	Outcrop
52b	13	o.s.	85	2	—	"	—	—	63*	Interbedded with charno-ckites and pyroxene-plagioclase schists
28	25	12	58	5	o.s.	"	27	1.813	78*	Outcrop
28a	13	60	27	o.s.	—	—	32	1.817	84*	Maculose relicts of paleo-some in shadow granites (specimen 28)
205a	20	5	69	6	—	o.s.	—	—	—	Interbedded with charno-ckites and quartzites

* These values are based on spectroscopic silicate analyses.

** [o.s. = optic sign.]

Spinel-sillimanite-quartz-garnet-cordierite varieties, largely feldspath-ized, are the most widespread in the paleosome of migmatites. Their textures are hetero-granoblastic, but the majority of minerals are lenti-cularly flattened. Garnet metablasts usually stand out by their large size, up to 5 mm. The cordierite metablasts are somewhat smaller, up to 2.5 mm. The grains of other minerals seldom exceed 0.5—0.6 mm. They are usually shapeless with ragged outlines, only sillimanite being locally columnar. Mineral replacements and reaction rims are widespread. Spinel and corundum, often forming aggregates with ore minerals, are overgrown by sillimanite and sapphirine. Spinel is especially often en-closed in a sillimanite envelope. In their turn, these minerals are over-grown by rims of cordierite or are embedded in it. Garnet often forms rims at the contacts between sillimanite or sapphirine and quartz. The relationship between garnet and cordierite is not quite clear. In places, there are hypersthene rims, some 0.5 mm wide, along their contacts. In turn, cordierite is intensively replaced by perthite and, in this case, cordierite relicts may be embedded within the K-feldspar; in such instances cordierite is simultaneously replaced by biotite. However, the most characteristic feature in the replacement of cordierite by K-feldspar is the transformation of cordierite grains into a fine symplektite of cordierite, quartz and hypersthene. When the rocks contain plagioclase, it is usually replaced by K-feldspar.

The spinel present is hercynite. Its ferruginosity in the rocks under consideration varies considerably (50 to 85 at.%). The variation of the iron content in garnet is also considerable (53–85 at.%), which corresponds almost perfectly to that of spinel. The characteristic refractive indices of sillimanite and sapphirine in these schists are presented in Table 29. Sillimanite often exhibits oblique extinction. Cordierite is always poly-synthetically twinned, and has a positive $2V$. Its ferruginosity, determined from the refractive index, is 24–41 at.%. The ferruginosity of biotite is also significantly variable (26–40 at.%). Perthite in the migmatite paleo-some differs in no respect from that in the metasome.

Shadow perthitic granites generally only contain garnet. Varieties containing spinel and garnet, sillimanite and garnet, sillimanite alone, or all these minerals together, are much less common. In the majority of cases, multimineral granites form intercalations with shadow garnet granite; in rare cases, they form separate units or occur as the metasome in coarsely-layered migmatites. Although rare, they deserve the closest attention, since their presence denotes a low alkali activity during the formation of the entire complex of perthitic granitoids.

Shadow garnet perthitic granites form thick units in the metamorphic complex of the Napier zone of Enderby Land. In extremely rare cases, they retain original relicts which are lenslike or of sheet form in section, and have a composition corresponding to feldspathized shadow garnet plagiogranites. The composition of the shadow granites near these rem-nants is distinguished by a somewhat higher plagioclase content. Blocks or lenses of Mg-Fe-Al or monomineral quartzite embedded in shadow granites may be regarded as remnants which were not readily lent to granitization. Shadow granites bearing these quartzites are enriched in quartz and occasionally contain scattered grains of high-alumina minerals (sillimanite, cordierite).

Garnet perthitic granites are white, light gray and gray in color and have a massive to slightly gneissic structure. The mineral composition is given in Table 30. Variations of the plagioclase and garnet contents range from a few scattered grains to 10%. The quartz content is 5–50% and the perthite content 40–95%. Fine booklets of biotite and chlorite replacing garnet occur sporadically in these rocks. Accessory minerals include rutile, zircon and magnetite. Epigenetically altered rocks contain epidote, zoisite, chlorite, sericite, clay minerals and iron oxides.

As with perthitic charnockites, these rocks include at least three textural varieties. The most widespread is a blastocataclastic type characterized by large perthite grains (1.5–2.5 mm), small irregular plagioclase and quartz grains (up to 0.5 mm) being jammed in the perthite interstices. The plagioclase and quartz grains have serrated boundaries. Plagioclase grains display traces of cataclasis, including bent twins, and wavy and "blocky" extinctions. Quartz occurs as small granulated grains, but locally also forms mosaic monomineral aggregates. Garnet grains are

TABLE 30. Mineral composition and characteristics of shadow perthitic granitoids containing sillimanite, spinel and garnet (Enderby Land)

Speci-men No.	Mineral composition, vol.%								Characteristics of minerals							Geological setting
	qz	plag	perth-ite	spin	sill	gar	biot	ore and acces-sory min-erals	An con-tent of plagio-clase	garnet		spinel		biotite		
										n	f at.%	n	f at.%	n_z	f at.%	
214a	25	8	66	—	1	—	o.s.**	o.s.	25	—	—	—	—	—	—	Metasome in layered migmatites
813v	18	—	77	—	5	—	—	—	—	—	—	—	—	—	—	Intercalations in inter-bedded perthitic garnet shadow granites and charnockites
795b	22	o.s.	78	—	+	+	—	—	—	—	—	—	—	—	—	Intercalations in a group of kinzigite layers
215b	o.s.	3	37	12	—	30	17	1	20	1.800*	70*	1.802	72	1.615*	28*	Intercalations in garnet perthitic shadow granites
155	32	3	57	2	—	5	—	1	28	1.791	68	—	—	—	—	Spinel-sillimanite perth-itic shadow granitoid unit
813g	7	—	53	1	15	23	1	1	—	1.792	70*	—	—	—	—	Intercalations in inter-bedded perthitic garnet shadow granites and charnockites

* These values are based on spectroscopic silicate analyses.
** [o.s. = optic sign.]

usually irregular, cracked or broken along edges and vary from 0.5 to 5 mm in diameter; they occur as metablasts (or porphyroblasts) within the hetero-granoblastic matrix. Wavy extinction is also occasionally observed in mesoperthite; this perthite rarely occurs in the fine-grained part of the rock (Figure 11). Less widespread is the granulitic texture formed by roughly lenticular quartz segregations (5—7 mm × 1—2 mm), irregularly distributed within the fine- and medium-grained mass of the other minerals. In the hetero-granoblastic texture, all mineral grains are irregular in shape, with ragged outlines. The mesoperthite and quartz grains (average 2 mm) are considerably larger than those of plagioclase (up to 0.5 mm) and garnet (0.3— 1 mm).

These textures are variously complicated by reactive relationships among the minerals. In the blastocataclastic texture, quartz grains corrode both garnet and plagioclase and contain their relicts as inclusions. Sporadic rounded mesoperthite grains and rutile needles also occur as inclusions. Fine-grained plagioclase is highly myrmekitized and forms serrated boundaries with perthite. Rare myrmekitized plagioclase grains are included in marginal zones of perthites, but retain their serrated boundaries. Rocks of this texture do not contain any other K-feldspar but perthite. The latter occasionally contains rutile needles. Certain garnet grains have broken edges, are corroded by quartz and contain plagioclase inclusions. Thin symplektitic aggregations with quartz locally develop along the edges of garnet. Aggregates of fine biotite flakes occur in rock and mineral cracks and near magnetite, clearly developed from garnet after cataclasis. In places, this biotite has a radial structure.

FIGURE 11. Shadow garnet perthitic granite with blastocataclastic texture (× 10, crossed nicols, thin section 813d).

In shadow garnet granites with hetero-granoblastic texture, quartz contains inclusions of perthite, zircon, rutile, garnet and plagioclase, and occasionally of an entire aggregate of these minerals. The plagioclase is highly myrmekitized and forms serrated boundaries with perthite. Perthite and plagioclase are intensively replaced by orthoclase. The edges of perthite grains contain rounded inclusions of quartz. Garnet grains are corroded by quartz and perthitic orthoclase. Garnet contains sporadic inclusions of quartz and zircon; biotite is often present. Rocks with this texture usually occur in the margins of the Napier zone or near faults. The highest-temperature equilibrium of minerals is found in granulitic texture rocks, characterized by an absence of inclusions in the quartz. Plagioclase is only slightly corroded by quartz and mesoperthite. Myrmekite in plagioclase is very rare. Garnet is euhedral.

In the majority of specimens, the plagioclase composition is oligoclase (An 25-30). With an increasing plagioclase content in relicts of the original rock, the anorthite content increases to 34-37% and locally reaches 55%. Maculose (nonequilibrium) structures are discernible in this basic plagioclase. Several thin sections of original rock relicts and shadow granites exhibit antiperthitic ingrowths in the plagioclase, emphasizing the enderbitic nature of the rocks. Twinning of plagioclase is very fine and indistinct, but is totally absent in myrmekitic grains.

The properties of the alkaline feldspar (perthite) are practically the same as those of the perthite in the shadow charnockites. The perthite in original rock relicts has a lower content of the plagioclase molecule than the perthite in the shadow granite host, although the basicity of plagioclase ingrowths remains approximately the same. This observation is in agreement with Barth's paleothermometer, according to which feldspars with the same albite distribution coefficient in coexisting plagioclase and alkaline feldspar may be formed at the same temperatures. Measured refracted indices of K-feldspar in perthite ($n_x = 1.521$, $n_z = 1.528$) indicate that it is Na-orthoclase; thus not all of the albite content is confined to the plagioclase ingrowths of perthite. According to $2V$ measurements (-60 to -80°), the K-feldspar of perthite is a triclinic orthoclase, fluctuating between slightly triclinic minerals and nearly true microclines. Indeed, a fairly distinct microcline crosshatching appears at the edges of orthoclase with large $2V$. The intergranular orthoclase locally observed in perthitic granites (up to 20% perthite) are apparently due to a more complete exsolution of perthite during the later amphibolite facies metamorphism.

The iron content of garnets, based on optical properties, is 60-87 at.%. The difference in the ferruginosities of garnet from granitized relicts and their shadow granite host possibly denotes different original compositions of these rocks. The average ferruginosity of garnet in perthitic granites is 71.5 at.%, considerably higher than that of garnets in shadow plagiogranites.

Shadow granites containing other aluminous minerals along with or instead of garnet, are texturally similar to the garnet varieties. Their mineral composition, listed in Table 31, indicates that they are also analogous to the garnet granites with respect to the composition of their

TABLE 31. Chemical composition of garnet shadow perthites from Enderby Land

Specimen No.

Component	179b wt%	179b at.%	179b R/Al	486a wt%	486a at.%	486a R/Al	179 wt%	179 at.%	179 R/Al	28 wt%	28 at.%	28 R/Al	28a wt%	28a at.%	28a R/Al	205a wt%	205a at.%	205a R/Al
SiO_2	61.38	57.9	30.1	73.56	69.1	4.49	74.40	70.2	4.74	73.47	69.5	4.48	74.23	70.3	4.88	74.72	70.2	4.88
TiO_2	0.52	0.3	0.02	0.20	0.2	0.01	0.14	0.1	0.01	0.14	0.1	—	0.10	—	—	0.10	—	—
Al_2O_3	17.16	19.2	1.00	13.97	15.4	1.00	13.35	14.8	1.00	13.88	15.5	1.00	12.83	14.4	1.00	13.06	14.4	1.00
Fe_2O_3	0.84	0.6	0.03	0.45	0.3	0.02	0.56	0.4	0.03	0.43	0.3	0.02	0.45	0.3	0.02	0.03	—	—
FeO	8.46	6.7	0.35	1.85	1.4	0.09	1.84	1.4	0.09	1.19	1.0	0.06	2.09	1.6	0.11	2.40	1.9	0.13
MnO	0.19	0.2	—	0.04	—	—	0.03	—	—	—	—	—	0.03	—	—	0.08	—	—
MgO	2.89	4.1	0.21	0.41	0.6	0.04	0.41	0.6	0.04	0.34	0.5	0.03	0.53	0.7	0.05	0.93	1.3	0.09
CaO	1.64	1.6	0.08	0.98	1.0	0.06	1.31	1.3	0.09	1.51	1.5	0.10	1.48	1.5	0.10	1.75	1.8	0.12
Na_2O	2.15	3.9	0.20	3.66	6.6	0.43	2.83	5.2	0.35	2.60	4.6	0.30	2.44	4.5	0.31	3.16	5.8	0.40
K_2O	4.50	5.4	0.28	4.50	5.4	0.35	4.97	6.0	0.41	5.72	6.9	0.45	5.31	6.5	0.45	3.74	4.5	0.31
P_2O_5	0.12	0.1	—	0.03	—	—	0.07	—	—	0.10	0.1	—	0.12	0.1	—	0.09	0.1	—
Loss on ignition	0.22	—	—	0.29	—	—	0.16	—	—	0.17	—	—	0.16	—	—	0.38	—	—
Σ	100.07	100.0	—	99.94	100.0	—	100.07	—	—	99.51	100.0	—	99.77	—	—	100.44	100.0	—
CuO										0.29			—					
Cr_2O_3										0.08			0.16	0.1				
NiO										0.04								

TABLE 31 (continued)

	Specimen No.					
	179b	486a	179	28	28a	205a
Numerical characteristics (after Zavaritskii)						
a	10.7	14.1	16.4	13.7	12.7	11.9
b	20.9	3.7	4.1	2.9	3.6	4.5
c	1.9	1.2	1.4	1.8	1.8	2.0
s	66.5	81.0	78.1	81.6	81.9	81.6
Q	+9.7	+32.6	+22.0	+34.0	+36.6	+37.4
f'	40.8	48.0	49.2	53.5	64.8	49.3
m'	22.2	16.0	15.4	18.6	24.1	33.3
c'	—	—	—	—	—	—
a'	37.0	36.0	35.4	27.9	11.1	17.4
Coordinates of the ACF diagram (after Eskola and Korzhinskii)						
A	43.7	52.6	52.8	55.9	46.5	45.7
C	7.4	16.1	18.7	22.9	20.9	19.1
F	48.9	31.3	28.2	21.2	32.6	35.2
Norm, % (after Barth)						
Albite	19.5	33.3	25.8	23.8	22.5	28.8
Anorthite	7.4	5.1	6.0	6.8	6.8	7.9
Orthoclase	27.1	27.0	29.8	34.6	31.9	22.3
Ortho-pyroxene	20.6	3.2	3.4	2.3	4.2	6.3
Magnetite	1.0	0.5	0.6	0.5	0.5	—
Ilmenite	0.7	0.3	0.2	0.2	0.1	0.1
Apatite	0.3	—	0.1	0.3	0.3	0.3
Quartz	16.6	29.3	32.8	30.5	32.8	33.3
Corundum	6.8	1.3	1.3	1.0	0.7	1.0
Chromite	—	—	—	—	0.2	—

Note. Modal composition of the rocks are given in Table 29.

salic portion. Textural relationships show that garnet developed later than spinel and sillimanite, since it contains numerous inclusions of these two minerals. Likewise, the sporadically present biotite is secondary relative to the garnet. The feldspars are closely similar to those in the garnet varieties with respect to composition and texture. The iron content of garnet is fairly constant (68—70 at.%). The spinel is somewhat more ferruginous than the coexisting garnet. Biotite present in a specimen containing both spinel and garnet has a low iron content, 26 at.%.

The chemical composition of shadow garnet granites is presented in Table 32. According to Zavaritskii's classification, they belong to rocks saturated in SiO_2, high in alkalis and saturated in alumina. Hence, they differ from the shadow garnet plagiogranites mainly in their higher alkalinity. Comparison of plagiogranites and granites with approximately the same Si : Al ratios reveals that the granites are higher in silica and potassium and lower in iron, magnesium and calcium; sodium contents are the same in both rocks. If plagiogranites are regarded as the original material of perthitic granites, then the chemical nature of the granitization is the same as that which operated in the Ca-Mg schists.

Garnet granites differ from shadow perthite charnockites mainly in their considerably smaller Ca : Al ratio (0.06—0.12). However, there are also other differences, e. g., the K : Al ratio is larger in garnet granites than in charnockites. Some granite varieties are several times richer in alumina than are charnockites. The a characteristic suggests that, on the whole, the granites are more alkaline than charnockites, while the lower c value denotes a lower Ca content in feldspar corresponding to the lower basicity of plagioclase in the granites in comparison to charnockites. The higher average a values in granites also indicate that their colored minerals are more aluminous than those in charnockites.

Thus, the differences between garnet granites and charnockites suggest the possibility that the former originated from the latter either due to prolonged granitization or to increasing potassium activity in the granitizing solutions. However, although these modes of origin for the shadow garnet granite are possible, they are not confirmed by geological observation, e. g., interlayered charnockites and granites in the same exposure. Furthermore, the alumina saturation of charnockites should lower and not raise the potassium activity. It is therefore more reasonable to assume that the shadow garnet granites originated from rocks with a moderate content of alumina, including shadow plagiogranites. In this case, the alumina content of the original rocks should decrease, which is in fact revealed by comparison of the normative composition of plagiogranites and perthitic granites. The marked deviations from the average contents of silica, alumina, iron and magnesium in certain specimens of shadow perthitic granites evidently points to different starting compositions of the original rock, which, in turn, also influences the grade of granitization. Such "anomalous" shadow granites are often closely interlayered with "normal" ones, supporting this hypothesis. The common chemical features of the "anomalous" and "normal" granites (same Ca : Al ratios and alkali contents) permits their classification in this group of rocks, apart from their mineralogical and textural features.

TABLE 32. Mineral composition and characteristics, and geological setting of the paleosome of coarsely layered migmatites of aluminous schists on Enderby Land

Specimen No.	qz	plag	Kfs	spin	sill	gar	hyp	spph	cord	biot	grph	coru	ore and accessory minerals	An content of plagioclase	garnet n	garnet f at.%	spinel n	spinel a (Å)	spinel f at.%	Geological setting
204	22	—	—	3	6	—	—	—	67	o.s.**	—	—	2	—	—	—	—	—	—	Interbedded with layers of quartzites and lenses of pyroxene-plagioclase schists
670	6	o.s.	13	3	3	—	—	—	65	7	—	o.s.	3	—	—	—	—	—	—	Interbedded with layers of quartzites
795a	29	—	27	o.s.	6	37	—	—	—	o.s.	—	—	1	—	1.813	85	1.817	—	85	Uniform migmatites
23	12	—	1	5	8	5	—	—	65	—	3	—	o.s.	—	1.774	59*	—	8.12	49.5	"
5—3	21	11	56	3	2	2	—	—	5	o.s.	—	—	"	26—32	1.772	53*	—	8.12*	52*	Xenolith in intrusive charnockites
769a	20	o.s.	—	4	13	32	—	6	25	*	—	—	"	—	—	—	—	±0.07	—	Interbedded with layers of quartzites
670a	20	—	10	1	8	17	o.s.	—	28	9	—	o.s.	7	—	1.770	61*	—	—	—	As above

TABLE 32 (continued)

Characteristics of minerals

Specimen No.	sillimanite n_z	sillimanite n_x	sillimanite 2V°	biotite n_z	biotite f, at.%	cordierite n_z	cordierite n_x	cordierite 2V°	cordierite f, at.%	sapphirine n_z	sapphirine n_x	sapphirine 2V°
204	—	—	—	—	—	—	—	—	—	—	—	—
670	—	—	—	1.646	40	1.546	1.536	+82	24	—	—	—
795a	1.679	1.657	+28	—	—	—	—	—	—	—	—	—
23	—	—	—	—	—	1.546	1.537	+83	24	—	—	—
5—3	—	—	—	—	—	1.550	1.540	+70	31	—	—	—
769a	—	—	—	—	—	1.554	1.547	+84	41	1.735	1.732	—70
670a	—	—	—	1.615	28*	1.546	1.536	+82	14*	—	—	—

* These values are based on spectroscopic silicate analyses.
** [o.s. = optic sign.]

Coarsely layered migmatites with granite metasomes were discovered after a fairly detailed investigation of the Bunger Oasis /57/ and encountered only very locally in the Rayner zone of Enderby Land and on Queen Maud Land. Their paleosome is distinguished by the constant presence of spinel, sillimanite, garnet, biotite, K-feldspar, plagioclase and quartz (Table 33). Appreciable amounts of cordierite (20—40%) occur sporadically, especially in specimens with low biotite contents. The feldspar content is fairly substantial (13—45%). K-feldspar predominates over plagioclase in the majority of cases. The quartz content is very variable, ranging from very low (5—8%) to nearly normal for granite (28—30%). The sillimanite contents are high (16—35%) and spinel forms 1—5%, garnet 15—17% and biotite 1—12% of the rock. The content of ore minerals is relatively high (3—8%). Accessory minerals include zircon and rutile.

Cordierite-free paleosome has a complex porphyro-lepidonematoblastic texture. Its texture depends on the distribution of sillimanite and garnet, bandlike aggregates being common. Sillimanite is represented by columnar crystals and needles 0.5—2 mm long, oriented in a parallel manner or form-ing sheaflike aggregates. The sillimanite-bearing bands contain a profusion of irregular K-feldspar segregations showing ragged boundaries with relict plagioclase grains. In places, K-feldspar corrodes and replaces sillimanite aggregates. Garnet aggregates consist of cracked grains (3—5 mm), elongated in one direction, with biotite flakes concentrated around them. Garnet grains are diablastic (containing inclusions of quartz, spinel, silli-manite and biotite). Occasionally there are glomeroblastic aggregates of garnet grains, up to 1 cm in size. The finest bands in the paleosome are composed of skeletal titanomagnetite grains together with spinel and biotite. Aggregates of dark-colored minerals, containing relicts of plagio-clase, are interlayered with lenticular quartz aggregates.

The cordierites-bearing paleosome has hetero- and glomerogranoblastic textures. The cordierite is concentrated in bands, although separate euhedral grains of the same mineral (0.3—0.6 mm) are scattered throughout the rock. The cordierite grains in the bands reach 2—3 mm in size, contain spinel inclusions and are cracked, the spaces being filled with ore. The cordierite is surrounded by a rim of biotite and pyrite. The cordierite-bearing rocks always contain garnet, but generally as scattered porphyro-glomeroblastic aggregates, in which the size of crystalline grains reaches 6—7 mm. In places the cordierite is distinctly replaced by garnet. A characteristic feature of this variety of paleosome is its high content of quartz (20—30%) and K-feldspar (up to 20%), while its plagioclase content is highly variable (3—20%). Quartz forms separate intercalations of ragged grains reaching 0.5—3.0 mm in size. K-feldspar is represented by xeno-blastic elongated segregations without any definite orientation. It contains fairly large quantities of fusiform perthitic inclusions as well as numerous relicts of corroded plagioclase lathes.

The texture of the paleosome of migmatites is reminiscent of banded high-alumina schists, probably due to the rhythmic nature of original clay-silt sediments which were transformed into the migmatites by regional metamorphism.

TABLE 33. Mineral composition and characteristics in coarsely layered migmatites of aluminous schists in the Bunger Oasis

Speci-men No.	Mineral composition, vol.%										Characteristics of minerals						
									Ore and accessory minerals	An content of plagioclase	garnet		cordierite			biotite	
	qz	plag	Kfs	spin	sill	gar	cord	biot			n	f at.%	n_z	n_x	f at.%	n_z	f at.%
Paleosome																	
144a	8	2	26	2	31	16	—	10	5	—	1.790	67	—	—	—	—	—
552	13	2	13	2	35	15	—	12	8	—	—	—	—	—	—	1.633	35
583v	5	25	20	2	16	16	—	12	4	—	—	—	—	—	·	—	—
303	30	3	10	1	17	16	20	3	3	28	—	—	1.540	1.530	14	—	—
305	20	20	20	1	—	15	20	1	3	27	1.780	61	1.546	1.536	20	—	—
228g*	25	3	33	5	6	17	8	o.s.**	3	33	1.785	64	1.537	1.531	12	—	—
Metasome																	
85b	32	30	36	—	—	—	—	1	1	25							
94b	45	20	30	—	2	—	—	2	1	27							
104b	27	35	30	—	—	—	—	6	2	25							
117a	25	25	45	—	—	—	—	4	1	29							
181	33	24	39	—	—	—	—	4	—	30							
242v	35	15	40	—	—	—	—	9	1	25							
338	28	30	40	—	—	2	—	—	—	—							

* Paleosome of migmatite from the Rayner zone of Enderby Land.
** [o.s. = optic sign.]

The anorthite content of plagioclase is constant (27—33%). Perthitic K-feldspar sometimes possesses a twin lattice. Greenish brown spinel is clearly a hercynite (specimen 228g, $n = 1.816$; $f = 84$ at.%). Sillimanite possesses the following optical constants: $n_z = 1.680$—1.681; $n_x = 1.660$—1.659; $2V = +26$ to $+28°$. Garnet has a low ferruginosity: $f = 61$—67 at.%. The iron content of cordierite, based on its refractive index, is 12—20 at.%, which is lower than the ferruginosity of cordierites from other high-alumina rocks of the granulite facies. The ferruginosity of biotites is also rather low (35 at.%).

The metasome of coarsely layered migmatites consists almost exclusive-ly of biotite granites (Table 33) which are fine- to medium-grained and show a characteristic yellowish pink color. The texture is most commonly granoblastic with elements of porphyroblastic and poikiloblastic textures; there is considerable evidence of replacement and intergrowth processes. The distribution of quartz in the metasome is heterogeneous, some portions of the rock being entirely composed by 3—5-mm xenoblastic grains, and others containing veinlike segregations penetrating the feldspar. The biotite content rarely reaches 10%, but is most commonly 2—3%. The metasome sporadically contains garnet and very rarely sillimanite. Ore minerals reach 1—3%. Accessory minerals include rutile, zircon, apatite, hercynite and cordierite. K-feldspar almost always predominates over plagioclase of constant composition (An 25—30). It is mainly represented by irregular segregations (2—6 mm) of microcline-microperthite lathes ($\perp(001)n_y = 11$—$13°$; $n_z = 1.525$; $n_x = 1.519$; $2V = -75$ to $-85°$). Segregations of this type contain inclusions of resorbed plagioclase grains. Myrmekitic intergrowths of plagioclase and quartz occur along the plagioclase-microcline contact. Aside from metablastic microcline, the granites contain small (1–2 mm) anhedral grains of soda orthoclase ($\perp(001)n_y = = 4$–$8°$; $2V = -48$ to $-60°$). All colored minerals, except biotite, are relicts.

Shadow granites and finely layered migmatites consist of the following two large groups: a) moderately aluminous varieties represented by biotite-garnet finely layered migmatites and shadow granites; b) high-alumina varieties represented only by finely layered migmatites containing spinel, sillimanite and cordierite in addition to the garnet and biotite. Finely layered migmatites and shadow granites of the first group occur almost everywhere in the granulite facies of the crystal-line basement, with the exception of the Napier zone of Enderby Land. The granulites which occur in the eastern part of the Rayner zone of Enderby Land occupy a special position among rocks of this group. The granulites of the Humboldt Mountains on Queen Maud Land, which outwardly resemble the Rayner zone granulites, developed from shadow charnockites and partially from enderbites during superimposed amphibolite facies meta-morphism. They are described in the chapter on polymetamorphism. Finely layered migmatites of the second group occur in the Bunger Oasis and on Queen Maud Land.

Biotite-garnet finely layered migmatites and shadow granites form extensive (tens and even hundreds of square kilometers) migmatite fields. Their total visible thickness is 1–3 km. Shadow granites are transitional to the finely layered migmatites and are concordantly inter-layered with them. They also form separate layers up to 1 km in thickness and comparatively thin (5–30 m) intercalations with migmatites. The migmatites are inequigranular pinkish gray or yellowish gray gneissic rocks with distinct banding. In shadow granites, the banding is only weakly discernible through the relatively homogeneous gneissic granite. The components of these rocks include quartz, plagioclase, K-feldspar, garnet and biotite, their relative quantities varying widely (Table 34). Rocks with high biotite contents also have high garnet contents and are thus melano-cratic. Rocks with low biotite contents (up to 5%) as a rule do not contain over 5% garnet. Although it is possible to differentiate between varieties with lower and higher grades of granitization by the plagioclase and K-feldspar relationships, they are essentially little different.

The texture of migmatites and shadow granites is characterized by the inequigranularity and nonuniform mineral distribution. Firstly, plagioclase is fine-grained in comparison with K-feldspar and quartz. Furthermore, the grain size of each mineral may vary significantly within a single thin section. Thus, plagioclase varies from 0.1 to 4.0 mm, quartz from 0.4 to 2.5 mm, and K-feldspar grains from 1.5 to 4.0 mm. In many cases K-feldspar forms porphyroblasts up to 1.0–2.0 cm across. The size of garnet grains is fairly constant within a given specimen; these are either small irregular grains (0.4–1.0 mm) commensurate with the other min-erals, or large euhedral metablasts with ragged crystal boundaries. Biotite occurs as platelets of 0.3–1.0 mm. The nonuniform distribution

TABLE 34. Mineral composition and characteristics in shadow garnet granitoids and finely layered migmatites

Specimen No.	Mineral composition, vol.%							Characteristics of minerals				Geological setting
	qz	plag	Kfs	gar	biot	ore and accessory minerals	An content of plagioclase	garnet		biotite		
								n	f at.%	n_z	f at.%	
Enderby Land												
836zh	30	30	35	o.s.*	3	2	35	—	—	—	—	Finely layered migmatites
836m	20	38	33	o.s.	6	3	35	—	—	—	—	As above
838	24	50	12	6	7	1	34	—	—	—	—	"
836v	32	22	25	9	12	o.s.	34	—	—	—	—	"
70	o.s.	32	25	27	15	"	33	1.791	68	—	—	Shadow granitoids interlayered with bifeldspar charnockites
49a	20	38	38	4	o.s.	"	40	—	74	—	—	Granulitic layers
49b	51	6	42	1	"	"	20	—	78	—	—	" "
Bunger Oasis												
538b	45	10	15	25	2	3	33	1.790	67	—	—	Finely layered migmatites
Queen Maud Land												
734a	37	18	40	2	2	1	27	1.782	62	1.678	55	Metasome of a garnet plagiogranite migmatite
756	30	10	35	5	20	1	26	—	—	1.650	42	Finely layered migmatites
736a	30	10	40	12	7	1	31	1.800	74	1.682	57	As above
736	30	32	20	5	10	3	27	—	—	1.665	49	"
850a	25	15	50	3	7	o.s.	29	1.808	80	—	—	Shadow granitoids
849	25	20	48	5	2	"	29	1.812	84	—	—	As above
827v	28	13	49	2	7	1	28	1.809	81	1.675	53	"
767	23	35	30	2	10	—	29	1.812	84	1.684	56	"
754	25	16	45	3	10	1	26	1.805	78	1.673	52	"

* [o.s. = optic sign.]

of the minerals in the rocks gives rise to monomineralic segregations of
K-feldspar, plagioclase, garnet and biotite. Fine-grained plagioclase areas
often contain biotite and garnet grains. Two textural forms, granulitic
and lepidogranoblastic, occur in these rocks. The granulitic texture is
characterized by approximately lenticular and even ribbonlike quartz grains
up to 2.5×5 mm in size. The other minerals are less commonly flattened.
The lepidogranoblastic texture exhibits subparallel biotite flakes together
with irregular blastic grains of the other minerals (Figure 12).

FIGURE 12. Shadow garnet bifeldspar granite (x 12, crossed nicols, thin section
228b).

These textural elements are considerably complicated by reactive relationships among the minerals. For example, K-feldspar replaces plagioclase in all specimens, with myrmekites formed at their contact; resorbed
plagioclase grains, often myrmekitized, are embedded in porphyroblasts
of K-feldspar. Indications of the replacement of plagioclase by quartz are
less distinct. In places plagioclase is replaced by biotite. Garnet is consistently replaced by biotite and somewhat less commonly by quartz.
Diablastic garnet grains most commonly contain rounded and oval inclusions of quartz and, less frequently, biotite, zircon and ore. Quartz forms
symplektitic intergrowths with biotite. Where biotite is embedded in quartz,
K-feldspar is also present. The textural relationships of minerals indicate
their paragenetic sequence and degree of recrystallization. It is clear that
granitization occurred later than biotitization. The latter was preceded
by cataclasis under abyssal conditions manifested as cracks in garnet,

bent twin planes and locally the disappearance of plagioclase twins, wavy extinction of plagioclase, and granulation of quartz grains. In contrast to these minerals, biotite and K-feldspar show no traces of cataclasis and recrystallization.

The plagioclase in these rocks varies from oligoclase (An 26) to andesine (An 47). On the average, the more basic plagioclase is found in rocks of Enderby Land and Bunger Oasis (An 33−35), while more acid plagioclase occurs in rocks of Queen Maud Land (An 26−31). The basicity of plagioclase declines with increasing migmatization and granitization of the rocks; this reduced An content is also apparently dependent on other factors (content of quartz and colored minerals, etc.). Thus, more acid plagioclase is found in leucocratic migmatites that are transitional to quartzites. In some cases some of the plagioclase grains contain sporadic antiperthitic ingrowths. K-feldspar is generally perthitic. The perthitic components are concentrated in the central portions of grains; these are lenticular, maculose or veinlike and account for 5−20 vol.% of the host-mineral grain. The host mineral in Enderby Land migmatites is soda orthoclase, partially microclinized along the crystal edges. Its refractive indices are: $n_x = 1.521$−1.525; $n_z = 1.527$−1.532; $2V = -57$ to $-82°$. The migmatites and shadow granites in the Bunger Oasis and Queen Maud Land contain two types of K-feldspar: a characteristically crosshatched microcline forming small grains ($2V = -83$ to $-84°$) and a non-crosshatched orthoclase transitional to soda-orthoclase, forming metablasts resorbed by the microcline ($2V = -64$ to $-67°$). These metablasts are also microclinized along the edges ($2V = -79$ to $-81°$). The refractive indices of orthoclase are: $n_x = 1.521$−1.522; $n_z = 1.526$−1.528. The ferruginosity of garnet is 62−84 at.%. The most iron-rich garnets ($f = 78$−84 at.%) were observed in shadow granites on Queen Maud Land. The finely layered migmatites from other regions of Antarctica contain garnets of approximately the same ferruginosity (62−74 at.%). The iron content of biotite is comparatively high in both the migmatites and shadow granites of Queen Maud Land (42−56 at.%); it is somewhat lower (37−44 at.%) in biotite from rocks on Enderby Land and the Bunger Oasis. Segregations of fine-grained sphene and chlorite aggregates occur locally in cracks within biotite. The accessory minerals in rocks of this group are usually zircon and monazite.

Saxon-type granulites in the Rayner zone of Enderby Land occur as separate lenticular sheetlike bodies with thickness ranging from tens to several hundred meters and extending over several kilometers. They are interbedded with layers of garnet-pyroxene-plagioclase schists and their migmatites. In places, the granulites contain dikes of metabasites transformed into garnet-pyroxene and garnet-pyroxene-plagioclase schists. The granulite layers form distinct, often tectonic contacts with other metamorphic rocks including finely layered migmatites and shadow granites.

The granulites are light gray, pinkish gray or pinkish yellowish. In places they are schistose with fine plications. Cleavage faces on granulite specimens exhibit a fine (0.5−2 mm) lineation consisting of altered quartz "strips" and feldspar lenticles separated by small, slightly flattened,

sub-euhedral red garnet. The mineral composition of granulites is given
in Table 34. The plagioclase content of Enderby Land granulites usually
does not exceed 10%, while K-feldspar often accounts for over 50% of
the rock. Quartz contents are high (20—50%). Garnet, the main colored
mineral, forms up to 4% of the rock, and biotite is sporadic. Ore veins
are also rare.

Granulites differ from garnet shadow granites and finely layered migmatites in their typical granulitic texture. Quartz ribbons averaging
1—8 mm in length and 0.15—0.5 mm in width sometimes extend through an
entire thin section. Between them are distinctly outlined lenses of small
microcline grains or large lenticular grains of perthitic orthoclase and
somewhat flattened euhedral garnet grains. It is important to note the
presence of two K-feldspars in the rock, the perthitic orthoclase and a
typically crosshatched microcline-perthite. Plagioclase is partially corroded by quartz, and forms myrmekites at the contact with orthoclase.
The latter is corroded, replaced by and containing ingrowths of microcline.
Orthoclase is clearly the earlier K-feldspar in the rock. Thin biotite flakes,
reaching up to 1 mm in length, occur at the contact between quartz ribbons
and garnet grains. Garnet grains are surrounded by biotite rims, while
separate maculose aggregates of biotite flakes are scattered throughout the
rock. The accessory minerals (zircon, monazite, apatite) occur in the
garnet and biotite aggregates. The composition of plagioclase varies
according to the content of K-feldspar in the rocks; from An 23 in rocks
with a predominance of K-feldspar to An 40 in rocks with equal amounts of
both feldspars. The garnet is usually highly ferruginous (74—78 at.%),
but this declines to 57—60 at.% in varieties with high basic plagioclase
contents.

The texture and composition of the garnet (including its high calcium
content) indicate that the granulites originated from garnet shadow granites
and finely layered migmatites that were strongly recrystallized under
conditions of unilateral pressures /58/. Excess pressure was probably
responsible for the excellent crosshatching manifested in the microcline
of these rocks.

The chemical composition of these rocks is given in Table 35. According
to Zavaritskii characteristics, they belong to rocks saturated in SiO_2 and
Al_2O_3 and moderately rich in alkalis. They differ from shadow garnet
plagiogranites in their higher contents of potassium and ferric iron and
lower contents of ferrous iron, magnesium and calcium. The contents of
silica, alumina and soda are approximately equal. The average silica
content is somewhat higher in the bifeldspar granites. Bifeldspar granites
with very low calcium and sodium (plagioclase) contents have high contents
of magnesium and iron (colored minerals). Since shadow garnet plagiogranites often form the paleosome of migmatized shadow garnet bifeldspar
granites, it is natural to assume, considering their geological setting and
composition, that the latter originated by granitization of the former. An
equally probable assumption is that the plagiogranites and granites formed
by selective melting of the rocks equivalent in composition to the combined
composition of plagiogranite and granite. This genesis for shadow

TABLE 35. Chemical composition of shadow garnet granitoids

Specimen No.

Component	836			836k			836i			838			836v		
	wt%	at.%	$\frac{R}{Al}$	wt%	at.%	$\frac{R}{Al}$	wt%	at.%	$\frac{R}{Al}$	wt%	at.%	$\frac{R}{Al}$	wt%	at.%	$\frac{R}{Al}$
SiO_2	75.57	72.0	4.74	70.22	67.0	4.35	71.90	68.4	4.44	74.66	70.6	4.80	68.97	66.8	5.10
TiO_2	—	—	—	0.46	0.3	0.02	0.40	0.3	0.02	0.16	0.1	0.01	0.89	0.6	0.05
Al_2O_3	13.51	15.2	1.00	13.78	15.4	1.00	13.80	15.4	1.00	13.22	14.7	1.00	11.45	13.1	1.00
Fe_2O_3	0.20	0.1	0.01	1.70	1.3	0.08	1.07	0.8	0.05	0.59	0.4	0.03	0.96	0.7	0.05
FeO	0.82	0.6	0.04	2.34	1.8	0.12	2.16	1.7	0.11	1.23	1.0	0.07	6.83	5.5	0.42
MnO	0.05	—	—	0.04	—	—	0.03	—	—	0.02	—	—	0.10	—	—
MgO	0.36	0.5	0.03	0.91	1.3	0.08	0.88	1.2	0.08	0.60	0.8	0.05	3.39	4.9	0.37
CaO	1.68	1.7	0.11	2.01	2.1	0.14	2.26	2.3	0.15	1.40	1.4	0.10	0.56	0.6	0.05
Na_2O	1.97	3.6	0.24	2.40	4.5	0.29	2.32	4.3	0.28	2.40	4.5	0.31	1.02	1.9	0.14
K_2O	5.21	6.3	0.41	5.10	6.2	0.40	4.55	5.5	0.36	5.47	6.5	0.44	4.63	5.8	0.44
P_2O_5	0.05	—	—	0.15	0.1	—	0.13	0.1	—	0.07	—	—	0.07	0.1	—
Loss on ignition	0.30	—	—	0.51	—	—	0.40	—	—	0.34	—	—	0.74	—	—
Σ	99.72	100.0	—	99.62	100.0	—	99.90	100.0	—	100.16	100.0	—	99.71	100.0	—

TABLE 35 (continued)

Component	734a			736			827v			754		
	wt%	at.%	$\frac{R}{Al}$	wt%	at.%	$\frac{R}{Al}$	wt%	at.%	$\frac{R}{Al}$	wt%	at.%	$\frac{R}{Al}$
SiO_2	74.25	69.5	4.54	69.95	66.3	4.17	73.94	70.2	4.84	71.79	67.7	4.29
TiO_2	0.12	—	—	0.47	0.3	0.02	0.22	0.2	0.01	0.32	0.2	0.01
Al_2O_3	13.95	15.3	1.00	14.23	15.9	1.00	13.03	14.5	1.00	14.28	15.8	1.00
Fe_2O_3	0.88	0.7	0.05	1.32	0.9	0.06	0.58	0.5	0.03	0.66	0.5	0.03
FeO	0.72	0.6	0.04	2.84	2.2	0.14	2.16	1.7	0.12	2.74	2.1	0.13
MnO	0.03	—	—	0.08	—	—	0.05	—	—	0.04	—	—
MgO	0.20	0.3	0.02	1.10	1.5	0.09	0.45	0.6	0.04	0.35	0.5	0.03
CaO	0.95	1.0	0.07	2.10	2.2	0.14	1.38	1.4	0.10	1.54	1.6	0.10
Na_2O	3.56	6.4	0.42	3.37	6.3	0.40	2.40	4.5	0.31	2.91	5.3	0.34
K_2O	5.26	6.2	0.41	3.70	4.4	0.28	5.30	6.4	0.44	5.27	6.3	0.40
P_2O_5	0.01	—	—	0.02	—	—	0.02	—	—	0.02	—	—
Loss on ignition	0.05	—	—	0.08	—	—	0.35	—	—	0.42	—	—
Σ	99.98	100.0	—	99.91	100.0	—	99.88	100.0	—	100.34	100.0	—

Specimen No.

TABLE 35 (continued)

	Specimen No.							
	836	836k	836i	838	836v	734a	736	828
Numerical characteristics (after Zavaritskii)								
a	11.4	12.5	11.6	12.7	8.4	14.8	12.5	12.5
b	3.5	5.9	5.2	3.6	16.9	2.7	6.6	4.2
c	2.0	2.4	2.7	1.6	0.6	1.1	2.5	1.7
s	83.1	79.2	80.5	82.1	74.1	81.4	78.4	81.6
Q	+41.4	+31.0	+35.1	+37.2	+30.8	+32.1	+29.3	+36.5
f'	24.5	61.4	53.0	45.5	40.7	53.6	56.5	59.4
m'	17.0	25.0	26.0	27.2	31.7	12.2	27.3	17.2
c'	—	—	—	—	—	—	—	—
a'	58.5	13.6	21.0	27.3	27.6	34.2	16.2	23.4
Coordinates of the ACF diagram (after Eskola and Korzhinskii)								
A	64.6	48.3	51.6	52.0	32.9	60.0	46.7	49.6
C	21.3	20.7	21.0	22.4	3.5	21.2	19.3	19.1
F	14.2	31.0	27.4	25.6	63.6	18.8	34.0	31.3
Norm, % (after Barth)								
Albite	18.0	22.3	21.4	22.1	9.8	32.0	30.9	22.2
Anorthite	8.0	9.5	10.6	6.5	2.0	4.8	10.7	7.1
Orthoclase	31.5	31.0	27.6	32.7	28.7	31.2	22.4	31.9
Orthopyroxene	2.1	4.2	4.6	2.9	19.0	0.9	6.1	3.9
Magnetite	0.2	1.8	1.2	0.7	1.0	1.0	1.4	0.7
Ilmenite	—	0.7	0.6	0.2	1.3	0.1	0.7	0.3
Apatite	0.2	0.3	0.3	0.1	0.3	—	—	—
Quartz	38.0	29.2	32.3	33.7	33.3	29.2	26.9	33.0
Corundum	2.0	1.0	1.4	1.1	4.6	0.8	0.9	0.9

Note. Modal compositions of the rocks are given in Table 34.

granitoids would explain their interlayering, which is the most common mode of their occurrence.

Shadow garnet bifeldspar granites are practically indistinguishable from shadow perthitic garnet granites with respect to composition. How - ever, a comparison of granites with the same Si : Al ratio reveals lower contents of iron and sodium in bifeldspar than in perthitic granites. Therefore, it is possible that perthitic granites may have been the rocks which were selectively melted to produce plagiogranites and bifeldspar granites. These rocks differ from shadow charnockites only in their consistent, though not very marked, saturation in alumina. Hence, it is concluded that heavily granitized varieties of Ca-Mg and aluminous schists become similar in composition, losing nearly all features of their initial composition. Crystallization of different varieties is probably dependent on the temperature conditions /44, 57/. Therefore, except for the relicts in shadow granites, it would be practically impossible to determine the rocks from which they formed.

Finely layered migmatites of high-alumina schists compose units which vary in thickness from tens of meters to 1−2 km. In general, they are interlayered with the biotite-garnet shadow granites and finely layered migmatites described above. Migmatites of high-alumina schists are represented by medium- to coarse-grained yellowish pink rocks with an irregular "streaky" appearance. They are usually hetero-granoblastic, often porphyrogranoblastic with very widespread mineral replacements and reaction rims. The mineral grains are xenoblastic, only sillimanite and garnet being idiomorphic. A characteristic feature of this rock is the nonuniform distribution of minerals. Quartz, for ex-ample, forms monomineralic lenticular intercalations. Quartz and K-feldspar form irregular, lenticular, veiny and maculose segregations. All the varieties of migmatite exhibit the replacement of plagioclase by K-feldspar and the replacement of garnet by biotite and quartz. Plagio-clase occurs in two generations; as small grains of 1−2 mm, which are replaced by K-feldspar, and as metablastic lathes (5−6 mm) filled with quartz inclusions. Plagioclase in the metablasts is usually more acid (by 10−15 An) than in small grains. Garnet also has two forms: small grains (0.5−1 mm), and metablasts (4−7 mm) filled with inclusions of quartz, biotite, sillimanite, spinel and ore.

The composition of migmatites (Table 36) always includes quartz, plagioclase, K-feldspar, garnet, ore and biotite. The following varieties can be distinguished with respect to the other aluminous minerals: 1) spinel-sillimanite-cordierite, 2) spinel-cordierite, 3) sillimanite-cordierite, and 4) sillimanite. The first three varieties are confined to the Bunger Oasis, while the sillimanite variety is more widespread on Queen Maud Land, where sillimanite-cordierite varieties occur to a limited extent. This regional distribution of the rocks denotes a higher temperature of metamorphism in the Bunger Oasis than on Queen Maud Land.

The mineral substitutions in the different migmatites exhibit the follow-ing features: In spinel-sillimanite-cordierite varieties, there is a distinct

TABLE 36. Mineral composition and characteristics of finely layered migmatites of high-alumina schists

Specimen No.	Mineral composition, vol.%											Characteristics of minerals								Geological setting
	qz	plag	Kfs	spin	sill	gar	hyp	cord	biot	ore and accessory minerals	An content of plagioclase	garnet n	garnet f at.%	cordierite n_z	cordierite n_x	cordierite f at.%	biotite n_z	biotite f at.%	
151	32	20	19	1	10	8	—	3	5	2	30	1.792	69	—	—	—	1.630	33	
105	30	13	13	2	6	12	—	6	16	2	27	1.780	61	1.540	1.530	14	1.630	33	
302	30	20	14	1	10	8	—	8	7	2	30	1.785	64	1.543	1.534	20	1.639	38	
157	18	13	o.s.*	4	4	5	—	50	2	4	41	1.788	66	—	—	—	—	—	
152v	35	25	38	1	—	17	—	—	18	3	40	1.786	65	—	—	—	1.622	30	Bunger Oasis
112v	20	12	18	—	—	18	—	3	6	1	25	1.792	69	—	—	—	1.626	31	
88b	37	20	22	2	—	11	—	10	—	—	26	—	—	1.549	1.538	29	—	—	
344	30	14	5	1	2	11	2	12	8	2	30	1.785	64	1.552	1.543	36	1.638	37	
453	20	10	11	—	4	3	—	50	5	6	39	—	—	1.549	1.537	29	—	—	
260b	30	40	5	—	6	15	—	—	1	1	38	1.790	67	—	—	—	—	—	
292	18	50	5	—	3	20	—	—	—	2	41	1.796	72	—	—	—	1.625	31	
153	33	5	15	—	5	30	—	—	9	2	41	—	—	—	—	—	1.626	31	
152b	15	3	55	—	1	18	—	—	4	2	24	1.780	61	—	—	—	—	—	
658	30	24	26	—	5	8	—	—	5	2	26	—	—	—	—	—	—	—	
862b	26	35	o.s.	—	1	15	—	—	21	1	30	—	—	—	—	—	1.641	39	
852a	13	30	o.s.	—	1	25	—	—	30	2	35	1.790	67	—	—	—	—	—	
857a	43	—	4	—	—	20	—	—	15	5	33	1.799	74	—	—	—	1.671	52	Queen Maud Land
843a	10	28	12	—	5	8	—	—	35	2	25	1.790	67	—	—	—	1.647	41	
799v	20	20	20	—	1	15	—	—	23	1	30	1.790	67	—	—	—	—	—	
814g	30	30	25	—	6	3	—	—	5	1	22	1.806	79	—	—	—	1.667	49	
146a	20	10	10	—	10	26	—	9	12	3	40	1.796	72	1.546	1.536	20	—	—	
193	29	12	41	—	3	2	—	8	3	2	30	—	—	1.550	1.542	31	—	—	Bunger Oasis
809	32	16	22	—	4	7	—	6	10	3	27	—	—	—	—	—	—	—	
827b	35	15	15	—	5	10	—	12	5	3	31	1.808	80	—	—	—	1.671	52	Queen Maud Land, 8% komerupine
800e	15	40	o.s.	—	1	10	—	—	32	2	39	1.781	61	—	—	—	1.627	32	
669	27	5	5	—	3	—	—	—	3	2	—	—	—	1.543	1.534	20	—	—	Bunger Oasis

* [o.s. = optic sign.]

replacement of the spinel + sillimanite association by the cordierite + garnet association, involving the formation of a new finely acicular variety of
sillimanite. In this case, reaction rims of sillimanite, cordierite and
garnet are formed around the spinel. There are obviously no sillimanite
rims around spinel in the spinel-cordierite variety. In both these varieties,
cordierite is replaced by garnet and biotite while sillimanite and cordierite
are replaced by K-feldspar. Cordierite is also replaced by garnet and
biotite in sillimanite-cordierite migmatites. The high=alumina minerals
reach the highest degree of equilibrium in sillimanite migmatites, where
there is only garnet formed later than sillimanite.

The An contents in plagioclase vary considerably, from 25 to 41% in the
Bunger Oasis migmatites and from 22 to 39% in the migmatites of Queen
Maud Land. K-feldspar in the Bunger Oasis migmatites is most frequently
represented by microperthitic Na-orthoclase ($\perp$ (001) n_y = 7–10°; $2V$ = –52
to –68°), which is often microclinized along the edges. In places, microcline
may replace an entire orthoclase grain. Perthitic ingrowths do not exceed
20 vol.% of the grain. In contrast, crosshatched microcline ($2V$ = –78 to –84°) is
more widespread in the migmatites of Queen Maud Land, whereas orthoclase
is less common. The iron content of garnet ranges from 61 to 80 at.%.
On the average, the ferruginosity of garnet is the lowest (65.4 at.%) in
spinel-bearing migmatites. Its average ferruginosity in sillimanite varieties is 68.5 at.% and this value is still higher in sillimanite-cordierite
varieties (76 at.%, two measurements). The garnets in Bunger Oasis rocks
have lower average iron contents (66.4 at.%) than those in Queen Maud Land
(71.3 at.%). The brown-green spinel in the migmatites is a hercynite, which
often occurs in intergrowths with ore minerals. The cordierite in migmatites is polysynthetically twinned and its ferruginosity is 14–36 at.%.
The ferruginosity of biotite is directly related to that of garnet. The least
ferruginous biotites occur in Bunger Oasis rocks (31–37 at.%, average
33 at.%), and the most ferruginous biotites in rocks of Queen Maud Land
(32–52 at.%, average 44 at.%). Thus, the iron contents of minerals suggest
that migmatites of Queen Maud Land were formed not only at lower temperatures than those in the Bunger Oasis, but also at a higher alkali
potential /34, 44/.

The chemical composition of the above-described migmatites is presented in Table 37. According to Zavaritskii characteristics, these rocks are
saturated in silica, moderately rich in alkalis and saturated in alumina.
A comparison of these rocks with shadow biotite-garnet granites and finely
layered migmatites (Table 35) demonstrates that the latter have much lower
alumina and higher silica contents. The finely layered migmatites of high-
alumina schists are lower in silica, alkalis (both sodium and potassium)
and calcium and richer in aluminum, ferric and ferrous iron, manganese
and magnesium than the shadow biotite-garnet granites.

It has been suggested that granitization of high-alumina schists produces
shadow biotite-garnet granites /58/. A comparison of the chemical composition of these granites with that of the finely layered migmatites of high-
alumina schists, revealed that the latter's transformation into biotite-
garnet granite was accompanied, in the first place, by an influx of SiO_2

TABLE 37. Chemical composition of finely layered migmatites of high-alumina schists in the Bunger Oasis

Compo-nent	Specimen No.														
	151			105			157			302			153		
	wt%	at.%	$\frac{R}{Al}$	wt%	at.%	$\frac{R}{Al}$	wt%	at.%	$\frac{R}{Al}$	wt%	at.%	$\frac{R}{Al}$	wt%	at.%	$\frac{R}{Al}$
SiO_2	67.59	65.0	3.65	67.91	65.8	4.11	59.65	57.0	3.04	66.69	64.3	3.40	60.34	58.2	2.58
TiO_2	1.07	0.8	0.05	0.83	0.6	0.04	1.18	0.9	0.05	1.04	0.8	0.04	0.92	0.6	0.03
Al_2O_3	15.74	17.8	1.00	13.88	16.0	1.00	16.64	18.8	1.00	16.62	18.9	1.00	20.02	22.6	1.00
Fe_2O_3	2.22	1.6	0.09	3.82	2.8	0.17	2.48	1.8	0.10	2.57	1.8	0.10	0.70	0.5	0.02
FeO	4.78	3.9	0.22	3.39	2.7	0.17	8.56	6.8	0.36	5.35	4.3	0.23	8.66	7.0	0.31
MnO	0.15	0.1	—	0.17	0.1	—	0.22	0.2	0.01	0.21	0.2	0.01	0.20	0.2	0.01
MgO	2.20	3.2	0.18	3.71	5.4	0.34	3.53	5.0	0.27	2.68	3.9	0.21	3.12	4.5	0.20
CaO	1.08	1.2	0.07	0.57	0.6	0.04	3.18	3.3	0.18	0.70	0.8	0.04	0.48	0.5	0.62
Na_2O	1.30	2.4	0.13	1.27	2.3	0.14	2.10	3.9	0.21	1.34	2.5	0.13	0.77	1.4	0.06
K_2O	3.28	4.0	0.22	2.98	3.7	0.23	1.88	2.3	0.12	1.93	2.4	0.13	3.70	4.5	0.20
P_2O_5	—	—	—	—	—	—	—	—	—	0.07	0.1	—	—	—	—
Loss on ignition	0.74	—	—	1.99	—	—	0.62	—	—	0.70	—	—	0.94	—	—
Σ	100.15	100.0	—	100.63	100.0	—	100.04	100.0	—	99.90	—	—	99.85	100.0	—

136 CH. II. GRANULITE FACIES

TABLE 37 (continued)

	Specimen No.				
	151	105	157	302	153
Numerical characteristics (after Zavaritskii)					
a	7.1	6.5	7.1	5.2	6.4
b	19.6	21.3	22.8	24.3	23.9
c	1.3	0.6	3.8	0.8	0.6
s	72.0	71.6	66.3	69.7	63.1
Q	+28.5	+29.6	+14.6	+28.2	+12.8
f'	31.4	28.6	44.4	28.0	27.5
m'	17.8	27.2	25.4	17.0	16.0
c'	—	—	—	—	—
a'	50.8	44.2	30.2	55.0	56.5
Coordinates of the ACF diagram (after Eskola and Korzhinskii)					
A	57.7	53.0	45.1	60.5	57.9
C	5.9	3.0	11.7	3.2	1.8
F	36.4	44.0	43.2	36.3	40.3
Norm, % (after Barth)					
Albite	12.1	11.7	19.5	12.5	7.2
Anorthite	5.8	2.9	16.4	2.9	2.6
Orthoclase	20.3	18.7	11.5	11.9	22.6
Orthopyroxene	11.0	12.4	20.5	13.5	21.5
Magnetite	2.4	4.2	2.8	2.8	0.7
Ilmenite	1.6	1.2	1.7	1.5	1.3
Apatite	—	—	—	0.3	—
Quartz	37.7	40.2	21.6	41.9	28.4
Corundum	9.1	8.7	6.0	12.9	15.7

Note. Modal compositions of the rocks are given in Table 36.

and a removal of Al_2O_3. However, the mobilities of these components are low in the high-temperature region. Moreover, any significant influx of calcium is likewise impossible since observations have established its relative loss in migmatites and granites. Therefore, in the author's opinion, the finely layered migmatites of high-alumina schists cannot have been converted to shadow biotite-garnet granite by granitization. In general, the ultrametamorphism of these schists ends in the stage of finely layered migmatites. Transformation of high-alumina schists into shadow granites is possible, in rare cases, as is attested by the development of the perthitic shadow granitoids. However, the specific features of high alumina rocks are also preserved in shadow granitoids, in which biotite and garnet are replaced by aluminous sillimanite, spinel and cordierite. These shadow granitoids may originate only at low alkalinity. Argillaceous sedimentary rocks were clearly the starting material for the migmatites of high-alumina schists. The fluctuations in the chemical composition of the migmatites from one specimen to another may be due to differences in their original compositions.

QUARTZITES

Quartzites are defined herein as rocks containing over 50—60% quartz. They are far from the most important rocks in the metamorphic series; however, they occur in many regions of Antarctica and, in some cases, determine certain of the properties of the local rock series. Quartzites are most extensive on Enderby Land, where nearly all their varieties which have to date been discovered in Antarctica are encountered. The majority of Antarctic quartzites are aluminous, a feature shown by the consistent presence of various high-alumina minerals. Nevertheless, some varieties are free of aluminous colored minerals. As a rule, quartz accounts for over 90 vol.% of these rocks, the remaining 10% being feldspars. An overwhelming majority of aluminous quartzites occur in series charac-terized by a predominance of granitized aluminous schists. Feldspathic quartzites usually occur in series of granitized Ca-Mg schists.

Aluminous quartzites most often form separate formations up to 500 m thick as well as thinner bedded units which are intercalated with aluminous schists. Less commonly, quartzites are interbedded with pyroxene-plagioclase schists; however, the latter are often present in quartzite beds as intercalations and lenses. Quartzites also form intercalations, up to 15 m thick, in shadow garnet granites or in groups of interbedded shadow charnockites and garnet granites. Together with aluminous schists, they sometimes form the paleosome of coarsely layered migmatites. However, aluminous quartzites essentially do not occur as relicts in shadow granites. This denotes that shadow granites were not formed from quartzites and that aluminous quartzites were absent from series giving rise to shadow granites.

The following varieties of quartzites are distinguished according to the stable associations of the high-alumina minerals: a) spinel-sillimanite, b) sillimanite, c) sillimanite-garnet, d) sillimanite-hypersthene, e) hypersthene-cordierite, and f) garnet.

Spinel-sillimanite quartzites occur mainly in the Napier zone of Enderby Land; they are fairly common in the Larsemann Oasis on the Ingrid Christensen coast and occur sporadically in the Bunger region. Sillimanite-hypersthene, hypersthene-cordierite and cordierite quartzites have only been observed in the Napier zone of Enderby Land. Sillimanite quartzites, generally occurring only to a very limited extent in Antarctica, have been reported from the Napier zone of Enderby Land, the Ingrid Christensen coast and Queen Maud Land (Humboldt Mountains). Garnet quartzites have been reported from Enderby Land and the Bunger Oasis. Garnet quartzites are the most widespread variety in the Bunger Oasis. Sillimanite-garnet quartzite occurs practically in all the regions of Antarctica with rocks of the granulite facies. It is especially common on Queed Maud Land and in the Rayner zone of Enderby Land.

FIGURE 13. Spinel-sillimanite quartzite, dark portions are spinel (X 12, regular light, thin section 23).

Spinel-sillimanite quartzites (Figure 13) are distinguished by their bluish gray color, nonuniform banding and heterogeneous distribution of rock-forming minerals. Aside from the ever-present quartz, spinel and sillimanite, they also contain feldspars (plagioclase and K-feldspar), cordierite, garnet, biotite, graphite, sapphirine, hypersthene and ore minerals (Tables 38 and 39). The most widespread accessory mineral of quartzites is rutile, which occurs as anhedral grains, prismatic crystals with cross-twins, and acicular aggregates. Oval and zoned zircon grains are frequently encountered.

The texture of the quartzites is very complex. Medium-grained grano-blastic textures deviate toward metablastic textures in the presence of columnar sillimanite and toward lepidoblastic textures in the presence of biotite and graphite. Together with these, complex diablastic aggregates of spinel, sillimanite, garnet, cordierite, quartz and feldspars also occur. Most commonly, spinel and sillimanite are overgrown by cordierite and garnet or are embedded in metablasts of these minerals. Similarly, spinel is overgrown by sillimanite and garnet by cordierite. These relationships possibly indicate two generations of sillimanite and cordier-ite. In the case of sillimanite, two generations can be distinctly established; the earlier generation is represented by elongated prismatic grains with rhombic cross sections, while the later stage appears mainly as rims around aggregates of ore minerals. Spinel forms acicular aggregates which overgrow the first generation. The two sillimanite generations differ from each other in their optical and chemical properties. Separate cordierite generations have not been established. Cordierite and garnet form fairly large metablasts (up to 3 mm), in which spinel and sillimanite are embedded. In places, plagioclase is replaced by cordierite which con-tains diffuse relicts of the feldspar; in other cases, these minerals are in equilibrium. In feldspathized varieties, a fine quartz-cordierite symplektite is formed at the contact of cordierite with K-feldspar. Cordierite is replaced by penninite and biotite. Garnet is corroded by quartz and more completely replaced by biotite. Plagioclase is replaced by K-feldspar. Hypersthene, which locally occurs in quartzites, like sapphirine, is apparently a bimetasomatic mineral which originated in the quartzite as the result of reactions at their contact with bipyroxene schists. These minerals are usually embedded in rims of cordierite grains and are replaced by the latter. The existence of numerous mutually substituting mineral phases in spinel-sillimanite quartzites emphasizes their nonequilibrium during metamorphism.

Spinel is grayish green or brownish gray-green in color and is a hercynite, similar to the spinel in migmatites of aluminous schists. Its ferruginosity is 47—54 at.%. Hercynite regularly forms complex aggre-gates with ore minerals. First-generation sillimanite has an anomalous oblique extinction (up to 10°) with respect to the prismatic faces. Its refractive indices are: $n_z = 1.678-1.679$; $n_x = 1.657-1.658$; $2V = +20$ to $+30°$. The refractive indices of the late sillimanite are 0.007 to 0.010 larger. Pinkish garnet is often diablastic due to inclusions of quartz, spinel and sillimanite. Its ferruginosity is higher than that of hercynite, but is directly proportional to the latter, varying from 52 at.% (the lowest known for granulitic rocks in Antarctica) to 65 at.%. Hypersthene has a high iron content whereas the polysynthetically twinned cordierite has a medium iron content. The composition and textural features of feldspars correspond to those in shadow perthitic granitoids, i.e., plagioclase is

TABLE 38. Mineral composition and characteristics, and geological setting of spinel-sillimanite quartzites from Enderby Land

Specimen No.	Mineral composition, vol.%													Characteristics of minerals							
	qz	plag	Kfs	spin	sill	gar	hyp	spph	cord	biot	grph	ore and accessory minerals	An content of plagioclase	garnet n	garnet f at.%	hypersthene n_z	hypersthene n_x	hypersthene f at.%	spinel n	spinel a (Å)	spinel f at.%
204g	72	20	+	4	+	—	—	—	2	—	—	2	56	—	—	—	—	—	—	—	—
209	60	6	—	+	5	—	—	—	7	7	2	5	—	—	—	—	—	—	—	—	—
202b	66	14	+	+	+	13	—	—	—	6	—	1	32	1.787	65	—	—	—	—	8.127± 0.008	54
792b	67	—	+	6	3	24	—	—	—	+	—	+	—	—	—	—	—	—	—	—	—
774a	43	1	21	+	1	32	—	—	—	+	—	2	—	—	—	—	—	—	—	—	—
183v	53	15	4	+	7	15	—	—	—	—	6	+	—	—	—	—	—	—	—	—	—
214	42	8	+	1	10	30	—	—	5	3	—	1	30	—	—	—	—	—	—	—	—
770a	70	4	10	2	1	10	—	—	3	—	—	+	37	1.765	52*	—	—	—	—	8.114± 0.007	47
769v	72	—	—	+	+	26	+	1	—	—	—	1	—	—	—	—	—	—	—	—	—
670v	62	+	5	+	9	11	1	—	5	5	—	2	—	—	—	—	—	—	—	—	—
796a	50	—	—	1	2	33	2	2	10	+	—	1	—	—	—	—	—	—	—	—	—
766b	57	4	20	1	—	2	1	—	15	—	—	+	32	1.780	60	1.726	1.711	50	—	—	—

TABLE 38 (continued)

Specimen No.	Characteristics of minerals							Geological setting
	sillimanite			cordierite				
	n_Z	n_X	$2V°$	n_Z	n_X	$2V°$	f at.%	
204 g	—	—	—	—	—	—	—	Group of interbedded quartzites and high-alumina schists, with lenses of pyroxene-plagioclase schists
209	—	—	—	—	—	—	—	Intercalations up to 15 m thick in shadow garnet granites
202 b	—	—	—	—	—	—	—	Group of quartzite beds
792 b	—	—	—	—	—	—	—	Interbedded with garnet quartzites and pyroxene-plagioclase schists
774a	—	—	—	—	—	—	—	Interbedded with pyroxene-plagioclase and pyroxene schists
183 v	—	—	—	—	—	—	—	Thin intercalations in a group of interbedded shadow garnet granites and charnockites
214	—	—	—	—	—	—	—	Paleosome of plicated layered migmatite with meso-perthitic sillimanite granite metasome
770a	1.678	1.658	+30	—	—	—	—	Paleosome of layered migmatite with shadow bifeldspar garnet metasome
769a	—	—	—	—	—	—	—	Group of interbedded quartzites and high-alumina schists
670 v	—	—	—	—	—	—	—	As above
796a	—	—	—	—	—	—	—	Group of quartzites beds with lenses of pyroxene schists
766b	—	—	—	1.543	1.535	—85	20	Group of quartzite beds about 300 m thick

TABLE 39. Mineral composition and characteristics in quartzites from various regions of Antarctica

Specimen No.	qz	plag	Kfs	spin	sill	gar	cord	biot	ore and accessory minerals	An content of plagioclase	garnet n	garnet f at.%	cordierite n_z	cordierite n_x	cordierite f at.%	biotite n_z	biotite f at.%
Bunger Oasis																	
48	77	3	2	2	2	10	1	2	3	—	—	—	—	—	—	—	—
230	60	15	—	2	—	5	15	—	—	38	—	—	1.546	1.536	24	—	—
929	62	5	13	—	2	15	—	2	1	—	1.790	67	—	—	—	—	—
Queen Maud Land																	
800 b	60	—	5	—	5	15	—	15	+	—	1.781	61	—	—	—	—	—
727 g	55	—	+	—	20	6	5	11	3	—	1.786	70*	—	—	—	—	—
801 a	60	15	20	—	3	—	2	—	+	26	—	—	—	—	—	—	—
Enderby Land																	
202 g	68	—	—	—	—	30	—	—	1								
202 e	45	10	12	—	—	20	—	12	1								
644	82	10	4	—	—	3	—	1	—								
Quartzitic rocks from Bunger Oasis																	
91	45	39	3	—	—	6	2	4	1	38	1.789	67	—	—	—	—	—
116 a	40	40	—	—	—	10	1	7	2	38	—	—	—	—	—	1.640	38
183	50	22	—	—	—	14	8	4	2	38	1.790	67	—	—	—	—	—
65 b	60	10	5	—	—	6	—	18	1	42	1.790	67	—	—	—	—	—
283	64	15	1	—	—	18	—	—	2	37	1.790	67	—	—	—	1.650	42
538 b	45	10	15	—	—	25	—	2	3	33	—	—	—	—	—	—	—

andesine—An 30—37 (rarely labradorite), and the K-feldspar is perthitic
Na-orthoclase.

In view of these textural and compositional features of spinel-sillimanite
quartzites, it may be assumed that the primary mineral association,
spinel-sillimanite-quartz, was replaced by the following later associations
during lower-temperature retrograde transformations: cordierite-
sillimanite-quartz, cordierite-garnet-quartz, cordierite-quartz, garnet-
sillimanite-quartz, garnet-quartz. Plagioclase, if present in the primary
association, is replaced by cordierite and a plagioclase with a lower An
content. The mineral composition of later associations, although dependent
on the temperature conditions, was undoubtedly also affected by the chemical composition of the rocks and by the pressure. Apparently, the change
in temperature conditions occurred during granitization of the country
rock; thus the later mineral associations in the quartzites may be regarded
as side-products of granitization.

Sillimanite quartzites occur in thin intercalations within beds
of garnet-sillimanite, hypersthene-sillimanite and spinel-sillimanite
quartzites. Apparently, they originated from rocks low in iron and magnesium, since they contain only traces of ore minerals, while the magnesian minerals are represented by cordierite (rarely up to 2%) or traces
of sapphirine. The major rock-forming minerals of these quartzites are
quartz and sillimanite, usually accounting for over 70% of the rock. Plagioclase is nearly always present, varying in content from traces to 15%.
Moreover, sillimanite quartzites are always feldspathized, containing up
to 25% K-feldspar (Table 40).

FIGURE 14. Biotitized garnet-sillimanite quartzite (x 30, regular light, thin
section 577a)

TABLE 40. Mineral composition and characteristics in sillimanite, sillimanite–garnet and sillimanite–hypersthene quartzites from Enderby Land

Specimen No.	Mineral composition, vol.%									Characteristics of minerals								Geological setting
	qz	plag	Kfs	sill	gar	hyp	spph	biot	ore and accessory minerals	An content of plagioclase	garnet n	garnet f at.%	hypersthene n_z	hypersthene n_x	hypersthene f at.%	biotite n_z	biotite f at.%	
Sillimanite quartzites																		
670b	73	2	5	20	—	—	—	—	o.s.*	—	—	—	—	—	—	—	—	Group of interbedded quartzites and high-alumina schists
459—1	67	2	26	5	—	—	—	—	· ·	—	—	—	—	—	—	—	—	Beds of sillimanite quartzites
459	86	—	6	7	—	—	o.s.	—	·*	—	—	—	—	—	—	—	—	" " "
171d	93	—	6	1	o.s.	—	—	—	o.s.	—	—	—	—	—	—	—	—	Intercalations within a group of interbedded bifeldspar garnet shadow granites with pyroxene-plagioclase schists
Sillimanite-garnet quartzites																		
577a	62	—	16	3	10	—	—	9	·	—	—	—	—	—	—	—	—	Intercalations within a group of beds of bifeldspar garnet shadow granites
656	54	—	20	7	18	—	—	o.s.	1	—	—	—	—	—	—	—	—	Beds of sillimanite-garnet quartzites with intercalations of pyroxene-plagioclase schists
475	67	5	8	4	15	—	—	—	1	35	—	—	—	—	—	—	—	As above
43	53	7	8	8	13	—	—	11	o.s.	67	—	—	—	—	—	—	—	Beds of various quartzites
Sillimanite-hypersthene quartzites																		
459a	57	35	—	2	—	4	—	2	o.s.	24	—	—	1.682	1.672	13	1.591	15	Intercalations within beds of sillimanite quartzites
459a—1	67	6	—	14	—	6	—	7	· ·	24	—	—	—	—	—	—	—	As above
185	50	—	32	5	—	8	—	5	· ·	—	—	—	1.706	1.694	28	1.600	20	Beds of sillimanite-hypersthene quartzites
72	65	—	—	12	18	5	—	—	·	—	1.778	59	1.700	1.688	22	—	—	Quartzites beds with intercalations of enderbites

* [o.s. = optic sign.]

Sillimanite quartzites generally exhibit a blastocataclastic texture superimposed over a nematogranoblastic texture; the latter is due to tabular sillimanite crystals $(0.2 \times 1.5$ mm) within granoblastic quartz and roughly lenticular feldspars (up to 2 mm). The feldspars are irregularly distributed and are usually grouped. The plagioclase and sillimanite exhibit wavy and "block" extinction. Quartz is granulated. Plagioclase, An 26−33, is replaced by K-feldspar, which is represented by perthitic orthoclase (Enderby Land) or microclinized perthitic orthoclase (Queen Maud Land). On Enderby Land, in addition to the tabular sillimanite, there are bundles of acicular sillimanite. Sillimanite needles are also found in quartz and mesoperthite. The second generation of sillimanite evidently owes its origin to a feldspathization of quartzites and a general lowering of the temperature.

Sillimanite-garnet quartzites (Figure 14) are feldspathized rocks. They occur as intercalations (up to 5 m thick) within groups of interbedded shadow charnockites and garnet granites. They also form scattered zones with diffuse outlines within garnet shadow granites. Lenses of sillimanite-garnet quartzites are also present in groups of interbedded garnet-bipyroxene shadow granites and calciphyres. Quartzite exposures exhibit distinct intercalations of pyroxene-plagioclase schists. The quartzites always contain quartz, K-feldspar, sillimanite, garnet, biotite and ore minerals. Plagioclase occurs sporadically (Table 40). Accessory minerals are zircon and rutile. Garnet is usually the predominant colored mineral.

The texture of the quartzites is determined by a subparallel distribution of biotite flakes, columnar sillimanite grains, flattened garnet grains and roughly lenticular quartz grains, with intergranular anhedral K-feldspar. In places, K-feldspar forms separate "strips." Both large and small granulated quartz lenses are present $(3 \times 10$ mm, and 1−2 mm, respectively). Small mosaic and broken quartz grains (0.2−1.0 mm) occur within the lenticular quartz. The tabular sillimanite grains $(2V = +26°)$ are generally small (0.1−0.5 mm) but a few larger grains $(0.3 \times 1.5$ mm) also occur. Flattened garnet grains reach 1×3 mm in size. In less cataclastic varieties, garnet forms sub-euhedral metablasts up to 2.5 mm in size, which contain numerous inclusions of rounded and irregular quartz grains, sillimanite needles and prisms and zircon granules. Depending on the distribution of the sillimanite needles, snowball garnets may occur as well as more complex forms indicating the translocation of grains during crystallization; the garnet itself forms metablasts which are discordant with respect to the gneissosity. Clearly, in this case, translocation "canceled" the stress which otherwise produced blastocataclastic textures. Feldspar grains are 0.1−1.5 mm and biotite flakes 1.5−2 mm in size. Garnet is replaced by biotite and quartz, occasionally forming symplektite intergrowths, while sillimanite is replaced by K-feldspar. In rare cases, garnet-sillimanite quartzites also contain cordierite. Cordierite and sillimanite in quartzites are commonly replaced by penninite; garnet and biotite are replaced by chlorite. The ferruginosity of garnet is 61−67 at.% which is higher than its ferruginosity in spinel-sillimanite quartzites. K-feldspar is usually microclinized orthoclase, exhibiting traces of typical microcline crosshatching along its margins ($2V = -84$ to $-85°$, $\perp (001) n_y = = 6-8°$).

Sillimanite-hypersthene quartzites (Figure 15) were encountered only in three exposures (isolated nunataks) on Enderby Land at the boundary of the Napier and Rayner zones. The sillimanite-hypersthene association is rare and deserves a detailed description.

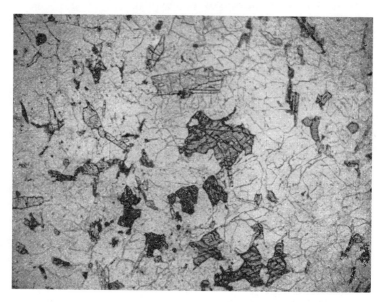

FIGURE 15. Sillimanite-hypersthene quartzite (x 15, regular light, thin section 135).

The sillimanite-pyroxene quartzites at rock station 459 are 100 m thick, with thin intercalations of sillimanite quartzites. Aside from sillimanite, bronzite and quartz, they contain plagioclase and biotite. The mineral composition is given in Table 40.

The rocks are white, and banded, due to the separation of sillimanite and plagioclase. Their texture is granoblastic, with glomeroblastic segregations of sillimanite and bronzite against a mesastasis of mosaic quartz forming grains up to 0.5 mm in diameter with scattered inclusions of sillimanite, bronzite and biotite. The plagioclase is scattered with the quartz, forming anhedral grains of the same size as the quartz. Bronzite is represented by 0.2—0.6 mm anhedral grains which locally develop short prisms. It is overgrown by sillimanite as a continuous rim or as bundles of acicular and tubular grains. Rutile granules occur within sillimanite aggregates, especially at the contact with bronzite. Biotite forms subhedral flakes (up to 0.4 mm), replaces sillimanite and bronzite, and contains their relics. Quartz corrodes bronzite, sillimanite and plagioclase.

Plagioclase (An 24) contains inclusions of sillimanite and rutile. It is often untwinned. The ferruginosity of the colored minerals is low, 13 at.% for bronzite and 15 at.% for biotite.

In rock station 185, sillimanite-hypersthene quartzites compose the paleosome of layered migmatites, the metasome being perthitic garnet granite. The total thickness of these migmatites beds is 10 m. The paleo- some contains much K-feldspar (32%) and some biotite (5%). Accessory minerals are zircon and rutile. The texture is granoblastic with lepido- nematogranoblastic elements. Hypersthene and sillimanite form discrete chains of grains. Aggregations of tabular sillimanite and an-subhedral hypersthene are rare. The various mineral grains have the following dimensions: quartz, 1—3 mm; K-feldspar, 0.3—0.6 mm; hypersthene, 0.5—1.5 mm; sillimanite, 0.1—1 mm, and biotite 0.1—0.6 mm.

Sillimanite and hypersthene are replaced by quartz and biotite; sillimanite is also replaced by K-feldspar. Quartz contains numerous inclusions of sillimanite, hypersthene and biotite. In turn, the hypersthene and sillimanite contain rounded quartz inclusions. The ferruginosity of hypersthene is 28 at.% and that of biotite, 20 at.%. K-feldspar is repre- sented by cryptoperthite and its optical properties correspond to a highly sodic orthoclase ($\perp(100)\,n_y$= 8°; $2V$ = −73 to −75°; n_x = 1.534; n_z = 1.542).

Beds of hypersthene-sillimanite quartzites observed at rock station 72 also contain 18% garnet. The quartzites contain intercalations of amphi- bolized garnet-pyroxene-plagioclase schists with sharp contacts, the visible overall thickness of this group of beds being 100 m. Hypersthene- sillimanite quartzites are brown in color and are massive. Their texture is characterized by flattened quartz grains (up to 2.5—5 mm long), and roughly lenticular accumulations of colored minerals parallel to and com- mensurate with the quartz lenses. Reaction garnet, replacing both silli- manite and hypersthene, develops on the edges of sillimanite and hyper- sthene grains. The garnet contains inclusions of sillimanite prisms and rounded quartz grains. All the minerals are corroded to varying degrees by quartz. The sillimanite and hypersthene grains are 0.1—1 mm and garnet grains up to 2 mm in size. Rutile is present as an accessory mineral, generally aggregates with sillimanite or imbedded in quartz. The ferruginosity of hypersthene is close to that of bronzite (f = 22 at.%); the ferruginosity of garnet is also low (f = 59 at.%).

Hypersthene-cordierite quartzites are widespread on Enderby Land. They compose large separate exposures or are interbedded with spinel-sillimanite quartzites and schists. The apparent thickness of these quartzites reaches hundreds of meters. Occasionally, the same beds contain lenses of pyroxene-plagioclase schists and enderbites. Macro- scopically, these are inequigranular, maculose and indistinctly banded rocks with massive structure; they are gray to light gray in color. The mineralogical composition of hypersthene-cordierite quartzites is listed in Table 41. It always includes quartz, hypersthene, cordierite and biotite. In rare cases, there are insignificant amounts of plagioclase, sapphirine and ore minerals. The quartzites are enriched in K-feldspar near pegmatite veins (ramification of migmatites). The mineral contents vary considerably. Rutile and zircon are the accessory minerals.

TABLE 41. Mineral composition and characteristics in hypersthene-cordierite quartzites from Enderby Land

Specimen No.	Mineral composition, vol.%									Characteristics of minerals									Geological setting
										hypersthene			biotite		cordierite				
	qz	plag	Kfs	hyp	spph	cord	biot	ore and accessory minerals	An content of plagioclase	n_z	n_x	f at.%	n_z	f at.%	n_z	n_x	$2V$	f at.%	
189	64	2	—	10	—	23	o.s.*	1	35	—	—	—	—	—	—	—	+80	—	Quartzite beds with lenses of pyroxene-plagioclase schists and veins of enderbite
189a	47	o.s.	o.s.	26	—	22	5	o.s.	—	—	—	—	—	—	—	—	—	—	As above
796b	97	—	—	2	—	1	o.s.	"	37	—	—	—	—	—	—	—	—	—	Quartzite beds with lenses of pyroxene schists
769b	92	—	—	4	1	3	"	"	—	—	—	—	—	—	—	—	—	—	Interbedded quartzites and high-alumina schists
459v	54	—	15	1	—	29	1	"	—	—	—	—	—	—	—	—	—82	—	Intercalations in sillimanite quartzites
473	50	—	18	3	—	25	3	1	—	—	—	—	—	—	—	—	—	—	Beds of hypersthene-cordierite quartzites
473b	46	—	35	1	—	16	2	o.s.	—	1.722	1.707	45	1.638	37	1.552	1.543	—85	36	As above
473v	46	—	—	20	—	30	1	3	—	—	—	—	—	—	—	—	—	—	" "
473e	38	—	—	14	—	43	3	2	—	1.708	1.696	30	1.615	26	1.543	1.534	+82	20	" "
210a	72	—	—	1	—	25	2	o.s.	—	—	—	—	—	—	—	—	—	—	Rocks with diffuse contacts in garnet charnockites

* [o.s. = optic sign.]

The distribution of minerals in quartzites and their grain sizes are markedly nonuniform. The quartz grains are roughly lenticular, 1—8 mm in size, and are granulated along the edges. This inhomogeneous mass of quartz forms the matrix for the various aggregates of other minerals. In some cases cordierite, hypersthene and sapphirine compose separate areas of irregular and lenticular shapes; these have the appearance of independent rocks. In other cases, raggedly shaped quartz lenses alternate with similar lenses of other minerals. In still other occurrences, there are alternating bands of melanocratic and colorless minerals, or the cordierite and hypersthene may be uniformly distributed throughout the rock mass. In feldspathized specimens, thin bands of K-feldspar alternate with those of quartz and cordierite. However, all these structures possess one feature in common, i. e., lenticular flattening of nearly all the minerals (granulitization), with rare exceptions in cases of hypersthene.

The cordierite grains are small (0.6—2 mm). This mineral often overgrows hypersthene and sapphirine, penetrating via cracks and forming rims up to 0.5 mm wide. Relics of these minerals occur in the cordierite in marginal rims consisting of a fine quartz-cordierite symplektite. The symplektite rims reach widths of 0.5 mm. Cordierite is replaced by pinite and fine-grained biotite. Hypersthene forms prismatic and anhedral grains with an average size of 0.3—0.7 mm; a few large hypersthene metablasts, up to 8 mm across, also occur. Hypersthene is replaced by biotite and quartz, which sometimes form symplektitic aggregates, as well as by cordierite. Sapphirine is separated from hypersthene by a cordierite rim. Plagioclase replaces quartz and cordierite symplektites. In feldspathized varieties, K-feldspar (microclinized perthite) forms anhedral grains (0.5—1 mm) which replace cordierite and plagioclase; myrmekitic quartz intergrowths are formed in the cordierite and plagioclase. Cordierite is generally polysynthetically twinned; wedge-shaped twins with planar ends are characteristic. The angle of the optical axes of cordierites in feldspathized quartzites is negative and that in nonfeldspathized quartzites is positive. Its iron content is 20—36 at.%. Hypersthene is markedly pleochroic and apparently aluminous, with a ferruginosity of 30—45 at.%. The ferruginosity of biotite is close to that of cordierite (26—37 at.%). Plagioclase (An 35—37) is antiperthitic.

Garnet quartzites are light gray or bluish gray in color. They are massive and locally a gneissic structure occurs due to parallel orientation of biotite flakes and lenticular segregations of feldspar. Garnet quartzites form thin intercalations among shadow garnet granites, shadow enderbites and spinel-sillimanite quartzites. They are sometimes boudinaged and lenticular. The mineral composition of garnet quartzites is presented in Table 39. Aside from garnet, ore and quartz, they often contain plagioclase and biotite, and sporadic amounts of cordierite. Some of the quartzites are feldspathized. Their texture is hetero-granoblastic, with subeuhedral corroded garnet metablasts measuring 5 mm or more. These stand out sharply against a background predominated by large serrated quartz grains. Feldspars are usually intergranular, their grain size seldom exceeding 0.8 mm. Parallel biotite flakes introduce a lepidogranoblastic textural element into the rock. In places, biotite overgrows the garnet, resulting in corona structures. Like garnet, cordierite forms metablasts, which are, however, considerably smaller. Plagioclase is antiperthitic oligoclase-andesine (An 27—38), while K-feldspar is a perthitic orthoclase or crosshatched microcline. The garnet is diablastic, and is pinkish in thin section. Its iron content is fairly constant (66—67 at.%). The iron content of biotite is higher in garnet quartzite (38—42 at.%) than in the majority of the other quartzites described above.

Feldspar quartzites do not form separate units but appear as lenses, up to 1.5 m thick and 2.5 m long, as well as thin intercalations (up to 1 m) within shadow granitoids. They apparently represent remnants of the original rock. These quartzites have been observed mainly on Enderby Land. They are light gray or bluish gray in color with a massive struc- ture; very locally, a gneissic structure occurs due to lenticular segrega- tions of feldspar. In addition to quartz, which accounts for 85—95% of the rock, they contain variable amounts of one (plagioclase) or two (plagioclase and orthoclase) feldspars (Table 42). Sporadic flakes of biotite and graphite are noted. Rutile and zircon, sometimes reaching 1% in content, are the accessory minerals. The presence of plagioclase in the quartzites is due to the initial composition of the rocks. However, its composition and texture resemble those of enderbites due to the enderbitization of plagioclase quartzites. K-feldspar formed during granitization. The extensive jointing of the quartzites and their consequent high permeability to various aqueous solutions in the epizone, resulted in the development of various secondary alteration products in the feldspars or in cracks; these include chlorite, sericite, zeolites, clinozoisite, fluorite, iron hydroxides and clay minerals.

TABLE 42. Mineral composition and geological setting of feldspar quartzites from Enderby Land

Speci-men No.	Mineral composition, vol.%						Geological setting
	qz	plag	Kfs	biot	grph	accessory minerals	
205b	95	—	4	—	—	1	Intercalation within interbedded shadow garnet mesoperthitic granites and charnockites
46a	95	2	3	—	—	o.s.*	Lenses in shadow bifeldspar charnockite
29g	88	12	—	—	—	"	Lenses in enderbite
281	96	4	—	o.s.	o.s.	"	Intercalations in shadow garnet bifeldspar granites

* [o.s. = optic sign.]

The texture of quartzites is hetero-granoblastic. Large quartz grains (2—4 mm) with serrated boundaries are predominant. They are sometimes granulated along their edges or in certain zones. The quartz often contains inclusions of rutile needles. The feldspars are generally intergranular with anhedral grains seldom exceeding 0.8 mm in diameter. The plagioclase is often replaced by K-feldspar, represented by antiperthitic oligoclase-andesine (An 27—31). K-feldspar presents a variety of compositions and textures. Two K-feldspars, perthite and orthoclase, are liable to occur even within a single specimen. In rocks with intensively manifested low-temperature mineralization, K-feldspar is represented by microcline. The structure and composition of quartzites confirm the opinion that these rocks do not readily lend themselves to granitization /21, 57/. It is possible to trace a distinct relationship between granitization and the composition of quartzites; aluminous quartzites are of a higher grade of granitization than feldspar quartzites. Among the aluminous varieties, those containing plagioclase often prove to be of a higher grade of granitization; this is due to the ease of addition of potassium into the feldspar structure, and not to the disintegration of the aluminous minerals and their subsequent replacement by feldspar.

METASOMATIC HIGH-ALUMINA ROCKS

As in the case of diopside rocks formed by bimetasomatic processes at contacts between calciphyres and shadow granitoids, unusual magnesian-ferruginous-aluminous crystalline rocks, with or without quartz, form at contacts between hypersthenites, bronzitites and orthopyroxene schists and shadow granitoids (saturated in alumina). These rocks occur locally in high-alumina ultrametamorphic series in the form of isolated lenses and thin intercalations (Table 43). The formation of these rocks clearly requires specific temperature and pressure conditions and accompanying metasomatosis; they are consequently rather rare in the metamorphic complex of East Antarctica. To date, they have been encountered in the Napier zone of Enderby Land with sporadic occurrences in the Bunger Oasis. The following five varieties of these rocks can be distinguished with respect to their mineral compositions: a) sillimanite-hypersthene-cordierite, b) spinel-hypersthene-cordierite, c) hypersthene-cordierite, d) spinel-hypersthene-garnet-cordierite, and e) garnet-hypersthene-cordierite.

All varieties contain biotite, and garnet-containing varieties contain plagioclase. These are generally formed at the contact between pyroxene-plagioclase schists and shadow granitoids. All spinel- and biotite-free varieties form on contact between pyroxenites and shadow granitoids. In rocks lacking in silica (garnet-free varieties), sapphirine occurs along with, or instead of, cordierite while hypersthene is accompanied by olivine; plagioclase occurs sporadically. Quartz and K-feldspar may occur in all varieties, but in extremely variable amounts. Besides the hypersthene-bearing varieties, metasomatic rocks may occasionally be represented by biotite-cordierite-quartz and biotite-sapphirine-cordierite assemblages.

Sillimanite-hypersthene-cordierite rocks often form relics in shadow garnet perthitic granites. The mineral composition of these rocks includes hypersthene, sillimanite, sapphirine, cordierite, biotite, quartz and K-feldspar, with prevalence of colored minerals (Table 43). Rutile and zircon are present as accessory minerals. In general, the rocks are nearly devoid of quartz; however, quartz appears at the contact with shadow granite in appreciable quantities. In these occurrences, sapphirine disappears and the colored minerals' content decreases. K-feldspar penetrates into the near-contact portion of the rock and along cracks.

The texture is controlled by a heterogeneous development of polygonal hypersthene grains, often poikilitic. Cordierite forms the matrix. Mica lepidoblasts, quartz segregations and numerous reactive relationships also occur. The size of hypersthene grains is 1—5 mm, but these are smaller, 0.4—1 mm, in near-contact varieties. Sillimanite is represented by lenticular grains up to 0.5 × 4 mm in size. Minute sillimanite prisms are usually embedded in cordierite. Sapphirine forms equidimensional or elongated polygonal grains up to 2.5—3 mm in size, often in symplektitic aggregates (2 mm) with cordierite. Sapphirine grains are up to 0.4 mm in diameter and irregular cordierite grains average 0.3—0.6 mm. Most commonly, cordierite forms an aggregate of small grains serving as a cement for the other minerals. Furthermore, cordierite rims often develop around hypersthene and sillimanite. Biotite is represented by flakes ranging from 0.3 to 3.5 mm. Quartz forms lenticular flattened grains (0.5 to 2.5 mm across). K-feldspar occurs in small anhedral grains (0.5— 1 mm). Hypersthene is corroded by sillimanite; sillimanite lathes penetrating the hypersthene are separated from it by a cordierite rim. Hypersthene relicts occur in the sillimanite. Hypersthene is resorbed by cordierite which penetrates along cleavage cracks and forms overgrowths. Fine quartz-cordierite symplektite forms at the cordierite-hypersthene boundary. Hypersthene is replaced by biotite along the edges and in cracks; it is resorbed by quartz in quartz-bearing varieties. Sillimanite is intensively corroded by sapphirine-cordierite and cordierite-sapphirine symplektite, and is also replaced by biotite. Sapphirine is entirely embedded in cordierite. There are inclusions of biotite, sillimanite, zircon and rutile within symplektitic aggregates of sapphirine and cordierite. Sapphirine is apparently replaced by biotite. In turn, cordierite is corroded by K-feldspar, resulting in a symplektite of quartz and cordierite. Biotite forms symplektitic aggregates with quartz and cordierite along its crystal boundaries (Figure 16).

The ferruginosity of hypersthene in these rocks (22—26 at.%) is significantly lower than that of biotite (32—37 at.%). The ferruginosity of cordierite is 16—20 at.% and the $2V$ of sillimanite is +27°. K-feldspar is represented by perthite. Rutile occurs as subeuhedral grains (up to 0.5 mm across); columnar crystals are up to 1 mm long, and oval and barrel-shaped crystals are 0.35 × 0.8 mm, 0.8 × 0.8 mm, and smaller. There are some completely transparent green grains. Inclusions of fine rutile needles and grains occur in biotite and quartz. The rutile content in the rock is about 1%.

Spinel-hypersthene-cordierite rocks are often associated with spinel-sillimanite quartzites. They stand out because of their brownish

TABLE 43. Metasomatic high-alumina rocks of the granulite facies from Enderby Land and the Bunger Oasis

Specimen No.	qz	plag	Kfs	spin	sill	gar	hyp	spph	cord	biot	grph	ore and accessory minerals	An content of plagioclase	garnet n	garnet f at.%	spinel n	spinel a(Å)	spinel f at.%	hypersthene n_z	hypersthene n_x	hypersthene f at.%
473d	—	—	—	—	—	—	58	—	27	14	—	1	—	—	—	—	—	—	1.708	1.696	30
5—2	—	—	—	—	—	—	50	—	25	8	—	—	20	—	—	—	—	—	—	—	—
820a	—	7	10	—	—	—	23	—	59	+	+	1	—	—	—	—	—	—	—	—	—
468e	42	24	4	—	—	—	7	—	18	—	—	1	44	—	—	—	—	—	—	—	—
208b	+	—	—	—	—	—	55	—	25	20	—	+	37	—	—	—	—	—	1.701	1.689	23
208v	55	22	+	—	—	—	15	—	6	2	—	+	—	—	—	—	—	—	1.712 / 1.700	1.700 / 1.688	34 / 22
208d	69	10	3	—	—	—	1	—	16	1	—	+	27	—	—	—	—	—	1.712 / 1.700	1.700 / 1.687	34 / 22
208k	2	—	—	—	—	—	50	—	42	6	—	+	—	—	—	—	—	—	1.692	1.680	17
208e	—	—	1.5	—	—	—	37	1.5	48	12	—	+	—	—	—	—	—	—	1.695	1.684	19
208g	—	—	2	2	—	—	29	4	40	25	—	+	—	—	—	—	—	—	1.694	1.683	18
204b	74	—	—	3	—	—	17	—	3	4	—	+	—	—	—	—	—	—	1.715	1.703	38
27a	35	—	8	0.5	—	—	2	—	47	4	—	+	—	—	—	—	—	—	1.712	1.700	34
27b	55	6	5	2	—	—	2.5	—	27	4	—	+	—	—	—	—	—	—	—	—	—
236a	—	—	10	2	—	—	30	—	52	5	—	1	—	—	—	—	—	—	1.696	1.684	20
755g	—	2	12	2	—	—	58	2	14	10	—	+	32	—	—	—	8.145± 0.004	60	1.715	1.702	34*

TABLE 43 (continued)

Speci-men No.	qz	plag	Kfs	spin	sill	gar	hyp	spph	cord	biot	grph	ore and accessory minerals	An content of plagio-clase	garnet n	garnet f at.%	spinel n	spinel a(Å)	spinel f at.%	hypersthene nz	hypersthene nx	hypersthene f at.%
760z	18	—	6	+	—	—	55	+	18	—	—	2	—	—	—	—	—	—	—	—	—
2081	—	—	—	6	—	—	17	50	—	27	—	+	—	—	—	1.719	—	0	1.666	1.658	1
210b	5	17	—	—	—	—	—	20	33	47	—	—	58	—	—	—	—	—	—	—	—
204d	30	4	1	3	—	34	23	—	16	+	—	1	25	—	—	—	—	—	—	—	—
210v	+	50	2	0.5	—	0.5	5	—	54	1.5	—	2.5	30	—	—	—	—	—	—	—	—
820v	—	—	—	3	—	4	3	—	38	—	+	2	—	—	—	—	8.13±0.003	53.5	1.742	1.726	61
906a	40	5	—	2	—	2	55	—	20	15	—	1	33	1.780	60	—	—	—	1.714	1.700	35
706	1	15	—	2	—	2	10	—	25	5	—	1	37	—	—	—	—	—	1.715	1.699	37
169b	3	5	38	—	—	38	3	—	12	3	—	+	37	1.793	70	—	—	—	1.720	1.705	43
169v	40	3	58	—	—	13	7	—	13	2	—	1	40	—	—	—	—	—	1.722	1.707	45
169g	—	19	—	—	—	17	2	—	20	1	—	1	38	—	—	—	—	—	—	—	—
666g	6	5	—	—	—	12	43	—	10	25	—	+	—	—	—	—	—	—	1.704	1.691	26
666v	+	+	—	—	—	53	2	—	7	30	+	2	35	—	—	—	—	—	—	—	—
165a	10	31	15	—	—	5	15	—	30	2	—	2	35	—	—	—	—	—	1.733	1.717	56
949	—	5	5	—	—	2	30	18	40	8	—	—	—	—	—	—	—	—	1.717	1.701	40
1—5	—	—	—	—	3	—	20	2	18	40	—	1	—	—	—	—	—	—	1.704	1.691	26
1—6	—	—	2	—	11	—	73	—	4	7	—	1	—	—	—	—	—	—	1.700	1.688	22
1—6—1	65	+	2	—	6	—	14	—	7	5	—	1	—	—	—	—	—	—	1.700	1.688	22

TABLE 43 (continued)

Specimen No.	biotite		cordierite				sapphirine			Geological setting
	n_z	f, at.%	n_z	n_x	$2V$	f at.%	n_z	n_x	$2V$	
473d	1.615	26	1.543	1.534	+82	20	—	—	—	Lenses of hypersthenites in quartzite and high-alumina schist beds
5–2	—	—	—	—	—	—	—	—	—	Contact of hypersthenite with intrusive charnockites
820a	—	—	—	—	—	—	—	—	—	Beds with veinlets of shadow garnet perthitic granite
468e	1.603	21	1.553	1.544	—	39	—	—	—	Xenolith in intrusive charnockite
208b	1.618	28	1.540	1.533	+80	14	—	—	—	Contact of bronzitite with mesoperthitic charnockites
208v	1.606	23	1.555	1.546	90	42	—	—	—	As above
208d	1.606	23	1.543	1.535	−82 +88	20	—	—	—	"
208k	—	10	—	—	−81	8.7	—	—	—	"
208e	1.591	8	1.538	1.531	+85	12	1.724	1.718	−60	"
208g	1.595	19	1.538	1.531	−85	13	1.724	1.718	−67	"
204b	—	—	—	—	—	—	—	—	—	Contact of pyroxene-plagioclase schists with high-alumina schists and spinel-sillimanite quartzites
27a	—	—	1.536	1.529	—	10	—	—	—	As above
27b	—	—	—	—	—	—	—	—	—	"
236a	—	—	—	—	—	—	—	—	—	Contact of pyroxene-plagioclase schists with shadow garnet perthitic granitoids
755g	1.619	21	1.543	1.535	+73	20	1.732	1.728	−54	Hypersthenites at contact of mesoperthitic shadow garnet granitoids and enderbites
760z	—	—	—	—	—	—	—	—	—	Contact of hypersthenites with shadow garnet mesoperthitic granites

TABLE 43 (continued)

Specimen No.	biotite		cordierite				sapphirine			Geological setting
	n_z	f, at.%	n_z	n_x	$2V$	f, at.%	n_z	n_x	$2V$	
2081	—	—	—	—	—	—	1.710	1.704	—	+ Ol (n_z = 1.671; n_x = 1.538; f = 0). Lens in mesoperthitic charnockite
210b	—	63	—	—	—	—	—	—	—	Block in garnet mesoperthitic charnockites
204d	—	—	—	—	—	8.5	—	—	—	Contact of pyroxene-plagioclase schists with kinzigite and spinel-sillimanite quartzite
210v	—	—	—	—	—	—	—	—	—	Schlieren in mesoperthitic garnet charnockites
820v	¦	—	1.551	1.541	—	33	—	—	—	Contact of specimen 820a with shadow garnet mesoperthitic granite
906a	1.635	36	—	—	—	—	—	—	—	Bunger Oasis
706	—	—	—	—	—	—	—	—	—	" "
169b	1.655	—	1.550	1.540	+85	—	—	—	—	Layers in shadow garnet mesoperthitic granites
169v	1.645	—	1.546	1.537	+87	31	—	—	—	As above
169g	—	—	—	—	—	24	—	—!	—	Contact of layers represented by specimens 169b and 169v with shadow garnet mesoperthitic granites
666g	1.639	38	1.554	1.547	+71	41	—	—	—!	Contact of pyroxene-plagioclase schists with shadow garnet mesoperthitic granite and kinzigites
666v	1.667	49	1.557	1.549	—84	50	—	—	—	As above
165a	—	—	—	—	—	—	—	—	—	Interbedded with shadow mesoperthitic garnet granites
949	1.628	32	1.543	1.534	—83	20	1.723	1.717	—68	Bunger Oasis
1—5	—	—	—	—	—	—	—	—	—	Altered hypersthenites in shadow garnet mesoperthitic granites
1—6	1.638	37	1.541	1.534	—80	16	1.719	1.713	—52	As above
1—6—1	1.638	37	1.541	1.534	—80	16	—	—	—	" "

color and black lenticular and maculose hypersthene segregations. These hypersthene rocks may form intercalations, 20 cm—2 m thick. Aside from spinel, hypersthene and cordierite, they often contain large amounts of quartz, biotite and K-feldspar. Plagioclase is local. Sapphirine occurs in quartz-free varieties. Accessory minerals are represented by rutile and zircon. Ore minerals occur sporadically. The rocks have a hetero-granoblastic texture, complicated by reactive interrelationships. Aggregates of colored minerals occur as blobs within large serrated quartz grains. Spinel is usually embedded in hypersthene and resembles relict grains; in general, it is surrounded by a thin film of cordierite. Spinel often occurs in complex aggregates with ore minerals, although it occasionally also forms separate grains. Cordierite replaces spinel and hypersthene, forming symplektite-like aggregates with these minerals. Large hypersthene grains, with a very strong pleochroism and anomalous interference colors, are highly aluminous varieties; hypersthene from symplektitic aggregates is devoid of these properties and apparently has a lower alumina content. Cordierite also replaces quartz. Biotite develops simultaneously from cordierite and hypersthene. The rock texture is further complicated by the appearance of plagioclase and K-feldspar which give rise to a thin cordierite-quartz symplektite along edges of feldspar (generally K-feldspar) (Figure 17).

The large number of mineral phases in the rocks and the complex, often contradictory, relationships of minerals observed in thin section, suggest that many minerals are represented by several generations. These generations differ in their chemical and textural properties, as in the case of hypersthene. Tracing the succession of generations is difficult without a large number of accurate chemical and optical measurements. Nevertheless, the nonequilibrium nature of the mineral association sequences is beyond doubt. Spinel is dark brownish green in color and is a hercynite. The iron content of hypersthene is 20—37 at.% and that of cordierite is 10—20 at.%. Biotite has a high content of titanium and alumina. The compositions of plagioclase and K-feldspar correspond to similar feldspars in shadow granitoids of the Napier zone. The An content of plagioclase is 32; K-feldspar is most commonly perthite. A second, nonperthitic K-feldspar also occurs; it develops interstitially, in cracks, and also participates in quartz-cordierite symplektites.

Hypersthene-cordierite rocks are formed at contacts of hypersthenite with aluminous quartzite and alumina-rich shadow granitoids. They mainly develop at the expense of hypersthenites, the remnants of which are very seldom preserved (they were encountered at the center of hypersthene-cordierite blocks in only one exposure). The hypersthene-cordierite rocks resemble metasomatic diopsidic rocks in many respects, both internally and in their mode of occurrence. They form lenses, foliated layers, boudinaged intercalations and rootless agmatitized bodies. They differ from diopsidic rocks in their brown or dark brown color and common fine "streaky" structure. The mineral composition of these rocks is given in Table 43. It always includes hypersthene, cordierite and biotite. Quartz (locally in large amounts) and K-feldspar occur in approximately one-half of the collected specimens. Plagioclase (in rocks enriched in quartz)

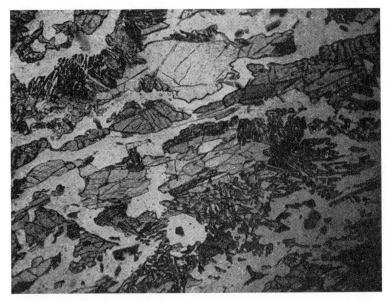

FIGURE 16.   Sillimanite-hypersthene-cordierite metasomatic rocks (× 12, regular light, thin section 1—6—1).

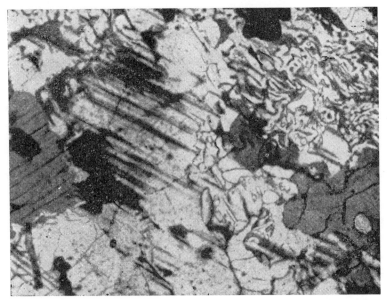

FIGURE 17.   Development of a quartz-cordierite symplektite in granitized spinel-hypersthene-cordierite metasomatic rock (× 30, crossed nicols, thin section 27a).

and sapphirine (exclusively in quartz-free rocks) occur sporadically. Rutile is the accessory mineral.

Rock station 208 is the representative site of the hypersthene-cordierite rocks and consists of agmatites. Gradual transitions from very coarse-grained bronzitites to banded medium-grained hypersthene-cordierite-quartz rocks can be traced in some of the agmatite blocks. Coarse-grained and very coarse-grained massive and finely banded (depending upon the degree of alteration) bronzitites usually possess a hetero-granoblastic or lepidogranoblastic texture, complicated by reactive relationships among the minerals. In specimens with predominant bronzite, this mineral contains poikiloblastic plagioclase with uneven extinction, indicating the replacement of the bronzite by plagioclase. Bronzite, in turn, is corroded by quartz and replaced by biotite along cracks. Cordierite appears in marginal portions of the blocks and corrodes bronzite, forming symplektite aggregates; the bronzite is altered in composition to hypersthene. Thus, the rocks contain two generations of orthopyroxene. Cordierite is in turn replaced by quartz, K-feldspar and biotite; as in the case of plagioclase, symplektite aggregates of cordierite with quartz formed during this process /35/. In sapphirine-bearing rocks the replacement of bronzite by sapphirine, which penetrates along cracks, is clear. However, a thin cordierite rim is always present at their contact. Sapphirine is corroded by cordierite and embedded in the latter. Relicts of sapphirine display indistinct outlines. Sapphirine is also corroded by biotite. At the contact with the host shadow granitoids, the rocks are enriched in quartz and microclinized orthoclase, the latter sometimes forming symplektitic aggregates with low-calcium plagioclase. A decrease in the orthopyroxene content is accompanied by an increase of biotite and cordierite in the rock, while a decrease in cordierite is accompanied by an increase in the quartz content.

The ferruginosity of orthopyroxene varies from the central portion of the rock bodies toward the periphery. In the central portion it is represented by bronzite with $f = 17-19$ at.%; this is superseded by hypersthene with $f = 22-23$ at.%; and finally it becomes hypersthene with $f = 30-34$ at.%. The last two generations of orthopyroxene may occur even in the same thin sections. Biotite and cordierite generations correspond to the same generations as hypersthene. The ferruginosity of biotite varies correspondingly from $10-19$ at.% to $21-23$ at.% and finally to $26-28$ at.%, while that of cordierite varies from $8-13$ at.% to $14-20$ at.% and finally to $39-42$ at.%. Plagioclase in hypersthene-cordierite rocks varies in its a An content from the center of the blocks $(47-48)$ toward their periphery $(27-32)$. Based on optical properties, K-feldspar, represented by perthitic microclinized orthoclase, contains some 46% of oligoclase-andesine in solid solution ($n_z = 1.528$; $n_x = 1.521$, $2V = -77$ to $-80°$). This corresponds to the perthite that is most widespread in the Napier zone (the content of perthitic ingrowths visible under the microscope varies from 25 to 45%). Rutile often occurs as sagenite (in hypersthene and quartz) which emphasizes the high-temperature nature of the primary mineral associations. Rutile grains appear where the ferruginosities increase.

Spinel-hypersthene-garnet-cordierite rocks are formed
at the contact of pyroxene-plagioclase schists with spinel-sillimanite
quartzites and schists as well as with alumina-rich shadow granites. They
always contain spinel, hypersthene, garnet, cordierite, plagioclase, biotite
and ore minerals, and sporadic quartz and K-feldspar (Table 43). Accessory
minerals are represented by rutile needles and zircon granules. The rocks
possess a hetero-granoblastic texture combined with reaction structures
of replacement and overgrowths. The mineral distribution is extremely
heterogeneous. Cordierite forms the rock "cement" in which hypersthene
grains and spinel + ore aggregates are embedded. Garnet rims the aggregates and forms metablasts containing relict hypersthene. Hypersthene is
also replaced by cordierite and biotite, being converted along the grain
edges to fine cordierite-hypersthene symplektites having higher ferruginosities. In turn, cordierite is converted to fine symplektite with quartz
at the contact of quartz and K-feldspar. Plagioclase is intensively corroded
by quartz, K-feldspar and especially quartz-cordierite symplektite. Quartz
corrodes practically all minerals with which it is in direct contact. Spinel
and ore are often separated from quartz by rims of cordierite and biotite.
Biotite replaces cordierite. The rock gives the impression that the spinel +
+ hypersthene + cordierite + plagioclase association is gradually replaced
by the garnet + biotite + K-feldspar + quartz association. The few available
measurements of refractive indices indicate the iron contents of the various
minerals. Biotite and hypersthene, of equally medium ferruginosity, are
associated with low-iron garnet. However, these measurements were
carried out by index of refraction liquids and it is therefore difficult to
establish which mineral generation was measured. In one case, these
rocks were discovered at the contact of hypersthene-cordierite rocks with
shadow garnet granitoids, which suggests that garnet and biotite appear as
a result of granitization of hypersthene-cordierite rocks.

Garnet-hypersthene-cordierite rocks compose layers within
shadow garnet granitoids and they also form rims around boudins of
hypersthene rocks embedded in shadow garnet plagiogranites. Similar to
the garnet-bearing rocks described above, they always contain plagioclase.
Generally, except for the absence of spinel, they are similar to the
preceding variety in their mineral composition. The textures of these
rocks are quite variable, including granoblastic, near-hornfels, blastocataclastic, and mortar (granulated interstitial cordierite and plagioclase)
varieties. The distribution of minerals is very heterogeneous. Garnet
forms large metablasts and apparently develops at the expense of
hypersthene-cordierite symplektite. In turn, garnet is replaced by biotite
and quartz. Inclusions in garnet include rounded quartz grains, ragged
biotite, cordierite-quartz symplektite and hypersthene. Hypersthene is
replaced by cordierite, where it is converted to a hypersthene-cordierite
symplektite, while cordierite and plagioclase are replaced by quartz,
K-feldspar and biotite, converted to a cordierite-quartz symplektite and
a myrmekitic plagioclase. Replacement of these minerals by K-feldspar
is especially intensive. Relicts of the replaced minerals often occur in
the K-feldspar. The plagioclase is an andesine (An = 35—40); the iron
contents of hypersthene, cordierite, biotite and garnet are the highest noted

for high-alumina metasomatic rocks. The K-feldspar is a microclinized soda orthoclase-perthite ($2V = -80°$; $n_x = 1.522$; $n_y = 1.526$; $n_z = 1.528$).

Rare metasomatic rocks include spinel-enstatite-forsterite-sapphirine-phlogopite, sapphirine-cordierite-phlogopite, and biotite-cordierite-quartz varieties. Their mineral composition, the characteristics of their minerals and their geological setting are presented in Table 43. All these rocks are distinguished by a low ferruginosity of their component minerals. Only the more interesting of these rocks, namely the spinel-enstatite-forsterite-sapphirine-phlogopite variety, will be discussed. The most important feature of this rock is the high magnesium content, the equally high alumina content and the very low silica content. The texture is lepidogranoblastic with metablastic enstatite. The enstatite is replaced by an unusual poly-synthetically twinned sapphirine. Olivine and spinel often occur in symplek-titic aggregates. Mica corrodes and replaces all other minerals. Thus, the initial forsterite-spinel association is replaced first by the enstatite-sapphirine association and then by mica.

Table 44 presents the chemical analyses of hypersthene-cordierite rocks and one analysis of the spinel-forsterite-enstatite-sapphirine-phlogopite rock (specimen 208l). Specimens 208b, v and d were taken from the same block, from the center outward. The series begins with specimen 208a (Table 3) and ends with specimen 208 (Table 22). The former is a quartz-plagioclase bronzitite from the very center of the block while the latter is a shadow mesoperthitic charnockite containing metasomatic rocks. Specimens 208e and g are sapphirine-bearing varieties of hypersthene-cordierite rock from another block in the same exposure. The chemical data suggest the following: 1) in the contact zone, charnockites are enriched in alumina, magnesium and iron and depleted in silica and alkalis; 2) hypersthenites are enriched in alumina and alkalis but depleted in silica, magnesium, iron and calcium. The most distinct compositional trends are shown by alumina, silica, magnesium and alkalis; their redistribution is mainly responsible for the bimetasomatic phenomena at the contact of these rocks.

These bimetasomatic phenomena are undoubtedly related to regional granitization of granulite facies rocks. Counterdiffusion of the components of reacting rocks, producing increasing skarn reactions, proceeds via slowly percolating granitizing pore melt-solutions in the direction toward the contact of rocks which are capable of interreacting at the high granitiza-tion temperature. Components of ascending solutions evidently participate in the formation of reaction zones. The composition of these solutions alters in relation to the components consumed in the formation of reaction zones; their concentration of components removed from the reaction zone increases. In the present case, silica and calcium are removed from the reaction zone while alkalis are introduced. Korzhinskii, who first re-ported and theoretically substantiated the phenomenon of bimetasomatosis, pointed out that the contacts of hyperbasites with silicate rocks are sites of high-temperature bimetasomatosis /32/. In higher parts of the crust, different metasomatic silica-poor rocks (nepheline, jadeite, vermiculite, talc, etc.) occur at the contacts with hyperbasites. An accumulation of

TABLE 44. Chemical composition of metasomatic high-alumina rocks from Enderby Land

Compo- nent	208b			208v			208d			208g			208e			208l		
	wt%	at.%	$\frac{R}{Al}$	wt%	at.%	$\frac{R}{Al}$	wt%	at.%	$\frac{R}{Al}$	wt%	at.%	$\frac{R}{Al}$	wt%	at.%	$\frac{R}{Al}$	wt%	at.%	$\frac{R}{Al}$
SiO_2	51.62	46.5	3.45	71.38	67.2	4.64	74.21	70.5	4.73	48.55	43.4	2.32	47.74	42.8	2.25	32.00	26.7	0.96
TiO_2	0.68	0.5	0.04	0.22	0.2	0.01	0.20	0.2	0.01	0.34	0.2	0.01	0.40	0.3	0.02	0.22	0.1	—
Al_2O_3	12.72	13.5	1.00	13.12	14.5	1.00	13.33	14.9	1.00	17.70	18.7	1.00	17.89	19.0	1.00	27.27	26.8	1.00
Fe_2O_3	1.51	1.0	0.07	0.87	0.6	0.04	0.55	0.4	0.03	1.39	0.9	0.05	1.82	1.2	0.06	0.63	0.4	0.01
FeO	7.79	5.9	0.44	3.39	2.7	0.19	2.69	2.2	0.15	6.47	4.8	0.26	5.68	4.3	0.23	0.83	0.5	0.02
MnO	0.20	0.2	0.01	0.04	—	—	0.04	—	—	0.11	—	—	0.10	—	—	—	—	—
MgO	20.10	27.0	2.00	4.96	6.9	0.48	4.33	6.2	0.42	21.68	28.9	1.54	21.16	28.2	1.48	33.57	41.7	1.56
CaO	1.90	1.8	0.13	2.60	2.6	0.18	1.42	1.4	0.09	0.14	0.2	0.01	—	—	—	—	—	—
Na_2O	1.08	1.9	0.14	2.25	4.1	0.28	1.53	2.8	0.19	0.21	0.3	0.02	0.30	0.5	0.03	0.18	0.3	0.01
K_2O	1.37	1.6	0.12	0.90	1.1	0.08	1.12	1.4	0.09	2.31	2.6	0.14	3.20	3.7	0.19	3.16	3.4	0.13
P_2O_5	0.12	0.1	—	0.07	—	—	0.05	—	—	0.09	—	—	0.07	—	—	0.10	0.1	—
Loss on ignition	0.95	—	—	0.29	—	—	0.47	—	—	1.19	—	—	1.59	—	—	2.19	—	—
Σ	100.04	100.0	—	100.09	100.0	—	92.94	100.0	—	100.18	100.0	—	99.95	100.0	—	100.15	100.0	—
Cr_2O_3	0.15			0.15	0.1					0.15	0.1							

TABLE 44 (continued)

	Specimen No.					
	208b	208v	208d	208g	208e	208l
Numerical characteristics (after Zavaritskii)						
a	3.7	5.8	4.5	3.0	4.4	3.8
b	43.6	16.0	17.9	51.8	50.6	68.3
c	2.0	2.9	1.5	0.2	0.0	0.0
s	50.7	75.3	76.1	45.0	45.0	27.9
Q	−8.0	+36.1	+41.7	−16.2	−18.8	−51.8
f'	17.4	22.9	15.5	11.6	11.3	1.4
m'	66.8	48.6	37.1	57.5	58.3	63.4
c'						
a'	15.8	28.5	47.4	30.9	30.4	35.2
Coordinates of the ACF diagram (after Eskola and Korzhinskii)						
A	22.4	43.2	52.4	31.7	31.2	35.4
C	4.1	12.1	7.0	0.4	0.0	—
F	73.5	44.7	40.6	67.9	68.8	64.6
Norm, % (after Barth)						
Albite	9.5	20.3	14.0	1.6	2.7	1.5
Anorthite	8.4	12.4	6.7	0.3	—	—
Orthoclase	7.8	5.6	6.8	12.8	18.3	16.8
Orthopyroxene	64.2	18.2	16.0	65.9	60.5	—
Clinopyroxene	—	—	—	—	—	—
Olivine	—	—	—	—	—	47.2
Spinel	—	—	—	—	4.5	31.2
Magnetite	1.5	0.9	0.6	1.4	1.8	0.6
Ilmenite	1.0	0.3	0.3	0.4	0.5	0.3
Apatite	0.3	0.2	0.2	0.2	—	0.1
Chlorite	—	0.2	—	0.2	—	—
Quartz	0.6	37.6	47.3	1.5	—	—
Corundum	6.7	4.3	8.1	15.7	11.7	2.3

Note. Modal compositions of the rocks are given in Table 43.

alumina, magnesium and iron in the bimetasomatic rocks described herein, suggests that these minerals may occur at contacts between hyperbasites and quartzites or shadow charnockites, in zones of granitization; such contacts are widespread on Enderby Land.

MINERALS OF THE GRANULITE FACIES

Mineralogical studies of the granulite facies concentrated particularly on orthopyroxenes and garnets, which are the critical minerals of this facies. The widespread occurrence of feldspar in the majority of rocks required chemical analyses in addition to optical measurements. Minerals atypical of the granulite facies, such as clinopyroxene, amphibole and biotite, are given a less exhaustive chemical description. The mineral compositions were largely examined by optical methods, but spectrographic and chemical analyses were also carried out. The results were used to construct correlation diagrams for the optical properties and ferruginosities of hypersthene and garnet; these diagrams were subsequently applied in the determination of the iron contents. The ferruginosity of clinopyroxene was determined from the well-known diagram provided by Hess and Muir, the ferruginosities of biotite and amphibole from the Drugova-Glebovitskii diagrams /22/ (for granulite facies rocks) and the ferruginosity of cordierite from Marakushev's diagram /43/. The composition of spinel was de- determined from the refractive indices and the crystal parameters, by means of the diagram provided by Deer, Howie and Zussmann /19/. Due to the small number of chemical analyses other methods were used to determine the chemical properties: the high purity of the monomineralic fraction, and the rapidity and accuracy ($\pm 4-7\%$) of spectroscopic analyses were the main factors governing the analytical methods. The spectroscopic analyses permitted multi-determination of minerals which make up only a few percent of the rocks. The relatively low accuracy of this analytical method is compensated by the high purity of the samples; thus only 50–100 mg of a monomineralic fraction was required instead of the 3–5 g required for wet chemical analyses.

The method used for computing the crystallochemical mineral formulas is given for each mineral. The standard computation features for all minerals are as follows. The formula amounts of cations were computed to the second decimal place. The common denominator was calculated from the sum of cations, with the exception of silicon in silicates, and silicon and aluminum in aluminosilicates, since these elements are determined with the least accuracy due to their high content and to their presence as mechanical impurities in the monomineralic fraction. After the analytical results were corrected for these elements, the chemical composition was scaled to 100%. The analysis yields data only for ferric iron, whereas the bulk of the iron in investigated minerals is in the ferrous state. Based on empirical data, the ferric iron plays a minor role in the granulite facies minerals, therefore the entire ferric iron content was

considered as ferrous iron. This was followed by the calculation of the
overall ferruginosity of the minerals $f = \dfrac{Fe}{Fe + Mg}$ and $F = \dfrac{Fe +}{Fe + Mg + Mn}$
and the formula amounts of cations. Chemical analyses data were used to
calculate the standard ferruginosity $\left(f_1 = \dfrac{FeO}{FeO + MgO} \right)$.

Orthopyroxenes

Hypersthenes are typical minerals of granulite facies rocks in
Antarctica, both those high in CaO (pyroxene-plagioclase schists) and
those low in this component (charnockites). Their iron contents vary
relative to the associated garnet, clinopyroxene, cordierite, biotite and
hornblende. Table 45 lists 25 analyses of orthopyroxene from different
mineral parageneses. High alumina contents, which are typical of all
granulite facies orthopyroxene, are consistently manifested in the schists
of Antarctica. Their Al_2O_3 content varies from 2.22 to 11.15 wt%. The
orthopyroxenes may be divided into the following two groups with respect
to their alumina contents: 1) orthopyroxenes from rocks high in alumina;
mostly metasomatic spinel-hypersthene-quartz, hypersthene-cordierite,
hypersthene-cordierite-garnet, and other varieties, as well as from certain
garnet-hypersthene enderbites with high garnet contents. Orthopyroxenes
from these rocks contain 7.04—11.14 wt% alumina; 2) orthopyroxenes from
rocks that are low in alumina, including an overwhelming majority of Ca—Mg
schists. The alumina content in the hypersthene varies from 2.22 to
6.80 wt% (usually 2.24—3.44) and is often independent of the alumina content
in the rocks. Indeed, in meta-ultrabasite (sample 798b), containing 3.34 wt%
alumina, it remains unchanged in the predominant bronzite, whereas in
pyroxene-plagioclase schists, enderbites and charnockites, containing as
much as 12—15 wt% alumina, the hypersthene contains only 2.5 wt% alumina
(samples 203g, 213a, 30 and others). However, in meta-ultrabasite,
hypersthene is the only mineral containing alumina; it has thus absorbed
the entire alumina content in the rock, whereas most of the alumina in the
pyroxene-plagioclase schists and shadow granitoids were consumed in the
formation of feldspar. Therefore, the authors share Howie's view /74/ that,
in these cases, the alumina content is the controlling factor at the moment
of crystallization of the mineral. Experimental investigations /5, 86/ have
shown that high pressures are conducive to the inclusion of certain amounts
of alumina in the structure of orthopyroxenes. On the one hand, Hess /102/,
Kuno /112/ and Howie /16/ determined that an admixture of alumina
diminishes the unit cell parameters and thus is dependent on pressure;
however, on the other hand, hypersthene, in many near-surface high-
temperature igneous and contact rocks contains nearly the same admixture
of alumina as in granulite facies rocks and consequently pressure in this
case apparently plays a minimal role, the high temperature being the major
factor.

TABLE 45.   Chemical composition of orthopyroxenes from granulite facies rocks on Enderby Land and in other regions of Antarctica

Component	798b wt% by analysis	798b correction	798b corrected analysis	56b wt% by analysis	56b correction	56b corrected analysis	153b wt% by analysis	153b correction	153b corrected analysis	203g wt% by analysis	203g correction	203g corrected analysis	236v wt% by analysis	236v correction	236v corrected analysis	213a wt% by analysis	213a correction	213a corrected analysis
SiO_2	54.71	−1.1	54.80	50.7	−4.4	50.05	51.86	−2.05	51.20	55.0	−1.2	53.16	52.2	−9.55	50.30	51.2	−7.4	49.40
TiO_2	0.17		0.17	0.2		0.22	0.34		0.35	0.2		0.20	0.3		0.35	0.2		0.23
Al_2O_3	3.37		3.44	2.1		2.27	3.66		3.76	2.3		2.27	2.7		3.18	2.3		2.59
Fe_2O_3	1.41		1.44	30.0		—	1.66		1.71	20.7		—	25.4		—	31.1		—
FeO	8.23		8.42	(27.15)		29.34	18.83		19.36	(18.7)		18.48	(22.85)		26.96	(28.2)		31.78
MnO	0.22		0.23	0.66		0.71	0.41		0.42	0.50		0.49	0.39		0.46	0.47		0.53
MgO	30.26		30.95	14.3		15.46	20.35		20.91	24.9		24.61	15.2		17.93	12.9		14.55
CaO	0.53		0.55	1.8		1.95	2.23		2.29	0.8		0.79	0.7		0.82	0.8		0.92
Σ	98.90		100.00	99.76		100.00	99.34		100.00	104.4		100.00	96.89		100.00	98.97		100.00
Constant	n_z	n_x	$2V$				n_z	n_x	$2V$	n_z	n_x	$2V$						
Value	1.687	1.677	−88				1.714	1.700	−60	1.708	1.696	−62						
F, at.%	14.9			50.9			35.6			29.4			45.4			54.5		
f_1, at.%	15.0			51.6			35.9			29.6			45.8			55.0		

Specimen No.

TABLE 45 (continued)

Component	41b wt% by analysis	41b correction	41b corrected analysis	42 wt% by analysis	42 correction	42 corrected analysis	40 wt% by analysis	40 correction	40 corrected analysis	213b wt% by analysis	213b correction	213b corrected analysis	232a wt% by analysis	232a correction	232a corrected analysis	30 wt% by analysis	30 correction	30 corrected analysis	29 wt% by analysis	29 correction	29 corrected analysis
SiO_2	52.0	−3.65	51.50	51.9	−5.6	49.90	52.2	−8.3	48.75	50.7	−9.25	48.43	52.5	−8.0	50.24	52.5	−11.65	49.70	53.1	−10,0	49.40
TiO_2	0.1		0.11	0.1		0.11	0.3		0.33	0.2		0.23	0.1		0.11	0.2		0.24	0.2		0.23
Al_2O_3	2.1		2.24	2.6		2.80	7.5		8.25	1.9		2.22	2.1		2.37	2.0		2.44	1.9		2.18
Fe_2O_3	26.4		—	30.4		—	20.9		—	37.1		—	29.0		—	28.4		—	32.3		—
FeO	(23.7)		25.21	(27.6)		29.73	(18.80)		20.90	(31.6)		36.92	(26.15)		29.45	(25.6)		31.17	(29.2)		33.43
MnO	0.29		0.31	0.41		0.44	0.30		0.33	0.25		0.29	0.52		0.59	0.32		0.39	0.35		0.40
MgO	18.2		19.35	14.3		15.40	18.9		21.00	9.7		11.33	14.1		15.89	12.5		15.21	12.2		13.90
CaO	1.2		1.88	1.5		1.62	0.4		0.44	0.5		0.58	1.2		1.35	0.7		0.85	0.4		0.46
Σ	100.29		100.00	101.21		100.00	100.50		100.00	100.35		100.00	99.52		100.00	96.62		100.00	100.45		100.00

Optical properties

	41b			42			40			213b			232a			30	29
Constant	n_z	n_x	$2V$	n_z	n_x	$2V$	n_z	n_x	$2V$	n_z	n_x	$2V$	n_z	n_x	$2V$		
Value	1.719	1.704	−51	1.728	1.714	−5.7	1.715	1.702	−70	1.749	1.732	−61	1.727	1.713	−62	—	—

	41b	42	40	213b	232a	30	29
F, at.%	42.0	51.6	35.7	64.4	50.5	53.1	57.1
f, at.%	42.2	52.0	35.8	64.6	51.0	53.4	57.3

TABLE 45 (continued)

Specimen No.

Component	208 wt% by analysis	208 correction	208 corrected analysis	175—1 wt% by analysis	175—1 correction	175—1 corrected analysis	33b wt% by analysis	33b correction	33b corrected analysis	473d wt% by analysis	473d correction	473d corrected analysis	755g wt% by analysis	755g correction	755g corrected analysis	820v wt% by analysis	820v correction	820v corrected analysis
SiO_2	51.5	-8.9	48.99	52.2	-11.9	48.10	48.5		49.90	49.9	-1.3	49.63	48.9	-3.25	47.55	47.2	-3.65	46.91
TiO_2	0.2		0.23	0.3		0.36	0.3		0.31	0.34		0.35	0.40		0.42	0.33		0.36
Al_2O_3	7.2		8.27	5.7		6.80	2.9		2.98	8.15		8.32	10.7		11.15	7.5		8.07
Fe_2O_3	20.5		—	25.3		—	30.8		—	1.99		2.03	21.0		—	30.5		—
FeO	(18.4)		21.15 (22.85)	(22.85)		27.30 (27.9)	(27.9)		28.71	15.10		15.42 (18.7)	(18.7)		19.45 (27.3)	(27.3)		29.39
MnO	0.18		0.21	0.10		0.12	0.14		0.14	0.80		0.82	0.31		0.32	0.30		0.32
MgO	18.0		20.69	14.0		16.72	16.70		17.19	22.72		23.19	20.0		20.80	13.9		14.95
CaO	0.4		0.46	0.5		0.60	0.75		0.77	0.24		0.24	0.30		0.31	—		—
Σ	97.98		100.00	98.10		100.00	100.09		100.00	99.24		100.00	101.61		100.00	99.73		100.00

Specimen	Constant	Value	F, at.%	f, at.%
208	n_z | n_x	1.713 | 1.698	36.2	36.3
175—1			47.5	47.5
33b			48.2	48.2
473d	n_z | n_x | $2V°$	1.708 | 1.696 | -80	29.0	29.4
755g	n_z | n_x | $2V°$	1.715 | 1.702 | -78	34.2	34.4
820v	n_z | n_x | $2V°$	1.729 | 1.715 | -65	52.1	52.4

TABLE 45 (continued)

Specimen No.

Component	306k Wt% by analysis	306k correction	306k corrected analysis	208i Wt% by analysis	208i correction	208i corrected analysis	208e Wt% by analysis	208e correction	208e corrected analysis	906a* Wt% by analysis	906a* correction	906a* corrected analysis	936* Wt% by analysis	936* correction	936* corrected analysis	204b Wt% by analysis	204b correction	204b corrected analysis
SiO_2	55.5	−7.8	52.44	54.2	−9.2	50.24	55.9	−7.95	52.44	48.35	−0.9	48.47	52.15	−2.15	51.10	50.2	−7.2	47.94
TiO_2	0.2		0.22	0.2		0.22	0.2		0.22	0.22		0.22	0.22		0.22	0.2		0.22
Al_2O_3	6.4		7.04	6.4		7.15	7.4		8.10	8.80		8.99	2.91		2.96	8.8		9.81
Fe_2O_3	10.8		—	18.8		—	11.7		—	4.60		4 70	1.72		1.76	21.7		—
FeO	(9.8)		10.77	(16.95)		18.93	(10.5)		11.48	16.11		16.44	21.30		21.80	(19.55)		21.80
MnO	0.16		0.18	0.21		0.23	0.18		0.20	0.23		0.23	0.62		0.63	0.23		0.26
MgO	26.3		28.91	20.5		22.89	24.9		27.23	20.50		20.95	19.30		19.77	17.6		19.62
CaO	0.4		0.44	0.3		0.34	0.3		0.33	—		—	1.70		1.74	0.3		0.33
Σ	99.76		100.0	100.61		100.00	100.58		100.00	98.81		100.00	99.92		100.00	99.03		99.98

Constant	306k n_z	306k n_x	306k $2V°$	208i n_z	208i n_x	208i $2V°$	208e n_z	208e n_x	208e $2V°$	906a* n_z	906a* n_x	936* n_z	936* n_x	204b n_z	204b n_x	204b $2V°$
Value	1.692	1.680	+80	1.710	1.698	−80	1.695	1.684	+87	1.714	1.700	1.718	1.704	1.715	1.703	90
F, at.%	17.2			31.6			19.0			35.6		39.5		38.2		
f_1, at.%	17.3			31.8			19.1			35.7		39.9		38.4		

Supplement to Table 45

Specimen No.	Approximate crystallochemical formulas of orthopyroxenes	Paragenesis	Designation of the rock
798 b	$(Ca_{0.01} Fe^{2+}_{0.13} Fe^{3+}_{0.02} Mg_{0.81} Al_{0.03}) [Si_{0.96} Al_{0.04}] O_3$	hyp + oliv + clpy + orem	Olivine-bipyroxene schists (meta-ultrabasite)
56b	$(Ca_{0.04} Fe_{0.48} Mn_{0.01} Mg_{0.45} Al_{0.02}) [Si_{0.97} Al_{0.03}] O_3$	hyp + clpy + plag + amph + orem + qz	Bipyroxene-plagioclase schists, amphibolized
153b	$(Ca_{0.04} Fe^{2+}_{0.30} Fe^{3+}_{0.02} Mg_{0.58} Al_{0.04}) [Si_{0.96} Al_{0.1}] O_3$	hyp + clpy + plag + biot + qz	Bipyroxene-plagioclase schists, biotitized
203g	$(Ca_{0.02} Fe_{0.28} Mn_{0.01} Mg_{0.67} Al_{0.02}) [Si_{0.97} Al_{0.03}] O_3$	hyp + clpy + plag + amph + biot + orem	Bipyroxene-plagioclase schists, amphibolized and biotitized
236v	$(Ca_{0.02} Fe_{0.43} Mn_{0.01} Mg_{0.51} Al_{0.03}) [Si_{0.96} Al_{0.04}] O_3$	hyp + plag + orem	Hypersthene-plagioclase schists
213a	$(Ca_{0.02} Fe_{0.52} Mn_{0.01} Mg_{0.42} Al_{0.03}) [Si_{0.97} Al_{0.03}] O_3$	hyp + plag + orem + qz + biot	As above
41b	$(Ca_{0.03} Fe_{0.40} Mg_{0.55} Al_{0.02}) [Si_{0.97} Al_{0.03}] O_3$	hyp + clpy + gar + plag + amph + orem	Garnet-bipyroxene-plagioclase schists
42	$(Ca_{0.03} Fe_{0.49} Mn_{0.01} Mg_{0.44} Al_{0.03}) [Si_{0.97} Al_{0.03}] O_3$	hyp + clpy + gar + plag + amph + orem	Garnet-bipyroxene-plagioclase schists
40	$(Fe_{0.33} Mg_{0.58} Al_{0.09}) [Si_{0.91} Al_{0.09}] O_3$	qz + plag + Kfs + hyp + gar + biot + orem	Garnet-hypersthene shadow granitoid
213b	$(Ca_{0.01} Fe_{0.62} Mg_{0.34} Al_{0.03}) [Si_{0.97} Al_{0.03}] O_3$	qz + plag + Kfs + hyp + gar + orem	As above
232a	$(Ca_{0.03} Fe_{0.48} Mn_{0.01} Mg_{0.46} Al_{0.03}) [Si_{0.97} Al_{0.03}] O_2$	qz + plag + Kfs + hyp + orem	Enderbite
30	$(Ca_{0.02} Fe_{0.51} Mg_{0.44} Al_{0.03}) [Si_{0.97} Al_{0.03}] O_3$	qz + plag + hyp + biot + amph	Enderbite, biotitized and amphibolized
29	$(Ca_{0.01} Fe_{0.55} Mn_{0.01} Mg_{0.41} Al_{0.02}) [Si_{0.97} Al_{0.03}] O_3$	qz + plag + hyp + orem	Enderbite

Supplement to Table 45 (continued)

	Approximate crystallochemical formulas of orthopyroxenes	Paragenesis	Designation of the rock
208	$(Ca_{0.01} Fe_{0.33} Mg_{0.57} Al_{0.09}) [Si_{0.91} Al_{0.09}] O_3$	qz + plag + mesoperthite + hyp	Mesoperthitic charnockite
175—1	$(Ca_{0.01} Fe_{0.43} Mg_{0.48} Al_{0.08}) [Si_{0.92} Al_{0.08}] O_3$	qz + plag + mesoperthite + hyp + orem	"
33b	$(Ca_{0.02} Fe_{0.46} Mg_{0.49} Al_{0.03}) [Si_{0.96} Al_{0.04}] O_3$	qz + plag + mesoperthite + hyp	"
473d	$(Fe^{2+}_{0.24} Fe^{3+}_{0.03} Mn_{0.01} Mg_{0.63} Al_{0.09}) [Si_{0.91} Al_{0.09}] O_3$	hyp + cord + biot + orem	Metasomatic rock
755g	$(Ca_{0.01} Fe_{0.30} Mg_{0.57} Al_{0.12}) [Si_{0.87} Ti_{0.01} Al_{0.12}] O_3$	hyp + cord + plag + biot + spin + spph + orem	"
820v	$(Fe_{0.47} Mg_{0.44} Al_{0.09}) [Si_{0.91} Al_{0.09}] O_3$	hyp + cord + plag + spin + gar + biot + orem	"
208k	$(Ca_{0.01} Fe_{0.16} Mg_{0.76} Al_{0.07}) [Si_{0.92} Al_{0.08}] O_3$	qz + hyp + cord + biot	"
208i	$(Ca_{0.01} Fe_{0.30} Mg_{0.62} Al_{0.07}) [Si_{0.92} Al_{0.08}] O_3$	qz + Kfs + hyp + cord + biot	"
208e	$(Ca_{0.01} Fe_{0.17} Mg_{0.74} Al_{0.08}) [Si_{0.91} Al_{0.09}] O_3$	hyp + spph + cord + biot + Kfs	"
906a*	$(Fe^{2+}_{0.25} Fe^{3+}_{0.07} Mg_{0.58} Al_{0.10}) [Si_{0.90} Al_{0.10}] O_3$	hyp + cord + gar + biot + plag + orem	"
936*	$(Ca_{0.04} Fe^{2+}_{0.34} Fe^{3+}_{0.03} Mn_{0.01} Mg_{0.55} Al_{0.03}) [Si_{0.96} Al_{0.04}] O_3$	hyp + clpy + plag + biot + qz + Kfs + orem	Bipyroxene-plagioclase schist
204b	$(Ca_{0.01} Fe_{0.34} Mg_{0.54} Al_{0.11}) [Si_{0.89} Al_{0.11}] O_3$	hyp + spin + cord + biot + qz	Metasomatic rock

Notes. 1. Asterisk indicates hypersthene from Bunger Oasis rocks. 2. The mineral and chemical compositions of the rocks are listed in Tables 2—25, 43 and 44.

Orthopyroxenes from rocks with high calcium contents (pyroxene-plagioclase and garnet-pyroxene schists) also have high calcium contents (0.80—2.29 wt%), whereas in rocks low in calcium, the Ca content in hypersthene does not exceed 0.60 wt%. The admixture of calcium in orthopyroxenes is usually controlled by their crystallization temperature /16/. Investigations of an artificial system $MgSiO_3$—$CaMgSiO_3$ conducted by Atlas /79/ and Schairer and Boyd /124/, led to the conclusion that the maximum number of Ca atoms per 6 oxygen atoms is 0.115 at 1100°C, 0.050 at 1000°C and 0.030 at 700°C. Therefore it may be assumed that the formation temperatures of orthopyroxenes (0.04—0.08 atoms Ca per 6 atoms oxygen) in rocks that are high in CaO were mostly above 1000°C, i. e., in the region of magmatic temperatures; this is in agreement with the data concerning the genesis of calcareous-magnesian schists and apparently testifies to their incomplete recrystallization under granulite facies conditions. It is clear that the calcium content in orthopyroxenes from rocks low in CaO cannot serve as a geothermometer, since the composition of orthopyroxene is directly influenced by the low calcium content in the rock itself. Lamellar segregations of clinopyroxene parallel to (001) which were repeatedly noted in orthopyroxene from rocks with high calcium contents (Figure 18) and from pyroxene-magnetite-quartz rocks, are very closely related to the calcium content in the orthopyroxene. Analogous ingrowths of clinopyroxenes have been described by Parras /117/ in certain rocks of high-grade metamorphism. The presence of clinopyroxene ingrowths in hypersthene also attests to the high formation temperature of the solid solution of these minerals and its exsolution in the slowly cooling crystals during metamorphism. Experimental investigations will be helpful in calibrating this geothermometer, resembling Barth's feldspar geothermometer. However, not all investigators are convinced that the lamellar structure of hypersthene originated from the parent solid solution of clinopyroxene as an independent phase in the host orthopyroxene. Some authors attribute this structure to translational gliding /98, 103/ and others to twinning /88, 93/. However, Hess /103/ concluded that the disturbance of orientation (translational gliding and bending) occurs in the host crystal of orthopyroxene, while lamellar segregations differ chemically from the containing crystal and possess the optical properties of diopside. Distinctly determinable lamellar segregations of clinopyroxene in hypersthene from pyroxene-magnetite-quartz schists were observed.

The most important index of the conditions of orthopyroxene formation is its iron content, i. e., the ratio of iron and magnesium ions. However, this depends upon many factors, the major ones being the chemical composition of rock, the temperature and the chemical potential of alkalis. These factors are largely mutually controlled. Research limited to 25 analyses of orthopyroxene from rocks of different compositions and genesis is not adequate for a conclusion on its iron content in rocks of certain types, due to the possibility of random deviations. In order to obtain broader data on the ferruginosity of hypersthenes, the authors constructed a diagram of refractive indices of hypersthene as a function of ferruginosity,

FIGURE 18. Lamellar segregations of clinopyroxene in hypersthene (x 40, crossed nicols, thin section 350a).

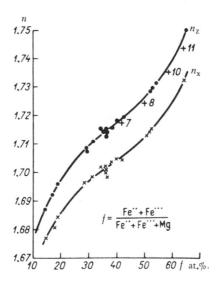

FIGURE 19. Refractive indices n_X and n_Z of orthopyroxenes in Antarctica as a function of their ferruginosity, f.

Upright crosses (+) mark the relationships for metamorphic pyroxenes from India and South Africa (based on the literature).

for Antarctic metamorphic rocks (Figure 19). The diagram was then used
to determine the ferruginosity of orthopyroxene (listed in the tables) from
refractive index measurements. The relationships between the optical
properties and chemical composition of orthopyroxenes were studied by
many investigators /97, 102, 119, 121, etc./. The established relationship
between the optical properties and the atomic ratio $Mg : (Fe^{2+} + Fe^{3+} + Mn)$
illustrated by the well-known diagram provided by Deer, Howie and
Zussman /16/, was based on studies of pyroxenes mainly from magmatic
rocks and, to a lesser extent, metamorphic rocks. It shows that the refractive indices vary linearly with the combined iron + manganese content
and that the index n_z increases approximately by 0.00125 per every atomic
percent of (Fe + Mn). At the same time, metamorphic hypersthenes are
known to possess a widely variable composition, an important part being
played, as already mentioned, by replacement of bivalent cations and silicon
by trivalent aluminum. The effect of the aluminum content on refractive
indices of orthopyroxenes was studied by Hess /102/ and Kuno /112/; both
concluded that for the composition En_{100}, the presence of 0.140−0.07 atom
aluminum per formula unit increases the index n_z by 0.005; however, the
effect is nullified when extrapolated to Fs_{100}. Hori /105/ demonstrated that
the presence of aluminum increases the n_z and decreases the n_x. Many
researchers /41, 76/ acknowledge that the compositional dependence of
the optical properties of orthopyroxenes varies from one region to another.
This is probably due to the metamorphic history of a given region as well
as to subtle structural alterations in the orthopyroxene which usually escape
the investigator's attention. Among others, an indication of a different
structure in orthopyroxene is provided by its anomalous oblique extinction
in many charnockitic and granulitic rocks from different regions of the
world /41, 54, 144/. For many rocks from Enderby Land /27, 144/, a
banded structure of hypersthene indicating the transition from hypersthene
to clinohypersthene was noted. Howie /16/ noted smaller unit cell parameters of metamorphic pyroxenes, which was attributed by him to the
inclusion of aluminum in the orthopyroxene structure.

The above data called for the construction of this diagram, which was
developed for the first time for the Antarctic rocks. The diagram also
takes into account the possibility of various systematic errors that may
be involved in measurements of refractive indices and in chemical analyses
performed by different researchers, a fact which is often neglected by
authors of such diagrams. In the present case, all measurements of refractive indices were performed by the same mineralogist, and all the
spectroscopic silicate analyses were carried out by the same analytical
chemist. Thus the diagram is suggested for the determination of ferruginosities of Antarctic metamorphic orthopyroxenes and possibly for orthopyroxenes from metamorphic rocks of the Southern Hemisphere (Gondwana).
Indeed, the points marked on the diagram (according to Deer et al. /16/) for
orthopyroxenes from Gondwana and for metamorphic rocks, lie very close
to the curve in the present diagram (Figure 19). An examination of the
diagram reveals that the refractive index in metamorphic rocks obeys a
more complex relationship than previously assumed /16, 41, 76/. A noteworthy feature is the variation in the birefringence of orthopyroxenes,

the maximum birefringence (0.014) occurring in the case of pyroxenes with a ferruginosity of 30—50 at.%. The value of birefringence declines with increasing iron and magnesium contents. The pyroxene samples with ferruginosities of 30—50 at.% include samples with the highest alumina content (6—8 wt%). It is thus clear that the variation in birefringence is due to this high alumina content. Apparently, the same circumstance also affects the refractive index growth rate, depending on the ferruginosity.

The ferruginosity determined from the diagram was used to calculate the average ferruginosity of orthopyroxenes for different types of granulite facies rocks in Antarctica (Table 46). The table clearly shows the dependence of the ferruginosity of hypersthene on the acidity-alkalinity of the rock, the hypersthene ferruginosity increasing with increasing acidity-alkalinity. The most highly ferruginous hyperstheses are found in shadow charnockites and the most highly magnesian hyperstheses in meta-ultra-basites. At the same time, there is a direct dependence on the rock composition. There is an inverse relationship between ferruginosity and temperature, but it is very weak.

TABLE 46. Mean overall ferruginosities of orthopyroxenes for granulite facies rocks in Antarctica

Rock	Ferruginosity of orthopyroxene, at.%	Number of investigated samples
Pyroxene-plagioclase schists	41.7	121
Shadow enderbites	48.6	59
Shadow charnockites	58.5	41
Meta-ultrabasites (magnesian schists)	25.4	11
Metasomatic high-alumina rocks	32.3	18

In the majority of pyroxene-plagioclase schists, in meta-ultrabasites and in metasomatic bronzitites, spinel-quartz-hypersthene and magnetite-quartz-pyroxene rocks, as well as partially in enderbites, the orthopyroxenes exhibit peculiar bands, their boundaries trending perpendicular to the jointing and to the long axes of grains. These bands have the appearance of twins with very smooth and distinct contacts. Such structures have been obtained experimentally by Turner et al. /133/, by subjecting specimens of enstatite pyroxenite to a pressure of 5 kbar at 500—800°C. Under these conditions, enstatite was inverted to clinoenstatite, which formed bands in the enstatite. The inversion proceeded more vigorously at 800°C. Turner provides examples of morphological forms analogous to those under consideration in natural formations. In other investigations, Riecker and Rooney /122/ produced similar structures in natural enstatite by subjecting it to high temperatures (500—1000°C) and high pressures (15—40 kbar) and to a stress of 5.5—15.0 kbar. Even stress of short duration produced clino-enstatite as bands in the enstatites trending perpendicular to the stress direction. In 1965, Boyd and England published the results of experiments on determination of inversion of orthoenstatite to clinoenstatite /4/. They derived the inversion curve equation $T = 630 + 2.6P$, where T is given in °C and P in kilobars.

In collating all experimental data, it should be noted that the transformation of enstatite into clinoenstatite in Turner's and Riecker's experiments was especially intensive in the stability field of enstatite determined by Boyd and England. The experiments suggest that the formation of banded structures in the hypersthene was due to the stress at high temperatures and pressures; this is also indicated by the fact that the banded structures of hypersthenes are especially distinct in schists with blastocataclastic textures. Taking into account the fact that banded orthopyroxenes are less common in enderbites and totally absent from charnockites, it may be stated with assurance that the stress in these rocks was most probably relieved by the flowing of the rocks themselves; this was impossible for the rigid blocks of schists, and the stress was probably relieved by deformations of mineral structures. However, clinohypersthenes have not yet been observed in natural rocks, although cases of oblique extinction in hypersthene have been reported, as mentioned above /41, 54/. Possibly, the relief of lateral stress in the presence of high temperatures and high pressures produced reverse inversion instantaneously. Boyd and England /4/ noted that preliminary experiments suggested a maximum of the hypersthene inversion region near 900°, i.e., considerably above the inversion of enstatite and ferrosillite.

To conclude this description of orthopyroxenes, it is worth describing the method used for computing the crystallochemical formulas listed in Table 45. This computation was based on the sum of bivalent cations and half of aluminum ions equated to one formula unit, thus: $Ca + Mn + Mg + Fe + 0.5Al = 1$. This denominator was used to calculate the formula amounts of iron, a correction being introduced for excess silica. In this case, the excess silica was due to the nearly identical hardness of the hypersthene and the agate mortar in which it was ground for analysis. The quantity of excess silica is especially large when small amounts of the mineral are ground, because of the direct friction of the pestle against the mortar bottom. Furthermore, there was a direct relationship between the crushing force and the amount of excess silica in analysis. The same phenomena are encountered in the grinding of garnet. The mineral formulas are only approximate because the computation of the component formula amounts is made only to the second decimal place.

Clinopyroxenes

Clinopyroxenes occur mainly in calcareous rocks of the granulite facies, including pyroxene-plagioclase schists, diopside rocks and calciphyres. They also appear in meta-ultrabasites and metasomatic pyroxene-quartz-magnetite rocks. They are much more rarely found (in small amounts) in enderbites and charnockites. Clinopyroxenes occur most extensively in

calcareous-magnesian schists and their migmatites, where they are found together with plagioclase, garnet and hypersthene. Their ferruginosities vary in
parallel with those of garnet and hypersthene.

Chemical studies were made of seven clinopyroxenes from rocks of the
granulite facies: two from pyroxene-plagioclase schists, four from garnet-
pyroxene-plagioclase schists and one from a diopside rock (Table 47). The
chemical composition of clinopyroxene from the diopside rock is included
in its petrographic description. Scaling of the analysis of this clinopyroxene
to its components yielded the following results: 92% diopside, 3% hedenbergite, 1% jadeite and 4% enstatite. Hence, even in a diopside rock of the
granulite facies, the diopside contains excess magnesium and iron, and
also aluminum, sodium and ferric iron, as against a somewhat low calcium
content. The ferruginosity of this diopside is 3.7 at.% — one of the lowest
values. A still larger amount of admixtures is found in clinopyroxenes
from schists. The listed crystallochemical formulas indicate that the clinopyroxenes from schists are mostly augites, and in one case, a salite
with high aluminum content (Figure 20). As pointed out by Howie /16/, this
composition for clinopyroxene is most probably due to increased solubility
of Mg and Fe^{2+} in diopside-hedenbergite at higher temperatures. Similar to
many other augites /16/, clinopyroxenes from schists in Antarctica contain
2.40—3.78 wt% alumina and 0.19—0.50 wt% titanium. They possibly contain
an admixture of ferric oxide which may be responsible for the silica deficit
/112/. An important factor which points to high pressures during the
crystallization of clinopyroxenes is the presence of 0.41—0.95 wt% Na_2O,
which is also responsible for their high alkalinity.

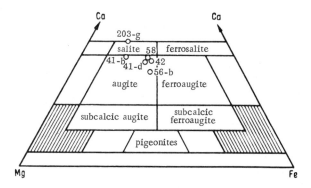

FIGURE 20. Nomenclature diagram by Hess and Poldervaart /120/ for clinopyroxenes
in the coordinates of Ca, Mg and (Fe^{2+} and Fe^{3+} + Mn) with the position of granulite
facies clinopyroxenes from Enderby Land.

After conversion to minals, it becomes clear that the clinopyroxenes
under consideration contain <50% of the wollastonite molecule (37—47%).
This deficit in the formation of pyroxene of the diopside-hedenbergite series

TABLE 47. Chemical composition of clinopyroxenes from Enderby Land schists

Component	58 wt% by analysis	58 correction	58 corrected analysis	41d wt% by analysis	41d correction	41d corrected analysis	41b wt% by analysis	41b correction	41b corrected analysis	42 wt% by analysis	42 correction	42 corrected analysis	56b wt% by analysis	56b correction	56b corrected analysis	203g wt% by analysis	203g correction	203g corrected analysis
SiO_2	50.0	+3.9	51.63	50.8	+3.0	51.75	50.5	+4.85	55.20	49.0	+0.4	50.82	48.7	+0.2	50.62	50.2	+1.6	51.51
TiO_2	0.3		0.29	0.2		0.19	0.2		0.19	0.3		0.31	0.4		0.41	0.5		0.50
Al_2O_3	3.0		2.87	2.5		2.40	3.2		3.02	3.5		3.61	2.8		2.90	3.8		3.78
Fe_2O_3	16.5		—	16.2		—	12.2		—	16.0		—	17.5		—	9.4		—
FeO	(14.8)		(14.20)	(14.5)		13.96	10.9		10.30	(14.4)		14.84	(15.8)		16.38	(8.5)		8.45
MnO	0.21		0.20	0.15		0.14	0.15		0.14	0.22		0.23	0.35		0.36	0.16		0.16
MgO	10.3		9.86	11.3		10.87	13.9		13.11	9.8		10.09	10.5		10.88	11.7		11.63
CaO	20.9		20.00	20.8		20.02	21.6		20.39	18.8		19.48	17.4		18.04	23.5		23.37
Na_2O	1.0		0.95	0.7		0.67	0.7		0.65	0.6		0.62	0.4		0.41	0.6		0.60
Σ	102.21		100.00	102.65		100.00	102.45		100.00	98.32		100.00	98.05		100.00	99.86		100.00

Simplified composition, minals

	58	41d	41b	42	56b	203g
Diopside	46	48	57	44	40	63
Hedenbergite	36	34	24	35	34	31
Enstatite	6	8	9	8	13	
Ferrosilite	5	5	5	8	10	2
Jadeite	7	5	5	5	3	4

Ferruginosity, at.%

	58	41d	41b	42	56b	203g
F	44.3	41.7	30.5	44.9	45.4	28.9
f	44.6	41.9	30.6	45.2	45.8	29.0

Content of the wollastonite molecule

	58	41d	41b	42	56b	203g
	40.5	40.5	40.5	39.5	37	47

Optical properties

	n_z	n_x	$2V°$
58	1.727	1.700	+57 —58
41d	1.725	1.698	+53
41b	1.716	1.690	+52 —55
42	1.724	1.697	+53 —55
56b	1.719	1.694	+53
203g	1.719	1.694	+53

Supplement to Table 47

Specimen No.	Approximate crystallochemical formula	Paragenesis	Designation of the rock
58	$(Na_{0.07} Ca_{0.81} Fe_{0.45} Mn_{0.01} Mg_{0.56} Al_{0.10})_2$ $[Si_{1.96} Ti_{0.01} Al_{0.03}]_2 O_6$	qz + plag + Kfs + clpy + amph + gar + orem	Garnet-clinopyroxene-plagioclase schist
41d	$(Na_{0.05} Ca_{0.81} Fe_{0.44} Mn_{0.01} Mg_{0.62} Al_{0.07})_2$ $[Si_{1.96} Ti_{0.01} Al_{0.03}]_2 O_6$	plag + hyp + clpy + amph + gar + orem	As above
41b	$(Na_{0.05} Ca_{0.81} Fe_{0.32} Mg_{0.73} Al_{0.09})_2$ $[Si_{1.95} Ti_{0.01} Al_{0.04}]_2 O_6$	plag + hyp + clpy + amph + gar + orem	Garnet-bipyroxene-plagioclase schist
42	$(Na_{0.05} Ca_{0.79} Fe_{0.47} Mn_{0.01} Mg_{0.57} Al_{0.11})_2$ $[Si_{1.94} Ti_{0.01} Al_{0.05}]_2 O_6$	plag + hyp + clpy + amph + gar + orem	Amphibolized garnet-bipyroxene schists
56b	$(Na_{0.03} Ca_{0.74} Mg_{0.62} Fe_{0.52} Mn_{0.01} Al_{0.08})_2$ $[Si_{1.94} Ti_{0.01} Al_{0.05}]_2 O_6$	hyp + clpy + plag + amph + qz + orem	Bipyroxene-plagioclase schist, amphibolized
203g	$(Na_{0.04} Ca_{0.94} Fe_{0.26} Mg_{0.85} Al_{0.11})_2$ $[Si_{1.93} Ti_{0.01} Al_{0.06}]_2 O_6$	hyp + clpy + plag + amph + biot + orem	Bipyroxene-plagioclase schist, biotitized

Note. The mineral and chemical compositions of the rocks are listed in Tables 4, 8, 10.

is replenished by hypersthene and jadeite molecules, amounting to 2—23 and 3—7%, respectively. The largest amounts of jadeite are found in clinopyroxenes from garnet-pyroxene-plagioclase schists (5—7%). Lamellar ingrowths of orthopyroxene found in certain clinopyroxenes are regarded as exsolution products of solid solution, the latter's composition being determined by the above numerical data on the content of minals in pyroxenes.

The overall ferruginosity of clinopyroxenes determined from their optical properties differs from the analytically determined ferruginosity by ±1—4 at.%. However, the discrepancy reaches 7 at.% in some pyroxenes of low ferruginosity. Such clinopyroxenes with relatively high refractive index and low ferruginosity have the largest content of aluminum (specimen 203g), although they are salites with respect to their calcium content. As a rule, the ferruginosity of these clinopyroxenes is extremely close to that of the coextant hypersthenes, i.e., it corresponds to the highest-temperature parageneses. Optical studies of clinopyroxenes yielded mean ferruginosities for certain rocks (Table 48).

TABLE 48. Mean ferruginosity of clinopyroxenes from metamorphites in Antarctica

Rock	Total ferruginosity, at.%	Number of determinations
Magnesian schists (meta-ultrabasites)	28	6
Pyroxene-plagioclase schists	34.4	71
Shadow enderbites	42.2	10
Shadow charnockites	62.5	2
Calciphyres and diopside rocks	20.4	17

It may be seen from Table 48 that the ferruginosity of clinopyroxene follows the same pattern as that of orthopyroxene. The crystallochemical formulas of clinopyroxene were computed on the assumption that the clinopyroxenes were solid solutions of diopside-hedenbergite, jadeite and aluminous hypersthene. Similar to the case of hypersthene and garnet, the computation was confined to bivalent cations and trivalent and monovalent cations that were isomorphic with them. In this case the computation formula must be

$$(Na + Al)_{jad} + (Ca + Mg + Fe)_{diop-heden} + (Mg + Fe + Al)_{hyp} = 2$$

or

$$Na + Ca + Mg + Mn + Fe + (Al = Na) + \tfrac{1}{2}(Al - Na) = 2,$$

corresponding to formula

$$1.5\,Na + Ca + Mg + Mn + Fe + 0.5\,Al = 2.$$

The common denominator determined by the formula was used to calculate
the coefficients for the ions. The analytical results were corrected for the
usual silica deficit, the correction varying from 0.2 to 4.85 wt% silica. As
yet, the cause of silica deficit is not clear, but it is within permissible error
of the method employed. At the same time, the available complete chemical
analyses of augites and salites from different regions of the world show the
presence of a silica deficit in a majority of cases /16/. This deficit is
often not compensated even by aluminum, titanium and ferric iron combined
(scaled to six molecules of oxygen). Furthermore, in this case, the valence
of the silicon-oxygen tetrahedra does not correspond to the valence of the
group of bivalent cations and the trivalent cations by which they are replaced. Therefore the recalculation method is preferable. On the other
hand, silicon deficit can indeed be compensated by ferric iron, the more so
since the deficit is larger in those clinopyroxenes relatively rich in sodium
(0.04—0.07 formula units). Usually, large amounts of ferric iron are
characteristic of Na varieties of augites. Therefore it is probable that
instead of, or along with, the jadeite molecule, the clinopyroxenes may also
contain the aegirine molecule. Unfortunately, the nature of silicate spectro-
scopy does not permit differentiation between ferrous and ferric iron, and
the authors are forced to regard the entire iron content as ferrous. The
clinopyroxene minals were calculated in a simplified manner. The entire
aluminum replacing bivalent cations remaining after the saturation of the
jadeite molecule was assumed to be included in the hypersthene. Incidentally,
even if it had happened to be regarded as included in the Tschermack
molecule, an equivalent amount of magnesium and iron for the formation
of hypersthene would have been liberated just the same. The author's
procedure, in which the minals were determined only to whole units, did
not permit consistently equal ferruginosity ratios in the minals of diopside-
hedenbergite and hypersthene.

Garnets

Garnets are among the most widespread and important minerals in the
granulite facies rocks. They serve as indicators for temperature and
pressure variations /35, 43/. On the other hand, however, the composition
of a garnet is largely dependent on that of the rock in which it occurs.
It should also be noted that studies of the chemical composition of garnet
encounter certain difficulties, since garnet may be present in rocks ranging
from the greenschist to the granulite facies. In the course of slow, gradual
regional metamorphism, the composition of garnet may vary not in its
entirety but gradually, beginning with the periphery and along cracks. The
existence of zonal garnets has been noted by many researchers /38, 143/.
In the case of continuous zonality, such zoning is barely discernible
in thin section, and therefore the chemical analysis of the monomineral
fraction yields averaged values for the composition of garnets (Figure 21).

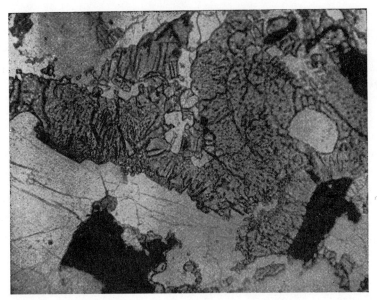

FIGURE 21. Zonal garnet in a garnet-hypersthene shadow granitoid (x 30, crossed nicols, thin section 38).

    Twenty-eight chemical and spectroscopic silicate analyses were carried out on garnets mainly from Enderby Land rocks. Garnets from other regions of Antarctica have been little studied (two analyses from Bunger Oasis rocks and two from Queen Maud Land). The chemical composition of garnet is listed in Tables 49—51. It may be stated that since the iron determined by spectroscopic silicate analysis is stated as ferric iron, then scaled to ferrous iron, the entire calcium component of garnet is considered as grossular. This is obviously correct, since it has been established statistically that the content of the andradite component in granulite facies garnet does not exceed 2% on the average /20, 35/ and can be ignored, since this amount of iron is within the analytical error. The limits of the contents of different components in granulite facies garnet in Antarctica are as follows: the most magnesian varieties contain 46% pyrope, the most ferruginous varieties 81% almandine, the most calcic varieties 26% grossular and the most manganiferous varieties 8% spessartite. At the same time, garnets of low ferruginosity (49% almandine) have the maximum magnesium contents; however, the reverse is not true, i. e., garnets with low magnesium contents (11% pyrope) do not have the maximum ferruginosity. Similarly, there is no general correlation, for all garnets, with respect to the contents of the other components. Therefore it is feasible to consider garnets from three fairly broad groups of rocks on account of the probability of discovering correlative properties of certain garnet components in relation to the composition and formation conditions of rocks. These groups of rocks are

TABLE 49. Chemical composition of garnets from high-alumina rocks of the granulite facies on Enderby Land

Component	792b wt% by analysis	792b correction	792b corrected analysis	813g wt% by analysis	813g correction	813g corrected analysis	670a wt% by analysis	670a correction	670a corrected analysis	769a wt% by analysis	769a correction	769a corrected analysis	770a wt% by analysis	770a correction	770a corrected analysis
SiO_2	44.4	−12.5	38.57	44.2	−9.9	38.43	43.6	−11.15	39.07	44.9	−12.1	39.66	41.8	−7.25	39.75
TiO_2	0.14		0.16	0.15		0.17	0.11		0.13	0.12		0.14	0.13		0.15
Al_2O_3	20.00	−1.9	21.88	21.5	−2.2	21.62	20.0	−1.6	22.16	20.6	−2.0	22.49	21.0	−1.55	22.38
Fe_2O_3	27.2		—	30.3		—	24.4		—	22.2		—	22.8		—
FeO	(24.48)		29.60	(27.27)		30.55	(21.96)		26.44	(19.98)		24.16	(20.52)		23.61
MnO	0.58		0.70	0.35		0.39	0.43		0.52	0.30		0.36	0.46		0.53
MgO	6.9		8.34	6.6		7.39	7.9		9.51	10.0		12.09	10.5		12.08
CaO	0.62		0.75	1.3		1.45	1.8		2.17	0.91		1.10	1.3		1.50
Σ	99.84		100.00	104.40		100.00	98.24		100.00	99.03		100.00	97.99		100.00

Physical properties

	792b			813g			670a			769a			770a		
a (Å)	11.51			11.52			11.52			11.51			11.51		
d, g/cm³	4.13			4.18			3.97			3.86			3.84		
N	1.787			1.792			1.770			1.772			1.765		

Composition, minals

	792b			813g			670a			769a			770a		
Pyrope	32			29			36			45			46		
Almandine	64			66			57			51			49		
Grossular	2			4			6			3			4		
Andradite	—			—			1			—			—		
Spessartite	2			1			—			1			1		

Ferruginosity, at.%

	792b			813g			670a			769a			770a		
F	65.5			69.2			60.5			52.6			51.1		
f	66.5			69.9			61.3			53.0			51.8		

TABLE 49 (continued)

Component	5–3			727g**			827b**			215b			305*		
	wt.% by analysis	correction	corrected analysis	wt.% by analysis	correction	corrected analysis	wt.% by analysis	correction	corrected analysis	wt.% by analysis	correction	corrected analysis	wt.% by analysis	correction	corrected analysis
SiO_2	42.6	−6.6	39.23	40.40	−7.0	38.20	38.51	−3.8	37.09	46.3	−17.0	38.28	40.87	−5.35	39.07
TiO_2	0.12		0.13	0.20		0.23	0.24		0.26	0.1		0.13	0.14		0.15
Al_2O_3	21.0	−0.6	22.23	20.90	−1.9	21.82	20.56	−0.75	21.10	19.4	−2.8	21.68	21.72	−1.5	22.21
Fe_2O_3	26.9		—	3.91	−3.91	—	1.27	−1.27	—	26.2		—	1.70	−1.70	—
FeO	(24.21)		26.38	23.80		27.36	34.06		36.30	(23.6)		30.83	22.65		24.93
MnO	0.48		0.52	0.44		0.70	0.70		0.75	0.45		0.59	2.10		2.31
MgO	9.6		10.46	5.60		6.45	3.21		3.42	5.7		7.45	9.36		10.32
CaO	0.96		1.05	4.71		5.43	1.03		1.08	0.8		1.04	0.91		1.01
Σ	101.66		100.00	99.96		100.00	99.58		100.00	98.95		100.00	99.55		100.00
Physical properties															
a (Å)		3.97			3.99			4.22			—			3.98	
d, g/cm³		1.774			1.786			1.808			1.799			1.780	
N															
Composition, minals															
Pyrope		40			25			14			29			39	
Almandine		56			59			81			67			53	
Grossular		3			15			3			3			3	
Andradite		—			—			2			1			—	
Spessartite		1			1			—						5	
Ferruginosity, at.%															
F		58.0			69.5			84.1			69.1			54.6	
f		58.8			70.4			85.7			69.9			57.6	

Specimen No.

Notes. 1. Asterisk marks garnet from Bunger Oasis rocks, and the double asterisk indicates those from Queen Maud Land. 2. The mineral composition of the rocks are listed in Tables 30, 32, 33, 36, 38, 39.

Supplement to Table 49

Specimen No.	Approximate crystallochemical formula	Paragenesis	Designation of rock
792b	$(Ca_{0.06}Fe_{1.92}Mn_{0.05}Mg_{0.97})_3\ Al_2\ [(Si_{2.99}Ti_{0.01})_3\ O_{12}]$	qz + mesoperthite + spin + sill + gar + biot + orem	High-alumina quartzite
813g	$(Ca_{0.12}Fe_{1.99}Mn_{0.03}Mg_{0.86})_3\ Al_2\ [(Si_{2.99}Ti_{0.01})_3\ O_{12}]$	qz + mesoperthite + spin + sill + gar + biot + orem	Perthitic shadow high-alumina granite
670a	$(Ca_{0.18}Fe_{1.71}Mn_{0.03}Mg_{1.08})_3\ Al_2\ [Si_3 O_{12}]$	qz + Kfs + spin + sill + gar + hyp + cord + biot + coru + orem	Coarsely layered migmatite of high-alumina schist
769a	$(Ca_{0.09}Fe_{1.53}Mn_{0.02}Mg_{1.36})_3\ Al_2\ [(Si_{2.99}Ti_{0.01})_3\ O_{12}]$	qz + plag + spin + sill + gar + spph + cord + biot + orem	As above
770a	$(Ca_{0.12}Fe_{1.47}Mn_{0.04}Mg_{1.37})_3\ Al_2\ [(Si_{2.99}Ti_{0.01})_3\ O_{12}]$	qz + plag + Kfs + spin + sill + gar + cord	High-alumina quartzite
5—3	$(Ca_{0.09}Fe_{1.69}Mn_{0.03}Mg_{1.19})_3\ Al_2\ [(Si_{2.99}Ti_{0.01})_3\ O_{12}]$	qz + plag + Kfs + spin + sill + gar + cord + biot + orem	Xenolith of a high-alumina schist in intrusive charnockites
727g	$(Ca_{0.45}Fe_{1.77}Mn_{0.03}Mg_{0.75})_3\ Al_2\ [(Si_{2.99}Ti_{0.01})_3\ O_{12}]$	qz + sill + gar + cord + biot + orem	High-alumina quartzite
827b	$(Ca_{0.09}Fe_{2.45}Mn_{0.05}Mg_{0.41})_3\ Al_2\ [(Si_{2.98}Ti_{0.02})_3\ O_{12}]$	qz + plag + Kfs + sill + gar + cord + biot + orem	Thinly layered migmatite of a high-alumina schist
215b	$(Ca_{0.09}Fe_{2.01}Mn_{0.04}Mg_{0.86})_3\ Al_2\ [Si_3 O_{12}]$	qz + plag + mesoperthite + spin + gar + biot + orem	Perthitic shadow high-alumina granitoid
305	$(Ca_{0.08}Fe_{1.59}Mn_{0.15}Mg_{1.18})_3\ Al_2\ [(Si_{2.99}Ti_{0.01})_3\ O_{12}]$	qz + plag + Kfs + spin + gar + cord + biot + orem	Coarsely layered migmatite of high-alumina schist

TABLE 50. Chemical composition of garnets from moderately aluminous (low-calcium) rocks of the granulite facies on Enderby Land

Component	179g wt% by analysis	179g correction	179g corrected analysis	179b wt% by analysis	179b correction	179b corrected analysis	179 wt% by analysis	179 correction	179 corrected analysis	21 wt% by analysis	21 correction	21 corrected analysis	28 wt% by analysis	28 correction	28 corrected analysis	28a wt% by analysis	28a correction	28a corrected analysis
SiO_2	43.2	−7.2	39.21	37.7	−1.7	38.88	38.2	−3.2	39.03	45.0	−14.1	39.00	45.6	−12.3	37.80	44.8	−14.5	37.43
TiO_2	0.12		0.13	0.14		0.15	0.12		0.13	0.1		0.12	0.2		0.23	0.1		0.12
Al_2O_3	21.4	−1.05	22.16	19.9		21.50	19.8		22.08	20.5	−2.5	22.00	19.0		21.58	19.7	−2.5	21.30
Fe_2O_3	25.8		—	29.1		0.54	26.4		—	25.2		—	30.6		—	30.1		—
FeO	(23.2)		25.29(26.19)	(26.19)		27.81(23.76)	(23.76)		26.49(22.7)	(22.7)		27.80(27.70)	(27.70)		31.46(27.2)	(27.2)		33.60
MnO	0.51		0.56	0.59		0.64	0.70		0.78	0.27		0.32	0.46		0.52	0.91		1.13
MgO	9.0		9.81	7.7		8.32	8.3		9.26	7.7		9.42	4.50		5.11	2.9		3.58
CaO	2.6		2.84	2.0		2.16	2.0		2.23	1.1		1.34	2.9		3.30	2.3		2.84
Σ	102.63		100.00	97.13		100.00	95.52		100.00	100.87		100.00	103.26		100.00	100.81		100.00

Physical properties

	179g	179b	179	21	28	28a
a (Å)	11.50	11.514	11.507	—	—	—
d, g/cm³	—	—	—	—	—	—
N	1.783	1.780	1.791	—	1.813	1.817

Composition, minals

	179g	179b	179	21	28	28a
Pyrope	37	32	35	36	31	15
Almandine	54	60	57	60	69	75
Grossular	8	5	6	4	9	8
Andradite	—	—	—	—	—	—
Spessartite	1	1	2	—	1	2

Ferruginosity, at.%

	179g	179b	179	21	28	28a
F	58.4	63.9	60.5	61.8	76.4	83.8
f	59.2	65.0	61.6	62.3	77.5	84.0

TABLE 50 (continued)

MINERALS OF THE GRANULITE FACIES

Component	202g analysis by wt%	202g correction	202g corrected analysis	52b analysis by wt%	52b correction	52b corrected analysis	179a analysis by wt%	179a correction	179a corrected analysis	213b analysis by wt%	213b correction	213b corrected analysis	765a analysis by wt%	765a correction	765a corrected analysis	765b analysis by wt%	765b correction	765b corrected analysis
SiO_2	43.6	−11.0	38.72	44.9	−10.6	38.80	40.10	−2.7	38.90	42.3	−7.5	37.45	38.7	−3.9	37.54	34.6	−1.4	37.54
TiO_2	0.1		0.12	0.1		0.11	0.13		0.15				0.13		0.14	0.12		0.14
Al_2O_3	20.8	−2.3	21.97	20.3	−0.8	22.04	20.60		21.60	20.0	−0.3	21.53	19.8	−0.1	21.24	21.9	−3.2	21.15
Fe_2O_3	27.1		—	27.2		—	27.10		0.50	33.3		—	30.7		—	30.9		—
FeO	(24.40)		29.00	(24.4)		27.61	(24.40)		25.50	(30.1)		32.35	(27.63)		29.95	(27.81)		31.45
MnO	0.29		0.34	1.10		1.24	0.45		0.45	0.75		0.81	3.4		3.68	2.7		3.05
MgO	7.2		8.54	8.1		9.17	8.10		8.50	2.7		2.91	4.4		4.74	3.1		3.50
CaO	1.1		1.31	0.9		1.03	4.30		4.50	4.6		4.95	2.5		2.71	2.8		3.17
Σ	100.19		100.00	102.60		100.00	100.78		100.00	103.65		100.00	99.63		100.00	96.12		100.00

Physical properties

	202g	52b	179a	213b	765a	765b
a (Å)	—	—	11.512	—	11.56	11.55
d, g/cm³	—	—	—	—	—	—
N			1.782	1.809	1.796	1.803

Composition, minals

	202g	52b	179a	213b	765a	765b
Pyrope	33	35	33	11	18	14
Almandine	62	59	54	72	66	70
Grossular	4	3	10	14	8	9
Andradite	—	—	2	—	—	—
Spessartite	1	3	1	3	8	7

Ferruginosity, at.%

	202g	52b	179a	213b	765a	765b
F	65.0	61.1	62.1	84.2	71.0	77.1
f	65.5	62 8	62.7	86.1	78.0	83.4

TABLE 50 (continued)

Component	478b			40			406b*			162			49a			49b		
	wt% by analysis	correction	corrected analysis	wt% by analysis	correction	corrected analysis	wt% by analysis	correction	corrected analysis	wt% by analysis	correction	corrected analysis	wt% by analysis	correction	corrected analysis	wt% by analysis	correction	corrected analysis
SiO_2	40.5	−6.3	38.35	46.2	−12.4	39.55	40.34	−4.6	39.25	46.8	−12.6	38.93	41.2	−4.1	38.36	44.5	−10.8	37.80
TiO_2	0.14		0.16	0.1		0.12	0.14		0.15	0.1		0.11	<0.1		0.1	<0.1		—
Al_2O_3	21.6	−2.2	21.75	20.4	−1.3	22.35	22.85	−3.2	21.58	19.6	−0.2	22.08	19.4	+1.6	21.70	20.4	−1.3	21.40
Fe_2O_3	29.5		—	23.3			1.59	−0.75	0.92	26.5		—	28.0		—	31.6		—
FeO	(26.55)		29.77	(21.0)		24.55	23.19		25.46	(23.85)		27.16	(25.3)		26.15	(28.45)		31.90
MnO	1.0		1.12	0.59		0.69	0.58		0.64	0.48		0.56	1.28		1.32	1.16		1.30
MgO	6.3		7.06	9.7		11.34	9.98		10.96	8.1		9.22	4.9		5.05	4.4		4.90
CaO	1.6		1.79	1.2		1.40	0.95		1.04	1.7		1.94	7.1		7.32	2.2		2.70
Σ	100.64		100.00	101.49		100.00	99.62		100.00	103.28		100.00	101.98		100.00	104.36		100.00

Physical properties

a (Å)	11.52			—			—			—								
d, g/cm^3	3.99			—			4.00			3.93								
N	1.790			1.775			1.782			1.784								

Composition, minals

Pyrope	28			43			42			36			20			19		
Almandine	65			52			54			58			57			71		
Grossular	5			4			—			5			20			7		
Andradite	—			—			3			—			—			—		
Spessartite	2			1			1			1			3			3		

Ferruginosity, at.%

F	68.4			54.0			56.6			61.5			71.6			75.8		
f	70.3			54.8			56.5			62.4			74.4			78.4		

Notes. 1. Asterisk indicates garnet from Bunger Oasis. 2. The mineral and chemical compositions of the rocks are listed in Tables 24, 25, 26, 27, 28, 29, 34, 35.

Supplement to Table 50

Specimen No.	Approximate crystallochemical formula	Paragenesis	Designation of rock
179g	$(Ca_{0.24}Fe_{1.62}Mn_{0.03}Mg_{1.11})_3 [Si_3O_{12}]$	qz + plag + Kfs + gar + biot + orem	Shadow biotite-garnet plagiogranite
179b	$(Ca_{0.21}Fe_{1.80}Mn_{0.03}Mg_{0.96})_3 (Fe_{0.04}Al_{1.96})_2 [(Si_{2.99}Ti_{0.01})_3 O_{12}]$	qz + plag + Kfs + gar + orem	Shadow garnet mesoperthitic granite
179	$(Ca_{0.18}Fe_{1.71}Mn_{0.06}Mg_{1.05})_3 Al_2 [Si_3O_{12}]$	qz + plag + mesoperthite + gar + orem	As above
21	$(Ca_{0.11}Fe_{1.79}Mn_{0.02}Mg_{1.08})_3 Al_2 [Si_3O_{12}]$	qz + plag + mesoperthite + gar + biot + orem	Biotitized shadow garnet mesoperthitic granite
28	$(Ca_{0.28}Fe_{2.07}Mn_{0.04}Mg_{0.62})_3 Al_2 [(Si_{2.98}Ti_{0.02})_3 O_{12}]$	qz + plag + Kfs + gar + orem	Shadow garnet mesoperthitic granite
28a	$(Ca_{0.24}Fe_{2.26}Mn_{0.07}Mg_{0.43})_3 Al_2 [Si_3O_{12}]$	qz + plag + Kfs + gar	Granitized shadow garnet plagiogranite
202g	$(Ca_{0.11}Fe_{1.88}Mn_{0.02}Mg_{0.99})_3 Al_2 [Si_3O_{12}]$	qz + gar	Garnet quartzite
52b	$(Ca_{0.09}Fe_{1.78}Mn_{0.08}Mg_{1.05})_3 Al_2 [Si_3O_{12}]$	qz + plag + mesoperthite + gar	Shadow garnet mesoperthitic granite
179a	$(Ca_{0.36}Fe_{1.62}Mn_{0.03}Mg_{0.99})_3 (Fe_{0.04}Al_{1.96})_2 [(Si_{2.99}Ti_{0.01})_3 O_{12}]$	qz + plag + Kfs + hyp + gar + biot	Biotitized garnet-hypersthene shadow plagiogranite (enderbite)
213b	$(Ca_{0.43}Fe_{2.16}Mn_{0.06}Mg_{0.35})_3 Al_2 [Si_3O_{12}]$	qz + plag + Kfs + hyp + gar + orem	Garnet-hypersthene shadow plagiogranite (enderbite)

Supplement to Table 50 (continued)

Specimen No.	Approximate crystallochemical formula	Paragenesis	Designation of rock
765a	$(Ca_{0.24}Fe_{1.98}Mn_{0.24}Mg_{0.54})_3 Al_2 [(Si_{2.99}Ti_{0.01})_3^{++} O_{12}]$	qz + plag + Kfs + hyp + gar + orem	Garnet-hypersthene shadow granites (charnockite)
765b	$(Ca_{0.27}Fe_{2.10}Mn_{0.21}Mg_{0.42})_3 Al_2 [(Si_{2.99}Ti_{0.01})_3 O_{12}]$	qz + plag + Kfs + hyp + gar + orem	Garnet-hypersthene shadow granitoid
478b	$(Ca_{0.15}Fe_{1.95}Mn_{0.07}Mg_{0.83})_3 Al_2 [(Si_{2.99}Ti_{0.01})_3 O_{12}]$	qz + plag + Kfs + hyp + gar + biot + orem	As above
40	$(Ca_{0.11}Fe_{1.56}Mn_{0.04}Mg_{1.29})_3 Al_2 [Si_3 O_{12}]$	qz + plag + Kfs + hyp + gar + biot + orem	" "
406b	$(Ca_{0.09}Fe_{1.62}Mn_{0.04}Mg_{1.25})_3 (Fe_{0.05}Al_{1.95}) [(Si_{2.99}Ti_{0.01})_3 O_{12}]$	qz + plag + hyp + gar + biot + orem	Migmatite paleosome, intermediate in composition between schist and enderbite
162	$(Ca_{0.16}Fe_{1.74}Mn_{0.04}Mg_{1.06})_3 Al_2 [(Si_{2.99}Ti_{0.01})_3 O_{12}]$	qz + mesoperthite + hyp + gar + biot + orem	Garnet-hypersthene shadow meso-perthitic granite (charnockite)
49a	$(Ca_{0.61}Fe_{1.71}Mn_{0.09}Mg_{0.59})_3 Al_2 [Si_3 O_{12}]$	qz + plag + Kfs + gar	Saxon-type granulite
49b	$(Ca_{0.21}Fe_{2.12}Mn_{0.09}Mg_{0.58})_3 Al_2 [Si_3 O_{12}]$	qz + plag + Kfs + gar	" " "

TABLE 51. Chemical composition of garnets from calcium-rich granulite facies rocks of Enderby Land

	Specimen No.											
	58			41d			41b			42		
Component	wt% by analysis	correction	corrected analysis	wt% by analysis	correction	corrected analysis	wt% by analysis	correction	corrected analysis	wt% by analysis	correction	corrected analysis
SiO_2	41.4	−6.3	38.09	42.3	−6.9	38.17	45.5	−11.2	38.70	42.2	−6.0	38.40
TiO_2	0.1	−1.3	0.12	0.1	−0.9	0.11	0.1	−0.5	0.11	0.1	+0.1	0.11
Al_2O_3	21.2		21.60	21.0		21.67	20.0		22.00	20.4		21.90
Fe_2O_3	26.8		—	27.7		—	24.0		—	26.8		—
FeO	(24.15)		26.20	(25.0)		26.96	(21.55)		24.30	(24.15)		25.92
MnO	1.1		1.19	0.64		0.69	0.67		0.76	0.89		0.95
MgO	3.4		3.69	4.00		4.31	5.8		6.55	5.8		6.12
CaO	8.4		9.11	7.5		8.09	6.7		7.58	6.2		6.60
Σ	102.0		100.00	103.24		100.00	102.77		100.0	102.39		100.00

Physical properties

	58	41d	41b	42
a (Å)	—	—	—	—
d, g/cm³				
N	1.798	1.796	1.789	1.790

Composition, minals

	58	41d	41b	42
Pyrope	14	17	25	24
Almandine	57	59	52	56
Grossular	26	22	21	18
Andradite	—	—	—	—
Spessartite	3	2	2	2

Ferruginosity, at.%

	58	41d	41b	42
F	77.1	76.2	66.2	68.2
f	79.9	78.3	67.6	70.0

Supplement to Table 51

Specimen No.	Approximate crystallochemical formulas	Paragenesis	Designation of rock
58	$(Ca_{0.77}Fe_{1.72}Mn_{0.08}Mg_{0.43})_3 \, Al_2 \, [Si_3 O_{12}]$	qz + plag + Kfs + clpy + amph + gar + orem	Garnet-clinopyroxene-plagioclase schist
41d	$(Ca_{0.68}Fe_{1.77}Mn_{0.05}Mg_{0.50})_3 \, Al_2 \, [Si_3 O_{12}]$	plag + hyp + clpy + amph + gar + orem	Garnet-clinopyroxene-plagioclase schist
41b	$(Ca_{0.63}Fe_{1.57}Mn_{0.05}Mg_{0.75})_3 \, Al_2 \, [Si_3 O_{12}]$	plag + hyp + clpy + amph + gar + orem	Garnet-bipyroxene-plagioclase schist
42	$(Ca_{0.55}Fe_{1.67}Mn_{0.06}Mg_{0.72})_3 \, Al_2 \, [Si_3 O_{12}]$	plag + hyp + clpy + amph + gar + orem	Amphibolized garnet-bipyroxene-plagioclase schist

Note. The mineral and chemical compositions of the rocks are presented in Tables 10 and 11.

as follows: 1) high-alumina rocks containing, in addition to garnet, other high-alumina minerals (sillimanite, cordierite, spinel); these rocks are usually low in calcium; 2) moderately aluminous varieties that are relatively low in calcium, the colored minerals of which, in addition to the garnet, include biotite and hypersthene; 3) rocks rich in calcium, in which ortho-pyroxene and clinopyroxene or clinopyroxene alone occur in addition to the garnet. In the first two groups, the garnet occurs in a paragenesis with quartz, whereas in rocks of the third group it may occur both in quartz-free and quartz-bearing rocks. On the average, the ferruginosity of garnet is the lowest in the first group of rocks, 61.6 at.% (ranging from 51.8 to 69.9 at.%). The garnets contain 29—46% pyrope, 49—67% almandine, 2—6% grossular and 1—2% spessartite, and hence have a lower manganese and calcium content than all other garnets. Because of the low content of the other components, the correlation between the content of pyrope and alman-dine is very strong and inversely proportional. Garnets of the highest ferruginosity and consequently also those lowest in magnesium, occur in the most granitized varieties (shadow perthitic granitoids).

In the second group of rocks, the mean ferruginosity of garnets is 69.3 at.% (ranging from 54.8 to 86.1 at.%). Garnets in this group contain 11—43% pyrope, 52—81% almandine, 3—20% grossular and 0—8% spessartite. They contain the most ferruginous garnets of the granulite facies in Antarctica (77—86 at.%). Garnets with the highest ferruginosity occur in rocks with the highest grade of granitization, i. e., shadow perthitic granit-oids. However, it must be emphasized that they must be low in calcium, since calcium-rich garnets in this group of rocks are also of high ferru-ginosity. Such garnets occur in rocks that have been only slightly affected by granitization as well as in enderbitized varieties. Garnets from this group, in general, have higher calcium contents than garnets from the above group. The increase in the calcium content of garnets is accompanied by an increase in their manganese content. The highest calcium contents occur in garnets from granulites (up to 20% grossular). Remarkably, garnet from garnet schists in the same exposure as garnet-hypersthene schists (the garnet of which contains considerable amounts of the calcium component, 12% grossular + andradite) likewise has a high calcium content, 5—8% grossular (exposure 179a, b, g). This indicates that the calcium content in the garnet was possibly affected by thermodynamic conditions (apparently, pressure), instead of the composition of the rocks. Garnets with the highest manganese contents (specimens 765a, b) occur in shadow granitoids located near the zone of high-temperature diaphthoresis indicated by unakitized intrusive granitoids /68/ in the north of Enderby Land penin-sula. The rocks containing this garnet, however, do not have a high man-ganese content, and therefore the high manganese content in the garnet could be due to its origin at a lower temperature than the other garnets from the same group of rocks; this is in agreement with the geological setting of the rocks containing the manganiferous garnets.

Since the majority of analyses were performed on garnets from moderately aluminous rocks of low calcium content, it is possible to undertake a determi-nation of the composition of garnets in different metamorphic zones of

Enderby Land. The highest magnesium contents are found in garnets from the Napier metamorphic zone (mean ferruginosity, 67.6 at.%). The lowest magnesium contents are found in garnets from the Rayner zone (mean ferruginosity, 75.4 at.%). The difference in the iron content of garnet is related to a variation in the depth conditions, as was demonstrated by Marakushev /43/. Hence, the metamorphism in the Napier zone took place at a greater depth than that in the Rayner zone.

Correlation of the composition of any two components in garnets from rocks of the second group reveals a weaker interdependence than in rocks of the first group. This is due to replacement of magnesium by calcium, and of iron by manganese and calcium. This evidently indicates not only that garnets of the group in question were formed at different depths but also at different temperatures and pressures.

In calcium-rich rocks (third group) the ferruginosity of garnet is still higher than in the preceding groups, averaging 73.9 at.% (from 67.6 to 79.9 at.%). The garnets of these rocks contain 14—25% pyrope, 52—59% almandine, 18—26% grossular and 2—3% spessartite. Thus, along with the high ferruginosity, the distinctive features of these garnets include their high content of grossular and low content of almandine (nearly the same as in low-ferruginosity garnets from high-alumina rocks). Apparently, the ferruginosity of garnets in these rocks is high not because of the replacement of magnesium by iron, but because of its replacement by calcium. It is difficult to carry out a correlation of the relative contents of the various components in these garnets due to the inadequate data. However, there is an apparent correlation between pyrope and grossular. It should be noted that calcium-rich garnets (Gross + Andr > 10%) from all paragenetic types exhibit the following common property: if the composition of the garnets is plotted on the Pyr–Alm + Spes–Gros + Andr diagram (Figure 22), most of the high-calcium garnets lie parallel to the Pyr–Gros + Andr side of the triangle. Thus, their almandine contents are similar, but they differ significantly with respect to pyrope or calcium components. On the other hand, low-calcium garnets plot parallel to the Pyr–Alm + Spes side, i. e., for similar Ca contents, their pyrope and almandine contents are interdependent. Since high-calcium garnets are not confined to high-calcium rocks but also occur in low-calcium rocks, it is clear that the calcium content of Antarctic garnets is a function of thermodynamic conditions.

As pointed out by many investigators /2, 15, 62/, the calcium contents in garnets increases with diminishing grade of metamorphism. Indeed, high-calcium garnets have been encountered only in polymetamorphic zones, with high-temperature diaphthoresis of the amphibolite facies superimposed on the granulite facies rock (Rayner zone of Enderby Land and on Queen Maud Land). However, the geologic setting and structure of the rocks containing the high-calcium garnet attest to high pressures during the formation of these rocks. As indicated above, the Ca^{2+} ion is isomorphic with the Mg^{2+} ion in garnets of such rocks. The replacement by the large calcium ion (ionic radius = 1.04 kX) of the small magnesium ions (ionic radius = 0.74 kX) instead of the larger ions of iron (ionic radius = 0.80 kX) and manganese (ionic radius = 0.91 kX) undoubtedly indicates superpressures (stress)

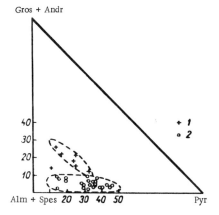

FIGURE 22. Composition of garnets (in minals) from granulite facies rocks of Antarctica:

1) high-calcium garnets; 2) low-calcium garnets.

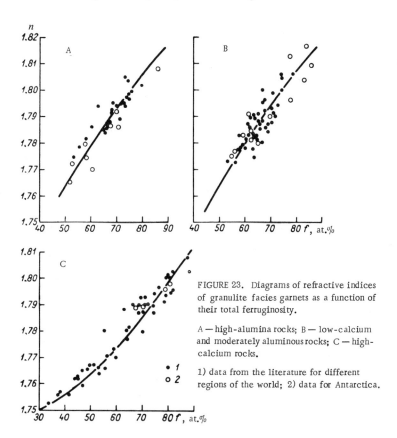

FIGURE 23. Diagrams of refractive indices of granulite facies garnets as a function of their total ferruginosity.

A — high-alumina rocks; B — low-calcium and moderately aluminous rocks; C — high-calcium rocks.

1) data from the literature for different regions of the world; 2) data for Antarctica.

during the formation of high-calcium garnets in Antarctica.* Presumably, the superpressure conditions may determine the isomorphism of iron and manganese in zones of lower temperatures.

Garnet is the most highly ferruginous mineral in quartz-bearing metamorphic rocks of the granulite facies. Its ferruginosity depends on the rock composition, on its formation temperature and depth and on the chemical potential of alkalis. Characterization of the ferruginosity of garnets in rocks of different alkalinities from different regions of Antarctica (in order to compare the formation depths of granulite facies rocks) requires the use of their refractive indices. The authors are not fully satisfied with the currently available diagrams depicting the refractive index of garnet as a function of its total ferruginosity because of their failure to take into account the data on Antarctic garnets and also because they either encompass garnets from all metamorphic facies /72, 35/ or else incompletely encompass the granulite facies rocks /41, 143/. Unfortunately, the relatively small number of analyses of garnets from Antarctic rocks of different compositions prevented the development of a diagram for granulite facies garnet from Antarctica (as for hypersthenes). Therefore use was made of numerous analytical data on garnets available in the literature /8, 29, 35, 39, 40, 41, 43, 62, 70, 143/ and by adding the Antarctic data, three diagrams were constructed (Figure 23). Diagram A (for high-alumina rocks) was based on 40 analyses (analytical accuracy, ±5 at.%, and ±3 at.% in 88% of cases). Diagram B (for low-calcium and moderately aluminous rocks) was based on 65 analyses (analytical accuracy, ±6 at.%, and ±3 at.% in 77% of cases). Diagram C was based on 55 analyses (analytical accuracy ±6 at.% and ±3 at.% in 85% of cases). The last diagram also includes garnets from calcium-rich eclogites and eclogitized gabbros. Values obtained from these diagrams permit the characterization of garnets from different regions and rock types of Antarctica. It should be noted that garnets from granulites are more accurately determined from curve C, because of their high Ca content.

The mean ferruginosity of garnets is given in Tables 52 and 53, which clearly indicate that 1) the ferruginosity of garnet increases from high-alumina rocks to moderately aluminous and low-calcium rocks to high-calcium rocks; 2) the ferruginosity of garnets increases with increasing alkali contents in the rock (mainly potassium) so that the lowest ferruginosity is found in garnets from weakly feldspathized rocks in every group, while the highest ferruginosity is found in garnets from shadow granitoids; 3) the ferruginosity of garnets decreases with increasing depth and temperature of a given paragenesis — e. g., garnets from biotite-bearing assemblages proved to be more ferruginous than those from hypersthene-bearing assemblages, other conditions being equal; 4) the ferruginosity of garnet in every paragenetic assemblage increases in the following direction: Napier zone of Enderby Land — Rayner zone of Enderby Land — Bunger Oasis — Queen Maud Land. Hence, the depth of metamorphism is greatest in the Napier zone of Enderby Land and smallest on Queen

---

* Ionic radii from Belov and Bokii /14/.

TABLE 52. Mean ferruginosity of garnets (at.%) from different groups of rocks (optical and chemical data)

Group of rocks	Mean ferruginosity	Number of determinations	Region of Antarctica
High-alumina quartzites	61.9	8	Enderby Land, Queen Maud Land, Bunger Oasis
High-alumina migmatites	67.0	24	As above
High-alumina shadow granites	69.3	3	Enderby Land
Shadow biotite-garnet plagiogranites	63.8	14	Enderby Land, Queen Maud Land, Bunger Oasis
Shadow mesoperthitic garnet granites	69.3	9	Enderby Land
Shadow biotite-garnet bifeldspar granites	75.5	11	Enderby Land, Queen Maud Land, Bunger Oasis
Shadow garnet-hypersthene granitoids	69.5	21	As above
Garnet-bipyroxene schists	74.2	23	Enderby Land, Queen Maud Land
Garnet quartzites	66.8	4	Enderby Land, Bunger Oasis

TABLE 53. Mean ferruginosity of garnets (at.%) from different regions of Antarctica (optical and chemical data)

Enderby Land						Bunger Oasis		Queen Maud Land		Paragenesis
Napier zone		Rayner zone		Both zones						
mean ferruginosity	number of determinations	mean ferruginosity	number of determinations	mean ferruginosity	number of determinations	mean ferruginosity	number of determinations	mean ferruginosity	number of determinations	
63.3	11	64.0	1	63.4	12	66.2	15	69.8	8	High-alumina rocks
70.1	21	72.5	6	70.7	27	63.7	18	73.4	13	Low-calcium, moderately aluminous rocks
—	—	74.5	11	74.5	11	—	—	74.0	12	High-calcium rocks
67.8	32	73.2	18	69.8	50	64.9	33	72.8	33	All mineral parageneses

Note. Mean ferruginosity of granulite facies garnet in Antarctica is 69.2 at.%.

Maud Land. Attention is attracted by the somewhat low ferruginosity of garnets from high-calcium rocks of Queen Maud Land, in comparison to garnets from similar rocks on Enderby Land, indicating greater depths of metamorphism in similar zones on Queen Maud Land. This is explained by the fact that the high-calcium rocks in both regions are localized in certain zones distinguished by high unilateral pressure.

The method used for conversion of the spectroscopic silicate analyses of garnet is as follows: the calculation is done for the sum of cations Mg^{2+}, Fe^{2+}, Mn^{2+}, Ca^{2+}, equal to three formula units. The entire ferric iron is scaled to ferrous iron and computed for almandine, since the content of the andradite molecule in granulite facies garnet is usually insignificant /62/. Only in rare cases, when the amount of aluminum ions fell short of two formula units, part of the iron was regarded as ferric and combined in the grossular molecule along with calcium. Calculation of the common denominator was followed by calculation of the amounts of aluminum and silicon necessary for filling the corresponding sites in the structure, assuming that titanium replaced silicon isomorphously /62/. Usually, the resultant excess of silicon and aluminum (as in the calculation of chemical silicate analyses from data of many authors /62/) was determined in wt%, and the analytical results were corrected for this and then scaled to 100%. The excess of silicon and aluminum in garnet is due to the presence of fine sillimanite needles and quartz granules that cannot be mechanically separated. Moreover, excess silicon is produced by grinding the garnet in an agate mortar, its hardness being much higher than that of agates. The described conversion method yields satisfactory crystallochemical formulas for garnet.

Feldspars

Feldspars in rocks of the granulite facies are represented by four chemical types, plagioclases, antiperthitic plagioclases, perthites and K-Na-feldspars. Nearly all of the perthitic feldspars are considered to be the result of exsolution of solid solutions and only in rare cases does the possibility exist that certain antiperthitic ingrowths in plagioclase originated by direct replacement during granitization. Furthermore, a comparison of the results of chemical and optical methods for the determination of the composition reveals that certain of the feldspars still remain in solid solutions, although partial exsolution has taken place.

Plagioclases, in all modifications for all the granulite facies rocks, were measured on Fedorov's stage, and the results have been listed in several tables. Therefore, the following discussion will be limited to an examination of mean values of the plagioclase composition for rocks of different types and from different regions of Antarctica, as well as certain chemical features of antiperthitic plagioclases from enderbites. Where zonal plagioclases occur extensively, the average plagioclase composition was computed for the peripheral zones, because the latter are in equilibrium

with the surrounding minerals. The composition of plagioclases from
granulite facies rocks of Antarctica (Table 54) depends on the composition
of the rock and on the degree and nature of its granitization. Indeed, a
comparison of the corresponding varieties of granitization series of high-
calcium, moderately aluminous and high-alumina rocks from any region of
Antarctica, reveals a decrease in the basicity of plagioclase with decreasing
calcium content in the rock. The basicity of plagioclase declines with increasing grade of granitization, as can be seen in all granitization series.
Essentially, soda granitization solutions diminish the basicity of plagioclase
more markedly than do essentially potassic solutions, as is readily seen by
comparing the basicities of plagioclases from pyroxene-plagioclase schists
and enderbites (as well as enderbites and charnockites on Enderby Land).
In cases of a marked predominance of essentially potassic granitization
solutions, the basicity of plagioclase in granitized rocks may even increase,
either owing to the loss of sodium (established by a comparison of the
chemical analyses of perthitic and bifeldspar charnockites) or by selective
fusion of the "minimal melt." The composition of the latter is determined
by the Q:Ab:Or ratios which best suit a given temperature and other external conditions /11/. Apparently, both phenomena occur concurrently and
therefore the composition of plagioclases in charnockites of the Bunger
Oasis and Queen Maud Land is more basic than in enderbites of the same
regions. It should be noted that the plagioclase from garnet-bipyroxene-
plagioclase schists are more acid than those from pyroxene-plagioclase
schists, in spite of the identical chemical composition of these rocks. The
difference in the plagioclase basicity is evidently due to thermodynamic
conditions responsible for redistribution of potassium between garnet and
plagioclase. In this respect the major part was probably played by high
pressure, which affected the formation of the association of garnet-
bipyroxene-plagioclase schists.

  As is known from the petrography of the rocks, the majority of the
plagioclases contain antiperthite ingrowths; this is particularly noted in
enderbites. As pointed out by Deer et al. /18/, antiperthitic plagioclases
are characteristic of granulite facies rocks and were formed by exsolution
from a plagioclase—K-feldspar solid solution. Sen /126/ showed that the
potassium content in a plagioclase is related to the formation temperature
and is independent of either the Ab:An ratio in the plagioclase or the potassium content of the rock (melt) during crystallization. According to Sen,
plagioclase of the amphibolite facies averages 0.9 wt% K_2O)(from 0.6 to
2.3%); that in rocks of the granulite facies averages 4.0 wt% (0.6—7.6%),
and that in some igneous rocks, 6.5 wt% (4.4—11.5%). The plagioclase
in enderbites from Enderby Land contains 1.3—3.2 wt% K_2O (by flame
photometry, specimen 232a, Table 16), i. e., it lies completely within the
range of the granulite facies. A simple calculation shows that the plagioclase from enderbites contains 11—20% of the orthoclase molecule, while
the plagioclase in specimen 232a contains 36% anorthite (Table 16).

  Alkaline feldspars of the granulite facies in Antarctica fall into two
groups, perthites and perthite-bearing K-feldspars. The perthite-bearing
K-feldspars in granulite facies rocks are common in nearly all regions of

TABLE 54. Mean composition of plagioclases from granulite facies rocks

Rock	Enderby Land		Bunger Oasis		Queen Maud Land		Entire Antarctica	
	mean compositions	number of determinations	mean compositions	number of determinations	mean compositions	number of determinations	mean compositions	number of determinations
Pyroxene-plagioclase schists	54.4	49	55.0	66	50.9	17	54.3	132
Rocks of intermediate composition between pyroxene-plagioclase schists and enderbites	—	—	51.9	30	—	—	51.9	30
Enderbites	37.3	22	34.2	19	29.3	3	35.4	44
Perthitic charnockites	31.7	11	—	—	—	—	31.7	11
Bifeldspar charnockites	28.5	4	38.2	10	30.0	3	34.5	17
Shadow garnet-hypersthene granitoids	33.0	11	36.6	15	32.0	3	34.8	29
Garnet-bipyroxene-plagioclase schists	42.5	13	38.0	2	35.3	17	38.4	32
Shadow biotite-garnet plagiogranites	36.0	6	31.8	8	31.3	3	33.2	17
Shadow perthitic garnet granites	30.5	6	—	—	—	—	30.5	6
Shadow bifeldspar biotite-garnet granites	34.2	5	33.0	1	28.0	9	30.4	15
"Saxon" granulites	30.0	2	—	—	33.0	?	—	—
High-alumina migmatites with perthitic metasome	29.0	2	—	—	—	—	29.0	2
High-alumina migmatites with bifeldspar metasome	—	—	32.2	20	30.6	8	31.7	28
High-alumina shadow perthitic granites	26.5	3	—	—	—	—	26.5	3
High-alumina quartzites	37.2	11	38.0	4	26.0	1	36.7	16
Garnet quartzites	—	—	37.3	3	—	—	37.3	3
Metasome of migmatites of pyroxene-plagioclase schists	38.0	3	30.8	4	26.0	2	32.1	9
Metasome of migmatites of high-alumina schists	—	—	26.8	6	—	—	26.8	6
Perthite ingrowths in perthitic charnockites	30.1	11	—	—	—	—	30.1	11

Antarctica. Perthites are the predominant component of shadow granitoids and metasomes of migmatites only in the Napier zone of Enderby Land. Therefore, much work was concentrated on these inadequately studied alkaline feldspars. Flame photometry was used to study the composition of ten perthites from three types of shadow granitoids — from garnet-hypersthene granites, charnockites and garnet granites (Table 55). Perthites from enderbites proved to have the highest calcium content and, at the same time, the lowest potassium content (specimens 232a, 30 and 29). Perthites from charnockites have high potassium contents and low calcium contents (specimens 22a, 33b and 208). Perthite from garnet granites (specimens 28, 28a, 21, 211) is low in calcium and high in alkalis, especially potassium. Computation for minals of perthites (Table 55) shows that they are liable to contain 1—18% anorthite, 39—52% albite and 36—58% orthoclase. Further exsolution and homogenization of perthites gradually convert them to perthite-bearing K-feldspar. The temperature interval for exsolution of solid solutions of perthite composition determined from Barth's well-known stability diagram for the system albite-orthoclase /81/ is 650—740°C, provided that the plagioclase component is represented by albite. However, the exsolution temperature increases considerably in the presence of anorthite in the solid solution /18/, and therefore the exsolution temperatures of the perthites under consideration must be higher.

It was previously established that alkaline feldspar in the granulite facies in Antarctica may be present in the following three structural states: 1) slightly triclinized orthoclase; 2) intermediate microcline; 3) almost completely triclinized microcline. Triclinization of orthoclase is readily observable in thin sections as the development and quality of the microcline crosshatching. In the majority of cases, the microclinization of orthoclase proceeds from grain margins. Microclinized antiperthitic ingrowths in plagioclase were occasionally observed. Weakly triclinized orthoclase is common in perthites, but even then in zones close to faults (in the periphery of the Napier zone), whereas microclinization of perthitic orthoclase is quite distinct near intrusive rocks. In the rest of Antarctica, one encounters mainly intermediate microcline (or partially triclinized orthoclase) with an indistinct crosshatching, often confined to a part of the grain. However, the triclinization increases in polymetamorphic zones that form a transition to the amphibolite facies (for instance, Queen Maud Land, western Enderby Land), and the granulites and rocks that are interbedded with them contain two K-feldspars; a fully triclinized microcline with well-developed cross-hatching and orthoclase, in which the microcline crosshatching is weakly manifested only locally along grain edges.

Refractive determinations of relatively homogeneous orthoclase and cryptoperthitic orthoclase from bifeldspar shadow granitoids and migmatite metasome of the same composition, reveal the following data: 1) for Enderby Land, they range from $n_z = 1.527-1.530$ and $n_x = 1.521-1.523$, corresponding to 25—45% Ab (+ An) by Tuttle's diagram /134/; 2) for Queen Maud Land and the Bunger Oasis, $n_z = 1.526-1.528$ and $n_x = 1.521-1.522$, corresponding to 22—32% Ab (+ An). The refractive indices for analyzed cryptomesoperthite from specimen 208 are $n_z = 1.532$, $n_x = 1.525$. Since every percent of

TABLE 55. Chemical composition of perthites (solid solutions of feldspars) from shadow granitoids of the granulite facies on Enderby Land

Component	Specimen No.												
	232a	30	29	162	215	175–1	22a	33b	203	28	28a	21	211
	Contents of alkalis and lime, %												
CaO	4.1	4.9	3.7	3.6	2.9	2.3	0.8	0.7	0.4	0.8	0.5	0.6	0.2
Na_2O	4.3	5.2	6.4	4.5	4.8	5.4	4.7	4.0	3.8	5.0	3.9	7.8	6.6
K_2O	1.3	2.4	3.2	7.2	5.5	7.4	6.7	11.1	13.4	8.6	8.6	10.5	11.8
	Composition, minals												
Anorthite	31	29	19	18	16	11	5	3	2	4	3	2	1
Albite	58	55	61	40	48	47	49	34	29	45	39	52	46
Orthoclase	11	16	20	42	36	42	46	63	69	51	58	46	53

Supplement to Table 55

Specimen No.	Approximate crystallochemical formula	Paragenesis	Designation of rocks
232a	$Ca_{0.31}Na_{0.58}K_{0.11}Al_{1.31}Si_{2.89}O_8$	qz + plag + Kfs + hyp + orem	Enderbite
30	$Ca_{0.28}Na_{0.55}K_{0.16}Al_{1.28}Si_{2.72}O_8$	qz + plag + hyp + biot + amph	Biotitized and amphibolized enderbite
29	$Ca_{0.19}Na_{0.61}K_{0.20}Al_{1.19}Si_{2.81}O_8$	qz + plag + hyp + orem	Enderbite
162	$Ca_{0.18}Na_{0.40}K_{0.42}Al_{1.18}Si_{2.82}O_8$	qz + plag + mesoperthite + hyp + gar + orem	Shadow garnet-hypersthene granitoid
215	$Ca_{0.16}Na_{0.48}K_{0.38}Al_{1.16}Si_{2.84}O_8$	qz + plag + mesoperthite + hyp + gar + biot + orem	As above
175—1	$Ca_{0.11}Na_{0.47}K_{0.42}Al_{1.11}Si_{2.89}O_8$	qz + plag + mesoperthite + hyp + orem	Perthitic charnockite
22-a	$Ca_{0.05}Na_{0.49}K_{0.46}Al_{1.04}Si_{2.96}O_8$	qz + mesoperthite + hyp + biot	"
33b	$Ca_{0.03}Na_{0.34}K_{0.63}Al_{1.03}Si_{2.97}O_8$	qz + plag + mesoperthite + hyp	"
208	$Ca_{0.02}Na_{0.29}K_{0.89}Al_{1.02}Si_{2.98}O_8$	qz + plag + mesoperthite + hyp	"
28	$Ca_{0.04}Na_{0.45}K_{0.51}Al_{1.04}Si_{2.96}O_8$	qz + plag + mesoperthite + gar + orem	Shadow perthitic garnet granite
28a	$Ca_{0.03}Na_{0.39}K_{0.58}Al_{1.03}Si_{2.97}O_8$	qz + plag + mesoperthite + gar	As above
21	$Ca_{0.02}Na_{0.52}K_{0.46}Al_{1.02}Si_{2.98}O_8$	qz + plag + mesoperthite + gar + biot + orem	"
211	$Ca_{0.01}Na_{0.46}K_{0.53}Al_{1.01}Si_{2.99}O_8$	qz + plag + mesoperthite + gar + orem	"

Note. The mineral and chemical compositions of the rocks are presented in Tables 16, 18, 20, 22, 24, 27, 29, 31.

anorthite in the solid solution increases the refractive index of albite
(see analysis 208 and Table 56), it may be assumed that the optically
determined albite content of the cryptoperthite (56%) compares satisfactorily
with the analytically determined value.

    In conclusion, it should be noted that investigations of alkaline feldspars
show that the highest-temperature varieties (perthites) occur in the Napier
zone of Enderby Land, and the lowest-temperature varieties (microclines)
on Queen Maud Land.

Biotites

    Studies of biotite from granulite facies rocks from Antarctica are only
now beginning with only seven mineral analyses being available (Table 56).
The analyses were scaled by the method suggested by Borneman-
Starynkevich for chemical analyses of biotites /6/. Four biotites (specimens 210b, 208e, 203k, 755g) are from high-alumina metasomatic rocks.
Their ferruginosities are 6.3—10.1 at.% which is close to pure phlogopite.
Two biotites were obtained from high-alumina low-calcium schists (specimens 215b and 670a) and the remaining biotites (478b) from shadow
garnet-hypersthene granitoid. With the exception of low-ferruginous
biotites (only very slightly colored), all biotites are light brown to slightly
orange in color. The orange pleochroic tinge is assumed to be related to
the presence of titanium at a low degree of iron oxidation. A slightly orange
pleochroic tinge is displayed by many biotites from granulite facies rocks in
Antarctica. With respect to titanium, the first two biotites belong to those
of the amphibolite facies, and the remaining specimens to biotites of the
granulite facies /9, 35, 70/. However, with respect to their alumina
contents, the biotites under consideration belong to varieties intermediate
between the granulite and amphibolite facies.

    When the composition of biotites from granulite facies rocks (established
by many authors /9, 20, 35/) is applied to the biotites under consideration,
it is seen that the mineral did not originate under granulite facies conditions. On the contrary, all observations of the development of biotite in
granulite facies rocks testify to its secondary development from other
minerals such as hypersthene and garnet. Therefore, no doubt arises
concerning the relationship of the development of biotite to repeated metamorphism of granulite facies rocks under amphibolite facies conditions.

    In the authors' opinion, the specific composition of the biotite is due to
the composition of the granulite facies rocks and the minerals from which
the biotites develop. Rutile, which is a characteristic accessory mineral
in high-alumina rocks, is present in the form of needles in hypersthene and
garnet and passes into the replacing biotite. Alumina is often already
concentrated in well-"packed" minerals and it is released for biotites only
with difficulty. The somewhat low water content of quasi-granulite biotites
/20/ is also readily explicable by the very low water content of granulite
facies rocks. The ferruginosity of biotites was determined from refractive

TABLE 56. Chemical composition of biotites from granulite facies rocks on Enderby Land

Component	210b wt% by analysis	210b corrected analysis	208e wt% by analysis	208e corrected analysis	208k wt% by analysis	208k corrected analysis	755g wt% by analysis	755g corrected analysis	215b wt% by analysis	215b corrected analysis	670a wt% by analysis	670a corrected analysis	478b wt% by analysis	478b corrected analysis
SiO_2	40.3	40.46	42.7	42.55	42.1	42.39	41.0	38.80	40.8	41.08	36.3	33.25	40.7	39.06
TiO_2	1.7	1.71	1.3	1.30	4.3	4.33	5.0	4.73	4.5	4.53	3.8	4.00	3.6	3.46
Al_2O_3	15.6	15.66	15.8	15.75	14.2	14.30	20.0	18.93	15.2	15.30	16.5	17.39	20.1	19.29
Fe_2O_3	3.6	—	4.4	—	4.8	—	10.0	—	10.6	—	12.7	—	15.5	—
FeO	(3.3)	3.31	(4.0)	3.99	(4.3)	4.33	(9.05)	8.56	(9.5)	9.56	(11.35)	11.96	(13.95)	13.39
MnO	0.02	0.02	0.02	0.02	0.02	0.02	0.04	0.04	0.03	0.03	0.02	0.02	0.02	0.02
MgO	27.5	27.60	25.0	24.92	21.6	21.75	19.0	17.98	18.3	18.42	16.3	17.18	14.8	14.20
CaO	—	—	—	—	—	—	0.34	0.31	—	—	сл.	—	сл.	—
Na_2O	1.0	1.00	0.8	0.80	0.5	0.50	0.4	0.38	0.9	0.91	0.43	0.45	0.57	0.55
K_2O	10.2	10.24	10.7	10.67	12.3	12.38	10.85	10.27	10.1	10.17	10.2	10.75	10.45	10.03
Σ	99.92	100.00	100.72	100.00	99.82	100.00	106.63	100.00	100.43	100.00	96.25	100.00	105.74	100.00
$n_z = n_y$ / f	6.3		1.591 / 8.3		10.1		1.619 / 21.1		1.615 / 22.6		1.615 / 28.1		1.638 / 34.6	

Supplement to Table 56

Specimen No.	Approximate crystallochemical formula	Paragenesis	Designation of rock
210b	$(K_{0.87}Na_{0.13})_{1.00} (Mg_{2.76}Fe_{0.19}Ti_{0.04}Al_{0.01})_{3.00} [Si_{2.72}Ti_{0.05}Al_{1.23}]_{4.00} O_{12}$	spph + cord + biot	Metasomatic rocks
208e	$(K_{0.93}Na_{0.07})_{1.00} (Mg_{2.53}Fe_{0.23}Ti_{0.07}Al_{0.16})_{3.00} [Si_{2.30}Al_{1.10}]_{4.00} O_{12}$	hyp + spph + cord + biot + Kfs	As above
208k	$(K_{1.13}Na_{0.07})_{1.20} (Mg_{2.30}Fe_{0.26}Ti_{0.23}Al_{0.21})_{3.00} [Si_{3.02}Al_{0.98}]_{4.00} O_{12}$	hyp + cord + biot	"
755g	$(K_{0.93}Na_{0.05}Ca_{0.02})_{1.00} (Mg_{1.90}Fe_{0.51}Ti_{0.25}Al_{0.34})_{3.00} [Si_{2.76}Al_{1.24}]_{4.00} O_{12}$	hyp + spin + spph + cord + biot + plag + Kfs	"
215b	$(K_{0.92}Na_{0.13})_{1.05} (Mg_{1.96}Fe_{0.57}Ti_{0.24}Al_{0.23})_{3.00} [Si_{2.94}Al_{1.05}]_{4.00} O_{12}$	gar + spin + biot + qz + plag + mesoperthite + orem	Shadow mesoperthitic granitoid
670a	$(K_{0.98}Na_{0.08})_{1.04} (Mg_{1.84}Fe_{0.72}Ti_{0.22}Al_{0.22})_{3.00} [Si_{2.75}Al_{1.25}]_{4.00} O_{12}$	spin + sill + gar + hyp + cord + biot + coru + qz + Kfs + orem	High-alumina schist
478b	$(K_{0.92}Na_{0.08})_{1.00} (Mg_{1.53}Fe_{0.81}Ti_{0.19}Al_{0.47})_{3.00} [Si_{2.83}Al_{1.17}]_{4.00} O_{12}$	qz + plag + Kfs + hyp + gar + biot + orem	Shadow garnet-hyper- sthene granitoid

N o t e . The mineral compositions of the rocks are listed in Tables 25, 31, 33, 45.

indices using the diagram provided by Drugova and Glebovitskii /22/. In the general case, the ferruginosity of biotite may be assumed to vary in direct proportion to the variation in the ferruginosity of the coexisting granulite facies minerals, and therefore we shall not dwell on the ferruginosities of biotites from different rocks and different regions of Antarctica, particularly since the ferruginosity of biotite as determined from its optical properties may often differ from its actual value.

Amphiboles

As yet, only three analyses are available for amphiboles from the granulite facies rocks of Antarctica, two from garnet-pyroxene-plagioclase schists (specimens 41d and 42) and one from pyroxene-plagioclase schists (specimen 326a; Table 57). The latest works dealing with the paragenetic types of amphiboles /20, 22, 35/ testify that amphiboles from the granulite facies rocks differ from those from the amphibolite facies rocks in their mean contents of aluminum, total alkalis, titanium and OH. Thus, Dobretsov et al. /20/ provide the following average content and standard deviations of these elements in the crystallochemical formula of calcic amphiboles in the actinolite-hornblende series (Table 58). A comparison of data given in Tables 57 and 58 shows that the amphiboles under consideration are closest to those from rocks of doubtful granulite facies and amphibolite facies with hypersthene. On the other hand, studies of thin sections reveal that in the majority of cases, a secondary origin of amphiboles in the granulite facies rocks of Antarctica, relative to pyroxenes and plagioclase, is beyond doubt. From the literature /20/, it is also known that the primary nature of amphiboles from granulite facies rocks is often doubtful. Therefore, the appearance of amphibole in granulite facies rocks is considered to be a superimposed process related to amphibolite facies granitization or to a regressive stage of granulite facies metamorphism. It is clear that the composition of amphibole in such cases is specific, since it formed from granulite facies minerals (pyroxenes, plagioclases), and not from greenschist facies minerals (as is the case in progressive metamorphism). It may also be noted that typical amphiboles of amphibolite facies and amphiboles from granulite facies are not so markedly different as in the case of garnet. Furthermore, amphiboles formed in basic igneous rocks approach the composition of amphiboles from the granulite facies rocks /16/. This provides an indirect proof that amphiboles are apparently not formed under granulite facies conditions but under other conditions at lower temperatures.

TABLE 57. Chemical composition of amphiboles from granulite facies rocks in Antarctica

Component	Specimen No.					
	41d		42		326a	
	wt% by analysis	corrected analysis	wt% by analysis	corrected analysis	wt% by analysis	corrected analysis
SiO_2	41.3	40.94	41.0	42.27	44.62	44.54
TiO_2	4.6	4.56	3.8	3.92	2.00	2.00
Al_2O_3	13.0	12.88	11.8	12.17	11.20	11.18
Fe_2O_3	22.7	—	20.4	—	2.55	2.54
FeO	(20.40)	20.22	(18.55)	19.13	9.14	9.12
MnO	0.09	0.09	0.13	0.13	0.14	0.14
MgO	6.8	6.74	7.9	8.15	13.44	13.42
CaO	9.8	9.71	10.0	10.31	12.14	12.12
Na_2O	2.2	2.18	1.8	1.86	1.61	1.61
K_2O	2.7	2.68	2.0	2.06	1.15	1.15
Loss on ignition	—	—	—		2.19	2.18
Σ	103.19	100.00	98.83	100.00	100.18	100.00

Optical properties

n_z	1.710		1.710		1.673	
n_x	1.685		1.685		1.650	
2V			from -82 to $-83°$			

Ferruginosity

F	62.5		56.6	32.2
f	62.7		56.8	32.3
f^1				27.6

Supplement to Table 57

Specimen No.	Approximate crystallochemical formula	Paragenesis	Designation of rock
41d	$(K_{0.52}Na_{0.62}Ca_{1.56})_{2.70}$ $(Fe_{2.54}$ $Mg_{1.51}Mn_{0.01}Ti_{0.52}Al_{0.41})_{4.99}$ $[Si_{6.14}Al_{1.86}]_{8.00}$ $O_{22}(OH)_2$	plag + hyp + + clpy + amph + + gar + orem	Garnet-clinopyroxene-plagioclase schist
42	$(K_{0.39}Na_{0.53}Ca_{1.63})_{2.55}$ $(Fe_{2.34}$ $Mg_{1.80}Mn_{0.02}Ti_{0.44}Al_{0.40})_{5.00}$ $[Si_{6.26}Al_{1.74}]_{8.00}$ $O_{24}(OH)_2$	plag + hyp + + clpy + amph + + gar + orem	Garnet-bipyroxene-plagioclase schist
326a	$(K_{0.22}Na_{0.46}Ca_{1.90})_{2.58}$ $(Fe^{2+}_{1.11}$ $Fe^{3+}_{0.28}Mg_{2.93}Mn_{0.02}Ti_{0.22}$ $Al_{0.44})_{5.00}$ $(Si_{6.51}Al_{1.49})_{8.00}$ $(O_{21.86}OH_{0.14})_{22}$ $(OH)_2$	hyp + clpy + + amph + plag + + orem	Bipyroxene-plagioclase schist

Notes. 1. Specimen 326a came from the Bunger Oasis, the rest from Enderby Land.
2. The mineral and chemical compositions are listed in Tables 10 and 11.

TABLE 58. Mean content and standard deviation of elements in the crystallochemical formula of calcic amphiboles (after Dobretsov et al. /20/)

Facies	Ti		Al		Al^{IV}		Al^{VI}		Na + K	
	mean content	standard deviation	mean content	standard deviation	mean content	standard deviation	mean content	standard deviation	mean content	standard deviation
Rocks of the granulite facies	0.21	0.12	2.09	0.33	1.63	0.30	0.45	0.32	0.71	0.17
Rocks of doubtful granulite and amphibolite facies with hypersthene	0.25	0.05	2.23	0.23	1.69	0.15	0.53	0.11	0.73	0.08
All rocks of the granulite facies	0.23	0.09	2.16	0.29	1.66	0.24	0.49	0.24	0.72	0.13
Rocks of the amphibolite facies (without hypersthene)	0.15	0.07	2.06	0.22	1.64	0.24	0.42	0.25	0.67	0.17
As above, without granite-gneisses	0.16	0.07	2.05	0.22	1.56	0.22	0.50	0.24	0.59	0.13
Granite-gneisses	0.16	0.09	2.12	0.21	1.88	0.12	0.24	0.12	0.87	0.09
Rocks of the amphibolite facies with quartz	0.16	0.08	2.17	0.32	1.73	0.26	0.44	0.33	0.71	0.17

FORMATION TEMPERATURES OF
METAMORPHIC ASSOCIATIONS

Since pyroxenes and garnet are typomorphic minerals of metamorphic
rocks of the granulite facies, Kretz's hypersthene-clinopyroxene thermometer /74, 111/ and Perchuk's garnet-pyroxene thermometers /51, 52/
were used to determine the formation temperatures of the granulite facies
rocks. The hypersthene-clinopyroxene thermometer is independent and
the most suitable for the determination of the temperatures of this mineral
association. Unfortunately, the hypersthene-clinopyroxene association is
almost entirely confined to pyroxene-plagioclase schists and is very rarely
found in enderbites and charnockites. Furthermore, the hypersthene-
clinopyroxene thermometer has been calibrated to within the interval
600–1400°C, and the high-temperature portion of this range (1200–1400°C)
is the least accurately calibrated. However, as stated above, the accuracy
of the determinations of pyroxene ferruginosity from optical data is fairly
high, making it possible to apply statistical methods for the detection of
temperature peaks. Therefore, the hypersthene-clinopyroxene thermometer
was the principle thermometer for the granulite facies.

The garnet-pyroxene thermometers are calibrated by using the biotite-
garnet, amphibole-garnet, amphibole-clinopyroxene and hypersthene-
amphibole thermometers. Therefore the garnet-pyroxene thermometers
essentially indicate the temperature of origin of biotite and amphibole in
the pyroxenes + garnet association. A secondary genesis of biotite and
amphibole in the granulite facies rocks of Antarctica is most common.
These thermometers are therefore used to determine mineral associations
of the amphibolite facies superimposed on the granulite facies. They are
convenient for temperature measurements of the bifeldspar charnockite
(hornblende-granulite) subfacies, which is closest to the amphibolite facies
with respect to its mineral paragenesis. The most accurate of the garnet-
pyroxene thermometers is the garnet-hypersthene-clinopyroxene thermometer, but its application is limited by the high-pressure association, which
is rarely encountered. As already shown, optical determinations of the
magnesium and iron contents satisfy the thermometric accuracy. This
thermometer is supplemented by the garnet-amphibole, clinopyroxene-
amphibole, hypersthene-amphibole and garnet-biotite thermometers; however, these are not used unless the chemical composition of amphibole and
biotite is known, since optical determinations of their magnesium and iron
contents are liable to be erroneous, as is indicated by investigations of
amphiboles and biotites carried out by Korikovskii, Drugova and Glebovitskii,
and others /8, 22, 35/. Moreover, their application is confined to a definite
composition of amphibole and biotite. The association of garnet with
hypersthene and clinopyroxene also permits the determination of pressure,
in addition to temperature. The garnet-hypersthene-clinopyroxene barometer is independent, and determines the pressures necessary for the
formation of this association.

On the basis of the available analyses of alkaline feldspars and determinations of the composition of coexistent plagioclases, it is possible to determine

the exsolution temperature of perthite by means of Barth's two-feldspar
thermometer and stability diagram for the albite-orthoclase system /81, 82/.

The hypersthene-clinopyroxene thermometer was used in determinations
of 73 temperatures in the 600—1400°C interval (from optical and chemical
data). The results of measurements were compiled in histograms for different regions and for the overall crystalline basement (Figure 24). The
histogram for Enderby Land displays two peaks, in the 1100—1200°C and
900—1000°C intervals. There are a fairly large number of intermediate
values in the 1000—1100°C interval. The majority of temperatures of the
hypersthene-clinopyroxene association from enderbites and enderbitized
schists from the Napier zone on Enderby Land lie in the 1100—1200°C interval, while temperatures of this association from slightly feldspathized
enderbites and pyroxene-plagioclase schists of the Napier zone on Enderby
Land lie in the 1000—1100°C interval. Temperatures of the association
from perthitic charnockites and charnockitized schists lie in the 900—
1000°C interval. A comparison of these numerical data with the temperatures determined by means of Barth's two-feldspar thermometer (Table 59)
defines temperatures of 900—1000°C for perthitic charnockites; the
temperatures for perthites with a low content of anorthite (from proper
perthitic charnockites and granites) have temperatures ranging from 900
to 990°C, perthites with higher anorthite contents (from perthitic charnockites approaching enderbites) lie within the 1100—1200°C temperature range.
Hence the 1100—1200°C interval may be accepted for the enderbitization
temperature, and the 900—1000°C interval as the charnockitization temperature. Barth's thermometer indicates a temperature of 750°C for some
perthitic charnockites forming a transition to bifeldspar charnockites
(Table 59). It is of interest to note that this temperature interval (700—
800°C) also exists in the histogram of temperatures determined by means
of the hypersthene-clinopyroxene thermometer for Rayner zone samples,
whereas the formation of bifeldspar charnockites is most strongly manifested on Enderby Land. Using other mineralogical thermometers, the
temperatures corresponding to biotitization and amphibolization of rocks
in the Rayner zone lie within the 640—790°C interval (Table 59), while
biotitization and amphibolization in the marginal portions of the Napier
zone lie in the 660—810°C interval. Since biotitization and amphibolization
are processes completing the genesis of bifeldspar charnockites, the 700—
800°C interval may be adopted as the formation temperature of bifeldspar
charnockites. The 600—700°C interval probably marked completion of the
regional metamorphic processes on Enderby Land. The exsolution temperatures of perthites vary from 650 to 750°C, with rare exceptions (Table 59).
As suggested above, the bifeldspar charnockites on Enderby Land originated
from perthitic charnockites with complete exsolution of perthite accelerated
by the influx of potassium. This assumption is confirmed by temperature
measurements.

Since the temperatures indicated by the hypersthene-clinopyroxene
thermometer on Enderby Land do not fall below 700°C, this temperature
may be regarded as the lower temperature boundary of the granulite facies
on Enderby Land. The upper temperature boundary should apparently be

TABLE 59. Formation temperatures of Enderby Land rocks (°C) determined from chemical analyses of the minerals

Specimen No.	Perchuk thermometers						Two-feldspar thermometer (Barth)	Exsolution temperature of perthites (after Barth)	Designation of rock
	Hypersthene-clinopyroxene thermometer (Kretz)	garnet-pyroxene thermometer	garnet-amphibole thermometer	clinopyroxene-amphibole thermometer	hypersthene-amphibole thermometer	garnet-biotite thermometer			
41b	840	640	—	—	—	—	—	—	Hypersthene-garnet-clinopyroxene-plagioclase schists with amphiboles
42	1267	750	795	—	—	—	—	—	As above
41d	—	—	770	790	770	—	—	—	Amphibolized clinopyroxene-plagioclase schist
478b	—	690	—	—	—	640	—	—	Biotitized shadow clinopyroxene granitoid
215b	—	—	—	—	—	780	—	—	Biotitized shadow spinel-garnet perthitic granite
670a	—	—	—	—	—	660	—	—	High-alumina schist (biotitized)
56b	1336	—	—	—	—	—	—	—	Pyroxene-plagioclase schist
203g	1500	—	—	—	—	—	—	—	As above
213b	—	665	—	—	—	—	—	—	Biotitized shadow garnet-hypersthene granitoids
40	—	785	—	—	—	—	—	—	As above
162	—	810	—	—	—	—	1100	730	Biotitized shadow garnet-hypersthene granite (mesoperthitic)
215	—	—	—	—	—	—	1200	750	Shadow garnet-hypersthene perthitic granite
208	—	—	—	—	—	—	750	560	Shadow perthitic charnockite, transitional to bifeldspar charnockite
28	—	—	—	—	—	—	920	690	Shadow garnet perthitic granite
28a	—	—	—	—	—	—	900	650	As above
21	—	—	—	—	—	—	990	720	As above

N o t e .   Perchuk thermometers indicate the formation temperature of biotite and/or amphibole in the corresponding mineral associations.

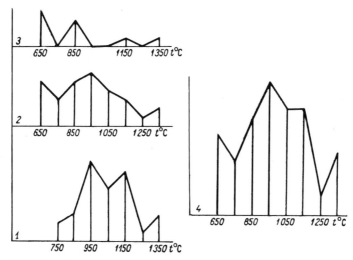

FIGURE 24. Histograms of temperatures determined by means of the hypersthene-clinopyroxene thermometer for crystalline basement metamorphic rocks of the Antarctic Platform:

1) Enderby Land; 2) Bunger Oasis; 3) Queen Maud Land; 4) granulite facies of Antarctica.

drawn at 1200°C, which limits enderbitization, the first process occurring in rocks under conditions of the granulite facies. However, the hypersthene-clinopyroxene thermometer also indicates temperatures above 1250°C in rocks described as pyroxene-plagioclase schists. K_D^{Mg} in the hypersthene-clinopyroxene association fluctuates from 0.78 to 1.48 (Table 60). These rocks are evidently metabasites which did not undergo complete recrystallization under the granulite facies conditions (beginning with enderbitization), but intruded after the enderbitization. However, it cannot be stated that for higher temperatures of the hypersthene-clinopyroxene association (with respect to the enderbitization temperature), metabasite formation takes place later, since the temperature is also controlled by the composition of rocks. The more basic the rock, the higher the temperature at which it crystallizes from magma. This is also confirmed by the K_D^{Mg} values determined in magnesian schists (Table 60), which fluctuate between 1.25 and 2.32. The analytical data for minerals were applied to determine high temperatures for three specimens of metabasites (Table 61). The rock represented by specimen 42 was found to have been included after the formation of perthitic charnockites but before the formation of bifeldspar charnockites (its temperature is 1267°C). However, the formation conditions of pyroxene-plagioclase schists, the temperature of which is above the lower temperature boundary of enderbites, require more detailed studies and they are not discussed further in this work.

TABLE 60. Distribution coefficient of magnesium (K_D^{Mg}) between coexistent hypersthene and clinopyroxene from some Enderby Land schists

Specimen No.	f_{hyp}	f_{clpy}	K_D^{Mg}	Remarks
798b	15*	29	2.32	Olivine-hypersthene-clinopyroxene schists
58—1	20	25	1.33	(meta-ultrabasites)
485b	16	29	2.14	
356a	18	24	1.44	
155b	32	37	1.25	
798d	15	24	1.79	
153b	36*	42	1.29	Pyroxene-plagioclase schists (metabasites)
802b	37	32	0.80	
777v	25	33	1.48	
63—1	32	35	1.14	
800b	30	32	1.10	
812a	37	34	0.88	
156a	42	36	0.78	
167a	41	46	1.23	
343b	52	47	0.82	
383a	38	40	1.09	

Notes. 1. The ferruginosity of pyroxenes was determined from optical constants.
2. The asterisk indicates that the ferruginosity was determined from the chemical analysis of hypersthene.

TABLE 61. Pressure and temperature of garnet-hypersthene-clinopyroxene mineral associations (determined from Perchuk's diagram /52/)

Specimen No.	f_{hyp}	f_{clpy}	f_{gar}	$K_D^{Mg}{}_{gar-hyp}$	$K_D^{Mg}{}_{gar-clpy}$	P, kbar	Temperature by the hypersthene-clinopyroxene thermometer, °C
\multicolumn{8}{c}{Enderby Land}							
416*	42.0	30.5	67.5	0.34	0.21	11.6	840
42*	52.0	45.0	70.0	0.46	0.35	10.0	1267
41v	56.0	48.0	78.0	0.36	0.26	10.4	1160
58d	55.0	49.0	79.0	0.35	0.25	11.1	1039
41e	32.0	24.0	62.0	0.29	0.19	9.8	965
\multicolumn{8}{c}{Queen Maud Land}							
794d	52.0	37.0	73.0	0.40	0.22	4.3	662
856b	48.0	33.0	66.0	0.48	0.25	6.0	650
864v	58.0	46.0	76.0	0.44	0.27	6.0	840
863b	64.0	52.0	76.0	0.56	0.34	9.9	810
830b	44.0	37.0	70.0	0.34	0.25	11.8	1200
830	42.0	37.0	70.0	0.31	0.25	13.0	1400

Note. The asterisk indicates that the ferruginosity was determined by chemical analysis.

Without dwelling in detail on the temperature histograms obtained by means of the hypersthene-clinopyroxene thermometer for rocks in the Bunger Oasis and Queed Maud Land, the following should be noted: 1) Aside from the temperatures corresponding to those of the hypersthene-clinopyroxene association on Enderby Land, the temperature histogram for the Bunger Oasis exhibits a peak in the 600—700°C interval, corresponding to the formation temperatures of bifeldspar charnockites of the Bunger Oasis. 2) The inflection in the 800—900°C interval corresponds to the formation of rocks with a composition intermediate between enderbites and pyroxene-plagioclase schists in the Bunger Oasis. 3) The inflection in the 700—800°C interval corresponds to the formation temperature of bifeldspar charnockites on Enderby Land, and reflects the formation temperatures of the Bunger Oasis enderbites. 4) A peak in the 900—1000°C interval corresponds to the formation temperature of perthitic charnockites on Enderby Land, and reflects the most widespread crystallization temperature of the pyroxene-plagioclase schists. A large quantity of these also crystallized at temperatures of 1000—1100, 1100—1200°C and higher (Figure 24). The histogram for Queen Maud Land exhibits two substantial peaks; in the 600—700°C interval (formation of bifeldspar charnockites) and in the 800—900°C interval (crystallization temperature of the majority of pyroxene-plagioclase schists on Queen Maud Land) (Figure 24).

The histogram for the overall crystalline basement of Antarctica (temperatures determined by means of the hypersthene-clinopyroxene thermometer; Figure 24) indicated that the metamorphic events of the granulite facies range over the temperature interval of 600 to 1200°C; the majority of metamorphic events fall in the following intervals: 1100—1200°C, 1000—1100°C, 900—1000°C, 800—900°C and 600—700°C. The combined diagram of temperatures determined by different methods for different regions in the crystalline basement (Figure 25) indicates that the metamorphism in the granulite facies took place at higher temperatures on Enderby Land and lower temperatures in the Bunger Oasis and on Queen Maud Land. On the other hand, metamorphism that should be classified with the amphibolite facies (by nature of its manifestations) occurred at a relatively lower temperature on Queen Maud Land than in the Bunger Oasis and on Enderby Land.

In conclusion, the pressure determinations are described. Judging from the garnet-hypersthene-clinopyroxene barometer, the formation of this association on Enderby Land required pressures of 9.8—11.6 kbar (hypersthene-clinopyroxene temperatures interval of 840—1300°C), while on Queen Maud Land it falls in two intervals — 4.3—6 kbar and 9.9—13 kbar (Table 61); the first pressure interval corresponds to the hypersthene-clinopyroxene temperature interval of 650—840°C, and the second, to the 810—1400°C interval. It is probable that the formation of the garnet-hypersthene-clinopyroxene association on Queen Maud Land proceeded in at least two stages, one of which corresponds to the formation of the same association on Enderby Land while the other occurred under polymetamorphic conditions. This subject, together with the disposition of different stages of mineral associations on Queen Maud Land, calls for further consideration.

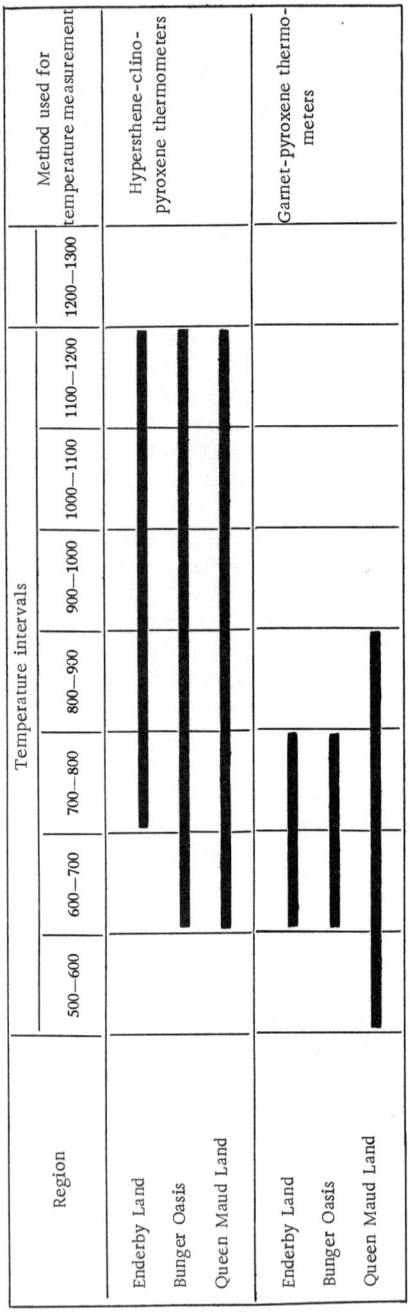

Temperature intervals

Region	500—600	600—700	700—800	800—900	900—1000	1000—1100	1100—1200	1200—1300	Method used for temperature measurement
Enderby Land			████████████████████████████████████						Hypersthene-clino-pyroxene thermometers
Bunger Oasis		██							
Queen Maud Land		██							
Enderby Land		███							Garnet-pyroxene thermometers
Bunger Oasis		███							
Queen Maud Land	██████████████████████████████████								

FIGURE 25. Temperatures of mineral associations of the crystalline basement of Antarctica

MINERAL ASSOCIATIONS OF THE
GRANULITE FACIES

The determination of facies is based on equilibrium mineral associations. Application of the facies principle is based on the detection of stable associations /68/ which originate under certain invariable metamorphic conditions. In describing the rocks, it was demonstrated that their real mineral composition was not formed during a single metamorphic stage, but came about as a result of a repeated metamorphic process under a variety of physicochemical conditions. Aside from vertical and lateral temperature and pressure variations, granitization processes took place, which are related to the variations of the major metamorphic parameters. Processes of regional granitization include bimetasomatosis (described as a contact effect between rocks high in calcium and ferromagnesian components with those high in alumina, silica and alkalis). The same type of phenomena also includes formation of "incompatible" minerals, especially in carbonates and high-alumina rocks due to solutions acting over a small distance. The "incompatible" minerals include quartz and alkaline feldspars on the one hand, and some high-alumina minerals (such as spinel, sapphirine, cordierite, corundum) and olivine on the other. Residual granitization phenomena also include the formation of hysterogenetic hydrated minerals which are locally abundant, providing that the composition of rocks in which they originated is close to their own. In the latter case, the most common phenomenon is the development of hornblende from pyroxene-plagioclase schists, since the compositions of hornblende and the schists often lie at the same point on the ACF diagram. Another circumstance impeding detection of stable mineral associations is that many rocks do not reflect the delay in metachronic crystallization.

Nevertheless, painstaking studies of rock structures, real mineral associations and ACF diagrams revealed stable mineral associations of the granulite facies in Antarctica. In the present book, the authors avoid discussion of analysis of rare mineral associations, not because they lack interest (on the contrary, they are given major attention in the petrographic descriptions), but because they occur only rarely and in small areas.

In view of the setting of metamorphic rocks in Antarctica, it is important to determine the facies from the most widespread rock types, such as pyroxene-plagioclase schists and various shadow calcareous and aluminous granitoids. The rare mineral associations composing carbonate rocks and the associated calcareous-silicate formations, magnesian schists and quartzites are listed in Table 62. They clearly deserve more attention in future investigations.

To date, three groups of stable mineral associations in pyroxene-plagioclase schists and shadow granitoids have been detected. Each group was found to be highly localized in certain zones of the crystalline basement of Antarctica.

The mineral associations of the first group are: a) for pyroxene-plagioclase schists: $plag_{37-82} + hyp_{30-54} + clpy_{32-46} + (qz) + (Kfs)$; $plag_{42-82} + hyp_{24-54} + (qz) + (Kfs)$; b) for enderbites: $qz + plag_{31-51} + hyp_{41-57} + clpy_{33-34} + Kfs$; $qz + plag_{30-47} + hyp_{37-54} + (Kfs)$; c) for charnockites: $qz + perthite + hyp_{37-72} + (plag_{20-36}) + (clpy)$; d) for garnet and garnet-hypersthene shadow

TABLE 62. Mineral associations of the granulite facies in the crystalline basement of Antarctica

Rocks	Mineral associations		
	Enderby Land	Bunger Oasis	Queen Maud Land
Calciphyres and associated calcareous-silicate rocks	dol + calc dol + calc + oliv$_{0-10}$ + spin$_{0-2}$ dol + calc + oliv$_{0-10}$ + spin$_{0-2}$ + dioP$_{0-9}$ dol + calc + oliv$_{0-10}$ + spin$_{0-2}$ + dioP$_{0-15}$ + phl dol + calc + oliv$_{0-10}$ + dioP$_{0-9}$ dol + calc + oliv + diop + amph oliv + spin + coru . spin + diop + plag + amph + carb spin + diop + plag + amph + phl diop + scap	dol + calc dol + calc + oliv$_5$ + spin$_{1-4}$ + diop$_9$ dol + calc + oliv$_5$ + spin$_{3-4}$ + diop + phl dol + calc + oliv$_2$ + spin$_{1-2}$ + diop$_{15}$ + phl$_3$ + gros dol + calc + oliv$_{10}$ + spin$_3$ + diop + phl$_4$ + amph + gar + scap dol + calc + oliv$_3$ + phl$_4$ spin + diop$_{3-12}$ + plag + phl$_{6-7}$ + (amph) + (carb) diop$_{12}$ + plag$_{69-78}$ + phl + (carb) diop$_{14}$ + plag$_{54}$ + qz diop$_{5\ 34}$ + scap$_{20-68}$ + carb + (qz)	dol + calc dol + calc + oliv$_0$ + spin$_0$ dol + calc + hum + spin$_0$ dol + calc + hum + dioP$_{25}$ + plag$_{80}$ dol + calc + hum + dioP$_{25}$ + plag$_{80}$ diop$_{21-40}$ + plag$_{70-92}$ + phl$_{10}$ + (carb) + (qz) diop + plag$_{92}$ + scap + carb diop$_{33}$ + plag$_{75}$ + amph + carb + qz diop$_{26}$ + scap$_{79-81}$ + (qz) diop$_{30}$ + scap + amph + carb
Magnesian schists (meta-ultrabasites)	oliv$_{14-28}$ + orpy$_{15-20}$ + clpy$_{21-29}$ + cumm$_{15-61}$ + (biot$_{23-41}$) + (plag) orpy$_{15-32}$ + clpy$_{24-37}$ + biot$_{24-28}$ + (cumm$_{66}$) + (plag) orpy + clpy + gar orpy + clpy + gar + cumm + biot + (plag$_{38}$) orpy + biot + plag$_{33}$ + (qz)		oliv$_{10}$ + orpy$_{13}$ + clpy + cumm$_{53}$ + biot$_{25}$ + plag orpy$_{41}$ + clpy + cumm + plag$_{51}$ orpy$_{28}$ + cumm orpy$_{54}$ + cumm + biot + plag orpy$_{27}$ + biot + plag + gar
Pyroxene-plagioclase schists	plag$_{37-82}$ + hyP$_{30-54}$ + clpy$_{32-46}$ + (qz) + (Kfs)	plag$_{33-77}$ + hyP$_{31-54}$ + clpy$_{25-42}$ + (qz)	plag$_{33-79}$ + hyP$_{36-57}$ + clpy$_{23-51}$ + (horn$_{25-56}$) + (biot$_{37-47}$) + (qz)

Garnet-pyroxene-plagioclase schists	plag$_{31-90}$ + hyp$_{25-59}$ + clpy$_{32-48}$ + (horn$_{38-65}$) + (biot$_{24-52}$) + (qz) + (Kfs) plag$_{42-82}$ + hyp$_{24-54}$ + (qz) + (Kfs) plag$_{38-46}$ + hyp$_{41-46}$ + biot$_{36}$ + (horn$_{44}$) + (qz) + (Kfs) plag$_{37-46}$ + clpy$_{37}$ + horn$_{48}$ + biot$_{44}$ + (qz) + (Kfs)	plag$_{32-79}$ + hyp$_{24-55}$ + clpy$_{21-45}$ + (horn$_{34-59}$) + (biot$_{30-61}$) + (qz) + (Kfs) plag$_{41-80}$ + hyp$_{29-52}$ + (horn$_{36}$) + (biot$_{35-38}$) + (qz) + (Kfs)	plag$_{33}$ + clpy$_{40}$ + biot$_{49}$ + qz
Enderbites and rocks intermediate between pyroxene-plagioclase schists and enderbites	plag$_{30-47}$ + clpy$_{40-49}$ + gar$_{74-80}$ + horn$_{35-60}$ + (qz) + (Kfs) + (biot$_{54}$) plag$_{26-80}$ + hyp$_{22-57}$ + clpy$_{24-55}$ + gar$_{52-79}$ + horn$_{50-73}$ + (biot$_{43-50}$) + (qz) + (Kfs)	plag$_{36-40}$hyp$_{54}$ + clpy$_{29}$ + gar + horn + biot + qz + (Kfs)	plag$_{34-57}$ + clpy$_{29-51}$ + gar$_{67-84}$ + (horn$_{45-62}$) + (biot$_{49-53}$) + (qz) + (Kfs) plag$_{30-31}$ + hyp$_{52-64}$ + clpy$_{33-52}$ + gar$_{66-79}$ + horn$_{50-62}$ + (biot$_{47-58}$) + (qz) + (Kfs)
Charnockites	qz + plag$_{31-51}$ + hyp$_{42-57}$ + clpy$_{33-44}$ + Kfs + (horn$_{63}$) qz + plag$_{29-47}$ + hyp$_{36-57}$ + Kfs + (biot$_{37-47}$)	qz + plag$_{27-67}$ + hyp$_{38-74}$ + clpy$_{32-50}$ + (horn$_{59}$) + (biot$_{38-49}$) + (Kfs) qz + plag$_{25-72}$ + hyp$_{35-64}$ + (biot$_{37-51}$) + (Kfs)	qz + plag$_{28}$ + hyp$_{42}$ + clpy$_{37-47}$ + horn$_{52}$ + biot$_{42-44}$ + Kfs qz + plag$_{33}$ + clpy$_{40}$ + biot$_{49}$ + Kfs
	qz + perthite + hyp$_{37-72}$ + (plag$_{20-36}$) + (clpy$_{52}$) + (biot) qz + plag$_{22-36}$ + Kfs + hyp$_{61-76}$ + (clpy$_{73}$) + (horn) + (biot)	qz + plag$_{28-50}$ + Kfs + hyp$_{51-65}$ + (clpy) + (horn$_{57}$) + (biot$_{43}$)	qz + plag + Kfs + hyp$_{73}$ + horn$_{61-94}$ + biot$_{51-86}$ + (clpy)
Garnet-hypersthene shadow granitoids	qz + plag$_{28-48}$ + hyp$_{29-82}$ + gar$_{62-83}$ + (biot$_{28-37}$) + (Kfs)	qz + plag$_{32-40}$ + hyp$_{36-57}$ + gar$_{61-69}$ + (biot$_{44}$) + (Kfs)	qz + plag$_{28-36}$ + hyp$_{59-73}$ + gar$_{77-83}$ + biot$_{48-54}$ + Kfs
Garnet shadow granitoids	qz + plag$_{30-50}$ + gar$_{59-83}$ + biot + (Kfs) qz + perthite + gar$_{62-84}$ + (plag$_{25-35}$) + (biot) qz + plag$_{20-40}$ + Kfs + gar$_{68-78}$ + biot	qz + plag$_{29-39}$ + gar$_{60-66}$ + biot$_{30-51}$ + (Kfs) qz + plag$_{33}$ + Kfs + gar$_{67}$ + biot	qz + plag$_{29-35}$ + gar$_{58-60}$ + biot$_{35-52}$ + (Kfs) qz + plag$_{26-31}$ + Kfs + gar$_{82-84}$ + biot$_{42-57}$
Aluminous schists and their migmatites and shadow granites	qz + spin$_{49-82}$ + sill + cord$_{14-31}$ + (gar$_{53-85}$) + (biot$_{28-40}$) + (plag$_{26-32}$) + (Kfs)	qz + plag$_{27-41}$ + Kfs + spin + sill + gar$_{61-69}$ + biot$_{33-38}$ + (cord$_{14-20}$)	qz + plag$_{22-35}$ + Kfs + sill + gar$_{67-80}$ + biot$_{39-52}$ + (cord)

TABLE 62 (continued)

Rocks	Mineral associations		
	Enderby Land	Bunger Oasis	Queen Maud Land
Aluminous schists and their migmatites and shadow granites	qz + perthite + sill + (plag$_{25}$) + (gar) qz + perthite + spin$_{72}$ + gar$_{68-70}$ + (biot$_{23}$) + (plag$_{20-28}$) + (sill) qz + plag$_{33}$ + Kfs + spin + sill + gar$_{64}$ + cord$_{12}$ + biot qz + spin$_{47-54}$ + sill + (gar$_{52-66}$) + (cord) + (biot) + (grph) + (plag$_{30-56}$) + (Kfs) qz + spin + sill + gar + hyp + (cord) + (spph) + (biot) + (Kfs)	qz + plag$_{25-40}$ + Kfs + spin + gar$_{61-69}$ + cord$_{20-36}$ + biot$_{30-38}$ qz + plag$_{27}$ + Kfs + sill + biot qz + plag$_{21-41}$ + Kfs + sill + gar$_{61-72}$ + biot$_{31-37}$ + (cord$_{20-31}$) qz + plag + Kfs + sill + biot + cord$_{20}$ qz + plag$_{33-42}$ + gar$_{67}$ + (spin) + (sill) + (cord$_{24}$) + (biot$_{38-42}$) + (Kfs)	qz + plag$_{39}$ + Kfs + sill + gar$_{61}$ + biot$_{32}$ + komerupine qz + sill + gar$_{61-70}$ + biot + (Kfs) + (cord)
Quartzites	qz + plag$_{32}$ + Kfs + spin + gar$_{60}$ + hyp$_{50}$ + cord$_{20}$ qz + hyp$_{30-45}$ + cord$_{20-36}$ + (plag$_{35-37}$) + (Kfs) + (spph) + (biot$_{26-37}$) qz + Kfs + sill + (gar) + (spph) + (plag$_{35-67}$) + (biot) qz + sill + hyp$_{13-28}$ + (gar$_{59}$) + (biot$_{15-20}$) + (plag$_{24}$) + (Kfs) qz + gar$_{66}$ + (plag) + (Kfs) + (biot) qz + plag + (Kfs) + (grph) + (biot) qz + Kfs		qz + plag$_{26}$ + Kfs + sill + cord

Note. The numerical subscripts denote the An content in plagioclase, the meionite molecule content in scapolite, and total ferruginosity (at.%) in other minerals.

granites: qz + perthite + gar_{62-84} + $(plag_{24-35})$; qz + $plag_{28-48}$ + hyp_{37-65} +
+ gar_{62-83} + (perthite or Kfs); e) for high-alumina shadow granites:
qz + perthite + $spin_{72}$ + gar_{68-70} + $(plag_{20-28})$; qz + perthite + sill + $(plag_{25})$ +
+ (gar). These mineral associations are depicted in Figure 26, which
indicates the chemical compositions of rocks representing these associations.

Mineral associations of the second group are 1) for pyroxene-plagioclase
schists: $plag_{40-80}$ + hyp_{29-52} + $biot_{35-38}$ + (qz) + (Kfs); $plag_{72}$ + hyp_{31} + $horn_{36}$;
$plag_{33}$ + $clpy_{40}$ + $biot_{49}$ + qz; b) for enderbites: qz + $plag_{25-72}$ + hyp_{35-64} +
+ $biot_{37-51}$ + Kfs; qz + $plag_{33}$ + $clpy_{40}$ + $biot_{49}$ + Kfs; c) for charnockites:
qz + $plag_{22-50}$ + Kfs + hyp_{51-76} + $biot_{43}$; d) for garnet plagiogranites:
qz + $plag_{29-50}$ + gar_{58-83} + $biot_{30-52}$ + Kfs; e) for shadow garnet granites:
qz + Kfs + $plag_{20\;40}$ + gar_{62-84} + $biot_{42-57}$; f) for high alumina shadow granites: qz + Kfs + $plag_{27}$ + sill + biot. These mineral associations are depicted in Figure 26, together with the chemical composition of rocks and
accompanying stable associations.

Mineral associations of the third group are a) for pyroxene-plagioclase
schists: $plag_{34-47}$ + $clpy_{49}$ + gar_{79-80} + (qz) + (Kfs); b) for shadow garnet
granitoids: qz + Kfs + $plag_{20-40}$ + gar_{74-78} + (biot). Mineral associations of
this group are depicted in Figure 26, together with the chemical composition
of rocks (including unstable associations). An analysis of the mineral
associations from the first toward the third group indicates a simplification
of their composition and a narrowing of the compositional range of minerals
due to the fewer mineral associations in the second and third groups.

Mineral associations of the first group are widespread only in the Napier
zone of Enderby Land; they occur sporadically in the Rayner zone of
Enderby Land and in the Bunger Oasis and have not been encountered on
Queen Maud Land. On the other hand, the second group is more common
in the Bunger Oasis, Queen Maud Land and in the Rayner zone of Enderby
Land, but occurs only to a very limited extent in the peripheries of the
Napier zone in Enderby Land. Mineral associations of the third group are
localized in tectonic zones to the east of Enderby Land (along the Wilma
and Robert Glaciers) and along Queen Maud Land (Humboldt Mountains).
It cannot be assumed, however, that the composition of rocks in the regions
characterized by these mineral associations is limited only to these
associations. Unstable mineral associations are extremely widespread
(considerably more widespread than the stable associations, the latter being
only a particular case of the former), as is indicated by data given in Table 62
and by observations of rock structures.

On the basis of the above thermometric and piezometric investigations, the
established groups of stable mineral associations permit the determination
of three subfacies of the granulite facies, formerly known as the pyroxene-
granulite subfacies, hornblende-granulite subfacies /71/ and granulite
subfacies with clinopyroxene and almandine /135, 136/. The first is the
highest-temperature facies, the second is a lower-temperature facies,
while the third facies is characterized by high pressures generated by stress.
The extent of the granulite subfacies occurrence is given in Appendices 1
and 2. The typical occurrence of the pyroxene-granulite subfacies is in the
Napier zone of Enderby Land and that of the hornblende-granulite subfacies

is in the Bunger Oasis. The close similarity of the temperatures of the hornblende-granulite subfacies to those of the amphibolite facies /68, 70/ explains the extensive occurrence of unstable mineral associations, since the cooling of selective melts liberates a certain quantity of water which, at relatively low temperatures, produces additional phases, which are characteristic of the amphibolite facies. The higher temperatures determined in the Rayner zone and also sporadic occurrence of perthitic charnockites and even enderbites within its boundaries, prompted the authors to place these in the region where hornblende-granulite subfacies conditions are superimposed on the metamorphic rocks of the pyroxene-granulite subfacies. On Queen Maud Land and in the extreme west of Enderby Land, stable mineral associations of calcareous-magnesian rocks are usually represented by hypersthene-free clinopyroxene-bearing associations of high alkalinity. This high (potassic) alkalinity develops during granitization and is characteristic of the amphibolite facies, as will be shown below. This feature, as well as the extensive occurrence of unstable mineral associations of the granulite facies in the regions under consideration, indicates that these occurrences resulted from the superposition of the amphibolite facies on mineral parageneses of the granulite facies. Typical occurrences of this kind will be discussed below.

In order to examine the effects of alkali potentials on the formation of mineral parageneses under the granulite facies conditions on Enderby Land, diagrams of the chemical potentials of alkalis for the most widespread rocks were constructed (according to Korzhinskii /33/). For diagrams of the chemical potentials of alkalis for the pyroxene-granulite subfacies of calcareous and moderately aluminous rocks (Figure 27), the following conditions were assumed: T and P, constants; completely mobile components, K_2O and Na_2O; excess component, SiO_2; inert components, Al_2O_3, CaO and isomorphous components, MgO, FeO. Under these conditions, an association of five minerals is nonvariant and is represented in the diagram by a certain point. This pentamineral association is as follows: garnet (gar) + hypersthene (hyp) + clinopyroxene (clpy) + plagioclase (plag) + perthite (orcl). Although this has not yet been established for the pyroxene-granulite subfacies, it is theoretically possible since all five minerals form tetramineral monovariant parageneses. The following simplified mineral compositions were assumed: gar — $(Mg, Fe)_3Al_2[Si_3O_{12}]$; hyp — $(Mg, Fe)SiO_3$; clpy — $Ca(Mg, Fe)Si_2O_6$; plag, An 33 — $(2NaAlSi_3O_8 \cdot CaAl_2Si_2O_8)$; orcl — $(4KAlSi_3O_8 \cdot CaSl_2Si_2O_8)$.

In Figure 27, five divariant fields are delimited, every one of which is characterized by a single-valued correlation between the mineral composition and the ratio of the three inert components. Every field corresponds to a certain metasomatic facies /33/. Indeed, studies of the rocks revealed three of the five facies, denoted by the fields 1, 2 and 3. The first field corresponds to the facies in enderbites, the second field to that in perthitic charnockites, and the third field corresponds to the facies in clinopyroxene perthitic shadow granites (occurring rarely due to the absence of rocks with suitable chemical compositions). The reason for not encountering facies 4 and 5 is also clear. These facies can originate only at a lower Na_2O potential than in the facies of enderbites; however, enderbitization was the most widespread regional process on Enderby Land, as already shown. The relatively rare occurrence of clinopyroxene-bearing chanockites on Enderby Land also finds an explanation, i. e., the diagram shows that these rocks formed at a very high potassium and medium sodium potentials. The extensive occurrence of garnet-hypersthene perthitic shadow granitoids transitional from enderbites to charnockites (fields 1, 2 and 3) and the very limited occurrence of garnet plagiogneisses (fields 1, 2 and the diop reaction) are likewise distinctly illustrated on the diagram. On the basis of the diagram in Figure 27, it is possible to predict still undetected parageneses in the pyroxene-granulite subfacies.

The conditions assumed for constructing the diagram of the chemical potentials of alkalis for the hornblende-granulite subfacies (Figure 28) were the same as those assumed for the pyroxene-granulite subfacies. In order to emphasize the characteristic features of the diagrams in Figures 28 and 27, the following feldspar compositions were assumed for the latter: orthoclase without an admixture of the plagioclase molecule (orcl — $KAlSi_3O_8$) and plagioclase with An 20 (plag — $4NaAlSi_3O_8 \cdot CaAl_2Si_2O_8$). In the diagram of Figure 28, field 1 corresponds to metasomatic facies of enderbites, field 2 to charnockites proper, field 3 to diopside shadow granites, field 4 to diopside-garnet shadow granites, and field 5 to diopside-garnet plagiogneisses. Rocks of the first three metasomatic facies have been encountered ubiquitously on Enderby Land, but those of the fourth and fifth facies have only been tentatively traced in the southeast of Enderby Land (in the region of the Wilma and Robert Glaciers).

Comparison of the above-examined diagrams for two subfacies of the granulite facies leads to the following conclusions: 1) only fields 1 are the same size for both subfacies, denoting equal and widespread occurrence of enderbites in these subfacies; 2) field 2 of charnockites proper is narrower than field 2 of perthitic charnockites, confirming the relatively less widespread occurrence of the former in the hornblende-granulite subfacies; 3) field 3 in the diagram for the hornblende-granulite subfacies is more than double the size of field 3 in the diagram for the pyroxene-granulite subfacies, denoting a considerably more widespread occurrence of the former subfacies and of charnockitoids containing clinopyroxene with or instead of hypersthene; 4) the difference in the dimensions of the 4th and 5th fields suggests a more widespread occurrence of clinopyroxene-garnet shadow granitoids in the granulite subfacies in comparison to the clinopyroxene-garnet plagiogneisses; the relative areal exposures of these rocks are reversed in the hornblende-granulite subfacies. On the whole, the association of clinopyroxene with garnet and feldspars in the pyroxene-granulite subfacies must exist over a broader range of K_2O content than in the hornblende-granulite subfacies, since in the latter, garnet should disappear at a high K_2O content, as is seen in Figure 28 (fields 3 and 2); 5) sillimanite-bearing associations can exist in the hornblende-granulite subfacies within a significantly narrower range of the chemical composition than in the pyroxene-granulite subfacies, and sillimanite must be gradually but completely replaced by orthoclase at lower temperatures; the disappearance of the ferruginous-magnesian garnet

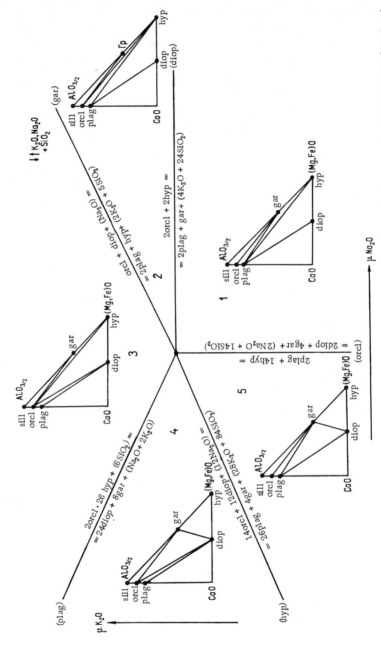

FIGURE 27. Diagram of the mineral parageneses of calcareous and moderately aluminous rocks in relation to the chemical potentials of Na₂O and K₂O for the pyroxene-granulite subfacies.

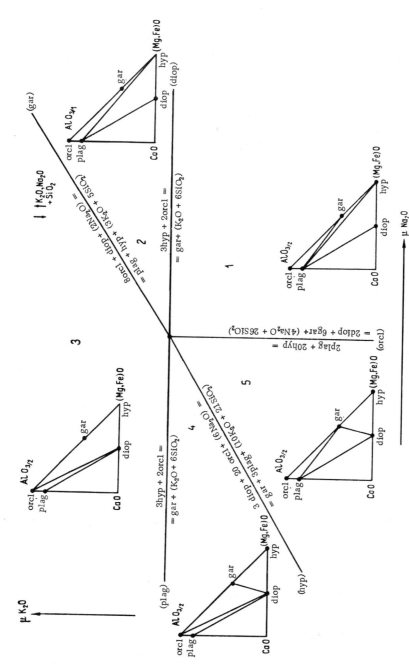

FIGURE 28. Diagram of the mineral parageneses of calcareous and moderate alumina rocks in relation to the chemical potentials of Na_2O and K_2O for the hornblende-granulite subfacies.

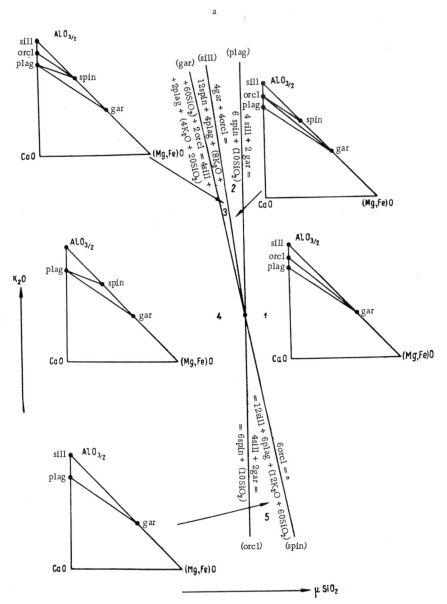

FIGURE 29. Diagram of the parageneses of high-alumina rocks in relation to the chemical

a) for the pyroxene-granulite subfacies; b) for the hornblende-granulite subfacies.

b

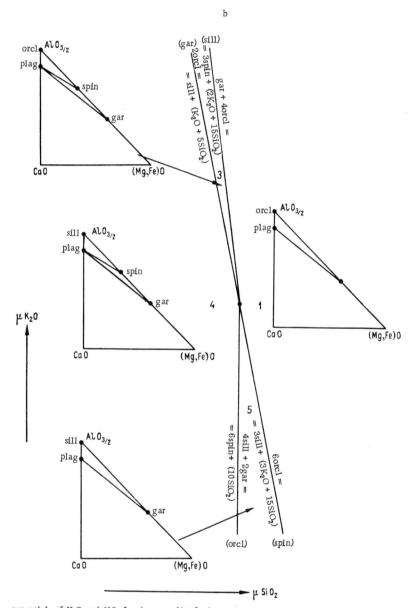

potentials of K$_2$O and SiO$_2$ for the granulite facies:

in fields 2 and 3 (Figure 28) testifies to a higher K_2O potential in the hornblende-granulite subfacies in comparison to the pyroxene-granulite subfacies; 6) a comparison of the paragenetic triangles in analogous fields in the diagrams of Figures 27 and 28 reveals a difference of the calcium content in the garnet related to the magnitude of the chemical potentials of K_2O and Ca_2O; thus, the Ca content of garnet in field 1 may be higher in the pyroxene-granulite subfacies; it is the same for both subfacies in fields 4 and 5, whereas in field 3 the Ca content of garnet in the hornblende-granulite subfacies must be higher than that in the pyroxene-granulite subfacies.

For the investigation of high-alumina rocks in the formation of which a very important part is played by the influx of potassium, the chemical potentials of potassium and silicon were taken as the coordinates. The chemical potential of silicon (although it is present in excess) was taken as a coordinate because of the variability of its content in spinel-bearing rocks (Table 62). The following conditions were assumed for construction of the diagram of the chemical potentials of K_2O and SiO_2: 1) T and P, constants; 2) Na_2O was assumed to be a fully mobile component with a constant potential; 3) K_2O and SiO_2 essentially fully mobile components; 4) Al_2O_3, CaO, (Mg, Fe)O, essentially inert components: pentamineral paragenesis: sill + plag + orcl + gar + spin. The spinel and sillimanite were assumed to have the formular compositions, and the remaining minerals are treated as in the preceding diagrams. From the diagrams in Figure 29a, b, it is distinctly seen that the parageneses of shadow granitoids with spinel are only possible at a low silicon potential. To put it differently, the influx of silica during the formation of shadow granitoids is limited, confirming the assumption concerning the low mobility of silica under the granulite facies conditions as indicated in the description of the granulite facies rocks. The unusually wide fields 1 and 4 indicate that their parageneses are possible at infinitely wide variations of the potassium potential, while the limited size of fields 2, 3 and 5 emphasizes the low mobility of silica as well as the rare occurrence of the parageneses indicated in these fields. Nevertheless, they were discovered (Table 62), and therefore these mineral parageneses may be regarded as critical for the pyroxene-granulite subfacies. In Figure 29b, field 2 disappears because of the impossibility of the parageneses of spinel with garnet and orthoclase and the high potassium potential that is characteristic of the hornblende-granulite subfacies.

Chapter III

POLYMETAMORPHIC FORMATIONS

Blocks of the crystalline basement of the Antarctic Platform which mainly outcrop on the East Antarctica coast are dominated by metamorphic strata of the granulite facies. However, many crystalline basement blocks in the western half of East Antarctica, and especially on Queen Maud Land from Tottanfjella (Tottan Hills) to the Yamato Mountains, are composed of polymetamorphic strata in which the granulite facies rocks underwent superimposed metamorphism in the amphibolite facies. This occurred simultaneously with the formation of monometamorphic amphibolite facies rocks in the adjacent peripheral zones. At this stage of the Antarctic investigations, the following regions are known to be dominated by polymetamorphic rocks: 1) the Humboldt Mountains and Petermann Range (11—13°E) on Queen Maud Land; 2) central part of Queen Maud Land beginning with the Shcherbakov Range (10°30' E) and ending at the Preuschoff Range (4°E); 3) peripheries of the Sør Rondane and Yamato Mountains in the east of Queen Maud Land; 4) Shackleton Glacier region (97—99°E) on Queen Mary Land. There is no doubt that polymetamorphic strata occur also in other areas on the coast of East Antarctica, but they have been only little studied. This also applies to the Mirny Observatory area, where metamorphics (agmatites) have been preserved in skialiths within charnockites. It should be emphasized that, as a rule, intrusive and apointrusive massifs of charnockitic rocks are widespread near polymetamorphic strata.

GEOLOGY AND PETROLOGY OF THE HUMBOLDT MOUNTAINS AND PETERMANN RANGE

Polymetamorphic rocks in the crystalline basement of the Antarctic Platform were best studied in the Humboldt Mountains and Petermann Range, where a geological survey at a scale 1:200,000 was carried out in 1967 in a well-exposed region over an area of 1500 km^2 (Appendix 3). Therefore a detailed description of the geology and petrology of these mountains will shed some light on the formation processes of polymetamorphics, particularly in that they occur in conjunction with charnockitic massifs of complex structures, as well with blocks of monometamorphic rocks of the amphibolite facies. As a result, this chapter diverges somewhat from the general style of this monograph in that it describes specific geological series and bodies (composition and origin) instead of groups of rocks of the same metamorphic facies, as in the other chapters. A description of this kind offers the additional advantage of permitting a direct comparison of the polymetamorphic and monometamorphic rocks of different metamorphic facies, revealing their most essential differences with respect to composition and origin as well as geological setting.

Geological-tectonic structure of the region

At present, the Humboldt Mountains and Petermann Range are block structures located within reactivated crystalline basement rocks of the ancient Antarctic Platform /59/*. The complex mosaic of block mountains is distinguished by the alternation of outcropping uplifted blocks and subsided blocks buried under thick (0.3—0.8 km) continental ice sheets; the total areas of the two types of blocks are approximately the same. The investigated region includes 12 major uplifted blocks, usually trending E—W. Four of these form independent block ranges separated by mountain glaciers. Dimensions of the blocks vary very considerably, from tens of square kilometers up to 600 km². Large blocks are built of smaller blocks, the widths of which are relatively consistent. The faults delimiting the blocks were reactivated during the Meso-Cenozoic, as in other regions of Antarctica /13/. They are apparently normal strike-slip faults with vertical dips. Dislocations along the vertical component of faults do not usually exceed the ice thickness in the fault troughs.

The following three types of blocks can be distinguished by their structural-facies features: 1) those composed of metamorphic rocks of the amphibolite facies; 2) those composed of granulite facies rocks, repeatedly metamorphosed under amphibolite facies conditions; 3) those composed of charnockites and anorthosites. The first group includes the blocks of Mt. Insel, Mt. Sudovikov, Mt. Sphinx, Mt. Dyke, and the Bardin Range, making up a NW striking zone distinguished by the homogeneous composition of its rocks and geological structures. To the east of this zone, the majority of the second group of blocks are composed of intrusive formations. West of it, the largest blocks in the Humboldt Mountains are largely composed of polymetamorphic rocks. Their initial metamorphism under granulite facies conditions was related to older structures of the central massif type, and their final metamorphism took place under amphibolite facies conditions, which was superimposed on rocks of central massifs; it furthermore caused primary metamorphism in rocks of the younger structures which surrounded the central massifs. The anorthosite blocks belong to old structures, since a distinct amphibolite facies metamorphism was superimposed on these rocks, while charnockites are relatively younger, having been formed as a

---

* Here and throughout the monograph, the tectonic-magmatic reactivity is defined as a fundamental tectonic rearrangement of the oldest blocks in the crystalline basement accompanied by the penetration of basaltic and regenerated granitic magmas and also by the development of migmatization and granitization process and the appearance of new mineral associations of the amphibolite facies superimposed on the initial granulite facies rocks.

result of superimposed amphibolite facies metamorphism. Hence, the Humboldt Mountains and Petermann Range expose a heterogeneous crystalline basement distinguished by central massifs of polymetamorphic strata surrounded by blocks of amphibolite facies strata.

The Gorki and Rosa Luxemburg ranges block in the Humboldt Mountains has an area of 600 km^2 and is the largest in the region. According to the bedding of metamorphic rocks of different initial compositions and their granitized and migmatized varieties, the rocks in the block can be differentiated into the following three suites grouped by the authors as the Humboldt Series (from younger to older): 1) the Luxemburg Suite (over 2800 m thick); 2) the Schüssel Suite (about 4000 m thick); 3) the Gorki Suite (over 2200 m thick). The thicknesses of suites were determined from the profile; the Luxemburg and Gorki Suites respectively lie at the top and base of the Humboldt Series. Thus, the thickness of the entire Humboldt Series in this block is over 9000 m. A nearly continuous profile of this suite was studied on the eastern slopes of the range. The high stratigraphic setting of the Luxemburg Suite is indicated by its occurrence in the core of the Humboldt syncline exposed in this block. The limbs of this fold compose the remaining two suites. The span of the Humboldt syncline is about 30 km. Its axis strikes ~E—W along the edge of the Gorki and Luxemburg ranges, along some 26 km. The syncline has been dislocated along its axis by a fault having an amplitude of the order of 1.5 km, which is reflected in the relief of the linear edges of the ridges. The northern limb of the syncline has been uplifted above the southern limb along this fault. The trough of the syncline is undulating, but on the whole it rises more rapidly to the west than to the east and, consequently, the outcrop areas of older suites increase westward. The trough undulation is most pronounced in the Schüssel Suite in the region of Mt. Mechnikov, Mt. Altar and Mt. Kurchatov. The Humboldt syncline, if regarded as an elementary fold, is an oblique open fold of the parallel type /1/. The rocks in the syncline dip at angles of 60—80° and 25—50° in its southern and northern limbs, respectively, in the area of the maximum plunge of the trough, and at angles of 30—60° and 15—40°, respectively, in the area of its westward uplift. Rocks of the Luxemburg Suite dip fairly symmetrically, the most marked asymmetry of the fold beginning in the Schüssel Suite. The rocks dip at angles of 7—40° at the closure of the fold. The trough becomes less steep toward the fold core, and consequently it has a "troughlike" shape in section along the strike.

The limbs of the Humboldt syncline are complicated by oblique and inverted folds and flexures of the second and third orders. The axial planes of these folds dip concordantly with the dip of rocks in the limbs (toward the syncline core). The dips of axial planes decrease in the direction toward the syncline limbs. The largest inversions of the axial planes of third-order folds occur in the northern limb of the syncline. Third-order folds and flexures are clearly visible in exposures, represented by linear open flexure folds. The stratigraphic relationships of the suites are also confirmed by their setting in the third-order folds. Thus, the Schüssel Suite in the central portion of Rosa Luxemburg Range composes the core of an upright, somewhat similar syncline with a normal closure and limb-to-limb span of about 700 m. Rocks of the Gorki Suite are exposed in an oblique anticline that is conjugate with the above syncline, inverted 40° southward (dip of axial plane is 5°), with limb-to-limb span of about 900 m complicated by a syncline with a span of about 80 m. With respect to the type of layering in fold bands, the majority of third-order folds belong to brachystructures with the fold limbs dipping to different sides. Such folds are especially characteristic for areas with a predominance of a single suite. On the other hand, in borderline areas, there are linear structures of the third order, as is the case at the boundary between the Schüssel and Gorki, and Schüssel and Luxemburg suites. In the majority of cases, axes of second- and third-order structures are subparallel to the Humboldt syncline axis, deviations being traceable only in the northern-most portion of the northern limb of the syncline.

Rocks of the Luxemburg Suite have thin partings parallel to the stratification as well as migmatite banding. On the whole, rocks in the southern limb of the Humboldt syncline are monoclinally bedded. Only very rarely do they contain small flexures with spans of up to 5—7 m, broken in their central portion by nearly vertical upthrow faults of amplitudes not exceeding a few meters. Zones of such faults are filled with blastomylonites of the containing rocks. Blastesis of the mylonites corresponds to the level of low-grade amphibolite facies. Small oblique concentric linear drag folds with spans of up to 1 m were observed in the near-axial portion in the southern limb of the Humboldt syncline in partially migmatized rocks of the Luxemburg Suite. The southern, more gently sloping limbs of these anticlines are transected along the banding by veinlets of pegmatitic granite, probably syngenetic with the folds. The axes of these folds are subparallel to the axis of the major syncline. The formation and morphology of these folds, and also the above-described flexures, are related to insufficient plasticity of the relatively homogeneous matter during the folding; the filling of cracks by pegmatite attests to its lower formation temperature in comparison to the vein material of migmatites formed still under the conditions of the granulite facies. Thus, the formation of minor folded forms in this suite was probably related to the metamorphic period of the superimposed amphibolite facies. Bending was the principal formation factor for the minor folds. Small lenticular boudins of meta-ultrabasites up to 2.5 m long and 0.3—0.4 m thick occur in the central part of the Luxemburg Suite profile in the southern limb of the Humboldt syncline. The boudins have indistinct contacts. The inner crystallizational schistosity coincides with the gneissosity of the host rocks. Spaces between the boudins are filled by comparatively leucocratic schists.

In the northern limb of the Humboldt syncline, the lower part of the Luxemburg Suite consists of 30—35% basic schists and 65—70% migmatites, strongly cataclastic and converted to granulitic rocks. The former occur in boudinaged beds 0.3—7.0 m thick (average thickness 2 m) and the latter in beds 0.5—3.0 m thick. The rocks are monolithic. Part of the Luxumburg Suite is distinguished by a combination of relatively large folds with spans of 50—300 m and small-scale plications. An example of such folds is found in the southern part of the Gorki Range where it joins the Rosa Luxemburg Range. The limb-to-limb span of these folds ranges from a few meters to 70 m and their amplitude reaches 70 m. The folds are isoclinal and they are inverted toward 225°. The axial plane is arculate. The folds display a complex undulating shape. A characteristic feature is the presence of comparatively leucocratic garnet-bearing rocks in the nose of folds.

The pyroxene-amphibole-plagioclase schists participating in these folds are
boudinaged in a "ladder" pattern, the angular and plicated boudins being
shifted toward the curves of anticlines.   The spaces between the boudins
are filled with granulitic rocks, "flowing," as it were, around the boudins.
The fold limbs exhibit small random plications with amplitudes ranging from a
few centimeters to tens of centimeters.   The folds are broken by fissures
localized in their limbs, the rocks having been cataclastized along these
fissures.   The vertical amplitude of the movement reaches 5 m.   The formation of such folds is related to the differentiated, variable state of matter during
the entire process, which reacted differently to the movements of the ultrametamorphic period.   A characteristic feature of such folds is the random arrangement of their axes.   In relation to these folds, there are local, still
smaller folds in certain intercalations ("fragmentary" folding related to the
mobile state of matter); their formation suggests a twice-repeated "soften-
ing" of the rocks.   In the upper part of the Luxemburg Suite, only 10—15 % of
the rocks are boudinaged or exhibit disjointed layers and beds of biotite-
amphibole-pyroxene-plagioclase schists; the rest are granulitic migmatites.
In this case, there are only small plications and drag folds with spans of
1—1.5 m, to complicate the bedding of rocks, which is, on the whole, monotonous.   The axes of small folds are subparallel to those of the third-order
folds.   Their amplitudes reach 2 m.   The anticlines are similar (almost
angular, oblique), while the synclines are box-shaped.   Their axial planes
dip away from the cores of third-order synclines.   The steep limbs are
often separated along the stratification by pegmatitic veinlets or filled
cracks, which appear to be syngenetic with the folding.

   The Schüssel Suite has a more variable composition than the foregoing
suite and a correspondingly larger variety of small structural forms.   The
bedding of rocks is monoclinal in the southern limb of the Humboldt syncline
in approximately one-half of the Schüssel Suite exposures; the other half
contains folds with spans of 30—180 m.   The folds are usually oblique,
inverted southward, of the parallel type, with normal curves.   The synclines
are occasionally box-shaped.   The anticlines are represented by isoclines
with disharmonic strata.   Fracture zones are common, but the movement
along them only rarely reaches 50 m, and is usually limited to only a few
meters.   The fracture zones are located in flexures and steep limbs of
anticlines of the fifth—sixth order.   The majority of these folds were formed
by bending, corresponding to a relatively rigid state of the metamorphic
strata.   Isoclinal and box folds, corresponding to a more plastic state of
matter, occur at the top of the suite at the contact with the Luxemburg Suite.
The bottom of the Schüssel Suite at the contact with the Gorki Suite contains
a fairly large quantity (15—20 vol. % of the strata) of lenticular boudins of
basic schists; the host granulites "flow" aroung the boudins.   The size of
boudins does not exceed 0.5 × 20 m.   In the northern limb of the Humboldt
syncline, the groups of Schüssel Suite beds are 200—300 m thick (composed
of finely layered rocks).   They are crumpled into oblique concentric folds
with ordinary curves and limb-to-limb spans of 10—30 m.   The fold axes
undulate from horizontal to inclined (25°).   The limbs dip at 40—55°.   The
curves of folds are often complicated by fissures filled with pegmatitic
granites.   The axes of these folds are oriented parallel to those of the third-
order folds.   Inversion of small folds toward the axial portions of third-
order anticlines is traceable.   The folds gradually peter out and folded beds

alternate with monoclinal beds 300—500 m thick. Plications and small drag folds, as well as ptygmatic folds, are extremely rare; the axial planes of ptygmatic folds are oriented parallel to the strike of the rocks. All rocks of the suite under consideration, except the carbonates, are dominated by augen lenticular structures, granulitic structures, schistosity along the lamination and fine parting, while quartzites even exhibit fracture cleavage. In the authors' opinion, the structural-textural features combined with the described forms of small-scale folding and minor faulting indicate at least two stages of differential movements. This is also confirmed by observations of the boudinage structures in beds of calciphyres and marbles. On the one hand, marble and calciphyre beds were themselves subjected to boudinage and form beady and lenticular bodies up to 50—70 m in size, with the gneissosity of the host rocks "flowing" around them; i. e., the marbles and calciphyres in places underwent rigid deformation and the host rocks plastic deformation. On the other hand, the calciphyre boudins themselves often contain small angular boudins (similar to the matrix of agmatites) of diopside rocks, the interboudin spaces being filled either with silicified calciphyres or with granitic veinlets. In this case, the calciphyres acted as plastic rocks, changing their mineralogical composition. Moreover, the calciphyres become so "softened" that they were rheomorphically injected into the host rocks, forming "eruptive" breccias with calcite cement. Simultaneously, the calciphyres were recrystallized. Thus, observations of the boudinage structures related to the calciphyres permit the establishment of three stages of differential movements.

Small-scale plications with microfold spans of 3—4 cm and amplitudes of 10—25 cm, often occur in the shadow biotite-garnet granites of the Gorki Suite. The dip direction of their axial planes coincides with the gneissosity of the rocks. The microfolds are isoclinal and similar. There are thickenings in the curves of folds, both in the melanocratic and the leucocratic intercalations. Granitic ptygmatite and vertical veinlets without distinct contacts are superimposed on these folds. The ptygmatitic folds are analogous to the microfolds with respect to dimensions and morphology. The largest folds of this type were observed only in the upper portion of the suite, near its contact with the Schüssel Suite. They are represented by isoclinal folds with limb-to-limb spans of up to 3.5 m and asymmetric, rounded curves. The axial planes of these folds dip vertically. Along the steeper northern limbs of synclines there are shear zones along the stratification; granite veinlets penetrate via these shears. Metabasites and basic schists in the Gorki Suite in the majority of cases form irregularly lenticular to angular-rounded boudins up to 5 m in diameter. On the whole, the gneissosity of the host rocks "flows" around the boudins. The interboudin spaces are of complex shape and are filled with pegmatites or granitic rock. Calciphyres and diopside rocks often occur in blocks and slabs oriented across the strike of the host rocks. At the same time, the host shadow granites display steep flexures with spans of up to 3 m, transected along their curves by faults filled with blastomylonites or fine-grained granitic rocks with ill-defined boundaries, in which migmatitic lenticular banding is oriented parallel to the veinlets. Movements along the flexural faults reach 10—12 m. The absence of folds of the fourth—fifth order is a characteristic feature of the Gorki Suite. The axes of small folds in the upper part of the suite are parallel to the axes of the second-order folds. The trends of the axes of small folds vary in the lower portions of the suite. Apparently, the small-scale structures of the Gorki Suite have retained the impression of the plastic state of matter which reacted differently to differential movements of several diastrophic stages during their formation. A small quantity of rigid rocks were boudinaged. Formation of flexures, larger folds and faults syngenetic with the folds is distinctly related to differential movements of the superimposed metamorphism of the amphibolite facies. However, these movements within the Gorki Suite are manifested less distinctly than in the upper suites. In comparison with the latter, the Gorki Suite includes multiple vein formations of several intrusive stages, since gneissified granitic veins were observed in addition to the massive veins.

Small intrusions of charnockitoids occur in marginal portions of the block of the Gorki and Rosa Luxemburg ranges. The geological setting at contacts between older polymetamorphic rocks and monometamorphic rocks of the amphibolite facies is typical of the localization of postorogenic intrusions /69/. The geological setting of anorthosites in this block remains obscure, due to the fact that their contacts were not observed.

The following data are based on a description of the structures of the Humboldt Mountains block:

1. The relative constancy and the thickness of the suites in the Humboldt Series and the composition of their constituent rocks suggest that the accumulation of primary sediments took place in a nondifferentiated, slowly downwarping basin different from typical geosynclines.

2. The principal structure of the region, i. e., the Humboldt syncline, is simple in spite of the complexity of associated small-scale structures; the suites of the Humboldt Series are concordantly bedded in both limbs of the syncline. The textural-structural features and morphology of the small-scale structures are dependent on the physical properties of the rocks during the period of deformation. All suites and their structures had a multistage genesis.

3. The textural-structural elements of rocks and small dislocations are similar in all suites, except for the lower strata of the Gorki Suite in the block margins. Granulitic, augen and lenticular structures are characteristic of a majority of rocks, signifying that the formation or transformation of these rocks took place under conditions of compression and low plasticity. This also explains the small-scale faults accompanied by blastomylonites which, as a rule, are located in the limbs of small folds and flexures.

4. The base of overlying and upper portion of underlying suites exhibit morphologically similar small-scale folds as well as some similarity in the composition of the rocks. Boudins, lenses or intercalations of metabasites, meta-ultrabasites and metavolcanics transformed into basic schists, as well as boudinaged beds of calciphyres, are concentrated in the lower horizons of suites.

5. Three stages of differential tectonic movements are assumed. The main and earliest stage created the major structures in the region (including the Humboldt syncline) during the period of regional metamorphism in the granulite facies. The next stage, occurring soon after it, was related to ultrametamorphism, which tended to complicate the major structures by the

addition of small-scale structural forms, mostly related to plastic deformations. The latest, third stage related to superimposed amphibolite facies
metamorphism occurred predominantly in rigid rocks. Thus, the tectonic
movements of all stages were differential and occurred at dissimilar physical
states of the rocks, resulting in structural disharmony manifested most
markedly in the northern limb of the Humboldt syncline. The tectonic
movements during the amphibolite facies metamorphism are manifested
differently in separate parts of the block and were accompanied by unilateral
compression of the strata (stress) which resulted in the formation of granulites. These occur extensively in the Schüssel Suite and in the adjacent
strata of other suites.

   The Mt. Insel, Mt. Sphinx, and Mt. Dyke blocks and the
Bardin Range have been less thoroughly studied because of poor exposures
in comparison to the Humboldt Mountains. It is therefore difficult to determine their general structure. However, this can apparently be represented
as a synclinorium zone due, among others, to the relatively few granitoid
intrusions. These blocks are composed of migmatites and shadow granites,
all of the amphibolite facies (together termed the Insel Series) with visible
thickness of at least 7 km. In the Mt. Insel and Mt. Sudovikov blocks, the
strata generally dip monoclinally toward the SW. Small-scale plications
with considerable variations in the nature of fold bends are extremely
widespread. The predominant forms are similar folds of the first and second
types /1/, which are usually isoclinal. The limb-to-limb span of microfolds
is 10—20 cm with an amplitude of up to 40 cm. Exposures of migmatites also
exhibit larger folds (with spans of up to 200 m); these are recumbent with
normal fold bends which are locally angular. Their axial dispositions are
variable but generally parallel to the major folds. The limbs of these folds
are complicated by numerous similar drag microfolds with amplitudes of
up to 20 cm and axial planes dipping toward the bends in the major folds.
Boudins in the major rocks of the Insel Series are lenticular (0.3 — 0.4 ×
× 0.2 — 1.5 m) and discordant, probably indicating rotation. Isolated boudins
are numerous. The overall SE strike of the structures in the Insel Series
is preserved in the Mt. Sphinx and Mt. Dyke blocks and in the Bardin Range.
There are also second-order linear folds (spans of up to 3 km). The limbs
are undulant and the axial trends are irregular. There is evidence of compression and diapiric movements in the cores which consist of shadow
granites (similar to the central part of Mt. Sphinx). The dip of the limbs
of the second-order folds is highly variable, generally ranging from 30° to
90°, the steeper limbs generally occurring in overturned folds. Such folds
are very uncharacteristic of the internal structures of beds in the Humboldt
Series. Small-scale folding in these rocks is characterized by 1) parallel
overturned folds with ordinary fold bends (limb span and amplitude
3—4 m) and by 2) similar overturned folds of the second type with acute
bends (span up to 40 cm, amplitude up to 1 m). The former probably are
flow folds, and the latter plastic drag folds. Folds of both types are superimposed by ptygmatic folds with similar axial planes, which occur
parallel to the migmatitic banding or are vertical. Their average limb
spans are 5 cm and the amplitudes reach 20 cm. The ptygmatic folds are
similar to the isoclinal folds with normal folds bends. Ptygmatic folds often
occur in the cores of second-order anticlines. Boudins of basic schists
form lenticular bodies several meters thick which are concordant with the

host gneisses. A characteristic feature of the Insel Series is the large
number of boudinaged dykelike bodies (gently discordant to semicon-
cordant) of metabasites and meta-ultrabasites (up to 10 vol. % of the strata).
These bodies measure 0.5—4 m in thickness and have an angular-blocky, rectan-
gular shape. The interboudin spaces, also with complex shapes, are commonly occupied by migmatized biotite-amphibole plagiogneisses, and locally
by granitic material with a high quartz content. The larger bodies of metabasites and meta-ultrabasites are 10—80 m thick and give rise to reticulate
migmatites. The characteristic third-order structures in the Insel Series
form agmatitic isometric bodies built of granitoids in the Bardin Ridge.
The size of paleosome blocks is 2—20 m, while the metasome (variable
composition) forms 2—40-m thick veins. Diapiric movements are indicated
by the presence in the marginal portions of blocks of the host rocks. On
the whole, it should be noted that the structural forms in blocks of the Insel
Series mostly indicate a plastic state (flowage of rocks), with the exception
of meta-intrusives which are transformed into boudinaged structures. This
is also indicated by the absence of granulitic structures in the rocks, the
extreme rarity of augen-lenticular migmatites and the absence of blastomylonites. In contrast to the Humboldt Series, no indications of several
tectonic stages have been discovered in the Insel Series.

The Mt. Sinitsyn block is composed of gneissic anorthosites, among
which more or less massive rocks occur only in isolated areas. In the
southern part of the block, the gneissosity strikes NE and dips 30° SE; in the
northern part, the gneiss strikes NW and dips 40° SW. The gneissosity often
crosscuts (at up to 90°) bands of melanocratic anorthosites and gabbro-
norites. The gneissic structure in the anorthosites originated during their
recrystallization under amphibolite facies conditions with a unilateral
pressure; i.e., under the same conditions as the Humboldt Series granulites.

The Krasovskii Range, Mt. Shvedov, Mt. Curie and Mt.
Contact blocks are largely composed of charnockites, relict beds of
polymetamorphic rocks and anorthosites. The first two blocks cover an
area of 120—150 km^2 each, while the last three are only 15—25 km^2. The ice-
filled depressions which separate these blocks are possibly composed of
charnockites; in this case the entire massif would exceed 500 km^2. The
massif, in its present-day erosional exposure, has a very complex, extremely
irregular configuration. The charnockites have intrusive relationships to
the surrounding polymetamorphic strata, although no clear traces of contact
metamorphism have been observed. The relationship between the charnockites and anorthosites is complex; the latter are appreciably feldspathized
and fractured at the contact, and isolated large blocks have been preserved
within the charnockites. The charnockites are represented by coarse- to
very coarse-grained massive rocks which underwent cataclasm but were
not gneissified. Their most characteristic feature is the complex relationship
of different varieties ranging from slightly feldspathized gabbro-norites
through diorite-syenites and syenites and granosyenites. All these varieties
often occur concurrently in the same rocky exposures, forming gradual
transitions between one another. In places, the diorite-syenites and syenites
and especially the granosyenites individually form fairly large massiflike
areas. Intrusive contact between all these charnockitic varieties was not
observed; their boundaries are generally rather diffuse. In the authors'
opinion, the charnockitic series are mobilized block intrusions of gabbroids,

part of the ancient complex of the crystalline basement which underwent superimposed metamorphism, which transformed the gabbroids into charnockites. This transformation process, which involved partial melts during the superimposed stage of regional metamorphism together with tectonism, may be defined as typical of granitization. It should be noted that numerous granitic veins, the vein material of agmatites and, lastly, the granitic bodies cross-cutting all the other rocks in the region, are products of the same partial melts.

To conclude this geological description, the following important structural features of the Humboldt Mountains and Petermann Range should be emphasized: 1) the presence of two structural complexes forming the crystalline basement of the Antarctic Platform; 2) the presence of postorogenic block intrusions of charnockites which largely originated from intrusions of gabbroids of the lower structural stage of the crystalline basement; 3) the presence of two regional metamorphic stages — the fundamental stage (probably Upper Archean) occurred under granulite facies conditions and the superimposed stage (probably Lower Proterozoic), under amphibolite facies conditions; 4) the formation of a large concordant body of granulites from granitized rocks of the lower structural stage, which originated under the conditions of stress during the formation of the upper structural stage; 5) the extensive participation of profuse partial melts which originated as a result of the superimposed amphibolite facies metamorphism and were responsible for the charnockitization of the gabbroids and the formation of the abundant granitoid vein series and of agmatites.

This review of the geological-tectonic setting of the region will be followed by a description of the metamorphic suites and series composing the crystalline basement within the Humboldt Mountains and Petermann Range. The intrusive rocks will be described in Chapter V (dealing with charnockites with the exception of granitized agmatized Insel Series gabbroids which have been so strongly altered that they may be described together with the other metamorphics of this series).

Luxemburg Suite

The Luxemburg Suite, which occurs in the core of the synclinal structure, possesses a definite composition differing from that of the other suites in the limbs. It is mainly composed of layered migmatites, with bipyroxene crystalline paleosome rocks altered to different degrees, and granitoids, with sporadic pyroxene relicts and neogenic garnet, forming the metasome. The migmatites are largely cataclastic and are often transformed into garnet-bearing mylonites. The migmatites regularly include boudinaged bodies of metabasites and ultra-matabasites, usually transformed to strongly amphibolized bipyroxene-plagioclase schists. The suite lacks shadow granitoids, calciphyres and quartzites, although these are common in all the other suites in the region.

Bipyroxene schists (intensely amphibolized) formed at the expense of boudinaged sheets of basites. In outcrop, these intrusive bodies are represented by lenses or rounded boudins 3—7 m in diameter. When occurring in migmatites, chains of such boudins extend over hundreds of meters;

in mylonites, the boudins are "stretched," highly schistose and cataclastic
(Figure 30).   The schists, colored dark gray to black, occasionally present
a near-massive habit and medium-grained texture.   They are most often
heterogranoblastic with elements of relict prismatic texture.   They consist
of some 50% basic plagioclase, An 47 to 65 (Table 63).   The plagioclase
content is markedly lower in meta-ultrabasites and the An content increases
to 70.   The other half of the rock consists of colored minerals, with amphiboles predominating over pyroxenes, and orthopyroxene over clinopyroxene.
Titanomagnetite is the only accessory mineral.   There is a slight but
constant admixture of biotite.   A characteristic feature of these schists is
the somewhat high (in comparison to the original basites) ferruginosity of
colored minerals, 40—50% in amphiboles and orthopyroxenes and approximately 10% less in clinopyroxenes.

FIGURE 30.   Boudins and fractured layers of bipyroxene schists within
mylonites formed from migmatites.   Luxemburg Suite, exposure 73.

Migmatites are the most widespread rock in the Luxemburg Suite,
where they often form strata 300—500 m thick.   The prevalent coarsely
layered migmatites have paleosome layers 10—50 cm thick and metasome
layers up to 30 cm thick, the former being somewhat more abundant than

the latter (Figure 31). In places the layered migmatites have been converted to peculiar agmatites, in which fragments of the former have been cemented by leucogranitic veins. The paleosome is represented by dark gray bipyroxene schists, amphibolized and biotitized to varying degrees, with orthopyroxene in a better state of preservation than clinopyroxene. The mineral content varies considerably (Table 63): 20—60% plagioclase and 5—65% hornblende. The amount of preserved pyroxenes is related to that of hornblende. This is especially true of orthopyroxenes (1—15%), whereas clinopyroxenes have often been fully replaced by amphiboles. Generally, amphibolization of the paleosome is the leading process in migmatization. The composition of the plagioclase is subject to marked changes due to the partial recrystallization of the paleosome during migmatization. Beside the nearly prismatic zoned plates of basic plagioclase (An 73 in the center, An 49 in the margins) there are azonal grains of andesine, An 29—36. The ferruginosity of colored minerals is somewhat higher than in the metabasites (up to 52% in pyroxenes, up to 50% in amphiboles, up to 62% in biotites), but it never reaches the ferruginosity of colored minerals in the shadow granites. The metasome is light gray with a yellowish tinge, consisting of fine-grained shadow granitoids containing relicts of pyroxenes as well as amphibole, whereas biotite and sporadic garnet probably developed during migmatization. Morphologically, the metasome is a product of injection. Its composition is nonuniform, the two branches — plagiogranitic and granitic — being distinctly differentiated. The plagiogranitic material contains relicts of pyroxenes, whereas the granitic material contains only biotite and garnet.

FIGURE 31. Microfolded layered migmatites of bipyroxene schists, Luxemburg Suite, exposure 81.

The composition of plagioclase in both varieties is the same and is constant, with the anorthite content showing small fluctuations between 27 and 30% (dropping to 18% only in the most leucocratic rocks). The quartz content is highly variable (15—35%) depending on the nature of its segregations which form comparatively large aggregates, up to 5—7 mm; these enrich the rock nonuniformly, often investing it with a granulitic habit (Figure 32). K-feldspar is usually represented by microcline, its irregular grains corroding the plagioclase and producing profuse myrmekite. Plagiogranitic metasome is characteristic only for layered migmatites. It is entirely granitic in the agmatites formed from the migmatites.

FIGURE 32. Migmatite of bipyroxene-plagioclase schists. Narrow granulitic strips of quartz are visible. Luxemburg Suite. Thin section 271a (×8, crossed nicols).

TABLE 63. Mineral composition and characteristics of Luxemburg Suite rocks

Specimen no.	Composition											
	K-feldspar	plagioclase	quartz	orthopyroxene	clinopyroxene	amphibole	biotite	garnet	ore minerals	apatite	zircon	An content of plagioclase
												Amphibolized
67v		5		43		52						52
73a		55		10	10	20	3		2			51
73b		50		10	7	30	1		2			47
73e		52	o.s.+	22	—	22	1		3			65
263b		50		10	10	26	2		2			39
												Migmatites from
												Paleo
67		50	1	11	9	25	1		3			29
67b		60		14	16	4			4	2		36
81		50		15	—	24	10	o.s.	1			c++—73
												m++—49
												azonal
271a		20	4	1		65	8		2			55—41
												Meta
												a) plagio
67a	—	65	13	5	10	2	3		2			27
271a	—	68	30	1	—	o.s.	1			o.s.		29
												b) gran
81g	25	33	28				3	8	2	1		30
81a	40	20	37				1	2				18
												Cataclasites and mylonites
73v	15	33	17				17	13	3	2	o.s.	
73d	13	40	20				10	15	2	o.s.	"	24
263	20	25	25				6*	20	3	1	"	27
263v	35	30	26				2	6	1	o.s.	"	
263d	30	30	18				5	14	2	1	"	28
												Vein
73	46	14	35				1	3	1	o.s.		25
81v		60	24				13	3	o.s.	"	o.s.	25

* Note. Here and henceforth asterisks indicate minerals for which quantitative spectroscopic

\+ [o.s. = optic sign.]

++ [c. = central, m = marginal portions of grains.]

Mineral constants											
orthopyroxene			clinopyroxene			amphibole			biotite		garnet
n_z	n_x	ferruginosity, at. %	n_z	n_x	ferruginosity, at. %	n_z	n_x	ferruginosity, at. %	n_z	ferruginosity, at. %	n

bipyroxene schists

n_z	n_x	ferr.	n_z	n_x	ferr.	n_z	n_x	ferr.	n_z	ferr.	n
1.702	1.690	30				1.674	1.652	31			
1.720	1.706	46	1.716	1.689	33	1.681	1.656	37			
1.725	1.710	48	1.718	1.692	37	1.686	1.661	43			
1.720	1.706	46				1.687	1.662	44			
1.725	1.710	48	1.718	1.692	37	1.686	1.661	40	1.643	47	

bipyroxene schists

s o m e

n_z	n_x	ferr.	n_z	n_x	ferr.	n_z	n_x	ferr.	n_z	ferr.	n
1.719	1.705	44	1.720	1.694	41	1.694	1.672	52			
1.725	1.710	48				1.692	1.665	47	1.646	49	
1.730	1.715	52				1.687	1.662	41	1.662	62	

s o m e
granitic

n_z	n_x	ferr.	n_z	n_x	ferr.	n_z	n_x	ferr.	n_z	ferr.	n
1.718	1.704	43	1.721	1.694	42				1.646	49	

itic

(from migmatites)

n_z	n_x	ferr.	n_z	n_x	ferr.	n_z	n_x	ferr.	n_z	ferr.	n
									1.648	51	1.790
									1.658	58	1.790
									1.660	60	

granites

analysis was performed.

Cataclasites and mylonites are fairly widespread. In the suite dominated by migmatites, an overwhelming majority of these stress rocks are formed at their expense. Mylonitization considerably alters not only the habit and structure of rocks but also their mineral composition. Recrystallization renders the mylonites nearly plastic, often enveloping rigid boudins and lenses of metabasites (Figure 29), resulting in light colored, almost white, finely banded, fine-grained rocks exhibiting distinctly visible individual feldspar grains and also lenticular quartz aggregates elongated in one direction. Their structure is most frequently mylonitic, complicated by porphyroclasts and fine-grained aggregates. The mylonite matrix, with granules of some 0.01 mm in size, preserves a considerable quantity of clastic plagioclase grains (0.5—1 mm) and isometric garnet (1—3 mm). K-feldspar grains (0.5—2 mm) of a most intricate form are indicative of recrystallization. The mineral composition of mylonitized migmatites is fairly consistent, although the contents of individual minerals are variable: 25—40% plagioclase, 15—35% K-feldspar, 15—25% quartz, 2—17% biotite and 5—20% garnet. Together with relict, accessory and ore minerals, there is a constant admixture of apatite (1—2%) and very small grains of zircon. The cataclasites and mylonites do not contain pyroxenes or hornblende.

Granite veins occur only to a limited extent in the suite under consideration. They are most commonly concordant, rarely discordant, and their thickness varies from 30 to 60 cm. The following differentiation may be made with respect to their composition: a) older veins of plagiogranites, heavily cataclastized and even mylonitized and hence banded; b) veins of younger, relatively lightly cataclastized alaskite granites. Characteristically, the plagiogranite veins exhibit only a high biotite content (up to 15%) and the presence of garnet, although the narrow endocontact melanocratic fringes consist of up to 50% pyroxenes and amphiboles. These veins have preserved relatively large (2—3 mm) porphyroclasts of oligoclase (An 25). K-feldspar is absent. On the other hand, nearly one half of the alaskite veins are composed of fractured microline, while the oligoclase is relict. They also have a very low content of colored minerals, with a prevalence of garnet, and only an insignificant admixture of biotite.

Schüssel Suite

The Schüssel Suite is composed of unique rocks which occur only in this suite, clearly reflecting the characteristic features of the primary granulite and superimposed amphibolite facies. Over one half of the total volume of the suite consists of unusual granulites formed from layered migmatites and shadow granitoids (mainly ultrametagenic charnockites and less commonly enderbites). Such rocks contain relict associations of granulite facies minerals coexisting with the newly formed amphibolite facies minerals; the latter often completely displace minerals of the former association. During the superimposition of the amphibolite facies, the rocks were recrystallized under stress at depths appropriate to the facies. A small part (up to 15 vol. %) of the suite is composed of polymigmatites. The content of calciphyres and quartzites is even lower. The latter form

sheets of a few meters to tens of meters in thickness and are often strongly
boudinaged. Finally, among the granulites sheets of metabasites occur,
which were transformed into strongly amphibolized and biotitized bipyroxene
schists (up to biotite-bearing amphibolites).

Granulites are the marker rocks in the Schüssel Suite. Judging from
their colored mineral content (relict pyroxenes and neogenic amphibole,
biotite and garnet), they may be arbitrarily subdivided into melanocratic
(25—30%), mesotype (15—20%) and leucocratic (up to 10% colored minerals).
The melanocratic granulites were apparently finely layered migmatites prior
to granulation; the leucocratic granulites were shadow granites, and the
mesotype granulites were intermediate formations. Recrystallization
not only obliterated the primary textures and structures of the migmatites
and shadow granites, but was moreover accompanied by a gradual disappearance of pyroxenes and also partially of amphiboles (replaced by garnet and
biotite). As a result, two types of granulites were formed: a) bipyroxene-
garnet granulites and, b) biotite-garnet granulites. Both types occur
together in the same exposures, but more commonly they form independent
layers, tens of meters thick. The more thorough the recrystallization, the
smaller is the amount of relict pyroxenes, which disappear in the lightest-
colored and most garnet-enriched varieties. It is therefore preferable to
provide separate descriptions of these two types of granulites, the more so
since the biotite-garnet granulites possibly were partially formed at the
expense of granitized aluminous schists.

Bipyroxene-garnet granulites, usually containing amphibole and sporadically a small admixture of biotite, resemble light-colored finely layered
migmatites in their external appearance. They are strongly schistose, and
consequently thin partings are common in outcrops. Basically these are
fine- and very fine-grained, fairly dense rocks with porphyroblastic textures.
Granulitic textures, mainly due to parallel ribbon-lenticular quartz segregations, developed against the general background of heterogranoblastic
textures with predominantly small (0.3—0.7 mm), irregular mineral grains.
The granulitic texture is to a certain extent disturbed by garnet porphyroblasts
(1—3 mm, rarely up to 1 cm) and also irregular segregations of K-feldspar
(2—3 mm). The colored minerals usually form catenary aggregates. Pyroxene grains are often skeletal due to an abundance of inclusions and ingrowths
(in particular, quartz or ore minerals) The grain size of the pyroxene varies
between 0.1 and 0.7 mm, while amphibole grains with prismatic outlines
reach 1—1.5 mm (Figure 33). Plagiogranitic varieties, which can be distinguished among the granulites, play a very subordinate role. Their
composition resembles that of enderbites, although their pyroxenes have
only been partially preserved. The prevailing colored minerals are
biotite and garnet (15—30%). Plagiogranitic granulites form isolated
layers of variable thickness (1—10 m) among normal granulites.

Enderbitic granulites (Table 64) are distinguished by a predominance
of antiperthitic plagioclase (40—65 %) with a highly variable An content,
from 27 to 46. Fine-grained plagioclase aggregates with a grain size of
up to 0.3—0.5 mm are common. The aggregates often contain broken
tabular grains, generally of albite, up to 1 mm in size, with bent polysynthetic
twins. The quartz content is 15—30% in a variety of segregations, including
mosaic aggregates of small grains, metablastic relatively large grains and

finely lenticular (filiform) aggregates stretched in one direction; consequently the typical granulitic texture in the rocks is not very distinct. K-feldspar occurs sporadically and in small amounts (2—6 %). The amount of antiper-thitic ingrowths in the plagioclase is also relatively small. The ferruginosity of colored minerals is close to that of the minerals in the paleosome of the migmatites; 54—62 % in orthopyroxene and 63—67 % in biotites coexisting with the orthopyroxene. A low ferruginosity (29—47%) is found only in biotites of a later generation (diaphthoritic). Along with these occur isometric garnet grains (1—2 mm) with irregular outlines, also of low ferruginosity in com-parison to garnets of all other granulite varieties. Plagiogranitic granulites approach melanocratic varieties in their colored mineral content. The recrystallization was incomplete, and the newly formed minerals are more often diaphthoritic. On the whole, such granulites constitute intermediate varieties between the migmatites and granulites.

FIGURE 33. Shadow granite transformed into granulite (thin section 280, ×11, crossed nicols).

Bipyroxene-garnet granulites with alkaline K-feldspars originate from ultrametagenic charnockites and similar migmatites, which underwent relatively deep-seated recrystallization under unilateral pressure (stress); this resulted in rocks with specific granulitic textures and also with a nonequilibrium mineral association of the granulite and superimposed amphibolite facies. The former have been considerably reworked during amphibolite facies metamorphism. The composition of these granulites is fairly characteristic (Table 64); their plagioclase content is variable (20—40%) with a stable An content: oligoclase, An 25—30 and less commonly An 21—24. They also contain 15—25% each of perthitic K-feldspar and quartz. Clinopyroxene (3—10%) is more common than orthopyroxene (2—5%); both pyroxenes possess a distinctly high ferruginosity; 60—70% for ortho-pyroxene, 55—75% for clinopyroxene, which is in general the largest for metamorphic rocks in the region. The secondary minerals include horn-blende, garnet and biotite; their secondary character is manifested in the segregation forms. The nearly black common hornblende (3—8%) occurs in prismatic grains up to 2 mm in length, which are often diablastic due to an abundance of ore inclusions and less abundant relicts of pyroxene. Its ferruginosity reaches 70%. The dark red (pink in thin sections) garnet (10—15%) is represented by isometric, often porphyroblastic segregations of 1—2 mm (occasionally up to 1 cm), generally with irregular baylike outlines and a diablastic texture due to an abundance of small inclusions of pyroxenes and quartz ingrowths; the ferruginosity of the garnet is 70—30%. Up to 1—3% fine biotite flakes (0.5—1.0 mm) are usually associated with amphibole laths which penetrate into the garnet and pyroxenes via cracks and which contain symplektitic quartz ingrowths; their ferruginosity is high, reaching 78%. Accessory minerals of these granulites are very specific. The predominant accessory mineral is titanomagnetite occurring in small irregular grains (occasionally replaced by sphene), amounting to 3—6%. Minute, often broken apatite crystallites (1—2%) and sporadic zircon granules (0.2—0.5 mm), often of a clastic habit, are ubiquitous. The range of acces-sory minerals reflects the nature of the parent rocks of the granulites in question (basic schists and plagiogneisses) which are enriched in ore minerals and also indicates intensive granitization of the granulites which contain apatite and zircon. The latter minerals are not recrystallized during granulation, but are fractured.

The biotite-garnet granulites do not include any plagiogranitic varieties. They are often finely interbedded with bipyroxene-garnet varieties, but more commonly form independent beds, tens of meters thick. Their colored mineral content varies from 10 to 30%; it is thus possible to differentiate between melanocratic, mesotype and leucocratic varieties, with distinct ribbon structures of quartz aggregates and extremely minute (generally less than 0.1 mm and rarely up to 0.3 mm) matrix grains. Garnet porphyroblasts (2—3 mm) and xenoblastic segregations of perthitic K-feldspar (1—2 mm) are disseminated throughout the matrix. Fine-grained, light-colored rocks (white, pale pinkish yellow and pale gray) with disseminated bright red garnet crystallites are limited to the Schüssel Suite and form its marker horizons. The granulites (Table 64) display considerable fluctuations of the rock-forming minerals, especially colored minerals, depending on the degree of their recrystallization. The K-feldspar content (microcline or perthitic orthoclase, triclinized to varying degrees) varies from 15 to 55%;

TABLE 64. Mineral composition and characteristics of rocks in the Schüssel Suite

Amphibolized and biotitized

Specimen No.	K-feldspar	plagioclase	quartz	orthopyroxene	clinopyroxene	amphibole	biotite	garnet	carbonate	scapolite	ore mineral	apatite	sphene	zircon	rutile
558v		50		19*	5*	22*	3				1				
819v		45	5	3	13	12	20				2				
820a		50	1	3	18	4	18				5	1			
823b		45		43	9						3				
91g		58	1	9	12	8	5				4	3			
565		55	1	16*	12*	3	7				4	2			
809b		50		14	9	13	12				2	o.s.+			
824v		55	2	o.s.	2	18	18				3	2			

Amphi

Specimen No.	K-feldspar	plagioclase	quartz	orthopyroxene	clinopyroxene	amphibole	biotite	garnet	carbonate	scapolite	ore mineral	apatite	sphene	zircon	rutile
553b		10	7			50	10				13	10			
819g		40			o.s.	50*	6				3	1			
820b		42			"	55	3								
560b		45	5		"	23	22				2	1	2		

Migmatites from metamorphosed

Paleo

Specimen No.	K-feldspar	plagioclase	quartz	orthopyroxene	clinopyroxene	amphibole	biotite	garnet	carbonate	scapolite	ore mineral	apatite	sphene	zircon	rutile
65	10	40	21				8	6	10			3	2		
64	1	50	23			2	9	6	5			3	1		
64a	2	45	3			17*	23*	5*	4*			1	o.s.		
64v		58	25			7	5	2				2	1		
64g		13				42	12		25			6	2		
76		54	2	7		10	20	3				4			
77		50	22					14*	12*			1	1			o.s.
78a	3	50	3	4		16	2	20				2	o.s.	o.s.	
78g		65		6		8	8	7				4	2		
79	5	50	20				3	16				3	2		1	
80a	o.s.	45	12			18	2	20				2	1			o.s.
292-1		28	14					28	30							»
822a	10	37	18				10	6	13			4	2			»
98a	5	60	5	2		10		16				2	o.s.			»
573a	2	36	10			10	3	5	25			4	3		2	
823a	8	42	6	6		8		5	15			6	4		

Paleosome of agmatites

Specimen No.	K-feldspar	plagioclase	quartz	orthopyroxene	clinopyroxene	amphibole	biotite	garnet	carbonate	scapolite	ore mineral	apatite	sphene	zircon	rutile
74g		45				10	o.s.	40*				5				
99a		53		35*			11*					1				
233		45	1	13*	22*	13	2*					4				

An content of plagioclase	orthopyroxene			clinopyroxene			amphibole			biotite		garnet
	n_z	n_x	ferrugino-sity, at. %	n_z	n_x	ferrugino-sity, at. %	n_z	n_x	ferrugino-sity, at. %	n_z	ferrugino-sity, at. %	n
bipyroxene schists												
37	1.712	1.698	38	1.712	1.686	28	1.668	1.643	25			
53	1.730	1.715	52	1.719	1.694	38	1.688	1.664	43	1.646	49	
	1.737	1.721	57	1.723	1.696	45				1.655	56	
50				1.722	1.697	44	1.701	1.677	55			
34	1.738	1.722	58	1.726	1.699	49	1.700	1.675	54	1.670	67	
39	1.721	1.706	46	1.718	1.690	37	1.695	1.670	50	1.654	55	
c^{++}–65	1.724	1.709	47	1.715	1.686	32	1.680	1.654	35	1.654	55	
m^{++}–80												
46				1.710	1.685	25	1.674	1.650	31	1.654	55	
bolites												
—												
50												
53							1.686	1.660	40			
45							1.678	1.651	34			
bipyroxene schists												
some												
31												
34				1.718	1.693	37	1.698	1.674	52	1.657	58	1.785
34				1.716	1.690	33	1.694	1.670	48	1.655	56	1.782
38				1.720	1.694	41	1.697	1.672	51	1.655	56	1.780
				1.720	1.694	41	1.697	1.672	51			1.782
	1.745	1.729	64	1.725	1.699	46	1.708	1.684	61			
56										1.638	43	1.788
42	1.744	1.728	64	1.721	1.695	42				1.672	69	
37	1.734	1.719	57	1.718	1.692	37	1.685	1.661	40	1.650	52	
42				1.718	1.692	37				1.666	64	
37										1.626	34	1.785
38	1.730	1.715	52	1.716	1.690	33				1.654	55	
37				1.725	1.699	48				1.671	69	1.795
41	1.728	1.713	50	1.720	1.695	41	1.693	1.670	56	1.654	55	1.790
(schists from metabasites)												
80—88							1.674	1.650	31	1.627	35	1.780
80—86	1.708	1.695	34				1.682	1.658	37	1.620	29	
79—80	1.729	1.714	51	1.719	1.693	38	1.660	1.633	18			

TABLE 64 (continued)

Specimen No.	Composition														
	K-feldspar	plagioclase	quartz	orthopyroxene	clinopyroxene	amphibole	biotite	garnet	carbonate	scapolite	ore mineral	apatite	sphene	zircon	rutile
Meta															
65b	20	40	14				5	17			1	1			2
98		67	7				6	18			o.s.				2
99	1	53	30				3	12							
64b	14	45	28				6	2			4	1		o.s.	
74b	33	30	25				1	10						»	1
76a	40	28	23				2	6			1			»	
77a	45	26	20				3	6			o.s.			»	
78a	40	20	27				3	10			»				
79a	50	12	15			7	15				1		o.s.	o.s.	
80b	26	30	35				3	5			1		»		
99v	32	32	24				o.s.	11			1			o.s.	o.s.
292	44	30	20					6							
822	37	25	28				5	4			1			o.s.	
Metasome															
233a		59	22	5		1	8		o.s.		3	2		o.s.	
233b	17	40	28		o.s.		14	o.s.			1	o.s.		»	
Finely layered migmatites and shadow															
Plagiogranitic															
821a		60	24	10*		o.s.	4*				2	o.s.			
91	4	53	30	2	o.s.	»	11					»		o.s.	
558a		65	16		12		11				2	1	4	»	
558b	6	45	22	o.s.		10	1	10			4	2		»	
66		56	27				4	10				2			1
74		50	25			o.s.	13	12*			o.s.	o.s.		o.s.	
74d		40	25	o.s.			15	18			2		»		
99g	2	50	13				14	16			3	2			
279b	3	63	6		15	4	1	3			3	2			
Granitic															
a) Bipyroxene-garnet															
277b	12	45	8	4	10	3	o.s.	11			5	2		o.s.	
278	15	40	7	5	7	7		13			4	2		»	
278a	12	45	7	5	7	7		13			3	1		»	
279	30	30	11		7	2		15			3	2			
553	23	27	22	—	7	2	o.s.	14			4	1		o.s.	
555	18	30	20	—	8	3		17			3	1		»	
557	20	27	20	3*	6*	4*	1	12*			5	2		»	
557a	23	30	20	2	4	6		10			3	2			
558	15	38	20		3	6	1	10			5	2			
559	18	33	20	2	7	3		10			5	2		o.s.	
559a	13	45	15			15		6			4	2		»	
560a	10	26	18	3	10		3	22			6	2		»	

An content of plagioclase	orthopyroxene			clinopyroxene			amphibole			biotite		garnet
	n_z	n_x	ferrugino-sity, at. %	n_z	n_x	ferrugino-sity, at. %	n_z	n_x	ferrugino-sity, at. %	n_z	ferrugino-sity, at. %	n
some												
30												
20												
38										1.624	33	1.764
24										1.642	46	1.780
										1.646	49	1.795
27												—
34							1.711	1.687	65	1.660	59	1.803
										1.672	69	
33												
of agmatites												
38	1.747	1.730	66							1.670	67	
35												

granitoids transformed into granulites

c o m p o s i t i o n

An content of plagioclase	n_z	n_x	ferr.	n_z	n_x	ferr.	n_z	n_x	ferr.	n_z	ferr.	n
32	1.732	1.717	54							1.670	67	
27	1.742	1.726	62							1.665	63	
40												
27												
35—38										1.620	29	1.770
46										1.643	47	1.788
38										1.627	35	1.785
35				1.735	1.709	64						1.804

c o m p o s i t i o n

varieties

An content of plagioclase	n_z	n_x	ferr.	n_z	n_x	ferr.	n_z	n_x	ferr.	n_z	ferr.	n
30	1.746	1.730	64	1.731	1.706	57	1.704	1.680	58			1.795
28	1.751	1.734	69	1.730	1.705	56	1.706	1.682	59			1.795
28	1.750	1.733	68	1.732	1.707	59	1.707	1.683	60			1.799
31				1.739	1.714	71						1.799
28				1.732	1.707	59	1.706	1.686	59			1.799
29												
30	1.740	1.724	60	1.730	1.705	56	1.708	1.683	61			1.795
27												
30												
29												
29												
30	1.738	1.722	58	1.724	1.697	46				1.665	63	1.792

TABLE 64 (continued)

Specimen No.	Composition														
	K-feldspar	plagioclase	quartz	orthopyroxene	clinopyroxene	amphibole	biotite	garnet	carbonate	scapolite	ore mineral	apatite	sphene	zircon	rutile
560g	18	27	15	4	10		3	15			6	2		o.s.	
570	24	30	22		7	1		13			2	1		"	
571	20	35	20		3	8	2	6			4	2		"	
572	20	30	19		6	3	o.s.	17			4	1		"	
573	20	25	20		6	6	2	15			4	2			
814a	23	27	22		7	4		14			2	1		o.s.	
815	22	25	20		8	4		18			2	1		"	
816	22	30	13	3*	7*	5*	1	15*			3	1		"	
816v	13	40	20		5	7		10			4	1		"	
817	20	36	18		3	7	1	10			4	1		"	
818	25	28	18		3	12		10			3	1		"	
818a	26	27	15	2	5	7		12			4	2	o.s.	"	
820	22	33	20		5		4	13			2	1		"	
823	22	35	15	3	7	2	o.s.	12			3	1		"	
567	44	11	16		6	7*	1	12*			2	1		"	
568b	27	22	15		5	7	3	16			3	2			
280	20	40	26	1	2	2	1	7			1	o.s.		o.s.	
565a	12	45	25	8*			5	3*			2			"	

b) Biotite-garnet

Specimen No.	K-feldspar	plagioclase	quartz	orthopyroxene	clinopyroxene	amphibole	biotite	garnet	carbonate	scapolite	ore mineral	apatite	sphene	zircon	rutile
74a	20	25	25				20	10			o.s.	2		o.s.	
78e	35	25	15	o.s.		17	5	—			1	2		"	
277a	30	26	18			15	2	5			3	1		"	
556d	10	45	24			12	6				1	2		"	
561b	30	30	18				5	15			2	o.s.		"	
824	15	30	17			13	12	7			2	2	1		1
824a	40	16	20	1		15	5				2	1			o.s.
824g	40	10	17				10*	20*			2	1		"	
819	10	40	25				10*	12*			2	1		"	
819a	18	32	23				12	13			1	1		"	
91a	18	40	20			7	13				2	o.s.		"	
100	33	28	28				3	7			1	1		"	
100a	30	23	28				7	10			1	o.s.		"	
100b	32	28	26				3	10			1	o.s.		"	
100g	38	24	30				2	6			o.s.	"		"	
556	18	40	25			4	7	3			1	2		"	
560	30	20	34				2	13			1			"	
561	27	35	20				8	6			2	2		"	
571b	55	13	20			7	3				2	o.s.		"	
564	52	17	20			6	2				2	"	o.s.	"	
277	48	3	47			o.s.	1				1				

	Minerals characteristics											
	orthopyroxene			clinopyroxene			amphibole			biotite		garnet
An content of plagioclase	n_z	n_x	ferruginosity, at. %	n_z	n_x	ferruginosity, at. %	n_z	n_x	ferruginosity, at. %	n_z	ferruginosity, at. %	n
31												
24				1.742	1.716	75						
28				1.731	1.706	57						
25				1.734	1.710	63	1.710	1.689	63			1.802
							-1.715	-1.693	69			
30				1.731	1.706	57	1.705	1.681	59			1.795
25				1.728	1.703	52	1.706	1.686	59			
27				1.740	1.716	72	1.720	1.700	87			1.802
29	1.748	1.731	66	1.733	1.707	61	1.707	1.683	60			1.795
27												
28				1.727	1.702	50	1.703	1.680	57			1.795
24				1.729	1.704	54	1.708	1.684	61			1.819
	1.747	1.731	65	1.730	1.705	56						1.795
30				1.723	1.696	45						1.792
	1.754	1.737	71	1.730	1.705	56	1.710	1.685	64			1.795
27				1.737	1.710	67	1.712	1.688	66			1.804
27	1.752	1.735	70	1.730	1.705	56	1.711	1.687	65	1.685	78	1.795
21	1.732	1.717	55							1.660	59	1.795

varieties

										1.650	52	1.799
24							1.709	1.685	63			1.795
31												
28												
29				1.736	1.711	66	1.711	1.687	65			1 803
30										1.663	61	1.795
28										1.650	52	1 795
29												
28												
										1.650	52	1.800
27												
30										1.656	57	1.795
27												
25												

TABLE 64 (continued)

Specimen No.	K-feldspar	plagioclase	quartz	orthopyroxene	clinopyroxene	amphibole	biotite	garnet	carbonate	scapolite	ore mineral	apatite	sphene	zircon	rutile
											Composition				
556a	40	28	27			o.s.	3					2			
569	65	26	1				2					5			
809	15	50	28				7							o.s.	
824b	50		45				1	2			2				
818b	43	15	37					5			o.s.			„	

Calci

Specimen No.	K-feldspar	plagioclase	quartz	orthopyroxene	clinopyroxene	amphibole	biotite	garnet	carbonate	scapolite	ore mineral	apatite	sphene	zircon	rutile
66a		4			90		3		o.s.				1		
78b		2			50		46		„	20		2			
79v					78	o.s.	1		„	20		1	o.s.		
79g		5			80		o.s.		„	15					
79d		1			70				1	26			2		
80		1			70				2	25			2		
278b			3		30			13	1	26			o.s.		
278v		15	10		18	1			2	50		1	3		
280a		3			90				o.s.	6		1			
556b		o.s.			90	10			„	o.s.					
556v		7			80	6	2		„	3					
819d		1	1		14	5	2		70	6		o.s.	1		
815a					5	4	3		65	o.s.					
815v					80		1		9	10			o.s.		
98g	3	7			45	1			7	35	2		„		
98d			2		5				5	32			1		
568					50	2	3		33	10			2		
568v			7		25				o.s.	57	2	1	8		

Quart

Specimen No.	K-feldspar	plagioclase	quartz	orthopyroxene	clinopyroxene	amphibole	biotite	garnet	carbonate	scapolite	ore mineral	apatite	sphene	zircon	rutile
78	10	2	87		o.s.		1				o.s.				o.s.
79b	12	2	85	o.s.							1				„
571a	25	9	65											1	

Granitic

Specimen No.	K-feldspar	plagioclase	quartz	orthopyroxene	clinopyroxene	amphibole	biotite	garnet	carbonate	scapolite	ore mineral	apatite	sphene	zircon	rutile
77b	8	35	37				3	15*				2			
809a	20	50	30				o.s.								
553a	25	40	25			1	4	2			3	o.s.		o.s.	
568g	25	36	35				4						o.s.		
74v	52	15	28				o.s.	3			2				
91v	50	20	25				5								
98b	54	21	20				5							o.s.	

Notes. Specimen 819a, monazite, o.s.; specimen 278b, wollastonite, 27%, n_Z = 1.632, n_X = 1.618; specimen n_O = 1.663, forsterite 22%, n_Z = 1.677, n_X = 1.643; specimen 98d, wollastonite, 55%, n_Z = 1.632, n_X = 1.618;

+ [o.s. = optic sign.]
++ [c & m = central and marginal portions of grains, respectively.]

An content of plagioclase	orthopyroxene			clinopyroxene			amphibole			biotite		garnet
	n_z	n_x	ferruginosity, at. %	n_z	n_x	ferruginosity, at. %	n_z	n_x	ferruginosity, at. %	n_z	ferruginosity, at. %	n
30 / 25										1.645	48	1.808
phyres												
80				1.724	1.697	46	1.695	1.673	50	1.650	52	
				1.703	1.678	13				Phlogopite 1.594	12	
37				1.732	1.705	60						
							Actinolite 1.645	1.619	24			
							Cummingtonite 1.656	1.632	20	Phlogopite 1.578	6	
94				1.728	1.700	52						
				1.708	1.680	21						
zites												
veins												
31												1.782
30												
26												
24												

556v, humite, 2 %; specimen 819d, calcite, n_O = 1.663; specimen 815a, spinel, 1 %, calcite, specimen 568, calcite, n_O = 1.658, scapolite, n_O = 1.587, n_e = 1.553 (~ 85 % meionite molecule).

oligoclase-andesine (An 24—31) 20—40%; quartz 20—30%; and garnet 5—20%. Amphibole, 4—17%, has been preserved in places, mostly in the melanocratic varieties. However, where granitization is strong, the amphibole is replaced by biotite. Pyroxenes are essentially absent, except for rare clinopyroxene relicts. The ferruginosities of the principal colored minerals are relatively high, 52—61% for biotite, 65—70% for amphibole and 83—90% for garnet. The accessory minerals are similar to those already described for the pyroxene-garnet granulites. However, the biotite-garnet varieties have a considerably smaller ore mineral content, a larger content of apatite and zircon and, most important, they contain sporadic grains of monazite.

An analysis of the geological setting, structure and composition of Schüssel Suite granulites in their entirety yields the following characteristic features: a) the occurrence of granulite strata with a total thickness of up to 4 km in the form of a large nearly E-W lenticular body extending over some 30 km; b) a very fine-grained mosaic structure for the bulk of granulites; ribbon-lenticular quartz aggregates and garnet porphyroblasts occur in this mosaic; c) a largely granitic composition of the granulites, combining mineral associations of the granulite and amphibolite facies; this suggests that the original rocks for the majority of granulites were shadow granitoids of charnockitic (less frequently enderbitic) composition and closely similar to migmatites. A confirmation of this is based on their granitic composition and also on the nature of the minerals, particularly the high ferruginosity of the colored minerals of the granulites — relict pyroxenes and neogenic amphiboles, garnets and biotites, usually originating during granitization of basic and near-basic rocks.

The granulites in the mountains of Saxony and Bohemia, the classic location in which they were first studied /137/, are metamorphic rocks consisting of a fine-grained feldspar-quartz mosaic with an extremely variable content of femic minerals. It is thus possible to differentiate felsic, intermediate and mafic varieties. Ribbon or lenticular quartz grains and aggregates are a characteristic feature of the granulites. The typical feldspar is usually perthitic, whereas plagioclase may be antiperthitic. Orthopyroxenes are represented mostly by ferrohypersthene, and clino-pyroxenes by salite. Almandine is prevalent among the garnets. Some beds of felsic granulites also contain cordierite and kyanite in addition to the garnet. In descriptions of Saxon granulites, it is emphasized that they are by no means rocks of the "granulite facies" of regional metamorphism, although historically the facies derived its name from these granulites. Hence, the justified suggestion that the terms should be revised, since granulite is often identified with the granulite facies in geological literature, leading to serious misunderstandings. In fact, the granulites are a specific rock group occurring in the crystalline basement of platforms formed in the presence of the most intensive tectonic movements, with which disjunc-tive dislocations are predominantly associated, not only in the vertical but also in the horizontal planes. The tectonic origin of granulite is attested to, in the first place, by their structure—paratectonites of orthorhombic and monoclinic symmetries. Thus, the granulite body in the Saxon Mountains is a tectonic lens located along an abyssal lineament extending over hundreds of kilometers. The body was squeezed out (uplifted) from great depths during the Caledonian tectogenetic epoch, probably in a partially plastic state. The movement was accompanied by a recrystallization of the rocks,

which became especially intense in the final stages. It is conditionally
assumed that the original rocks for the Saxon granulites were predominantly
the oldest terrigenous sediments with sheets of metabasites transformed
into granulite facies schists, which were converted to amphibolite facies
rocks by the tectonic squeezing out of the granulite body (as a diapir).

The Schüssel Suite granulites are likewise regarded by the authors as
paratectonites. They originated during the older (pre-Riphean) tectogenesis,
which was responsible for activation of the crystalline basement of the
Antarctic Platform in the central region of Queen Maud Land. Apparently,
the original rocks were ultrametagenic shadow granitoids closely similar to
migmatites of the charnockitic variety, subjected to intensive recrystallization probably without any substantial influx or loss of elements. They were
thus transformed into very fine-grained granulites with profuse new mineral
development (garnet and partially amphibole and biotite). Their texture was
converted from the usual heterogranoblastic to granulitic. At the same
time, one cannot rule out the possibility that the granulites originated by
granitization, followed by granulation of paragneisses, which may have given
rise to biotite-garnet granulites without pyroxene relicts. The metabasite
sheets and the beds of calciphyres and quartzites included among the
granulites were also recrystallized and repeatedly metamorphosed. This
is reflected in their parageneses — a nonequilibrium combination of
mineral associations of the granulite and amphibolite facies. This is borne
out by the following description of various rocks which were encountered
in the granulite strata.

Metabasites which were transformed into amphibolized and biotitized
bipyroxene schists and amphibolites, occur ubiquitously in the granulites in
the form of sheets (often boudinaged) 0.5—20.0 m thick. The metabasites
are appreciably cataclastized, recrystallized and repeatedly metamorphosed.
They are represented by dark gray to black fine- and medium-grained
schists with heterogranoblastic textures, continuously disturbed by cataclasis. The size of isometric and irregular grains varies from 0.5 to 2.5 mm.
The crystalline habit has been retained by broken plagioclase laths with
broad polysynthetic twins; prismatic amphibole grains, often diablastic
due to the abundant inclusions of pyroxenes and ore minerals, approach
porphyroblasts in their shape and size (3—4 mm). On the other hand, the
relict pyroxene grains present a variety of very irregular shapes, including
baylike, tortuous, skeletal, clastic, etc. Schists (Table 64) formed from
metabasites consist of plagioclases (up to 50%) ranging from An 34 to An 53;
labradorites which have been disanorthitized only to a relatively slight
degree. The rest of the rock consists of various colored minerals, in places
with prevalence of amphibole; some varieties are therefore represented by
biotitized amphibolites. However, pyroxenes are more common in the rocks
under discussion: 3—20% orthopyroxenes with ferruginosity of 38—58% and
9—43% clinopyroxene with ferruginosity of 25—49%. Such significant fluctuations in the pyroxene content reflect the different degrees of recrystallization of the metabasites, resulting in the development of 3—22% amphibole
and nearly the same amount of biotite, as well as sporadic quartz (5%).
In such cases, the ferruginosity of secondary colored minerals is usually
somewhat higher than that of relict pyroxenes: 40—55% for amphibole and
55—67% for biotite. A characteristic feature is the absence of K-feldspar
and garnet which appear only in the rare cases of migmatization of these

rocks. Certain features of the original rocks, characteristic of gabbroids, are preserved. In view of their occurrence within formerly shadow charnockites and enderbites which were transformed into paratectonites (granulites), the "stability" of these rocks in the granitization process is surprising. However, the metabasites under consideration bear distinct traces of double metamorphism: a) under granulite facies conditions, when they were transformed into bipyroxene-labradorite schists, and b) under amphibolite facies conditions, when they were intensively amphibolized and biotitized, up to the development of typical amphibolites.

Migmatites occur in fairly thick (100—200 m) units fringing the granulite body. Morphologically, they belong to coarsely layered varieties (Figure 34), the alternating layers of paleosome (heavily altered pyroxene-bearing schists) and metasome (granites) varying from 30 cm to 1 m in thickness. However, normal layered migmatites with layers of a few centimeters in thickness are not too rare. Different varieties of layered migmatites alternate with one another. They locally appear to be agmatitic. However, typical agmatites more commonly develop from boudinaged bodies of metabasites, where the boudins are embedded mainly in a plagiogranitic metasome. The paleosome layers are composed of gray and dark gray, fine- to medium-grained schists of granoblastic textures (with elements of heteroblastic and porphyroblastic textures) which are often cataclastized. The fine (0.3—0.5 mm) mosaic grains of the paleosome consist of plagioclase and quartz, although 2-mm long plagioclase laths with antiperthitic ingrowths have been preserved in places. Large (up to 3 mm) lenticular quartz segregations, together with the coarse plagioclase, produce an overall impression of limited granulation. As always, the most xenoblastic forms are exhibited by the pyroxene grains, which vary widely in size from 0.2 to 1mm. Prismatic (2 mm) amphibole grains and rounded isometric garnet grains, of the same size, but with irregular and often rugged boundaries, are often encountered. The paleosome of coarsely layered migmatites (Table 64), which displays a strong similarity to the paleosome of the heavily altered metabasites, differs from the latter in its considerable content of nearly ubiquitous quartz (usually 10—25%) and the frequent occurrence of garnet (5—25%); there is a simultaneous decrease in the pyroxene content, particularly orthopyroxenes, which have been preserved only in a few migmatite specimens in amounts of 2—7%. The paleosome has a somewhat higher content of clinopyroxenes (10—15%), but even these are not consistently present. This is in contrast to the ubiquitous amphibole (5—20%) and biotite (10—20%). K-feldspar occurs sporadically (3—10%). The principal paleosome mineral is plagioclase of variable composition, An 34 to An 56 (rare), usually composing about one half of the rocks. The ferruginosity of orthopyroxenes is high (56—64%) and that of amphiboles and biotites replacing the pyroxene is usually higher still (up to 60—70%). The iron content of clinopyroxenes is low (33—46%) since the more ferruginous varieties are replaced by amphibole.

The metasome of migmatites is fairly uniform and often cannot be distinguished from granulites in its external appearance. This is due to its mosaic matrix and thin parallel lenticular quartz segregations. It has a granoblastic texture with marked granulitic elements. The grains average 0.3—0.6 mm in diameter, with garnet grains standing out due to their relatively large size (1—2 mm). Normal granites predominate over plagiogranites

in the metasome, although the principal-mineral content in such rocks
renders their classification as granites somewhat arbitrary. Thus, they
usually contain 15—25% quartz, 20—60% plagioclase (An 20—38), 15—50%
K-feldspar, with only biotite (2—15%) and garnet (5—10%) as the main
colored minerals. Sporadic amphibole relicts have a high ferruginosity
(77%) whereas the iron contents of biotites and garnets are extremely
variable, (33—69% and 60—70%, respectively). This variability probably
denotes superimposed crystallization of these migmatites, producing a
nonequilibrium association of minerals of different compositions.

FIGURE 34. Coarsely layered migmatites replacing bipyroxene schists, Schüssel Suite,
exposure 77.

Calciphyres form beds with a considerable variation in thickness,
1—2 m for boudinaged and 50—100 m for cataclastic beds. The former often
occur in association with quartzite layers. The calciphyres are represented
by inequigranular (most commonly coarse-grained) rocks of maculose
structure with porphyrogranoblastic textures due to large diopside crystals.
Their color is variegated, white and green, and less commonly uniform,
pinkish gray and pale yellow. The calciphyres in bedrock exposures have
undergone disintegration at the surface to form a gritty mass. They possess
distinct relict granulite and superimposed amphibolite mineral associations.
Their persistent minerals are diopside (salite), carbonate (calcite) and
scapolite (mostly meionite)(Table 64). Clinopyroxene is prevalent in the
majority of investigated specimens, 70—90%, and its content drops to
5—15% in only a few sporadic occurrences. Most often, it accounts for one
half of the rock. A variable ferruginosity of the pyroxene is a characteristic feature; salites and ferrosalites with a ferruginosity of 50—60% are
widespread along with diopsides of ferruginosity 13—21%. It should be
emphasized that the ferruginosity of diopsides in the typical granulite facies

calciphyres occurring in many regions of East Antarctica is 5—20% /57/, reaching 50% and more only in the course of recrystallization under amphibolite facies conditions, as is the case in the Schüssel Suite calciphyres. In the latter, cummingtonite and wollastonite occur with the ferrosalite in the same paragenesis. The content of scapolite is 20—35%, rarely more. The amount of preserved carbonates is small, 1—7% rarely reaching 60—70%. All other minerals—quartz, plagioclase, amphibole, mica, titanomagnetite and sphene—occur sporadically, totalling 1—5%, and rarely 10%, while the content of wollastonite is 27 and in places 55%. A few calciphyre specimens contain preserved forsterite and spinel.

It should be noted that many of these minerals frequently have unusual compositions, especially in different beds of calciphyres which underwent nonuniform recrystallization under the amphibolite facies conditions. Thus, besides the very basic plagioclases, An 80 and An 94, there are andesines, An 35—37, and in these specimens, the contents of plagioclase and quartz are doubled or even tripled. Cummingtonite and even actinolite (ferruginosity 20—24%) occur together with common hornblende, with a ferruginosity of 58%. Phlogopite (ferruginosity 6—12%) occurs with diopsides of low ferruginosity, while biotite (ferruginosity 52%) occurs with ferrosalites. Wollastonite likewise occurs in calciphyres with ferrosalites, and not with diopside. On the whole, there is a distinct pattern of nonequilibrium mineral associations in the schists occurring together with calciphyres, ranging from forsterite to phlogopite, from anorthite to andesine, and from diopside to ferrosalite, which are in some cases largely or completely replaced by wollastonite.

Quartzites, in beds 1—5 m thick, often occur together with calciphyres. With the latter, they are typical formerly sedimentary rocks in shadow pyroxene-bearing granitoids, which were transformed into granulites.

The quartzites are white and pinkish-yellowish, medium-grained rocks of a nearly monomineralic composition, except for superimposed feldspathization (K-feldspar up to 10—25%). Their principal mineral is quartz (65—90%), followed by K-feldspar, a small admixture of acid andesine (2—9%) and comparatively rare biotite flakes, ore grains and minute clastic crystallites of zircon.

Granitic veins, accounting for 3—10 vol. % of the exposures, play a significant part in almost one half of Schüssel Suite outcrops. They are best preserved in migmatites, investing them with an agmatitic appearance. Although the veins are often appreciably cataclastized, they preserve the form of the youngest intrusions in granulites and migmatites. The veins are composed by medium- and coarse-grained rocks of various light shades (pale gray, yellowish, pinkish, cream, etc.), most frequently with porphyroblastic textures disturbed by cataclasis. The porphyroblasts are mainly plagioclase laths with rugged outlines, and irregularly shaped quartz grains of 4—6 mm. Microcline (most commonly with a distinct crosshatching) occurs in very irregular and elongated veins of 1—2 mm filling interstices. Some areas are heavily cataclastized and converted to a finely crushed mass of quartz-feldspar mosaic aggregates. Garnet grains of isometric habit (2—4 mm) assume the character of porphyroblasts in these mosaic aggregates. As a rule, the veins are leucocratic (Table 64), with a fringe of amphibole, biotite and garnet occasionally forming only in selvages. In the veins themselves, biotite is usually present (3—5 %), while garnet and amphibole occur sporadically. In addition ore grains (2—3 %) and disseminated granules of apatite, zircon and sphene total about 1 %. The principal minerals in the veins are feldspar and quartz, and their different contents may provide a basis for an arbitrary differentiation of plagiogranite, granite and granosyenite varieties. Such veins probably are products of crystallization in partial melts which formed during the superimposed stage of the amphibolite facies metamorphism. Besides independent veins, these melts also produced the metasome of agmatites, often forming at the expense of older layered migmatites and even shadow granitoids.

In concluding the description of the Schüssel Suite, it is necessary to emphasize that its rocks bear vivid evidence of at least two stages of regional metamorphism; the last stage (especially widespread in the crystalline basement of central Queen Maud Land) invested the rocks with the structure observed in the present-day erosional section. During the early stage, which formed the lower structural series of the crystalline basement of the Antarctic Platform (tentatively regarded as Upper Archean by analogy with the other continents in the southern hemisphere), occurred the regional metamorphism of the granulite facies, possibly completed under conditions of higher grades of the amphibolite facies. During this stage, thick strata of volcanogenic rocks in mobile zones of the basement produced schists of basic compositions as well as various plagiogneisses. These were then transformed (partially or completely) into shadow granitoids and migmatites, mostly of the charnockitic varieties. During the superimposed stage of regional metamorphism, which probably took place in the Lower Proterozoic (?), and certainly in pre-Riphean time, the migmatites and shadow granitoids in the stress-dominated abyssal fault zone were transformed into granulites, while schists of basic composition were transformed into amphibolites and agmatites. Rocks such as the calciphyres which, at first glance, do not appear to have undergone any significant alterations, actually became dominated by nonequilibrium mineral associations of the relict granulite and superimposed amphibolite facies.

Gorki Suite

The constituent rocks of the Gorki Suite differ significantly from those of the Schüssel Suite. Although the Gorki Suite, too, is dominated by migmatites and shadow granites, these were formed from primary sediments and not from volcanogenic rocks. They include rocks transformed into high-alumina schists which therefore contain, along with biotite and garnet, sillimanite and cordierite instead of the pyroxene and amphibole. Graphite is present in some varieties. Therefore, the ultrametagenic rocks in the Gorki Suite are of granitic composition instead of charnockitic as in the Schüssel Suite. Characteristically, the range of all the other rocks, accounting for less than 20 vol. % of the Gorki Suite, is the same as in the Schüssel Suite. Thus, sheets of strongly altered metabasites, as well as calciphyre and quartzite beds, occur with the biotite-garnet shadow granites in the Gorki Suite. The veins in both suites are very similar.

Migmatites of the Gorki Suite (Table 65) differ from those of the Schüssel Suite by a predominance of layered (especially finely layered) varieties, the absence of pyroxenes (even in the paleosome), the presence of cordierite and sillimanite, the low content of colored minerals (biotite and garnet), the stable composition of the plagioclase, which does not rise above An 30—31, and the ubiquitous gradual transition of migmatites to shadow granites even within the boundaries of one bedrock exposure (Figure 35). As a rule, the intercalations of paleosome and metasome in these migmatites vary in thickness from a few millimeters to several centimeters, and it is only rarely that paleosome layers attain thicknesses of tens of centimeters. The volume of the paleosome is somewhat less than that of the metasome. The paleosome is considerably more melano-cratic than the metasome. It is coarse-grained, whereas the metasome is fine-grained, often with granulated quartz segregations. Such migmatites, where fractured, are in places converted to agmatites. The granite veinlets vary considerably in thickness and account for 20—30 vol. % of the rock.

FIGURE 35. Cataclastized finely layered migmatites with biotite-garnet paleosome, Gorki Suite, exposure 65.

Both components of the migmatites are prevalently granoblastic, with an addition of nematolepidoblastic elements in the paleosome and porphyro-blastic and granulitic elements in the metasome.   The paleosome is most commonly dominated (up to 60—70%) by acid andesine An 26—31, but some varieties are rich in sillimanite (up to 30%).   The contents of quartz and microcline are extremely variable; quartz varies from 1 to 30% and micro-cline from sporadic grains to 25%; consequently, aside from the plagiogneiss paleosome, some migmatites contain quartz-free alumina schists as their paleosome.   The prevalent colored mineral is usually biotite.   Garnet occurs locally with a highly variable content (5 to 30%).   The ferruginosities of these minerals are high: 51—68% in biotite and 80—90% in garnet.   In rare cases, the paleosome contains appreciable amounts of amphibole (up to 15%), spinel (up to 3%) and accessory minerals such as apatite, zircon and orthite.   On the whole, the migmatite paleosome is distinguished by an extremely variable mineral composition, which likewise reflects its initial sedimentary-terrigenous origin (Figure 36).   The composition of the meta-some is considerably more stable, although the contents of individual minerals, especially feldspars, are very variable.   Plagiogranitic, granitic

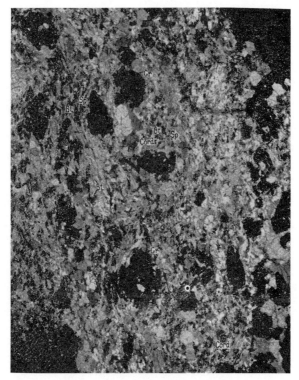

FIGURE 36. Cataclastized migmatite paleosome with sillimanite and cordierite. Augen structure, lepidogranoblastic fundamental pattern. Gorki Suite (thin section 92, × 11, crossed nicols).

TABLE 65. Mineral composition and characteristics of rocks of the Gorki Suite

Migmatites from biotite-garnet and biotite (sporadically with cordierite

Specimen No.	K-feldspar	plagioclase	quartz	orthopyroxene	clinopyroxene	amphibole	biotite	garnet	carbonate	scapolite	cordierite	sillimanite	ore mineral	apatite	sphene	zircon	rutile
Paleo																	
94		26	1				30	13				30					
235	o.s.+	34	34				18	9			5	o.s.	o.s.			o.s.	
61b	„	38	30				16*	14*					2				
62	„	60	15				25									o.s.	
63	„	70	5		15		10										
275		65	5				30										
65	25	33	3			8	6	20						3	2		
92	20	15	o.s.				20	22			15		4	1		o.s.	
Meta																	
a) plagio																	
43d		60	30				3	3	4				o.s.				
92b	6	55	37				2										
92v	8	55	37				o.s.						o.s.				
94a		55	30				10	5									
b) gra																	
65v	14	16	37				2*	15*			3	12	1			o.s.	
92a	40	30	25				4	1					o.s.			„	
61a	60	18	20				2										
61g	55	17	16				9	3						o.s.			
62a	58	20	18				2	2							o.s.		
235a	22	32	35				2	3			6						
235b	20	20	42				12	2			4		o.s.				
275	73	7	10				10										
Finely layered migmatites																	
a) plagio																	
43e		42	32				15	10					1			o.s.	
62b		65	25				10	o.s.						o.s.	o.s.	„	
72		50	27				15	3						3	2	„	
95zh	5	57	18				18						o.s.	o.s.			
96	1	59	25				4	5			3				1	5	1
276v	1	59	14				18						o.s.	3	5	o.s.	
288a	3	50	35				7	5					„	o.s.		„	
94b	8	27	35				13	7		o.s.	10						

	Mineral characteristics												
	orthopyroxene			clinopyroxene			amphibole			biotite		garnet
An content of plagioclase	n_z	n_x	ferrugino-sity, at. %	n_z	n_x	ferrugino-sity, at. %	n_z	n_z	ferrugino-sity, at. %	n_z	ferrugino-sity, at. %	n
and sillimanite) plagiogneisses and schists												
some												
26												
26												
31										1.672	68	1.795
31												
27							1.684	1.660	47	1.649	51	
31												
29												1.810
some												
granitic												
nitic												
30										1.655	55	1.782
27												
25										1.650	51	1.806
24												
and shadow granites												
granitic												
30												
24												
31												
24												
31												
31												
28												
										1.660	59	1.806

TABLE 65 (continued)

Specimen No.	K-feldspar	plagioclase	quartz	orthopyroxene	clinopyroxene	amphibole	biotite	garnet	carbonate	scapolite	cordierite	sillimanite	ore mineral	apatite	sphene	zircon	rutile
													Composition				

Finely layered migmatites

b) gra

Specimen No.	K-feldspar	plagioclase	quartz	orthopyroxene	clinopyroxene	amphibole	biotite	garnet	carbonate	scapolite	cordierite	sillimanite	ore mineral	apatite	sphene	zircon	rutile
275g	12	50	20				9	6					2	1		o.s.	
95g	12	33	40				5	8					2				
60g	15	60	19				2	3					1		o.s.		
243b	15	30	20				18	1				14	2			o.s.	
276b	15	30	30				7	13					3	1		1	
61	20	40	25				10	3					1	1			
63b	57	4	30				7	2								o.s.	
71	50	14	22			1	7	4					1	1		"	
72a	23	30	15				25						4	3		"	
72b	18	22	25				10*	16*				7	2			"	
95	35	2	35				3	18				5	2				o.s.
95e	50	22	20				5	2					1		o.s.	o.s.	
95z	52	20	22				2	3					1				
235i	45	3	45				5						2				
275v	34	32	18				8	4					2	2			
275d	45	8	20				4	13*				8	2				o.s.
276d	36	20	24				8	5				5	2				
276g	53	13	18				6	8				1	1	1	o.s.	o.s.	o.s.
276e	47	10	20				15	5				2	1				"
288b	25	33	25				15	2					o.s.	o.s.		o.s.	
552	60		15				10	5			o.s.	5	1				
563	26	5	38				5	7			5	10	2				2

Melanocratic rocks (paleosome

Specimen No.	K-feldspar	plagioclase	quartz	orthopyroxene	clinopyroxene	amphibole	biotite	garnet	carbonate	scapolite	cordierite	sillimanite	ore mineral	apatite	sphene	zircon	rutile
60e			15				18	63					4				
95b		12	20				3	50			10		3	o.s.		2	
97v	7	40	10				15	28					o.s.				o.s.
243b—1	10	15	20				18	22				14	1	o.s.		o.s.	
279a		15	o.s.	17*	5		1	55*					5	2			
279b	3	60	2	15	8		4	3					3	2			
96a		5	36				3	50			3		3	o.s.			
96d		60	7				25	5	o.s.				2	1			
95d		13				75	10						2	o.s.			

	Mineral characteristics											
	orthopyroxene			clinopyroxene			amphibole			biotite		garnet
An content of plagioclase	n_z	n_x	ferruginosity, at. %	n_z	n_x	ferruginosity, at. %	n_z	n_x	ferruginosity, at. %	n_z	ferruginosity, at. %	n

and shadow granites

nitic

29												
31										1.647	49	1.803
24										1.660	59	1.809
26												
21												
25							1.722	1.698	84	1.692	82	1.809
30												
26										1.653	53	1.799
										1.660	59	1.795
										1.665	62	1.795
										1.646	48	1.785
										1.650	51	·1.799
34												
27												

relicts in shadow granite)

										1.627	36	1.790
70												
35				1.727	1.700	51	1.704	1.680	65			1.803
				1.735	1.709	64						1.804

TABLE 65 (continued)

Quart[zites]

Specimen No.	K-feldspar	plagioclase	quartz	orthopyroxene	clinopyroxene	amphibole	biotite	garnet	carbonate	scapolite	cordierite	sillimanite	ore mineral	apatite	sphene	zircon	rutile
63a		27	71				2										o.s.
96g	10	3	87				o.s.										o.s.
235v		26	70				2							1	o.s.	1	
97d			95									5					
290a	6	3	60				10	13			3	5					
552a	48		49				1	1				1					

Calci[phyres]

Specimen No.	K-feldspar	plagioclase	quartz	orthopyroxene	clinopyroxene	amphibole	biotite	garnet	carbonate	scapolite	cordierite	sillimanite	ore mineral	apatite	sphene	zircon	rutile
43		5		93		2							o.s.				
43a		2	3	85	10	o.s.											
43b		2		98		•											
92d	o.s.	3	13	40	3				2	34				1	4		
92e	3	15	12	20	3				10	35					2		
94g		17	4	75	1				1	o.s.					2		
94d				60		40											
235g				o.s.		1			95				o.s.				
235d				o.s.					70								
235e		3		95		1			o.s.					1			
235zh				50	2					47							
235z	o.s.			o.s.				43	10	3							
275b		2		75		22			1								
276a		1		91*					2	5					1		
96v		2		17		2			75	1				1	2		

Heavily silicified [quartzites]

Specimen No.	K-feldspar	plagioclase	quartz	orthopyroxene	clinopyroxene	amphibole	biotite	garnet	carbonate	scapolite	cordierite	sillimanite	ore mineral	apatite	sphene	zircon	rutile
276	18		50		5	3	1		3	18		o.s.			2		

Metabasites and meta-ultrabasites, in places

Specimen No.	K-feldspar	plagioclase	quartz	orthopyroxene	clinopyroxene	amphibole	biotite	garnet	carbonate	scapolite	cordierite	sillimanite	ore mineral	apatite	sphene	zircon	rutile
43zh	5	54	3		13	—	22						3	o.s.			
43z		68	2		10		2	o.s.					5				
60d		32	3	5	22	4	1	28					5				
95a		55	2	10	25	5	o.s.						3	o.s.			
95i		40		2		45*	13*										
95l		50		9	10	18	10						3	o.s.			

An content of plagioclase	orthopyroxene			clinopyroxene			amphibole			biotite		garnet
	n_z	n_x	ferruginosity, at. %	n_z	n_x	ferruginosity, at. %	n_z	n_x	ferruginosity, at. %	n_z	ferruginosity, at. %	n
zites												
20												
23												
25										1.654	54	
										1.612	25	1.760
phyres												
37												
35												
93				1.706	1.676	19				Phlogopite		
				1.718	1.689	37				1.594	12	
				1.706	1.679	19						
				1.734	1.708	62						
				1.714	1.684	31						
and feldspathized calciphyre												
				1.713	1.685	30						
transformed into amphibolites												
30				1.718	1.691	37				1.628	36	1.795
35	1.731	1.716	54	1.720	1.693	41				1.650	51	1.780
	1.727	1.712	50	1.714	1.688	31	1.686	1.663	48			
57	1.726	1.710	49	1.712	1.683	28	1.688	1.663	50			
77	1.714	1.700	41	1.668—1.674	1.643—1.648	30—37	1.630	1.630	38			
61	1.722	1.707	47	1.706	1.680	19	1.662	1.638	24	1.640	44	

TABLE 65 (continued)

Specimen No.	K-feldspar	plagioclase	quartz	orthopyroxene	clinopyroxene	amphibole	biotite	garnet	carbonate	scapolite	cordierite	sillimanite	ore mineral	apatite	sphene	zircon	rutile
												Composition →					
250a	10		39		50								1				
288	60	13	20*	o.s.			3	o.s.					3	1			
552b	48	2	16	14	1		14						5				
60v	65	5			20		8						2	o.s.			
96b	50	15	3				10	20					2				o.s.
96zh	40	o.s.	a.s.	15	21		22						2		o.s.		
96z	50	"	8	10	10		20						2	o.s.			

Meta

a) grano

Specimen No.	K-feldspar	plagioclase	quartz	orthopyroxene	clinopyroxene	amphibole	biotite	garnet	carbonate	scapolite	cordierite	sillimanite	ore mineral	apatite	sphene	zircon	rutile
92g		13	50	15			10	7						5	o.s.		o.s.	

b) plagio

Specimen No.	K-feldspar	plagioclase	quartz	orthopyroxene	clinopyroxene	amphibole	biotite	garnet	carbonate	scapolite	cordierite	sillimanite	ore mineral	apatite	sphene	zircon	rutile
250b		59	35			o.s.	5						o.s.	1			
279v	2	50	48						o.s.								

c) grano

Specimen No.	K-feldspar	plagioclase	quartz	orthopyroxene	clinopyroxene	amphibole	biotite	garnet	carbonate	scapolite	cordierite	sillimanite	ore mineral	apatite	sphene	zircon	rutile
95v	54	25	15				5						o.s.	o.s.		o.s.	
253	63	10	20				7						"	"		o.s.	
43g	72	8	20	o.s.									"	"		"	

d) gran

Specimen No.	K-feldspar	plagioclase	quartz	orthopyroxene	clinopyroxene	amphibole	biotite	garnet	carbonate	scapolite	cordierite	sillimanite	ore mineral	apatite	sphene	zircon	rutile
60a	40	15	35				10						o.s.				
95k	30	45	20				2	3						o.s.			
97g	32	30	28				10										
563a	47	22	27				3							o.s.	o.s.		

Notes. Specimen 235, cordierite, n_z = 1.553, n_x = 1.541; specimen 62, orthite, o.s.; specimen 92, sillimanite, orthite, o.s.; specimen 235a, cordierite; n_z = 1.552, n_x = 1.541; specimen 235b, cordierite, n_z = 1.553, n_x = 1.541; specimen 276v, orthite, o.s. < 1%; specimen 72a, orthite, o.s. < 1%; specimen 72b, sillimanite, n_z = 1.677, specimen 552, graphite, 4%; specimen 563, cordierite, n_z = 1.550, n_x = 1.539, sillimanite, n_z = 1.677, n_x = 1.657; cordierite, n_z = 1.540, n_x = 1.532; specimen 235g, spinel, 2%, n = 1.726, humite, 2%, n_z = 1.675, n_x = 1.643; 276 scapolite, n_o = 1.584, n_e = 1.552; specimen 250a, spinel, o.s. up to 1%; specimen 563a, muscovite, 1%.
+[o.s. = optic sign.]

An content of plagioclase	orthopyroxene			clinopyroxene			amphibole			biotite		garnet
	n_z	n_x	ferrugino-sity, at. %	n_z	n_x	ferrugino-sity, at. %	n_z	n_x	ferrugino-sity, at. %	n_z	ferrugino-sity, at. %	n
93	1.697	1.685	25				1.672	1.648	33			
38	1.723	1.708	48							1.654	54	1.790
47	1.729	1.714	51	1.716	1.690	33				1.661	60	
32							1.680	1.656	41	1.634	41	
36	1.714	1.700	41							1.630	38	1.777
53				1.716	1.690	33	1.674	1.650	37	1.650	51	
	1.718	1.704	43	1.711	1.684	27	1.681	1.657	43	1.642	46	

some

diorite

| 30 | | | | | | | 1.709 | 1.685 | 71 | 1.673 | 69 | |

granites

| 23 | | | | | | | | | | 1.660 | 59 | |

syenites

ites

| 20 | | | | | | | | | | 1.674 | 70 | |
| 26 | | | | | | | | | | 1.640 | 43 | |

n_z = 1.677, n_x = 1.657, spinel 3%; n = 1.806, cordierite; n_z = 1.554, n_x = 1.545; specimen 43d, specimen 72, orthite, o.s., < 1%; specimen 95 zh, sericite 2%; specimen 96, graphite 1%; n_x = 1.657; specimen 275v, orthite, o.s. < 1%; specimen 275d, sillimanite, n_z = 1.677, n_x = 1.657; specimen 235v, graphite, o.s. up to 1%; specimen 290a, sillimanite, n_z = 1.677, n_x = 1.657, specimen 235d, calcite, n_o = 1.663, forsterite 30%; specimen 235z, wollastonite 42%; specimen and granosyenitic varieties are distinguishable. Cordierite and sillimanite occur much less frequently than in the matrix, probably due to their insta- bility during the crystallization of the partial melts. Titanomagnetite and its alteration product sphene, as well as rutile, apatite, zircon and orthite, are rare accessories.

Repeated migmatization produces agmatites, mostly in layered migmatites, but occasionally in strongly altered metabasites. Leucocratic granite forms the metasome. This results in a decreased total quantity of colored minerals in the agmatites, which gradually approach shadow granites; they exhibit a relatively high content of unusual maculose melanocratic schlieren, which are paleosome relicts. The schlieren are especially high in garnet (high ferruginosity, 80—85%) and biotite (ferruginosity, 60%); some aggregates have preserved clinopyroxenes with ferruginosities of 51—64% and amphi- bole with a ferruginosity of 68%. Others have preserved sillimanite and cordierite. These melanocratic aggregates within shadow granitoids have a high content of ore minerals (up to 5%) and apatite (up to 2%). The prin- cipal salic mineral (10—60%) is plagioclase, An 35—95. The quartz contents are likewise variable (10—35%) while K-feldspar is sporadic. Shadow gra- nites with an appreciable content of melanocratic aggregates usually occur near contacts with agmatites. The formation of such agmatites is related to the superimposed stage of regional metamorphism under amphibolite facies conditions.

Further granitization transforms the migmatites into shadow granitoids in which the content of colored minerals rises to 25% while the quartz content falls to 15—20%. Moreover, some rocks contain a very small ad- mixture of K-feldspar and must be classified with the plagiogranites, whereas others, on the other hand, contain microcline with an admixture of plagioclase and belong to the granosyenites. Garnet cannot, of course, be a persistent or principal colored mineral in magmatic granites. This is also true of sillimanite, cordierite and graphite which are sporadic in ultra- metagenic shadow granitoids. The latter more commonly resemble granite- gneisses; their banded structure is inherited from layered migmatites. As a rule, they are represented by light-colored (pinkish yellow and grayish pink), fine-grained, less commonly medium-grained rocks, which are locally fairly massive. Augenlike segregations of K-feldspar and garnet 3—8 mm in size exhibit the appearance of porphyroblasts. The paleosome grains do not exceed 1—2 mm, averaging 0.3—0.6 mm. Not infrequently, certain shadow granites contain intricate melanocratic accumulations, usually extend- ing linearly for a few decimeters. These paleosome relicts present a great variety of forms, including maculose, banded, lenticular-bent, and grouped together, all with irregular outlines. Their distribution is very hetero- geneous. The shadow granitoids possess heterogranoblastic textures with fragments exhibiting porphyroblastic and lepidoblastic textures with distinct corrosion-metasomatic features due to the substitution of some minerals by others (Figure 37). "Healed" cracks in filled intricate and fine segregations of K-feldspar and quartz are also present. Features of recrystallization and cataclasis are distinctly visible, but they do not produce granulites which are very characteristic of the Schüssel Suite.

FIGURE 37. Shadow granite from sillimanite-biotite-garnet plagiogneiss.
A large garnet poikiloporphyroblast is seen in the bottom left corner (Gorki
Suite, thin section 72b, ×11, crossed nicols).

The mineral composition of shadow granitoids is fairly constant, although
quantitative fluctuations of individual minerals are considerable (Table 65).
Plagioclase, An 25—30, is present as small (0.2—0.5 mm), isometric and
tubular grains, corroded by other minerals. K-feldspar is usually represented by microcline (more often with indistinct crosshatching) which is
always appreciably more xenoblastic than the plagioclase. Quartz segregations are distinctly metablastic. All salic minerals form ingrowths in
one another: K-feldspar forms antiperthitic ingrowths in plagioclase, quartz
is myrmekitic in plagioclase, while plagioclase forms perthitic ingrowths
in K-feldspar. These features indicate a close interrelationship of these
minerals during rock formation. The colored minerals are monotonous,
being limited to biotite and garnet. Biotite occurs as fine flakes 0.2—0.5 mm
long, oriented in one direction. In general they are uniformly disseminated
throughout the rock. However, the linearity of the flakes is often "inter-
rupted" by glomero-aggregates of biotite often associated with sillimanite
and cordierite and also surrounding the crystalline garnet grains. The

fine biotite flakes are less frequently accompanied by larger biotite grains up to 2 mm long. Very characteristically, the two generations of biotite differ in their ferruginosities, 81—82% for the larger grains and 48—62% in the most widespread diaphthoritic flakes and their aggregates. The extremely rare relict granules of amphibole also have a high ferruginosity (up to 90%). Garnet is one of the most characteristic minerals in shadow granitoids in which it occurs ubiquitously but in extremely variable amounts ranging from 2 to 17%. Garnet is most commonly present in the form of crystalline grains with ragged outlines, since it is usually corroded by biotite flakes and contains biotite and quartz ingrowths. The garnet grains present a great variety of grain sizes, ranging from 0.2 to 3 mm, and occasionally up to 1 cm. They are commonly cracked and broken: the cracks have been "healed" by biotite flakes and filiform quartz segregations. There are two varieties of garnets with different ferruginosities, 66—72 and 80—90%. The latter are the highest iron contents of garnets in rocks of the investigated region. It is difficult to determine the sequence of separation of these two varieties of garnet. However, in general, the larger and less disintegrated grains have higher ferruginosities. It should be emphasized that the colored minerals in shadow granitoids possess a higher ferruginosity than the paleosome of migmatites. At the same time, the secondary colored minerals developing in granitoids always have a low ferruginosity. Unique in shadow granitoids are high-alumina minerals such as cordierite and sillimanite which became unstable during granitization (particularly cordierite). Their content in granite therefore decreases appreciably in comparison, for example, with the paleosome of migmatites. Cordierite, in fact, becomes a rare mineral. It usually occurs around garnet crystals or forms grains of xenoblastic outlines, 0.3—0.5 mm in size, permeated by fine quartz ingrowths and biotite flakes. Sillimanite is better preserved than cordierite; its content in shadow granitoids varies from 1 to 10%. It forms prismatic or isometric grains 0.1—1 mm long. Occasionally, there are large (up to 5 mm) porphyroblastic grains. Fine sillimanite needles are included in plagioclase and locally in garnet grains. Sillimanite is often replaced by a biotite aggregate; relict granules of the former are preserved in the latter. The sillimanite is also replaced by muscovite. An unusual accessory mineral in these granitoids is graphite, its content in some specimens reaching 1—4%. Graphite forms thin opaque flakes with frayed edges, 0.3—0.5 mm long. Another ubiquitous accessory mineral is titanomagnetite (1—4%), often accompanied by sphene and rutile. There are appreciable amounts (1—2%) of apatite crystallites; sporadic zircon grains, sometimes probably clastic, are always present. Rare orthite crystallites occur only in shadow granitoids.

Shadow granitoids display traces of two stages of regional metamorphism. The initial stage produced the finely layered migmatites from sedimentary-terrigenous strata under granulite facies conditions. The end stage transformed the latter into a variety of shadow granitoids under amphibolite facies conditions, giving rise to a biotite-garnet association gradually displacing the relict cordierite-sillimanite association which is unstable under the new conditions. Recrystallization of finely layered migmatites is related to the final stage of metamorphism, but it probably occurred under hydrostatic rather than unilateral pressure, in the abyssal fault zone.

The shadow granitoids were thus not transformed into granulites, unlike similar rocks of the Schüssel Suite.

Metabasites and meta-ultrabasites in the Gorki Suite occur within migmatites and shadow granites (Figure 38) and represent pre-granitization relicts. However, they were transformed into bipyroxene schists, amphibolized and biotitized to varying degrees and, in places, also enriched in garnet. In comparison to analogous Schüssel Suite rocks, the Gorki Suite metabasites are much more highly altered, enriched with quartz, have a higher content of colored minerals, mainly secondary minerals such as amphibole, biotite and garnet (garnet is absent from the Schüssel Suite metabasites). Metabasites of the Gorki Suite differ little from analogous rocks of the Schüssel Suite with respect to bedding, thickness of the sheets, structure, texture and mineral composition. It should be emphasized that the extremely nonuniform composition of the metabasites is due to appreciable fluctuations in the contents of rock-forming minerals (Table 65). These represent a nonequilibrium association formed under the conditions of the granulite and superimposed amphibolite facies.

FIGURE 38. Boudins of metabasites (2 m) in layered migmatites. Both are intersected by thin veinlets of granite (Gorki Suite, exposure 95).

Calciphyres are more common in the Gorki Suite than in the Schüssel Suite, although the thickness of their boudinaged sheets is not large (usually a few meters and sometimes a few tens of meters). They differ little from analogous rocks in the Schüssel Suite with respect to their bedding and structure. The principal difference is probably the significant predominance in the Gorki Suite calciphyres of clinopyroxene (salite series) occurring in crystalline grains 1—2 mm in size, and less commonly in metablasts of up

1 cm. A large number of varieties are almost entirely composed of clinopyroxene, with only isolated layers composed predominantly of calcite
(nearly pure marbles). As a rule, the central portions of many calciphyre
boudins are composed of salites and their peripheral portions of calcite.
The mineral composition of calciphyres is extremely variable (Table 65),
even the content of the principal rock-forming mineral clinopyroxene varies
from 5 to 98 %. However, the most characteristic feature is the frequent
simultaneous presence in a single specimen of two clinopyroxene varieties,
differing markedly in their ferruginosities, i. e., relict grains of pale green
color with a ferruginosity of 19 %, and grayish green grains with a ferruginosity of up to 37 %. Larger metablasts of later origin and of deep green
color, formed by the recrystallization of small grains, have a ferruginosity
of up to 62 %. The variable composition of pyroxenes is augmented by the
presence of other minerals of the nonequilibrium association, i. e., forsterite, humite and spinel, as well as newly formed wollastonite and scapolite
(occasionally grossular). Such mineral associations provide a vivid testi-
mony to the nonequilibrium nature of the parageneses of the granulite and
amphibolite facies; the former paragenesis becomes unstable and is gradually replaced by the latter. The situation is likewise reflected in the
variability of the composition of plagioclase, ranging from newly formed
andesine, An 35—37, to relict anorthite, An 93. Occasionally, the calciphyres contain an admixture of quartz and still less frequently of microcline. Their content increases considerably at the contact with granite
veins.

Quartzites are much more widespread in the Gorki Suite than in the
Schüssel Suite. They occur in comparatively thin beds (1—7 m) within migmatites and shadow granitoids, but are themselves only very slightly granitized. Quartzites of the Gorki Suite contain a richer minor mineral
association in comparison to the more homogeneous Schüssel Suite quartzites.
The former, for example, often contain garnet and sillimanite along with
the biotite, whereas the latter always contain biotite alone. The quartzites
reflect the composition of their containing metamorphic strata. In the
Schüssel Suite, where they occur within granulated shadow charnockites,
the quartzites contain pyroxene granules and a small admixture of biotite;
in the Gorki Suite, where they occur with meta-sedimentary rocks (aluminous
schists and shadow granites), quartzites contain 1—13 % garnet, 1—15 %
sillimanite, 1—10 % biotite and sporadically up to 3 % cordierite. Quartz is
the principal mineral of these rocks. It occurs in small granules 0.2—
1.0 mm in size, lenticular segregations and irregular monomineralic grains
(2—4 mm). In places, the quartzite is completely recrystallized and
constitutes an aggregate of uniformly oriented, thin lenticules enriched in
microcline and oligoclase (An 20—25).

Veins in the Gorki Suite form a greater variety of rock types than in
the Schüssel Suite. In addition to the predominant granites, they often
contain granosyenites and plagiogranites and in some places, granodiorites.
Each of these rocks forms independent veins; the formation sequence
is difficult to establish since they usually occur in different host rocks, in
different exposures. The composition of the veins is close to that of the
host rocks in the majority of cases, e. g., if the metasome of migmatites
is granosyenite or plagiogranite, the veins are of the same composition.

Notwithstanding their different compositions, all veins are composed of
leucocratic rocks and their only persistent dark component is biotite (3—10%).
Occasionally the veins contain garnet and then only in host rocks rich in
that mineral.   The vein rocks are often porphyroblastic due to the presence
of large K-feldspar laths.   Porphyroclastic textures are imparted to some
veins by cataclasis.

In concluding the description of the Gorki Suite, it should be emphasized
that, although it possesses several features in common with the Schüssel Suite,
it differs from the latter in the composition of the principal rocks.   The
common features of the two suites are as follows: a) significant prevalence
of migmatites and shadow granitoids over all the other rocks, attesting to
formation of the crystalline basement under conditions of fairly deep, and
high-temperature metamorphism with considerable development of ultrametamorphic processes; b) ubiquitous development of nonequilibrium
mineral associations; c) presence of rocks that are resistant to granitization, including metabasites, calciphyres and quartzites, another characteristic feature of which are nonequilibrium associations of minerals of the
granulite and superimposed amphibolite facies.   However, the differences
between the two suites are more significant: a) Schüssel Suite migmatites
and shadow granitoids are charnockitic, and consequently the pyroxenes
occur together with amphibole and garnet of the pyrope-almandine series;
whereas the characteristic minerals of analogous rocks in the Gorki Suite
(aluminous specialization) include sillimanite, cordierite and garnet of the
almandine series with an admixture of grossular and only partially of
pyrope molecules, as well as biotite and unique graphite.   These attest to
differences in the original materials of the ultrametagenic rocks — volcanogenic rocks of magmatic origin for the Schüssel Suite, terrigenous-chemo-
genic rocks for the Gorki Suite; b) ultrametagenic rocks in the Schüssel
Suite have been transformed into granulites of paratectonic origin, whereas
analogous rocks in the Gorki Suite are relatively slightly granulated.   This
indicates special conditions at the concluding stage in the formation of the
Schüssel Suite, i. e., in an abyssal fault zone dominated by stress, whereas
the Gorki Suite rocks in the same stage were subjected only to hydrostatic
pressure; c) analogous rocks in the two suites, such as calciphyres and
quartzites, exhibit certain differences.   They are more heavily altered
and contain sillimanite, cordierite and graphite in the Gorki Suite.

A comparative description of the Schüssel and Gorki suites provides the
most vivid expression of the characteristic features of rocks of polymetamorphic genesis.   Therefore, considerable attention was given to their
description in the region of the Humboldt Mountains.   The following is a
brief description of rocks in other regions of the crystalline basement with
typical metamorphic formations.   They have been much less studied than those
in the Humboldt Mountains region and the differences between them and the
latter are slight.   The examination of the geological structure in the
Humboldt Mountains will be concluded with a detailed description of the
Insel Series composed of monometamorphic rocks of the amphibolite facies.

POLYMETAMORPHIC ROCKS IN OTHER
REGIONS OF EAST ANTARCTICA

Close to the Humboldt Mountains (20 km to the west), on the other side
of a broad ice-filled mountain valley, occurs the more than 30-km long,
~ E-W trending (across the strike of rocks) Shcherbakov Range (10°30' E).
This contains a profile of polymetamorphic strata similar to that of the
Humboldt Mountains. The center is occupied by the thickest group of rocks
(7—8 km) composed predominantly of garnet-biotite shadow granites, partially
converted to granulites. These contain frequent relict beds of partially
granulated bipyroxene-garnet shadow granites. The thickness of such
intercalations reaches tens of meters. The suite contains rare boudinaged
intercalations of calciphyres and metabasites as well as quartzites. The
composition of the suite has much in common with the Schüssel Suite in the
Humboldt Mountains. The garnet-biotite shadow granites possess a gneissoid
structure and granoblastic texture with granulitic elements. They consist
of oligoclase and microcline (20—25 % each), quartz (30 %), biotite (8—10 %)
and garnet (10—15 %). Microcline is predominant (50 %) in some varieties
and oligoclase (40 %) in others. The accessory minerals include sphene,
apatite and zircon. There are numerous intercalations of another type of
shadow granites, containing relicts of high-iron orthopyroxene (2—3 %) and
clinopyroxene (3—8 %) along with garnet (10—15 %) and an insignificant
admixture of biotite (1 %). The quartz content is low (15—25 %). On the
whole, these rocks have an almost equal content of oligoclase, An 23—26,
and microcline and are ultrametagenic charnockites with distinct granulitic
textures. Another group of strata in the Shcherbakov Range occurs along
the periphery, with an undetermined thickness. A characteristic feature of
its composition is the predominance of migmatites, with high-alumina
minerals, over shadow granites. The most abundant of these are sillimanite
(5—10 %) and garnet (8—15 %). A thin intercalation very rich in andalusite
was encountered in one case. The andalusites are prophyroblastic, up to
1 cm in size, with inclusions of quartz and small sillimanite needles.
Andalusite porphyroblasts ($n_z = 1.645$; $n_x = 1.636$) are embedded in a quartz-
feldspar matrix devoid of garnet and sillimanite. The migmatite paleosome,
together with the high-alumina minerals, has a considerable biotite content,
which is rare in shadow granites. The shadow granites include both normal
and plagioclase types, and certain varieties are granosyenites. The shadow
granites contain intrusive bodies of amphibolized metabasites, boudinaged
beds of calciphyres, and quartzites. In all these features, the strata are
similar to the Gorki Suite of the Humboldt Mountains. On the whole, the
two groups of strata constitute a series similar to the Humboldt Series
which is characteristic for the polymetamorphic rocks.

Farther west, over a distance of 250 km, blocks of metamorphic rocks
are less frequent than blocks of intrusive charnockites, probably rheomorphic in origin. The former appear as polymetamorphic strata, the profiles
of which resemble the Humboldt Series, although they also form anticlinal
structures in addition to the synclines. Some areas within the polymetamorphic rocks contain relicts of the granulite facies parageneses. North
of the mountain ranges there are some nunataks composed exclusively of
amphibolite facies rocks. Supracrustal rocks of this composition occur in

the western regions of Queen Maud Land (4°E — 2°W). These are dominated
by blocks of typical monometamorphic rocks of the amphibolite facies,
without charnockite intrusions. On the whole, the central part of Queen
Maud Land provides an example of block mountains in mobile regions of
the Upper Archean crystalline basement which underwent an intensive
tectometamorphic rearrangement during the Early Proterozoic. The development of the polymetamorphic rocks is due to this reactivation.

The Yamato Mountains are block structures, forming five rocky summits
separated by ice and small nunataks extending submeridionally for over 50 km.
Polymetamorphic rocks are exposed in only two peripheral blocks, between
which there are migmatites and plagiogneisses of the amphibolite facies. Polymetamorphic rocks have been encountered only on the periphery of the Sør
Rondane Mountains, at the following locations: 1) in the extreme SW, in the
upper reaches of the Borchgrevink Glacier (21°30'E), and 2) in the extreme
NE, on the margin of the Oberstbreen Glacier (27°20'E), these relicts form
groups of low nunataks. Between them, for a distance of nearly 200 km,
there are numerous blocks composed of monometamorphic rocks of the
amphibolite facies intruded by metagabbroic and granitic rocks. Polymetamorphic rocks also build the isolated Botnnuten Peak, situated 150 km
NE of the Yamato Mountains in the easternmost part of Queen Maud Land.
All these blocks of metamorphic rocks, in spite of their considerable terri-
torial separation, have identical geological settings in the peripheral portions
of large blocks of monometamorphic rocks. Their rock compositions are
also similar, exhibiting a relatively low grade of migmatization and
granitization.

A characteristic feature of the polymetamorphic rocks of the Yamato
and Sør Rondane Mountains is the prevalence of the following two types of
plagiogneisses, fairly often (particularly in the Sør Rondane Mountains)
alternating in beds several meters thick in the same exposures: a) bipyroxene plagiogneisses (often considerably biotitized and less commonly
amphibolized), not infrequently transformed into migmatites and shadow
granites of a charnockitic variety; b) biotite-garnet plagiogneisses (occasionally with amphibole), usually only migmatized. The blocks of polymetamorphic rocks almost always contain calciphyres, mainly consisting of
diopside and scapolite. The ferruginosity of diopside reaches 40% in some
specimens. The bipyroxene plagiogneiss usually forms the paleosome of
migmatites, with 40—60% andesine (An 36—45), 10—20% quartz, 3—15% orthopyroxene (ferruginosity, 45—50%), 0—20% clinopyroxene (ferruginosity,
37—45%), with a total of 5—25% biotite plus amphibole depending on the
pyroxene which they replace. In places, the migmatites form a gradual
transition to shadow granites (charnockitic). The paleosome of migmatites
is initially appreciably feldspathized, then transformed into a rock with a
predominance of microcline-perthite over oligoclase-andesine. Its quartz
content reaches 25—30%, and pyroxene is decreased by 1/2—2/3 while its
ferruginosity increases by 15—20%. Amphibole nearly disappears, and
biotite becomes the leading colored mineral (with a ferruginosity of 60—70%).
The biotite-garnet plagiogneisses are most commonly the paleosome of
layered migmatites. They mainly consist of oligoclase-andesine (An 23—31)
with varying admixtures of K-feldspar, quartz (up to 20—30%) and colored
minerals. Garnet forms only a small admixture in varieties dominated by
amphibole and biotite, but its content reaches 20% when the amphibole and/or

biotite contents are much reduced. Although the garnet content of these migmatites is high in some areas, they never contain sillimanite or cordierite. Therefore it appears that the amphibolite facies minerals, namely biotite and amphibole on the one hand, and garnet on the other, do not develop from high-alumina minerals, but from pyroxenes and more basic plagioclases. Thus the biotite-garnet plagiogneisses are the final products of recrystallization of the parent bipyroxene plagiogneisses under amphibolite facies conditions, i. e., products of polymetamorphism. On the whole, the rare blocks of polymetamorphic rocks in the Sør Rondane and Yamato mountains somewhat resemble the Schüssel Suite rocks in their composition, but differ from that suite in that they are only slightly granulated. Probably, granulation of rocks is not a regional process within the crystalline basement but takes place in local zones of abyssal faults dominated by stress. All the other dominant rocks of the Yamato and Sør Rondane Mountains are typical amphibolite facies formations.

As many as five small nunataks are exposed on the periphery of the Shackleton Glacier. Many of these are composed of a variety of plagiogneisses and their migmatites formed in two metamorphic stages, so that they have been transformed into polymetamorphic rocks. Characteristically, the latter are nowhere transformed into typical shadow granites or granulites. The polymetamorphic rocks are predominantly migmatites. Biotitized hypersthene plagiogneisses form the paleosome of layered migmatites on Davis Peninsula and Alligator Island /57/. They contain 50—60% oligoclase-andesine (An 27—32), 20—30% quartz, 5—10% hypersthene (ferruginosity, 45—58%) and 6—10% biotite (ferruginosity, 55—60%). The paleosome of agmatites is most commonly represented by amphibolites, with relicts of pyroxenes or by appreciably amphibolized bipyroxene schists with plagioclase-andesine (An 40—45) and pyroxenes; orthopyroxenes ($f = 40\%$) and clinopyroxene ($f = 32\%$). The metasome of migmatites on Alligator Island has equal contents of oligoclase, microcline and quartz, while the predominant colored mineral is biotite (7—10%). There are rare relicts of highly ferruginous orthopyroxene. The metasome of migmatites on Davis Peninsula has a plagiogranitic composition, with nearly 60% acid andesine and a small admixture of microcline, up to 30% quartz and 10% biotite, with pyroxene relicts.

INSEL SERIES

The northern margins of the Humboldt Mountains and Petermann Range as well as their center contain a group of migmatites and shadow granites of the amphibolite facies. These are in contact with the polymetamorphic Humboldt Series along the abyssal fault. The metamorphic strata of the amphibolite facies have a combined visible thickness of at least 6—7 km. They are exposed in blocks in the northern margins of the mountains with areas of 50—60 km^2, and also form a large block in the center of the region with an area of up to 150 km^2. Although the profile is heterogeneous, the strata in question cannot be differentiated into suites, and have therefore been designated in their entirety as the Insel Series — after Mount Insel which provides the most complete profile of this group of strata. The time of formation of the Insel Series, its setting in the crystalline basement, and its relationship with the granulite facies series have not yet been definitely established. The part played in the formation of the strata by superimposed metamorphism related to later stages of the tectono-magmatic activization of the crystalline basement, for example, during the Late Baikal epoch, still remains obscure. It may only be assumed that the Insel Series was formed at lesser depths and at lower temperatures than the principal basement rocks of the granulite facies and that its formation conditions were analogous to those of the metamorphic strata in the western part of Queen Maud Land, in the Sør Rondane Mountains, in the western part of Enderby Land (Prince Olav Coast) and other regions with extensive occurrence of typical amphibolite facies rocks. All these strata may compose the upper stage of the crystalline basement, its blocks coming in contact with those of the lower stage due to their translocation from different depths along regional faults. The possibility that the blocks of amphibolite and granulite facies rocks were formed simultaneously in different structural-facies zones (and hence their different grades of metamorphism) cannot be ruled out. The superimposed metamorphism of later epochs related to reactivization of the crystalline basement has possibly been reflected in the appearance of mineral associations of the epidote-amphibolite facies in rocks of the amphibolite facies, some traces of which are also present in the Insel Series. Several indications (described further on) suggest that the metamorphic strata of the Insel Series were never subjected to granulite facies conditions and that the leading mineral parageneses of the amphibolite facies are primary and in equilibrium.

The various migmatites and shadow granites formed from the amphibole-biotite and biotite plagiogneisses and partially also amphibolites, are markedly predominant in the Insel Series. Boudinaged bodies of amphibolites, calciphyres and quartzites account for about 5%. A similar volume within the Insel Series is occupied by granitoid veins. Intrusive formations within the Insel Series are represented by sporadic stocks and dikes of granitized gabbroids and small fissures filling bodies of biotite-amphibole granitoids. Characteristically, the series contains a very small amount of high-alumina rocks with very low contents of such minerals as sillimanite; cordierite and spinel are totally absent. It is therefore natural that the series does not contain any bipyroxene schists, migmatites and shadow granitoids of enderbitic-charnockitic varieties.

Layered migmatites are the predominant rocks in the Insel Series (Figure 39); finely and coarsely layered varieties often alternate even within a single exposure. The finely layered varieties usually have a garnet-biotite paleosome and the coarsely layered varieties, a biotite-amphibole paleosome. In the former, thin paleosome intercalations (up to 1 cm thick) account for about $1/3$ of the rock volume; in the latter, the layers are 0.5—1 m thick and form about one-half of the rock. The paleosome most commonly consists of fine-grained and medium-grained, fairly melanocratic biotite-amphibole plagiogneisses, of light gray and gray color, with lepidoheterogranoblastic textures and schistose structures (Figure 40). The size and shape of grains vary widely, including isometric plagioclase grains (0.5—1.5 mm), prismatic amphibole laths (1—2 mm) and xenoblastic and oval quartz segregations

(0.5—3 mm). A very characteristic feature of these plagiogneisses (Table 65) is the paragenesis of andesine, An 30—38 (seldom up to An 46), with ordinary hornblende of ferruginosity 46—60% with an admixture of biotite (ferruginosity 55—70%) and in places also rare salite (ferruginosity 41—45%). Together with these primary minerals, there locally occur secondary amphiboles of the cummingtonite-grünerite series which completely replace clinopyroxene. These amphiboles are accompanied by biotite of low ferruginosity (38%) which is also a secondary mineral. The paleosome often consists almost entirely of amphibole and andesine with an admixture of quartz (10—15%), biotite (2—10%), and accessory minerals— mostly titanomagnetite (2—3%), sphene (1—2%) and apatite (1—2%). There are also rare grains of zircon and orthite. In places, the paleosome has higher contents of quartz (up to 20%) and biotite (up to 15%). Such varieties also have higher contents of zircon and orthite. On the whole, this paleosome approaches andesite in composition. Characteristically, such paleosome lacks K-feldspar and garnet, although these are present in the metasome. Another, less common

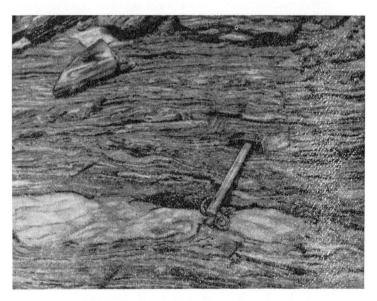

FIGURE 39. Typical finely layered migmatite with a biotite-garnet paleosome (Insel Series, exposure 49).

garnet-biotite paleosome type exhibits a very fine-grained texture. Its composition (Table 66) includes a comparatively acid plagioclase, An 26—28, accompanied by a high content of quartz (20—30%) and biotite (up to 25%). Also present is garnet (4—10%) of high ferruginosity, while accessory minerals are rare. On the whole, this type of paleosome is more often characteristic of finely layered migmatites. It is an acid rock, though of sedimentary-terrigenous rather than magmatic origin. A third type of paleosome, which is characteristic of agmatites, is represented by amphibole-biotite gneisses differing from the paleosome of coarsely layered migmatites in their constant content of K-feldspar. The colored minerals in this paleosome have high ferruginosities (62—69%), while the prevalent accessory mineral is sphene (3—4%) which in places completely replaces the ore mineral. Plagioclase is characterized by a variable composition, ranging from An 24 to An 35 even in a single specimen. Zoning is common, with different zones varying in An content by up to 10%. In places, the paleosome of agmatites is a finely layered migmatite with a plagiogranitic metasome. Biotite is the only colored mineral, making up 1—4% of the metasome and up to 50% of the paleosome. It is possible that, in this case repeated migmatization of the plagiogneisses took place, producing first the finely layered migmatites, then the agmatite. Both processes, however, occurred under amphibolite facies conditions.

FIGURE 40. Fractured finely layered migmatite from plagiogneiss, Insel Series. A leucocratic coarse-grained intercalation representing the metasome occurs in the center. (Thin section 82a, ×8, crossed nicols).

TABLE 66. Mineral composition and characteristics, Insel Series

Paleosome of layered migmatites

a) biotite-amphibole

Specimen No.	K-feldspar	plagioclase	quartz	clinopyroxene	amphibole	biotite	garnet	carbonate	scapolite	ore mineral	apatite	sphene	zircon	orthite	An content of plagioclase	cpx n_x	cpx n_z	cpx ferruginosity, at.%	amph n_x	amph n_z	amph ferruginosity, at.%	biot n_x	biot ferruginosity, at.%	garnet n
82b		50	5		25	20				o.s.*	o.s.				32				1.695	1.661	57	1.632	38	
46		48			45	4				3				o.s.	In places, c**–28				1.692	1.668	54			
52		40	20		12	38					1	o.s.	1		33									
84		70	8			7				2	1		o.s.	»	35									
84v		45	13	7	23*	9*				1	o.s.	2			34				1.684	1.654	58	1.659	59	
257		45		2	50*	3									29	1.720	1.694	41	1.692	1.667	54	1.675	70	
257a		40	5		55	2				3	o.s.				31				1.697	1.673	59			
257b		67			25	1				2					25									
284		48	13	7	10	16				3	2	1			38				1.702	1.672	75			
285		47	10		30	10				2	1				35				1.705	1.683	68	1.655	55	
850		40	15		25	14				4	2		o.s.		38	1.723	1.695	45	1.686	1.662	49			
807d		45	22		18	14				1	o.s.	o.s.			46				1.682	1.658	44	1.650	52	

Cummingtonite (amphibole of specimens 84v, 257, 257a); Grünerite (amphibole of specimens 284, 285, 850, 807d).

b) garnet-biotite

Specimen No.	K-feldspar	plagioclase	quartz	clinopyroxene	amphibole	biotite	garnet	carbonate	scapolite	ore mineral	apatite	sphene	zircon	orthite	An content of plagioclase	cpx n_x	cpx n_z	cpx ferruginosity, at.%	amph n_x	amph n_z	amph ferruginosity, at.%	biot n_x	biot ferruginosity, at.%	garnet n
47v		60	13			27	o.s.			o.s.	o.s.	o.s.			28							1.658	58	1.806
48		34	30			25	10			»	»	»	o.s.		26									
241		65	20			10	4				1		o.s.		28									

TABLE 66 (continued)

Specimen No.	K-feldspar	plagioclase	quartz	clinopyroxene	amphibole	biotite	garnet	carbonate	scapolite	ore mineral	apatite	sphene	zircon	orthite	An content of plagioclase	clinopyroxene n_x	clinopyroxene n_z	clinopyroxene ferrugino-sity, at.%	amphibole n_x	amphibole n_z	amphibole ferrugino-sity, at.%	biotite n_x	biotite ferrugino-sity, at.%	garnet n
Paleosome of agmatites																								
537a	25	52	10		14	12				1	o.s.	o.s.		o.s.	24 In places, c – 30				1.704	1.680	66	1.663	62	
538	6	40	16			20					o.s.	4		o.s.	26									
538a	18	45	17		6	11				3	o.s.	3			c – 34									
808	7	28	20		18	18				3	3	3		o.s.	m** – 25 35									
Including finely layered migmatites																								
a) paleosome																								
49v	50		37			13				o.s.					35									
240	25		25			50																		
b) metasome																								
49v	57		42			1									30									
240	60		34			4				2														

TABLE 66 (continued)

Specimen No.	Composition														An content of plagioclase	Mineral characteristics								
																clinopyroxene			amphibole			biotite		garnet
	K-feldspar	plagioclase	quartz	clinopyroxene	amphibole	biotite	garnet	carbonate	scapolite	ore mineral	apatite	sphene	zircon	orthite		n_x	n_z	ferrugino-sity, at.%	n_x	n_z	ferrugino-sity, at.%	n_x	ferrugino-sity, at.%	n
Metasome of migmatites																								
a) plagiogranitic																								
46a		43	43		2	10				2					21									
237g		70	14		2	12				2					18				Grünerite 1.703	1.673	75	1.670	67	
286v	15	50	30			2									25							1.672	68	
b) granitic																								
47	28	28	35			6	3						o.s.		25									
47a	33	33	25			8	1				o.s.	o.s.	»	o.s.	28									
48b	65	12	20		o.s.	12	2																	
52a	39	25	20			11				o.s.	o.s.	o.s.	o.s.	o.s.	28									
84a	38	16	35			2	o.s.						o.s.	o.s.	25									
241	60	18	20			5				1	1													
284—1	55	14	22		2	10					2	1												
286b	30	25	27			12	o.s.						o.s.		28									
807g	25	27	35				6			o.s.	o.s.			o.s.	29									
Metasome in agmatites																								
a) plagiogranitic																								
49a	o.s.	44	45			10	.			o.s.	o.s.	o.s.	o.s.	o.s.	30									
49b		72	25			3				»	»	»	»	»	30									
240a		60	35			5				»	o.s.	o.s.	o.s.	o.s.	30									

TABLE 66 (continued)

b) granitic

Specimen No.	K-feldspar	plagioclase	quartz	clinopyroxene	amphibole	biotite	garnet	carbonate	scapolite	ore mineral	apatite	sphene	zircon	orthite	An content of plagioclase	clinopyroxene n_x	clinopyroxene n_z	clinopyroxene ferruginosity, at.%	amphibole n_x	amphibole n_z	amphibole ferruginosity, at.%	biotite n_x	biotite ferruginosity, at.%	garnet n
537	70	8	20			2*				o.s.	o.s.		o.s.		22									
538b	40	32	18			8				"					25									
538v	48	15	35			1						1			28									
808a	38	38	20			4				o.s.												1.660	59	

Finely layered migmatites and shadow granites (from plagiogneisses and amphibolites)

a) plagiogranitic composition

Specimen No.	K-feldspar	plagioclase	quartz	clinopyroxene	amphibole	biotite	garnet	carbonate	scapolite	ore mineral	apatite	sphene	zircon	orthite	An content of plagioclase	clinopyroxene n_x	clinopyroxene n_z	clinopyroxene ferruginosity, at.%	amphibole n_x	amphibole n_z	amphibole ferruginosity, at.%	biotite n_x	biotite ferruginosity, at.%	garnet n
83b		45	40			10	5*			1			o.s.		24									
83v	2	50	35			9	5								25									
238	8	58	35		o.s.	5	o.s.					o.s.			27									
238a		63	17		o.s.	12	"				1	o.s.			36									
286a	13	45	25			13	3				1			1	28									
591		50	33			15									34									
830a	15	37	25		1	16	5			o.s.					37 (In places, m — 45)							1.647	49	1.803
51v		37	33			30	o.s.				o.s.	a.s.												
534b	4	38	20			31	7*			1	"	"	"		28							1.660	59	1.806
540a	7	58	12			15	5				2	"	"		28							1.674	70	1.795
540b		54	20			20	2			2	2		"		39							1.663	62	1.809
805g		47	33			15				2			"		23							1.674	70	1.809
806	3	47	35			13	"				o.s.		"	o.s.	25							1.664	62	1.813

TABLE 66 (continued)

b) granitic composition

Specimen No.	Composition																Mineral characteristics								
	K-feldspar	plagioclase	quartz	clinopyroxene	amphibole	biotite	garnet	carbonate	scapolite	ore mineral	apatite	sphene	zircon	orthite	An content of plagioclase	clinopyroxene n_x	clinopyroxene n_z	clinopyroxene ferruginosity, at.%	amphibole n_x	amphibole n_z	amphibole ferruginosity, at.%	biotite n_x	biotite ferruginosity, at.%	garnet n
50	40	18	32		8*	6*	4*			o.s.	o.s.		o.s.		17				1.678	1.654	41	1.664	62	1.813
51	65	7	18		7	10*				″	o.s.	o.s.	″		30				1.707	1.683	69	1.641	45	1.795
82	30	30	20			12*	3				1		″		30							1.675	70	1.807
82a	20	35	22			18	3*						1		28									
83	30	30	23		2	6	2			2	o.s.	o.s.	o.s.		26							1.656	56	
238b	59	8	22			9				1	″	″	″	o.s.	28									
242a	66	15	13			6					″		″		26									
242b	57	15	18			9					″		″	o.s.	28									
273	30	30	32			10				o.s.	″		″		27							1.650	52	
284a	29	30	27			9	o.s.			1			″	o.s.	25									
285b	30	30	27			13	o.s.					o.s.	″		22									
540	40	28	22			10	4				o.s.		″		20									
534a	63	6	15		1	15	1				2		″		28				1.722	1.698	84	1.654	55	1.809
541	32	32	22			2					1		″		24							1.690	81	
537d	25	35	20			18					1		″											
590	33	30	25			10							″		21									
535	67	7	30			4					o.s.	o.s.	″											
833	28	27	30			15							″											
833a	40	18	25			17					″		″		25									
833b	60	15	25			3*					″		″		23									
834	30	36	20			14*	2						″	o.s.								1.663	62	

TABLE 66 (continued)

Specimen No.	K-feldspar	plagioclase	quartz	clinopyroxene	amphibole	biotite	garnet	carbonate	scapolite	ore mineral	apatite	sphene	zircon	orthite	An content of plagioclase	cpx n_x	cpx n_z	cpx ferrug., at.%	amph n_x	amph n_z	amph ferrug., at.%	biot n_x	biot ferrug., at.%	garnet n

Amphibolites

a) boudinaged bodies

50v		35	7	o.s.	52*	6*				o.s.	o.s.				c.,—65—50 m.,—70—85				1.678	1.654	41	1.630	37	
52b		40	5	20	33	2				»		o.s.	o.s.		71	1.712	1.684	28	1.664 / 1.652	1.640 / 1.626	29 / 33	1.625	33	
591a		36	4	o.s.	48	7				4	1	1			42				1.678	1.653	41			
590a		35	6	3	50	4				1	o.s.				c.,—35 m.,—45	1.718	1.690	36	1.692	1.667	54			
285a		30	10	o.s.	50*	4				3	1	2			80									
241a		45	7	o.s.	30*	18				o.s.	o.s.	o.s.			41				1.681	1.655	44	1.644	47	

(Actinolite — for 52b amphibole)

b) relicts in shadow granites

805a		20	30		5	45				o.s.	o.s.	o.s.			95									
83a		27	28		25*	20									79—82				1.667	1.639	41	1.625	33	
807v		30	3		27	40				o.s.	o.s.				50				1.672	1.649	34	1.620	29	
286		43	17		25	15									c.,—71—78 m.,—62				1.662	1.635	24			
540v		35	33		7	25									89									
806a		28	27		2	40				3		o.s.	o.s.		72									

(Cummingtonite — for shadow granite amphiboles)

TABLE 66 (continued)

Specimen No.	K-feldspar	plagioclase	quartz	clinopyroxene	amphibole	biotite	garnet	carbonate	scapolite	ore mineral	apatite	sphene	zircon	orthite	An content of plagioclase	cpx n_x	cpx n_z	cpx ferrugino-sity, at.%	amph n_x	amph n_z	amph ferrugino-sity, at.%	biot n_x	biot ferrugino-sity, at.%	garnet n
Calciphyres																								
284b			40	26	2				28	o.s.		2				1.702	1.729	55	1.664	1.687	50			
284v	3	8	2	85	5			1	6			1				1.698	1.725	48	1.663	1.686	49			
537b		2	1	50	5	2		13	12			2												
537v			8	20	2		33	20	10	o.s.	o.s.	1		1										
Quartzites																								
285g		34	50			13	13			o.s.	o.s.				30									
285e		34	50			16	3			"	"				c,−31 m,−27									
534v		14	85	o.s.	2	1				o.s.	o.s.				30				1.692	1.715	78			
237v	7	27	60			3		1		o.s.	o.s.				29							1.670	67	
Vein granitoids																								
a) plagiogranites																								
46v		64	30		1	4				1	o.s.		o.s.	o.s.	21									
50b		60	35			4									29							1.650	52	
84b		70	22			8									30							1.650	52	

TABLE 66 (continued)

b) granites

Specimen No.	K-feldspar	plagioclase	quartz	clinopyroxene	amphibole	biotite	garnet	carbonate	scapolite	ore mineral	apatite	sphene	zircon	orthite	An content of plagioclase	clinopyroxene n_x	clinopyroxene n_z	clinopyroxene ferrugino-sity, at. %	amphibole n_x	amphibole n_z	amphibole ferrugino-sity, at. %	garnet n_x	garnet ferrugino-sity, at. %	biotite n
50a	49	25	23			2				2	o.s.				24									
51b	39	30	25			6	o.s.			o.s.	o.s.	o.s.	o.s.	o.s.	22									
82v	31	25	25			17				:	=	:	=	1	23									
82g	35	23	28			13					=		=	1	27									
84g	34	30	22			13				1	=		=									1.674	70	
284g	62	8	25			5				1				1										
290b	30	26	28			12						o.s.	o.s.	o.s.										
806b	51	17	28			3									23									

c) granosyenites

Specimen No.	K-feldspar	plagioclase	quartz	clinopyroxene	amphibole	biotite	garnet	carbonate	scapolite	ore mineral	apatite	sphene	zircon	orthite	An content of plagioclase	garnet n_x	garnet ferrugino-sity, at. %
51g	51	23	17			8				1	o.s.	o.s.	o.s.	o.s.	25		
534	52	30	16			2	o.s.			o.s.	o.s.				24	1.668	65
808b	70	7	18			5									24		

Notes. Specimen 286v, muscovite, 3%; specimen 48b, muscovite, 1%; specimen 538b, radioactive mineral (?), 2%; specimen 83, muscovite, 3%; specimen 534a, muscovite, 1%; specimen 284b, orthite, $n_z = 1.712$, $n_x = 1.703$; specimen 537b, clinozoisite, 4%, $n_z = 1.718$, $n_x = 1.708$; specimen 537v, clinozoisite, 4%; calcite, $n_0 = 1.658$.

* [o.s. = optic sign.]

** [c and m = central and marginal portions of grains, respectively.]

The metasome of migmatites is plagiogranitic and granitic in composition. The latter considerably predominates over the former (Table 66). The metasome content in the layered migmatites averages double that in agmatites. Plagiogranitic metasome forms fine- and medium-grained gneissic shadow granites. Its texture is lepidogranoblastic with grains of 0.5—3.0 mm (the largest grains are quartz xenoblasts). The colored minerals have high ferruginosities, 67—75%, and form rugged-banded aggregates with a linear orientation. A paragenesis of oligoclase, An 18—25, with grünerite and highly ferruginous biotite is characteristic. The quartz content varies from 15 to 40%, with a corresponding variation in the plagioclase content. Appreciable amounts of K-feldspar (up to 15%) appear irregularly. The accessories are ore minerals except for minute relict granules of clinopyroxene. This variable composition of the metasome suggests the participation of metasomatic processes in its formation. The composition of the plagiogranitic metasome is similar to that of the veins. The fine-to medium-grained rocks are massive with a granoblastic texture. Porphyroblastic elements are due to the presence of plagioclase laths up to 1 cm in size. Generally, the grain size is 0.5—3 mm; the larger grains are plagioclase and the smaller ones are quartz. The association of acid andesine, An 30, with quartz (25—30%) (normal for granites) and a relatively high iron content in biotite is characteristic. The veins contain a variety of accessory minerals ranging from sphene to orthite although their amount is very small. The granitic metasome is similar in all migmatite varieties. However, it resembles shadow granite in the layered migmatites and fine- grained massive granite in the agmatites. It must be emphasized that the metasome of layered migmatites often contains a highly ferruginous garnet and sporadic relict amphibole granules which are absent from the metasome of agmatites. Possibly, the shadow granites of layered migmatites were formed metasomatically, whereas the metasome of agmatites crystallized from a melt. A characteristic feature of granitic metasome is the prevalence of microcline over oligoclase (An 22—28); thus, some varieties correspond in composition to granosyenites, particularly since quartz varies from 20 to 35%. The colored minerals are represented mainly by biotite, but its content in the metasome of layered migmatites is double that in the granite metasome of agmatite. The ferruginosity of biotite reaches 60%. Garnets occur only in shadow granites, where they vary in content, from sporadic grains to 6%; this is certainly less than the garnet content in the migmatite paleosome. The character of the metasome suggests the possibility of nonsimultaneous formation of the layered migmatites and agmatites, the latter being superimposed on the former.

Shadow granitoids of the Insel Series are distinguished by the fairly important role played in their composition by melanocratic varieties resembling finely layered migmatites. However, both rocks are so closely interbedded in the same outcrops that it is practically impossible to differentiate between them. Possibly, the finely layered migmatites are the paleosome from which the shadow granitoids, represented by gneissic medium-grained rocks, light gray and light yellow (less frequently pink) in color, were formed. Melanocratic, mostly biotite-amphibole aggregates, form maculose, lenticular and "frayed" accumulations, ranging from a few centimeters to several decimeters in size. These are irregularly distributed in

the rock.   The texture is heterogranoblastic with lepidoblastic or porphyroblastic elements.   The size and shape of the rock-forming mineral grains
present a great variety, ranging from 0.5 to 4 mm, the larger xenoblastic
grains being neogenic microline and quartz.   Less common are prismatic
and euhedral grains of amphibole and garnet.   The size of euhedral plagioclase grains does not exceed 1 mm, which is also the length of fine biotite
flakes and quartz grains in mosaic aggregates.   Cataclasis is noted throughout,
although it is less intensive than in other suites of the Humboldt Mountains
(Figure 41).

FIGURE 41. Biotite shadow granite with heterogranoblastic texture. The quartz
is slightly granulated. (Insel Series, thin section 273, × 11, crossed nicols).

The shadow granitoids form two varieties with respect to composition:
plagiogranites, and granites with trends toward granosyenites.   The first
type is usually represented by more melanocratic rocks, approaching finely
layered migmatites.   Characteristically, both types of shadow granitoids
are often interbedded in the same outcrops in the form of diffuse sheets
forming gradual transitions between each other.   The plagioclase in granites

is stable and is represented by oligoclase, An 23—28, with only slight
variations, whereas the plagioclase in plagiogranites is distinguished by
an extremely unstable composition fluctuating between oligoclase, An 24—25,
and basic andesine, An 45—48, which display a reverse metamorphic zonality.
The An content is 10% higher in the rims than in the center. The plagiogranitic
varieties have a very unstable mineral composition and widely fluctuating
ferruginosities of the colored minerals (Table 66). Thus, the plagioclase
content (of unstable composition) fluctuates between 37 and 63%, and the
quartz content varies correspondingly from 17 to 40%. Microcline is
sporadic (2—15%). Plagioclase forms small euhedral grains and porphyroblastic laths. It is always corroded by shapeless quartz segregations and
in places by microcline veins which fill cracks in the porphyroblasts. In
places, there are lenticular-ribbon quartz aggregates, linearly oriented,
imparting a granulitic texture to the rock. The main colored mineral is
biotite with a ferruginosity of 48—70%. This forms aggregates up to 1 mm
in size and separate flakes up to 2—3 mm long. Prismatic hornblende grains
are locally preserved (occasionally in appreciable amounts); as a rule, they
are replaced by biotite. Garnet is nearly ubiquitous in the plagiogranites,
but it does not exceed 5—7% in content (usually less). Its ferruginosity is
75—90%. Isometric garnet grains are corroded by biotite flakes, within
which they are embedded. A great variety of accessory minerals are present
in small amounts. Apatite is somewhat more abundant than the others,
although zircon and orthite are likewise found, although sporadically. Ore
minerals have been preserved only in insignificant amounts, but sphene
appears in their place.

A characteristic feature of shadow granites proper is an appreciable
prevalence of microline over plagioclase and of the latter over quartz
(Table 66). Unlike the shadow plagiogranites, they are rich in metasomatic
substitution elements. Plagioclase has a relict appearance, although its
content is still significant, 10—35%. It usually occurs in small (0.3—1.5 mm)
nearly euhedral grains, markedly corroded by microcline and quartz. Plagioclase porphyroblasts practically disappear, being intensively corroded by
microcline and quartz. Both these minerals form anhedral segregations,
0.5—3 mm in size and occasionally up to 5 — 7 mm. The content of microcline
(often twinned) fluctuates from 20 to 65%, whereas the content of quartz is
more stable (20—30%). Resorbed plagioclase relicts occur in the microcline porphyroblasts. In places, the quartz segregations assume a lenticular-
ribbon shape, imparting granulitic textures to the rock. The prevalent
colored mineral is biotite, its content varying from 3 to 18% and its ferruginosity from 45 to 80%, depending on the degree of metasomatism of the
shadow granite. Hornblende relicts, with a ferruginosity of 40—80%, and a
small amount of tiny garnet grains (2—3%) with a variable but fairly high
ferruginosity (80—90%) occur sporadically. There is an occasional small
admixture of muscovite. The accessory minerals include small amounts of
ubiquitous apatite and zircon and sporadic ore and sphene. Such granites
were formed from biotite-amphibole plagiogneisses granitized under amphibolite facies conditions. The granitization mainly resulted in an enrichment
in K-feldspar. They may also have originated from layered migmatites,
and in this case it is difficult to determine whether the process was related
to a single or two consecutive metamorphic stages.

Amphibolites in the Insel Series play the same role as metabasites and bipyroxene schists derived from them in the other suites of the Humboldt Mountains, formed under granulite and superimposed amphibolite facies conditions. The amphibolites compose fairly large sheets up to 100—120 m thick, but more commonly form stocks and dikes. They occur as fairly massive (dark gray to black) medium-to fine-grained schists. Their texture is commonly granoblastic with relicts of a granular texture. They are composed mainly of prismatic (1—3 mm) and smaller euhedral grains of amphibole and plagioclase (0.5—1 mm). The interstices are filled with xenoblastic quartz granules and aggregates of biotite flakes, partly replacing the primary minerals. Large amphibole grains display a poikiloblastic texture due to profuse small inclusions of quartz and biotite (Figure 42). About one half of the rock is composed of ordinary hornblende with a relatively low ferruginosity (40—54%), replaced locally by a secondary actinolite having a ferruginosity of up to 30%. Relict clinopyroxene grains of still lower ferruginosity, 28—36%, often occur within the prismatic hornblende aggregates. Presumably, pyroxene was the major rock-forming mineral in the original rock; its replacement by amphibole resulted from recrystallization under amphibolite facies conditions. About one-third of the rock volume consists of plagioclases with an extremely variable composition, ranging from andesine, An 40, to anorthite, An 85, even within a single specimen. There is a marked reverse metamorphic zonation, with increased basicity in the marginal zones of plagioclase grains; bytownite-anorthite, An 70—85, in the rims and labradorite, An 50—65, at the center. Even highly altered grains consist of andesine — An 35 at the center and An 45 in the rim. These sharp fluctuations in the plagioclase composition indicate intensive recrystallization accompanied by "disanorthitization" of the plagioclase. Quartz is an ubiquitous but relatively minor admixture (5—10%). Its appearance is also possibly related to recrystallization and alteration and not to superimposed silicic metasomatism. Aggregates of biotite flakes form a similar admixture, although their content locally reaches 18% (generally 2—5%). The biotite occurs almost exclusively along the edges of amphibole grains and its ferruginosity is still lower than that of the amphibole (33—47%), again indicating its secondary nature. The ore mineral frequently occurs with sphene; their combined content is 2—5%. The only other accessory mineral is apatite; zircon and orthite, which are common in shadow granitoids, are absent from the amphibolites. Relicts of amphibolite boudins occur within finely layered migmatites and shadow granites. They form wedged-out sheets, lenses, "horsetails" and diffuse patches several meters in size. These melanocratic relicts have a considerably higher content of secondary biotite, sometimes even exceeding that of hornblende. The ore minerals disappear. Secondary cummingtonite appears with hornblende instead of actinolite as in large bodies of amphibolites. The amphibolites under discussion are exclusively confined to the Insel Series and do not occur in the other metamorphic strata of the Humboldt Mountains and Petermann Range. They are typical metamorphic schists formed in amphibolite facies from magmatic rocks of basic composition.

Calciphyres form comparatively small beds which are fairly well preserved among layered migmatites and shadow granites. Their thickness varies from 20 cm to 1.5 m, and they can be traced over tens of meters along strike.   In places, the calciphyres are highly silicified and in such cases contain orthite crystallites.   Their structure is similar to calciphyres occurring in other suites of the Humboldt Mountains formed under poly-metamorphic conditions, but their composition is somewhat different (Table 66).   Firstly, the clinopyroxene, which is predominant in these cal-ciphyres (20—85 %), is always a salite (approaching ferrosalite — ferrugino-sity, 48 — 55 %), whereas calciphyres of the granulite facies contain diopside; a more ferruginous clinopyroxene is restricted to zones of superim-posed metamorphism of the amphibolite facies.   Another characteristic feature is the persistent presence of small amounts (2—5 %) of ordinary hornblende, with a ferruginosity that is almost the same as that of salite. Ubiquitous sphene is the only accessory mineral.   Their third characteristic feature is the local intense silicification.   The fourth feature is an ubiquitous admixture of clinozoisite occurring within calcite-scapolite aggregates, usually accounting for one-third of the rock volume.

FIGURE 42. Amphibolite from the Insel Series, displaying poikiloblastic texture of amphibole grains (dark). (Thin section 590a, × 8, crossed nicols).

Quartzites occur to a very limited extent in the Insel Series, forming intercalations only a few decimeters thick. An outstanding feature of these quartzites is the high plagioclase (An 27—31) content and the presence of biotite. Thus, they may be designated as quartzite-gneisses (Table 66). Most commonly, these rocks contain 50% quartz, 35% plagioclase and >10% of comparatively highly ferruginous (67%) biotite, with an admixture of still more ferruginous (81%) hornblende and even sporadic grains of ferrosalite. The K-feldspar content is small and far from ubiquitous. Another feature of the quartzites is the high degree of recrystallization resulting in coarser grains. This is especially noticeable in varieties containing 70—80% quartz which forms large xenoblastic grains up to 1 cm in size. Accessory minerals include ore granules and apatite crystallites.

Granitoid veins occur in almost all rock exposures of the Insel Series, accounting for 2—8% of their volume. They resemble the veins of the Humboldt Series with respect to form and composition. On the other hand, their mineral associations are closest to the amphibolite facies paragenesis. The veins are represented by plagiogranites, granites and granosyenites. This differentiation is essentially based on the feldspar and quartz contents. The composition of these minerals is the same in all the varieties, and this also applies to the colored and accessory minerals (Table 66). Granitoid veins, 20 cm to 2 m thick, are usually composed of fine-grained and medium-grained cataclastized rocks, which are coarse-grained in granosyenite varieties, where they assume pegmatitic habits due to large (1—3 cm) microcline porphyroblasts containing abundant perthite ingrowths. Typical pegmatite veins have not been encountered in Insel Series rocks.

The composition of the prevalent fine-grained granite veins is fairly stable; oligoclase, An 22—27, predominates over microcline almost everywhere, whereas the quartz content is almost normal for granites, 22—28%. The only colored mineral (barring the very rare garnet grains) is biotite of ferruginosity 65—70%. The range of accessory minerals is fairly stable, and includes 1—2% ore, 1% apatite and zircon crystallites (combined), up to 1% orthite (somewhat high) and sporadic sphene surrounding the ore. The basicity of plagioclase rises to An 35 in the earliest plagiogranite veins, the content of biotite declines to 4—5% with a ferruginosity not exceeding 52%, and there is a considerable decrease in the accessory mineral content. On the other hand, in the latest granosyenite veins, plagioclase has been replaced by K-feldspar to a considerable extent, the quartz content has decreased, and the content of accessory minerals has increased. This composition is due not only to their direct crystallization from partial melts but also to their subsequent metasomatism by residual alkaline solutions. This is also the cause for the porphyroblastic nature of microcline and the pegmatitic habit of the veins. The metasomatism of the veins is manifested only in narrow (3—8 cm) melanocratic selvage bands. These bands are composed of biotite plus garnet (~50%). Later segregations of microcline corrode all other minerals.

The Insel Series contains the following sporadic intrusions: a) granitized gabbroids transformed into rocks having compositions similar to quartz diorites and even granosyenites; amphibole and biotite are the colored minerals; b) amphibole-biotite and biotite granitoids; mostly granites with variations toward granodiorites and granosyenites. The granitoids will be described in the chapter dealing with charnockitic intrusions of the Humboldt Mountains and Petermann Range, since in places they are spatially related to these rocks and also bear some similarity to them. The gabbroids are described here, as a good example of granitization of basic magmatic rocks under amphibolite facies conditions. Two discordant bodies of granitized gabbroids were encountered in Insel Series strata on the Bardin Ridge. These are steep, dome-shaped massifs with an area 5—6 km^2. Granitized gabbroids in outcrops exhibit agmatitic features, being transected by a network of granite veins composing up to 10—15 vol. % of the rocks. Dikes of gabbroids, transformed into amphibolites, have already been described. The contacts of the intrusive bodies with the host migmatites and shadow granites exhibit an abundance of veins. Extremely thin apophyses of these veins permeate the endomorphic gabbroids, modifying the composition of the latter to such an extent that they assume the form of ramified migmatites. In general, the contacts of granitized gabbroids with host rocks are fairly distinct, although contact effects of the former on the latter have not been encountered, probably because they were obliterated by superimposed granitization processes.

Granitized gabbroids have been transformed mainly into peculiar dioritelike rocks, mostly quartz-bearing and in places also considerably feldspathized. They are represented by greenish-tinged, dark gray, medium- and coarse-grained, usually massive rocks, with local banded and trachytic structures. Their texture is most commonly porphyroblastic with a fine-grained matrix; in places they are hypidiomorphogranular and occasionally even relict-ophitic. The size of matrix grains is 1—5 mm, while the K-feldspar porphyroblasts reach 1—2 cm in size, and are often oriented parallel to the porphyroblasts of granite veins. Plagioclase grains retain their prismatic shape, although they are usually corroded by xenoblastic segregations of quartz and microcline. Sporadic prismatic amphibole grains are euhedral, but they are permeated by biotite flakes and contain quartz ingrowths and ore inclusions, resulting in a diablastic texture. Accumulations of biotite flakes, 1—2 mm long, separate prismatic plagioclase grains which are embedded in them. The composition of rocks is extremely variable. Their plagioclase content (An 25—45) ranges from 20 to 50 %. The microcline content is usually small, 1—3 %, although it reaches 30—35 % in a few varieties. Sometimes, 1—2-cm laths with distinct crosshatching are formed together with ragged segregations; in this case, the rock assumes the composition of a granosyenite. Quartz is ubiquitous (5—20 %). The most characteristic feature of granitized gabbroids is the content of the colored minerals of which biotite (10—20 %) predominates over amphibole (5—10 %). Apparently, hornblende becomes unstable in granitization and is replaced by biotite, while pyroxene disappears altogether. Another characteristic feature is the content of the accessory minerals: sphene (2—4 %), apatite (1—2 %), and rare rounded zircon crystallites. Intensive net veining in the gabbroids (agmatitization) and their granitization are a single process occurring under conditions of the medium-grade amphibolite facies. This also resulted in the instability of pyroxenes and partly also of amphiboles. Garnets are not formed at all, while the colored minerals are limited to biotite of a moderate ferruginosity.

MINERALS OF METAMORPHIC ROCKS IN THE
HUMBOLDT MOUNTAINS AND PETERMANN RANGE

The following rock-forming minerals, of varying compositions, are characteristic of the metamorphic rocks in the region: orthopyroxenes, clinopyroxenes, hornblendes, biotites, garnets and plagioclases. Seventy-one quantitative spectroscopic analyses were performed on the colored minerals from very small samples (10—20 mg) permitting the preparation of fairly homogeneous fractions of every mineral. However, the computations of the components of complex minerals and the derivation of their crystallochemical formulas required corrections for the silicon and aluminum contents, and the scaling of the analyses to 100%, i. e., converting the analysis to an "ideal" form. These corrections proved necessary only for pyroxenes and garnets and are listed in the pertinent column of every table. The spectroscopic analyses did not differentiate between ferrous and ferric iron and therefore the total content of this element in the form of Fe_2O_3 was converted to FeO, since the ferric minerals contain ferrous iron almost exclusively. The morphology and dimensions of minerals as well as their interrelationships are presented in the description of the rocks and are therefore not considered here.

Orthopyroxenes are typomorphic minerals for the Schüssel and Luxemburg Suites, but are limited to intrusive bodies of metabasites in the Gorki Suite. Eight spectroscopic analyses (Table 67) permit the differentiation of two types of orthopyroxenes, which are characteristic for: a) amphibolized bipyroxene schists (including those in the paleosome of migmatites) and b) granulites. The two types of pyroxenes differ firstly in their ferruginosities. The ferruginosity of the former is 39—46% (32—45% for migmatites), and that of the latter 54—64%, increasing by 20% in the granulites. This is reflected by the content of the enstatite and ferrosilite molecules in the two types, i.e., 48—63% enstatite and 30—42% ferrosilite in schists, and 30—43% enstatite and 50—58% ferrosilite in granulites. These variations underscore the difference between the formation conditions of the different types of orthopyroxenes. The calcium content of pyroxenes is 1.2—4.3%. This element is assumed to be included in the diopside molecule, because very fine ingrowths of clinopyroxene (possibly as a result of recrystallization of the mineral) are often found in orthopyroxene. There is 1.3—3.9% aluminum which is probably a component of Tschermak's hypothetical molecule although, in fact, the position of aluminum within the orthopyroxene structure remains obscure. It may only be noted that the aluminum content in orthopyroxene of the Schüssel Suite rocks is standard for this mineral and does not attain its value (9—12%) in orthopyroxenes that are in paragenesis with high-alumina minerals. Therefore, the original rocks of the Schüssel Suite were volcanogenic and not sedimentary since granulite facies metamorphism produces high-alumina orthopyroxene in the latter. The contents of calcium and aluminum are interrelated; as the former increases, the latter decreases, providing an indirect indication of the primary volcanogenic composition of the Schüssel Suite. In the Gorki Suite, the orthopyroxenes are confined to metabasite that has been transformed into amphibolized bipyroxene schist. The ferruginosity of pyroxene is comparatively low (42%), corresponding to that of analogous schists in other suites. The contents of aluminum and calcium are very low, and in this respect the mineral is close to its classic type.

TABLE 67. Orthopyroxenes of metamorphic rocks

Schüssel Suite

Component	specimen 558v, amphibolized bipyroxene schist			specimen 565, amphibolized bipyroxene schist			specimen 99a, paleosome of migmatite from bipyroxene schist			specimen 233, matrix of migmatite from bipyroxene schist			specimen 821a, shadow plagiogranite transformed into granulite		
	wt. %	correction	corrected analysis	wt. %	correction	corrected analysis	wt. %	correction	corrected analysis	wt. %	correction	corrected analysis	wt. %	correction	corrected analysis
SiO_2	59.5	−15.0	52.1	52.2	−7.6	51.2	55.0	−6.1	51.9	53.0	−8.6	51.0	53.1	−11.3	48.8
TiO_2	0.1		0.1	0.2		0.2	0.2		0.2	0.3		0.3	0.4		0.5
Al_2O_3	1.4		1.6	1.6		1.8	3.9		4.1	1.7		1.9	3.1		3.6
Fe_2O_3	21.1			25.6			20.0			25.3			29.1		
(FeO)	(19.0)		22.3	(23.0)		26.4	(18.0)		19.1	(22.8)		26.2	(26.2)		30.5
MgO	16.6		19.5	15.3		17.5	21.5		22.8	15.5		17.8	12.3		14.4
MnO	0.84		0.9	0.45		0.5	0.34		0.3	0.51		0.6	0.67		0.8
CaO	3.0		3.5	2.1		2.4	1.5		1.6	1.9		2.2	1.2		1.4
K_2O	<0.3			0.1			<0.3			0.1			1.3		
Na_2O	0.1			0.1			<0.1			0.1			0.3		
Σ	102.6		100.0	97.6		100.0	102.4		100.0	98.4		100.0	101.5		100.0

Component composition, %

Tschermak's molecule	4	4	7	4	7
Diopside	10	6	—	4	—
Ferrosilite	35	42	30	42	50
Enstatite	51	48	63	50	43

Ferruginosity, at. %

f { by composition	39	46	32	45	54
{ by refractive index	38	46	34	51	54

TABLE 67 (continued)

Component	Schüssel Suite specimen 557, granulite from shadow granite wt.%	correction	corrected analysis	specimen 816, granulite from shadow granite wt.%	correction	corrected analysis	Gorki Suite specimen 288, metabasite wt.%	correction	corrected analysis	Orthopyroxenes according to Deer /16/ No. 12	No. 13
SiO_2	53.0	−8.4	49.6	52.0	−9.2	48.2	51.5	−0.9	52.7	48.29	53.20
TiO_2	0.4		0.4	0.3		0.3	0.2		0.2	0.40	0.13
Al_2O_3	1.3		1.4	2.4		2.7	<1.5		—	2.83	1.15
Fe_2O_3	30.2		30.3	34.4		34.9	26.7		25.5	1.23	—
(FeO)	(27.2)		12.7	(31.0)		11.2	(24.0)		20.2	33.67	21.64
MgO	11.4			9.9			19.0			10.77	22.50
MnO	0.7		0.8	0.37		0.4	0.48		0.5	0.67	0.78
CaO	4.3		4.8	2.0		2.3	0.8		0.9	2.29	0.82
K_2O	0.6			0.6			0.1			0.03	
Na_2O	0.1			<0.1			0.2			0.04	
Σ	99.3		100.0	101.4		100.0	99.3		100.0	100.22	100.22

Component composition, %

Tschermak's molecule	4			6			—				
Diopside	16			4			4				
Ferrosilite	50			58			40				
Enstatite	30			32			56				

Ferrosinosity, at. %

f % { by composition	57			64			42			64	35
{ by refractive index	60			66			46			64	35

Supplement to Table 67

Crystallochemical formulas

Specimen 558v $(Fe_{0.35} \ Mg_{0.54} \ Mn_{0.02} \ Ca_{0.07} \ Al_{0.02})_{1.00} \ [(Si_{0.98} \ Al_{0.02})_{1.00}O_3]$

,,   565 $(Fe_{0.42} \ Mg_{0.50} \ Mn_{0.01} \ Ca_{0.05} \ Al_{0.02})_{1.00} \ [(Si_{0.98} \ Al_{0.02})_{1.00} \ O_3]$

,,   99a $(Fe_{0.30} \ Mg_{0.62} \ Mn_{0.01} \ Ca_{0.03} \ Al_{0.04})_{1.00} \ [(Si_{0.85} \ Al_{0.05})_{1.00} \ O_3]$

,,   233 $(Fe_{0.42} \ Mg_{0.51} \ Mn_{0.01} \ Ca_{0.04} \ Al_{0.02})_{1.00} \ [(Si_{0.97} \ Ti_{0.01} \ Al_{0.02})_{1.00} \ O_3]$

,,   821a $(Fe_{0.50} \ Mg_{0.42} \ Mn_{0.01} \ Ca_{0.03} \ Al_{0.04})_{1.00} \ [(Si_{0.95} \ Ti_{0.01} \ Al_{0.04})_{1.00} \ O_3]$

,,   557 $(Fe_{0.50} \ Mg_{0.37} \ Mn_{0.01} \ Ca_{0.10} \ Al_{0.02})_{1.00} \ [(Si_{0.98} \ Al_{0.02})_{1.00} \ O_3]$

,,   816 $(Fe_{0.58} \ Mg_{0.33} \ Mn_{0.01} \ Ca_{0.05} \ Al_{0.03})_{1.00} \ [(Si_{0.96} \ Ti_{0.01} \ Al_{0.03})_{1.00} \ O_3]$

,,   288 $(Fe_{0.40} \ Mg_{0.57} \ Mn_{0.01} \ Ca_{0.02})_{1.00} \ [Si \ O_3]$

Notes. 1) Analyses of orthopyroxenes, according to Deer /16/, are indicated for minerals from bipyroxene granulite (No. 12, p. 29) and from amphibolite (No. 5, p. 28). 2) Al_2O_3 was ignored in the analysis of specimen 288 because of analytical inaccuracy.

It is very useful to compare these analyses with the chemical analyses of two orthopyroxenes from metamorphic rocks taken from Deer /16/. The composition of pyroxene from granulite according to Deer is very similar to the composition of orthopyroxenes from granulites from the Schüssel Suite, especially the more typical ones (e.g., specimen 816). The composition of the orthopyroxenes from amphibolized bipyroxene schists is equally close to that of orthopyroxenes from amphibolite (from Deer). For determination of the metamorphic facies, it is useful to compare the crystallochemical formulas for the Schüssel Suite orthopyroxenes with the typical orthopyroxenes described by Dobretsov /10/. The orthopyroxenes from Schüssel Suite rocks are found to follow two of Dobretsov's types; specimen No. 6a corresponds to his amphibole-bipyroxene gneisses which are analogous to the present analyses of pyroxene from schists (specimens 558v, 656, 99a and 233), while No. 10 corresponds to his charnockites that are analogous to our analyses of pyroxene from granulites represented by specimens 821a, 557 and 816. Both types were classified by Dobretsov with mineral associations of the granulite facies, but the presence of hornblende, in the authors' opinion, indicates a typical example of minerals of polymetamorphic genesis produced by superposition of the high-temperature amphibolite facies over mineral associations of the granulite facies.

Clinopyroxenes (Table 68) are characteristic of metamorphic rocks of the same suites as orthopyroxenes. They vary most in Schüssel Suite rocks, whereas in the Gorki Suite pyroxenes occur only in calciphyres and very rarely in relicts of specific shadow granitoids. Six spectroscopic

TABLE 68. Clinopyroxenes of metamorphic rocks

Component	specimen 558v, amphibolized bipyroxene schist wt.%	correction	corrected analysis	specimen 565, amphibolized bipyroxene schist wt.%	correction	corrected analysis	specimen 64a, paleosome of migmatite from bipyroxene schist wt.%	correction	corrected analysis	specimen 233, paleosome of migmatite from bipyroxene schist wt.%	correction	corrected analysis	specimen 816, granulite from shadow granite wt.%	correction	corrected analysis	specimen 557, granulite from shadow granite wt.%	correction	corrected analysis
						Schüssel Suite												
SiO_2	53.0	+0.5	52.5	50.6	−2.8	51.2	52.2	+1.0	51.8	50.6	−3.0	51.0	49.7	−7.1	48.2	50.4	−2.4	49.8
TiO_2	0.2		0.2	0.8		0.9	0.2		0.2	0.8		0.9	1.3		1.5	0.8		0.8
Al_2O_3	2.0		2.0	2.8		3.0	3.6		3.5	2.8		3.0	4.0		4.5	3.5		3.6
Fe_2O_3	8.5			12.8			11.6			13.0			18.5			18.9		
(FeO)	(7.6)		7.4	(11.5)		12.3	(10.4)		10.1	(11.7)		12.5	(16.7)		18.9	(17.0)		17.7
MgO	13.2		13.0	11.2		12.0	13.3		13.0	11.5		12.3	8.0		9.1	9.7		10.1
MnO	0.33		0.3	0.21		0.2	0.49		0.5	0.24		0.2	0.17		0.2	0.32		0.3
CaO	24.6		24.1	18.6		19.9	21.0		20.4	18.4		19.7	15.3		17.3	16.6		17.2
Na_2O	<0.6		0.6	0.5		0.5	0.5		0.5	0.4		0.4	0.3		0.3	0.5		0.5
K_2O	0.5	−1	0.5	0.4			<0.6			0.2			1.0		0.3	1.1		0.5
Σ	102.3		100.0	97.9		100.0	102.9		100.0	97.9		100.0	98.3		100.0	101.8		100.0
Component composition																		
Jadeite	4			6			3			4			3			4		
Tschermak's molecule	2			1			6			3			9			6		
Hedenbergite	23			29			25			28			34			32		
Diopside	70			50			51			49			29			33		
Ferrosilite				5			4			6			13			12		
Enstatite	1			9			11			10			12			13		
						Ferruginosity, at.%												
f { by composition	25			37			31			36			54			50		
by refractive index	28			37			33			38			61			56		

TABLE 68 (continued)

Component	Gorki Suite — specimen 279a, paleosome relicts in shadow granite			specimen 276a², (colorless), calciphyres			specimen 276a' (green)			specimen 68b (brownish), calciphyres at contact with charnockites			specimen 68b (pale green), calciphyres at contact with charnockites			Clinopyroxenes according to Deer — No. 27 (p. 60), salite from amphibolite	No.34 (p. 131), augite from hypersthene granulite	No. 3 (p. 134), ferro-augite from pyroxene granulite
	wt. %	correction	corrected analysis	wt. %	correction	corrected analysis	wt. %	correction	corrected analysis	wt. %	correction	corrected analysis	wt. %	correction	corrected analysis			
SiO_2	48.0	+3.4	49.8	48.2	+5.2	53.2	49.6	+2.1	50.9	49.7	+4.9	52.4	50.0	+4.0	52.4	50.02	50.09	49.8
TiO_2	0.6		0.6	0.2		0.2	0.3		0.3	0.3		0.3	0.2		0.2	0.41	0.30	0.16
Al_2O_3	3.2		3.1	1.7		1.7	2.3		2.2	3.1		3.0	2.4		2.3	1.98	2.86	2.50
Fe_2O_3	21.7		—	7.2		—	17.0		—	8.6		—	8.2		—	2.67	1.32	2.95
(FeO)	(19.5)		18.9	(6.5)		6.5	(15.3)		15.1	(7.7)		7.4	(7.4)		7.2	9.72	14.09	16.60
MgO	6.0		5.8	13.9		13.8	8.5		8.4	13.2		12.7	13.0		12.6	9.84	10.51	8.60
MnO	0.17		0.2	0.12		0.1	0.22		0.2	0.11		0.1	0.12		0.1	0.83	0.24	0.28
CaO	21.4		20.7	24.2		24.1	22.8		22.4	24.5		23.5	25.6		24.9	23.74	20.11	18.66
Na_2O	0.9		0.9	0.4		0.4	0.5		0.5	0.6		0.6	0.3		0.3	0.12	0.39	0.50
K_2O	0.3			<0.1			0.3			<0.1			0.1			0.08	0.18	0.05
																H_2O+1.58		
Σ	102.3		100.0	95.8		100.0	101.5		100.0	100.1		100.0	99.8		100.0	100.62	100.19	100.10

Component composition

	279a	276a²	276a'	68b (brownish)	68b (pale green)	No.27	No.34	No.3
Jadeite	7	3	3	4	2			
Tschermak's molecule	4	1	1	5	5			
Hedenbergite	54	20	47	22	22			
Diopside	29	75	46	67	71			
Ferrosilite	4	—	1	—	—			
Enstatite	2	1	2	2	—			

Ferruginosity, at. %

	279a	276a²	276a'	68b (brownish)	68b (pale green)	No.27	No.34	No.3
f { by composition	65	21	50	25	24	41	45	56
{ by refractive index	51		62	—		35	40	56

Supplement to Table 68

Crystallochemical formulas

Specimen 558v $(Na_{0.04} \ Ca_{0.95} \ Fe_{0.23} \ Mg_{0.71} \ Mn_{0.01} \ Al_{0.06})_{2.00} \ [(Si_{1.96} \ Ti_{0.01} \ Al_{0.03})_{2.00} \ O_6]$

„ 565 $(Na_{0.06} \ Ca_{0.80} \ Fe_{0.39} \ Mg_{0.67} \ Mn_{0.01} \ Al_{0.07})_{2.00} \ [(Si_{1.93} \ Ti_{0.02} \ Al_{0.05})_{2.00} \ O_6]$

„ 64a $(Na_{0.03} \ Ca_{0.82} \ Fe_{0.32} \ Mg_{0.72} \ Mn_{0.02} \ Al_{0.09} \ )_{2.00} \ [(Si_{1.93} \ Ti_{0.01} Al_{0.06})_{2.00} \ O_6]$

„ 233 $(Na_{0.04} \ Ca_{0.80} \ Fe_{0.39} \ Mg_{0.69} \ Mn_{0.01} \ Al_{0.07})_{2.00} \ [(Si_{1.93} \ Ti_{0.02} \ Al_{0.05})_{2.00} \ O_6]$

„ 816 $(Na_{0.03} \ Ca_{0.72} \ Fe_{0.61} \ Mg_{0.52} \ Al_{0.12})_{2.00} \ [(Si_{1.87} \ Ti_{0.04} \ Al_{0.09})_{2.00} \ O_6]$

„ 557 $(Na_{0.04} \ Ca_{0.71} \ Fe_{0.56} \ Mg_{0.58} \ Mn_{0.01} \ Al_{0.10})_{2.00} \ [(Si_{92} \ Ti_{0.02} \ Al_{0.06})_{2.00} \ O_6)$

„ 279a $(Na_{0.07} \ Ca_{0.87} \ Fe_{0.61} \ Mg_{0.34} \ Al_{0.11})_{2.00} \ [(Si_{1.95} \ Ti_{0.02} \ Al_{0.03})_{2.00} \ O_6]$

„ 276a   (1) $(Na_{0.03} \ Ca_{0.94} \ Fe_{0.49} \ Mg_{0.49} \ Mn_{0.01} \ Al_{0.04})_{2.00} \ [(Si_{1.93} \ Ti_{0.01} \ Al_{0.01})_{2.00} \ O_6]$

„ 276a   (2) $(Na_{0.03} \ Ca_{0.96} \ Fe_{0.20} \ Mg_{0.76} \ Al_{0.05})_{2.00} \ [(Si_{1.97} \ Ti_{0.01} \ Al_{0.02})_{2.00} \ O_6]$

„ 68b   (1) $(Na_{0.04} \ Ca_{0.94} \ Fe_{0.23} \ Mg_{0.70} \ Al_{0.09})_{2.00} \ [(Si_{1.95} \ Ti_{0.01} \ Al_{0.04})_{2.00} \ O_6]$

„ 68b   (2) $(Na_{0.02} \ Ca_{0.99} \ Fe_{0.22} \ Mg_{0.70} \ Al_{0.07})_{2.00} \ [(Si_{1.95} \ Ti_{0.01} \ Al_{0.04})_{2.00} \ O_6]$

analyses of clinopyroxenes describe three Schüssel Suite rocks; i.e., 1) amphibolized bipyroxene schists, 2) paleosome of migmatite that are closely similar to these schists and 3) the widespread granulites. The clinopyroxenes in the first two rocks are the closest to salites, and in the third rock to ferroaugites. It must be emphasized that the pyroxene varieties were determined herein rather tentatively, mainly by the Fe+Mg/Ca ratio. Four analyses of clinopyroxenes from Gorki Suite calciphyres belong to salites and ferrosalites. The only analysis of clinopyroxene from melanocratic schlieren in shadow granites of the Gorki Suite approaches ferroaugite.

All eleven analyses of clinopyroxenes fall into the following three distinct groups with respect to ferruginosity: 1) those with relatively low ferruginosity (21—25%), found in diopsides of calciphyres and bipyroxene schists only slightly affected by recrystallization; 2) those with medium ferruginosity (31—37%), found in salites or augites of appreciably recrystallized bipyroxene schists and especially paleosomes of bipyroxene migmatites; 3) those of high ferruginosity (50—65%), found in ferroaugites of granulites and relicts in shadow granitoids and (which is especially interesting) ferrosilites of strongly recrystallized calciphyres under amphibolite facies conditions, where diopside relicts (with ferruginosity of only 21%) have been preserved alongside the clinopyroxenes. It should be emphasized that this agreement of ferruginosities was determined spectroscopically and from refractive indices; it is much less satisfactory for clinopyroxenes than for orthopyroxenes. The discrepancies are as much as ±10%, especially for highly ferruginous varieties, whereas the results for varieties of low and medium ferruginosities are in satisfactory agreement, the discrepancies being within 2—3%. It is of interest to note that Deer's /16/ high-quality chemical analyses of clinopyroxenes likewise reveal considerable differences between the ferruginosity values determined analytically and from refractive indices. A comparison of the spectroscopic analyses of the Schüssel Suite pyroxenes with Deer's chemical analyses of clinopyroxenes from metamorphic rocks revealed a pronounced resemblance between the salite and ferroaugite from a granulite (after Deer) and clinopyroxenes from the Schüssel Suite granulites. This is still another confirmation of the appropriateness of dividing the clinopyroxenes into salitic and augitic series.

The component composition of clinopyroxenes is considerably more complex than that of orthopyroxenes. The clinopyroxenes consist of at least six components, the ratio of diopside and hedenbergite molecules being probably the most important factor. This ratio varies approximately from 4 to 1, and is only 1/2 for the most ferruginous pyroxene, i.e., the content of the hedenbergite molecule is double that of the diopside molecule. Nevertheless, there is no direct relationship between the ferruginosity of clinopyroxenes and the ratios of dioposide and hedenbergite molecules, because the pyroxenes under consideration often contain appreciable amounts of the ferrosilite or enstatite molecule. This possibly indicates that the minerals in question are solid solutions of orthopyroxene in clinopyroxene, particularly since ingrowths of the former were observed in certain specimens. On the other hand, a deficit in calcium may indicate the pigeonitic nature of the pyroxene and may be unrelated to the presence of ferrosilite-enstatite molecules. The appreciable admixture of jadeite and Tschermak's molecule in some pyroxene specimens indicates that the mineral belongs to the augite series.

Of considerable interest is a comparison of the composition of two varieties of pyroxenes occurring together in the same calciphyre specimen (27a); the less ferruginous and nearly colorless (in thin sections) variety is replaced by the highly ferruginous green variety. Characteristically, their compositions differ mainly with respect to magnesium and iron, whereas the contents of other elements are nearly the same. The colorless variety contains 6.5% FeO and 13.8% MgO, whereas the green variety contains 15.1% FeO and 8.4% MgO. The difference between the combined contents of these elements is compensated by the higher silica content in the colorless variety. A noteworthy feature is the high content of alkali in the green variety, which is at least double that in the colorless variety. Although the accuracy of spectroscopic determinations of small amounts of alkalis is low, nevertheless it is possible to state that the increase in ferruginosity of the pyroxenes in calciphyres during recrystallization occurred under conditions of alkaline metasomatism. The highest content of alkalis was determined in the clinopyroxenes of granulites formed from shadow charnockites, and the participation of alkaline metasomatism in their formation is certain. The content of alumina in clinopyroxenes (1.7—4.5%) is close to its content in orthopyroxenes (1.3—3.9%) and it is therefore incorrect to distinguish an augitic series of clinopyroxenes solely on the basis of their alumina content, as was done formerly. Apparently, it is much more important to establish a significant excess of the sum Mg + Fe over calcium, classifying such pyroxenes as augites, and as ferroaugites in the case of marked predominance of iron.

Spectroscopic analyses of clinopyroxenes reveal the following consistencies: a) the lowest ferruginosity occurs in diopside from slightly altered calciphyres of the granulite facies; their recrystallization under the amphibolite facies conditions raises their ferruginosity more than double, while the ratios of all the other components remain as before. Consequently, the mineral is transformed into a ferrosilite; b) the lowest ferruginosity of augites is characteristic of bipyroxene schists, and it is nearly doubled when these are transformed into granulated shadow granites; it reaches its maximum in the heavily reworked melanocratic relicts from shadow granites, where the pyroxenes are represented by ferroaugites. For determination of metamorphic facies it is useful to compare these pyroxenes with the composition of typical clinopyroxenes given by Dobretsov /20/. Clinopyroxenes from strongly amphibolized bipyroxene schists (including the paleosome of migmatites, analyses 565, 64a and 233) are equally close to bipyroxene gneisses (type 6) and to amphibolites (type 6b). Clinopyroxenes in granulated shadow granites (analyses 816 and 557) are similar to charnockites (type 14), but differ in their distinctly lower contents of calcium and, in part, of magnesium and their high iron content. The same differences are characteristic of calciphyres, especially those which underwent recrystallization under amphibolite facies conditions (analysis 276a[1]); they contain nearly twice as much magnesium and 2.5 times more iron. It is probable that the differences between these pyroxenes and the typical clinopyroxenes in granulite facies rocks are due to their recrystallization under high-grade amphibolite facies conditions.

A m p h i b o l e s occur in rocks of all suites of the Humboldt Mountains irrespective of their polymetamorphic or monometamorphic nature. Their analyses (14) are therefore of special interest. All amphiboles (Table 69) are represented by common hornblende, but their compositions differ depending on their origin. The only exception is one analysis of amphibole (specimen 83a) which is a cummingtonite; it occurs as a relict mineral only in rocks of the Insel Series.

One group of hornblendes is characteristic of polymetamorphic shadow charnockites transformed into Schüssel Suite granulites (specimens 557, 816, and 867). They differ from all the other varieties in the following respects: a) a maximum ferruginosity 62—76%, and consequently the highest FeO content, 21—26%, and the lowest MgO content, 4.6—7.5%, as compared to the usual 10—16% FeO and 9—15% MgO; b) a somewhat high CaO content, 8.5—10.6%, as compared to 11—13% in the other varieties; c) a high TiO_2 content, 4—5%, as compared to the usual 1—2% and even less; d) a high content of alkalis, 1.0—2.4% Na_2O and 2.2—3.1% K_2O, whereas alkali contents in hornblendes of the amphibolite facies rocks do not usually exceed 1.5% each; e) a decrease of silica by 2—5%.

Thus, hornblendes of shadow granitoids that underwent granulite facies metamorphism, and were then transformed into granulites (under amphibolite facies conditions), differ from the average composition of common hornblendes in their higher content of titanium and alkalis (especially potassium)

TABLE 69. Amphiboles of metamorphic rocks

Component	Schüssel Suite												Gorki Suite		Insel Suite			
	specimen 558v, amphibolized bipyroxene schist		specimen 819g, amphibolite from pyroxene schist		specimen 64a, paleosome of migmatite from bipyroxene schist		specimen 557, granulite from shadow granite		specimen 816, granulite from shadow granite		specimen 567, granulite from shadow granite		specimen 95i, metabasite transformed into amphibolite		specimen 50v, amphibolite		specimen 241a, amphibolite	
	wt %	corrected analysis	wt %	corrected analysis	wt %	corrected analysis	wt %	corrected analysis	wt %	corrected analysis	wt %	corrected analysis	wt %	corrected analysis	wt %	corrected analysis	wt %	corrected analysis
SiO_2	45.1	46.1	39.4	40.5	42.6	42.3	40.0	40.1	41.6	41.3	36.8	37.5	45.8	46.8	48.5	48.7	48.4	48.6
TiO_2	0.9	0.9	3.3	3.4	1.5	1.5	5.6	5.6	4.1	4.1	5.0	5.1	0.9	0.9	0.8	0.8	1.2	1.2
Al_2O_3	11.2	11.4	14.0	14.3	12.5	12.4	11.3	11.3	11.9	11.8	10.7	10.9	10.9	11.2	9.2	9.2	11.1	11.2
Fe_2O_3	10.9	—	17.6	—	18.6	—	24.0	—	25.9	—	28.9	—	17.4	—	15.3	—	18.1	—
(FeO)	(9.8)	10.0	(15.8)	16.2	(16.7)	16.6	(21.6)	21.6	(23.3)	23.1	(26.0)	26.5	(15.7)	16.0	(13.8)	13.9	(16.3)	16.4
MgO	15.3	15.6	11.0	11.3	13.0	12.9	7.5	7.5	7.1	7.1	4.6	4.7	10.9	11.2	12.0	12.1	9.6	9.6
MnO	0.17	0.2	0.23	0.2	0.36	0.4	0.21	0.2	0.1	0.1	0.1	0.1	0.27	0.3	0.36	0.4	0.44	0.4
CaO	12.1	12.4	10.1	10.4	10.6	10.5	10.0	10.0	8.5	8.4	10.4	10.6	10.9	11.2	12.5	12.6	9.9	10.0
Na_2O	1.2	1.2	0.7	0.7	1.0	1.0	0.9	0.9	1.0	1.0	2.4	2.4	1.2	1.2	1.0	1.0	1.3	1.3
K_2O	2.2	2.2	2.9	3.0	2.4	2.4	2.8	2.8	3.1	3.1	2.2	2.2	1.2	1.2	1.3	1.3	1.3	1.3
Σ	99.1	100.0	99.2	100.0	102.6	100.0	102.3	100.0	103.3	100.0	101.1	100.0	99.5	100.0	101.0	100.0	101.3	100.0
Ferruginosity, at. % — By composition	26		45		42		62		65		76		45		39		49	
By refractive index	25		40		48		61		60		66		67		41		46	

TABLE 69 (continued)

Components	Insel Suite											Amphiboles according to Deer /16/		
	specimen 84v, paleosome of migmatite		specimen 237, paleosome of migmatite		specimen 46, paleosome of migmatite		specimen 82, shadow granite		specimen 83a, cummingtonite from biotitic amphibolite		specimen 31, (p. 304), clinopyroxene amphibolite	specimen 32 (p. 304), granulite	specimen 16 (p. 300), hornblende schist	specimen 4 (p. 256), cummingtonite from amphibolite
	wt%	corrected analysis	wt%	corrected analysis	wt%	corrected analysis	wt%	corrected analysis	wt%	corrected analysis				
SiO_2	44.8	47.1	43.5	44.8	42.2	42.8	48.0	47.0	53.0	57.4	44.36	42.24	48.83	52.05
TiO_2	1.7	1.8	1.0	1.0	1.7	1.7	0.5	0.5	0.6	0.6	1.26	2.76	0.78	0.60
Al_2O_3	9.4	9.9	10.4	10.7	10.4	10.6	9.1	8.9	2.8	3.0	11.69	10.47	6.58	0.77
Fe_2O_3	19.5	18.4	23.9	22.1	24.4	22.3	18.6	16.3	21.8	21.2	1.29	4.04	1.02	3.40
(FeO)	(17.5)	(17.5)	(21.5)		(22.0)		(16.7)		(19.6)		16.63	16.06	12.76	22.35
MgO	8.4	8.8	8.0	8.2	7.6	7.7	11.9	11.6	14.1	15.3	9.71	9.22	13.98	15.26
MnO	0.32	0.3	0.39	0.4	0.44	0.4	0.48	0.5	0.67	0.8	0.43	0.28	0.34	1.41
CaO	10.5	11.0	10.8	11.1	11.2	11.4	13.2	12.9	1.0	1.1	11.82	11.23	12.88	1.89
Na_2O	1.0	1.1	1.0	1.0	1.8	1.8	0.9	0.9	0.2	0.2	0.79	1.44	0.58	0.21
K_2O	1.5	1.6	0.7	0.7	1.3	1.3	1.4	1.4	0.4	0.4	0.50	0.89	0.28	0.07
H_2O^+											1.67			1.98
Σ	95.1	100.0	97.3	100.0	101.0	100.0	104.1	100.0	94.6	100.0	100.27	99.40	100.07	99.99
Ferruginosity, at.%														
By composition	54		60		62		44		44		51	55	35	48
By refractive index	47		59		55		41		41		42	57	30	41

Supplement to Table 69

Crystallochemical formulas

Specimen 558v $(Ca_{1.87} K_{0.40} Na_{0.33})_{2.60} (Fe_{1.18} Mg_{3.29} Mn_{0.02} Al_{0.51})_{5.00} [(Si_{6.51} Al_{1.40} Ti_{0.09})_{8.00} O_{22}] (OH)_2$

„   819g $(Ca_{1.60} K_{0.55} Na_{0.19})_{2.34} (Fe_{1.95} Mg_{2.42} Mn_{0.03} Al_{0.60})_{5.00} [(Si_{5.81} Al_{1.83} Ti_{0.36})_{8.00} O_{22}] (OH)_2$

„   64a $(Ca_{1.60} K_{0.42} Na_{0.27})_{2.29} (Fe_{1.97} Mg_{2.73} Mn_{0.04} Al_{0.26})_{5.00} [(Si_{6.01} Al_{1.83} Ti_{0.16})_{8.00} O_{22}] (OH)_2$

„   557 $(Ca_{1.60} K_{0.54} Na_{0.27})_{2.41} (Fe_{2.70} Mg_{1.67} Mn_{0.03} Al_{0.60})_{5.00} [(Si_{5.98} Al_{1.39} Ti_{0.63})_{8.00} O_{22}] (OH)_2$

„   816 $(Ca_{1.34} K_{0.58} Na_{0.28})_{2.20} (Fe_{2.84} Mg_{1.55} Mn_{0.02} Al_{0.59})_{5.00} [(Si_{6.09} Al_{1.46} Ti_{0.45})_{8.00} O_{22}] (OH)_2$

„   567 $(Ca_{1.74} K_{0.53} Na_{0.73})_{3.00} (Fe_{3.45} Mg_{1.09} Mn_{0.01} Al_{0.45})_{5.00} [(Si_{5.85} Al_{1.55} Ti_{0.60})_{8.00} O_{22}] (OH)_2$

„   95i $(Ca_{1.70} K_{0.23} Na_{0.33})_{2.26} (Fe_{1.91} Mg_{2.37} Mn_{0.04} Al_{0.88})_{5.00} [(Si_{6.70} Al_{1.20} Ti_{0.10})_{8.00} O_{22}] (OH)_2$

„   50v $(Ca_{1.94} K_{0.24} Na_{0.28})_{2.46} (Fe_{1.67} Mg_{2.59} Mn_{0.04} Al_{0.70})_{5.00} [(Si_{7.04} Al_{0.87} Ti_{0.09})_{8.00} O_{22}] (OH)_2$

„   241a $(Ca_{1.52} K_{0.24} Na_{0.36})_{2.12} (Fe_{1.95} Mg_{2.05} Mn_{0.05} Al_{0.95})_{5.00} [(Si_{6.94} Al_{0.93} Ti_{0.13})_{8.00} O_{22}] (OH)_2$

„   84v $(Ca_{1.73} K_{0.30} Na_{0.30})_{2.33} (Fe_{2.26} Mg_{1.92} Mn_{0.04} Al_{0.78})_{5.00} [(Si_{6.89} Al_{0.92} Ti_{0.19})_{8.00} O_{22}] (OH)_2$

„   237 $(Ca_{1.74} K_{0.13} Na_{0.29})_{2.16} (Fe_{2.69} Mg_{1.78} Mn_{0.05} Al_{0.48})_{5.00} [(Si_{6.52} Al_{1.36} Ti_{0.12})_{8.00} O_{22}] (OH)_2$

„   46 $(Ca_{1.82} K_{0.25} Na_{0.53})_{2.60} (Fe_{2.78} Mg_{1.72} Mn_{0.05} Al_{0.45})_{5.00} [(Si_{6.40} Al_{1.41} Ti_{0.19})_{8.00} O_{22}] (OH)_2$

„   82 $(Ca_{2.01} K_{0.26} Na_{0.26})_{2.53} (Fe_{1.99} Mg_{2.53} Mn_{0.06} Al_{0.42})_{5.00} [(Si_{6.85} Al_{1.10} Ti_{0.05})_{8.00} O_{22}] (OH)_2$

N o t e. The total ferruginosity of amphiboles was determined from the refractive index by means of the diagrams provided by Drugova and Glebovitskii /22/. Amphibole in Schüssel Suite rocks was determined by means of the diagram for the granulite facies rocks, while amphibole in rocks of the Gorki and Insel Suites was determined by means of the diagram for the amphibolite facies rocks.

and their lower content of calcium and silica. Such hornblendes are fairly close to Deer's analysis No. 32 (amphibole extracted from granulite) /16/. Characteristically, hornblende (specimen 82) in shadow granite formed under amphibolite facies conditions does not possess all these properties and is considerably closer to the hornblende from amphibole schist (see Deer's analysis No. 16). The composition of hornblendes in metabasites, bipyroxene schists, and in the paleosome of migmatites depends on the intensity of amphibolization of these rocks under conditions of the super-imposed amphibolite facies. Thus, the initial stage of amphibolization of bipyroxene schists (specimen 558v) is responsible for a low total ferru-ginosity (26%) and a low titanium content (up to 1%) in the hornblende. Yet, the same rocks which were transformed into amphibolite (specimen 819g) contain hornblende with a ferruginosity of 45% and with 3.3% titanium. The composition of hornblende in the paleosome of migmatites exhibits an approximately similar modification; the higher the migmatization grade of a rock, the higher is the iron content of the mineral and the lower is its magnesium content. The contents of other elements in hornblendes are little altered during all these transformations, with the exception of silica, which decreases with increasing ferruginosity of the mineral.

The hornblendes in Insel Series rocks of the amphibolite facies also possess other features that are different from hornblendes in polymetamorphic suites. They attain the maximum ferruginosity in migmatite paleosomes (54—62%), whereas their ferruginosity in shadow granites is lower (44%), rising only in certain specific shadow granites of metasomatic origin. This suggests a limited role of metasomatic processes in the formation of a majority of Insel Series shadow granites, but eutectic melts are more important in this respect. The situation is reversed in the formation of polymetamorphics, in which alkaline metasomatism plays a leading role. Thus, hornblende in polymetamorphic rocks forms a mineral series with steadily increasing ferruginosities, originating from slightly amphibolized bipyroxene schists (26%) through amphibolites and the paleosome of migmatites (42—45%) to shadow granites transformed into granulites (62—76%). Hornblende in monometamorphic rocks of the amphibolite facies increases in ferruginosity only from amphibolites (39%) to the paleosome of migmatites (52%), whereas the ferruginosity of hornblende in shadow granites decreases. The difference in the composition of hornblendes in different facies of metamorphism is also underscored by certain other features: amphibolite facies hornblendes have a lower alumina content (9—11%) than amphibole from polymetamorphic rocks (11—14%), and their contents of titanium (0.5—1.5%) and alkalis (2—3%) are likewise lower than in polymetamorphic rocks (1.5—5.5% TiO_2, 3—4.5% total alkalis). These differences in composition for hornblendes in different facies of metamorphism can be explained by the nature of the original rocks and their metamorphic conditions. Polymetamorphic shadow granitoids probably formed from volcanogenic rocks by regional granulite facies metamorphism. Shadow granites (volcanogenic origin) originating under the amphibolite facies conditions were transformed into granulites under the influence of stress (in the abyssal fault zone). Monometamorphic rocks of the amphibolite facies may have been formed from either volcanogenic or sedimentary-terrigenous sediments, followed by granitization, including the interaction between the plagiogneiss paleosomes and eutectic melts.

The presence of secondary cummingtonite in the amphibolites and paleosomes of Insel Series migmatites is indicative of its replacement of hornblende. A comparison of the analysis of minerals in specimen 83a with Deer's cummingtonite No. 4 /16/ revealed that the amphibole was a typical cummingtonite. It should be noted that this cummingtonite, which belongs to products of the epidote-amphibolite or even greenschist facies, does not occur in rocks of the polymetamorphic suites in the region.

Before comparing the amphiboles with typical hornblendes, it is necessary to point out that the average composition of the latter is relatively constant in rocks of the granulite and amphibolite facies (Sobolev /20/), especially in view of standard deviations from average values. However, there is an increase in ferruginosity and a corresponding decrease in the magnesian content in amphibolite facies hornblendes in comparison to those of the granulite facies (Table 70). In this respect, amphibole from Schüssel Suite granulated charnockites is considerably closer to the amphibolite facies hornblende. This holds true even when considering that the crystallochemical formulas of the amphiboles always yield high values for the ferrous iron content, since the spectroscopic analyses do not differentiate between ferrous and ferric iron, and the total iron content is scaled to ferrous iron. Amphiboles of bipyroxene schists are probably closer to typical granulite facies hornblendes, especially with respect to the Fe : Mg ratio, although they hardly differ from amphibolite facies hornblendes with respect to the contents of other elements. Significantly, the hornblende from typical Insel Series amphibolites is considerably closer in composition to granulite facies amphibole; however, in the paleosome of migmatites from the same suite it is nearly analogous to amphibolite facies amphibole. There is thus an apparent unreliability in the determination of facies of hornblendes from their composition.

A comparison of the amphiboles under discussion with typical hornblendes of the granulite and amphibolite facies, indicates that our amphiboles from polymetamorphic rocks usually contain less silica and sodium and more titanium and potassium than the granulite facies amphiboles. All other deviations (Table 70) permit a differentiation between hornblendes from monometamorphic and polymetamorphic rocks. Their differences from the typical types are also explained by the original composition of the rocks (e. g., high titanium contents) and by the high grade of granitization which distinguishes the polymetamorphic rocks.

B i o t i t e s have been investigated from different rocks of all the suites of the crystalline strata of the Humboldt Mountains and Petermann Range. The total of 19 spectroscopic analyses reveals certain consistencies in the composition of different varieties of the mineral in relation to the composition and origin of rocks in which it occurs (Table 71). In the first place, attention is attracted by the difference between biotites in polymetamorphic and monometamorphic rocks. Titanium contents are 3—8% in the former and 1.9—3.7% in the latter. Potassium contents are 7—11% in the former and 6—8.5% in the latter. In contrast, the content of iron is on the whole higher in the biotites from the monometamorphic rocks of the Insel Series (18—28%) than in biotites of the polymetamorphic rocks (10—23%). Similar consistencies also exist in the case of common hornblendes, and they may therefore be regarded as decisive for the determination of the nature of metamorphism. In the polymetamorphic Schüssel Suite, the total ferruginosity of biotites is 25—63%, rising gradually from the paleosome of migmatites to granulated shadow granites. In the monometamorphic Insel Series, the ferruginosity of biotite likewise increases from biotitized amphibolites (43—44%), to the paleosome of migmatites (57%) and finally to shadow granites (73—76%). Shadow granites (specimen 82) constitute an exception, due to the interaction of melts and paleosome. The ferruginosity of their biotite is only 47%. The ferruginosity of hornblende in the same shadow granite is also low (44%). One analysis (specimen 263) characterizes a secondary biotite from a cataclastized migmatite of the Luxemburg Suite formed from bipyroxene schists. Its ferruginosity is fairly high, 66%, which is higher than that of pyroxenes.

It is useful to compare the composition of these biotites (Table 72) with the typical composition of biotites according to Ushakova /20/. With respect to the contents of most elements, the biotites of migmatites and shadow granites of the Schüssel Suite are fairly close to the typical biotites of group No. 2, but they are considerably closer to group No. 9 with respect to the Mg : Fe ratio; they thus occupy an intermediate position between biotites

TABLE 70. Comparative characteristics of hornblendes

Rock types	Si	Ti	Al	Fe	Mg	Ca	Na	K	Mn
Polymetamorphic rocks									
Amphibolized bipyroxene schists and paleosome of migmatites (specimens 558v, 819g, 64a)	5.81—6.51	0.09—0.36	1.91—2.43	1.18—1.97	2.42—3.29	1.60—1.87	0.19—0.33	0.42—0.55	0.02—0.04
Granulated shadow granites with pyroxenes and amphiboles (specimens 557, 816, and 567)	5.85—6.09	0.45—0.63	1.99—2.05	2.70—3.45	1.09—1.67	1.34—1.74	0.27—0.73	0.53—0.58	0.01—0.03
Granulite facies rocks, Sobolev's type No. 1	6.34±0.23	0.23±0.09	2.16±0.29	1.61±0.33	2.39±0.57	1.82±0.14	0.51±0.12	0.22±0.10	0.02±0.01
Monometamorphic rocks									
Amphibolites (specimens 50v and 241a)	6.94—7.04	0.09—0.13	1.57—1.88	1.67—1.95	2.05—2.59	1.52—1.94	0.28—0.36	0.24	0.04—0.05
Paleosome of migmatites (specimens 84a, 237 and 46)	6.40—6.89	0.12—0.19	1.70—1,88	2.26—2.78	1.72—1.92	1.73—1.82	0.29—0.53	0.13—0.30	0.04—0.05
Amphibolite facies rocks without hypersthene, Sobolev's type No. 1	6.35±0.24	0.15±0.07	2.06±0.22	2.04±0.61	1.85±0.77	1.81±0.14	0.44±0.11	0.23±0.11	0.06±0.04
Amphibolite facies rocks with quartz, Sobolev's type No. 5	6.27±0.26	0.16±0.08	2.17±0.32	2.28±0.64	1.48±0.76	1.77±0.14	0.45±0.10	0.26±0.11	0.07±0.05

Note. The tabulated values are the coefficients in crystallochemical formulas of the minerals.

TABLE 71. Biotites of metamorphic rocks

Component	Luxemburg Suite specimen 263, cataclastized migmatite		specimen 99a, paleosome of agmatite		specimen 77, paleosome of migmatite		specimen 64a, paleosome of migmatite		specimen 233, paleosome of agmatite		Schüssel specimen 819, granulite from shadow granite	
	wt %	corrected analysis	wt %	corrected analysis	wt %	corrected analysis	wt %	corrected analysis	wt %	corrected analysis	wt %	corrected analysis
SiO_2	40.7	41.4	41.1	42.1	38.0	38.4	38.0	39.1	40.1	42.5	37.8	38.0
TiO_2	2.8	2.8	3.9	4.0	4.6	4.6	3.8	3.9	5.0	5.3	5 0	5.0
Al_2O_3	15.8	16.1	14.8	15.2	17.4	17.6	14.0	14.4	12.7	13.5	17.5	17.5
Fe_2O_3	26.0	—	11.2		17.4		18.5		20.9	—	20.4	
(FeO)	(23.4)	23.8	(10.1)	10.4	(15.7)	15.9	(16.6)	17.1	(18.8)	20.0	(18.4)	18.5
MgO	6.8	6.9	16.6	17.0	12.0	12.1	12.0	12.4	11.3	12.0	9.3	9.3
MnO	0.29	0.3	0.05	—	0.04	—	0.13	0.1	0.1	0.1	0.03	—
CaO	0.4	0.4	0.4	0.4	0.5	0.5	1.4	1.4	0.7	0.7	0.3	0.3
Na_2O	0.4	0.4	0.1	0.1	0.2	0.2	0.5	0.5	0.2	0.2	0.4	0.4
K_2O	7.8	7.9	10.5	10.8	10.6	10.7	10.8	11.1	5.4	5.7	11.0	11.0
Σ	101.0	100.0	98.6	100.0	100.7	100.0	99.1	100.0	96.4	100.0	101.7	100.0
f, %, by composition	66		25		42		44		48		53	
f, %, by refractive index	59		29		42		55		49		51	

							Insel

Component	specimen 83a, biotitic amphibolite		specimen 50v, amphibolite		specimen 82, shadow granite		specimen 81v, paleosome of migmatite	
	wt %	corrected analysis	wt %	corrected analysis	wt %	corrected analysis	wt %	corrected analysis
SiO_2	39.6	42.3	40.3	41.9	42.4	43.1	40.6	41.3
TiO_2	1.9	2.0	2.6	2.7	2.1	2.2	3.6	3.7
Al_2O_3	16.2	17.3	15.6	16.2	14.9	15.2	14.0	14.3
Fe_2O_3	18.7		18.6		20.6		25.6	
(FeO)	(16.8)	18.0	(16.7)	17.4	(18.5)	18.8	(23.0)	23.4
MgO	12.7	13.6	11.9	12.4	11.9	12.1	9.9	10.1
MnO	0.07	0.1	0.1	0.1	0.2	0.2	0.2	0.2
CaO	<0.5	—	0.4	0.4	0.5	0.5	<0.5	
Na_2O	0.4	0.4	0.5	0.5	0.4	0.4	0.3	0.3
K_2O	5.9	6.3	8.1	8.4	7.4	7.5	6.6	6.7
Σ	95.5	100.0	98.1	100.0	100.4	100.0	100.8	100.0
f, %, by composition	43		44		47		57	
f, %, by refractive index	33		37		46		50	

Suite					Gorki Suite						
specimen 824, granulite from shadow granite		specimen 821v, granulite from shadow plagio-granite		specimen 95i, metabasite		specimen 65v, metasome of migmatite (with cordierite and sillimanite)		specimen 72b, shadow granite (with sillimanite)		specimen 61b, paleosome of migmatite	
wt %	corrected analysis	wt %	corrected analysis	wt %	corrected analysis	wt %	corrected analysis	wt %	corrected analysis	wt %	corrected analysis
36.8	37.8	37.0	38.6	37.2	40.6	40.3	44.2	40.7	42.2	38.7	39.8
5.4	5.5	8.4	8.8	2.1	2.3	2.8	3.1	3.2	3.3	5.4	5.6
14.9	15.3	12.6	13.2	16.0	17.5	14.4	15.8	18.9	19.6	15.0	15.4
24.6		25.0		15.8		16.7		21.3	—	25.7	
(22.1)	22.7	(22.5)	23.5	(14.2)	15.5	(15.0)	16.4	(19.2)	19.3	(23.1)	23.8
8.7	8.9	7.4	7.7	13.1	14.3	10.7	11.7	6.8	7.1	7.5	7.7
0.03		0.1	0.1	0.05	—	0.04	—	0.05	0.1	0.06	0.1
< 0.5	0.4	0.4	0.4	0.7	0.8	0.4	0.4	0.1	0.1	0.3	0.3
0.5	0.5	0.6	0.6	0.9	1.0	0.6	0.7	0.7	0.7	0.3	0.3
8.7	8.9	6.8	7.1	7.3	8.0	7.0	7.7	6.7	7.0	6.8	7.0
99.6	100.0	98.3	100.0	93.2	100.0	92.9	100.0	98.5	100.0	99.8	100.0
59		63		38		44		61		63	
61		67		37		55		53		68	

Suite							
specimen 834, shadow granite		specimen 537, metasome in agmatites		specimen 50, shadow granite		Biotites according to Deer et al. /17/	
wt %	corrected analysis	wt %	corrected analysis	wt %	corrected analysis	wt %	corrected analysis
36.5	37.6	39.2	39.7	36.1	37.2	35.42	35.03
2.2	2.3	3.6	3.7	2.8	2.9	3.15	2.56
16.1	16.6	13.9	14.1	18.0	18.5	19.04	20.38
30.8		30.4		30.8		2.70	1.08
(27.7)	28.6	(27.4)	27.8	(27.7)	28.5	16.11	20.41
5.6	5.8	5.2	5.3	5.0	5.1	9.56	7.11
0.28	0.3	0.3	0.3	0.15	0.2	0.25	0.02
< 0.5		0.3	0.3	0.1	0.1	0.24	0.17
0.4	0.4	0.2	0.2	0.2	0.2	0.40	0.96
8.2	8.4	8.5	8.6	7.1	7.3	9.30	8.62
						HO+ 3.48	3.60
100.1	100.0	101.6	100.0	100.2	100.0	99.65	100.01
73		75		76		52	63
63		59		63		49	46

Supplement to Table 71

Crystallochemical formulas

Specimen 72b
$$(K_{0.65}Na_{0.10}Ca_{0.01})_{0.76} (Mg_{0.78}Fe_{1.22}Mn_{0.01}Ti_{0.18}Al_{0.81})_{3.00} [(Si_{3.11}Al_{0.89})_{4.00}O_{10}] (OH)_2$$

" 61b
$$(K_{0.67}Na_{0.05}Ca_{0.02})_{0.74} (Mg_{0.86}Fe_{1.49}Ti_{0.31}Al_{0.34})_{3.00} [(Si_{2.88}Al_{1.02})_{4.00}O_{10}] (OH)_2$$

" 83a
$$(K_{0.57}Na_{0.05})_{0.62} (Mg_{1.42}Fe_{1.06}Ti_{0.11}Al_{0.41})_{3.00} [(Si_{2.98}Al_{1.02})_{4.00}O_{10}] (OH)_2$$

" 50v
$$(K_{0.78}Na_{0.07}Ca_{0.03})_{0.88} (Mg_{1.34}Fe_{1.06}Ti_{0.15}Al_{0.45})_{3.00} [(Si_{3.06}Al_{0.94})_{4.00}O_{10}] (OH)_2$$

" 82
$$(K_{0.70}Na_{0.05}Ca_{0.04})_{0.79} (Mg_{1.31}Fe_{1.14}Mn_{0.01}Ti_{0.12}Al_{0.42})_{3.00} [(Si_{3.13}Al_{0.87})_{4.00}O_{10}] (OH)_2$$

" 84v
$$(K_{0.63}Na_{0.04})_{0.67} (Mg_{1.10}Fe_{1.43}Mn_{0.01}Ti_{0.20}Al_{0.26})_{3.00} [(Si_{3.03}Al_{0.97})_{4.00}O_{10}] (OH)_2$$

" 834
$$(K_{0.82}Na_{0.06})_{0.88} Mg_{0.66}Fe_{1.82}Mn_{0.02}Ti_{0.13}Al_{0.37})_{3.00} [(Si_{2.88}Al_{1.12})_{4.00}O_{10}] (OH)_2$$

" 537
$$[K_{0.85}Na_{0.03}Ca_{0.02})_{0.30} (Mg_{0.81}Fe_{1.80}Mn_{0.02}Ti_{0.21}Al_{0.36})_{3.00} [(Si_{3.08}Al_{0.92})_{4.00}O_{10}] (OH)_2$$

" 50
$$(K_{0.70}Na_{0.03}Ca_{0.01})_{0.74} (Mg_{0.58}Fe_{1.79}Mn_{0.01}Ti_{0.16}Al_{0.46})_{3.00} [(Si_{2.81}Al_{1.19})_{4.00}O_{10}] (OH)_2$$

" 263
$$(K_{0.76}Na_{0.06}Ca_{0.03})_{0.85} (Mg_{0.78}Fe_{1.49}Mn_{0.02}Ti_{0.16}Al_{0.55})_{3.00} [(Si_{3.12}Al_{0.88})_{4.00}O_{10}] (OH)_2$$

" 99a
$$(K_{0.99}Na_{0.02}Ca_{0.03})_{1.04} (Mg_{1.83}Fe_{0.62}Ti_{0.22}Al_{0.33})_{3.00} [(Si_{3.04}Al_{0.86})_{4.00}O_{10}[(OH)_2$$

" 77
$$(K_{1.01}Na_{0.03}Ca_{0.04})_{1.08} Mg_{1.33}Fe_{0.98}Ti_{0.26}Al_{0.41})_{3.00} [(Si_{2.88}Al_{1.14})_{4.00}O_{10}] (OH)_2$$

" 64a
$$(K_{1.08}Na_{0.07}Ca_{0.12})_{1.27} (Mg_{1.40}Fe_{1.09}Mn_{0.01}Ti_{0.23}Al_{0.27})_{3.00} [(Si_{2.98}Al_{1.02})_{4.00}O_{10}] (OH)_2$$

" 233
$$(K_{0.52}Na_{0.03}Ca_{0.06})_{0.61} Mg_{1.29}Fe_{1.20}Ti_{0.29}Al_{0.22})_{3.00} [(Si_{3.07}Al_{0.83})_{4.00}O_{10}] (OH)_2$$

" 819
$$(K_{1.07}Na_{0.05}Ca_{0.02})_{1.14} (Mg_{1.06}Fe_{1.18}Ti_{0.29}Al_{0.47})_{3.00} [(Si_{2.89}Al_{1.11})_{4.00}O_{10}] (OH)_2$$

" 824g
$$(K_{0.86}Na_{0.07}Ca_{0.03})_{0.96} (Mg_{1.01}Fe_{1.44}Ti_{0.32}Al_{0.23})_{3.00} \cdot [(Si_{2.87}Al_{1.13})_{4.00}O_{10}] (OH)_2$$

" 821a
$$(K_{0.69}Na_{0.09}Ca_{0.03})_{0.81} (Mg_{0.88}Fe_{1.49}Ti_{0.50}Al_{0.13})_{3.00} [(Si_{2.94}Al_{1.06})_{4.00}O_{10}] (OH)_2$$

" 95i
$$(K_{0.73}Na_{0.14}Ca_{0.06})_{0.93} (Mg_{1.53}Fe_{0.94}Mn_{0.01}Ti_{0.12}Al_{0.40})_{3.00} [(Si_{2.92}Al_{1.08})_{4.00}O_{10}] (OH)_2$$

" 65v
$$(K_{0.71}Na_{0.10}Ca_{0.03})_{0.84} (Mg_{1.27}Fe_{1.00}Ti_{0.17}Al_{0.56})_{3.00} [(Si_{3.21}Al_{0.79})_{4.00}O_{10}] (OH)_2$$

Note. The composition of biotites according to Deer is given for a quartz-biotite gneiss (No. 9) and for garnet-sillimanite-mica schists (No. 12).

TABLE 72. Comparative characteristics of biotites

Rock types and parageneses	Si	Al	Ti	Fe	Mn	Mg	Ca	Na	K
Polymetamorphic rocks									
Paleosome of Schüssel Suite migmatites (specimens 77, 64a, 233)	2.860—3.07	1.150—1.550	0.230—0.290	0.980—1.200	0.010	1.290—1.400	0.040—0.060	0.030—0.070	0.520—1.080
Granulated shadow granites (Schüssel Suite charnockites) (specimens 819, 824g, 821a)	2.870—2.940	1.190—1.580	0.290—0.500	1.180—1.490	None	0.880—1.060	0.020—0.030	0.050—0.090	0.690—1.070
Hyp + biot + plag + gar + horn ± mi + Kfs +qz; Ushavokova's group No.2	2.737±0.078	1.353±0.082	0.245±0.049	0.916±0.173	0.005±0.004	1.542±0.229	0.048±0.043	0.091±0.091	0.806±0.109
Monometamorphic rocks									
Insel Series amphibolites (specimens 83a and 50v)	2.980—3.060	1.190—1.430	0.110—0.150	1.060—1.065	None	1.340—1.420	0.030	0.050—0.070	0.570—0.780
Paleosome of Insel Series migmatites (specimen 84v)	3.030	1.230	0.200	1.430	0.010	1.100	None	0.040	0.630
Shadow granites from Insel Series (specimens 834, 537 and 50)	2.880—3.080	1.280—1.490	0.130—0.210	1.790—1.820	0.010—0.020	0.580—0.660	0.010—0.020	0.030—0.060	0.700—0.850
Biot + horn + plag + Kfs + qz; Ushakova's group No.10	2.741±0.100	1.366±0.123	0.144±0.043	0.980±0.198	0.017±0.015	1.403±0.145	0.063±0.048	0.051±0.035	0.808±0.102
Gar + biot + horn + plag + Kfs + qz; Ushakova's group No.9	2.723±0.089	1.453±0.128	0.164±0.088	1.220±0.260	0.007±0.004	1.184±0.296	0.047±0.031	0.080±0.073	0.761±0.097

Note. The values of coefficients in the crystallochemical formulas of the minerals are indicated.

TABLE 73. Garnets of metamorphic rocks

Schüssel Suite

Component	specimen 64a, paleosome of migmatites			specimen 74, migmatite			specimen 74g, paleosome of migmatites			specimen 77, paleosome of migmatites			specimen 819, granulite from shadow granite		
	wt %	correction,	corrected analysis	wt %	correction,	corrected analysis	wt %	correction,	corrected analysis	wt %	correction,	corrected analysis	wt %	correction,	corrected analysis
SiO_2	42.1	−2.3	39.1	41.8	−2.8	38.8	41.3	−0.9	38.9	40.9	−1.9	37.9	42.0	−3.7	38.5
TiO_2	0.1		0.1	0.1		0.1	0.1		0.1	0.2		0.2	0.2		0.2
Al_2O_3	19.8	+2.6	22.0	19.9	+2.1	21.9	18.2	+4.6	22.0	19.4	+2.7	21.5	20.2	+1.5	21.8
Fe_2O_3	23.9			30.9		—	28.2			33.0			29.8		
(FeO)	(21.5)		21.1	(27.8)		27.7	(25.4)		24.5	(30.0)		29.2	(26.0)		26.9
MgO	6.9		6.8	8.6		8.6	7.3		7.0	5.4		5.3	6.3		6.3
MnO	1.9		1.9	0.5		0.5	0.5		0.5	0.56		0.6	0.5		0.5
CaO	9.2		9.0	2.4		2.4	7.3		7.0	5.5		5.3	5.8		5.8
Na_2O	0.3			0.1			0.1			0.1			0.2		
K_2O	<0.6			<0.6			<0.6			<0.6			<0.6		
Σ	104.2		100.0	104.2		100.0	103.0		100.0	105.0		100.0	105.6		100.0
Grossular	25			7			19			15			16		
Almandine	45			59			53			64			59		
Pyrope	26			33			27			20			24		
Spessartite	4			1			1			1			1		
$f\%$ by composition	64			64			66			75			71		
N	1.782			1.788			1.780			1.788			1.795		

TABLE 73 (continued)

Schüssel Suite

Component	specimen 77b, vein plagiogranite			specimen 565a, granulite from shadow granite			specimen 824g, granulite from shadow granite			specimen 557, granulite from shadow granite			specimen 816, granulite from shadow granite			specimen 567, granulite from shadow granite		
	wt %	correction, wt %	corrected analysis	wt %	correction, wt %	corrected analysis	wt %	correction, wt %	corrected analysis	wt %	correction, wt %	corrected analysis	wt %	correction, wt %	corrected analysis	wt %	correction, wt %	corrected analysis
SiO_2	42.0	−4.3	38.7	42.2	−7.4	38.2	42.1	−5.3	38.3	44.5	−10.4	38.0	41.6	−4.6	37.7	40.7	−5.3	37.5
TiO_2	0.1		0.1	0.1		0.1	0.2		0.2	0.2		0.2	0.2		0.2	0.2		0.2
Al_2O_3	20.6	+0.7	21.9	19.2	+0.5	21.6	20.5	+0.4	21.8	20.6	−1.2	21.6	19.5	+1.4	21.3	19.6	+0.5	21.3
Fe_2O_3	31.6		—	30.3		—	27.6		—	26.7		—	31.7		—	30.4		—
(FeO)	28.4		29.1	(27.3)		29.9	(24.8)		25.8	(24.0)		26.8	(28.5)		29.1	(27.4)		29.0
MgO	7.8		8.0	5.2		5.7	4.7		4.9	3.7		4.1	3.2		3.3	1.6		1.7
MnO	0.48		0.5	0.79		0.9	0.47		0.5	1.3		1.5	1.0		1.0	0.56		0.6
CaO	1.7		1.7	3.3		3.6	8.1		8.5	7.0		7.8	7.2		7.4	9.2		9.7
Na_2O	0.1			0.1			0.4			0.6			0.1			0.2		
K_2O	0.6			0.2			0.2			0.2			0.6			0.3		
Σ	104.3		100.0	101.4		100.0	104.3		100.0	104.2		100.0	104.4		100.0	102.8		100.0

Component composition, %

Grossular	5			10			24			22			21			28		
Almandine	63			66			56			59			64			64		
Pyrope	31			22			19			16			13			7		
Spessartite	1			2			1			3			2			1		
f, % by composition	67			75			75			78			83			90		
N	1.782			1.795			1.795			1.795			1.795			1.803		

TABLE 73 (continued)

| | Gorki Suite | | | | | | | | | Insel Series | | | | | |
| | specimen 65v, migmatite (with sillimanite and cordierite) | | | specimen 275d, shadow granite | | | specimen 72b, shadow granite | | | specimen 61b, relicts of paleosome in shadow granite | | | specimen 278a, relicts of paleosome in shadow granite | | |
Component	wt %	correction, %	corrected analysis	wt %	correction, %	corrected analysis	wt %	correction, %	corrected analysis	wt %	correction, %	corrected analysis	wt %	correction, %	corrected analysis
SiO_2	40.7	−4.3	38.9	41.5	−3.9	38.4	42.6	−8.1	38.1	45.2	−9.9	37.9	44.1	−7.3	37.8
TiO_2	0.1		0.1	0.1		0.1	0.1		0.1	0.2		0.2	0.2		0.2
Al_2O_3	21.4	−0.8	22.0	20.4	+0.9	21.8	20.7	−1.1	21.7	19.9	+0.2	21.6	17.6	+3.3	21.4
Fe_2O_3	24.6		—	33.2		—	31.3		—	27.6		—	30.4		—
(FeO)	(22.1)		23.6	(29.9)		30.5	(28.2)		31.1	(24.8)		26.6	(27.4)		28.1
MgO	6.3		6.7	7.4		7.6	6.0		6.6	3.8		4.1	2.6		2.6
MnO	1.0		1.1	0.3		0.3	1.0		1.1	2.1		2.3	0.8		0.8
CaO	7.1		7.6	1.3		1.3	1.2		1.3	6.8		7.3	8.9		9.1
Na_2O	0.6			<0.1			0.2			0.3			0.4		
K_2O	0.3			<0.6			0.7			—			0.3		
Σ	102.1		100.0	104.2		100.0	103.8		100.0	105.9		100.0	105.3		100.0
Grossular			21			4			4			20			26
Almandine			51			66			68			59			61
Pyrope			26			29			26			16			11
Spessartite			2			1			2			5			2
f, % by composition			66			70			72			79			85
N			1.782			1.785			1.799			1.795			1.803

TABLE 73 (continued)

Component	specimen 50, shadow granite wt %	correction, wt %	corrected analysis	specimen 83, shadow granite wt %	correction, wt %	corrected analysis	specimen 83b, shadow plagiogranite wt %	correction, wt %	corrected analysis	specimen 534b, melanocratic shadow plagiogranite wt %	correction, wt %	corrected analysis	Almandine garnet No. 5 (p.106) (from pyroxene granulite)	Almandine garnet No. 7 (p.106) (from garnet-biotite gneiss)
SiO_2	40.6	−9.2	36.6	45.0	−14.7	37.6	43.2	−11.4	37.5	45.2	−14.1	36.9	37.33	38.03
TiO_2	0.4		0.5	0.2		0.3	0.2		0.2	0.2		0.2	0.02	—
Al_2O_3	20.2	−2.3	20.9	18.4	−1.2	21.4	19.9	−1.9	21.2	16.8	+0.8	20.9	20.96	22.05
Fe_2O_3	33.2		—	27.2			31.3			31.7			0.68	0.88
(FeO)	(29.9)		34.9	(24.5)		30.4	(28.2)		33.2	(28.5)		33.9	30.58	29.17
MgO	1.9		2.2	3.7		4.6	3.8		4.5	1.5		1.8	1.25	6.49
MnO	2.5		2.9	1.8		2.2	1.6		1.9	2.1		2.5	2.19	1.57
CaO	1.7		2.0	2.8		3.5	1.3		1.5	3.2		3.8	7.05	1.80
Na_2O	0.4			0.5			0.5			0.5			0.03	
K_2O	1.4			0.7			0.6			0.6				
Σ	102.3		100.0	100.3		100.0	102.4		100.0	101.8		100.0	100.09	99.99
Grossular			6			10			4			11	18.5	2.5
Almandine			78			67			74			76	71.4	68.0
Pyrope			9			18			18			7	5.0	25.9
Spessartite			7			5			4			6	5.1	3.6
f, % by composition			90			79			81			92	93	72
N		1.813			1.807			1.803			1.809		1.803	1.793

Supplement to Table 73

Crystallochemical formulas

Specimen 64a	$(Ca_{0.74}Fe_{1.36}Mg_{0.78}Mn_{0.12})_{3.00}$ $Al_{2.00}[Si_{3.00}O_{12}]$
„ 74	$(Ca_{0.20}Mg_{0.98}Fe_{1.79}Mn_{0.03})_{3.00}$ $Al_{2.00}[Si_{3.00}O_{12}]$
„ 74g	$(Ca_{0.58}Fe_{1.58}Mg_{0.81}Mn_{0.03})_{3.00}$ $Al_{2.00}[Si_{3.00}O_{12}]$
„ 77b	$(Ca_{0.14}Fe_{1.90}Mg_{0.93}Mn_{0.03})_{3.00}$ $Al_{2.00}[Si_{3.00}O_{12}]$
„ 819	$(Ca_{0.48}Fe_{1.76}Mg_{0.73}Mn_{0.03})_{3.00}$ $Al_{2.00}[(Si_{2.98}Ti_{0.01})_{3.00}O_{12}]$
„ 77	$(Ca_{0.45}Fe_{1.90}Mg_{0.61}Mn_{0.04})_{3.00}$ $Al_{2.00}[(Si_{2.99}Ti_{0.01})_{3.00}O_{12}]$
„ 565a	$(Ca_{0.30}Fe_{1.97}Mg_{0.87}Mn_{0.06})_{3.00}$ $Al_{2.00}[Si_{3.00}O_{12}]$
„ 824g	$(Ca_{0.71}Fe_{1.69}Mg_{0.57}Mn_{0.03})_{3.00}$ $Al_{2.00}[(Si_{2.99}Ti_{0.01})_{3.00}O_{12}]$
„ 557	$(Ca_{0.66}Fe_{1.77}Mg_{0.48}Mn_{0.09})_{3.00}$ $Al_{2.00}[(Si_{2.93}Ti_{0.02})_{3.00}O_{12}]$
„ 816	$(Ca_{0.62}Fe_{1.93}Mg_{0.38}Mn_{0.07})_{3.00}$ $Al_{2.00}[(Si_{2.99}Ti_{0.01})_{3.00}O_{12}]$
„ 567	$(Ca_{0.83}Fe_{1.93}Mg_{0.20}Mn_{0.04})_{3.00}$ $Al_{2.00}[(Si_{2.98}Ti_{0.02})_{3.00}O_{12}]$
„ 65v	$(Ca_{0.63}Fe_{1.53}Mg_{0.77}Mn_{0.07})_{3.00}$ $Al_{2.00}[Si_{3.00}O_{12}]$
„ 275d	$(Ca_{0.11}Fe_{1.99}Mg_{0.88}Mn_{0.02})_{3.00}$ $Al_{2.00}[Si_{3.00}O_{12}]$
„ 72b	$(Ca_{0.11}Fe_{2.04}Mg_{0.78}Mn_{0.07})_{3.00}$ $Al_{2.00}[(Si_{2.99}Ti_{0.01})_{3.00}O_{12}]$
„ 61b	$(Ca_{0.61}Fe_{1.76}Mg_{0.48}Mn_{0.15})_{3.00}$ $Al_{2.00}[(Si_{2.99}Ti_{0.01})_{3.00}O_{12}]$
„ 279a	$(Ca_{0.78}Fe_{1.85}Mg_{0.32}Mn_{0.05})_{3.00}$ $Al_{2.00}[(Si_{2.99}Ti_{0.01})_{3.00}O_{12}]$
„ 50	$(Ca_{0.17}Fe_{2.36}Mg_{0.27}Mn_{0.20})_{3.00}$ $Al_{2.00}[(Si_{2.97}Ti_{0.03})_{3.00}O_{12}]$
„ 83	$(Ca_{0.30}Fe_{2.01}Mg_{0.54}Mn_{0.15})_{3.00}$ $Al_{2.00}[(Si_{2.98}Ti_{0.02})_{3.00}O_{12}]$
„ 83b	$(Ca_{0.13}Fe_{2.21}Mg_{0.53}Mn_{0.13})_{3.00}$ $Al_{2.00}[(Si_{2.93}Ti_{0.02})_{3.00}O_{12}]$
„ 534b	$(Ca_{0.33}Fe_{2.29}Mg_{0.21}Mn_{0.17})_{3.00}$ $Al_{2.00}[(Si_{2.98}Ti_{0.02})_{3.00}O_{12}]$

of the granulite and amphibolite facies. An important feature is the high titanium and silica contents and low calcium and sodium contents in biotites of Schüssel Suite rocks, even relative to the granulite facies biotites, probably due to their polymetamorphic nature. Biotites of Insel Series amphibolites are similar in composition to biotites of group No. 10, typical of the amphibolite facies. However, there is a higher content of silica and a lower calcium and potassium content in the former. Biotites from migmatites and especially from shadow granites of the Insel Series are close in composition to biotites of group No. 9 (amphibolite facies), but the former have considerably higher iron and silica contents and lower aluminum, magnesium, calcium and sodium contents, due to their high granitization grade. This comparison permits a differentiation between two groups of biotites, i.e., those occurring in polymetamorphic and monometamorphic rocks. Furthermore, the composition of biotites within each group varies appreciably in relation to the migmatization and granitization of the rocks, which result in an increase in ferruginosity and alkalinity and decrease in magnesium and calcium contents. In concluding this description of biotites, it is necessary to emphasize the considerable discrepancy (5—16 %) between the ferruginosity determined by analytical and by refractive index methods. In approximately half of the analyzed specimens, the ferruginosity determined from the refractive index was too low, especially for highly ferruginous biotites. Therefore, the use of diagrams provided for the determination of ferruginosity in biotites from their refractive index is unreliable and it is

preferable to take account of the facies characteristics of biotites in
metamorphic rocks.

Garnets of different compositions and facies vary according to the
nature of the rock and its metamorphic facies, as is indicated by the 20
spectroscopic analyses presented in Table 73. It is interesting in this
respect to note that the almandine content in garnets varies as follows:
a) 45—66 % in the polymetamorphic (originally volcanogenic) Schüssel Suite;
b) 51—66 % in the polymetamorphic (originally sedimentary) Gorki Suite;
and c) 67—78 % in the metamorphic Insel Series of the amphibolite facies.
Thus amphibolite facies conditions produced the garnet containing the
maximum content of almandine. The total ferruginosity of garnet varies
correspondingly, 64—78 % in the Schüssel Suite, 66—85 % in the Gorki Suite,
and 79—92 % in the Insel Series. The garnets resemble the hornblendes and
biotites with respect to ferruginosity variations.

It is of interest to examine the garnet series in different rocks of the
Schüssel Suite, from the paleosome of migmatites to shadow granitoids
transformed into granulites. The contents of the almandine molecule vary
from 45 % in weakly recrystallized migmatite paleosome to 53—59 % in
strongly recrystallized paleosome, and to 64 % in completely recrystallized
paleosome, which is close to the composition of garnet in granulites where
the contents of the almandine molecule reaches 66 %. The difference between
the compositions of garnets in rocks of Gorki Suite and Insel Series is less
distinct because the analyzed garnets were taken predominantly from shadow
granites. Nevertheless, the content of the almandine molecule in the Gorki
Suite migmatite is 51 %, but it reaches 68 % in shadow granite; the values
for the Insel Suite are 60 and 74 % respectively. Thus, the higher the migmatization and granitization grade of rocks, the higher is the content of almandine molecule in garnets. In this respect, the garnets follow the same
trend as the other colored minerals of metamorphic rocks. The situation
is more complicated with regard to the contents of the pyrope and grossular
molecules, the pyrope varying from 7 to 33 % (more commonly from 20 to
30 %) and the grossular from 5 to 25 % (more commonly 20—25 %), in garnets
of Schüssel Suite rocks. For the Gorki Suite the corresponding values are:
pyrope, 11—26 % (more commonly 10—25 %) and grossular, 4—26 % (more
commonly 20—25 %); and for the Insel Series: pyrope, 7—18 % and grossular,
4—11 %. On the whole, the content of the pyrope and partially of the grossular molecules in garnets of rocks from the monometamorphic amphibolite
facies is lower than their contents in garnets of polymetamorphic rocks.
To put it differently, garnets of monometamorphic rocks have a more uniform
composition and the admixtures to the dominant almandine molecule are
small, whereas in garnets of polymetamorphic rocks the contents of almandine and the other components are often equal. An exception is the admixture
of the spessartite molecule which amounts to only 1—3 % in garnets of polymetamorphic rocks as compared to 4—7 % in those of monometamorphic rocks.

A comparison of the chemical analyses of garnets from different rocks
according to Deer /16/ with the "corrected analyses" of the garnets under
discussion reveals high degrees of similarity. Thus, garnet from pyroxene
granulite (according to Deer) is similar to that of the Schüssel Suite granulite
(specimen 567), and garnet from garnet-biotite gneiss (according to Deer) is
similar to garnet from shadow granite of the Gorki Suite (specimen 72b).
An attempt at constructing graphs of refractive index as a function of garnet

ferruginosity (in particular, the content of the almandine molecule) failed. Indeed, a comparison of the refractive indices and total ferruginosities of garnets (Table 73) does not reveal any distinct relationship between these parameters. For example, the refractive index, $n = 1.795$, was the same in garnets with ferruginosities of 71 % and 83 %, while the refractive index $n = 1.803$ was determined in garnets with total ferruginosities of 81 % and 90 %. Specific gravity determinations are of no avail, since garnets with low refractive indices often have higher specific gravities than those with high refractive indices, and vice versa. This situation is probably due to the multicomponent composition of garnets and the variable ratios of the components. The determination of the compositions of garnets from refractive indices is therefore as a rule unreliable. However the upward trend of refractive index with increasing total ferruginosity of garnets should be emphasized. Thus, garnets with ferruginosities of up to 50 % most commonly have refractive indices of 1.790—1.799, those with ferruginosities of up to 80 % have indices of 1.800—1.899 and those with ferruginosities of up to 90 % have indices of 1.800—1.810. Consequently, it is possible, on the whole, to consider the refractive indices for tentatively establishing the total ferruginosity.

For a more lucid depiction of the dissimilarities in the composition of garnets from different rocks and metamorphic facies, it is useful to compare the garnets from the different suites of the Humboldt Mountains (Table 74) with typical garnet compositions according to Sobolev /20/. Garnets from the paleosome of Schüssel Suite migmatites are almost analogous to garnets from bipyroxene-plagioclase rocks of type No. 9, belonging to the granulite facies. However, Schüssel Suite granulites occupy an intermediate position between granulites No. 5 (the granulite facies) and those of types Nos. 13 and 15 (the amphibolite facies). This is reflected in the low content of the pyrope molecule and the high content of the grossular molecule in the garnets of these granulites in comparison to Sobolev's granulites. It is further reflected in the high total ferruginosity of the former in comparison to the latter. The ferruginosity of the Sobolev granulite garnet is even higher than that of garnets of any granulite facies rocks described herein and is similar to that of the amphibolite facies garnets. At the same time, garnets of shadow granites from aluminous rocks of the Gorki Suite are very similar to those in cordierite-bearing gneisses of type 6, while the paleosome relicts in the former are nearly analogous to garnets of amphibolites No. 15. On the whole, the garnets of polymetamorphic rocks occupy an intermediate position between the typical garnets from the granulite and amphibolite facies. A different pattern is exhibited by the monometamorphic rocks. Thus, garnets of Insel Series shadow granites are similar to those of type No. 13 biotite gneisses, belonging to the amphibolite facies. This similarity is not confined to the major components but also extends to the total ferruginosities. Hence, the garnets provide an even more striking confirmation (than do other minerals) of the existence of two metamorphic rock types in the strata of the Humboldt Mountains and Petermann Range: 1) polymetamorphic rocks, composing the syncline of the Humboldt Mountains, and 2) monometamorphic rocks, composing blocks on the northern peaks of the Humboldt Mountains and on the Bardin Range (the Insel Series). In concluding the comparative description of garnets, it should be noted that the contents of

TABLE 74. Comparative characteristics of garnets

Rock type	Pyrope	Almandine	Spessartite	Grossular	Ferrugino-sity, %
Polymetamorphic rocks					
Paleosome of migmatites of the Schüssel Suite (specimens 64a, 74, 74g and 77)	20—33	45—64	1—4	7—25	64—75
Schüssel Suite granulites (specimens 812,565a, 824g, 557, 816)	13—24	56—64	1—3	10—24	71—83
Bipyroxene-plagioclase rocks, according to Sobolev, type No. 9	26 ± 12.5	53 ± 10.4	2.1 ± 1.2	16.4 ± 3.4	67 ± 15
Granulites, according to Sobolev, type No.5	35 ± 9	58.2 ± 9.2	1.4 ± 1.6	4.6 ± 2.3	63 ± 10
Paleosome of migmatites of the Gorki Suite (specimen 65v)	25	51	2	21	65
Shadow granites of the Gorki Suite (specimens 275d, 72b)	26—29	66—68	1—2	4	70—72
Paleosome relicts in a shadow granite of the Gorki Suite (specimens 64b and 279a)	11—16	59—61	2—5	20—26	79—85
Cordierite-bearing gneisses, according to Sobolev, type No. 6	27.8 ± 4.5	65.8 ± 3.4	1.8 ± 1.5	2.5 ± 2.4	71 ± 5'
Monometamorphic rocks					
Shadow granites of the Insel Series (specimens 50, 83, 83b, 534b)	7—18	67—78	4—7	4—11	79—92
Granites, biotite gneisses, according to Sobolev, type No. 13	17.8 ± 8.2	71.5 ± 7.6	5.1 ± 4.9	4.0 ± 3.5	81 ± 8
Amphibolites and amphibole gneisses, according to Sobolev, type No. 15	14.1 ± 4.2	59.8 ± 5.2	4.3 ± 5.2	18.6 ± 5.4	80 ± 6

the andradite component were not considered, since the spectroscopic analyses of garnets do not differentiate between ferrous and ferric iron. However, based on a comparison with the typical garnets described by Sobolev, the contents of the andradite molecule vary only from 1 to 3%. This is the possible extent of the increase in grossular and the decrease in almandine contents of the garnets described herein. Nevertheless, even considering this factor, the conclusions presented above, based on a comparison with typical garnets, remain valid.

Plagioclase characterizes the composition and genesis of rocks in each suite (based on measurements of more than 200 grains on the Fedorov stage).

An examination of Table 75 reveals that the composition of plagioclase in veins of all suites is nearly basic, indicating that the veins were formed under similar conditions. The veins are probably a crystallization product of a partial melt which originated during intensive tectonic activization of the crystalline basement. Plagioclases in shadow granitoids are fairly similar to one another; nevertheless in general, the plagioclases of the Schüssel Suite granitoids are more basic, especially relative to those of

TABLE 75. Composition of plagioclases in metamorphic rocks

Rocks	Suite			
	Luxemburg	Schüssel	Gorki	Insel
Bipyroxene schists and metabasites.....	39—65	34—53	30—77	41—80 amphibolites
Paleosome of migmatites	29—55	31—42	26—31	25—36
Metasome of migmatites	27—30	22—38	22—30	21—30
Shadow granitoids	None	24—40	21—31	23—36
Granitoid veins	25	24—31	23—30	23—30

Note. The An content in plagioclase is given exclusive of extreme values.

Gorki Suite shadow granites. This is probably due to the original composition of the rocks which were prevalently volcanogenic for the Schüssel Suite but terrigenous for the Gorki Suite. The composition of plagioclases in migmatites is also related to the composition of the original rocks. Plagioclases in the paleosome of migmatites in the Schüssel Suite have an average An content 10% higher than those in the paleosome of Gorki Suite migmatites. A similar trend is discernible in the metasome of migmatites, although the more acid varieties have plagioclases of the same composition.

Still more basic plagioclases occur in the paleosome of migmatites in the Luxemburg Suite, which is devoid of shadow granites. The widest fluctuations in the composition of plagioclase are characteristic of metamorphosed basic rocks transformed into bipyroxene schists in the Luxemburg, Schüssel and Gorki Suites and in the Insel Series amphibolites. In this respect, the strong, though nonuniform, recrystallization of rocks, resulting in the presence of labradorites and even bytownite relicts along with the newly formed andesines, must be considered. On the whole, a characteristic feature of the metamorphic rocks of the Humboldt Mountains and Petermann Range, irrespective of their facies, is a significant predominance of andesines over all the other varieties. Acid andesines are found in rocks of sedimentary origin, and intermediate and basic andesines in rocks of volcanic origin. This plagioclase composition is most characteristic of metamorphism under amphibolite facies conditions, irrespective of whether the facies is primary or superimposed on granulite facies rocks. The basicity of plagioclase decreases gradually from metabasites and schists to their migmatites and further to shadow granites. Another characteristic feature is the fact that the basicity of plagioclase is always higher in the paleosome of migmatites than in the metasome (in all the suites). The difference between the compositions of plagioclases in the paleosome and metasome is the lowest in the Gorki Suite, denoting their origin from a single source. In the other suites, the paleosome and metasome originated from different rock types. Thus, their An contents differ by some 10%.

A comparison of the mineral associations of four different polymetamorphic rocks from the Schüssel Suite (Table 76) indicates that, in spite of the very different composition of the rocks under comparison, the composition of their plagioclases is fairly uniform, varying within An 29—37. This

signifies a superimposed recrystallization under amphibolite facies conditions, rendering the composition of plagioclases in basic schists similar
to that in their migmatites and shadow granites.

TABLE 76. Comparative characteristics of total ferruginosity in coexistent minerals of different rocks in the
Schüssel Suite (according to quantitative spectroscopic analyses)

Rocks	Orthopy-roxene	Clinopy-roxene	Hornblende	Biotite	Garnet	An content of plagioclase
Amphibolized bipyroxene ; schist (specimen 558v)	39	25	26	—	—	37
Weakly recrystallized bipyroxene schist in the paleosome of agma-tite (specimen 233)	45	36	37	48	—	—
Strongly recrystallized garnet-bearing pyroxene schist in the paleosome of a layered mig-matite (specimen 64a)	—	31	42	44	64	34
Shadow granitoid transformed into granulite (specimen 557)..	57	50	62	—	78	30
Shadow granitoid transformed into granulite (specimen 816)..	64	54	65	—	83	29

Notes. 1. See Table 64 for the mineral compositions of the specimens. 2. The composition of shadow
granitoids approaches that of granodioites; their biotite content is negligible ($\approx 1\%$), while their content
of garnet is relatively high (12—15%).

Clinopyroxenes always have lower ferruginosities than orthopyroxenes
(by 7—14%) the difference diminishing gradually with increasing total
ferruginosities of both pyroxenes. As a rule, orthopyroxenes are replaced
by biotite and clinopyroxenes by hornblende during recrystallization and
granitization of basic schists under polymetamorphic conditions. In this
case, the ferruginosity of orthopyroxenes in the newly generated tetramineral
association is equal to (or somewhat lower than) the ferruginosity of biotites,
while the ferruginosity of clinopyroxenes is close to that of hornblende. All
four minerals coexist almost to the highest ferruginosity values, then the
unstable pyroxenes are almost completely replaced by biotite and hornblende.
The same effect may be achieved by regressive metamorphism unrelated to
granitization of basic schists, when pyroxenes of any (even relatively low)
ferruginosity are replaced by biotite and hornblende. However, in this case,
the ferruginosity of the latter two minerals is lower than that of the coexisting pyroxenes. In the initial stages of granitization of basic schists, along
with an increase in the ferruginosity of pyroxenes, hornblende and garnet
are formed instead of biotite; in general, the garnet replaces the orthopyroxene. In this case, the ferruginosity of hornblendes and garnets coexisting with pyroxenes is significantly higher than the ferruginosity of the
pyroxenes. Such associations of pyroxenes with garnet are produced at
high granitization temperatures and relatively low alkalinity in the initial
stages of the process. The development of granitization processes under
amphibolite facies conditions and an increase in the alkalinity of solutions

result in the replacement of the garnet by biotite in shadow granites and finely layered migmatites. On the whole, the mineral associations of the Schüssel Suite are unstable and the coexistence of minerals of different metamorphic facies is possible when the ferruginosities of these minerals are very similar. If the ferruginosities of the minerals are altered by granitization, the pyroxenes are largely replaced by hornblende and biotite (or garnet). This is confirmed by dozens of determinations of mineral ferruginosities in different rocks of the Schüssel Suite, based on refractive . indices and consequently less accurate. Therefore the pattern of the inter-relationships between the minerals is less clear than in the case of spectro-scopic analyses.

It is of interest to compare the ferruginosities of hornblende and biotite, the two main colored minerals in the Insel Series. The ferruginosities of both minerals are nearly the same (Table 77); the biotite ferruginosity is only slightly higher (by 3—5%), indicating similar formation conditions. Characteristically, the ferruginosity of colored minerals in the paleosome of migmatites of the amphibolite facies often proves to be higher than that in some shadow granites. This has already been mentioned in the descriptions of individual minerals; the suggested explanation is the higher degree of alkaline metasomatic recrystallization involved in the formation of mig-matite paleosomes, and, in contrast, the decisive role of crystallization from a eutectic melt in the formation of shadow granites.

TABLE 77. Ferruginosities of hornblende and biotite from Insel Series rocks

Rock	Hornblende	Biotite
Amphibolite (specimen 50v)	39	44
Migmatite paleosome (specimen 84v) ..	54	57
Shadow granite (specimen 82)	44	47

It is useful to summarize this examination of the composition of rock-forming minerals in the metamorphic strata of the Humboldt Mountains and Petermann Range by considering the differences between the polymetamor-phic and monometamorphic rocks, as depicted in Table 78.

The characteristic mineral associations and compositions in the polyme-tamorphic and monometamorphic rocks permit their separation, in spite of the common formation conditions partly in the concluding and partly in the main metamorphic stages. The two groups of rocks differ in their charac-teristic minerals, but even the same minerals (and this is especially important) have different compositions in each group of rocks. However, the trend of metamorphic processes is the same in both the polymetamorphic and monometamorphic rocks, and a similar range of rock types is present in both groups. Migmatites and shadow granites, which considerably pre-dominate over the original schists and closely similar plagiogneisses (with respect to the composition), are formed in the crystalline basement under conditions of the granulite facies and the primary and superimposed amphi-bolite facies. It should be noted that various metasomatic granitization

TABLE 78. Comparative characteristics of polymetamorphic and monometamorphic rocks

Minerals	Polymetamorphic rocks of the granulite and superimposed amphibolite facies	Monometamorphic rocks of the amphibolite facies
Orthopyroxenes	1. Gradual increase of ferruginosity from basic schists — to their migmatites — to shadow granites 2. Gradual replacement by biotite (or garnet in the case of low alkalinity of metasomatic solutions), rendering primary pyroxenes relict 3. Complete replacement by biotite on completion of metasomatic recrystallization under amphibolite facies conditions	
Clinopyroxenes	1. The lowest ferruginosity — in diopsides from granulite facies calciphyres; the ferruginosity is doubled during recrystallization under amphibolite facies conditions 2. Lowest ferruginosity in augites of basic schists, gradually increasing to the extent of nearly double on formation of granulated shadow granites	1. Present only in amphibolites and calciphyres, the salites of which have a ferruginosity equal to that found in highly recrystallized calciphyres of polymetamorphic rocks 2. Very rare in agmatites from amphibolites and absent in shadow granites
Hornblendes	1. Gradual increase of ferruginosity and the degree of replacement of clinopyroxenes, from basic schists to granulated shadow granites. At ferruginosities > 80%, the clinopyroxene is totally replaced by hornblende 2. Increase in the content of titanium and alkalis and also in places of the total ferruginosity, in shadow granites in comparison to analogous amphibolite facies rocks	1. Slight increase in ferruginosity from amphibolites to shadow granites produced by partial melts; the ferruginosity is doubled in migmatites 2. Low contents of aluminum, titanium and alkalis
Biotites	1. Gradual increase of ferruginosity and degree of replacement of orthopyroxenes, from basic schists and plagiogneisses through migmatites to shadow granites (to complete replacement) 2. High titanium and potassium contents, especially in shadow granites	1. Higher ferruginosity in migmatites in comparison to shadow granites produced by interaction between partial melt and paleosome 2. High iron content
Garnets	1. Content of the almandine molecule, 45—66%; total ferruginosity, 64—78% 2. High content of the pyrope molecule in comparison to the amphibolite facies garnets	1. Content of almandine molecule, 67—78%; total ferruginosity, 79—92% 2. Low content of the pyrope molecule
Plagioclases	1. Considerable variation in the composition of the mineral in migmatites and shadow granites, in including both the paleosome and metasome 2. Stable composition of the mineral in veins and the same composition as in amphibolite facies rocks	1. Relative stability of the minerals in migmatites and shadow granites 2. Stable composition of the mineral in veins

processes play a significantly more important role under conditions of the granulite and superimposed amphibolite facies. Eutectic melts seem to be the main granitization agent under amphibolite facies conditions, while metasomatic recrystallization features largely in the formation of the migmatite paleosomes. The most sensitive reaction to superimposition of the metamorphic facies is exhibited by the calciphyres, or more precisely their clinopyroxenes, when the rock is found to contain pyroxenes of both the granulite and amphibolite facies. However, minerals of both metamorphic facies also coexist in other rocks of different metamorphic origin, where the granulite facies minerals are always relicts. Adapting to the new conditions of the superimposed amphibolite facies, the granulite facies minerals (and especially the pyroxenes) increase their ferruginosity, while the garnets increase their content of the almandine molecule. Nevertheless, these associations must be regarded as nonequilibrium, since in the case of total recrystallization of the granulite facies rocks under the new amphibolite facies conditions, the granulite facies minerals which reach a maximum ferruginosity are completely replaced by amphibolite facies minerals. Primary amphibolite facies minerals never reach such high ferruginosities as do their analogs in rocks of polymetamorphic genesis. However, rocks of both types equally undergo granitization.

Mineral associations of polymetamorphic rocks are on the whole unstable, in contrast to those of monometamorphic rocks which are stable within a single metamorphic subfacies. To conclude this description of the minerals of metamorphic rocks, it is worthwhile emphasizing the importance of chemical analyses for determination of genesis, formation conditions and original composition of these rocks. Chemical rock analyses (and especially of the widespread migmatites and shadow granites) reflect random ratios of elements, depending on the amounts of paleosome and metasome as well as on their granitization grade. Therefore chemical analyses of polymetamorphic rocks were not carried out.

Chapter IV

AMPHIBOLITE FACIES

The amphibolite facies in the crystalline basement of the Antarctic Platform has been less thoroughly studied than the granulite facies. These rocks
present a considerably greater variety in mineralogy, structure and chemical features than the granulite facies rocks. Nevertheless, amphibolite
facies rocks must be described according to the regions in which they occur,
instead of genetic groups, because the latter have not yet been identified.

The largest regions with amphibolite facies rocks in Antarctica are the
Humboldt Moutains and Petermann Range, Prince Olav Coast, Sor Rondane
and Yamato mountains, western Queen Maud Land and the Lambert Glacier
area. Amphibolite facies rocks are also known from the Vestfold and
Grearson oases.

Amphibolite facies rocks of the Humboldt Mountains and Petermann
Range have already been described in Chapter III together with the polymetamorphic rocks for convenience of comparison. All the other amphibolite facies rocks are described below.

ROCKS OF THE PRINCE OLAV COAST

The following rocks on the Prince Olav Coast can be distinguished with
respect to their mineral compositions: a) amphibolites; b) biotite plagiogneisses; c) biotite-garnet plagiogneisses; d) high-alumina schists and
plagiogneisses; e) gedrite- and cummingtonite-bearing rocks.

A m p h i b o l i t e s form bedded units with thicknesses of tens of meters
(less commonly a few hundreds of meters) or else occur in thinner lenses
within granitized biotite plagiogneisses. The amphibolites usually have a
comparatively uniform, weakly banded structure. In places, the amphibolites
present alternations of more melanocratic varieties with subordinate leucocratic intercalations and biotite plagiogneisses, sometimes appreciably
granitized. Leucoamphibolites are cataclastized. They feature lenticular
or ribbon-shaped quartz segregations, a diffuse reverse zonality in the
plagioclase and newly formed epidote, scapolite and calcite. These transformations were classified as regional metamorphism of a lower grade
of the amphibolite facies. Clinopyroxene-bearing, biotitized and granitized
varieties can be distinguished among the amphibolites with reference to the composition (Table 79). The clinopyroxene-bearing amphibolites are segregated in
small lenses or diffuse "spots" within weakly biotitized amphibolites and stand
out due to their more massive structure and black color. A microscopic

TABLE 79. Mineral composition of amphibolites from Prince Olav Coast

Specimen No.	quartz	plagioclase	microcline	clinopyroxene	amphibole	biotite	ore mineral	epidote	accessory minerals	An content of plagioclase	cpx n_z	cpx n_x	cpx $2V°$	cpx f, at.%	amph n_z	amph n_x	amph $2V°$	amph f, at.%	biotite n_z	biotite f, at.%	microcline n_z	epidote n_z	epidote n_x	chlorite $2V°$	chlorite n_z	Geological setting
211d	—	26	—	8	60	—	2	—	2 o.s.*	50—82	1.717	1.691	+56	33	1.686	1.666	—69	49	—	—	—	1.765	1.738	—78	1.620	Chlorite, sericite, scapolite—4%. Pocket-shaped segregation in an amphibolite intercalation in biotite plagiogneiss
201b	1	54	—	—	28	17	—	—	•	30—34	—	—	—	—	1.690	1.670	—65—68	53	1.640	47	—	—	—	—	—	Lens in biotite plagiogneiss
201v	10	47	—	—	18	25	—	—	•	28	—	—	—	—	1.690	1.670	—58	53	1.648	53	—	—	—	—	—	As above, marginal portion of lens
206	8	50	—	—	10	13	3	—	•	30—40	—	—	—	—	1.684	1.664	—65	47	1.636	44	—	—	—	—	—	Amphibolite beds
211g	17	43	—	—	15	25	—	—	•	28	—	—	—	—	1.691	1.672	—57	54	1.560	63	—	—	—	—	—	Lens in granitized amphibolite
211b	8	52	—	—	25	13	—	2	2	32—33	—	—	—	—	1.701	1.682	—41	63	1.659	62	—	—	—	—	—	Intercalation in biotite plagiogneiss
206a	22	53	—	—	10	13	2	—	o.s.	32—38	—	—	—	—	1.684	1.664	—64	47	1.636	44	—	—	—	—	—	Amphibolite beds, interlayered with amphibolites represented by specimen 206
211v	25	28	15	—	18	10	—	4	•	28—29	—	—	—	—	1.701	1.682	—41	63	1.659	62	1.530	—	—	—78	—	Granitized area in amphibolite represented by specimen 211b
226	15	45	7	—	13	18	—	2	—	33	—	—	—	—	1.700	1.681	—	62	1.660	63	1.530	—	—	—	—	Beds of granitized amphibolites
228	—	47	13	—	20	18	—	1	1	37—38	—	—	—	—	1.697	1.678	—48	59	1.654	58	—	—	—	—	—	As above
228a	—	48	13	—	30	5	—	—	1	35—40	—	—	—	—	1.705	1.685	—46	67	1.660	63	1.529	—	—	—	—	Calcite, 3%

Note. The ferruginosities of hornblende and biotite were determined from curve II of the diagram provided by Drugova and Glebovitskii /22/.

* [o.s. = optic sign.]

examination distinctly establishes the relict nature of clinopyroxene and its intensive replacement by hornblende along cracks and on the periphery of grains. At the same time, these amphibolites have preserved complex diablastic aggregates of clinopyroxene with plagioclase. These features suggest a considerably more extensive initial occurrence of clinopyroxenes in the amphibolites under consideration. The original rocks were probably gabbroic.

Biotitized amphibolites occur in marginal portions of amphibolite lenses or in zones at contacts with biotite plagiogneisses. They often bear traces of the late development of biotite on the periphery or along cracks in hornblende and around ore grains.

The clinopyroxene-bearing amphibolites lack both biotite and quartz. Amphibole is essentially the only colored mineral in the pyroxeneless amphibolites, while quartz, present to the extent of a few percent, is often segregated in small, rounded intrusions in the hornblende or in symplektite aggregates with hornblende. In the biotitized varieties, newly formed biotite, at the expense of hornblende, has little effect on the contents of plagioclase and quartz, although the latter occasionally reaches 10% or more. Therefore, biotitization of amphibolites may be regarded as the initial stage in their granitization.

The granitized varieties occur to only a limited extent, forming small, "stretched" lenses in granitized biotite plagiogneisses or diffuse "spots" with irregular outlines in marginal portions of amphibolite beds. They stand out from the surrounding amphibolites by their inequigranular nature and coarser grain size and also by a more intensive layered manifestation of biotitization. Microscopic examination of granitized amphibolites distinctly reveals, in places, an intermittent-banded distribution of the microcline developing mostly from plagioclase and containing small relict inclusions of the latter. The inclusions are often surrounded by diffuse albite rims containing myrmekites. Besides feldspathization of amphibolites that are nearly devoid of quartz, the development of microcline also occurs in biotitized, quartz-bearing rocks.

The texture of amphibolites is heterogranoblastic. The mosaic aggregate of plagioclase (with 1—2-mm grains) contains somewhat larger (up to 4—5 mm) hornblende with small inclusions of plagioclase and quartz, so that the texture of these rocks approaches poikiloblastic. Marginal portions of such poikiloblasts in places contain symplektite aggregates of hornblende with quartz. In biotitized varieties, the predominant development of biotite in the form of subparallel flakes invests the rocks with a secondary lepidogranoblastic texture. All varieties of amphibolites underwent secondary transformations at a lower grade of the amphibolite facies under stress, which produced a cataclasis of the amphibolites in the initial stage of their transformation. Therefore blastocataclastic textures are common for repeatedly metamorphosed amphibolites. Ribbon-shaped newly formed quartz in leucoamphibolites gives rise to a granulite texture. Epidote predominantly replaces hornblende, while sericite replaces plagioclase in the marginal portions of grains. The superimposed associations are especially distinct in clinopyroxene-bearing amphibolites. In this case, ribbon-shaped quartz is absent, but epidotization, scapolitization, sericitization and calcitization are more intensive. These processes are also fairly distinctly observed in other amphibolite varieties, although to a lesser degree. Epidote replaces clinopyroxene and hornblende, while scapolite and sericite replace plagioclase. In many cases, epidote and scapolite form complex diablastic aggregates with mutual inclusions fully inherited from the corresponding forms of clinopyroxene-plagioclase aggregates. Scapolitization of plagioclase is accompanied by the development of reverse zonality. Calcite forms along small cracks at grain contacts. There is also a relatively weak chloritization of biotite.

Plagioclase of little altered amphibolites contains 30—35% anorthite. The basicity of biotite-enriched varieties decreases to oligoclase, An 28, and remains the same in feldspathized amphibolites outside the marginal albitic or myrmekitic fringes which are extremely characteristic for these varieties. In the case of repeated metamorphism, plagioclase of An 30—35 acquires a diffuse, zoned structure and its basicity increases from the central portions to the periphery of the grains (to andesine, An 38—40). Bytownite, An 80—90, develops in the marginal portions of zoned grains in scapolitized amphibolites. K-feldspar occurs as crosshatched microcline in all cases; the microcline is practically devoid of the albite component, as indicated by the refractive indices. The clinopyroxene is slightly greenish in thin section without any noticeable pleochroism. It corresponds to salite with ferruginosity 33 at.%. The amphibole is common hornblende, pleochroic from bluish green along n_z' to yellowish green along n_x', with a ferruginosity of 47—54 at.%. The ferruginosity of hornblende does not undergo any significant changes in clinopyroxene-bearing or in biotitized varieties. This fact suggests 1) more extensive original occurrence of clinopyroxene in amphibolites, the mineral being completely replaced by hornblende, and 2) instability of amphibole during biotitization and feldspathization. The hornblende in feldspathized amphibolites has a high ferruginosity (59—67 at.%). The ferruginosity of amphibole decreases somewhat (down to 47 at.%) in zones of silicification and other secondary alterations, and it undergoes incomplete recrystallization manifesting itself in the diffuse block structure of individual large grains. In only slightly altered varieties the biotite, which is pleochroic to dark brown along n_z', has nearly the same ferruginosity as the associated amphibolite. However, considerable biotitization somewhat raises the ferruginosity of biotite (to 63 at.%), similar to feldspathized varieties. The ferruginosities of biotite and amphibole are closely similar in repeatedly metamorphosed amphibolites. The slight decrease in their ferruginosities is compensated by finely disseminated magnetite separated out during recrystallization; in places, this accounts for as much as 2—3 vol.% of the rock. The accessory minerals, besides magnetite, include apatite (in small rounded or columnar grains) and sphene (in segregations having irregular shapes at grain contacts).

The chemical compositions of different varieties of amphibolites are given in Table 80. Granitization (biotitization) is weakest in the case of amphibolites with a low Si : Al ratio (low silica content, the alumina contents being approximately the same) and it is strongest in amphibolites with a high Si : Al ratio. The alkali contents of biotitized and granitized amphibolites are the same, but the former have higher contents of ferrous iron,

TABLE 80. Chemical composition of amphibolites from the Prince Olav Coast

Component	Specimen No.											
	211d			211g			211b			211v		
	wt%	at.%	R/Al	wt%	at.%	R/Al	wt%	at.%	R/Al	wt%	at.%	R/Al
SiO$_2$	43.39	41.2	2.38	55.61	52.1	2.76	56.44	53.5	2.91	61.14	57.8	3.26
TiO$_2$	0.56	0.4	0.02	0.88	0.6	0.03	1.02	0.7	0.04	0.48	0.3	0.02
Al$_2$O$_3$	15.50	17.3	1.00	17.06	18.9	1.00	16.57	18.4	1.00	15.95	17.7	1.00
Fe$_2$O$_3$	4.31	3.1	0.18	2.12	1.5	0.08	2.68	1.9	0.10	2.04	1.4	0.08
FeO	8.87	7.0	0.40	5.83	4.6	0.24	5.73	4.5	0.24	4.49	3.6	0.20
MnO	0.35	0.3	—	0.16	0.1	—	0.19	0.2	—	0.15	0.1	—
MgO	9.48	13.5	0.78	4.86	6.8	0.36	3.61	5.1	0.28	2.87	4.0	0.23
CaO	12.16	12.4	0.72	4.32	4.3	0.23	6.01	6.1	0.33	5.31	5.4	0.31
Na$_2$O	1.67	3.0	0.17	4.03	7.3	0.39	3.63	6.6	0.36	3.80	6.9	0.39
K$_2$O	1.41	1.7	0.10	3.12	3.7	0.20	2.41	2.8	0.15	2.28	2.7	0.15
P$_2$O$_5$	0.10	0.1	—	0.21	0.1	—	0.26	0.2	—	0.23	0.1	—
Loss on ignition	2.09	—	—	1.63	—	—	1.23	—	—	1.31	—	—
Σ	99.89	100.0	—	99.83	100.0	—	99.78	100.0	—	100.05	100.0	—

	Specimen No.			
	211d	211g	211b	211a
Numerical characteristics (after Zavaritskii)				
a	5.7	13.6	11.7	11.7
b	36.2	16.4	16.3	12.7
c	7.6	5.0	5.5	5.0
s	50.5	65.0	66.5	70.6
Q	−18.0	−2.2	+4.1	+12.8
f'	34.7	46.2	50.0	48.8
m'	44.9	50.8	38.0	38.0
c'	20.4	3.0	12.0	13.2
a'	—	—	—	—
Coordinates on the ACF diagram (after Eskola and Korzhinskii)				
A	27.6	33.2	35.1	38.2
C	27.0	18.3	24.5	25.4
F	45.4	48.5	39.4	36.4
Norm, % (after Barth)				
Albite	3.7	36.6	33.2	34.6
Anorthite	31.5	19.6	22.4	20.3
Orthoclase	8.6	18.6	14.2	13.6
Orthopyroxene	2.7	19.7	13.6	11.0
Clinopyroxene	23.7	0.9	5.2	4.5
Magnetite	4.6	2.2	2.9	2.2
Ilmenite	0.8	1.2	1.5	0.7
Apatite	0.3	0.3	0.5	0.3
Quartz	—	0.9	6.6	12.8
Nepheline	6.8	—	—	—
Olivine	17.3	—	—	—

Note. Modal composition of the rocks is listed in Table 79.

magnesium and manganese. These elements are obviously lost during granitization. Chemical analogs of the investigated amphibolites are magmatic rocks of the andesite-basalt or gabbro-diorite series. The only notable features are the high contents of potassium and ferrous iron in comparison to the corresponding intermediate magmatic rocks /65, 75/. In the granulite facies, pyroxene-plagioclase schists and melanocratic enderbites are the closest to amphibolites in their composition. They differ from the amphibolites mainly in their lower contents of manganese, ferric iron and potassium and their higher contents of titanium, ferrous iron and magnesium. The sodium content of enderbitized schists is distinctly higher than that in the amphibolites. On the other hand, the potassium content of bipyroxene schists is higher. Thus, the ferrous iron content in the amphibolites is intermediate between that of the corresponding magmatic rocks and granulite facies rocks, but their potassium content is higher than in all the other rocks. This observation is in agreement with the opinion of the majority of researchers in metamorphic geology concerning the concentration of potassium and the high oxygen potential in the amphibolite facies /35, 43/.

Biotite plagiogneisses are among the more widespread metamorphic rocks on the Prince Olav Coast. They are predominant in the Olav Series and contain intercalations and beds of amphibolites. They are often interlayered with biotite-garnet plagiogneisses of the Hinode Series and only infrequently contain intercalations of amphibolites with cummingtonite and gedrite. These rocks stand out distinctly by their light, slightly grayish or pinkish color. In relatively weakly granitized varieties of biotite plagiogneisses, distinct banded structures related to an enrichment of biotite in thin bands (a few centimeters wide) are common. They also display a distinct gneissosity coinciding with the banding, manifested in a parallel orientation of the biotite flakes. The banding is almost completely obliterated in strongly granitized varieties, whereas the gneissosity remains distinct. The maximum heterogeneity in the composition of biotite plagiogneisses is produced by the nonuniform distribution of biotite and dissimilar granitization grades of rocks. Mesotype varieties consisting of 55—75% plagioclase, up to 25% quartz and 10—15% biotite, are the most widespread among the plagiogneisses free of or with small amounts of K-feldspar. The comparatively rare melanocratic varieties contain up to 30—40% biotite but only up to 10% quartz. The content of K-feldspar increases up to 30—35% in higher grades of granitization, mainly at the expense of plagioclase. Granitized plagiogneisses contain up to 30% quartz and 5—10% biotite (Table 81). The accessory minerals are represented by apatite, zircon and magnetite.

Weakly granitized varieties of plagiogneiss exhibit well-developed lepidogranoblastic textures due to a subparallel distribution of small biotite flakes (up to 1 mm) in a mosaic plagioclase-quartz aggregate. In the narrow zones at contacts with amphibolites, the biotite plagiogneisses contain relicts of hornblende replaced by biotite along cracks and from the periphery of grains. The textures of granitized varieties are complicated by the appearance of somewhat larger (up to 4—5 mm) metablasts or aggregates of K-feldspar grains distinctly replacing the plagioclase. Contacts between the K-feldspar and the replaced plagioclase display diffuse rims of albite and partially of myrmekite. In varieties with the strongest granitization, the lepidogranoblastic textures of plagiogneisses are largely obliterated. These are replaced by metablastic textures related to the development of K-feldspar. Like the amphibolites, the plagiogneisses display signs of repeated metamorphism, especially in melanocratic plagiogneisses. They exhibit well-developed cataclasis and recrystallization, resulting in coarser, up to 3—5-mm lenticular quartz segregations in the fine-grained matrix (average grain size about 0.7 mm). In this case the biotite becomes diablastic and contains small rounded inclusions of quartz or, less commonly, forms symplektitic aggregates with the latter. It also occasionally contains magnetite grains with plagioclase and quartz inclusions, imparting a sideronitic texture. Other features include the development of epidote, calcite and sericite along fine cracks in plagioclase, relatively large muscovite crystals in K-feldspar, and the partial chloritization of biotite. All secondary alterations are rather limited and do not obliterate the main features of previously formed textures in plagiogneiss.

TABLE 81. Mineral composition of biotite plagiogneisses from the Prince Olav Coast

Specimen No.	Mineral composition, vol. %				Characteristics of minerals					Geological setting
					An content of plagioclase	biotite		microcline		
	quartz	plagioclase	microcline	biotite		n_z	f	n_z	n_x	
201v	25	65	—	10	28	1.656	69	—	—	Near contact with biotitic amphibolite
201	24	60	3	13	22, 23	1.660	63			Same beds, slightly granitized plagiogneiss
201g	20	50	15	15	19	1.658	61	1.530	1.523	Same beds, granitized plagiogneiss
211	30	35	26	9	18—10	1.667	67	1.530	1.523	Beds of strongly granitized plagiogneisses

Plagioclase, in the least altered varieties of plagiogneiss, contains 28—30% anorthite. Its basicity decreases to oligoclase, An 18—20, in granitized varieties. On the other hand, its basicity increases to andesine, An 38—40, in zones of blastocataclasis and in silicified layers. The superimposed nature of such alterations is clearly manifested in comparatively large plagioclase porphyroclasts with diffuse reversed zonality, with a composition varying from An 20—33 to An 39—40. The basicity of recrystallized finer-grained plagioclase corresponds to the marginal zone of larger grains. The development of sericite and muscovite is accompanied by a significant decrease in

.the basicity of plagioclase, down to albite-oligoclase, An 9—12. The biotite
is pleochroic to dark brown along n_z. Its ferruginosity is 60—67 at.%, the
lower values referring to nongranitized and the higher to granitized plagiogneisses. K-feldspar is exclusively represented by crosshatched microcline,
corresponding to microcline from granitized amphibolites in its refractive
indices.

Biotite-garnet plagiogneisses form beds and intercalations of various
overall thicknesses in biotite plagiogneisses, and occasionally separate
exposures. A common phenomenon is layered biotite-garnet plagiogneiss
migmatite. Shadow biotite granites form the metasome and correspond
in structure and composition to strongly granitized biotite plagiogneisses.
The paleosome of migmatites is often granitized, merging with the metasome
and forming areas of shadow garnet granites. The biotite-garnet plagiogneisses are gray, medium-grained, gneissic and finely eutaxitic rocks.
The banding is due to narrow intermittent strips, up to 5—10 cm wide, enriched in biotite and garnet. It is obliterated in granitized varieties, whereas
the gneissosity is preserved. The most widespread plagiogneisses are the
leucocratic varieties containing 3—9% garnet, 2—13% biotite, 55—65% plagioclase and 20—35% quartz (Table 82). The biotite content increases to 40%
in melanocratic varieties, but the contents of the other minerals decrease:
quartz down to 3%, and garnet down to sporadic grains. The quantitative
alterations in granitized varieties consist in a decrease of plagioclase
(down to 5%) due to its replacement by microcline which varies from 2 to
40%. There is a simultaneous decrease in colored minerals. The accessory
minerals include apatite and zircon.

The texture of the plagiogneiss is most commonly lepidogranoblastic or
porphyroblastic (garnet porphyroblasts); the lepidogranoblastic elements
average 0.5—1 mm in size. The garnet porphyroblasts (up to 4 mm) are
euhedral and diablastic due to quartz and biotite inclusions in the central
portions of grains (Figure 43). The structure of granitized varieties is
complicated by intergranular and metablastic microcline replacing the
plagioclase. The lepidogranoblastic texture is thus obliterated by the
metablastic texture. The mineral grains are corroded, assuming serrate
and rugged outlines. Garnet is replaced by biotite. Some areas of plagiogneisses manifest signs of repeated metamorphism, including blastocataclasis, the formation of lenticular mosaic quartz segregations, the replacement of plagioclase and microcline by sericite and muscovite, and the
replacement of biotite by muscovite, fibrolite and chlorite. Aggregates
of sericite accumulate in the intergranular space. Fibrolite forms sheaflike acicular aggregates penetrating the biotite along cleavage cracks.
Staurolite is sporadic and there is an increase in magnetite. Cataclastized
groups of plagiogneiss beds are transected by veins of pegmatites, their
contacts exhibiting the development of fibrolite. Andesine-oligoclase,
An 27—30, is characteristic of nongranitized plagiogneiss, and plagioclase
with An 10—24 is common in granitized plagiogneiss. The basicity of
plagioclase increases to andesine, An 40, in blastocataclastic zones. It
decreases with the development of sericite and muscovite, to albite-
oligoclase, An 10—12. Microcline is represented by distinctly crosshatched

TABLE 82. Mineral composition of biotite-garnet plagiogneisses from the Prince Olav Coast

Specimen No.	Mineral composition, vol.%									An content of plagioclase	Geological setting
	quartz	plagioclase	microcline	garnet	biotite	magnetite	fibrolite	sericite	accessory minerals		
278	33	58	—	7	2	o.s.*	—	—	—	30	Biotite-garnet plagiogneisses
279v	20	64	—	7	9	"	—	—	o.s.	38	As above
275v	33	55	—	2	7	2	—	1	"	27	" "
205b	19	60	—	5	12	3	—	—	1	33	" "
220a	35	43	—	3	13	2	—	4	—	12	1-m intercalations in beds of biotite plagiogneisses
243b	8	50	—	o.s.	42	—	—	—	o.s.	39	3-m layer in contact with biotite plagiogneisses
509	12	44	—	"	40	3	1	—	"	40	25-m intercalation in granitized biotite plagiogneisses. Blastocataclastic zone
279d	20	56	2	9	13	—	—	—	—	28	Granitized area in plagiogneiss beds, represented by specimen 279v
213a	33	37	23	o.s.	7	—	—	o.s.	o.s.	24	Beds of granitized biotite-garnet plagiogneisses
575a	23	5	42	1	25	—	o.s.	4	"	10	Beds of granitized biotite-garnet plagiogneisses

Note. A single grain of staurolite was found in specimen 575a.

* [o.s. = optic sign.]

grains. The microcline and biotite are similar in nature to those in amphibolites.

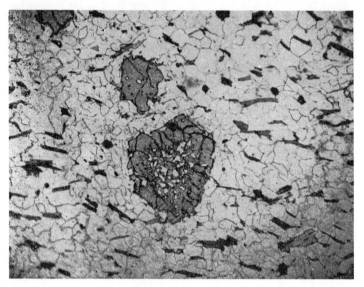

FIGURE 43. Biotite-garnet plagiogneiss (thin section 270v, × 15, regular light).

The high-alumina schists include b i o t i t e - s i l l i m a n i t e, g a r n e t-
b i o t i t e - s i l l i m a n i t e and c o r d i e r i t e - b i o t i t e - s i l l i m a n i t e
varieties. They compose intermittent, sometimes fairly thick intercalations
(up to 30 m) within biotite plagiogneisses. As a rule, they are cataclastized,
recrystallized, and transected by muscovite-bearing pegmatite veins.

In general, these are dark-colored, coarse-grained schistose rocks, with
widely varying contents of the rock-forming minerals (Table 83). The
majority contain variable amounts of both quartz and plagioclase, but certain
varieties are devoid or contain only insignificant amounts of one of these
minerals, mostly irrespective of the grade of feldspathization. However,
in some cases, the plagioclase content quite obviously decreases with an
increasing content of K-feldspar, which replaces it. Certain cordierite-
bearing schists are feldspar-free and their quartz content is only 1%.
Sillimanite and biotite are consistent components of all these rocks, varying
from 3 to 25%. The content of cordierite is 5—25% and that of garnet ranges
from sporadic grains to 25%. Considerable changes in the content of
colored minerals occur due to the secondary development of fibrolite
and muscovite, causing a fairly appreciable decrease in plagioclase, microcline, cordierite and biotite. On the other hand, these secondary minerals
are accompanied by an increase in the total content of sillimanite, fibrolite
and magnetite. The secondary minerals also include staurolite and kyanite,
which are present in the same biotite-cordierite-quartz specimens (up to 3%).

High-alumina schists possess a very complex, metablastic texture, which includes elements of granoblastic, lepidogranoblastic, porphyroblastic, poikiloporphyroblastic and blastocataclastic textures. However, the principal noteworthy point is the nature of the development of minerals of the superimposed stage of metamorphism. There is a distinct development of pseudomorphs of fibrolite after sillimanite, microcline, plagioclase and cordierite, and along cleavage cracks in biotite. Occasionally, staurolite and kyanite appear together with fibrolite at the expense of cordierite and biotite. The fibrolite is represented by sheaflike and glomerular aggregates of needles and filiform crystals. Staurolite and kyanite form irregular grains. The replacement of biotite and cordierite by fibrolite liberates considerable amounts of magnetite. The formation of magnetite also accompanies the replacement of cordierite by muscovite (sericite). Muscovite and sericite also intensively replace plagioclase and microcline. The An content in plagioclase is 24—35%. The microcline possesses a fine crosshatching. The ferruginosity of biotite, which is pleochroic to dark brown, is fairly constant in schists of different compositions (44 at.%). Cordierite is twinned and has a high ferruginosity (31 at.%). The sillimanite and fibrolite differ in compositions, as well as morphologically (Table 83).

The high-alumina schists contain two distinct mineral associations: 1) the early association represented by biotite and one of the high-alumina minerals — sillimanite, cordierite or garnet, and 2) the later association represented by fibrolite, kyanite, staurolite and muscovite. Quartz and plagioclase may be present in both associations, depending on the basicity. K-feldspar belongs to the early association, while magnetite belongs mainly to the late association.

Some rock varieties in the Hinode Series (Appendix 2) contain amphiboles of the anthophyllite-gedrite or cummingtonite-grünerite series. Usually, such rocks occur in thin (0.5—10 m) intercalations among biotite and biotite-garnet plagiogneiss, but often are found together with amphibolites. As a rule, areas with such rocks are saturated with concordant and discordant pegmatite veins. There are two groups differing in their appearance and composition but occurring in close association (even in the same exposures), i. e., cummingtonite- and gedrite-bearing hornblende amphibolites and gedrite rocks. The gedrite and cummingtonite amphibolites do not differ externally from cataclastized and partially recrystallized amphibolites. They are black, medium-grained schistose rocks and form the thickest and most consistent intercalations. Their contents of minerals (Table 84) fluctuate very considerably. The ubiquitous minerals include plagioclase (5—7%), hornblende (ranging from sporadic grains to 30%), quartz (3—20%), ferromagnesian amphibole (5—30%), biotite (ranging from sporadic flakes to 15%), and magnetite (1—6%). Accessory minerals are zircon, rutile and apatite. Approximately one-half of the specimens contain garnet, from sporadic grains up to 45%. In garnet-enriched varieties, the plagioclase content is markedly low, whereas it is the dominant mineral in garnet-free rocks. Besides garnet, there are in places other high-alumina minerals, including 2—5% cordierite and sporadic grains of kyanite and staurolite. Some specimens are intensively chloritized. Structurally and in their external

TABLE 83. Mineral composition of biotite-sillimanite and biotite-cordierite schists and plagiogneisses from the Prince Olav Coast

Specimen No.	Mineral composition, %											Characteristics of minerals										Geological setting
												sillimanite		fibrolite		cordierite				biotite		
	quartz	plagioclase	K-feldspar	sillimanite + fibrolite	cordierite	garnet	biotite	magnetite	muscovite + sericite	accessory minerals	An content of plagioclase	n_z	n_x	n_z	n_x	n_z	n_x	$2V°$	f at.%	n_z	f at.%	
204g	10	3	—	69	—	—	8	10	—	o.s.*	—	1.683	1.661	1.673	1.651	—	—	—	—	1.636	44	Intermittent intercalations in biotite plagiogneiss
204k	o.s.	35	—	32	—	—	15	13	5	•	25	—	—	—	—	—	—	—	—	—	—	As above
264d	44	40	—	8	—	—	3	o.s.	5	—	30	—	—	—	—	—	—	—	—	—	—	Intercalation of blastocataclastized rocks in biotite plagiogneiss
525b	17	3	60	10	—	—	7	—	3	o.s.	—	—	—	—	—	—	—	—	—	—	—	Overlying granitized biotite plagiogneiss
557	20	45	14	4	—	—	14	o.s.	3	•	29	—	—	—	—	—	—	—	—	—	—	Isolated exposure, 20 × 30 m²
204	2	12	—	33	—	25	20	8	—	•	34	—	—	—	—	—	—	—	—	—	—	Intermittent intercalations in biotite plagiogneiss
204o	1	—	—	10	62	—	5	15	7	•	—	—	—	—	—	1.550	1.540	+89	31	1.636	44	As above
545	35	35	—	6	10	o.s.	10	4	4	•	35	1.680	1.659	—	—	—	—	—	—	1.636	44	" "
573g	50	2	—	o.s.	20	—	25	—	—	—	24	—	—	—	—	—	—	—	—	—	—	30-m-thick intercalation in biotite plagiogneiss

Note. Specimen 573g contains 3% kyanite and sporadic grains of staurolite.

* [o.s. = optic sign.]

appearance, these rocks are close to the above-described biotitized amphibolites, but the ordinary lepidogranonematoblastic texture has been modified by cataclasis and recrystallization, accompanied by the development of secondary minerals. The average grain size of hornblende, azonal plagioclase and biotite is 0.5—1 mm. Glomeroblastic accumulations of these minerals, in which the larger grains are surrounded by smaller ones, are common. Quartz also forms monomineral lenticular mosaic segregations. Ferromagnesian amphibole (Figure 44) and euhedral diablastic garnet, with grains reaching 10 mm in size, develop from glomeroblastic hornblende concentrations at the edges, along cracks and in the form of large (1.5—4 mm) columnar metablasts. The garnet includes quartz, hornblende, biotite and ore. Garnet idioblasts are more commonly formed at the boundary of plagioclase and amphiboles or biotite and amphiboles. Glomeroblastic concentrations of small azonal plagioclase grains give rise to plagioclase metablasts with reverse irregular zonation, containing numerous rounded and polygonal quartz granules. Granules of staurolite and cordierite are found to be of later origin than the ferromagnesian amphibole; they penetrate into the amphibole along cracks. Cordierite also replaces plagioclase. Thus, the rocks contain two distinct mineral associations, the early one being represented by hornblende, azonal plagioclase and biotite, and the later by ferromagnesian amphibole, zonal plagioclase, staurolite and cordierite (apparently, kyanite and muscovite occasionally appear in these rocks).

FIGURE 44. Gedrite metablasts in hornblende amphibolite (thin section 278a, ×15, crossed nicols).

TABLE 84. Mineral composition of gedrite- and cummingtonite-bearing rocks from Prince Olav Coast

Specimen No.	quartz	plagioclase	hornblende	gedrite or cummingtonite	biotite	garnet	cordierite	staurolite	chlorite	magnetite	accessory minerals	An content of plagioclase	n_z	n_x	$cn_z°$	$2V°$	f, at.%
265b	20	64	4	7	o.s.*	—	—	—	—	5	—	42—77	—	—	19	−79	—
243v	8	48	30	4	7	o.s.	—	—	—	3	—	35	—	—	23	−75	—
278a	4	40	26	28	o.s.	—	5	—	—	2	—	29	1.681	1.659	17—18	−77	43
204b	15	30	30	13	4	o.s.	2	—	—	3	—	37—80	1.679	1.658	20	−82	41
204	15	30	30	16	5	38	—	o.s.	—	2	o.s.	43—76	1.679	1.657	14	−81	41
279g	12	8	20	16	4	23	—	—	—	2	—	—	—	—	—	—	—
279a	10	23	26	o.s.	12	45	—	—	6	6	—	55—94	1.682	1.658	11	−85	44
278v	10	4	18	15	5	o.s.	—	—	—	3	—	60	1.679	1.657	14	−83	41
535	18	67	o.s.	5	11	—	—	o.s.	o.s.	4	o.s.	40	—	—	—	−80	—
520	7	64	—	12	14	—	—	o.s.	24	34	—	27	—	—	—	—	—
573v	3	52	—	12	8	—	—	4	—	1	o.s.	—	—	—	—	—	—
278g	10	12	6	52	6	8	—	—	—	2	•	55	1.680	1.656	—	−80	42
278b	26	—	—	62	2	—	4	1	—	—	—	—	—	—	—	—	—

Characteristics of minerals: hornblende

* [o.s. = optic sign.]

TABLE 84 (continued)

Speci-men No.	Characteristics of minerals									Geological setting
	gedrite or cummingtonite					biotite		staurolite		
	n_z	n_x	$c \wedge n_z°$	$2V°$	f, at,%	$n_z = n_y$	f, at,%	n_z	n_x	
265b	1.677	1.657	0	+73	43	—	—	—	—	Beds underlying the amphibolites
243v	—	—	20	+79	32	—	—	—	—	2.5-m intercalation at the boundary of amphibolites and biotite plagiogneisses
278a	1.670	1.643	16—17	+86	44	—	—	—	—	3-m intercalations in biotite-garnet plagiogneiss
204b	1.666	1.647	0	+72	30	—	—	—	—	Beds overlying the biotite plagiogneiss
204	1.673	1.651	0	+73	38	1.622	33	—	—	As above
279g	—	—	—	—	—	1.659	63	—	—	Alternating with biotite plagiogneisses
279a	—	—	—	—	—	1.649	54	—	—	As above
278v	1.682	1.663	0	—	51	1.624	34	—	—	3-m intercalations in biotite-garnet plagiogneiss
535	1.672	1.652	0	+76	37	1.634	43	—	—	10-m intercalation in biotite plagiogneiss
520	1.679	1.657	0	+76	47	—	—	—	—	Interbedded with biotite leucoplagiogneiss
573v	1.673	1.653	0	—	38	1.620	31	—	—	0.5—0.7-m intercalations in biotite plagiogneiss
278g	1.677	1.658	5	+80	43	1.622	33	1.759	1.745	Lenticular intercalations in rocks represented by specimen 278a
278b	1.675	1.655	0	+80	40	—	—	1.755	1.741	As above

Notes. 1. Specimen 520 contains 3% muscovite. 2. Specimen 573v contains sporadic grains of kyanite, and specimen 278b contains 5% kyanite. The optical properties of kyanite in specimen 278b are $n_z = 1.729$, $n_x = 1.713$. There are cross cleavage and parallel twins (100). 3. The ferruginosities of cummingtonite and gedrite were determined by means of diagrams provided by Deer et al. /16/.

Plagioclase in the majority of amphibolites is polysynthetically twinned and displays maculose or diffuse zonality. The marginal zones are bytownites, An 76—80, and the central, andesine, An 37—43. Azonal plagioclases are represented by andesine, An 29—39. Rocks with azonal plagioclase or with zonal, garnet-bearing plagioclase have a low content of quartz (4—12%). The hornblende is strongly pleochroic to bluish green along n_z' ; its ferruginosity is nearly constant at 41—44 at. %. The ferromagnesian amphiboles are nearly colorless and weakly pleochroic to light brown along n_z'. In the majority of specimens, they are represented by orthorhombic varieties, but monoclinic cummingtonites occurred in two cases. The ferruginosity of these amphiboles varies from 30 to 47 at. %. With rare exceptions, the ferruginosity of ferromagnesian amphiboles approximately corresponds to that of the coexisting hornblende. The ferruginosity of biotite is subject to considerable variations, from 31—63 at. %, apparently due to the presence of two generations of biotite.

The second group of gedrite-bearing types is represented by coarse-grained, massive rocks which form thin sheets and lenses or pockets up to 0.5 m² in biotite-garnet and biotite plagiogneisses with intercalations of the above-described gedrite-bearing amphibolites. The principal components of these rocks are ferromagnesian amphiboles, accounting for over 50% of the volume (Table 84). Furthermore, they always contain quartz (10—25%), biotite (2—6%) and staurolite (1—4%). In places, plagioclase, hornblende, garnet, cordierite, kyanite and magnetite may occur. The rocks have very inequigranular, granoblastic textures. Metablasts of gedrite up to 15 × 8 mm, and quartz up to 5 × 2 mm, stand out. The granular dimensions of the other minerals range from 0.5 to 1.5 mm. The mineral ratios are analogous to those described for the amphibolites. Cordierite occurs in lenticular segregations, "flowing around" the gedrite and is apparently in equilibrium with plagioclase and gedrite, while biotite develops along cracks in the latter. The nature of the minerals is analogous to their nature in the amphibolites, but the plagioclase is exclusively represented by azonal grains of high basicity (labradorite, An 55). The staurolite is markedly pleochroic in tones of lemon yellow. Its idioblastic grains are zonal; twins are parallel to the elongation.

In summarizing the description of ferromagnesian amphibole-bearing rocks, the role played by ferromagnesian metasomatosis in their formation should be noted /91/. The metasomatosis undoubtedly participated in the transformation of amphibolites, the final product being coarse-grained gedrite rocks. The formation of the latter is apparently related to super-imposed metamorphism manifested throughout the Prince Olav Coast and reflected in the rocks not only in the magnesian metasomatosis, but also in the crystallization of the staurolite and kyanite. A relationship between repeated metamorphism and pegmatite formation is likewise obvious.

ROCKS OF THE LAMBERT GLACIER REGION

The following varieties of amphibolite facies rocks are distinguished in the Lambert Glacier region: 1) hornblende amphibolites, 2) cummingtonite amphibolites, 3) biotite-hornblende plagiogneisses, 4) staurolite-garnet quartzites and 5) biotite granites. Besides these rocks, Trail /131/ and Trail et al. /132/ found garnet-biotite-hornblende and hornblende plagiogneisses and amphibolites, chloritized epidote-garnet-hornblende and epidote-quartz-biotite-feldspar gneisses and plagiogneisses as well as tremolite-quartz marbles and epidote-mica-hornblende gneisses. Since no petrographic data are available on these rocks, the present description will be limited to the first five groups of rocks noted above.*

Amphibolites occurring as boudins in granites consist of 60% grass-green common hornblende ($n_z - 1.686-1.690$; $n_x = 1.662-1.666$; $cn_z = 19°$; $2V$, from -54 to -61°; $f = 48-52$ at.%), biotite ($n_z \sim n_y = 1.654$; $f = 58$ at.%), 25% oligoclase-andesine (No. 30), 5% quartz and clinopyroxene ($n_z = 1.722$; $n_x = 1.695$; $cn_z = 42°$; $f \cong 41$ at.%), with magnetite and sphene as the accessory minerals. The amphibolites are schistose. Their grain size is 0.5-1 mm with a lepidogranoblastic texture. The clinopyroxene is replaced by hornblende with which it forms complex aggregates. The biotite largely replaces amphibole. Biotitization of the amphibolites may be regarded as the initial stage of granitization. Amphibolites from separate beds consist of bluish green hornblende ($n_z = 1.680-1.688$; $n_x = 1.656-1.666$; $cn_z = 20°$; $2V$, -65 to -70°; $f = 42-50$ at.%) and plagioclase (An 32-40). Also present are 1-8% quartz, up to 7% greenish brown biotite ($n_z \approx n_y = 1.636-1.664$; $f = 42-63$ at.%), and small relict grains of clinopyroxene which are colorless in thin section ($n_z = 1.714$; $n_x = 1.689$; $f \cong 30$ at.%). Magnetite, sphene and apatite are the accessory minerals. The amphibolites also contain sericite, epidote, chlorite and albite as secondary minerals, but only to a limited extent. The low ferruginosity of the colored minerals in the amphibolites under consideration, in comparison to amphibolites from boudins in granites, may be due to a lower grade of granitization. These amphibolites are dark green, medium-grained rocks with a linear-parallel structure; their texture is granoblastic with nematoblastic elements.

Cummingtonite amphibolites consist of 90% colorless cummingtonite ($n_z = 1.648$; $n_x = 1.622$; $cn_z = 16°$; $2V = +82°$; $f = 23$ at.%) and 10% biotite ($n_z \approx n_y = 1.632$; $f = 40$ at.%). They possess a lepidonematogranoblastic texture and a schistose structure.

Biotite-hornblende plagiogneisses are uniform fine- and medium-grained gray rocks. Their average mineral composition is as follows: 45% plagioclase (oligoclase, An 25-30), 40% quartz, 5% bluish-green hornblende ($n_z = 1.703$; $n_x = 1.684$; $f \cong 65$ at.%), and 8% brown biotite ($n_z \approx n_y = 1.660$; $f = 59$ at.%). The accessory minerals include sphene, apatite and magnetite. Sporadic skeletal garnet grains in aggregates with plagioclase and quartz were detected in one specimen. The plagiogneisses contain a total of 2% secondary minerals, including epidote, calcite and chlorite.

* The descriptions of the rocks are based on Solov'ev's data.

Staurolite-garnet-biotite quartzites are gray and medium-grained. They contain 90% quartz, 5% biotite ($n_z \approx n_y$= 1.645; f = 51 at.%), 1% staurolite (n_z = 1.754; n_x = 1.743), 2% garnet (f = 87 at.%, Table 85), 1% plagioclase (~An 30). Magnetite and graphite are accessories and chlorite and sericite are secondary. Their texture is granoblastic. Garnet forms small subhedral crystals; their central portions are packed with small quartz and plagioclase inclusions. Staurolite forms independent xenoblastic segregations. Chlorite (n_y = 1.631) partially replaces biotite.

TABLE 85. Chemical composition of garnet in staurolite-garnet-biotite quartzite of Mt. Patrick (Lambert Glacier region), specimen 14e

Component	Wt% by analysis	Correction	Corrected analysis
SiO_2	40.51	−7.95	36.70
TiO_2	0.04		0.05
Al_2O_3	20.25	−3.30	19.14
Fe_2O_3	2.30		2.60
FeO	31.62		35.70
MnO	0.92		1.04
MgO	2.15		2.43
CaO	2.07		2.34
K_2O	0.15	−0.15	—
Na_2O	0.22	−0.22	—
Loss on ignition	0.09	−0.09	—
Σ	100.32		100.00

Minals: 81% almandine, 9.7% pyrope, 2.3% spessartite; n (garnet) = 1.819. Crystallochemical formula: $(Fe^{2+}_{2.43}Mg_{0.29}Mn_{0.07}Ca_{0.21})_3(Al_{1.85}Fe^{3+}_{0.15})_2[Si_3O_{12}]$.

Biotite granites consist of 45—55% microcline, 30—40% quartz, 11% oligoclase (An 26) and 4% biotite of varying degrees of chloritization ($n_z \cong n_y$ =1.684; $f \cong 80$ at.%). The accessory minerals include magnetite, apatite, sphene and fluorite. The plagioclase content increases to 70% in contact with beds of schist, at the expense of quartz (15%) and microcline (6%). The rocks at the contact of amphibolites and biotite granites were apparently produced by the partial granitization of the former. The biotite granites have a heterogranoblastic texture and are gneissic. Quartz and microcline form segregation accumulations. The nature of the bedding in the granites is obscure.

The biotite granites of Mt. Patrick (Lambert Glacier region) described above differ little from similar granites of the Grove Nunataks, represented by fairly uniform rocks with gneissic and finely banded structures; they are medium-grained and gray. The structure is due to the presence of fine intermittently banded biotite segregations. The granites consist of 25—34% quartz, 4—17% oligoclase (An 21—26), 45—60% microcline, and 2—5% biotite ($n_z \cong n_y$ =1.660—1.670; f= 59—67 at.%). The accessory minerals include magnetite, monazite, zircon and apatite. The granites exhibit a granoblastic or porphyroblastic texture with distinct blastocataclastic elements. The

TABLE 86. Chemical composition of metamorphics of granitic composition in the region of the Lambert Glacier and Grove Nunataks

Component	Region and Specimen No.						Modal composition of specimens, vol.%		
	Mt. Patrick (Lambert Glacier region), specimen 13			Grove Nunataks, specimen 7					
	wt%	at.%	$\frac{R}{Al}$	wt%	at.%	$\frac{R}{Al}$	mineral	specimen 13	specimen 7
SiO_2	75.86	73.9	5.86	74.04	69.9	4.95			
TiO_2	0.27	0.2	0.02	0.20	0.2	0.01			
Al_2O_3	10.91	12.6	1.00	12.68	14.1	1.00	Quartz	40	30
Fe_2O_3	1.46	1.1	0.09	1.20	0.8	0.06	Plagioclase	11	12
Cr_2O_3	0.02		—	—	—	—			
FeO	2.20	1.8	0.14	1.65	1.3	0.09	Microcline	45	55
MnO	0.05	0.1	—	0.02	—	—			
MgO	0.30	0.4	0.03	0.47	0.6	0.04			
CaO	0.50	0.5	0.04	1.18	1.2	0.08	Biotite	4	2
Na_2O	3.72	4.5	0.36	3.15	5.7	0.40			
K_2O	3.79	4.6	0.37	5.09	6.1	0.43	Magnetite	o.s.*	1
P_2O_5	0.11	0.1	—	0.13	0.1	—			
F	0.02	0.1	—	—	—	—			
Cl	0.07	0.1	—	—	—	—			
Loss on ignition	0.38	—	—	0.21	—	—			
Σ	99.66	100.0	—		100.0	—			

	Specimen No.	
	specimen 13	specimen 7
Numerical characteristics (after Zavaritskii)		
a	13.1	13.9
b	3.9	3.2
c	0.5	1.3
s	82.5	81.6
Q	+38.3	+34.1
f'	80.3	72.5
m'	11.5	21.6
c'	8.2	5.9
a'	—	—
Norm, % (after Barth)		
Albite	34.3	28.8
Anorthite	2.0	5.1
Orthoclase	22.8	30.4
Orthopyroxene	3.1	2.7
Magnetite	1.5	1.2
Ilmenite	0.2	0.3
Apatite	0.3	0.3
Quartz	35.5	31.0
Sphene	0.3	—
Corundum	—	0.2

* [o.s. = optic sign.]

porphyroblasts are microcline grains, up to 1 × 2 cm in size. The plagioclase is distinctly replaced by quartz and microcline.

The genesis of the granites can be partially determined from their
chemical composition (Table 86), which is similar in granites of both
regions in question; however, the granites of the Grove Nunataks have a
higher alkalinity, due to their higher Ca content /32/ and more favorable
Al : Si ratio in the rocks. The higher content of ferrous iron and magnesium in the Mt. Patrick granites reflects their higher biotite content,
while the lower content of calcium and alkalis reflects their low feldspar
content. Scaling of the analyses of the granites to the normal composition
reveals their significantly higher content of plagioclase, in particular albite,
and a lower content of orthoclase. This may be partly explained by inaccuracy of the visual count in thin sections; this is due to the large
dimensions of the microcline grains and partly to the fact that the albite
forms a solid solution with the microcline. Therefore, microcline
apparently contains 15—25% albite. Microcline in the granites of the
Grove Nunataks probably has a lower content of albite than the microcline
in the Mt. Patrick granites, while the contents of albite in the plagioclase
are nearly the same in both granites; these relationships are in accord
with Barth's principle /81, 82/, i. e., granites of the Grove Nunataks may
be of lower temperature than those of Mt. Patrick. Other noteworthy features
are the high content of silica, low content of alumina and high alkalinity of
both granites. These compositional features are uncharacteristic of
normal magmatic granites, occurring only in alkaline granites /65/ that
are devoid of alkaline colored minerals. In the authors' opinion, this
indicates an ultrametamorphic rather than a magmatic genesis of the
granites in question. For this reason they are regarded in this monograph
as formations of the amphibolite facies of metamorphism and have been
conditionally classified with the shadow granites.

ROCKS OF THE YAMATO MOUNTAINS

Rocks of the amphibolite facies compose some blocks in the Yamato
Mountains. Other, adjacent blocks are of the granulite facies with superimposed amphibolite facies, resulting in polymetamorphic rocks similar
to the suites of the Humboldt Mountains. The amphibolite facies rocks in
the Yamato Mountains have a uniform composition. Only two types
can be differentiated: 1) biotitized and feldspathized amphibolites occurring
within the migmatite strata of massifs "D," "G" and "E" /110/, where
they appear as the paleosome of agmatites and as skialiths in shadow
biotite-amphibole granites; 2) shadow biotite-amphibole granites partially
generated by granitization of amphibolites but mainly by granitization of
biotite-amphibole plagiogneisses.

Amphibolites of the Yamato Mountains possess several distinctive
features; they most commonly occur as the paleosome of migmatites
(Table 87). Their texture is lepidogranoblastic. In varieties with low

feldspathization grades, the plagioclase grains are characterized by their large size (up to 2 mm), occurring within a matrix of grain size 0.4—1 mm. With increasing K-feldspar and biotite contents, the plagioclase content decreases and quartz appears. Plagioclase is replaced by K-feldspar and quartz, while common hornblende is replaced by bluish green amphibole, biotite and magnetite. Quartz and K-feldspar develop interstitially. Biotite forms symplektite aggregates with quartz. The composition of plagioclase is fairly uniform. Its basicity varies from An 24 to An 28. K-feldspar is perthitic; the perthite ingrowths (lenses and beads, less commonly fine rods) account for 10 vol.% of the grains. Some grains display a distinct microcline crosshatching. Amphibole is mostly represented by green hornblende, with ferruginosity 49 at.% in specimens of low feldspathization grade. Biotite is pleochroic in ordinary shades up to dark brown along n_z'; its ferruginosity is 48 at.% in varieties with low feldspathization grades, and in this respect it does not differ from the amphibole.

The content of metasome in the agmatites of amphibolites is 35—90%. It is finely banded exhibiting a gradual transition to finely layered migmatites of biotite and biotite-amphibole plagiogneisses to shadow granites. The bands differ only with respect to the contents of plagioclase and colored minerals. The agmatite metasome was evidently formed from the finely layered migmatites and will therefore be considered in this section. It makes up from 13 to 20% of the rock. Plagioclase forms 5—30%, while K-feldspar is the predominant mineral (45—75%). Biotite is ubiquitous, varying in content from 1.5 to 9%. Approximately one half of the investigated specimens also contain amphibole, locally making up about 4% of the rock. The usual accessory minerals are sphene, zircon, orthite and apatite. Ore minerals are always present (up to 3%). The texture of these rocks is heterogranoblastic, with a transition in some areas to granoblastic or porphyroblastic (with K-feldspar porphyroblasts). A characteristic feature is the preferred orientation of mica or accumulations of dark-colored minerals and roughly lenticular quartz segregations. Quartz and K-feldspar usually have the largest grain size — 1—6 mm. The average size of plagioclase grains is 0.5—1 mm. Biotite and amphibole occur only as small grains, up to 1 mm. Amphibole is consistently replaced by biotite, while plagioclase is replaced by K-feldspar and quartz. Myrmekitized plagioclase is surrounded by albite. Biotite and quartz form symplektitic aggregates. Plagioclase has wavy extinction, and a regular, continuous or maculose zonation. Its An content varies only from An 24 to An 27. The K-feldspar is a perthitic microcline, with 10—40% perthite in the form of lenses and beads. The perthitic ingrowths are composed of albite. Microcline crosshatching is in evidence in all grains, to varying degrees, from indistinct microcline twins with an intensification of gridiron habit in the small cracked zones to crosshatching that is well formed throughout the grain. K-feldspar exhibits sericitization and pelitization. Amphibole is represented exclusively by common hornblende, which is pleochroic to a deep green color along n_z'; $cn_z' = 15$—$21°$. The biotite is pleochroic in ordinary shades of color up to dark brown along n_z' and is replaced by flakey

TABLE 87. Mineral composition of amphibolite facies rocks in the Yamato Mountains

Specimen No.	Mineral composition, %										An content of plagioclase	Characteristics of minerals						Geological setting of specimens and designation of rock
							accessory minerals					amphibole				biotite		
	quartz	plagioclase	K-feldspar	amphibole	biotite	ore mineral	sphene	zircon	apatite	others		n_z	n_x	$-2V°$	f at.%	n_z	f at.%	
201b	—	62	5	18	13	1.5	—	—	0.5	—	24—25	1.686	1.662	74	49	1.642	48	Paleosome of agmatite. Amphiboles of low feldspathization grade
201v	15	5	75	1.5	1.5	1.5	o.s.	o.s.	o.s.	Chevkinite, orthite	24—25	—	—	—	—	—	—	Metasome of agmatite. Biotite-amphibolite granosyenite
2	7	41	12	25	10	0.7	—	—	0.34	—	27	—	—	—	—	—	—	Paleosome of agmatite. Granitized amphibolite
2a	16	30	43	o.s.	8	2	o.s.	o.s.	1	—	25	—	—	—	—	—	—	Metasome of agmatite. Amphibole-biotite granosyenite
2b	1.5	23	23	25	22	3	—	—	2.5	—	27	—	—	—	—	—	—	Paleosome of agmatite. Granitized amphibolite
2g	16	20	58	—	2.5	1.5	o.s.	o.s.	—	Orthite, 0.5%	27	—	—	—	—	—	—	Metasome of agmatite. Biotite leucogranosyenite
201g,d	15	13	62	20	4	3	0.2	"	0.8	Calcite	25—26	—	—	—	—	—	—	Finely layered migmatite of biotite-amphibole gneiss with amphibolite skialiths

*[o.s. = optic sign.]

TABLE 87 (continued)

Specimen No.	quartz	plagioclase	K-feldspar	amphibole	biotite	ore mineral	sphene	zircon	apatite	others	An content of plagioclase	amphibole n_z	amphibole n_x	amphibole $-2V°$	amphibole f at.%	biotite n_z	biotite f at.%	Geological setting of specimens and designation of rock
201 e	18	29	47	—	4	2	o.s.*	o.s.	o.s.	Orthite, chevkinite	—	—	—	—	—	—	—	Finely layered migmatite of granitized biotite plagiogneis with amphibolite skialiths
YD—320	20.6	29.6	44.4	0.4	3.5	0.2	"	"	"	1.1?	—	—	—	—	—	—	—	Shadow granites with amphibolite skialiths
YD—335	15.7	21.5	52.9	—	8.5	0.9	"	"	0.3	0.1?	—	—	—	—	—	—	—	As above
YC—310	11.8	32.4	41.1	25	8.3	1.5	0.8	0.1	0.3	1.1?	—	1.691	—	66	54	1.656	60	Shadow biotite-amphibole granites composing massif "C"
YB—278	17.0	27.3	45.3	6.6	3.1	0.1	0.5	o.s.	0.1	—	—	—	—	—	—	—	—	Shadow biotite-amphibole granite composing massif "B"
505	24	25	39.7	3	4	0.5	0.2	0.1	1.5	—	24—25	1.707	1.683	52	69	1.665	67	As above
YB—261	5.4	18.6	51.3	8.7	6.4	0.9	0.1	0.5	0.2	1.3?	—	1.709	—	56	71	1.660	63	" "
YD—224	27.9	18.6	51.3	1.5	0.2	o.s.	o.s.	o.s.	o.s.	0.7?	—	—	—	—	—	—	—	Shadow biotite-amphibole granite from massif "D"

* [o.s. = optic sign.]

chlorite and sericite resulting in the separation of needles and small flakey disseminations of an opaque mineral. Japanese geologists encountered sparsely disseminated molybdenite in some specimens of such granitoids /110/.

Shadow biotite-amphibole granites form nebulitic (massifs "C" and "D") or banded and augen structures (massif "B") /110/. Banded structures are not very distinct; nevertheless, fine alternations of mafic (granosyenite) and felsic (granite) laminae, 5 mm thick, are discernible. Augen segregations of K-feldspar scattered in some parts of these granite gneisses exhibit the habit of porphyroclasts. The characteristic features of the mineral composition of these rocks are as follows: a) both amphibole and biotite are always present; b) K-feldspar is always more abundant than plagioclase; c) accessory minerals are sphene, zircon, apatite and magnetite.

The texture of the granite is heterogranoblastic and sometimes porphyroblastic; it is almost the same as the texture of the agmatic metasome. Quartz grains are roughly lenticular (2—3.5 mm), although small grains (0.2—1.5 mm), often intergranular, are also numerous. K-feldspar grains (1—2.5 mm; porphyroblasts, 10—20 mm) are always larger than plagioclase grains (0.2—2 mm), while biotite (0.2—1.3 mm), forming small intergranular flakes, is more abundant than amphibole (0.1—0.7 mm). K-feldspar porphyroblasts are surrounded by small plagioclase and quartz grains. Plagioclase is replaced by K-feldspar and corroded by quartz and biotite. Japanese investigators detected sporadic clinopyroxene grains of high ferruginosity in the shadow granites. The An content of plagioclase ranges from An 18 to An 25. It has a wavy extinction and bent twin facies. K-feldspar is represented by microcline and microcline-perthite. In large grains, the microcline crosshatching is most distinct along cracks. There is a secondary development of albite in the intricately ramifying veinlets and along edges of microcline grains. Amphibole is represented by bluish green hornblende and has a high ferruginosity (69—71 at. %); the ferruginosity of the coexisting brown biotite is somewhat lower (63—67 at. %). However, there are also exceptions where the ferruginosity of grass-green amphibole (54 at. %) is lower than that of the brown biotite (60 at. %).

The chemical composition of the shadow granites of the Yamato Mountains is listed in Table 88. The majority of shadow granitoids belong to rocks that are saturated in silica and rich in alkalis. The rocks richest in alkalis are also richer in mafic elements, approaching the composition of granosyenites. Specimen YB-261 has a somewhat exceptional composition for this group, since it represents rocks that are only slightly saturated in SiO_2 but are rich in alkalis, i. e., rocks that are intermediate between shadow granitoids and alkaline syenites. Another noteworthy feature is the high calcium content of the shadow granite and, often, a fairly considerable predominance of sodium over potassium, making it possible to classify these granites with the alkaline type /65/. It may thus be assumed that the granitoids under consideration were formed by granitization of basic or intermediate rocks having a high content of CaO and other base compounds. This also explains the high alkalinity of the granites in accordance with

TABLE 88. Chemical composition of shadow biotite-amphibole granites from the Yamato Mountains (after Kizaki) /110/

Specimen No.

Component	YD-320			YD-335			YC-310			YB-278			YB-261			YD-224		
	wt%	at.%	$\frac{R}{Al}$	wt%	at.%	$\frac{R}{Al}$	wt%	at.%	$\frac{R}{Al}$	wt%	at.%	$\frac{R}{Al}$	wt%	at.%	$\frac{R}{Al}$	wt%	at.%	$\frac{R}{Al}$
SiO_2	73.13	67.8	4.51	71.25	65.9	3.81	69.29	64.7	4.35	71.51	67.2	4.67	61.69	56.0	3.52	77.24	71.3	5.44
TiO_2	0.24	0.2	0.01	traces	—	—	0.64	0.4	0.03	0.54	0.4	0.03	1.39	1.0	0.06	0.14	0.1	—
Al_2O_3	13.78	15.0	1.00	15.84	17.3	1.00	13.53	14.9	1.00	13.32	14.7	1.00	14.86	15.9	1.00	11.96	13.1	1.00
Fe_2O_3	0.55	0.4	0.03	0.16	0.1	—	2.06	1.4	0.09	1.23	0.8	0.05	3.23	2.2	0.14	0.92	0.7	0.05
FeO	1.08	0.8	0.05	0.16	0.1	—	1.77	1.4	0.09	1.42	1.1	0.07	3.40	2.6	0.16	0.49	0.4	0.03
MnO	traces	—	—	traces	—	—	0.02	—	—	0.01	—	—	0.07	—	—	traces	—	—
MgO	0.55	0.7	0.05	traces	—	—	0.83	1.2	0.08	0.74	1.0	0.07	2.03	2.8	0.18	0.11	0.2	0.01
CaO	1.75	1.7	0.11	2.31	2.3	0.13	2.09	2.1	0.14	1.93	2.0	0.14	3.25	3.2	0.20	1.12	1.1	0.08
Na_2O	3.58	6.4	0.43	3.77	6.8	0.39	4.25	7.7	0.52	3.49	6.3	0.43	3.90	6.9	0.43	3.75	6.6	0.50
K_2O	4.99	6.0	0.40	6.13	7.3	0.42	4.39	5.3	0.36	4.92	5.9	0.40	5.29	6.1	0.38	3.34	4.0	0.31
P_2O_5	0.09	0.1	—	0.32	0.2	0.01	0.31	0.2	0.01	0.16	0.1	—	0.50	0.4	0.03	0.03	—	—
H_2O+	0.14	0.9	—	traces	—	—	0.11	0.7	—	0.08	0.5	—	0.48	2.9	—	0.42	2.5	—
H_2O-	0.18	—	—	0.15	—	—	0.17	—	—	0.42	—	—	0.47	—	—	0.22	—	—
CO_2	0.06	—	—	0.15	—	—	0.34	—	—	0.13	—	—	traces	—	—	0.26	—	—
Σ	100.12	100.0	—	100.24	100.0	—	99.80	100.0	—	99.90	100.0	—	100.56	100.0	—	100.09	100.0	—

TABLE 88 (continued)

	YD-320	YD-355	YC-310	YB-278	YB-261	YD-224
			Numerical characteristics (after Zavaritskii)			
a	14.7	17.0	15.4	14.4	16.1	12.0
b	2.7	1.1	6.1	4.4	11.2	1.7
c	1.6	2.0	1.1	1.4	2.1	1.3
s	81.0	79.9	77.4	79.8	70.6	84.4
Q	+34.0	+23.8	+15.8	+29.4	+6.9	+42.3
f'	53.7	25.0	54.4	52.3	53.6	76.0
m'	31.7	0.0	22.8	27.7	30.7	12.0
c'	14.6	75.0	22.8	20.0	15.7	12.0
		Coordinates on the ACF diagram (after Eskola and Korzhinskii)				
A	44.0	57.5	28.8	38.2	25.2	48.3
C	29.0	40.5	32.2	29.6	27.6	33.4
F	27.0	1.9	39.0	32.2	47.2	18.3
			Norm, % (after Barth)			
Albite	32.9	33.9	38.7	31.8	35.5	34.8
Anorthite	6.7	8.0	4.8	6.2	7.6	4.3
Orthoclase	29.8	36.4	26.6	29.5	31.5	20.4
Orthopyroxene	2.1	0.1	1.2	1.6	4.7	—
Clinopyroxene	0.9	—	3.4	2.1	4.3	0.7
Magnetite	0.6	0.2	2.1	1.3	3.4	1.0
Ilmenite	0.3	—	0.9	0.8	1.9	0.2
Apatite	0.3	0.6	0.6	0.3	1.1	—
Quartz	26.4	20.1	21.8	26.4	10.0	38.4
Wollastonite	—	0.7	—	—	—	0.2

Note. The modal composition of analyzed specimens is given in Table 87.

Korzhinskii's theory /32/ that interactions with rocks containing strong base compounds still further increase the alkalinity of alkaline solutions. Ultimately this results in syenitization of such rocks.

Analysis of the petrographic and petrochemical features of the rocks in the Yamato Mountains inevitably leads to the conclusion that they all originated by metamorphism of sedimentary-volcanogenic formations with high calcium contents, i. e., either basic igneous rocks or graywackes. The presence of carbonate sediments in the strata is also possible. The leading role in the original rocks probably belongs to the graywackes, because sufficient contents of silica and also of calcium could only accumulate in terrigenous formations; the basaltic series contain much less silica than the rocks under consideration, and they are also distinguished by a prevalence of ferromagnesian calcic components, in contrast to the rocks under consideration (in which these relationships are reversed). These features of the amphibolite facies rocks in the Yamato Mountains indicate that the metamorphic and ultrametamorphic processes took place under conditions of the high-grade amphibolite facies, at high alkali activity.

ROCKS OF THE SØR RONDANE MOUNTAINS

Rocks that were metamorphosed in the amphibolite facies form an overwhelming majority of exposures in the Sør Rondane Mountains. They can be differentiated into 1) biotite-amphibole plagiogneisses and their migmatites, 2) amphibolites and 3) marbles and calciphyres.

Biotite-amphibole plagiogneisses form a thick series of beds in the Sør Rondane Mountains. Their structure is banded, beds of plagiogneisses proper alternating with beds of feldspathized plagiogneisses or gneisses. The thicknesses of both types of beds vary from a few centimeters to a few decimeters. This results in layers resembling coarsely layered migmatites. Generally, migmatites are predominant, forming large areal exposures. Layered migmatites are the most widespread variety, with a weakly feldspathized biotite-amphibole plagiogneiss paleosome and a gneissic biotite granitoid metasome. The thickness of the metasome varies widely, from 5 cm to 1 m. The thickest metasome forms bulges up to 4 m in diameter. In places, the layered migmatites occur together with ramified and maculose varieties. Some areas of migmatite exposures are composed of unusual agmatites, the metasome of which was formed by metasomatic reworking of the paleosome, i. e., biotite-amphibole plagiogneiss. This metasome is represented by biotite granitoids, locally containing relics of hornblende and forming gradual transitions to the biotite-amphibole paleosome. Injection veinlets of pegmatitic granites are sometimes seen in the central part of the metasome. The size of the agmatite blocks is 5—15 m, while metasomatically reworked zones reach thicknesses of 4—5 m.

The differences between the mineral compositions of the gneisses and plagiogneisses mainly consist in the replacement of plagioclase by K-feldspar.

Furthermore, plagiogneisses occasionally contain appreciable amounts of clinopyroxene, especially near amphibolite intercalations. Otherwise, the gneisses and plagiogneisses are nearly identical in their mineral composi- tions (Table 89). On the other hand, the textures of these rocks are unique. The texture of plagiogneiss is lepidogranoblastic. However, plagioclase idioblasts, 2—3 mm in size, and "spots" of crystalline amphibole aggregates occur in a matrix of fine- and medium-grained quartz, plagioclase, amphi- bole and biotite (0.5—1.5 mm). The texture of the gneisses is heterolepido- granoblastic. The felsic minerals are separated in independent bands alter- nating with irregularly banded aggregates of mafic minerals. In the leuco- cratic bands, the most idioblastic habit is noted for plagioclase laths ranging in size from 0.4 to 1.5 mm. These are the result of recrystallization of previously cataclastized plagioclase grains, as is indicated by small in- completely recrystallized irregular plagioclase granules surrounding the larger idioblasts. The most xenoblastic habit is exhibited by small (0.3—0.5 mm) grains and larger, often lenticular segregations of quartz (up to 3—4 mm). Irregular microcline metablasts are considerably larger (2—3 mm) than the plagioclase laths, although smaller microcline grains (0.3—0.6 mm) also occur; these surround the metablasts and fill the interstices between the plagioclase laths. A prominent feature of the melanocratic bands are prismatic hornblende grains, 1—2 mm in size, often diablastic, with ingrowths of ore minerals, sphene and quartz. The biotite is secondary with respect to the hornblende, replacing the latter along the edges and cracks. Fine biotite flakes permeate all other rock-forming minerals.

The plagioclase in plagiogneiss contains up to 38% anorthite but, in general, the An content ranges from An 25 to An 30. Similar plagioclase also occurs in the gneisses, which suggests that the presence of microcline in the gneisses is not due to granitization, but to the original composition of the rocks. Even the ferruginosities of colored minerals are nearly the same in the gneisses and plagiogneisses. The ferruginosity of dark green hornblende is 60—67 at.% and the ferruginosity of brown biotite is always less than that of the hornblende, i. e., 52—55 at.%. The ferruginosity of clinopyroxene is 43 at.%. K-feldspar is represented in the gneisses by cross- hatched microcline. The characteristic accessory minerals are sphene and apatite, rarely zircon. It must be emphasized that the biotite-amphibole gneisses and plagiogneisses remain unchanged everywhere, even when forming the paleosome of migmatites.

The metasome of layered and ramified migmatites is the same in both its mineral composition and structural features. The entire variation of the metasome is due solely to fluctuations in the contents of microcline and quartz, and therefore its composition varies within the limits of granodiorite— granite—granosyenite (Table 89). Biotite, the only colored mineral, is limit- ed to 1—7 vol.% of the rocks. Its content increases to 16% only rarely in veins. As in the case of the paleosome, the accessory minerals are represented by apatite and zircon, with orthite instead of sphene. The metasome has a granoblastic texture. Irregular large microcline grains (2—7 mm), sometimes granulated along their edges, and smaller corroded plagioclase

TABLE 89. Mineral composition of the biotite-amphibole plagiogneisses and their migmatites in the Sør Rondane Mountains

Specimen No.	Mineral composition, vol.%										An content of plagioclase	Characteristics of minerals								Remarks
	quartz	plagioclase	K-feldspar	clino-pyroxene	amphibole	biotite	ore minerals	epidote + calcite	sphene	apatite		clinopyroxene n_z	n_x	f at.%	amphibole n_z	n_x	f at.%	biotite n_z	f at.%	
523	20	47	—	—	13	17	1	o.s.	2	o.s.*	25—26	—	—	—	—	—	—	—	—	Plagiogneiss
527	10	42	1	—	30	14	o.s.	o.s.	2	1	28—31	—	—	—	—	—	—	—	—	
19b	15	55	—	10	15	1	—	2	2	o.s.	25—26	1.723	1.698	43	1.698	1.678	60	—	—	Plagiogneiss, paleosome of layered migmatites
19	22	50	—	—	16	10	—	2	—	•	26—30	—	—	—	1.703	1.684	66	—	—	As above, low-grade felspathization
28a	15	45	o.s.	—	28	10	—	—	2	—	24—27	—	—	—	1.705	1.683	67	1.650	55	
14	25	40	5	—	15	10	3	3	1	1	36—38	—	—	—	1.700	1.687	62	1.645	52	Plagiogneiss, paleosome of layered migmatites
510	20	63	o.s.	—	9	5	o.s.	—	o.s.	o.s.	29—34	—	—	—	—	—	—	—	—	Gneiss interbedded with plagiogneisses
518	18	36	15	—	17	13	—	—	1	•	26—30	—	—	—	—	—	—	—	—	As above
209d	12	33	30	—	2	20	•	—	1	2	31	—	—	—	—	—	—	—	—	Mylonitized plagiogneiss
219	26	50	—	—	12	9	—	3	o.s.	o.s.	26—27	—	—	—	1.714	1.692	78	—	—	
219b	24	46	—	—	13	10	—	1	0,5	0,5	28	—	—	—	1.714	0.692	78	—	—	Biotite granite, metasome of layered migmatite
28	30	23	40	—	—	7	—	—	—	o.s.	—	—	—	—	—	—	—	—	—	
14a	12	10	75	—	—	3	1	—	—	—	—	—	—	—	—	—	—	—	—	Biotite granosyenite, metasome of layered migmatite
510b	12	62	25	—	—	1	1	—	—	—	12—14	—	—	—	—	—	—	—	—	Leucogranodiorite, metasome of layered migmatite
518b	33	22	42	—	—	2	1	—	—	—	25	—	—	—	—	—	—	—	—	Metasome of ramified migmatite
6a	30	46	20	—	—	3	1	—	—	—	17	—	—	—	—	—	—	—	—	As above
10e	28	25	28	—	—	16	—	—	—	—		—	—	—	—	—	—	—	—	
516a	30	28	36	—	—	6	—	—	—	—	21	—	—	—	—	—	—	—	—	
216	32	57	o.s.	—	—	10	1	—	1	o.s.	25	—	—	—	—	—	—	—	—	Metasomatic agmatite, metasome of plagiogneiss
224	22	60	3	—	—	10	2	2	1	•	18—19	—	—	—	—	—	—	—	—	As above
529a	30	44	14	—	—	12	—	—	—	•	22—24	—	—	—	—	—	—	—	—	
516	25	45	18	—	—	11	o.s.	—	—	•	27—28	—	—	—	—	—	—	1.655	67	
207g	30	30	32	—	—	8	—	—	—	•	22—24	—	—	—	—	—	—	—	—	

Notes. 1. Specimen 219b contains 5% garnet (n = 1.803, f = 83 at.%). 2. Specimen 516 contains 1% hornblende. 3. Specimen 10e contains 3% garnet (n = 1.799, d = 4—13 g/cm³, f = 80 at.%).

* [o.s. = optic sign.]

laths (1—3 mm), often myrmekitized, form the bulk of the metasome in the migmatites. Among these minerals are xenoblastic quartz grains, 0.3—1.0 mm in size. Biotite is disseminated throughout the rock in maculose aggregates. Plagioclase has a higher alkalinity than in the paleosome. It usually contains 12—20% anorthite, but is sometimes represented by oligoclase, An 22—25, in cross-cutting veins. The K-feldspar is a crosshatched microcline.

In view of the similarity between the migmatite plaeosome and non-migmatized plagiogneisses, distinct contacts between the metasome and paleosome, similarity in the composition of metasome veins in layered and ramified migmatites, as well as mineral and structural features of vein granitoids, the described migmatites are considered to be entirely injective. However, the metasome veins were conductors of alkali solutions and sometimes responsible for mixed, injective-metasomatic migmatites.

The agmatite metasome consists of shadow biotite granitoids. These are fine- to medium-grained, indistinctly banded rocks, light yellow or grayish in color. Their mineral composition is fairly constant, except for variations in the composition of feldspars; these are sometimes represented almost exclusively by plagioclase but in other locations, the content of K-feldspar exceeds that of plagioclase. There are also a continuous series of intermediate varieties between these extremes. The limits of the contents of the main rock-forming minerals are: quartz 22—32%, feldspars 57—63% and biotite 6—12%. There are also ore minerals, which range in content from sporadic grains to 2%. The accessory minerals are zircon and apatite. Sphene and hornblende occur sporadically. The texture of these shadow granitoids is porphyrogranoblastic, the porphyroblasts consisting of either oligoclase (laths, 2—4 mm) in plagiogranites or microcline (metablasts, 2—5 mm) in granites. The matrix has a grain size of 0.1—0.7 mm, and consists of quartz, biotite and feldspars, with ribbon and lenticular quartz grains up to 4 mm long. Plagioclase is replaced by microcline, and myrmekitized albite develops at the boundary of these minerals. The plagioclase contains 27—28% anorthite in granites with hornblende relicts, but in all other cases it is less basic (An 17—25) than that in the paleosome, its composition approaching the plagioclase in the injective metasome of migmatites. The ferruginosity of biotite (67 at.%) is higher than its ferruginosity in the paleosome of agmatites. The microcline has a distinctly crosshatched habit.

Two chemical analyses of biotite-amphibolite plagiogneiss (specimen 19) and shadow biotite plagiogranite (specimen 244) (Table 90) are available. These rocks were obtained from different areas in the Sør Rondane Mountains and are genetically unrelated (as is also borne out by the different Si : Al ratios); nevertheless a comparison of the atomic ratios of elements to aluminum distinctly denotes the chemical changes that must occur in biotite-amphibole plagiogneisses in their transformation into biotite plagiogranites. These chemical changes include a decrease in the contents of titanium, iron, manganese, magnesium and calcium, and an increase in the contents of sodium and silicon, which is characteristic of granitization processes. Thus, the metasomatic genesis of the metasome

TABLE 90. Chemical composition of biotite-amphibole and biotite plagiogneiss from the Sør Rondane Mountains

Component	Specimen No.					
	19			224		
	wt%	at.%	$\frac{R}{Al}$	wt%	at.%	$\frac{R}{Al}$
SiO_2	63.70	60.4	3.62	75.86	71.2	5.05
TiO_2	0.60	0.4	0.02	0.16	0.1	0.01
Al_2O_3	14.95	16.7	1.00	12.73	14.1	1.0
Fe_2O_3	3.40	2.4	0.14	0.74	0.5	0.04
FeO	4.15	3.3	0.20	1.26	1.0	0.07
MnO	0.12	0.1	0.01	0.01	—	—
MgO	1.96	2.8	0.17	0.61	0.8	0.06
CaO	4.61	4.6	0.28	2.81	2.8	0.20
Na_2O	4.00	7.4	0.44	4.49	8.2	0.58
K_2O	1.47	1.7	0.10	0.87	1.1	0.08
P_2O_5	0.24	0.2	0.01	0.11	0.1	0.01
Loss on ignition	0.88	—	—	0.38	—	—
Σ	100.08	100.0	—	100.03	100.0	—

	Specimen No.	
	19	224

Numerical characteristics (after Zavaritskii)

	19	224
a	11.0	10.9
b	11.4	3.3
c	4.5	2.7
s	73.1	83.1
Q	+19.7	+41.7
f'	60.8	54.6
m'	29.5	30.0
c'	9.7	16.0

Coordinates on the ACF diagram (after Eskola and Korzhinskii)

A	41.0	50.6
C	25.5	29.8
F	33.5	19.6

Norm, % (after Barth)

Albite	37.0	41.2
Anorthite	18.8	12.0
Orthoclase	8.8	5.4
Hypersthene	7.7	2.6
Clinopyroxene	2.5	0.9
Magnetite	3.6	0.7
Ilmenite	0.9	0.2
Apatite	0.5	0.3
Quartz	20.2	36.7

Note. The modal composition of analyzed specimens is presented in Table 89.

of agmatites, derived from biotite-amphibole plagiogneisses, has been established from their geological, mineralogical and chemical features.

It is difficult to name a chemical analog of the amphibole-biotite plagiogneiss among the igneous rocks; only dacites and quartz diorites may approach them with regard to composition /65/. In view of the widespread occurrence of biotite-amphibole plagiogneisses and gneisses, their layered structure, interbedding with marbles and calciphyres and also their chemical composition, a sedimentary origin is strongly suggested. The description of biotite-amphibole plagiogneisses and gneisses would be incomplete without a mention of cataclastized and mylonitized varieties. All varieties of gneisses and their migmatites have been affected by these processes, which involve partial recrystallization and the appearance of newly formed epidote, chlorite, sericite and carbonate. These processes raise the ferruginosity of amphibole up to 78 at.%.

Amphibolites, as a rule, occur as separate sheet bodies, 1—5 m thick, among a variety of rocks, including plagiogneisses, migmatites and marbles. They are represented by gray and dark gray schistose, fine- to medium-grained rocks. From the composition, it is possible to distinguish varieties containing clinopyroxene as well as biotitized and weakly granitized amphibolites (Table 91). Plagioclase, hornblende and ore are ubiquitous components of all varieties of amphibolites. Quartz, up to 10%, is common; it is essentially absent only from clinopyroxene-bearing varieties. The latter's amphibole content is lower, due to the intensive biotitization and feldspathization of the amphibolites. Sphene and apatite are the characteristic accessory minerals. The secondary minerals include epidote, carbonate, sericite and rarely actinolite.

The texture of amphibolites is heterogranoblastic and that of biotitized amphibolites is lepidogranoblastic. There are diablastic hornblende metablasts up to 2 mm in size, with inclusions of biotite, epidote, sphene and ore. Clinopyroxene is sometimes replaced by hornblende. Biotite formed later, since its fine flakes permeate amphibole, plagioclase and clinopyroxene. A nearly identical role is played by quartz, often forming symplektite aggregates with the biotite. Feldspathized amphibolites contain sporadic metablasts of microcline replacing plagioclase. The An content in the plagioclase reaches 50—57% in varieties where the latter's content exceeds 60%. In such varieties (especially epidotized amphibolites), large plagioclase metablasts exhibit reverse and maculose zonation, the An content increasing by 10—15% from the center of grains toward their margins. In other amphibolites, plagioclase is represented by andesine ranging from An 22 to An 45. The ferruginosity of clinopyroxene is fairly constant (38—41%). The ferruginosity of amphibole (green and bluish green) is always higher than that of clinopyroxene. The lowest ferruginosity of hornblende occurs in amphibolites with high contents of this mineral (35—37 at.%), and the highest in clinopyroxene-bearing varieties (56—59 at.%). In other cases, the ferruginosity of hornblende is 40—42 at.%. A few specimens of amphibolites contain garnet with a ferruginosity of 80 at.%. The garnet is possibly calcic.

TABLE 91. Mineral composition of amphibolites from the Sør Rondane Mountains

Specimen No.	Mineral composition, vol.%										An content of plagioclase	clinopyroxene				amphibole		
	quartz	plagioclase	K-feldspar	clino-pyroxene	amphi-bole	biotite	ore minerals	epidote + calcite	sphene	apatite		n_z	n_x	$2V°$	f at.%	n_z	n_x	f at.%
207v	o.s.*	45	—	11	38	6	o.s.	—	—	o.s.	27	1.722	1.696	+57	41	1.696	1.672	59
524	—	54	—	15	5	23	2	—	o.s.	1	26—27	1.720	1.695	+58	38	—	—	—
209	2	70	—	—	17	10	—	—	1	o.s.	50—57	—	—	—	—	1.681	1.662	43
209v	7	60	—	—	18	7	1	7	o.s.	—	35—49	—	—	—	—	1.684	1.664	49
524m	—	68	7	18	6	o.s.	1	—	*	—	41—43	1.722	1.696	+57	41	1.693	1.678	56
11b	5	30	—	—	63	—	1	—	1	—	26—27	—	—	—	—	1.674	1.552	37
11	4	15	—	—	78	2	1	—	—	—	23—25	—	—	—	—	1.672	1.650	35
6v	7	43	—	—	50	—	o.s.	o.s.	o.s.	o.s.	22—24	—	—	—	—	1.680	1.660	42
521n	10	18	—	—	27	24	9	—	*	8	30—31	—	—	—	—	1.680		—
510v	5	30	—	—	54	10	—	—	1	—	35—37	—	—	—	—	—	—	—

Notes. 1. Specimen 209v contains actinolite ($n_z = 1.652$; $n_x = 1.626$; $f = 34$ at.%) as well as the hornblende. Specimen 524i contains 4% garnet ($n = 1.799$, $f = 80$ at.%). 3. The ferruginosities of actinolite and tremolite were determined by the diagram provided by Deer et al. /16/.
* [o.s. = optic sign.]

TABLE 92. Chemical composition of amphibolites from the Sør Rondane Mountains

Component	Specimen No.					
	510v			209		
	wt%	at.%	$\dfrac{R}{Al}$	wt%	at.%	$\dfrac{R}{Al}$
SiO_2	49.12	45.7	2.75	51.86	47.8	1.80
TiO_2	0.84	0.6	0.04	0.52	0.3	0.01
Al_2O_3	15.13	16.6	1.00	24.44	26.5	1.00
Fe_2O_3	3.50	2.5	0.15	1.74	1.2	0.05
FeO	6.82	5.3	0.32	2.65	2.1	0.08
MnO	0.19	0.2	0.01	0.06	0.1	—
MgO	8.67	12.0	0.72	2.21	3.0	0.11
CaO	9.45	9.4	0.57	10.41	10.2	0.39
Na_2O	3.20	5.8	0.35	4.35	7.8	0.29
K_2O	1.48	1.8	0.11	0.78	0.9	0.03
P_2O_5.	0.20	0.1	0.01	0.16	0.1	—
Loss on ignition	1.71	—	—	1.14	—	—
Σ	100.31	100.0	—	100.62	100.0	—

	Specimen No.	
	510	209

Numerical characteristics (after Zavaritskii)

a	9.1	11.8
b	29.9	10.5
c	5.4	12.1
s	55.6	65.6
Q	−12.4	−4.5
f'	31.9	43.2
m'	48.3	39.6
c'	19.8	17.2

Coordinates on the ACF diagram (after Eskola and Korzhinskii)

A	25.0	53.7
C	26.3	30.8
F	48.7	15.5

Norm, % (after Barth)

Albite	26.3	38.7
Anorthite	22.5	44.5
Orthoclase	8.9	4.7
Olivine	16.3	4.6
Clinopyroxene	19.2	4.7
Magnetite	3.7	1.8
Ilmenite	1.1	0.7
Apatite	0.3	0.3
Nepheline	1.7	—

Note. The modal composition of analyzed specimens is given in Table 91.

The chemical composition of two specimens of amphibolite (510v — rich in amphibole, and 209 — rich in plagioclase) is given in Table 92. Their mineral differences are excellently reflected by the chemical composition. of the rocks. Thus, the composition of amphibolite enriched in hornblende scarcely differs from the average composition of certain basalts. Remarkably, the plagioclase-rich amphibolites have a composition nearly identical to that of average anorthosites /65/. Apparently, basalts and anorthosites could be the original rocks for the amphibolites. The alumina-rich amphibolite probably originated from sedimentary rocks (marls).

In concluding this description of the amphibolites, their very low grade of granitization, even amidst migmatites, should be noted. This is one of the characteristic features of amphibolites from the Sør Rondane Mountains, as well as of other similar amphibolite facies rocks.

Marbles and calciphyres form sheets (1—5 m thick) in biotite-amphibole plagiogneisses and in migmatites derived from amphibolites. A marble layer in the north of the Vengen Spur reaches a thickness of 100 m, but includes fractured amphibolite bodies. Sheets of carbonate rocks in migmatites are often boudinaged, usually with lenticular or rounded boudins. Bimetasomatic salite and salite-plagioclase rocks develop at contacts between calciphyres and migmatite metasome. Very similar rocks, in the form of lenses, are also often encountered within marble sheets. In this case, the original rocks may have had an unusual composition, approaching marls. Garnet-bearing skarns develop at contacts of calciphyres with intrusive granites. Weakly mineralized white marbles (Table 93) contain calcite (n_o = 1.660—1.664) with a very small admixture of the magnesite molecule (up to 10%), diopside, plagioclase, hornblende, epidote, sphene and quartz. Their texture is heterogranoblastic; the size of calcite grains is 1—8 mm and that of the remaining grains is 1—2 mm. The calciphyres are yellowish green, intermittently banded or maculose, owing to the accumulation of silicates within the carbonate mass. Aside from calcite (Table 93), the calciphyres also contain considerable amounts of salite (f = 45 at.%) and scapolite. There are small admixtures of sphene, hornblende, epidote and quartz. Scapolite most commonly forms fine-grained mosaic aggregates separate from pyroxene; scapolite metablasts (5—6 mm) with inclusions of salite grains occur locally. The rocks are heterogranoblastic, with glomeroblastic segregations of salite and scapolite.

The diopside rocks (plagioclase-diopside, scapolite-diopside) consist mainly of diopside with a Ca content of ~30 at.% (Table 93). Small grains of scapolite, andesine — An 29—32, calcite, sphene, quartz and graphite occur between large diopside grains (2—6 mm). All varieties of diopside rocks exhibit amphibolization of pyroxene along grain boundaries and in cracks. The amphibole is represented by actinolite (f = 52 at.%). The inclusions in marbles have an amphibole-salite-plagioclase composition and a granoblastic texture. Besides the enumerated minerals, they also contain calcite, sphene, apatite, ore, microcline and quartz. The quartz content occasionally reaches 17%, and the rock thus approaches a plagiogneiss. The ferruginosity of the dark-colored minerals is high. Pyroxene is represented by ferrosalite with f = 60 at.%, and amphibole by hornblende with f = 60—73 at.%.

TABLE 93. Mineral composition of calciphyres and diopside rocks in the Sør Rondane Mountains

Speci-men No.	Mineral composition, vol.%												Characteristics of minerals								Remarks
	carbonate	diopside	plagioclase	scapolite	amphibole	garnet	epidote	sphene	apatite	quartz	K-feldspar	An content of plagioclase	diopside n_z	diopside n_x	diopside f at.%	amphibole n_z	amphibole n_x	amphibole f at.%	garnet n	garnet d_4/cm	
8a	90	1	1	—	2	—	3	o.s.*		2	—	—	—	—	—	—	—	—	—	—	Weakly mineralized marble containing 1% biotite
516d	23	34	—	37	2	—	4	—		2	—	—	1.723	1.696	45	—	—	—	—	—	Scapolite-diopside calciphyre
10a	12	50	—	28	—	—	—	2		8	—	—	—	—	—	—	—	—	—	—	As above
524g	24	15	10	4	—	6	—	1	5	17	18	—	—	—	—	—	—	—	1.750	3.64	Scapolite-diopside calciphyres, enriched in grossular, quartz and feldspar — at contact with granitoids
524e	6	42	—	—	2	25	—	—		15	10	—	1.743	1.716	77	—	—	—	—	—	Rock at the contact of calciphyre and granitoid
524d	—	13	12	—	—	15	—	o.s.		30	30	—	1.732	1.704	60	—	—	—	1.748	—	As above
516g	4	76	—	—	10	—	—	—		10	—	—	1.713	1.686	30	1.667	1.643	52	—	—	Diopside rock. Amphibole is represented by actinolite
516v	5	64	13	—	6	—	—	—		12	—	29—32	—	—	—	—	—	—	—	—	Plagioclase-diopside rock, containing sporadic biotite flakes
524n	—	88	6	—	5	—	1	2		—	—	—	—	—	—	—	—	—	—	—	Plagioclase-diopside rock, containing 1% graphite
10v	—	88	—	—	8	—	1	1		17	—	—	1.732	1.705	60	1.712	1.687	73	—	—	Diopside rock
8b	3	22	48	3	8	—	2	2		—	—	27	—	—	—	—	—	—	—	—	Inclusion in marble. Amphibole is brown. (2V of pyroxene = +58°)
8v	—	18	50	—	20	—	1	1	1	2	6	—	—	—	—	1.698	1.674	60	—	—	Inclusion in marble. Dark green amphibole. The rock contains 2% ore minerals.

Note. The garnet in specimen 524g contains approximately 88% of the grossular molecule, while specimen 524d is 90% grossular.

* [o.s. = optic sign.]

Ferrosalite is replaced by hornblende. The plagioclase has the composition of oligoclase (An 27).

Skarn calciphyres differ from other calcic rocks in their mineral composition (and in their extremely inequigranular texture). Besides the carbonate, ferrosalite ($f = 60-77$ at.%), plagioclase, amphibole, scapolite, sphene and quartz, which also occur in other calciphyre varieties, the skarns contain garnet (88–90% grossular plus andradite) and microcline, together accounting for 25–45% of the rock. The quartz contents are high (15–30%). Apatite occurs sporadically, accounting for up to 5 vol.% of the rock. The texture of the skarns is also very complex. Their garnet occurs in 1–3-mm rounded grains with ragged outlines; it is often diablastic, due to numerous inclusions of quartz and feldspar granules. Some garnet grains are skeletal and form maculose aggregates or narrow rims around pyroxene. Plagioclase occurs in maculose segregations in which its small grains (0.5–1 mm) and sporadic laths (3 mm) occur side by side with xenoblastic segregations of K-feldspar. Quartz occurs together with feldspar in very small grains (0.3–0.5 mm), but there are also crystalline grains up to 6 mm in size with inclusions of skeletal garnet and pyroxene granules. Pyroxene forms prismatic grains, 1–3 mm in size, and is corroded by quartz-feldspar segregations.

ROCKS OF WESTERN QUEEN MAUD LAND*

In western Queen Maud Land (Preuschoff and Bundermann ranges, the Hedden, Paulsen, Barkley and Herrmann mountains, and the Gburek Peaks), there are the following three widespread groups of amphibolite facies rocks: 1) migmatized biotite-amphibole plagiogneisses, 2) migmatized fibrolite-garnet and biotite-garnet plagiogneisses and quartzites, and 3) carbonate rocks (marbles).

Biotite-amphibole plagiogneisses, free of all traces of migmatization, occur to a very limited extent among migmatized varieties. They are represented by fine- to medium-grained rocks with greenish gray color. Their texture is nemato- and lepidogranoblastic. Plagioclase is represented by oligoclase-andesine, An 27–30 (Table 94). The colored minerals are highly ferruginous; the ferruginosity of dark green hornblende is 65–70 at.% and that of brown biotite is 67–76 at.%.

Migmatized biotite-amphibole plagiogneisses are characterized by a prevalence of the paleosome over the metasome. Layered migmatites are the most widespread variety, although they occur together with ramified vein migmatites. Externally and structurally, the paleosome of migmatites scarcely differs from nonmigmatized plagiogneisses. However, it contains appreciable amounts of microcline replacing plagioclase (Table 94). Rims of myrmekitized albite develop along the boundaries of these minerals. The ferruginosity of colored minerals in the migmatite paleosome varies

---

* This section is based on the data collected by Ravich.

TABLE 94. Mineral composition of biotite-amphibole plagiogneisses, their migmatites and shadow granites in the western mountains of Queen Maud Land

Specimen No.	Mineral composition, vol.%						Characteristics of minerals						Remarks
	quartz	plagio-clase	K-feldspar	amphi-bole	biotite	ore and accessory minerals	An content of plagio-clase	amphibole n_z	amphibole n_x	amphibole f at.%	biotite n_z	biotite f at.%	
820a	20	40	—	10	25	5	30	1.706	1.682	68	1.675	73	Biotite-amphibole plagiogneisses
738a	30	22	—	25	15	8	27	1.702	1.682	65	1.665	67	"
738	30	41	—	12	15	2	27	1.708	1.687	70	1.677	76	"
733	25	30	—	30	10	5	30	1.705	1.687	67	1.677	76	"
Migmatites of biotite-amphibole plagiogneisses													
824g	20	37	10	10	20	3	30	1.700	1.680	62	1.680	78	Paleosome of migmatite
824	33	40	15	—	12	—	30				1.665	67	Metasome of migmatite, the paleosome of which is represented by specimen 824g
809	15	47	5	15	15	3	30	1.700	1.680	62	1.660	63	Paleosome of migmatite
809b	20	37	20	1	15	7	30				1.670	71	Metasome of migmatite, the paleosome of which is represented by specimen 809
786	20	48	—	2	28	2	30				1.659	62	Paleosome of migmatite
786v	30	33	25	—	12	—	30				1.671	72	Metasome of migmatite, the paleosome of which is represented by specimen 786
755	12	30	—	20	30	8	30	1.697	1.673	60	1.659	62	Paleosome of migmatite
755a	25	25	43	—	5	2	23				1.665	67	Metasome of migmatite, the paleosome of which is represented by specimen 755
731a	10	30	20	20	20	—	27	1.720	1.700	82	1.694	90	Paleosome of migmatite
731b	25	40	20	—	10	5	25				1.670	71	Metasome of migmatite, the paleosome of which is represented by specimen 731a
Shadow biotite-amphibole granites (granitized plagiogneisses)													
784	30	18	40	2	10	o.s.* 3	26	1.714	1.690	78	1.688	85	Shadow biotite granite
770b	20	20	40	9	8	—	26				1.684	82	
766v	25	30	40	—	5	—	24				1.684	82	
750a	25	21	30	8	10	6	26	1.716	1.695	79	1.674	73	
750	25	27	25	8	12	3	25	1.714	1.693	78	1.682	80	
743	18	18	40	2	12	3	23	1.714	1.693	78	1.690	86	

* [o.s. = optic sign.]

widely, whereas the basicity of plagioclase is essentially constant. The plagioclase is represented by oligoclase-andesine, An 27—30. The ferruginosity of hornblende is 60—82 at.% and that of biotite is 62—90 at.%. It is important to note that, in general, the high ferruginosity of colored minerals in plagiogneisses is related to the high content of ore minerals, i. e., to the high ferruginosity of the rocks themselves. Ore minerals often account for 5—8 vol.% of the rocks, both in the paleosome of migmatites and in non-migmatized plagiogneisses. The following consistency can be traced, although not very distinctly: the more abundant the ore minerals in a rock, the lower is the ferruginosity of its colored minerals.

The metasome of migmatites consists of biotite granite. In places it contains granules of amphibole and ore. The texture of medium-grained metasome is granoblastic. Plagioclase is replaced by microcline. Augen varieties are sometimes encountered. The composition of plagioclase is the same as in the paleosome; less commonly, it is somewhat more alkaline. The ferruginosity of biotite is usually lower (67—72 at.%) than that in the paleosome.

The migmatites contain concordant sheets of shadow biotite-amphibole granites, with thicknesses ranging from a few tens to several hundreds of meters, and rarely up to 1 km. They form a part of the migmatite fields. Shadow granites are represented by comparatively dense, medium-grained rocks, of yellowish pink or grayish yellow color. Their structure is gneissic. In places, they exhibit shadow migmatitic banding and relicts of skialiths of a biotite-amphibole plagiogneiss. The mineral composition of shadow granites is presented in Table 94. It is distinguished by a quartz content of 20—30%, and by the prevalence of K-feldspar over plagioclase and of biotite over amphibole. The content of ore minerals reaches 6%. Locally amphibole is absent. The texture of shadow granites is granoblastic or porphyroblastic; the porphyroblasts are irregular microcline grains. The microcline replaces plagioclase; rims of myrmekitized albite form along their contact. The biotite is secondary with respect to amphibole and plagioclase. The plagioclase is represented by oligoclase, An 23—26. The ferruginosity of colored minerals in shadow granites is always 8—12% higher than in plagiogneisses. The ferruginosity of hornblende is fairly constant, 78—79 at.%; that of biotite ranges from 73 to 86 at.% and is almost always higher than that of hornblende. K-feldspar is a crosshatched microcline, as in other amphibolite facies rocks of Antarctica. Apatite, sphene and zircon are the accessory minerals in all varieties of biotite-amphibole plagiogneisses. The zircon content increases during granitization and migmatization.

The chemical analyses of the paleosome and metasome of migmatites are given in Table 95; these indicate that the metasome is not a derivative of the biotite-amphibole plagiogneiss. It differs from the paleosome in the Si : Al ratio, and moreover, the paleosome often contains more alkalis, including potassium, than the metasome. The chemical composition of the metasome lies within the granite-granodiorite series. The high ferruginosity of the biotite-amphibole plagiogneisses, their slight saturation in silica and their high alkalinity should be emphasized. These chemical features of the plagiogneiss provide an excellent reflection of its mineral composition, including the high contents of ore minerals and biotite, the low basicity of plagioclase, etc.

Quartzites and aluminous plagiogneisses are important for the determination of the nature of the amphibolite facies metamorphism. Unfortunately, they have not yet been thoroughly studied. It is only known that the majority are distinguished by two types of associations, those of fibrolite with garnet and biotite and those of garnet with biotite. These rocks are everywhere feldspathized and the K-feldspar is represented by microcline. An unusual group of cataclastized quartzite beds containing kyanite (some 100 m thick) was encountered on Midbresraben Hill in the Penck Trough. These quartzites contain up to 80—85% large (up to 1 cm) poikiloblastic quartz grains with inclusions of prismatic kyanite (3—6 mm long), totaling not over 7—8%. Plagioclase granules and relict cordierite grains account for approximately the same amount. Fibrolite aggregates occur locally. The optical properties of kyanites are $n_z = 1.727 \pm 0.003$, $2V = -78°$. The primary fibrolite and cordierite quartzites are presumed to have undergone diaphthoresis under conditions of lower-grade amphibolite facies.

Marbles occur in concordant sheets, 20—300 m thick, within biotite-amphibole plagiogneisses. Together with the latter, they are crumpled into folds and transected by leucocratic granite and plagiogranite veins. Reaction rims and pockets of salite and salite-plagioclase rocks develop in calciphyres in contact with these veins. The salite-plagioclase rocks also compose intercalations 10—30 cm thick within the calciphyres. These intercalations possibly resulted from the initial composition of the carbonate beds. Contacts of marbles with the host migmatites exhibit reactive bimetasomatic fringes of phlogopite-tremolite and tremolite rocks, their thicknesses varying from a few centimeters to 20 cm.

Beds of snow-white marbles are comparatively rare, and their thickness does not exceed 15 m. Locally, they are enriched in graphite at their contacts. By far the larger part of marbles is mineralized and contains 2—17% silicate minerals (Table 96). They are dirty white in color and medium- to coarse-grained. Dark spots are accumulations of silicate minerals represented by plagioclase, salite, actinolite and epidote. Phlogopite and quartz occur sporadically. The presence of disseminated grains of sphene and ore is characteristic of many areas. The carbonates may be differentiated by composition into calcite-dolomite and dolomite marbles; the former are more common and they contain approximately equal amounts of calcite and dolomite. Calcite is comparatively rare in dolomite marbles. The marbles possess an equigranular granoblastic texture, with alternating medium- and coarse-grained bands. The dolomite grains are rhombic while calcite is more xenomorphic; the latter occurs interstitially and contains dolomite inclusions. Graphite, which occurs locally in the marbles, forms thin elongated platelets, up to 1 mm long, uniformly disseminated within carbonate grains (2—3%).

Marbles with an admixture of silicate minerals are often heterogranoblastic. Coarse-grained areas, with carbonates up to 1 cm and larger,

TABLE 95. Chemical composition of migmatites of biotite-amphibole plagiogneisses in the western mountains of Queen Maud Land

Compo-nent	786 (paleosome)			786v (metasome)			731a (paleosome)			731b (metasome)		
	wt%	at.%	$\frac{R}{Al}$	wt%	at.%	$\frac{R}{Al}$	wt%	at.%	$\frac{R}{Al}$	wt%	at.%	$\frac{R}{Al}$
SiO_2	60.27	56.7	3.12	72.45	68.4	4.53	62.50	59.0	3.49	68.50	64.1	3.93
TiO_2	1.03	0.7	0.04	0.22	0.2	0.01	0.64	0.5	0.03	0.51	0.3	0.02
Al_2O_3	16.35	18.2	1.00	13.58	15.1	1.00	15.22	16.9	1.00	14.87	16.3	1.00
Fe_2O_3	0.94	0.7	0.04	traces	—	—	3.29	2.4	0.14	1.10	0.8	0.05
FeO	5.60	4.4	0.24	2.74	2.1	0.14	5.36	4.2	0.25	2.78	2.2	0.13
MnO	0.10	0.1	0.01	traces	—	—	0.18	0.2	0.01	0.09	0.1	0.01
MgO	2.81	3.9	0.21	0.36	0.5	0.03	0.62	0.8	0.05	1.03	1.5	0.05
CaO	4.66	4.7	0.26	1.33	1.3	0.09	2.86	2.9	0.17	2.27	2.2	0.13
Na_2O	3.68	6.7	0.37	3.19	5.9	0.39	3.74	6.9	0.41	4.52	8.2	0.50
K_2O	2.70	3.3	0.18	5.40	6.5	0.43	5.10	6.1	0.36	3.55	4.2	0.20
P_2O_5	0.76	0.6	0.03	traces	—	—	0.04	0.1	0.01	0.06	0.1	0.0
Loss on ignition	0.97	—	—	0.56	—	—	0.45	—	—	0.54	—	—
Σ	99.87	100.0	—	99.83	100.0	—	99.99	100.0	—	99.82	100.0	—

	Specimen No.			
	786 (paleosome)	786v (metasome)	731a (paleosome)	731b (metasome)
Numerical characteristics (after Zavaritskii)				
a	12.3	14.5	15.7	14.9
b	11.9	3.3	10.3	5.7
c	5.0	1.5	2.4	2.4
s	70.8	80.7	71.6	77.0
Q	+5.1	+29.1	+1.5	+18.5
f'	53.2	77.5	79.4	63.5
m'	40.4	18.4	10.0	30.6
c'	6.4	—	10.0	5.9
a'	—	4.1	—	—
Coordinates on the ACF diagram (after Eskola and Korzhinskii)				
A	38.4	40.7	32.4	39.8
C	22.1	19.5	23.9	22.7
F	39.5	39.8	43.7	37.5
Norm, % (after Barth)				
Albite	33.7	29.5	34.3	41.0
Anorthite	18.9	6.5	9.8	9.8
Orthoclase	16.4	32.3	30.6	21.1
Hypersthene	14.6	5.3	5.7	5.6
Clinopyroxene	—	—	3.2	0.7
Magnetite	1.0	—	3.6	1.2
Ilmenite	1.5	0.3	0.9	0.7
Apatite	1.5	—	0.2	0.2
Quartz	11.8	26.0	11.7	19.7
Corundum	0.6	0.1	—	—

Note. The modal composition of the rocks is given in Table 94.

often appear in a medium-grained matrix. The form of carbonate minerals is the same as in pure marbles. Silicate minerals often form aggregates of small grains, 0.1—0.4 mm in diameter. Plagioclase and clinopyroxene occur in xenoblastic grains. Actinolite occurs as small elongated prismatic partially terminated crystallites and locally forms cruciform aggregates. Locally, it replaces salite. Epidote is inequigranular and has an irregular shape, in places forming small concentrations. Epidote also develops in cracks in salite and sometimes forms micro-segregations in cracks of plagioclase grains. In some areas, epidote and actinolite produce close intergrowths; they are also locally intergrown with small segregations of quartz. Some carbonate grains contain inclusions of plagioclase, clinopyroxene, sphene and ore minerals. Plagioclase is represented by oligoclase-andesine, An 29—30, and clinopyroxene-salite (ferruginosity, 60 at.%) occurs in the most highly mineralized areas. The ferruginosity of actinolite is 47 at.%. Phlogopite is nearly free of iron. The composition of epidote approaches that of pistacite ($n_z = 1.732$, $n_x = 1.716$).

In some marble sheets which are transected by leucogranite veins, there are quartz-muscovite pockets up to 30—40 cm in size. These are composed of quartz grains in a variety of sizes, sometimes euhedral, with aggregates of randomly oriented muscovite flakes. The muscovite ($n_z = 1.595$) is represented by silvery-white flakes of the magnesian variety (picrophengite). Light green flakes of ordinary muscovite were found in comminuted rock. Some muscovite-quartz lenticules have a zonal structure; the central zone is dominated by quartz with an admixture of carbonate and muscovite, while the marginal zone consists of a fine-grained carbonate-muscovite-quartz rock. The muscovite-quartz pockets are associated with minor mineralization, including tourmaline, monazite, pyrite and graphite.

Clinopyroxene accounts for over 70% of the plagioclase-pyroxene rocks, the remainder being plagioclase. Carbonates, quartz, pale yellow amphibole and rarely microcline occur locally in small amounts (Table 96). The rocks are heterogranoblastic. Pyroxene and plagioclase grains, with a variety of grain sizes, are randomly distributed. Plagioclase aggregates rarely form veinlets in pyroxene crystallites. Plagioclase probably crystallizes after the pyroxene which is replaced by pale green amphibole. Large pyroxene grains contain fine ingrowths of carbonate, phlogopite and microcline. Clinopyroxene is represented by ferrosilite ($f = 61$ at.%) and plagioclase by andesine (An 35).

Phlogopite-tremolite and tremolite rocks are layered and schistose. The latter contain a significant amount of carbonate in addition to the tremolite and phlogopite; the rock thus approaches the composition of calciphyre (Table 96). The dimensions of the elongated prismatic.grains of tremolite and the flakes of phlogopite are 0.5—1 $\times$ 2 $\times$ 3 mm. Carbonate grains form aggregates with tremolite grains, usually located in widened cleavage cracks. The colorless tremolites contain very little iron, while the ferruginosity of phlogopite is 6 at.%. The tremolite rock consists almost entirely of subparallel elongated, prismatic tremolite grains, with an addition of only sporadic, though fairly large irregular grains of ore and sphene.

TABLE 96. Mineral composition of marbles and associated diopside-plagioclase rocks in the western mountains of Queen Maud Land

Speci-men No.	Mineral composition, vol.%								Characteristics of minerals												Rock
	carbonate	diopside	plagioclase	amphibole	phlogopite	epidote	sphene + ore minerals	quartz	An content of plagioclase	clinopyroxene				phlogopite		amphibole					
										n_z	n_x	$2V°$	f at.%	n_z	f at.%	n_z	n_x	$c\,n_z$	$2V°$	f at.%	
118v	91	2	2	2	1	1	1	—	29	—	—	—	—	1.562	0	—	—	—	—	—	Mineralized marble
115v	90	2	2	2	—	3	1	—	—	1.719	1.691	+58	39	—	—	1.662	1.635	18	—80	47	Mineralized marble; amphibole is represented by actinolite
115a	83	6	8	1	—	—	2	—	30	1.732	1.704	+61	60	—	—	—	—	—	—	—	Mineralized marble
120v	17	—	—	75	8	—	—	—	—	—	—	—	—	1.585	6	1.628	1.602	22	—82	1	Schistose phlogopite-tremolite calciphyre
120a	2	77	17	3	—	—	—	1	35	1.733	1.705	+60	61	—	—	—	—	—	—	—	Salite-plagioclase rock

ROCKS OF THE GREARSON AND VESTFOLD OASES

A variety of amphibole facies rocks occur in the northern half of the
Grearson Oasis. Their relationships with the strata of granulite facies
rocks have not been established. There is a variety of plagiogneisses
containing high-alumina minerals, with interbedded sheets of amphibolites
several meters thick /57/.

Biotite-cordierite plagiogneisses are represented by gray
and light gray medium-grained gneissic rocks. They are always rich in
quartz, 45—60%; in addition 15—25% plagioclase, 10—30% cordierite and
2—10% biotite also occur. Garnet (not over 6%) and microcline (1—10%)
occur sporadically. The plagiogneisses are heterogranoblastic and their
grain size is 1—3 mm. Quartz and cordierite form lenticular aggregates
of irregular grains. Cordierite and garnet often contain ingrowths of
biotite and quartz. Microcline replaces plagioclase. Myrmekitized oligoclase, An 13—16, is formed at the boundaries of these minerals. Generally,
plagioclase is represented by andesine, An 35—37. The ferruginosity of
cordierite is extremely high, 56 at.% ($n_z = 1.561$; $n_x = 1.550$); it is replaced
by chlorite. Garnet, associated with cordierites, consists mainly of
almandine ($n = 1.794$).

Sillimanite-biotite plagiogneisses differ from the cordierite-
biotite variety in their lighter color and more distinct banding. They consist
of 30—40% quartz, 40—45% plagioclase, 2—10% sillimanite, 5—15% biotite
and 2—3% cordierite. They often contain 2—5% garnet and 3—10% microcline. The plagiogneisses are porphyroblastic, with a lepidonematogranoblastic inequigranular matrix. Large irregular plagioclase metablasts,
5—7 mm, occur in places. Quartz forms granulated lenticular segregations,
while sillimanite is represented by fibrolite aggregates. The garnet is
diablastic. Where the cordierite or fibrolite content increases to 40—60%,
the plagiogneisses are converted to schists with only 20—30% quartz and
sporadic occurrence of plagioclase. Such rocks have a high content of ore
minerals (5—8%), biotite (10—15%) and garnet (2—3%). These schists and
plagiogneisses undoubtedly evolved from terrigenous sedimentary rocks;
the original rocks were evidently sandstones in the case of plagiogneisses
and siltstones or shales in the case of the schists.

Biotite plagiogneisses are gray and medium-grained. They
consist of 30—40% quartz, 40—50% plagioclase, 12—20% biotite and 1—3% ore
minerals. Microcline occurs sporadically (2—8%). The accessory minerals
include zircon, monazite, orthite and rutile. The rocks are lepidogranoblastic; garnet metablasts, 2—4 mm, and lenticular segregations of
granulated quartz, 5—8 mm, occur in a fine-grained matrix (0.5—1 mm). All
the other minerals are poikiloblastic with numerous quartz ingrowths.
Microcline develops interstitially and replaces plagioclase. The latter is
represented by andesine, An 32—37, while the ferruginosity of biotite is
51 at.% ($n_z = 1.645$). The chemical composition of biotite plagiogneiss is
presented in Table 97. The plagiogneiss approaches granites in its silica
and alumina content, but is close to gabbro in its alkali content. It is difficult
to name a magmatic analog of this plagiogneiss, and therefore the plagiogneisses are assumed to have originated from sandstones.

TABLE 97. Chemical composition of plagiogneisses from the Vestfold and Grearson Oases

Component	Biotite plagiogneiss (Grearson Oasis)			Biotite-hornblende plagiogneiss (Vestfold Oasis)		
	wt%	at.%	$\dfrac{R}{Al}$	wt%	at.%	$\dfrac{R}{Al}$
SiO_2	71.22	68.5	4.89	50.70	47.8	2.35
TiO_2	0.73	0.5	0.04	1.63	1.1	0.06
Al_2O_3	12.33	14.0	1.00	18.32	20.3	1.00
Fe_2O_3	1.77	1.3	0.09	3.25	2.3	0.11
FeO	4.26	3.4	0.24	7.87	6.2	0.31
MnO	0.13	0.1	0.01	0.17	0.1	—
MgO	2.12	3.1	0.22	3.81	5.3	0.26
CaO	2.05	2.1	0.15	7.28	7.4	0.36
Na_2O	2.23	4.1	0.29	4.25	7.8	0.38
K_2O	2.30	2.8	0.20	1.13	1.4	0.07
P_2O_5	0.18	0.1	0.01	0.38	0.3	0.02
Loss on ignition	0.87	—	—	1.32		
Σ	100.19	100.0	—	100.11	100.0	

	Biotite plagiogneiss (Grearson Oasis)	Biotite-hornblende plagiogneiss (Vestfold Oasis)
Numerical characteristics (after Zavaritskii)		
a	7.8	11.5
b	12.1	19.9
c	2.4	7.0
s	77.7	61.6
Q	+37.4	−6.8
f′	44.6	54.8
m′	28.5	33.7
c′	—	11.5
a′	26.9	
Coordinates on the ACF diagram (after Eskola and Korzhinskii)		
A	44.9	36.9
C	13.3	24.6
F	41.7	38.5

Mineral composition of the rocks, vol.%

Component	Normative	Modal	Normative	Modal
Albite	20.5	30.5 (An 37)	39.0	44 (An 37)
Anorthite	9.5		27.8	
Orthoclase	14.0	8 (microcline)	7.0	
Orthopyroxene	10.8		10.0	
Magnetite	2.0	1.5 (titanomagnetite)	3.5	3.5 (titanomagnetite)
Ilmenite	1.0		2.2	
Apatite	0.3	0.5	0.8	0.5
Quartz	38.6	27.5	—	10
Biotite		12.0	—	16
Hornblende		—	—	26
Corundum	3.3		—	—
Clinopyroxene	—	—	5.2	—
Olivine	—	—	4.5	—

Garnet-biotite plagiogneisses differ little from biotite plagiogneisses. They contain 5—25% garnet; their contents of biotite (6—10%)
and plagioclase (20—25%) are lower, and their quartz content increases to
50—60%. The lepidogranoblastic texture of the biotite plagiogneiss is
in this case complicated by diablastic porphyroblasts of garnet, 5—10 mm
in size. The garnet ($n = 1.784$) is represented mainly by almandine. In
some areas of the Grearson Oasis, the plagiogneiss has been converted to
finely layered migmatites. The plagiogneiss in the paleosome is strongly
feldspathized and biotitized. The metasome is remarkably uniform. It
is represented by alaskitic granites, in which only the contents of microcline
(40—50%) and quartz (20—30%) are variable, while the contents of plagioclase
(20—30%) and ore (1—2%) are comparatively stable. There are only sporadic
grains of biotite, sillimanite, cordierite and garnet. The plagioclase is an
oligoclase, An 21—25. The metasome is porphyrogranoblastic, with microcline in the porphyroblasts. Plagioclase is replaced by microcline.

Amphibolites in the Grearson Oasis are greenish black, medium-
grained and consist almost entirely of common hornblende (93—95%) with a
ferruginosity of 27 at.% ($n_z = 1.666$; $n_x = 1.644$; $2V = -80°$; $cn_z = 18°$).
Biotite (2—3%), talc, epidote and actinolite needles develop on the hornblende.
Titanomagnetite forms glomero-accumulations with rims of brownish sphene
and biotite. Sphene and apatite are accessory minerals. Large amphibole
grains sometimes contain inclusions of quartz granules. On the whole, the
texture may be described as granoblastic.

A group of biotite-amphibole plagiogneiss beds with a composition
approaching that of amphibolites, is exposed in the north of the Vestfold
Oasis on the coast of Tryne Fjord. They are represented by dark gray,
fine-grained granoblastic rocks consisting of 18—23% quartz, 5—40%
andesine (An 34—37), 23—28% common hornblende, 13—16% biotite, 3—4%
ore minerals and accessory apatite. The biotite and hornblende are
replaced by epidote, plagioclase by clinozoisite. The chemical composition
of the biotite-amphibole plagiogneiss is given in Table 97. It is essentially
little different from melanocratic biotite-amphibole plagiogneisses from
other regions in Antarctica. However, its high content of alumina and low
content of quartz are striking. No such composition is encountered among
magmatic rocks and therefore it probably originated from sedimentary
rocks. Within the biotite-amphibole plagiogneiss are sheets of actinolite
schists, consisting of 75% columnar actinolite, 25% labradorite (An 64—66),
10% biotite flakes and quartz granules. Their texture is nematogranoblastic.
These rocks may have originated from sedimentary silica-carbonate sheets.

METABASITES

Basic igneous rocks which underwent metamorphism under amphibolite
facies conditions merit special consideration. They have been best studied
on Queen Maud Land (in the Yamato and Sør Rondane Mountains and in the
west of Queen Maud Land), where they often occupy considerable areas
that are commensurate with those occupied by paragneiss complexes.

In the west of Queen Maud Land, metabasites form sheets and dike-like boudinaged bodies, usually 1—2 m thick but occasionally reaching 15—20 m. The chains of boudins extend over hundreds of meters, and the largest ones over 1—2 km. The size of boudins varies within a few meters, but lenticular blocks of metabasites, tens of meters in size, are fairly common. The boudins are mainly equidimensional and angular. Interboudin spaces are filled with plagiogneisses or their granitized varieties, and also by pegmatitic granites or pegmatites. Large metabasite bodies are locally transformed into agmatites, as a rule with injective but sometimes also with injective-metasomatic metasome. In the Sør Rondane Mountains, metamorphosed basic rocks form large massifs of hundreds of square kilometers, small stocks with areas of tens of square kilometers, sheet bodies and dikes. The majority of metabasites have been transformed into agmatites. Blocks of agmatites are irregularly angular, 1—10 m in size. They have been cemented by leucocratic granitoids, amounting to as much as 30 vol.% of the agmatites. Leucocratic granitoids occur as net-veins and also in lenses, 7—10 m long and several meters thick. They locally form even larger bodies with irregular outlines. The bedding of the blocks of basic rocks remains intact, and the metasome is mostly injective, although injective-metasomatic metasomes are fairly common. Syenitization of the metabasites appears to be associated with the metasomatic processes. Metabasites in the Yamato Mountains are mainly represented by dike-like bodies, agmatized and syenitized to a considerable extent. In this location, the host rocks of metabasites are shadow biotite and biotite-amphibole granitoids.

The metabasites of Queen Maud Land have a highly variable mineral composition (Table 98). This is due to changes under amphibolite facies conditions and is partly governed by their original composition. However, it is not yet possible to make a complete evaluation of these factors and therefore the metabasites are provisionally differentiated only according to quantitative-mineralogical criteria.

Metabasites in the western part of Queen Maud Land are divided as follows: 1) completely biotitized and amphibolized; 2) biotitized and amphibolized, but retaining relict clinopyroxenes; 3) those containing clinopyroxene, including amphibolized, biotitized and also feldspathized rocks. Some of the feldspathized rocks do not contain amphibole (Table 98). A majority of the investigated rocks contain various amounts of quartz, probably produced by replacement of silica-rich pyroxenes by hornblende and biotite, and also partly by granitization of metabasites. Ore minerals are present in all the metabasite varieties (1—8%). Sphene, apatite and rare zircon are accessory minerals. The secondary minerals related to cataclasis and partial recrystallization of ortho-amphibolites at lower temperatures are represented by epidote, carbonate, chlorite and sericite. The texture is lepidogranoblastic, with porphyroblastic and poikiloblastic elements. Clinopyroxenes are always replaced by hornblende and their grains exhibit ragged outlines. Amphibole often forms large diablastic, tabular metablasts. They contain numerous inclusions of ore, sphene, quartz, plagioclase and relicts of clinopyroxene. Amphibole is replaced by

TABLE 98. Mineral composition of metabasites from mountains in Queen Maud Land (metamorphosed under amphibolite facies conditions)

Specimen No.	quartz	plagioclase	K-feldspars	clinopyroxene	amphibole	biotite	ore minerals	epidote + carbonate	sphene	apatite	An content of plagioclase	cpx n_z	cpx n_x	cpx $2V°$	cpx f at.%	amph n_z	amph n_x	amph f at.%	biot. n_z	biot. f at.%	Remarks
727 v	5	20	—	—	50	15	5	—	—	—	—	—	—	—	—	1.682	1.658	44	—	—	Contains 5% garnet with n = 1.782, d_3 = 3.96 g/cm³, f = 73 at.%
Western part of Queen Maud Land																					
731	—	30	—	10	42	15	3	—	—	—	30	1.713	1.689	—	25	1.685	1.663	49	1.650	56	Metagabbroids in western mountains of Queen Maud Land contain sphene, apatite and zircon as accessory minerals; epidote, chlorite, carbonate and sericite as secondary minerals. Certain specimens containing different accessories and secondary minerals are not specified. There is 12% garnet with n = 1.788; d = 4.02 g/cm³; f = 80 at.%
743b	—	23	—	10	25	15	3	—	—	—	26	—	—	—	—	1.685	1.663	49	1.650	56	
850	—	50	—	—	25	14	2	—	—	—	30	—	—	—	—	1.683	1.657	45	1.662	65	
708b	5	40	—	—	47	5	1	—	—	—	25	—	—	—	—	1.700	1.675	62	1.648	53	
753g	—	15	—	—	35	49	4	—	—	—	30	—	—	—	—	1.696	1.673	59	1.657	60	
735b	20	26	—	—	20	18	1	—	—	—	26	—	—	—	—	1.692	1.668	55	1.670	71	
844b	20	35	—	—	30	14	—	—	—	—	30	—	—	—	—	1.708	1.686	70	1.675	73	
750v	5	—	15	25	—	50	8	—	—	—	—	1.714	1.688	—	28	—	—	—	1.627	37	
711a	10	5	20	15	25	22	7	—	—	—	23	1.711	1.686	—	24	1.655	1.631	18	1.616	28	
718v	10	15	25	3	20	30	—	—	—	—	—	—	—	—	—	1.668	1.648	30	1.630	39	
720v	15	15	20	3	20	25	2	—	—	—	25	1.708	1.683	—	20	—	—	—	1.627	37	
Sør Rondane Mountains																					
512	8	60	—	7	12	2	5	—	—	—	38–40	1.719	1.694	+57	36	1.704	1.680	67	—	—	Contains 6% hypersthene with n_z = 1.725; n_x = 1.710; f = 44 at.%
528b	2	15	—	56	15	—	—	—	4	8	26–27	1.711	1.685	+27	25	1.666	1.642	27	—	—	
528v	—	27	—	55	15	15	—	—	1	—	o.s.*37–40	1.720	1.694	+60	38	1.690	1.666	53	—	—	Contains 2% orthite
512b	18	55	—	—	18	5	4	—	—	—	—	—	—	—	—	1.704	1.680	67	—	—	Contains sporadic hypersthene grains with n_z = 1.725, n_x = 1.710, f = 44 at.%

TABLE 98 (continued)

Specimen No.	quartz	plagioclase	K-feldspars	clinopyroxene	amphibole	biotite	ore minerals	epidote + carbonate	sphene	apatite	An content of plagioclase	cpx n_z	cpx n_x	cpx $2V°$	cpx f at.%	amph n_z	amph n_x	amph f at.%	biotite n_z	biotite f at.%	Remarks
520	o.s.*	47	—	3	50	—	3	—	o.s.	o.s.	39—49	1.708	1.682	—	—	1.678	1.654	40	—	—	Contains tremolite with n_z = 1.650, n_x = 1.626, f = 30 at.%; and actinolite with n_z = 1.666, n_x = 1.642, f = 52 at.%
26g	8	15	35	o.s.	30	5	2	—	4	1	—	—	—	—	—	1.677	1.660	40	—	—	
222	5	10	52	6	12	7	—	—	3	5	—	1.723	1.698	—	43	1.670	1.648	32	—	—	
519a	o.s.	16	8	—	60	1	2	—	7	6	—	1.723	1.699	—	43	1.668	1.643	30	—	—	
522a	3	38	7	—	29	20	o.s.	—	2	1	56—65	—	—	—	—	1.697	1.674	60	—	—	Contains actinolite with n_z = 1.668, n_x = 1.642, f = 55 at.%
24	15	55	—	—	10	18	2	—	—	o.s.	32—35	—	—	—	—	1.665	1.638	27	1.645	51	
23	10	50	—	—	23	10	—	—	—	2	24—25	—	—	—	—	1.703	1.684	66	—	—	
26	10	20	28	—	30	7	—	—	3	1	10—15	—	—	—	—	1.673	—	36	1.604	22	
26a	10	20	50	—	12	5	—	—	2	1	0—1	—	—	—	—	1.672	1.653	35	—	—	
221	15	22	46	—	7	4	2	—	3	1	0—3	—	—	—	—	1.699	1.680	62	—	—	
25	15	60	—	—	15	8	o.s.	2	o.s.	o.s.	23—26	—	—	—	—	1.691	1.672	53	—	—	Contains sporadic grains of zircon
25a	20	25	35	—	10	5	2	7	3	•	—	—	—	—	—	1.697	1.682	60	—	—	Contains sporadic grains of orthite
25g	15	50	—	—	10	18	1	6	—	—	37—40	—	—	—	—	—	—	—	1.650	56	
Yamato Mountains																					
501b	—	23	8	33	—	35	—	—	—	0.5	25	1.714	1.690	+57	28	—	—	—	—	—	Contains sporadic grains of zircon
YC-318	—	6.8	42.6	10.1	o.s.	38.6	o.s.	—	—	0.8	20—25	1.710	—	+59	23	—	—	—	—	—	
503	—	15	40	20	1	20	3	—	—	1	20—25	1.720	1.655	+57	37	—	—	—	—	—	As above
YB-253	6.7	41.9	37.3	—	4.1	7.5	0.1	1.8	0.2	0.3	—	—	—	—	—	—	—	—	—	—	Contains 0.1% zircon
YC-307	11.0	9.9	51.5	—	15.0	8.6	0.4	0.3	1.6	1.4	—	—	—	—	—	—	—	—	—	—	Contains 0.3% zircon

* [o.s. = optic sign.]

biotite, and the latter includes relicts of amphibole, plagioclase, ore minerals and quartz. As a rule, plagioclase forms separate lenticular segregations with grains ranging in size from minute particles to 2 mm; this suggests that the transformation of metabasites under amphibolite facies conditions was preceded by blastocataclastic alterations including granulation of plagioclase. In feldspathized varieties, plagioclase is replaced by microcline, which, along with quartz, develops interstitially, but often also forms large metablasts. The ore minerals are fairly uniformly disseminated throughout the rock. They are sometimes overgrown by sphene, indicating their titanomagnetite nature.

Certain pyroxene-free metabasites (ortho-amphibolites) contain 5—12% garnet, apparently due to high-pressure conditions (stress). The refractive index and specific gravity of these garnets suggest that they contain 26—27% grossular, 15—20% pyrope and 54—58% almandine (Table 98). Plagioclase in ortho-amphibolites is represented by oligoclase, An 26—30. Its basicity decreases somewhat in feldspathized specimens to An 23—25. The ferruginosity of clinopyroxene is low (20—28 at.%). The ferruginosity of amphibole — green common hornblende — fluctuates; it is lowest in the feldspathized (18—30 at.%), medium in clinopyroxene-bearing (49 at.%) and high in pyroxene-free varieties (44—70 at.%). It is always higher than the ferruginosity of clinopyroxene. The ferruginosity of biotite is higher than that of amphibole; 28—39 at.% in feldspathized, 56 at.% in clinopyroxene-bearing and 53—73 at.% in pyroxene-free varieties. The low ferruginosity of minerals in feldspathized metabasites could be explained by their high content of magnetite and consequently high oxygen potential; ferruginosity is known to decrease with an increasing oxygen potential /43/.

The following varieties of metabasites can be differentiated in the Sør Rondane Mountains with respect to their mineral composition (Table 98): 1) Metabasites of a relatively low-grade metamorphism; characterized by either a high content of clinopyroxene or the presence of hypersthene relicts, with or without clinopyroxene, low-grade biotitization and a high content of either ore minerals, or sphene and apatite. In places, they have preserved the primary prismatic-granular texture, but are generally largely transformed into a heterogranoblastic texture with poikiloblastic and diablastic elements. The plagioclase contains 26—49% anorthite; the ferruginosities of the colored minerals are 44 at.% for hypersthene, 20—38 at.% for clinopyroxene, 27—67 at.% for hornblende. 2) Metabasites of high-grade amphibolization and biotitization, transformed into typical ortho-amphibolites. They are devoid of clinopyroxene, and their leading colored minerals are biotite and hornblende. Essentially they do not differ in any respect from the ortho-amphibolites of western Queen Maud Land. Their plagioclase contains 24—40% anorthite. The ferruginosity of hornblende is 27—66 at.% and that of biotite, 51—56 at.%. 3) Syenitized metabasites, sometimes linked by gradual transitions with ortho-amphibolites. Some of the varieties contain clinopyroxene relicts. These metabasites have a low content of biotite and always contain quartz, and significant amounts of sphene and apatite. They possess blastocataclastic, inequigranular textures. Plagioclase is distinctly replaced by microcline.

The plagioclase is often represented by albite, An 0—10, and less commonly
by oligoclase, An 10—15. The ferruginosity of relict clinopyroxene is
43 at. %, that of hornblende 32—62 at. % and that of biotite 22 at. %.

In the Yamato Mountains, in addition to ortho-amphibolites that are very
similar to those described above (from the Sør Rondane Mountains and
western Queen Maud Land), syenitized varieties are also present
(Table 98). They fall into two groups. The first group comprises metabasites without quartz. Their leading colored minerals are clinopyroxene
and biotite. The content of amphibole is very low (up to 1%). Feldspars
are concentrated in fine-grained mosaic aggregates. Biotite flakes often
form monomineralic aggregates. Within this lepidogranoblastic matrix,
in which small clinopyroxene grains also occur, larger grains of clinopyroxene form porphyroblasts. Clinopyroxene is intensively replaced by
biotite and some of its large grains by grayish green subalkaline hornblende.
Biotite and hornblende occur as spots in the clinopyroxene. The biotite is
indistinctly oriented. The An content of plagioclase lies within An 20—25.
It exhibits maculose and regular zonation. The ferruginosity of clinopyroxene is 23—37 at. % and that of biotite is 46—58 at. %. K-feldspar is
perthitic without the typical crosshatching. The second group includes quartz
metabasites without clinopyroxene. The colored minerals compose 25%
of the rocks and are represented by hornblende and biotite, the quantitative
ratios of which vary. They exhibit a characteristic complex fine-grained
granoblastic texture with blastocataclastic elements. Quartz occurs in
grains of 0.1—1 mm. Plagioclase, An 21—27, is replaced by K-feldspar and
occurs in grains of 0.1—1 mm diameter with maculose and substitution antiperthites occupying as much as 50 vol. % of grain. K-feldspar is a microcline with 30% perthite of the rod-veinlet type in the central portions of
grains. It penetrates into plagioclase along cracks. Amphibole, represented
by green hornblende, is replaced at its edges and along cracks by bluish
green amphibole and orange biotite. The colored minerals have been considerably altered and partially transformed into aggregates of zoisite,
chlorite and iron hydroxides. Apatite, zircon, ilmenite and sphene are the
common accessory minerals. The latter two are strongly leucoxenized.

The chemical composition of metabasites from the Sør Rondane and
Yamato Mountains is given in Table 99; specimens 512b and 520 represent
amphibolized metabasites with relict structures of the original rocks, while
the remaining specimens exhibit various grades of syenitization. Amphibolized metabasites do not exhibit any significant differences from basalts
and gabbros. Although the syenitized metabasites fall into the same category
of basic and intermediate igneous rocks (based on their content of mafic
components), they nevertheless differ significantly in their higher content
of alkalis and low content of anorthite. The colored minerals of syenitized
metabasites have a higher content of calcium than in ordinary metabasites,
and potassium predominates over sodium in the feldspathic portion of these
rocks. Their silica content is only slightly higher than that in nonmeta-
morphosed gabbros. Only in a few specimens (specimen 221) has granitization reached a very advanced stage; the contents of silica and other
components are similar to those in alkaline-earth granites. Metabasites

TABLE 99. Chemical composition of metabasites from rocks on Queen Maud Land

Specimen No.

Component	512b			520			26g			26			221		
	wt%	at.%	$\frac{R}{Al}$	wt%	at.%	$\frac{R}{Al}$	wt%	at.%	$\frac{R}{Al}$	wt%	at.%	$\frac{R}{Al}$	wt%	at.%	$\frac{R}{Al}$
SiO_2	61.24	57.9	3.27	50.94	47.6	2.80	52.76	50.5	3.35	54.38	51.6	3.48	68.64	64.6	4.09
TiO_2	0.64	0.4	0.02	0.32	0.2	0.01	1.28	0.9	0.06	1.20	0.9	0.06	0.40	0.3	0.02
Al_2O_3	15.86	17.7	1.00	15.50	17.0	1.00	13.47	15.1	1.00	13.27	14.8	1.00	14.29	15.8	1.00
Fe_2O_3	2.79	1.9	0.11	1.52	1.0	0.06	3.13	2.2	0.15	2.43	1.7	0.11	1.37	1.0	0.06
FeO	4.85	3.9	0.22	6.35	4.9	0.29	4.99	4.0	0.26	4.18	3.3	0.22	1.55	1.2	0.08
MnO	0.11	—	—	0.16	0.1	—	0.13	0.1	0.01	0.09	—	—	0.05	—	—
MgO	3.25	4.5	0.25	9.01	12.5	0.74	4.40	6.3	0.47	4.14	5.9	0.40	0.89	1.2	0.08
CaO	6.31	6.4	0.36	11.50	11.5	0.68	7.93	8.1	0.54	7.42	7.5	0.51	2.30	2.3	0.15
Na_2O	3.43	6.3	0.36	2.54	4.6	0.27	2.05	3.8	0.25	2.56	4.7	0.32	2.95	5.4	0.34
K_2O	0.71	0.8	0.05	0.47	0.5	0.03	6.86	8.3	0.55	6.86	8.3	0.56	6.72	8.0	0.51
P_2O_5	0.24	0.2	0.01	0.11	0.1	—	0.91	0.7	0.05	1.61	1.3	0.09	0.29	0.2	0.01
Loss on ignition	0.88	—	—	1.78	—	—	1.00	—	—	1.19	—	—	0.61	—	—
Σ	100.37	100.0	—	100.20	100.0	—	98.91	100.0	—	99.33	100.0	—	100.05	100.0	—
BaO	—	—	—	—	—	—	0.96	—	—	0.85	—	—	—	—	—

TABLE 99 (continued)

Specimen No.

Component	YC-318			YB-253			YC-307			YA-301			YC-238		
	wt%	at,%	R/Al	wt%	at,%	R/Al	wt%	at,%	R/Al	wt%	at,%	R/Al	wt%	at,%	R/Al
SiO_2	50.18	45.2	5.87	52.02	48.0	3.22	59.19	55.0	3.72	55.31	50.1	4.05	55.28	50.4	3.63
TiO_2	1.30	0.8	0.10	1.54	1.1	0.07	1.43	1.0	0.07	0.79	0.5	0.04	1.14	0.8	0.06
Al_2O_3	7.19	7.7	1.00	13.79	14.9	1.00	13.57	14.8	1.00	11.60	12.4	1.00	13.00	13.9	1.00
Fe_2O_3	6.91	4.6	0.60	2.32	1.6	0.11	3.62	2.6	0.18	1.70	1.2	0.10	2.07	1.4	0.10
FeO	6.81	5.1	0.66	5.27	4.0	0.27	3.95	3.1	0.21	6.04	4.6	0.37	5.01	3.9	0.28
MnO	0.18	0.1	0.01	0.12	—	—	0.15	0.1	0.01	0.14	0.1	0.01	0.10	—	—
MgO	9.21	12.4	1.61	5.25	7.2	0.48	2.51	3.4	0.23	6.54	8.8	0.71	6.18	8.3	0.60
CaO	7.48	7.2	0.93	6.91	6.8	0.46	4.44	4.4	0.30	6.56	6.4	0.52	5.77	5.6	0.40
Na_2O	1.89	3.3	0.43	2.64	4.8	0.32	3.06	5.6	0.38	2.55	4.5	0.36	2.94	5.2	0.37
K_2O	6.50	7.7	1.00	6.31	7.4	0.50	6.20	7.4	0.50	6.13	7.1	0.57	5.97	6.9	0.50
P_2O_5	1.36	1.1	0.14	1.10	0.9	0.06	0.92	0.6	0.04	1.06	0.8	0.06	0.89	0.7	0.05
Loss on ignition	0.85	5.1	—	0.53	3.3	—	0.32	2.0	—	0.59	3.5	—	0.48	2.9	—
Σ	99.86	100.0	—	97.80	100.0	—	99.36	100.0	—	99.01	100.0	—	98.83	100.0	—
BaO	—	—	—	—	—	—	—	—	—	—	—	—	—	—	—

TABLE 99 (continued)

Component	Specimen No.									
	512b	520	26g	26	221	YC-318	YB-253	YC-307	YA-301	YC-238
Numerical characteristics (after Zavaritskii)										
a	8.6	6.1	14.4	15.5	15.9	9.2	15.1	15.0	13.9	14.7
b	14.0	29.1	22.8	20.9	5.5	32.0	23.0	15.4	24.7	22.3
c	6.4	7.2	1.8	1.1	1.4	-3.4	1.7	1.1	0.5	1.1
s	71.0	57.6	61.0	62.5	77.2	55.4	60.6	67.8	60.9	61.9
Q	+10.8	-26.1	-29.6	-26.9	+17.1	-11.0	-11.1	+3.1	-6.5	-6.7
f'	50.7	25.3	33.0	29.1	48.8	26.5	30.9	45.1	28.5	28.5
m'	39.9	51.7	32.5	33.3	26.8	46.2	39.4	27.3	42.7	45.7
c'	9.4	23.0	34.5	37.6	24.4	27.3	29.7	27.6	28.8	25.8
Coordinates on the ACF diagram (after Eskola and Korzhinskii)										
A	41.6	29.2	13.6	9.8	33.6	0.0	13.2	15.0	3.9	8.9
C	25.0	28.1	38.0	40.5	32.0	29.2	32.6	33.9	30.8	28.6
F	33.4	42.7	48.4	49.7	34.4	70.8	54.2	51.1	65.3	62.5
Norm, % (after Barth)										
Albite	31.5	23.0	14.9	23.4	26.8	—	18.9	27.9	23.1	26.8
Anorthite	26.4	30.0	7.4	4.6	6.2	—	7.2	5.1	2.3	4.5
Orthoclase	4.0	2.5	41.6	41.3	40.1	38.7	38.4	37.6	36.9	35.7
Olivine	—	5.9	4.1	3.8	—	16.3	8.3	—	8.1	7.4
Hypersthene	12.5	15.1	—	0.6	1.9	23.6	—	4.0	5.1	4.6
Clinopyroxene	3.2	21.3	22.5	18.9	2.9	2.4	16.9	9.8	19.4	15.5
Magnetite	2.9	1.5	3.4	2.6	1.5	1.8	2.4	3.9	1.9	2.2
Ilmenite	0.9	0.4	1.8	1.7	0.6	2.8	2.2	2.1	1.1	1.6
Apatite	0.4	0.3	1.7	3.1	0.6	—	2.3	1.7	2.1	1.7
Quartz	18.2	—	—	—	19.4	0.7	—	7.9	—	—
Nepheline	—	—	2.6	—	—	0.5	3.4	—	—	—
Leucite	—	—	—	—	—	13.2	—	—	—	—
Acmite	—	—	—	—	—	—	—	—	—	—

Note. Modal composition of the rocks is presented in Table 98.

TABLE 100. Mineral composition of agmatite metasome (metabasites) in the eastern mountains of Queen Maud Land

Specimen No.	Mineral composition, vol.%							Characteristics of minerals				
	quartz	plagioclase	K-feldspar	amphibole	biotite	garnet	ore and accessory minerals	An content of plagioclase	biotite n_z	biotite f, at.%	garnet n	garnet f, at.%
Sør Rondane Mountains												
512e	50	42	—	—	4	1	3	23	—	—	1.802	82
520a	20	70	—	—	9	1	3	34	1.651	56	—	—
800a	30	45	12	1	9	—	3	23	—	—	—	—
24a	28	40	30	—	2	—	—	16	—	—	—	—
26b	30	28	40	—	1	—	1	16	1.640	48	—	—
222a	22	30	40	4	1	—	3	17—20	—	—	—	—
Yamato Mountains												
YB=265	24.2	24.1	46.8	—	3.6	—	1.8	—	—	—	—	—
YC=313	31.3	23.2	41.3	—	0.2	—	1.7	28	1.660	63	—	—
YD=333	26.7	21.1	40.1	0.8	10.6	—	0.7	—	—	—	—	—

Note. Amphibole — n_z = 1.686, n_x = 1.669, f = 49 at.%.

TABLE 101. Chemical composition of agmatite metasome (metabasites) in the eastern mountains of Queen Maud Land

Specimen No.

Compo-nent	520a			26b			YB-265			YC-313			YD-333			YA-292		
	wt%	at.%	R/Al	wt%	at.%	R/Al	wt%	at.%	R/Al	wt%	at.%	R/Al	wt%	at.%	R/Al	wt%	at.%	R/Al
SiO_2	72.50	67.9	4.07	74.60	69.4	4.69	72.06	68.0	4.35	71.63	67.7	4.43	70.80	66.0	4.61	59.78	52.6	3.51
TiO_2	0.16	0.1	0.01	0.04	—	—	0.44	0.3	0.02	0.24	0.2	0.01	0.64	0.4	0.03	1.49	1.0	0.07
Al_2O_3	15.21	16.7	1.00	13.52	14.8	1.00	13.97	15.4	1.00	13.76	15.3	1.00	13.04	14.3	1.00	14.49	15.0	1.00
Fe_2O_3	0.54	0.4	0.02	0.86	0.6	0.04	1.12	0.8	0.05	1.39	1.00	0.07	1.10	0.8	0.06	2.16	1.5	0.10
FeO	1.22	1.0	0.06	0.40	0.3	0.02	0.92	0.7	0.05	0.89	0.7	0.05	3.51	2.7	0.19	3.84	3.0	0.20
MnO	0.01	—	—	0.02	—	—	traces	—	—	traces	—	—	0.04	—	—	0.07	—	—
MgO	0.76	1.1	0.07	0.43	0.6	0.04	0.41	0.6	0.04	0.05	—	—	0.64	0.9	0.06	2.74	3.6	0.24
CaO	4.32	4.3	0.26	1.46	1.5	0.10	1.13	1.1	0.07	1.36	1.4	0.09	1.52	1.5	0.10	3.42	3.3	0.22
Na_2O	4.18	7.6	0.46	4.05	7.3	0.49	3.60	6.6	0.43	3.75	6.8	0.44	3.49	6.3	0.54	3.49	5.9	0.39
K_2O	0.71	0.8	0.05	4.49	5.4	0.37	5.36	6.4	0.42	5.51	6.6	0.43	4.20	5.0	0.35	6.47	7.2	0.48
P_2O_5	0.16	0.1	0.01	0.08	0.1	0.01	0.12	0.1	0.01	0.09	0.1	0.01	0.14	0.1	0.01	0.84	0.6	0.04
Loss on ignition	0.30	—	—	0.29	—	—	traces	—	—	0.04	0.2	—	0.31	2.1	—	1.10	6.2	—
Σ	100.07	100.0	—	100.24	100.0	—	99.13	100.0	—	98.71	100.0	—	99.43	100.0	—	99.89	100.0	—

TABLE 101 (continued)

			Specimen No.			
	520a	26g	YB-265	YC-313	YD-333	YA-292
Numerical characteristics (after Zavaritskii)						
a	10.1	14.9	15.3	15.9	13.5	16.9
b	3.1	2.4	2.7	2.6	5.3	13.0
c	5.0	1.2	1.4	1.1	1.8	1.2
s	81.8	81.5	80.6	80.4	79.4	68.9
Q	+40.3	+30.8	+29.2	+27.9	+30.0	+2.8
f'	52.2	47.2	65.0	76.9	79.7	42.2
m'	41.3	30.6	25.0	2.6	20.3	35.4
c'	6.5	22.2	—	20.5	0.0	22.4
a'	—	—	10.0	—	—	—
Coordinates on the ACF diagram (after Eskola and Korzhinskii)						
A	56.4	46.7	50.0	47.5	37.3	16.8
C	29.3	33.3	22.9	35.0	18.1	27.2
T	14.3	20.0	27.1	17.5	44.6	56.0
Norm, % (after Barth)						
Albite	38.0	36.5	33.0	34.0	32.0	31.5
Anorthite	20.5	5.3	4.5	4.8	6.5	5.2
Orthoclase	4.0	27.0	32.0	33.0	25.5	38.5
Orthopyroxene	3.6	0.8	1.2	—	5.6	7.4
Clinopyroxene	—	0.8	—	—	—	5.6
Magnetite	0.6	0.9	1.2	1.5	1.2	2.3
Ilmenite	0.2	—	0.6	0.4	1.0	2.2
Apatite	0.3	0.3	0.3	0.3	0.3	1.7
Quartz	32.7	28.4	26.6	25.6	27.4	5.6
Corundum	0.1	—	0.6	—	0.5	—
Wollastonite	—	—	—	0.4	—	—

Note. Modal composition of the rocks is given in Table 100.

may be contaminated by injective veins in such cases. In conclusion, it must be emphasized that although the metabasites may represent a variety of igneous rocks of the diorite-gabbro series, they are nevertheless inevitably syenitized under the high-alkalinity conditions in the high-grade amphibolite facies.

Tables 100 and 101 describe the metasome of metabasite agmatites. This metasome is essentially a leucocratic biotite-microcline granite, but there are also biotite-garnet plagiogranites and biotite-amphibole quartz syenites.

MINERAL ASSOCIATIONS OF THE
AMPHIBOLITE FACIES

In all regions of the amphibolite facies, there are two main rock groups: amphibolites, including ortho-amphibolites; and biotite plagiogneisses, as a rule migmatized and granitized. Somewhat less widespread are biotite-amphibole plagiogneisses exhibiting a considerably lower grade of granitization. The mineral associations suggest that the biotite-amphibole plagiogneisses and amphibolites are similar and were evidently formed under closely corresponding physicochemical conditions. There are also certain dissimilarities, particularly in the mineral associations of amphibolites which are largely metabasites. The metabasite associations present a great variety with respect to chemical composition, formation time and metamorphism. Amphibolites and biotite-amphibole plagiogneisses free of K-feldspar stand out from the more common rocks in the regions of the Lambert Glacier and the Grearson Oasis. The Grearson Oasis amphibolites are highly basic and escaped feldspathization because of their composition. The widespread occurrence of common brown biotite in the Lambert Glacier amphibolites suggests that they belong to the same facies as the other rocks, particularly since the amphibolites of these two regions are in direct contact with rocks containing an abundance of K-feldspar.

High-alumina rocks are much less widespread within the amphibolite facies formation. They occur in the west of Queen Maud Land, on the Prince Olav Coast and in the Grearson Oasis, where they form thick units together with biotite plagiogneisses. High-alumina rocks occur only sporadically in the Lambert Glacier region. Their comparison with other rocks is made difficult by the inadequate available data. The variety of their mineral associations is dependent not only on the original rock compositions but also on the degree of secondary alteration. Nevertheless, it is possible to trace general features of the amphibolite facies. Carbonate rocks, as well as rocks containing ferromagnesian amphibole, have been discovered in only two crystalline basement regions, on Prince Olav Coast and in the Lambert Glacier region (the latter in the Sør Rondane Mountains and in the west of Queen Maud Land). There is a striking similarity in the mineral associations of carbonate rocks and associated calcareous silicate formations. It is still too early to speak of similarity or dissimilarity in the case of rocks with ferromagnesian minerals, since rocks from the Lambert Glacier have been studied in only a few specimens from a single stratum.

The characteristic mineral associations of the amphibolite facies of the crystalline basement are given below.

The amphibolites are characterized by the following seven mineral associations:

1) $clpy_{20-43}$ + $horn_{18-52}$ + $biot_{22-63}$ + plag $_{0-82}$ + (qz) + (micr) + (act_{30-52});
2) $clpy_{20-37}$ + $biot_{28-53}$ + $plag_{20-25}$ + Kfs + (horn);
3) $clpy_{20-38}$ + $horn_{27-53}$ + $plag_{26-82}$ + (qz) + (act_{30-52});
4) $clpy_{20-28}$ + $horn_{18-30}$ + $biot_{28-39}$ + micr + qz;
5) $clpy_{20-28}$ + $biot_{28-39}$ + micr + qz;
6) $horn_{27-74}$ + $biot_{42-73}$ + $plag_{22-65}$ + (qz) + (gar_{30-73}) + (micr) + (act_{34-55});
7) $horn_{27}$ + biot.

The biotite-amphibole plagiogneisses are characterized by the following two mineral associations:

8) $clpy_{43}$ + $horn_{60}$ + biot + $plag_{25-26}$ + qz;
9) $horn_{54-83}$ + $biot_{52-90}$ + $plag_{23-38}$ + qz + (micr).

The biotite plagiogneisses likewise display two characteristic associations:

10) $biot_{52-60}$ + $plag_{28-37}$ + qz;
11) $biot_{59-72}$ + $plag_{12-37}$ + qz + micr + (horn) + (gar).

Aluminous plagiogneisses and schists are characterized by the following six associations:

12) gar + biot + $plag_{20-40}$ + qz + (micr) + (staur);
13) gar_{87} + $biot_{51}$ + staur + $plag_{30}$ + qz;
14) sill + biot + $plag_{25-30}$ + qz + (micr) + (gar);
15) sill + cord + biot + qz + $(plag_{24-35})$ + (gar) + (musc) + (kyan) + (staur);
16) $cord_{56}$ + $plag_{35-37}$ + biot + qz + (micr) + (gar);
17) kyan + plag + cord + qz + (sill).

The mineral associations of calciphyres consist of the following six groups:

18) calc + dol + dip_{39-60} + $(plag_{29-30})$ + (act) + (biot) + (horn) + (qz);
19) carb + trem + phl;
20) carb + diop + plag + horn;
21) $diop_{30}$ + $(plag_{29-32})$ + (act);
22) $diop_{60}$ + $plag_{27}$ + $horn_{60-73}$;
23) $diop_{60-71}$ + $gros_{88-90}$ + carb + qz + micr + (plag) + (act).

Rocks containing ferromagnesian amphiboles form the following four associations:

24) $cumm_{23}$ + biot;
25) gedrite $(cumm)_{30-51}$ + $horn_{41-44}$ + $biot_{33-63}$ + $plag_{29-94}$ + qz + (gar) + + (cord) + (staur);
26) $gedrite_{38-47}$ + $biot_{31}$ + $plag_{27}$ + qz + (kyan) + (staur) + (musc);
27) $gedrite_{40-43}$ + $biot_{33}$ + staur + qz + $(plag_{55})$ + (horn) + (cord) + (kyan).

The last association is clearly metasomatic.

Using ACF diagrams (Figure 45) and taking into account the real structural relationships of the minerals, these associations were divided into stable and unstable types.

Association 1 is unstable because of the presence of clinopyroxene (Figure 45a). Indeed, this association describes metabasites which have been incompletely recrystallized in the amphibolite facies and in which the clinopyroxene is replaced by hornblende and would disappear upon complete recrystallization. This association must be transformed into association 6. It may also undergo other transformations related to alkaline metasomatism. Thus, association 1 characterizes the transformation of gabbro into the amphibolite facies. The appearance of actinolite in the latter renders its instability certain; the actinolite replaces hornblende. Association 2 is unstable only in the presence of hornblende which replaces clinopyroxene. The presence of common hornblende indicates insufficient alkalinity of the rock. Without the hornblende, this association describes a peculiar subfacies of the amphibolite facies, unusual in its extremely high potassium potential. This association comprises the syenitized gabbros of the Yamato Mountains (Figure 45b). It remains unstable only in the presence of actinolite (replacing hornblende) and characterizes the clinopyroxene-bearing amphibolites of the Sør Rondane Mountains and Prince Olav Coast. The presence of actinolite in the association testifies to the superposition of lower-temperature conditions. Associations 4 and 5 are completely stable (Figure 45a), characterizing certain granitized metabasites in the western part of Queen Maud Land in which plagioclase has been completely replaced by K-feldspar. Association 6 is unstable due to the presence of garnet and/or actinolite. This is the most widespread association, representing the majority of amphibolites in all crystalline basement regions. The presence of reaction garnet indicates a transition to the high-pressure subfacies: thus an + biot = gar + horn. Actinolite indicates the same as in associations 1 and 3. Association 7 is stable and describes the Grearson Oasis amphibolites. Association 8 is unstable because of the presence of clinopyroxene and is close to association 1; it differs from the latter in persistent presence of quartz and the absence of microcline and actinolite. This association occurs, though rarely, in the biotite-amphibole plagiogneisses of the Sør Rondane Mountains. Association 9 is stable and characterizes an overwhelming majority of the biotite-amphibole plagiogneisses. It is close to association 6. Associations 10 and 11 are completely stable (Figure 45a). The former belong to biotite plagiogneisses and the latter to their granitized varieties and migmatite metasomes. Association 11 may also be unstable, due to the coexisting hornblende and garnet.

Associations 12 and 13 are unstable in the presence of staurolite, the appearance of which suggests a transition to a lower-temperature subfacies. In association 12, the staurolite obviously developed as a secondary mineral (Prince Olav Coast). The situation with association 13 is more complicated, because biotite can replace almandine, completely or partially. If the staurolite is recognized as a primary mineral, as is also seen from the rock texture, the instability will be controlled by the presence of either biotite or garnet. The amphibolite facies in the staurolite stage is distinguished by wide variations in hydration, and this is consequently the explanation for the instability of the almandine-biotite paragenesis. This also applies, however, to other rocks containing both biotite and garnet, which is

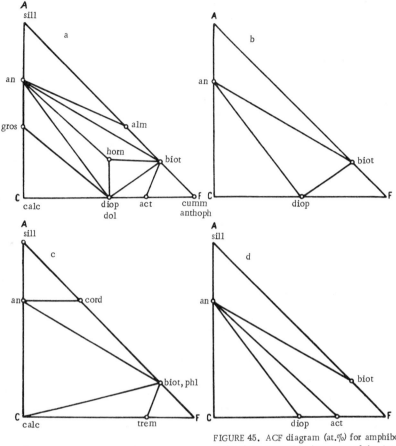

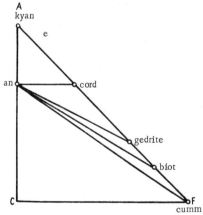

FIGURE 45. ACF diagram (at.%) for amphibolite facies rocks of the crystalline basement of the Antarctic Platform. Additional phases are quartz and microcline. The diagrams show stable mineral associations controlled by the composition of rocks:

a) amphibolites, metabasites, biotite-amphibole plagiogneisses and shadow granites, biotite plagiogneisses and shadow granites, garnet-biotite plagiogneisses and shadow granites, sillimanite-garnet plagiogneisses, schists and their migmatites, grossular and diopside calciphyres, marbles, diopside and diopside-plagioclase rocks, biotite-cummingtonite amphibolites; b) syenitized metabasites; c) sillimanite-cordierite and cordierite-biotite plagiogneisses, schists and their granitized varieties, tremolite-calcite-phlogopite rocks; d) sillimanite-biotite plagiogneisses, schists and their feldspathized varieties, diopside-amphibole rocks; e) kyanite-cordierite-plagioclase quartzites, gedrite-biotite-quartz-plagioclase rocks.

why the interrelationships between these minerals are often found to be reactive. The instability, however, can also be explained by the activity of potassium. A stable paragenesis of staurolite with garnet and plagioclase is shown in Figure 47. Association 14 is unstable (Figure 45d) only in the presence of garnet, while association 15 (Figure 45c) is extremely unstable, as is also denoted by complex textures of the rock. Its existence is due to the low activity of alkalis, with cordierite crystallizing in place of biotite or almandine. The instability of association 15 is also enhanced by the appearance of secondary, lower-temperature muscovite, kyanite and staurolite.

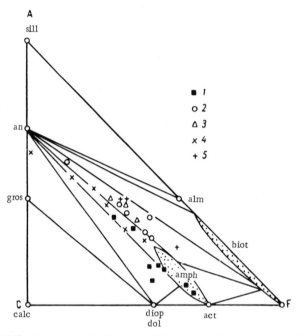

FIGURE 46. Paragenetic ACF diagram (at.%) for amphibolite facies rocks (sillimanite-almandine subfacies), with quartz and microcline as additional phases. The symbols indicate the compositions of analyzed rocks. The composition fields of amphibole and biotite are marked approximately, according to the literature /68/.

1) metabasites; 2) amphibolites; 3) biotite-amphibole plagiogneisses; 4) shadow biotite-amphibole granites; 5) shadow biotite granites and migmatite metasomes.

Association 16 may be unstable only in the presence of garnet (Figure 45c), and association 17 in the presence of sillimanite (Figure 45e). The mineral associations of marbles and calciphyres (18 and 20) are not stable in the presence of actinolite, biotite and hornblende (Figure 45a, b). Association 19 cannot exist in the presence of two carbonates. It probably formed under conditions approaching those of contact metamorphism, and this also applies

to the associations cord + biot + an and sill + cord + an (located together in
Figure 45c). Associations 21 and 22 are stable (Figure 45a, d), while association 23 is unstable in the presence of plagioclase and amphibole (Figure 45a, e). All the other associations are unstable, with the exception of
association 24. The formation of such associations is related, as was
demonstrated by Eskola /91/, to specific conditions of ferromagnesian
metasomatism. Therefore, hornblende in paragenesis with ferromagnesian
amphibole is unstable in the presence of plagioclase and biotite. The
mineral association becomes stable without hornblende, but is superimposed
by the lower-temperature kyanite, staurolite and muscovite.

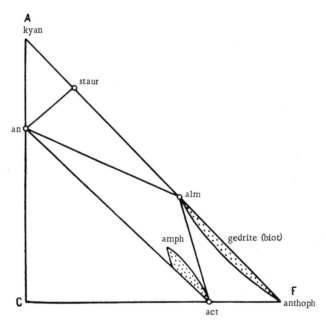

FIGURE 47. Paragenetic ACF diagram (at.%) for amphibolite facies rocks
(staurolite-kyanite subfacies), with SiO_2 as an additional phase. The
composition fields of amphibole and biotite are marked approximately,
according to the literature /68/.

The two real principal subfacies of the amphibolite facies that can be
distinguished on the basis of the stability of mineral associations in the
crystalline basement /68/ are the lower-temperature upper staurolite-
kyanite subfacies (Figure 47) and the high-temperature lower sillimanite-
almandine subfacies (Figure 46). The two subfacies can then be differentiat
ed by the extensive occurrence of ultrametamorphic processes in the
lower zone of the amphibolite facies, resulting in an abundance of shadow

microcline granites, providing satisfactory markers for the mapping of the occurrence of rocks of these subfacies. However, it is rather difficult to locate the sillimanite isograd because of the relatively limited occurrence of sillimanite-bearing rocks. Muscovite pegmatites are often genetically related to metamorphics of the staurolite-kyanite subfacies /10, 63/, and the occurrence of rocks of this subfacies can be mapped by means of these pegmatites. The majority of the regions of exposed crystalline basement of the amphibolite facies are rocks of the sillimanite-almandine subfacies. To date, the primary staurolite-kyanite subfacies has been established only for the region of the Lambert Glacier; however, even in that location, the determination is somewhat arbitrary because of the lack of sufficient observations. In contrast, the superposition of this subfacies on the sillimanite-almandine subfacies is distinctly observed on Prince Olav Coast and in western Queen Maud Land near the Penck Trough. Signs of super-position of lower-temperature associations are also observed in other regions with rocks of the sillimanite-almandine subfacies, including the secondary development of actinolite from hornblende and diopside, and the appearance of significant (up to 7%) amounts of epidote and muscovite. However, these minerals occur in many subfacies and consequently it is at present impossible to determine the subfacies to which they belong.

The paragenetic ACF diagrams (Figures 46 and 47) reflect real and possible parageneses of the amphibolite facies in the crystalline basement of the Antarctic Platform. When marked on the diagram, the available chemical analyses of rocks of the sillimanite-almandine subfacies fall precisely in the required paragenetic triangles, providing a reliable proof of the accuracy of the paragenetic diagram. To this diagram, it would be possible to add three other diagrams describing certain particular condi-tions in the sillimanite-almandine subfacies, including high alkalinity, high pressure (stress), and ferromagnesian metasomatism. The diagram of the staurolite-kyanite subfacies could be supplemented in the same way. How-ever, these particular parageneses have already been depicted in the ACF diagrams. Moreover, at present there are insufficient data for a more de-tailed differentiation of the amphibole facies of the crystalline basement of the Antarctic Platform.

Chapter V

FORMATION OF INTRUSIVE AND APOINTRUSIVE CHARNOCKITOIDS

Rocks of the charnockitoid family occurring in the crystalline basement of the Antarctic Platform are more extensive than all the other intrusive rocks combined. At present, the authors are aware of dozens of massifs of these rock types "saturating" the crystalline basement from Queen Maud Land to Adélie Land (0—145°E), over a distance of more than 7000 km.

The five most characteristic features of the intrusive charnockitoids in Antarctica are as follows: 1) occurrence in blocks of the Upper Archean composed of metamorphic rocks of the granulite facies which were, however, affected by subsequent stages of regional metamorphism and ultra-metamorphism under the amphibolite facies conditions; 2) spatial and, probably, genetic relation to intrusions of the gabbro-anorthosite group; 3) occurrence in zones of maximum tectonic activation of the crystalline basement; 4) formation of an overwhelming majority of the charnockitoids during periods of Proterozoic activations, i. e., Lower Proterozoic according to geological data, and at the Cambrian-Precambrian boundary according to absolute dating; 5) extensive variations in the size of intrusions, ranging from tens to several thousands of kilometers.

Charnockite intrusions were encountered and investigated with varying degrees of thoroughness in the following regions of East Antarctica (from west to east): 1) central Queen Maud Land (4—10°E); 2) Humboldt Mountains and Petermann Range on Queen Maud Land (11—13°E); 3) Enderby Land (45—56°E); 4) Mac-Robertson Land (60—70°E); 5) mountains surrounding the Amery Ice Shelf (67—73°E); 6) Vestfold Oasis on Ingrid Christensen Coast (78—79°E); 7) around the Mirny Observatory on Pravda Coast (93°E); 8) in the vicinity of Denman Glacier on Queen Maud Land (96—99°E); 9) Bunger Oasis on Knox Coast (100—102°E); 10) Windmill Islands off Budd Coast and in Grearson Oasis (110—111°E); 11) on islands in Henry Bay at the boundary of Sabrina and Banzare coasts (121°E).

Charnockites described within the metamorphic complex of Adélie Land have been compared by Beller /84/ with analogous rocks in South India. Although he does not describe their mode of occurrence, he mentions their apparently metamorphic genesis. Therefore, such charnockites may be regarded as ultrametagenic, but not intrusive.

The most detailed studies of charnockitic intrusions have been carried out in the vicinity of Mirny Observatory, in the Bunger Oasis, the Humboldt Mountains and Petermann Range, with geological surveys on scales of

1 : 10,000, 1 : 100,000 and 1 : 200,000, respectively. Geological mapping on a
scale of 1 : 1,000,000 was carried out on Queen Maud Land and Enderby
Land, and reconnaissance surveys were made in all other regions. The
charnockitic intrusions at Mirny and in the Bunger Oasis have been
described in detail in the monograph on the Precambrian in East Antarctica
/57/, in which only a brief description is given of the intrusions of the
Humboldt Mountains and Petermann Range, investigated in 1967. A comparison of the charnockitic intrusions which have been studied in detail will
permit the elucidation of the principal modes of formation of the intrusive
charnockitoids in East Antarctica.

INTRUSIONS OF THE HUMBOLDT MOUNTAINS
AND PETERMANN RANGE

The only massif in the northern part of the Humboldt Mountains lies
within Mount Insel and Mount Eck-Hörner, with an area of some 50 km².
As far as is known, the Petermann Range comprises two massifs respectively composing the Krasovskii Range (with Mount Shvedov and Mount Curie)
and the Zavaritskii Range. These may, however, prove to be a single
massif separated by an ice-filled mountain valley, 5—6 km wide. The
Krasovskii Massif has an area of some 200 km²; its fringes are separated
from the main massif by glacier valleys, 3—4 km wide. The Zavaritskii
Massif has an area over 100 km². However, if the two massifs should prove
to be a single body, then the total area must exceed 500 km², since in this
case a significant part of the massif would be under ice. Contacts with the
most migmatized and granitized schists are very rare and have therefore
been investigated only at a few points. Because of the nature of the exposures, the only direct contact that could be studied in detail was that in the
SE portion of Mount Eck-Hörner. Therefore the shape of massifs and their
mode of occurrence have not yet been accurately established but can only
be assumed from indirect data. Thus, the Eck-Hörner Massif has an
irregular domed shape and variable, mainly steep, bedding. Its line of
contact is always discordant with respect to the rocks into which it intrudes,
although the dip of the migmatites is similar to that of the contact planes
of the massif. The dip of contact planes is 70—80°, whereas the dip of the
host rocks varies from 45 to 70°. When the dip of the host rocks is 18—35°,
the dip of the contact plane is 40°, and the strike differs from that of the
host rocks by 30—40°. It is difficult to appraise the shape of the Krasovskii
and Zavaritskii massifs, since a considerable portion of these massifs is
concealed under a thick ice cover. On the whole, this massif also has a
dome shape but is considerably extended in a N-S direction at an angle of
40° relative to the strike of the host rocks. The eastern edge of the
Zavaritskii Massif, where it is in contact with metamorphosed anorthosites,
contains numerous anorthosite blocks of 5—200 m and larger, accounting
for at least 20% of the total mass of the marginal portions of the massif.
The exposures at the edge of the massif have the appearance of a giant

eruptive breccias. When the blocks of anorthosites reach a length of 1.5—
2 km along the strike, they alternate in a chaotic fashion with blocks of the
massif.

The massifs under consideration exhibit a wide range of rock compositions ranging from gabbroids to granitoids; only the acid varieties can be
designated as charnockites proper. Actually, the composition of rocks in
these massifs is so unusual that it is difficult to find the proper designation
for them in the existing classifications. With respect to their mineral
parageneses, they are the closest to charnockites and charnockitoid rocks,
whereas in their composition and ratios of chemical elements they form a
complex gamut of rocks ranging from gabbroids to low-grade feldspathization to subalkaline granitoids. The intermediate varieties correspond to
diorite-syenites and even syenites. As a rule, different rock varieties
alternate randomly, forming gradual transitions. Homogeneous areas in
various parts of the massif are formed only by the more acid varieties.
Intrusive contacts between different varieties were not observed anywhere
in the numerous exposures. Therefore, nonsimultaneous intrusions are
precluded. An exception is presented by anorthosites closely associated
with charnockite intrusions. They occur within the latter in the form of
tectonic blocks or xenoliths having the appearance of eruptive breccias. The
anorthosites do not form gradual transitions to the charnockite rocks. There are
two younger bodies of biotite-amphibolite granitoids, one of them with an
area of 15—20 km^2 crosscutting the Zavaritskii Massif, while the other, with an
area of 6 km^2, occurs within schists on the Bardin Range. Smaller granitoid
bodies have been encountered in the SW portion of the Eck-Hörner Massif
in anorthosites.

In view of the mineral composition of intrusive rocks in the Humboldt
Mountains and Petermann Range and their ratios of chemical elements,
they may be arbitrarily classified into the following groups: 1) anorthosites,
occurring within charnockitoids in tectonic blocks and xenoliths; 2) charnockitoids, subdivided into norites and gabbro-norites (metamorphosed),
gabbro-norite-diorite (feldspathized), diorite-syenites, syenites and granosyenites; 3) granitoid bodies cross-cutting the charnockitoids. The
differentiation of charnockitoids is arbitrary because of distinct transitions between nearly all varieties. The designations of the rocks are also
arbitrary, because the gabbro-norite and gabbro-diorite underwent metamorphism and various grades of feldspathization, and therefore cannot be
regarded as normal representatives of basic rocks. The formation of the
diorite-syenites, syenites and granosyenites was related to an intensification
in the grade of metamorphism and feldspathization of the same gabbroids,
resulting in a continuous series of rocks from gabbro-norites to granosyenites.

The presence of the charnockitoid series from gabbro-norites to granosyenites and the separation of the anorthosites are confirmed by the highly
varying compositions of the rocks in numerous exposures. The following
are some examples: a) an isolated rock at the SE edge of Mount Curie, not
over 0.5 km long and 200 m high (exposure 34), is composed of gabbroids
of a high metamorphic grade transformed into gabbro-diorites, diorite-
syenites and even syenites; b) a rock on the southern margin of Krasovskii

Range (exposure 38) is composed of very indistinctly separated grano-syenites and syenites; c) a rock at the SE tip of the Krasovskii Range (exposure 44) is composed mainly of syenites with considerable admixture of diffuse granosyenites which become more numerous toward the west (exposure 57); d) in the SE part of the Eck-Hörner Massif (exposure 575), gabbroids (norites) of a high metamorphic grade, transformed mainly into diorite-syenites, are in contact with porphyroblastic granosyenites. Although this contact is established by different colors of the rocks, no influences of one rock on the other have been observed; e) on the western slope of the Eck-Hörner Massif (exposure 57), there is a complex alternation of meta-morphosed anorthosites and feldspathized norites and diorite-syenites. It has the appearance of dike-like bodies of norite, 20—25 m thick, within the anorthosites; however, there is, in fact, a rhythmic banding, the anorthosite layers having a very low grade of feldspathization, while metanorites are transformed into diorite-syenite rocks; f) several exposures on the NE slope (543, 541, etc.) and spurs of the western slope, close to the center of the Zavaritskii Massif (exposures 586 and 587), are composed of biotite-amphibole granitoids, containing preserved blocks of metamorphosed anorthosites. The latter underwent blasto-metamorphism and deoxidation of plagioclase and are slightly feldspathized. In this case, it is apparent that the anorthosites are only slightly granitized even when they occur within intrusive bodies of granitoids.

Unusual fayalite-bearing plagiogranites, as yet encountered only on Mount Shvedov, may prove to be very rare ultimate products of the granitization of anorthosites, although the latter do not regularly lend themselves to graniti-zation.

Anorthosites

As early as 1961, a massif of anorthosites exposed over an area of at least 900 km^2 in the Wohlthat Mountains, 5—6 km east of the Petermann Range, was discovered. Isolated low rocky exposures of anorthosites were discovered in a glacier valley between this massif and the Zavaritskii charnockite massif. The anorthosite massif itself has already been described /58/. It is composed mostly of anorthosites containing 95—98% labradorite with an admixture of ortho- and clinopyroxenes as well as accessory minerals, which include magnetite, quartz, hornblende, etc., totaling 1—2%. The marginal facies of the massifs differ significantly from anorthosites of the central facies; their composition approaches that of norites and gabbro-norites, since they contain 10—30% ortho- and clinopyroxenes as well as 10—30% secondary minerals (quartz, K-feldspar, garnet, biotite and hornblende). The metamorphosed anorthosites described below occur mainly in blocks and xenoliths in the Zavaritskii charnockite massif. In the Eck-Hörner Massif, anorthosites of this kind are concentrated in the SW portion, where they alternate with metamorphosed norites. They differ from the Wohlthat Massif anorthosites in their somewhat higher grades of feldspathization and silicification, in the variable composition of plagioclase (ranging from acid andesine to labradorite), and a considerably higher content of secondary minerals (biotite, garnet and amphibole), which, in places, completely replace the pyroxenes. Although they exhibit distinct signs of metamorphism, the anorthosites have been preserved better than all other basic rocks in the region, in spite of being located within strongly granitized formations.

The anorthosites, exhibiting different grades of metamorphism, are generally variegated pale gray and grayish olive and display a complex combination of superimposed and relict structures and textures, further complicated by ubiquitous cataclasis. They exhibit banded, gneissic and augen structures depending on the arrangement of primary and especially secondary colored minerals. The latter are concentrated in banded and maculose aggregates or may be uniformly disseminated throughout the rock and, in this case, are linearly oriented. The texture of the anorthosites is a complex combination of prismatic-granular with porphyrogranoblastic and cataclastic elements (Figure 48). Besides cataclastized and fractured prismatic plagioclase laths, ranging in size from 2 to 8 mm, there are also granoblastic aggregates with grains of 0.1—0.5 mm. Within the latter, the plagioclase laths assume the habit of porphyroblasts. As a rule, the colored minerals form intricate aggregates ranging from a few mm to 20 cm which contain unusual schlieren of secondary hornblende, in places rimmed with crystalline garnet. Relict pyroxenes are present as xeno-blastic and skeletal grains. The larger orthopyroxene grains (up to 1 mm) are frequently surrounded by clinopyroxene or contain clinopyroxene ingrowths.

The composition (Table 102) of the majority of anorthosites is distinguished by a predominance of labradorite (80—95%) over all the other minerals. These include the pyroxenes (0—10%), as well as amphibole plus biotite (5—15%). Varieties approaching gabbro-norite-anorthosites contain andesine-labradorite (55—70%), while the colored minerals, besides the pyroxenes (0—15%), are represented by amphibole plus biotite (10—30%), and in places also by garnet (1—4%, rarely more). K-feldspar makes up 1—15% of the rock, but is often absent. Quartz is more widespread but in smaller amounts (1—9%). The range of accessory minerals is rather limited; in addition to the ore minerals, sphene and apatite are fairly common. The latter are more abundant in metamorphosed and feldspathized varieties, and locally contain fluorite.

The metamorphism of anorthosites is characterized by two processes: 1) development of amphibole and biotite (in places, of garnet), especially in varieties approaching gabbro-norite-anorthosites, and 2) feldspathization and silicification, common phenomena in blocks of anorthosites occurring within granitoids; in places, the anorthosites are also enriched in fluorite. The composition of plagioclase in the rocks under consideration varies from An 28 to 53. Pyroxenes and clinopyroxenes contain 56—62 and 35—60%, respectively, of the ferruginous components; the ferruginosity of hornblende is 34—58%, rising above 70% and up to 85% in feldspathized varieties. Along with relatively rare phlogopites, there are biotites with ferruginosities of

TABLE 102. Metamorphosed anorthosites

Specimen No.	K-feldspar	plagioclase	quartz	orthopyroxene	clinopyroxene	hornblende	biotite	ore mineral	apatite	zircon	sphene	garnet	orthite	An content of plagioclase	opx n_z	opx n_x	opx f,at.%	cpx n_z	cpx n_x	cpx f,at.%	hbl n_z	hbl n_x	hbl f,at.%	biotite $n_z - n_y$	biotite f,at.%	garnet n	garnet specific gravity	garnet almandine,%	Remarks
																													(Composition / Characteristics of minerals)
55a	—	90	—	8	10	5	2	—	o.s.	—	—	2	—	47—50	1.736	1.720	56	1.727	1.699	50	1.687	1.665	50	1.638	43	1.785		64	
56	—	80	—	—	5	—	—	1	—	—	—	—	—	48—50															
244v	—	82	1	—	—	2	1	2	—	—	1	7	—	39—41															
246	—	94	—	2	1	3	—	2	o.s.	—	—	—	—	51															
247	—	96	1	—	—	—	—	1	—	—	—	—	—	50—53															
247a	—	95	—	—	—	—	1	—	—	—	—	—	o.s.	53															
543e	7	85	—	—	6	3	4	1	—	—	1	—	—	50							1.674	1.648	38	1.645	49				Muscovite, 1%
545*	1	78	—	—	5	3	3	3	*	o.s.,**	—	—	—	50—52							1.693	1.671	58	1.630	36				
546*	1	85	—	—	1	—	1	2	*	—	—	—	—	50—53				1.716	1.690	35	1.676	1.650	39	1.662	64				
546d	—	96	5	—	—	1	—	1	—	—	—	—	—	50	1.738	1.722	58	1.724	1.698	47				1.648	52				
547	—	95	2	—	—	5	3	—	o.s.	—	1	—	—	57							1.685	1.662	48	1.612	17				Fluorite, 2%
548	—	93	—	—	—	12	2	1	—	—	—	—	—	50							1.685	1.662	48	1.660	62				
548a	—	86	2	—	—	—	3	3	—	—	2	—	—	51—53							1.668	1.642	34	1.614	20				
548zh	—	85	3	—	—	—	2	2	—	—	—	—	—	46—48										1.614	20				
549	1	95	1	—	—	1	—	2	o.s.	—	o.s.	18	—	50							1.719	1.696	85	1.612	17				
586d*	4	90	2	—	—	—	—	1	2	—	—	2	—	28—33	1.742	1.726	62				1.712	1.686	78	1.628	34				
578*	9	83	4	3	—	19	—	2	1	—	—	1	—	42	1.738	1.722	58				1.714	1.689	80	1.687	87				
576*	15	67	2	6	—	7	14	7	1	—	—	—	—	46							1.713	1.688	79	1.687	87				
577*	—	56	5	—	—	—	5	3	1	—	—	1	—	34	1.744	1.728	63	1.732	1.705	60	1.707	1.685	72	1.678	78				
53a	—	59	2	8	10	—	—	3	2	—	—	—	—	35—39	1.742	1.726	62	1.729	1.705	54	1.718	1.695	83	1.658	60	1.792, 1.799		72	Fluorite, 1%
53b	—	60	1	—	—	10	—	2	1	—	—	—	—	32—37							1.701	1.677	64	1.680	80	1.792, 1.799		72	
244	—	69	—	8	6	28	—	2	—	—	—	1	—	36							1.689	1.666	53	1.676	76				
244b	—	54	8	—	—	10	22	3	2	—	—	1	—	47—50										1.668	69	1.793		70	
541b	—	54	6	—	—	28	6	2	—	—	—	4	—											1.640	45	1.785, 1.803		72	

* The asterisk indicates specimens for which chemical analyses were performed.

** [o.s. = optic sign.]

52—69% and micas (approaching annites) with ferruginosities reaching 87%.
As a rule, the ferruginosity of colored minerals increases in anorthosite
blocks occurring within granitoids, probably due to the high alkalinity of the
environment in which the metamorphism of anorthosites took place. Only
the composition of garnets (in the anorthosite) remains more or less constant, with 70—72% (seldom less) of the almandine molecule, indicating
stability of its formation conditions. Garnets occur in anorthosites that
have been silicified but not feldspathized. The presence of garnet in
anorthosites which underwent high-grade metamorphism indicates their
formation at a certain stage of metamorphism: this would occur only in
high-alumina rocks in which the formation of alkaline feldspars essentially
does not take place under conditions of alkaline metamorphism.

FIGURE 48. Anorthosite (thin section 577, × 8, crossed nicols).

The wide range of variations in the composition of the majority of primary and secondary minerals in the anorthosites attests to a nonuniformity of metamorphism, which was undoubtedly superimposed and probably related to the formation of charnockitic rocks. However, on the whole, the chemical composition of anorthosites varies relatively little (Table 117). Thus, the silica content fluctuates from 52 to 57%, always slightly above its content in normal anorthosites (50%*). This is due to the silicification of the Petermann Range anorthosites. An even more characteristic feature of the group is its high content of alumina (22—27%) in comparison to all the other intrusive rocks in the region. This is very close to the alumina content in average anorthosites (28%). This provides still another indication of the inertness of alumina during metamorphism. The content of iron is subject to considerable variations, 0.5—2% Fe_2O_3 and 1—4.5% FeO, and is nearly always higher than in the average anorthosites (1.1% each for FeO and Fe_2O_3). On the other hand, the calcium content of the Antarctic anorthosites is always lower (8—10% CaO) than in average anorthosites (12.5%) due to the deanorthitization of plagioclase in the course of metamorphism. The same process is also responsible for the high content of alkalis (4—5.5% Na_2O, 1—2.3% K_2O), which is always higher than in the normal anorthosites (3.7% Na_2O, 0.7% K_2O). Hence, the change in the chemical composition of the rocks in question was, in general, not very drastic, notwithstanding the variable, though mainly high grade of metamorphism of the anorthosites. This metamorphism affected not only the structural characteristics of the rocks but also the compositions of the major rock-forming minerals (higher ferruginosity of pyroxenes, lower An content in plagioclase, development of secondary amphibole and biotite), and caused local feldspathization and silicification. The changes did not produce any new group of rocks, unlike the situation with gabbroids which are closely related to the anorthosites genetically and in their time of formation.

Charnockitoids

Metamorphosed gabbroids have been preserved only as relicts among anorthosites and diorite-syenites. In the former case, they form dike-like zones, 10—20 m wide, or less distinct small bodies in anorthosites, which "protected" them against granitization (more precisely syenitization). Larger bodies in diorite-syenites have been transformed into syenite-diorites, diffuse relicts of which are preserved at their contact with granosyenites.

The composition of the gabbroids is the closest to metamorphosed (slightly feldspathized and silicified) norite and gabbro-norite, with sparsely distributed pyroxenite schlieren (Figure 49). As a rule, they are represented by coarse- and medium-grained rocks, dark brownish gray

---

* The average chemical composition of rocks under consideration is compared with the average chemical composition of the major igneous rocks according to Tyrrel /23/.

FIGURE 49. Norite. Not distinct euhedral plagioclase (thin section 578g,
× 11, crossed nicols).

in color. The gabbro-norites in places show gradual transitions to
anorthosites; the latter are enriched in colored minerals. The structure
of metamorphosed gabbroids is most commonly maculose, less commonly
banded, depending on the arrangement of schlieren and banded aggregates
of colored minerals. It is affected by distinct cataclasis and blastosis.
The texture is most commonly heterogranoblastic with relicts of a gabbroic
texture. One of the most interesting elements of the primary texture of
the rocks are vermicular ingrowths of hypersthene permeating plagioclase
laths. Another characteristic feature is exsolution lamellae of clinopyroxene in orthopyroxene. The lamellar structure of pyroxenes is
affected by superimposed recrystallization resulting in allotriomorphogranular textures; the larger hypersthene grains are associated with
irregular inclusions of augite which also surround the hypersthene. In
the latter case, the ferruginosity of orthopyroxene increases considerably,

and hypersthenes of different ferruginosities coexist even within a single specimen. The rock texture is porphyroclastic, due to cataclasis; porphyroclasts consist of broken and corroded elongated prismatic plagioclase laths ranging in size from 3 mm to 1.5 cm. The colored minerals usually occur in fine-grained glomero-aggregates with irregular and skeletal grains of pyroxenes, 0.3—4 mm in size. The smaller grains formed due to fracturing. Xenoblastic amphibole granules and irregular biotite flakes replace the pyroxenes, relics of which occur ubiquitously within these secondary aggregates. A distinct recrystallization of the entire rock, with a profusion of K-feldspar ingrowths in the plagioclase laths, corroding the plagioclase grains and sometimes replacing them entirely, occurs locally. Quartz fills cracks in other minerals; together with late orthoclase, it heals traces of cataclasis. Furthermore, quartz forms serrated granules in recrystallized plagioclase aggregates.

The mineralogical composition of these gabbroids is unusual (Table 103). Plagioclase (andesine and labradorite) accounts for 40—70 vol.% of the rocks, but in some cases its content drops to 15%, reflecting transitions to anorthosites on the one hand and to pyroxenites on the other. The pyroxenes account for 20—35%, the content of orthopyroxene being considerably higher than that of clinopyroxene. Amphibole and biotite do not account for more than 5—10 vol.% of rocks, with rare exceptions. The content of ore is distinctly higher (5—12%) than in anorthosites; according to chemical analyses it is represented by titanomagnetite. A characteristic feature of these rocks is the nearly ubiquitous presence of K-feldspar and quartz, although in very moderate amounts (1—8 and 1—5%, respectively), as well as the high content of apatite (up to 3%). The composition of individual minerals vividly illustrates the difference between the rocks in question and average gabbros. Plagioclase ranges in composition from An 37 to An 66. Plagioclases with different contents of anorthite are frequently encountered within a single specimen, the relict laths being represented by An 48—50, while the recrystallized, smaller grains are represented by An 37. The ferruginosity of orthopyroxenes is considerably increased, 53—64% (even higher in exceptional cases) as compared to the ferruginosity of average gabbronorites, which is 35—40%. The same applies to clinopyroxenes. The ferruginosity of secondary colored minerals is, as a rule, also fairly high; 55—68% for hornblende, 60—71% for biotite (reduced to 30% or increased to 85% in rare cases).

The appearance of fayalite in the gabbroids under consideration deserves special attention. In this paragenesis, which is rare for such rocks, the fayalite coexists with a highly ferruginous clinopyroxene (86%), while orthopyroxene becomes unstable and occurs in small and sporadic relicts of high ferruginosity (72%). Fayalite, which is absent in anorthosites, first appears in metagabbroids, but then its contents increase and it occurs in nearly all other varieties of the charnockitoid series.

The unusual mineral composition of metagabbroids is reflected in the chemical analyses (Table 117), although on the whole they belong to rocks of the basic series. Thus, the silica content varies from 44 to 48%, as compared to 48% for the average composition of gabbro. The content of

TABLE 103. Metamorphosed gabbroids

Composition

Specimen No.	K-feldspar	plagioclase	quartz	fayalite	orthopyroxene	clinopyroxene	hornblende	biotite	ore mineral	apatite	zircon	sphene	garnet	orthite	An content of plagioclase
544*	1	55	2	—	24	4	3	3	5	3	—	—	—	—	50
548v	—	65	—	—	8	7	2	5	7	4	—	—	2	—	52¹ and 38²
575g	8	48	—	—	32	2	2	3	5	o.s.**	—	—	—	—	37—39
575d*	—	55	—	—	1	1	24	11	5	3	—	—	—	—	41
575e	6	16	—	—	68	4	1	2	9	o.s.	—	—	—	—	40—41
575zh	—	40	1	8	1	36	3	—	5	2	—	—	—	—	37
576a	—	63	—	—	13	—	2	8	12	—	—	—	—	—	66
578b	3	60	2	—	17	1	2	4	8	3	—	—	—	—	41—45
578v	3	52	2	—	20	2	2	6	10	3	—	—	—	—	41—42
578g*	2	49	2	—	23	2	2	5	12	3	—	—	—	—	55
586g	2	70	3	—	19	—	2	1	3	o.s.	—	—	—	—	48¹ 37²

Characteristics of minerals

Specimen No.	fayalite n_z	fayalite n_x	fayalite content, %	ortho-pyroxene n_z	ortho-pyroxene n_x	ortho-pyroxene f, at.%	clino-pyroxene n_z	clino-pyroxene n_x	clino-pyroxene f, at.%	hornblende n_z	hornblende n_x	hornblende f, at.%	biotite $n_z = n_y$	biotite f, at.%	Remarks
544*				1.731	1.716	53	1.722	1.695	42				1.662	64	
548v															¹laths ²small grains
575g				1.745	1.729	64	1.730	1.706	56				1.685	85	
575d*				1.732	1.717	54				1.678	1.654		1.665	66	
575e				1.733	1.717	55	1.726	1.702	49	1.602	1.668	55			
575zh	1.850	1.801	87	1.756	1.738	72	1.749	1.721	86						
576a				1.741	1.725	62									
578b				1.736	1.720	57				1.701	1.677	66	1.657	60	
578v				1.733	1.717	55				1.696	1.673	58	1.665	66	
578g*				1.737	1.721	58	1.721	1.696	41	1.702	1.680	68	1.668	69	
586g													1.670 / 1.625	71 / 31	¹laths ²small grains

* Chemical analysis.

** [o.s. = optic sign.]

alumina is low, 13—17% (nearly 18% in average gabbro). The iron content (Fe_2O_3) in the ore minerals is nearly the same as in average gabbro; however, the titanium content is several times higher (4—6% TiO_2) than in average gabbros (1% TiO_2). At the same time, there is a marked increase in the content of iron (FeO) in the colored minerals; 10—14% in the metagabbroids as compared to only 6% in the average gabbros. On the other hand, the calcium content of rocks under consideration is low; 8—9% CaO as compared to 11% in the average gabbros. This is due to the deanorthitization of plagioclase during metamorphism. The content of alkalis in metagabbroids remains nearly unchanged, otherwise they would not have retained their basic composition. However, the metamorphism involves a redistribution of the alkalis, resulting in the appearance of small amounts of orthoclase and biotite. Biotite is absent from associations with fayalite, which is possible under conditions of completely mobile behavior of the alkalis during the metamorphism of the gabbroids. At the same time, appearance of fayalite in the metagabbroids indicates that these rocks are related to all other rocks of the charnockite series, where fayalite is one of the typomorphic minerals. The high P_2O_5 content in the gabbroids, averaging 2%, as compared to not over 0.3% in the average gabbroids, should be noted. This also indicates the participation of volatile components along with highly mobile alkalis during metamorphism.

Thus, the comparatively rare "islands" of gabbroids preserved mainly within anorthosites and diorite-syenites carry distinct signs of recrystallization under conditions of alkaline metasomatism, investing the rocks with an unusual mineral composition. They have therefore all been designated as metamorphosed gabbroids, although the term might not be very appropriate, since the rocks essentially underwent an initial stage of granitization or, more precisely, charnockitization. All the other rocks in the charnockitoid series are likewise metamorphosed (syenitized) gabbroids. However, these processes were so intensive that they resulted in rocks that are qualitatively different from the original gabbroids. Therefore, in further discussion, they will not be collectively termed metamorphosed (granitized) gabbroids, which would be quite correct genetically, but will be designated according to their composition, which is closest (although never quite identical) to the corresponding intrusive rocks. This is the only approach to a differentiation of the continuous rock series, permitting an understanding of the essential nature of the mineralogical and chemical transformations undergone by these rocks in the course of regional metamorphism and related ultrametamorphism. At the same time, relict structural-mineralogical elements of the parent gabbroids can be traced in the majority of rocks, however markedly different from the original rocks.

Gabbro-norite-diorites (feldspathized) are very similar to the foregoing group of rocks. They were somewhat more strongly affected by granitization processes, which are scarcely traceable in the gabbroids. Rocks of both groups occur in the same exposures without distinct contacts. This is particularly in evidence in the SE tip of Mt. Curie. The gabbro-norite-diorites are more widespread than gabbro-norite in the massifs of the Petermann Range. The adopted designation of the group is rather arbitrary, because normal intrusive magmatic rocks characterized by an association of ortho- and clinopyroxenes with hornblende and biotite do not occur in nature. The group under consideration combines the minerals of gabbro-norites (pyroxenes) and diorites (hornblende); moreover, the chemical composition of these rocks is intermediate between gabbros and diorites. However, these rocks are similar to neither. Furthermore, the rocks contain quartz and K-feldspar in quantities that are unusual for either diorites or, especially, gabbros.

FIGURE 50. Cataclastized, feldspathized gabbro-norite-diorite with characteristic fine symplektitic aggregates of hornblende and quartz (thin section 36b, × 11, crossed nicols).

Feldspathized gabbro-norite-diorites are represented by medium- and coarse-grained rocks of dark brownish gray color. Their complex texture may, on the whole, be described as porphyrogranoblastic, since the prismatic grains of plagioclase (3—7 mm) and less abundant elongated prismatic pyroxene grains (2—4 mm) occur in a fine-grained (up to 1.5 mm) grano-blastic matrix consisting of the same minerals with the addition of xeno-blastic amphibole grains and biotite flakes (Figure 50). The latter, however, occasionally reach a length of 5—7 mm, acquiring the habit of porphyroblasts. In places, the prismatic plagioclase grains and the pyroxenes form areas with a typical gabbroid texture, separated by grano-blastic aggregates produced by the recrystallization of the larger crystals. K-feldspar penetrates cracks of minerals, often entirely replacing several prismatic plagioclase laths, resulting in large isometric grains of the K-feldspar, 7—8 mm in size. These contain relicts of the plagioclase laths. Quartz heals cracks and forms grains of a variety of sizes; in places, these are fractured into mosaic aggregates. Thus, the rock, with well-preserved textural relicts of gabbroids, underwent cataclasis and recrystallization, resulting in a finer-grained texture. Certain of the preserved minerals appear as porphyroblasts. However, the recrystallization also produced true porphyroblasts represented by K-feldspar and biotite.

The mineralogical composition of the gabbro-norite-diorites displays the following characteristic features (Table 104): a) stable composition of plagioclase represented by andesine, An 35—40 (with rare and insignificant variations) — it composes some 50—60% of the rock; b) significantly lower content of pyroxenes (2—20%) and higher content of amphibole plus biotite (20—40%); the former are considerably more abundant than the latter; c) stable contents of K-feldspar and quartz, 10—15%.

These features distinguish the rocks in question from metamorphosed gabbroids, in which the plagioclase composition varies over a range of ± An 30, and the quantitative ratio of primary pyroxenes to secondary biotites plus amphiboles is reversed, while K-feldspar and quartz occur only sporadically and in very limited amounts. A common feature of both groups of rocks is the relatively high ferruginosity of their colored minerals; this is highest in fayalite-bearing rocks, which are as scarce in this group as in the foregoing group. The content of apatite remains high (2—3%). It should be noted that titanomagnetite (locally together with sphene) and apatite are the only accessory minerals in these rocks. The chemical composition of the rocks (Table 117) exhibits elements of both diorites and gabbros. The content of silica is 51—55%, which is uncharacteristic of either diorites or gabbros. The content of alumina is 13—16%, and in this respect, the rocks are reminiscent of the diorites. On the other hand, the FeO content is 8—10%, much higher than in diorites and even in gabbros. The content of MgO is 3—5%, much closer to diorites than to gabbros. The rocks contain 6—7% CaO as do the diorites. The Na_2O content (2.5—3.0%) corresponds to the diorites, while the content of K_2O (2—3%) is somewhat higher than in the diorites and considerably higher than in the gabbros. On the whole, the chemical composition of the rocks in question approaches the diorites, but they have a very high content of iron in the colored minerals and of potassium in the feldspars.

Diorite-syenites are among the most widespread varieties in the granitized gabbroid series under consideration. They compose most of Mount Eck-Horner, the SE spur of Mount Curie, almost the entire Shvedov

TABLE 104. Gabbro-norite-diorites (feldspathized)

Specimen No.	Composition															Characteristics of minerals														Remarks
	K-feldspar	plagioclase	quartz	fayalite	orthopyroxene	clinopyroxene	hornblende	biotite	ore mineral	apatite	zircon	sphene	garnet	orthite	An content of plagioclase	fayalite n_z	fayalite n_x	fayalite content, %	ortho-pyroxene n_z	ortho-pyroxene n_x	ortho-pyroxene ferrugi-nosity, %	clino-pyroxene n_z	clino-pyroxene n_x	clino-pyroxene ferrugi-nosity, %	hornblende n_z	hornblende n_x	hornblende ferrugi-nosity, %	biotite $n_y = n_y$	biotite ferrugi-nosity, %	
34e	4	50	6	—	—	—	28	10	2	1	—	—	—	—	37										1.708	1.682	71	1.678	78	
34z	5	50	4	—	—	—	28	10	2	—	—	—	—	—	37										1.674	1.648	39			
36b*	1	52	7	—	—	—	12	20	3	1	—	3	—	—	28—35										1.694	1.670	57	1.660	62	
228*	9	68	3	—	9	2	—	3	4	2	—	—	—	—	40				1.736	1.720	57	1.725	1.700	48				1.684	84	
228zh*	7	61	4	—	6	1	10	6	3	2	—	—	—	—	32—36				1.741	1.725	62	1.730	1.706	56	1.701	1.674	66	1.674	74	
228z*	9	55	5	—	4	2	11	8	4	2	o.s.**	—	—	—	33				1.752	1.735	70	1.736	1.711	66	1.706	1.680	70	1.682	82	
229	8	50	7	—	1	1	20	15	2	1	—	—	—	—	34				1.750	1.734	68	1.734	1.710	63	1.704	1.679	69	1.680	80	
811*	3	50	8	7	—	2	20	—	2	—	—	—	—	—	40	1.862	1.812	94				1.718	1.694	38	1.686	1.664	49	1.660	61	Specimens 811, 823 and 836 are from Ravich's collection of 1961 /58/
823*	10	45	5	—	12	8	10	10	10	—	—	—	—	—	39				1.736	1.720	57	1.725	1.700	48				1.660	61	
836*	10	40	8	—	20	5	5	2	5	—	—	—	—	—	36															

* Chemical analysis.
** [o.s. = optic sign.]

Mountains and the southern extremities of the Krasovskii and Zavaritskii Ranges. All previously described groups of gabbroids also occur in these areas, forming gradual transitions with the diorite-syenite. It is thus difficult to distinguish between them in outcrop.

FIGURE 51. Diorite-syenite, heterocatablastic texture (thin section 546v, x 8, crossed nicols).

The diorite-syenite is represented by medium- and coarse-grained dark brown rocks. Their textures are very complex: relict gabbro textures, up to prismatic-granular, with superimposed metablasts due to cataclasis and feldspathization (Figure 51). The structure is massive, because such processes obliterate the banded nature of the parent gabbroids, rendering the rocks more homogeneous. This results in porphyrogranoblastic rocks in which the porphyroblasts consist of both relict plagioclase laths and more abundant newly formed K-feldspar. The former are deformed prismatic laths 3—7 mm in size, and the latter are irregular metablastic segregations 2—5 mm in size (sporadically reaching a length of 1 cm). Rare prismatic grains of pyroxene are up to 5—6 mm in length. These also resemble porphyroblasts, but are much less commonly preserved than the plagioclase. Large grains and laths of different minerals (including K-feldspar) account for 30—60 vol.% of the rocks. They are embedded in a relatively fine-grained fractured groundmass (0.5—2 mm) containing a profusion of quartz granules and intricate veinlets of K-feldspar. The plagioclases are subeuhedral but the pyroxenes are less satisfactorily preserved; partly replaced by secondary minerals thus acquiring skeletal forms. The pyroxenes are complexly interrelated; clinopyroxene forms numerous ingrowths in orthopyroxene, and the former often replaces the latter. Both pyroxenes have been replaced and rimmed by irregular segregations of amphiboles. Some amphibole laths, up to 5 mm long, also have the habit of porphyroblasts, with poikiloblastic quartz inclusions. Elongated prismatic plagioclase laths are often broken, producing small fragments (0.5—1 mm), slightly shifted with reference to one another. Their interstices are filled with quartz and amphibole. In general, amphibole forms aggregates with the less disturbed plagioclase laths. The aggregates are often accompanied by the deanorthitization of the plagioclase. Large grains of orthopyroxene on the whole preserve the relict prismatic forms, but they are replaced by ore minerals along cracks and are overgrown by amphibole around the edges. Some grains are permeated by fine flakes of biotite. Large K-feldspar segregations exhibit both well-crystallized forms and very intricate outlines; as a rule, they are represented by untwinned microperthites, only rarely with indistinct microcline crosshatching. Their edges contain numerous myrmekitic ingrowths and inclusions of small grains of plagioclase and even pyroxene. Undoubtedly, K-feldspar and quartz crystallize in the last stage, even after the cataclasis. The very complex combinations of textures (primary magmatic, cataclastic and metasomatic) with remarkable inequigranularity, suggest that their mineral associations originated at different depths and conditions. This, together with other features, precludes a normal magmatic genesis of these rocks.

The complex texture of diorite-syenites corresponds to their complex mineral composition (Table 105). A notable feature is the combination of microcline with andesine. Their combined contents in the rocks total 50—75% (individual contents are 20—60% and 15—50%, respectively). The content of feldspars is extremely variable; that of quartz is small and practically constant (3—8%). The composition of plagioclase varies from An 23 to An 40; even within the diffuse-zoned laths, the margins differ from the center by ±An 3—10. The content of the albite molecule (principally due to perthite ingrowths) in the K-feldspar is nearly constant, 27—28%. Associations of colored minerals, their contents varying significantly, are equally unusual for normal magmatic rocks. There are 2—22% (more commonly up to 10%) orthopyroxene, 1—27% clinopyroxene, 1—17% hornblende, and 1—5% biotite, depending on the content of pyroxenes which it replaces. Fayalite has been discovered in a few specimens, but in an association without orthopyroxene and with a maximum ferruginosity of

TABLE 105. Diorite-syenites

Specimen No.	K-feldspar	plagioclase	quartz	fayalite	orthopyroxene	clinopyroxene	hornblende	biotite	ore mineral	apatite	zircon	sphene	garnet	orthite	An content of plagioclase	fayalite n_z	fayalite n_x	content of fayalite, %	opx n_z	opx n_x	opx ferrug-nosity, %	cpx n_z	cpx n_x	cpx ferrug-nosity, at.%	hbl n_z	hbl n_x	hbl ferrug-nosity, at.%	bt $n_z=n_y$	bt ferrug-nosity, at.%	Remarks
36v*	36	35	4	—	5	—	15	1	2	2	o.s.**	—	—	—	40	—	—	—	1.752	1.735	70				1.708	1.682	71	1.680	80	
36g*	40	25	5	—	9	2	8	5	3	2	—	1	—	—	30—37	—	—	—	1.752	1.735	70				1.708	1.682	71	1.674	74	
59	35	40	3	3	3	4	14	—	1	—	—	—	—	—	30	1.855	1.806	89	1.769	1.750	84	1.735	1.710	64	1.715	1.689	80			The rock is close to syenites
93*	46	28	2	—	—	14	2	—	4	1	—	—	—	—	29							1.746	1.721	80	1.715	1.689	80			
228e*	40	33	6	—	2	1	13	2	2	1	—	—	—	—	32				1.754	1.737	72	1.736	1.711	66	1.709	1.683	72	1.682	82	Fluorite, 2%; $n = 1.434$; orthite, $n = 1.735$
249*	48	22	4	—	2	—	17	5	2	1	—	—	—	—	33				1.758	1.741	74				1.708	1.682	71	1.677	77	
546v*	45	25	8	—	—	—	10	4	2	—	—	—	—	4	23—24										1.723	1.698	91	1.685	85	
575b	24	23	3	—	12	28	5	—	5	—	—	—	—	—	40				1.754	1.737	72	1.755	1.730	95						
575v	24	46	—	—	22	2	1	—	4	1	—	—	—	—	33—37				1.742	1.726	63	1.752	1.726	90						Xenotime, 1%
575i	35	20	4	—	—	27	8	—	5	—	—	—	—	—	39—40							1.743	1.715	78	1.706	1.682	70			
578d	60	16	5	6	2	8	13	2	5	2	—	—	—	—	34—37	1.865	1.815	94				1.756	1.730	97	1.724	1.700	91	1.686	86	
592			4	—	—	9	2	—	3	—	—	—	—	—	25—27															The rock is close to syenites
592a*	20	51	4	—	10	4	5	—	4	2	—	—	—	—	30				1.757	1.739	74				1.708	1.682	71			
807*	40	28	5	—	8	1	13	2	3	—	—	—	—	—	32				1.753	1.740	71				1.709	1.683	72	1.680	80	From Ravich's collection

* Chemical analysis.

** [o.s. = optic sign.]

other colored minerals; 91—97% for the coexisting fayalite, hedenbergite and hastingsite. Generally, the ferruginosities of all colored minerals in the diorite-syenites are very high in comparison to other varieties of the rock series in question and only slightly lower than those noted for syenites; 70—84% for orthopyroxene, 64—97% for clinopyroxene, 71—91% for hornblende and 77—86% for biotite. Such high ferruginosities indicate a high alkalinity of the environment in which the rocks were formed. This alkalinity is also responsible for the coexistence of pyroxenes with amphibole and biotite, which generally belong to different mineral facies.

A noteworthy feature is the composition of the accessory minerals in the diorite-syenites. For the first time, orthite and fluorite occur along with the apatite, whereas the content of ore minerals (2—5%) decreases appreciably in comparison to the gabbroids. They are also dominated by titanomagnetite, in places occurring together with sphene. A characteristic feature is the absence of zircon and garnet; while the former appears in more acid varieties, the latter is generally unstable in this rock series.

The chemical composition of the syenite-diorites (Table 117) reflects their mineral composition and exhibits features that are characteristic of both the diorites and syenites. The content of iron in the syenite-diorite is even higher than in gabbroids, and it has no analogs among the normal magmatic rocks. The rocks in question contain 55—60% silica, which falls within the diorite-to-syenite SiO_2 range or even slightly exceeds it. On the other hand, the content of alumina (13—16%) is somewhat lower than its content in either diorites or syenites. The content of Fe_2O_3 (2—3%) does not exceed its content in the rocks under comparison, but the content of FeO, 8—9% (5% in leucocratic varieties), is considerably higher than the FeO content in the colored minerals not only of diorites and syenites, but even gabbros. At the same time, the content of MgO (1—2.5%) is lower, not only in comparison to the normal diorites (4.4%), but even relative to syenites (3.1%); this low MgO content, along with a high iron content, is a characteristic feature of the syenite-diorites, distinguishing them from any magmatic formations. The content of CaO (4.5—6%) is intermediate between diorites and syenites, and the same also applies to Na_2O (3—3.5%). However, the content of K_2O (3.5—5%) is considerably closer to the syenite than to the diorite. On the whole, the chemical composition of the syenite-diorites is close to the diorites and syenites in elements whose contents are nearly equal in both rock types (except, as stated above, for potassium).

Syenites form gradual transitions to diorite-syenites and occur together with them in the same rock exposures, although in smaller quantities.

The syenites also form a gradual transition to granosyenites, occurring together with the latter in exposures located at the contact of granosyenites with more basic rocks of the series under consideration. The syenites are represented by medium-grained porphyroblastic rocks of a characteristic brown color, as a rule lighter than the syenite-diorites. The rock structure is generally massive, but gneissic and in places maculose structures, due to heavy cataclasis and partial blastesis, also occur. Their texture is porphyroblastic with a granoblastic matrix (Figure 52). Relicts of the original matrix textures have been poorly preserved; they occur only as

FIGURE 52. Cataclastized biotite-amphibole syenite with porphyroblastic texture (thin section 44g, × 8, crossed nicols).

sporadic prismatic plagioclase (laths with profuse myrmekitic ingrowths
along their edges). However, there is a considerable predominance of
newly formed K-feldspar porphyroblasts, usually amounting to at least
one half of the volume of the rock. The textural pattern of the rocks is controlled by the prismatic and equigranular grains of K-feldspar, usually
5—6 mm in size but occasionally up to 1.5—2 cm. These are embedded
in a relatively fine-grained, recrystallized granoblastic mass, with grains
of 1.5—2.5 mm. The K-feldspar porphyroblasts often exhibit simple twins
and, less commonly, microcline crosshatching. In places, they contain a
profusion of poikiloblastic inclusions of plagioclase and quartz, 0.2—0.5 mm
in size, as well as fine perthite ingrowths. The matrix is dominated by
granoblastic aggregates of plagioclase, quartz and K-feldspar. Only small

TABLE 106. Syenites

Specimen No.	Composition															Characteristics of minerals													
	K-feldspar	plagioclase	quartz	fayalite	orthopyroxene	clinopyroxene	hornblende	biotite	ore mineral	apatite	zircon	sphene	garnet	orthite	An content of plagioclase	fayalite n_z	fayalite n_x	content of fayalite %	ortho-pyroxene n_z	ortho-pyroxene n_x	ferruginosity at%	clino-pyroxene n_z	clino-pyroxene n_x	ferruginosity at%	hornblende n_z	hornblende n_x	ferruginosity at%	biotite $n_z=n_y$	ferruginosity at%
38v	75	15	5	—	1	2	1	—	1	o.s.**	o.s.	—	—	—	29				1.769	1.750	84	1.746	1.721	80	1.715	1.690	80		
38b	87	5	4	1	—	—	1	1	1	•	—	—	—	—	27	1.855	1.806	89											
38v	78	7	8	1	—	—	2	2	2	•	—	—	—	—	27	1.865	1.815	94											
44*	71	11	4	—	—	—	10	3	1	—	o.s.	—	—	—	25										1.715	1.690	80	1.668	69
44a*	67	10	3	—	—	—	12	7	1	o.s.	•	—	—	—	25										1.720	1.695	87	1.691	90
44b	65	10	8	—	—	—	9	10	1	•	—	—	—	—	26										1.720	1.695	87	1.692	91
44v*	73	6	4	—	—	—	5	7	1	—	o.s.	—	—	—	27										1.720	1.694	87	1.692	91
44g*	62	14	8	—	—	—	8	1	—	—	—	—	—	—	28										1.720	1.695	89	1.692	91
70r	81	4	1	—	2	2	—	3	1	1	—	—	—	—	28							1.751	1.726	89	1.722	1.697	100	1.694	93
231b	73	6	4	—	1	—	12	3	2	1	o.s.	—	—	—	29										1.726	1.702	77		
231v	73	7	5	1	—	1	10	—	1	—	o.s.	—	—	—	28—32										1.711	1.686	80		
283*	76	15	4	—	—	—	2	4	1	1	o.s.	—	—	o.s.	30										1.715	1.690		1.678	78
283b*	70	15	3	—	—	—	6	2	1	o.s.	•	—	—	1	24—27													1.687	86
283v	75	16	4	—	—	—	2	2	1	—	—	—	—	—															
593	75	10	8	—	—	—	3	2	1	—	•	—	—	—											1.727	1.705	100	1.695	

Note: Orthite: $n_z = 1.775$; $n_x = 1.765$.

* Chemical analysis.

** [o. s. = optic sign.]

amounts of relict pyroxene and fayalite have been preserved. These are embedded in an aggregate of xenoblastic amphibole grains permeated by biotite flakes. The amphibole grains are often diablastic due to abundant inclusions of pyroxene and quartz. In places, prismatic amphibole grains reach 6 mm in size, where they assume the habit of porphyroblasts.

The mineral composition of the syenites differs markedly from that of the previously described rock groups (Table 106). In the first place, they are relatively leucocratic, and K-feldspar predominates considerably over all the other minerals combined, accounting for 62—87 vol.% of the rock. The content of plagioclase is only 10—15% and it is represented by a more acid variety (An 25—30) than in the above-described rocks. The syenites have a constant, though small quartz content (3—8%), and therefore may be termed quartzose. Clinopyroxenes and orthopyroxenes are highly ferruginous (80—90%) and have only been preserved in rare specimens; the content of either one does not exceed 1—2%. The contents of fayalite (ferruginosity, 86—94%) is also insignificant (1%). In contrast, highly ferruginous hornblende (ferruginosity, 80—100%) and biotite (ferruginosity, 86—93%) are ubiquitous; their contents are extremely variable (1—12% and 1—10%, respectively). The remarkably high ferruginosity of the colored minerals and the paragenesis of ferrosilite with hedenbergite, hastingsite and lepidomelane are among the most characteristic features of these syenites, testifying to the high alkalinity of the environment in which they were formed. Fayalite continues to coexist with hedenbergite but does not occur in paragenesis with ferrosilite, since the latter becomes unstable under highly alkaline conditions and is replaced by fayalite. Significantly, in a few cases, the ferruginosity of fayalite fluctuates even within a single specimen, indicating its nonequilibrium state. A characteristic feature of the accessory minerals in the syenites is the considerably reduced amount of ore segregations and apatite. On the other hand, the rocks often contain small crystalline grains of zircon and orthite.

The chemical composition of the syenites (Table 117) fully reflects their mineralogy and is the closest to the average syenites, although with the following two essential differences: a) a very high content of K_2O, 5—8%, as compared to up to 5% in the average syenite, and b) a very high content of iron in colored minerals, 6.5—7% FeO, decreasing to 3% in leucocratic varieties, as compared to not over 3% in the average syenites. These features are interrelated; the high ferruginosity of the colored minerals is only possible at a high potassium potential. The content of magnesium in the same minerals is rather low (1% MgO), due to their high iron content. In the average syenites, their MgO content is at least 3%. The silicification of the rocks results in a somewhat higher silica content (60—62%) than in the average syenites (58—59%). On the other hand, their Na_2O content (3—4%) corresponds to the average syenites (3.5%). The same applies to CaO, 3—4%, its content in the average syenites reaching up to 4.5%. Although the content of alumina in the syenites varies from 15 to 18%, its mean content corresponds to that for the average syenites, 16.5%.

Granosyenites differ from all the foregoing charnockitized rocks in their very coarse-grained texture due to prismatic K-feldspar crystals, 2—5 cm in size, accounting for $^1/_3$—$^1/_2$ of the volume of the rock. The granosyenites mainly compose the central portions of massifs, although they often form a direct contact with the host migmatized and granitized schists; e. g., in the north of the Eck-Hörner Massif and in the west of the Krasovskii Massif. The line of contact with the finer-grained charnockitoids is locally fairly distinct. However, they often form gradual transitions to syenites and diorite-syenites; their apparent separation as an individual unit is merely due to the presence of abundant and very large feldspar porphyroblasts. These impart to the rocks a habit that does not fit the common terminology; they are thus termed "giant-grained." The granosyenites are divided into light brown and light pinkish gray varieties, the former being somewhat finer-grained and with a smaller content of porphyroblasts than the latter. They also differ in their mineral compositions. The brown varieties sometimes contain pyroxene and almost always fayalite, whereas the gray varieties are devoid of these minerals. The color is apparently related to the degree of oxidation; the rocks are rendered light brown by a thin film of hydrated iron oxides developing predominantly in the pyroxene-fayalite granosyenites. The light gray color is found in rocks in which the colored minerals are limited to amphibole and biotite. Characteristically, the light gray and brown granosyenites alternate in the same exposure. In places, they are separated by a fairly distinct boundary traceable over hundreds of meters (Figure 53). This tends to complicate field work, since the boundary is often treated as a plane separating two rock types. More often, however, the two varieties form a complex pattern of very coarse pseudo-agmatites, possibly due to a nonuniform oxidation of the rocks along fissures.

FIGURE 53. Contact of light gray and brown granosyenites. The rock is 175 m high, exposure 33.

Granosyenites are represented by massive porphyroblastic rocks (Figure 54) of a very complex texture, due to a combination of its different elements. Formally it can be termed porphyro- or heterogranoblastic, with glomeroblastic concentrations of colored minerals (Figure 55); it actually consists of large (2—3 cm) porphyroblasts of K-feldspar embedded in a heterogeneous matrix consisting of: a) concentrations of prismatic laths of myrmekitized plagioclase, 2—4 mm in size, which are cataclastized and corroded by fine-grained quartz — K-feldspar segregations. The laths are probably relicts of the original matrix textures; b) fine-grained (0.3— 0.7 mm) granoblastic areas of plagioclase and quartz which are products of cataclasis and partial recrystallization of coarser-grained areas; c) glomeroblastic concentrations of amphibole and biotite in which are embedded xenomorphic, sometimes skeletal, granules of pyroxene and fayalite (0.3—1 mm). The textures are complicated by the following factors: presence of relict prismatic plagioclase laths, up to 2 cm long and 4—5 mm across, broken and packed with quartz ingrowths (porphyroblastic appearance); newly-formed, large (4—5 mm) amphibole laths with eroded rims, and euhedral quartz (3—7 mm) with the habit of porphyroblasts; inequigranular recrystallized areas composed of plagioclase grains and colored minerals which are xenoblastic and interpenetrating.

FIGURE 54. Porphyroblastic granosyenite with tail-like relicts of pyroxene amphibolites, exposure 31

Obviously, such textures, combining relict elements of basic intrusive magmatic rocks with corrosive-metasomatic elements and newly-formed porphyroblasts all complicated by cataclasis and blastesis, must belong to rocks of a very complex genesis.

FIGURE 55. Porphyroblastic granosyenite (thin section 31b, x 8,
crossed nicols)

K-feldspar porphyroblasts are represented by prismatic laths with
ragged boundaries. They are somewhat cataclastized. Simple twins occur
everywhere, while microcline crosshatching appears locally. Fused quartz
granules and relict plagioclase granules (0.5—0.8 mm), forming as much as
10—15% of the rock, are embedded in the porphyroblasts. Much less
common are poikiloblastic inclusions of irregular K-feldspar granules,
variously oriented within the host mineral of identical composition. The
presence of the two K-feldspar generations indicates a later formation of
the porphyroblasts. There is a profusion of microperthite ingrowths,
amounting to 5—30 vol.% of the host mineral. Myrmekite occurs ubiquitously at the contact of microperthite with plagioclase. These features suggest
fairly high-temperature formation conditions of the porphyroblasts:
>600°C. The colored minerals, as a rule, form glomero-aggregates, non-
uniformly disseminated through the rock. The principal component of

these aggregates is hornblende, occurring in prismatic grains with irregular outlines (1—3 mm). Symplektitic aggregates of amphibole with quartz are fairly common. Smaller relict granules of pyroxenes exhibiting ragged outlines, or locally, skeletal shapes, are embedded ubiquitously in the amphibole grains. Fayalite occurs in larger grains (up to 1 mm), and is often replaced along cracks by iron hydroxides and iddingsite. Biotite forms flakes with ragged outlines containing inclusions of accessory minerals, mainly zircon and orthite. It does not contain inclusions of pyroxene or fayalite, and it intersects all other colored minerals; it thus formed late. The colored minerals were undoubtedly formed in the following two stages: 1) pyroxene and somewhat later fayalite; 2) hornblende and biotite. The pyroxenes are intensively replaced by amphibole and, moreover, recrystallization under highly alkaline conditions rendered them highly ferruginous and sometimes also unstable; in the latter case, they are replaced by fayalites. The recrystallization process is completed by a total disappearance of the pyroxenes and fayalite; the rocks become hornblendic, lose their charnockitic elements and are converted to ordinary biotite-hornblende granosyenites. In order to emphasize the presence of a later cataclasis, it is worth noting the presence of narrow fracture zones in the granosyenites; these serve locally for the penetration of quartz and apatite veinlets. The granosyenites in these zones are shattered into small fragments cemented by a mylonite matrix. Fragments, 1—3 mm in size, are most commonly represented by individual minerals and less commonly by their aggregates, while the amount of fragments is nearly equal to the volume of the mylonitic matrix. The cracks in these cataclasites have been healed by carbonate veinlets.

The mineral composition of the granosyenites is very heterogeneous (Table 107); they are often composed of different colored minerals which occur in highly variable amounts. There are two varieties: 1) pyroxene-bearing and fayalite-bearing biotite-amphibole granosyenites; 2) biotite-amphibole granosyenites proper. The distribution of these varieties is not consistent, and they often occur in the same exposures. Nevertheless, the pyroxene-fayalite varieties are somewhat concentrated in the zones of transition between gabbroic-dioritic rocks and granosyenites. The content of salic minerals in these varieties is extremely variable, irrespective of their contents of colored minerals. This is especially characteristic in the case of K-feldspar, the content of which fluctuates from 30—70%. The content of plagioclase is 5—35%, and that of quartz is 10—20%. The composition of plagioclase is fairly stable, An 22—32 (most commonly, An 27—28). This is the most acid plagioclase in the charnockitoid series. Fayalite is present in approximately one-third of the investigated specimens to the extent of 1—4% (usually 3%). The pyroxenes have been much more rarely preserved; locally from 1 to 6%, but more often they are represented by sporadic relict granules. Nearly all the specimens contain 1—15% amphibole and 2—10% biotite, the content of the latter increasing in the varieties with a smaller amphibole content. The ferruginosities of all colored minerals are very high (not lower than those in syenites). Thus, the ferruginosity of fayalite is 93—94%, of orthopyroxene 81—84%, of clinopyroxene 77—95%, of hornblende 81—94% and of biotite 73—96%. A few specimens contain biotite of two generations, and in such cases the later generation, represented by fine flakes, is a magnesian variety (ferruginosity only 37%).

The high ferruginosity of colored minerals indicates that the grano-syenites are allied to diorite-syenite and syenite with respect to genesis. The range of accessory minerals is very characteristic. The ore minerals are again represented only by titanomagnetite (1—2%). Sphene appears in places, and its content may reach 3%. The content of apatite is moderate, up to 1%, and zircon crystallites occur fairly often in biotite. Orthite (up to 3%) and fluorite(1—4%) occur locally. Orthite and fluorite are especially characteristic of the granosyenites, signifying the appearance of a new association of accessory minerals which is almost unknown from other rocks in the series under consideration. Fluorite is represented by small (0.5 mm) irregular granules, variegated violet in color. The orthite is orange-brown, with small irregular grains (0.5—0.8 mm) occurring in close association with amphibole; a black rim of radioactive decay products forms on the latter's boundary.

It must be emphasized that of all rocks in the gabbroid-granitoid series, the fayalitic varieties of granosyenites are closest to charnockites. Compared with the foregoing groups, the granosyenites possess several very characteristic features distinguishing them from the other rocks of the series under consideration: a) fairly uniform concentrations, composing over one-half of the area of intrusive massifs; b) maximum quartz content along with alkalinity of feldspars; thus K-feldspar dominates over all the other minerals combined, while plagioclase assumes a relict nature and has the most acid composition; c) although they have a low content of colored minerals in comparison to the other rocks, they contain ubiquitous amphibole and biotite together with sporadic pyroxene and fayalite having the highest ferruginosities. Generally the pyroxenes are represented in porphyroblastic granosyenites only by relict granules, since they are intensively replaced by amphibole and especially biotite during the formation of these rocks; d) variable composition of the rock-forming minerals, mainly depending on the degree of development of K-feldspar porphyroblasts. These impart unique textures to the rock; e) specific association of accessory minerals, containing significant amounts of orthite and fluorite, in addition to the common apatite and zircon.

All these features are possibly a reflection of the formation conditions of this group of rocks, although it is genetically related to other varieties of the gabbroid-granitoid series.

The chemical composition of granosyenites (Table 117) reflects their mineral composition. The rock occupies an intermediate position between the average granodiorite and syenite (but closer to the former), although the contents of iron in the colored minerals and of potassium in the feldspars remains higher in the granosyenites. They contain nearly the same amount of silica (65—67%) as do the average granodiorites (66%), and 14—15.5% alumina as compared to about 15% in the average granodiorites. The granosyenites contain 2—5% ferrous iron (usually 4—5%) as compared to not over 3% in the average granodiorites and syenites. The MgO content

TABLE 107. Granosyenites

Specimen No.	K-feldspar	plagioclase	quartz	fayalite	orthopyroxene	clinopyroxene	hornblende	biotite	ore mineral	apatite	zircon	sphene	garnet	orthite	An content of plagioclase	n_z	n_x	content of fayalite, %
316*	48	15	20	3	—	—	8	4	1	o.s.†	o.s.	1	—	—	30	1.865	1.815	94
33	67	5	21	—	—	—	4	2	1	„	—	—	—	—	28			
33a	46	20	20	—	—	—	6	5	1	1	—	1	—	—	27			
33g	47	20	21	—	—	—	6	4	1	1	o.s.	—	—	—	27			
38*	50	16	20	—	—	—	7	4	2	1	„	—	—	—	27			
38a	50	18	18	3	—	—	5	4	2	o.s.	„	—	—	o.s.	27			
41a	65	10	18	—	—	—	3	2	1	1	„	—	—	—	28—30			
701	40	28	20	—	4	—	4	2	1	o.s.	„	—	—	—	27			
70o	38	14	17	—	—	5	15	5	2	2	„	2	—	o.s.	28			
89	70	10	15	—	—	—	4	1	o.s.	—	—	—	—	—	26			
230	68	7	16	—	—	—	—	9	—	o.s.	—	—	—	—	23			
231	38	31	16	3	o.s.	—	7	2	2	1	—	—	—	—	30			
231zh	67	14	10	—	—	—	4	3	2	o.s.	—	—	—	—	27			
231z	63	10	8	—	—	—	12	2	2	„	—	2	—	—	27			
236	62	11	14	3	—	—	6	2	2	„	—	—	—	—	28			
236a	61	8	13	—	—	—	8	7	2	„	—	—	—	—	24			
248	77	8	12	—	—	—	—	1	1	1	o.s.	—	—	o.s.	24—32			
248a	74	5	11	—	—	—	4	3	2	—	—	—	—	•	24			
296	65	12	20	—	—	—	1	1	1	o.s.	—	—	—	—	28			
246e	46	10	15	—	—	—	3	18	1	—	o.s.	—	—	3	27—28			
533	30	35	18	3	o.s.	4	8	—	2	o.s.	—	—	—	—	24	1.865	1.815	94
546zh	44	20	18	4	—	—	5	3	1	—	o.s.	—	—	3	22	1.865	1.815	94
548k	35	28	20	3	—	—	1	7	4	2	„	—	—	o.s.	28	1.862	1.813	93
548l	52	24	12	—	—	—	—	10	o.s.	—	„	—	—	•	22			
574d	50	20	14	3	—	4	8	—	1	—	„	—	—	—	24—30	1.862	1.813	93
581	65	20	10	1	o.s.	o.s.	3	—	1	o.s.	—	—	—	—	30	1.862	1.813	93
584	67	14	16	1	—	1	1	—	1	„	—	—	—	—	26			
585	66	12	18	1	—	—	1	1	1	—	—	—	—	—	23			
588	70	5	21	1	—	—	2	—	1	—	—	—	—	—	26			
588b	77	7	12	—	—	—	2	1	1	—	o.s.	—	—	—	27			
35a*	43	33	14	2	—	2	3	1	2	o.s.	„	—	—	o.s.	28			

† [o.s. = optic sign.]

Characteristics of minerals											Remarks
ortho-pyroxene			clino-pyroxene			hornblende			biotite		
n_z	n_x	ferruginosity, at.%	n_z	n_x	ferruginosity, at.%	n_z	n_x	ferruginosity, at.%	$n_z = n_y$	ferruginosity, at.%	
						1.722	1.697	90	1.682	82	
						1.719	1.694	86	1.684	84	
						1.719	1.695	86	1.693	93	
						1.717	1.693	82	1.680	80	
						1.715	1.690	81	1.675	75	
1.770	1.750	84							1.682	82	
			1.741	1.717	77	1.715	1.690	81			Granosyenite at a contact with shadow granites
						1.724	1.700	92	1.673	73	
1.765	1.746	81				1.714	1.688	80	1.682	82	
						1.717	1.692	82	1.682	82	
						1.721	1.697	89			
						1,720	1.695	87	1.694	93	
						1.720	1.695	87	1.697	96	
									1.682	82	
						1.725	1.703	92	1.684	84	Fluorite, 1%
						1.722	1.698	90	1.682	82	Fluorite, 4%
			1.750	1.725	87	1.722	1.696	90			
									1.694	93	Orthite, $n = 1.735$; fluorite, 2%, $n = 1.434$
			1,755	1,730	95	1.723	1.701	91	1.678	78	Fluorite, 2%
			1,746	1,721	80	1.718	1.693	83			
						1.718	1.693	83			
						1.725	1.700	92			
						1.727	1.702	94	1.695	94	Granosyenite at a contact with shadow granites
			1.756	1.730	96	1.728	1.704	95	1.699	98	Specimen from the 1961 collection

(1—1.5%) nearly corresponds to that in average granodiorites (1.8%). The content of CaO (2—3%) is somewhat lower than its usual value (3.8%) in average granodiorites. The same applies to Na$_2$O (3% in the granosyenites, and 3.5% in average granodiorites). The potassium content of the granosyenite is variable, 5—7% K$_2$O, whereas it does not exceed 5% even in average syenites (3% in average granodiorites). Thus the grano-syenites are fairly close to granodiorites in their chemical composition, except for their very high contents of ferrous iron and potassium, which are even somewhat higher than in syenites. The composition of the grano-syenites clearly reflects the nature of their genesis, which will be discussed further on.

Fayalite-bearing plagiogranites have as yet been encountered only on the northeastern slopes of Mount Shvedov in cliffs 150 m high, where they alternate with blocks of garnet-sillimanite-cordierite gneisses and shadow granites. The fayalite-bearing plagiogranites and blocks of shadow granites are the paleosome, while biotite-amphibole granites serve as the metasome in agmatitic formations. These rocks also form inde-pendent bodies alternating with one another. In this case, the fayalite plagio-granites are 5—30 m thick and locally boudinaged. The interboudin space is filled by biotite-amphibole granites. The latter are represented by the normal varieties of granitoids, similar to the rocks composing independent discordant bodies in the Bardin and Zavaritskii Ranges. The plagiogranites are closer to the brown granosyenites in their external appearance and in the composition of their colored minerals. They are probably of the same genetic category. Characteristically, they were mistaken for feldspathized leucocratic gabbroids in the field. Their peculiar plagiogranitic composi-tion is possibly due to their parent rocks which may have been anorthosites.

The fayalite-biotite plagiogranites are represented by massive medium- and coarse-grained brown rocks, highly cataclastized. Their texture is characterized by prismatic plagioclase laths (andesine, An 35—38), 3—5 mm in size, accounting for one-half of the rock volume. These laths lie in a granoblastic matrix consisting of fine-grained quartz with shattered plagio-clase grains and colored minerals of variable grain size ranging from 0.1 to 1 mm (Figure 56). Nevertheless, quartz forms xenoblastic grains, 6—8 mm in size, and contains inclusions of plagioclase laths. The total amount of quartz is large (30—35%). Cataclasis has most markedly affected the plagioclase laths, which are broken, exhibit deformed twins and are fractured along their edges. Fayalite (3—5%) forms irregular granules, 0.1—1 mm, with ore and serpentine-like products; biotite flakes develop along cracks in the fayalite. Biotite (9—10%) forms fine flakes up to 2 mm long, which also penetrate into other minerals. The biotite contains inclusions of ore granules and crystalline zircon grains. A noteworthy feature are the high and nearly equal ferruginosities of the coexistent fayalite ($n_z = 1.862$, $n_x = 1.812$; $f = 93\%$) and biotite ($n_z = 1.693$; $f = 92\%$). In this respect, these colored minerals are quite similar to those of the granosyenites. The rocks being described differ from the latter in the absence of K-feldspar and hornblende, and also in their high (double) content of quartz and a more basic composition of the plagioclase.

FIGURE 56. Plagiogranite with hypidiomorphogranular texture (thin section 57d, × 11, crossed nicols)

Chemically, the plagiogranites (Table 117) do not resemble any variety of the rocks in gabbroid-granitoid series. They contain 66—68% silica, which is closer to granodiorites than to granites, while their alumina content (13—14%) is close to that of the average granites (13%). Their content of MgO (0.4—0.8%) is closer to granites and that of CaO (3.5—4%) corresponds to granodiorites (3.8%). The contents of sodium (2.5—3% Na_2O) in the plagiogranites approaches its content in average granodiorites (3.5% Na_2O), but its potassium content (1.5% K_2O) is considerably lower than that in the granodiorites (2.8% K_2O). The ferrous iron content in the plagiogranites (5—8% FeO) is still very high, comparable with its content in average gabbros (6% FeO). Notwithstanding their high quartz content, the fayalite-biotite plagiogranites are closer in their chemical composition to granodiorites (or even to still more basic rocks) than to granites. This is especially true with reference to the very high iron content in the colored minerals, which is similar to that in average granodiorites. While the content of sodium is normal, attention is attracted by the very low content of potassium, suggesting that the rocks in question possibly originated from anorthosites. Furthermore, it should be noted that plagioclase in these plagiogranites is represented by a fairly basic andesine.

Granitoids

Amphibole-biotite and biotite granitoids form a small massif in the Zavaritskii Range, extending over nearly 10 km with a NE-SW trend, and transecting the charnockitoids. One of its most characteristic features is the profusion of fragments and blocks of embedded anorthosites. Another feature is an ubiquitous cataclasis of the rocks, imparting a gneissic structure to the granitoids, especially in the vicinity of anorthosites. The contact effects of one rock on the other are very limited. The anorthosites are slightly feldspathized and enriched in biotite, while the granitoids acquire sphene, which they usually lack. The line of contact is very irregular, and is indicative of the penetration of granitoids into the anorthosites. At the very contact, the granitoids become finer-grained, but there are no typical chilled contacts. Another massif in the Bardin Range trends NE-SW, but its length does not exceed 5 km. It transects the Insel Series crystalline rocks and is composed of coarse-grained biotite-oligoclase-microcline granite with high contents of fluorite and orthite. Characteristically, the host plagiogneisses also contain these accessory minerals at the contact with the granite.

The granitoids are represented by fine-, medium-, and locally coarse-grained rocks, light gray to pinkish gray in color. Their massive structure is often disturbed by cataclasis resulting in gneissic and maculose structures, the latter due to the glomerular arrangement of colored minerals. Textures have also been affected by cataclasis, which in places resulted in a porphyro-granoblastic appearance, obliterating the primary hypidiomorphogranular texture. The latter can nevertheless be traced (relict euhedral feldspars, Figure 57). Euhedral laths of K-feldspar and plagioclase, ranging from 3 mm to 1 cm, locally exhibit a porphyroblastic habit. They are embedded in a finer-grained matrix of the same minerals plus abundant quartz granules (0.2—0.7 mm). Biotite flakes, 1—2 mm long, form glomero-aggregates; in places, the biotite forms large crystals (3—5 mm), also appearing as porphyroblasts. In the rare specimens retaining a massive equigranular texture, the minerals have been so much deformed that the primary textural elements are nevertheless obliterated. The nonuniform mineralogical composition of these rocks renders them similar to granites which are transitional to both granodiorites and granosyenites (Table 108). The content of K-feldspar is especially variable, 15—60%; the lower contents occur in granodiorites to quartz-diorites. The latter have a low quartz content, 12—15%, and a high colored-mineral content, 20% (mainly biotite). These rocks are therefore termed quartz-diorites.

TABLE 108. Granitoids

Specimen No.	Composition											Characteristics of minerals						Remarks
	K-feldspar	plagioclase	quartz	hornblende	biotite	ore mineral	apatite	zircon	sphene	fluorite	orthite	An content of plagioclase	hornblende n_z	hornblende n_x	hornblende ferruginosity, at.%	biotite $n_z = n_y$	biotite ferruginosity, at.%	
57 g*	60	8	26	3	2	1	—	o.s.**	—	—	o.s.	27	1.718	1.696	82			
539*	50	17	18	—	13	1	o.s.	—	—	1	1	23—26				1.680	81	
543	35	22	23	—	12	—	2	—	4	o.s.	o.s.	30²) 34¹)						1) center; 2) margin (zoned plagioclase); carbonate, 2%
543 a	30	22	23	5	12	1	1	—	5	1	o.s.	28	1.709	1.689	72	1.670	71	
551*	20	38	15	3	20	2	1	—	3	—	1	28				1.660	62	
562	15	46	12	3	17	1	—	—	4	—	2	28¹) 35²)	1.702	1.679	68			1) edge (of a zoned plagioclase lath) 2) center
586*	65	11	18	—	5	o.s.	—	—	—	1	o.s.	26				1.682	82	
587*	60	12	17	5	3	1	—	o.s.	o.s.	—	1	28—29				1.670	71	Indications or orthite in the majority of specimens
58 b	57	10	18	—	13	1	o.s.	.	—	o.s.	1	27				1.675	75	

* Chemical analysis.
** [o.s. = optic sign.]

FIGURE 57. Fine-grained granite with a blastohypidiomorphogranular
texture (thin section 539, x 11, crossed nicols)

K-feldspars exhibit microcline crosshatching in nearly all specimens,
in the authors' opinion, as a result of ubiquitous cataclasis. The plagioclase
content varies from 10 to 40%, although it is commonly 10—20%, the
the rocks being similar to granosyenites. The quartz content in specimens
resembling granites is 18—26%, and on the whole, is somewhat low.

The composition of the plagioclase in the granitoids in direct contact
with the anorthosites deserves a special study. It appears that the granitoids contaminate a certain amount of fractured anorthosites, as is suggested
by the presence of labradorite laths; the plagioclase of granitoids is
usually represented by oligoclase. The colored minerals of granitoids
differ from the dark-colored associations of the charnockitoids, and for
this reason, the former have been regarded as a separate group of rocks.
Irrespective of the composition and content of salic minerals, the presence
of biotite, to the extent of 2—20%, is characteristic for all the granitoids

under consideration. Hornblende occurs sporadically (3—5%), generally together with biotite, in the more acid varieties of granitoids. Pyroxene and
fayalite are absent. Another distinctive feature of the colored minerals in
the granitoids is their uniform and moderately high ferruginosity, 60—80%,
distinctly setting them apart from the previously described charnockitoids
(the ferruginosity of the latter's more acid varieties is 80—100%).

The composition of the accessory minerals is very characteristic;
orthite and fluorite are nearly ubiquitous along with the common ore, apatite
and zircon. The presence of significant amounts of sphene (3—5%) in a few
specimens is due to contamination from the anorthosites at their mutual
contacts. The orthite content reaches 1—2%. It is represented by yellow and
orange, sub-euhedral grains, 0.2—1.5 mm in size, commonly occurring within
biotite. Fluorite forms minute, 0.1—0.2 mm, irregular granules within
glomero-aggregates of colored minerals.

Apparently, the unusual composition of the colored minerals, the nature
of the accessory minerals and the absence of the pyroxene-fayalite association indicate a different origin from that of other intrusive rocks in the
region. Granitoid genesis was probably related to partial melts produced in
considerable amounts during ultrametamorphism. These partial melts
originally corresponded to the quartz-feldspar eutectic. The ascent and
crystallization of this mobile melt resulted in contamination from the host
rocks and was followed by superimposed alkaline metasomatism. The resulting granitoids thus have variable compositions but with a distinct subalkaline trend. Biotite is the major colored mineral, and the accessories
include orthite and fluorite.

This explains the discordancy of the granitoids with respect to the host
rocks and to all other intrusive formations in the region. It may be assumed
that partial melts only rarely produced independent intrusions. Similar
melts largely interacted with older basic rocks, part of which underwent
recrystallization under conditions of alkaline metasomatism, producing
feldspathized gabbroids, diorites-syenites and syenites. The bulk of these
basic rocks, by interactions with the melts, was transformed in an even more
complicated manner into the relatively uniform "giant-grained" porphyroblastic granosyenites.

The chemical composition of the granitoids (Table 117) reflects all their
features and is on the whole different from the composition of any of the
previously described rocks. The majority approach average granites:
69.0—70.4% silica and 13—14% alumina, as compared to 72 and 13% respectively, in the average granites. Their contents of MgO (0.5—1%), CaO
(1.5—2%) and Na_2O (2.5—3%) are fairly close to those in average granites
(0.6, 1.5 and 3.5% respectively). At the same time, the contents of FeO
(2.5—3.5%) and K_2O (5—6%) are higher than those in the average granites,
which usually contain just under 2% FeO and 5% K_2O, and lower than in acid
varieties of charnockitoids. This feature also helps to distinguish the
granitoids from the charnockitoids. The more basic varieties of granitoids
are closest to granodiorites in their chemical composition (specimen 551),
notwithstanding the distinctly low contents of silica (62%), iron (up to 7%),
and potassium (over 4%) as compared to 66% SiO_2, 2.9% FeO and 2.8% K_2O

in the average granodiorites. The contents of all the other elements in the granitoids are similar to their contents in the granodiorites, with the exception of alumina, the content of which is 13.5% as compared to 15.3% in granodiorites. These chemical deviations in the granitoids which form independent bodies indicate a significant contamination of the original partial melt by material from the host rocks.

Veins and dikes

Veins and dikes of a variety of compositions are spatially associated with the charnockitoid series (Table 109). They include: 1) metamorphosed basic rocks (feldspathized and biotitized); 2) amphibole-biotite granodiorites; 3) amphibole-biotite and biotite granosyenites; 4) biotite granites; 5) pegmatites; 6) dolerites. This enumeration follows the presumed sequence of formation.

The veins characteristically lack rocks with a composition similar to gabbro-diorites, diorite-syenites and syenites, which are widespread within the charnockitoid intrusions. This may possibly be an indirect indication that these rock types were never molten and therefore could not have produced veins or dikes of analogous compositions. Another characteristic feature of these dikes and veins is the absence of the association of eulyte with hedenbergite and fayalite, noted in analogous intrusive rocks. This indicates that the vein material was different from the corresponding rocks of the charnockitoid massifs. The vein material was apparently derived mainly from mobile melts, slightly contaminated by the rocks into which they intruded. However, the corresponding charnockitoid rocks were originally gabbroid and were altered by metasomatic recrystallization and interaction with the partial melts; this resulted in the characteristic association of colored minerals in the charnockitoids, which is absent from the associated veins.

Dikes of metamorphosed basic rocks are extremely rare. One such dike was discovered in anorthosites on the eastern slope of the Zavaritskii Range. The dike (1 m thick) is boudinaged; the interboudin spaces are partly filled by granite veinlets and partly by fractured and highly metamorphosed anorthosite. The recrystallization invested the rocks with an inequigranular, banded structure and lepidogranoblastic texture. The profuse aggregates of colored minerals, which account for nearly $3/4$ of the rock volume, have preserved relict clinopyroxene grains (1 mm) in places replaced by hornblende. Characteristically, the ferruginosities of the colored minerals are comparatively low (40—43%). Sporadic lenticular and banded areas are almost entirely composed of euhedral plagioclase, An 46—50, with inclusions of biotite.

Another, even more highly altered porphyry dike was encountered among diorite-syenites on Mount Shvedov. Its fine-grained matrix is composed of minute (0.05—0.15 mm) granules of clinopyroxene embedded in aggregates of amphibole, biotite, plagioclase, K-feldspar and a little quartz (2—3%).

At least 20 vol.% of the rock is composed of deformed phenocrysts of plagioclase laths (2 $\times$ 5 mm) with an abundance of myrmekitic ingrowths and a rim of microcline-perthite. K-feldspar segregations with irregular outlines (crosshatched microcline) in the matrix are somewhat larger than the other grains. They replace plagioclase and were apparently produced by later feldspathization. These oldest dikes are transected by granitoid veins and, since they are probably genetically related to the gabbro-anorthosites, are similarly metamorphosed. In particular, they are feldspathized or strongly biotitized.

Granodiorite veins and dikes largely occur in anorthosites and are the least widespread among the granitoid veins. Their contacts with anorthosites are distinct; contact effects were obliterated by subsequent recrystallization and feldspathization. On the western slope of the Zavarits-kii Ridge, they are exclusively confined to large blocks of anorthosites occurring within granosyenites, into which the granodiorite veins do not penetrate. However, the granite veins cross-cutting them also transect anorthosites and granosyenites. This localization of the granodiorite veins indicates that they predate syenitization of gabbroids and possibly that they underwent feldspathization simultaneously with the latter, resulting in grano-syenites. Another characteristic feature of the granodiorite veins is their porphyritic texture. The phenocrysts are almost exclusively prismatic plagioclase laths. K-feldspar porphyroblasts, which occur in all other granitoid veins and pegmatites, are less abundant. This, together with other structural features, indicates that the granodiorite veins crystallized from a melt of similar composition. The granodiorite veins are usually 0.5—1 m thick and trend NW-SE. Sporadic straight veins, 1—3 m thick, are dike-like, although they show marked vertical dislocations. Medium-grained gray and dark gray rocks are maculose or gneissic. Their texture is inequi-granular with signs of cataclasis and recrystallization. An abundance of relict prismatic plagioclase laths, 3—5 mm long, is embedded together with K-feldspar and quartz in the granoblastic aggregates. These consist of equidimensional plagioclase, 0.5—1 mm, which in places is clearly derived from the laths, alternating with xenoblastic quartz and colored minerals. Plagioclase forms about $\frac{1}{2}$ of the rock volume, while K-feldspar and quartz respectively account for 10—12 and 15—20 vol.%. The content of colored minerals is approximately the same. The main colored mineral is amphi-bole which sometimes forms large prismatic grains (2—3 mm) with poikilitic ingrowths of feldspars. Biotite, second in abundance, usually consists of small irregular flakes, but also forms large laths, 2—3 mm long, with symplektitic quartz ingrowths. The ferruginosity of colored minerals is fairly high, 74% for amphibole and 85% for biotite. The plagioclase laths are zoned; the central parts are composed of basic andesine, An43, and the peripheral zones of oligoclase, An28. The main accessory mineral is apatite; crystalline granules of zircon are very rare. Ore minerals are accompanied by sphene.

A characteristic feature of the granitoid veins in anorthosites is an intense crumpling, and in giant-grained granosyenites, boudinage. In the latter case, the veins are broken into a series of lenses separated by

TABLE 109. Veins and dikes

Specimen No.	Rocks	K-feldspar	plagioclase	quartz	olivine	orthopyroxene	clinopyroxene	hornblende	biotite	ore mineral	apatite	zircon	sphene	garnet	orthite	An content of plagioclase	olivine n_z	olivine n_x	content of fayalite, %	clinopyroxene n_z	clinopyroxene n_x	clinopyroxene ferruginosity, %	hornblende n_z	hornblende n_x	hornblende ferruginosity, %	biotite n_z	biotite ferruginosity, %	Remarks
548b	Metamorphosed basic rock	—	32	—	—	—	24	7	28	1	2	—	6	—	—	46				1.720	1.694	40	1.680	1.655	43			
58b	Granodiorites	30	50	10	—	—	—	4	4	2	o.s.**	o.s.	—	—	—	28; 43*							1.710	1.685	74	1.685	85	Zoned laths
282v		30	45	15	—	—	—	—	10	—	—	—	—	—	o.s.	32—33										1.691	90	
543i		15	45	15	—	—	—	3	15	2	—	—	5	—	—	28												
227a	Granosyenites	70	10	15	—	—	—	—	4	—	1	—	—	—	o.s.	25—26										1.685	85	
227v		65	15	10	—	—	—	5	3	1	1	o.s.	—	—	1	24—28							1.722	1.697	90	1.687	87	
227v		65	5	18	—	—	—	—	—	—	—	—	—	—	o.s.	31												
31*	Granites	50	15	30	—	—	—	1	3	o.s.	o.s.	o.s.	—	—	1	26										1.680	80	Fluorite, 1%
236b		60	16	21	—	—	—	—	2	o.s.	—	—	—	—	•	25										1.684	84	Fluorite, 2%
236v		57	15	23	—	—	—	—	5	—	—	—	—	—	•	26										1.697	96	
551a		34	26	28	—	—	—	—	10	2	—	o.s.	—	—	•	27										1.693	92	Fluorite, 2%
586i		35	30	25	—	—	—	—	6	—	—	—	—	—	1											1.690	89	Fluorite, 1%
562a	Olivine dolerite	—	55	2	10	—	25	—	—	8	—	—	—	—	—	57¹); 40²)	1.792	1.750	59	1.726	1.700	49				1.689	88	1) grain center, 2) grain margin.

** [o.s. = optic sign.]

porphyroblastic granosyenites. Fine-grained granodiorites display a porphyritic texture with an allotriomorphogranular matrix. The elongated prismatic plagioclase laths are zoned, 3—5 mm long, and possess the habit of phenocrysts. The matrix is fine-grained (0.2—0.5 mm), consisting of a mosaic of plagioclase, quartz and unlatticed microperthite, as well as aggregates of diablastic amphibole, and biotite. The rock consists of 45—50% plagioclase, 15—30% K-feldspar, 10—15% quartz, 3—4% amphibole and 10—15% biotite. The accessory minerals, besides ore and sphene, include small crystals of apatite and less commonly, zircon. Unlike the thicker granodiorite dikes, the veins have an appreciably higher content of K-feldspar and biotite. The plagioclase is represented by acid andesine, An 28—33; in the larger laths (in dikes) it reaches An 45. The colored minerals are highly ferruginous (up to 90%). The granodiorite veins and dikes probably intruded into the anorthosites even before the formation of charnockitoids, and underwent boudinage and feldspathization simultaneously with the metamorphism of anorthosites.

Granosyenite veins and dikes are the most widespread, their overall quantity being equal to all other veins and dikes combined. They occur in a variety of rocks, but most commonly in giant-grained granosyenites, where they often account for 3—5 vol.% of outcrops. It is possible to distinguish two types of veins, depending on their dimensions and composition: 1) straight dike-like bodies, 2—8 m thick, composed of porphyroblastic coarse-grained rocks, and 2) twisting veins, 10 cm to 1 m thick, composed more commonly of aplitic rocks, but likewise containing K-feldspar porphyroblasts. Thick veins often possess an indistinct zonation. As a rule, they strike ~N-S over tens of meters, and dip to the west at angles of 25—60°. On the eastern slope of Mount Curie, a veinlike body, 3 m thick, is composed of coarse-grained relatively leucocratic porphyroblastic granosyenite. This is light pinkish-grayish in color in its central portion, with finer-grained melanocratic granosyenite on the periphery. The former consists of 65—70% K-feldspar (over half of which is in the form of porphyroblasts, 1—3 cm); 10—15% oligoclase-andesine, An 24—31; 10—15% quartz; and 5—10% colored minerals (amphibole and biotite). The fine-grained periphery has almost the same content of K-feldspar, which forms porphyroblasts, 5—7 mm in size, a smaller content of plagioclase (5—10%) and an equal content of quartz. The colored-mineral content increases to 15% (mainly biotite).

A N-S trending dike, 4 m thick, encountered on the eastern slope of the Zavaritskii Range, is composed of porphyritic biotite granosyenite. K-feldspar and quartz porphyroblasts (2—4 mm) account for nearly 40 vol.% of the rock. They are separated by a fine-grained granoblastic matrix consisting of the same minerals plus 13—15% oligoclase and 5% biotite. The grain size of the matrix does not exceed 0.2—0.3 mm. K-feldspar clearly replaces plagioclase, the latter being consistently embedded in the former as poikilitic ingrowths. Plagioclase laths, 2—3 mm long, which are corroded by microperthite, have been preserved in places. The dike is apparently intensively feldspathized and may have been originally composed of granodiorite. This alteration results in a decrease in the plagioclase content, the nearly total disappearance of its prismatic laths, the disappearance of amphibole and an overall decrease in the colored-mineral content.

In places, the granosyenite veins strike in a variety of directions. They are often appreciably cataclastized and gneissified. Their texture is porphyritic with an allotriomorphogranular matrix. The significantly smaller content of porphyroblasts in these veins, in comparison to the larger granosyenite veins, and their very fine-grained and relatively leucocratic matrix, result in aplite-like rocks (although the quartz content is variable, 8—18%). The main mineral is crosshatched microcline (70—80%), occurring as xenoblastic grains (0.1—1 mm) or less commonly as equidimensional euhedra (2—4 mm) with the habit of porphyroblasts. The interstices are occupied by still smaller myrmekitized plagioclase grains (making up not over 10%), small flakes of biotite and locally of amphibole (totaling 5%). The accessory minerals include apatite and zircon together with orthite and fluorite. The orthite forms small euhedral grains (0.5 mm), yellow-brown in color, with fine quartz ingrowths. Fluorite occurs as anhedral lilac-colored grains (0.3—0.5 mm). The presence of these two accessory minerals indicates a mineral association which occurs only in granitoids, but not in the more basic rocks (including syenite).

G r a n i t e s form comparatively small bodies, linear dikes and tortuous veins all of which cross-cut all other veins and rocks in the region, with the exception of dolerites and zoned pegmatites. The granite veins often account for 3—10 vol.% of intrusive rock exposures, although there are large granosyenite outcrops with very few veins. Nevertheless, even these exposures always contain at least a single granite vein, 20—30 cm thick. On the whole, the quantity of vein granites is fairly large and together with the large volume of similarly composed granite bodies in the Bardin and Zavaritskii Ranges, suggests a significant amount of granitic melt (possibly no less than 20 vol.% of all the intrusive rocks in the region). These melts produced not only separate bodies and veins, but also resulted in the formation of giant-grained granosyenites. Thus the quantity of melts produced in the course of superimposed ultrametamorphic processes during activation was quite sufficient for the recrystallization of gabbroids (and their metasomatic transformation into syenites) and also for the formation of granosyenites by a mixing of syenites with the granitic melts.

The texture and composition of the granites vary according to their shape. Coarse-grained porphyritic leucocratic granites are characteristic of large lenticular and irregular granite bodies (measuring tens and hundreds of meters); medium-grained granites and medium-grained porphyritic granites occur in dikes and larger veins; aplitic granites occur in narrow veins. A common feature of all these granites is their alaskitic nature due to the predominance of K-feldspar over plagioclase (often by a factor of 3—4) and the relatively low content of colored minerals (chiefly biotite). Characteristic of all granites is the absence of fayalite and pyroxene, the rarity of amphibole, and the presence of up to 2—3% accessory orthite and fluorite. Separate bodies are composed of fairly massive coarse-grained granites, light pinkish gray in color. They are generally inequigranular, since K-feldspar reaches up to 2—3 cm in length, and the other grains are only 2—8 mm. Outstanding among the latter are myrmekitized plagioclase laths, xenoblastic (often mosaic) granules of quartz, and small aggregates of biotite which contain the accessory minerals. Simple twins and microcline crosshatching in the K-feldspar are distorted and this mineral contains ingrowths of all the others. The composition of these granites is relatively simple: up to 50% K-feldspar, 15—20% oligoclase, An 25—26, 25—30% quartz, 3% biotite, 1% orthite and 2% fluorite. Granite veins, 1—3 mm thick, strike NE - SW and NW - SE with steep dips (40—70°) toward NW and SW respectively. They thus differ from the granosyenite veins which generally strike N - S and which they transect. They are composed of porphyritic, fine- and medium-grained light gray rocks. The veins are often appreciably gneissified and cataclastized, and consequently the primary hypidiomorphogranular texture of the rocks has been disturbed. The resulting textures are heterogranoblastic and sometimes even granulitic due to the presence of parallel, finely lenticular quartz aggregates. Although euhedral crosshatched microcline mainly forms the phenocrysts (5—10 mm in size), the rock also contains coarse euhedral plagioclase and quartz grains. These coarser grains constitute nearly one half of the rock, which, in this case, is hypidiomorphogranular. The rest of this rock is granoblastic, composed of smaller grains ($\leqslant$1—2 mm). It was possibly produced by fracturing of the hypidiomorphogranular aggregates. Such granites contain 50—60% microcline, 15—20% oligoclase, An 25—26, and have somewhat low contents of quartz (20—25%) and colored minerals (chiefly biotite, 5—8%). Accessory magnetite, apatite, zircon and orthite occur in sporadic grains, totaling <1%.

Granite dikes, 1—1.5 m thick, cross-cut all veins (including granite veins), with the exception of pegmatites. Most commonly, they strike NE and although they may be broken into separate blocks, they can generally be traced over tens of meters. The dikes are composed of medium- to coarse-grained massive rocks, light gray in color. Their texture is porphyritic, with an hypidiomorphogranular matrix affected by cataclasis. The porphyritic segregations, measuring 5—10 mm, contain euhedral prismatic laths of K-feldspar and plagioclase. The matrix is composed of K-feldspar, plagioclase (0.5—2 mm), quartz and biotite; lenticular quartz segregations may locally reach 5—6 mm in length. The composition of the granites is very uniform, with a small predominance of K-feldspar (35%) over oligoclase, An 25—27 (25—30%), plus quartz (25—28%) and biotite (5—10%). Accessory minerals are zircon, orthite and fluorite.

Relatively narrow (20—70 cm) granite veinlets frequently occur in 'giant-grained' granosyenites, but are also found in the other intrusive rocks. They strike randomly but always have gentle dips, 10—20°. They are composed of fine-grained rocks, with larger segregations (3—4 mm) of K-feldspar and quartz. Both the minerals account for as much as 90 vol.% of the rocks (25—30% quartz); the remaining 10% is formed by equal amounts of oligoclase and biotite. The main accessory mineral is orthite (<1%), together with rare fine-grained zircon (up to 0.03 mm). In some veinlets, fine parallel quartz segregations produce a granulitic texture, and the rock may be gneissic.

On the whole, the vein granites of the Humboldt Mountains and Petermann Range differ little from the normal granites (Table 109), although they possess the following two distinctive features: 1) a tendency to deviate in composition toward granosyenites and 2) a very high ferruginosity of the colored minerals, usually some 90% or higher. These features, i. e., high alkalinity and ferruginosity, are not confined to the veins, but occur in nearly all intrusive rocks in the region and especially in the acid varieties. Yet another characteristic feature of these veins is the presence of orthite and fluorite as the leading accessory minerals.

The chemical composition of granite veins has been determined only for lenticular bodies, in which they are represented by relatively leucocratic varieties. Therefore, their silica content is over 77%, as compared to not over 72% in average granites. The contents of other elements are close to those characteristic of average granites, with the exception of alumina (10—13% in average granites) and sodium oxide (2.3—3.5% in average granites). In the authors' opinion, the granite veins are largely crystallization products of a partial melt.

Pegmatite veins are comparatively rare, occurring mainly in diorite-syenites and syenites; none have been discovered in 'giant-grained' granosyenites and anorthosites. Their presence is possibly related to high-grade alkaline metasomatism, in which the older granite veins, recrystallizing in the solid state, acquire a zonation. The pegmatite veins are 2—5 m thick and the thickest veins exhibit the most marked zonation. The thickest pegmatite veins were encountered in the SE part of Mount Curie, where they occur in diorite-syenites, accounting for 3—5 vol.% of the rocks (no other vein types are present). The general structure of these veins is distinctly zonal, with a smokey quartz core, 1.5—2 m thick. This is surrounded by zones (up to 60—80 cm) of large (10—30 cm) K-feldspar crystals, followed, likewise on both sides, by graphic granite zones of the same thickness containing relatively large amphibole and biotite crystals. The outer rim (10 cm) consists of ~50% biotite plus amphibole, equal amounts of quartz plus oligoclase and 3—5% K-feldspar. Characteristically, the diorite-syenites, for a distance of 2—3 m from the vein, are enriched in large (3—5 cm) K-feldspar phenocrysts nearly ten times larger than the K-feldspar in the host diorite-syenite. These large porphyroblasts often compose 25 vol.% of the rocks, especially near the veins; they become sporadic at distances of 5—7 m from the contact. The large K-feldspar porphyroblasts impart the habit and composition of 'giant-grained' granosyenite to the diorite-syenite. However, the genesis of the large 'giant-grained' granosyenite bodies is quite different, particularly since they do not contain pegmatites.

Smaller pegmatite veins have fewer zones; they lack the quartz core, and are composed mainly of graphic granite with sporadic amphibole and biotite. Their content of accessory apatite and zircon is negligible, seemingly as if the pegmatites were 'sterile' with respect to these minerals. In places, fine cracks in the pegmatite veins are filled with aplitic graphic granite. The relationships between the pegmatites and other veins and dikes in the region have not been established, since the latter are generally lacking in the diorite-syenite and syenite.

In summary, the granitoid veins and dikes in the region of the Humboldt Mountains and Petermann Range form two principal varieties related to 1) recrystallization and feldspathization (prior to charnockitization) of older and basic veins occurring in anorthosites and gabbroid rocks, and 2) crystallization of partial melts in cracks in the charnockites followed by metasomatic feldspathization of both rocks.

Dolerite and gabbro-dolerite dikes are sporadic. Two dikes were examined, one occurring in granite and the other in 'giant-grained' granosyenites, where they transect granite veins and are probably the youngest formations. The first dike, 4 m thick, strikes 215° and dips 50° toward the SW. It consists of fresh olivine dolerite. The thickness and strike of the second dike were not determined. This dike is composed of gabbro-dolerite. The porphyritic olivine dolerite is medium-grained with a gabbro-ophitic texture. The matrix (0.5—1.0 mm) consists of clinopyroxene, olivine and ore, and the phenocrysts of prismatic plagioclase laths measuring 3—6 mm. Plagioclase accounts for 55 vol.% of the rock and is represented by zoned laths, with labradorite, An 57, at the center, and andesine, An 40, at the periphery. Clinopyroxene (titanoaugite) accounts for 25 vol.% of the rock; its ferruginosity is 49%. Euhedral olivine (0.3 mm) has a ferruginosity of 59%, and its content does not exceed 10%; it is intensively replaced by iddingsite. The content of titanomagnetite in the rock is also 10% and it is associated with clinopyroxene and olivine in the interstices of the plagioclase laths. A small amount of quartz (1—2%) is included in the other minerals.

The gabbro-dolerite is composed of dark-gray, medium-grained rocks with a typical gabbro-ophitic texture. One half of the rock is composed of larger (2 × 5 mm) prismatic laths of labradorite, An 54, with aggregates of smaller (1 mm) euhedral augite containing interstitial ore. Cinnamon-brown iddingsite is pseudomorphic after olivine. Fresh dolerite dikes are not related to the veins of specific granitoids, which accompany intrusions in the charnockitoid series. They are the youngest intrusives, probably genetically related to the Early Mesozoic trap formation of Antarctica.

Xenoliths and contact zones

Two types of xenoliths are distinguished; 1) sporadic, comparatively small fragments, measuring up to 1 m, mainly embedded within 'giant-grained' granosyenites, and 2) large fragments and blocks, measuring up to 100 m ("floating" pendants) embedded mainly in diorite-syenites or the youngest granites; chains of the blocks are similar to skialithic boudins.

Small xenoliths are represented by biotite-amphibole rocks, diopside rocks and cordierite-garnet-biotite plagiogneisses. Xenoliths of the biotite-amphibole rocks may form 1 to 2% of the Mount Curie granosyenite. They consist of subrounded to subangular, dark gray fragments measuring 0.2—1.0 m. In places, the xenoliths are linear and are intensively corroded by the host rock, thereby assuming diffuse outlines. Xenoliths often contain

sporadic K-feldspar porphyroblasts, 3—4 cm long, which also intersect the
xenolith-host rock contact. The composition of these xenoliths corresponds
to strongly metamorphosed and recrystallized amphibolites. One half of
the volume consists of fine-grained (0.2—0.3 mm) biotite-amphibole aggregates, and the other half of prismatic andesine laths, 1—2 mm long and
0.1—0.2 mm wide, containing colored-mineral inclusions. Irregular quartz
granules are ubiquitous (5—10%). Certain xenoliths have preserved a
relict texture similar to gabbro (prismatic granular). Other, rarer,
xenoliths in the 'giant-grained' granosyenites are boudins of diopside rocks,
0.5—2 m in diameter, which were encountered in several outcrops on the
eastern slope of the Zavaritskii Range. The boudins are composed of fine-
grained diopside aggregates with xenoblastic grains reaching 1—2 mm in
size. Other minerals include scapolite, calcite and plagioclase. Boudins
of diopside rocks are intersected by granite veinlets which also penetrate
into the host granosyenites. Characteristically, the granosyenites contain
xenoliths which were only weakly granitized. However, the basic rocks were
highly silicified, feldspathized, and biotitized. The composition of calciphyres has been little altered. The rare xenoliths in the Mount Shvedov
diorite-syenite have different compositions. The xenoliths occur in certain
bands within the diorite-syenites, suggesting remnants of specific beds in
the host rocks. The xenoliths are linear (0.5—1 m long and 0.1—0.2 m
wide) and are intruded by granite veinlets. They consist of a variety of
plagiogneisses with a prevalence of cordierite-garnet-biotite varieties,
sometimes with disintegrated hypersthene relics. Contacts with the host
diorite-syenites are diffuse. The xenolithic plagiogneisses are slightly
feldspathized but are intensively silicified. Their quartz content exceeds
40% and andesine, An 34, composes 35—37%. Cordierite-biotite-garnet
aggregates account for as much as 20%, the ferruginosity of the biotite
reaching 63% (Table 110). Only biotite, with vermicular quartz ingrowths,
appears to be a new crystallization product. All other colored minerals
are xenoblastic (0.3—0.8 mm). These plagiogneisses contain sporadic
disintegrated hypersthene, replaced by biotite and even by chlorite. Another
variety of plagiogneiss xenoliths has been feldspathized as well as silicified. The only mafic mineral is diopside (up to 20%), with accessory
sphene (2—3%) and apatite (1%). Carbonate aggregates develop within large
diopside grains. Such plagiogneisses possibly originated from calciphyres.

Large blocks were encountered in several exposures of metagabbroids,
diorite-syenites and locally granosyenites. Migmatite blocks (with calciphyres and quartzites) have been discovered in granites, where they may
form the paleosome of agmatites. Classic boudinaged blocks are abundant
in the charnockitoids occurring at the southern tip of the Zavaritskii Range
(Figure 58). Here, cliffs 300—350 m high and traceable over 2—3 km are
composed of uniform coarse-grained diorite-syenite (with a trend toward
syenite). They contain boudins of shadow granites and migmatites with
biotite-garnet paleosomes of various shapes and sizes. The latter form at
least 10 vol.% of the exposures. The boudins are most commonly ragged-
lenticular, linear (generally with an E-W trend) and form bands, 10—20 m
thick; the interboudin spaces are filled by diorite-syenite. Individual

TABLE 110. Xenoliths and rocks of exomorphic zones

Specimen No.	Rock	K-feldspar	plagioclase	quartz	fayalite	orthopyroxene	clinopyroxene	hornblende	biotite	ore mineral	apatite	zircon	sphene	garnet	orthite	An content of plagioclase
58v	Cordierite-garnet-biotite plagio-gneiss	—	36	40	—	1	—	—	10	1	o.s.**	—	—	8	—	34
57v*	Feldspathized biotite-cordierite-plagiogneiss	32	17	16	—	—	—	—	11	4	—	2	—	—	o.s.	27. 28
248b	Biotite-sillimanite-cordierite gneiss	40	—	33	—	—	—	—	3	2	—	—	—	2	—	
248v	Biotitized quartzite	—	5	79	—	—	—	—	15	1	—	o.s.	—	—	—	
281z	Diopside rock	—	5	—	—	—	95	—	—	—	—	o.s.	—	—	—	
249a*	Shadow granite	28	36	27	—	3	—	—	5	1	o.s.	—	—	—	—	
580g	Biotite-amphibole schist	—	47	2	—	—	—	25	20	3	2	—	1	—	—	29
70a	Biotite plagiogneiss with pyroxene relicts	1	60	21	—	5	1	—	12	—	o.s.	o.s.	—	—	—	25—28
70g	Calciphyre	3	—	—	—	—	45	—	—	—	—	.	2	—	—	
70zh	Shadow granite with garnet-biotite matrix	28	28	26	—	—	—	8	5	1	2	.	—	2	—	30
70z	Shadow granite with pyroxene-amphibole matrix	31	26	26	—	—	10	3	1	—	1	—	2	—	—	32
90	Slightly feldspathized bipyroxene schist	5	62	4	—	15	2	—	7	3	2	—	—	—	—	35—37
90a	Garnet-biotite plagiogneiss	—	38	31	—	—	—	—	18	1	o.s.	—	—	12	—	30—35
90g	Leucocratic shadow granite	50	18	30	—	—	—	—	1	o.s.	—	—	—	1	—	27

(Rows 70a–90g: Exomorphic zones)

* Chemical analysis.
** [o.s. = optic sign.]

TABLE 110 (continued)

Specimen No.	Rock	orthopyroxene n_z	orthopyroxene n_x	orthopyroxene ferruginosity, %	clinopyroxene n_z	clinopyroxene n_x	clinopyroxene ferruginosity, %	biotite n_z	biotite ferruginosity, %	garnet n	garnet contents of almandine, %	Remarks
58v	Cordierite-garnet-biotite plagiogneiss							1.662	63			Cordierite, 4%
57v*	Feldspathized biotite-cordierite-plagiogneiss											Cordierite 13%, $n_z=1.555$, $n_x=1.546$, sillimanite 2%, andalusite 3%, $n_z=1.642$, $n_x=1.632$
248b	Biotite-sillimanite-cordierite gneiss							1.658	60			Cordierite 15%, sillimanite 5%, $n_z=1.677$, $n_x=1.657$
248v	Biotitized quartzite							1.658	60			
281z	Diopside rock				1.708	1.679	22					
249a*	Shadow granite	1.748	1.732	68								
580g	Biotite-amphibole schist							1.665	66			

Exomorphic zones

Specimen No.	Rock	orthopyroxene n_z	orthopyroxene n_x	orthopyroxene ferruginosity, %	clinopyroxene n_z	clinopyroxene n_x	clinopyroxene ferruginosity, %	biotite n_z	biotite ferruginosity, %	garnet n	garnet contents of almandine, %	Remarks
70a	Biotite plagiogneiss with pyroxene relicts	1.736	1.720	57	1.722	1.694	42					
70g	Calciphyre											Wollastonite 20%, $n_z=1.632$, $n_x=1.618$, calcite 5%, scapolite 25%, $n_o=1.583$, $n_e=1.552$
70zh	Shadow granite with garnet-biotite matrix											
70z	Shadow granite with pyroxene-amphibole matrix	1.730	1.715	52	1.730	1.705	56	1.658	60			
90	Slightly feldspathized bipyroxene schist				1.721	1.696	41					
90a	Garnet-biotite plagiogneiss							1.675	75	1.799–1.806	77	
90g	Leucocratic shadow granite							1.675	75	1.799–1.806	77	

* Chemical analysis.

boudins are 20—100 m long and 5—10 m wide (sometimes more). The boudins form distinct contacts with the host diorite-syenites; this contact is generally discordant with the strike of the boudin layers. The layering of migmatites in the boudins is not disturbed; this layering generally strikes 240—260° with a dip of 50—70° to the SSW (Figure 59). The composition of the boudins is fairly constant throughout the huge exposure, with alternating leucocratic and melanocratic layers with thicknesses varying from 10 mm to 1.5 m. The former are 2—3 times more numerous than the latter and are composed of heteroblastic shadow granites with a considerable prevalence of microcline, up to 80%, over quartz (10—15%) and oligoclase, An 23 (5%). Biotite-garnet aggregates, in the form of thin intercalations, are limited to only 5% of the rock. The melanocratic layers are dominated by oligoclase, An 25 (up to 60%); they also contain 15% of quartz, but K-feldspar is absent. On the other hand, there is at least 30% of the biotite-garnet aggregate, and therefore the rock may be termed a melanocratic plagiogneiss. Contact effects of the diorite-syenites on these boudinage blocks are absent, except for the sporadic presence of large K-feldspar porphyroblasts. The boudinage blocks thus appear to form a tectonic contact with the charnockitoids. However, such blocks may prove to be skialiths.

Alternating bands of leucocratic fine-grained biotite-amphibole granites and fayalite-pyroxene syenites are exposed on the NE margin of the Mount Eck-Hörner Massif. The granite strata contain boudinaged calciphyre and shadow granite beds, 2—2.5 m thick, traced over 20—25 m along the strike. The beds form mechanical contacts with containing rocks. The calciphyres are represented by scapolite-diopside rocks with a minor admixture of plagioclase, quartz, calcite and sphene. Shadow granite xenoliths consist of equal amounts of oligoclase-andesine and K-feldspar and are distinguished by their high content of the biotite-amphibole aggregate (up to 20%) and low content of quartz (10—15%). No contact effects were noted at the host granite. The xenoliths contain granitoid veins which intrude the shadow gneissified granites and the calciphyre boudins as well. However, the veins do not enter the host massive granites or syenites.

Thin (5 m) migmatite beds, traceable over dozens of meters along strike, are skialithic in nature. These overlie irregular surfaces of uniform medium-grained diorite-syenites composing the rocks in the SE part of Mount Shvedov. The diorite-syenites have no apparent effect on the migmatites, although they penetrate into the latter in wedge-shaped forms, resulting in very irregular boundaries of the migmatite beds. Finely layered migmatites with a cordierite-biotite-garnet paleosome account for about one half of the rock; the other half is metasome composed of K-feldspar with minor quartz and oligoclase. The migmatite alternates with shadow granites having a similar mafic mineral content to the paleosome, i. e., hypersthene and biotite. The chemical analysis of this shadow granite (Table 117) indicates its similarity to average granodiorite, although it is somewhat oversaturated in silica (by 3%) and slightly enriched in potassium (by 0.8%) and iron (by 0.8%). The latter is due to the high ferruginosities of biotite and hypersthene (66—68%).

FIGURE 58. Outcrop 93, diorite-syenites with boudinaged layers of migmatite, up to 100 m high. Southern tip of the Zavaritskii Range.

FIGURE 59. Boudin of migmatite in diorite-syenite. Detail from outcrop 93.

Large skialithic blocks were found on Mount Insel and on the SE slope of the Zavaritskii Range. In the former location, uniform melanocratic granosyenites contain two lenses of granulite-like shadow granites with calciphyre boudins, 2—5 m thick, traceable along strike for at least 30—40 m. The banding (gneissosity) has not been disturbed in either lens. They strike 265° and dip 50—60° S. In the second location, a sheet of shadow granites (up to 20 m thick) containing small calciphyre boudins has been traced along strike for 40 m. This sheet strikes 240° and dips 30—40° SE, which coincides with trend of the layering in the host granosyenites. The shadow granites are intercalated with biotite-amphibole schists, quartzites and calciphyre boudins. The shadow granites are represented by unusual rocks consisting of 90—95% K-feldspar and quartz (in nearly equal quantities), with a small admixture of plagioclase (3—5%), amphibole and biotite (totaling 2—3%). Their most characteristic feature is the morphology of quartz segregations, which form subparallel fine-lenticular aggregates, investing the rock with the typical granulitic habit. Certain intercalations in the shadow granites are composed of biotite-amphibole rocks consisting of 50% colored-mineral aggregates with ferruginosities of 60%. Boudins of diopside rocks, measuring 0.2—1.0 m, are composed of 95% diopside with a ferruginosity of 22%; the remaining 5% consist of scapolite, plagioclase, calcite and sphene. In other blocks, shadow granite occurs as granite-gneiss, the oligoclase predominating over K-feldspar while the content of biotite-amphibole aggregates does not exceed 10%. Calciphyre boudins consist of 50% diopside, and 50% plagioclase plus scapolite. In these blocks as well, no contact effect of granosyenites was observed. In all cases, the ferruginosity of colored minerals in the skialiths and xenoliths is lower than that of analogous minerals in diorite-syenites and granosyenites.

An unusual group of agmatite-like beds is exposed on the NE slope of Mount Shvedov. The boudinaged bodies of fayalite-biotite plagiogranites occurring in normal biotite granites have been described. These granites also contain an abundance of sillimanite-cordierite-biotite plagiogneiss beds broken into blocks, and containing boudins of calciphyre and marble. The thicknesses of such strata range from a few meters to 20 m and they may be regarded as boudinaged skialiths or even as the paleosome of agmatites. It should be noted that these agmatites form over one half of the exposures on the NE slope of Mount Shvedov. The gneisses in these exposures have an unusual composition. They contain a considerable quantity of preserved sillimanite-biotite-cordierite aggregates (totaling up to 25%), and are enriched (up to 30%) in K-feldspar (mostly as porphyroblasts measuring up to 6—8 mm). They contain only some 20% oligoclase, An 27, and a similar quantity of quartz. These properties combine to produce an exceptional rock which may be designated as a melanocratic biotite-cordierite granosyenite. However, its most interesting feature is the range of accessory minerals, which include orthite and fluorite in association with zircon (up to 2%). Characteristically, in addition to the sillimanite, andalusite forms broad prismatic crystals measuring 1—1.5 mm, sometimes in symplektitic aggregates with the cordierite. The presence of neogenic andalusite is indicative of the contact effect of the granite on the former plagiogneiss. In addition to the andalusite, the latter were also enriched in K-feldspar and such rare accessory minerals as orthite and fluorite. The chemical composition of this gneiss (Table 117, specimen 57v) is unlike any igneous rock. It resembles granodiorite only with respect to its contents of silica and alumina. The magnesium and iron contents are several times higher, and the lime and alkali contents (components of feldspars) are several times lower than in average granodiorite.

On the whole, it is clear that the composition of xenoliths and blocks in intrusive charnockitoid rocks has been little altered in comparison to the host gneisses, calciphyres, migmatites and shadow granites. This indicates generally weak contact metamorphic effects during all formation stages. A somewhat more pronounced alteration occurs in the host metamorphic rocks due to the injection and crystallization of granite melts, which form the metasome of the agmatites.

Direct contacts between porphyroblastic granosyenites and host plagio-gneisses and shadow granites (containing calciphyre boudins and intercala-tions of quartzites) of different grades of migmatization were encountered on the SE edge of Mount Eck-Horner. Here, the nearly vertical outcrops form a comparatively low spur, some 500 m long and stretching almost across the strike of the rocks (exposure 70). The spur is composed of biotite-amphibole plagiogneiss beds containing relicts of pyroxenes, and with various grades of migmatization. Their total thickness is at least 300 m. The strike of the gneissosity and the parallel migmatite banding is ~N—S with a 45—70° dip toward the west. The plagiogneisses are distinguished by their high content of oligoclase, An 25—28 (60%), moderate content of quartz (20%) and the prevalence of biotite (12%) over other colored minerals including relicts of orthopyroxene (4%) and clinopyroxene (1%). Hornblende (2—3%) occurs locally. The ferruginosity of these colored minerals is moderate, 42—57% (Table 110), denoting the absence of contact effects of the granosyenite on the plagiogneiss. This is also indicated by the latter's negligible feldspathization (not over 1—2% K-feldspar). A lenti-cular body (up to 30 m in diameter) of shadow granites, concordant with the strike of plagiogneisses, was encountered in the latter. The plagio-gneisses consist of 40—50% crosshatched microcline, 20—30% quartz, 5—8% plagioclase relicts, 5—15% garnet and 1—7% biotite. Accessory minerals are titanomagnetite (with sphene inclusions) and apatite. The grano-syenites have no contact metamorphic effect on these shadow granites. Intercalations of boudinaged calciphyres, 1—2 m thick and composing up to 10 vol.% of the rock, occur with the shadow granites. The calciphyres con-sist of ~50% diopside and scapolite plus wollastonite. The calcite content is small (5—7%), and sphene is the only accessory minerals. The presence of considerable amounts of calcareous scapolite and wollastonite in the diopside calciphyes indicates their formation under amphibolite facies conditions. The calciphyres exhibit no signs of any contact influences from the grano-syenites.

Shadow granite beds, over 20 m thick, occur 30 m from the contact with the granosyenites. The shadow granites have a garnet-biotite-amphibole or amphibole-pyroxene matrix and contain intercalations of quartzites and

calciphyres 2—3 m thick. They are in direct contact with slightly migmatized plagiogneiss beds. The layered structures in these rocks are parallel.
The contact is fairly distinct and irregular; it strikes NE and dips steeply
toward the NW (nearly vertical). The contact is discordant. The composition of the shadow granites near the contact does not include any minerals
that would indicate a contact effect of the granosyenites. The granites
are heterogranoblastic with some elements of a granulitic texture due to
the ribbon-type quartz segregations. The rock consists of ~85% acid
andesine (An 30—32) and approximately equal amounts of microcline and
quartz. The colored-mineral content is 15%. In some cases these include
biotite, amphibole and garnet; in other occurrences, clinopyroxene and
amphibole (without garnet) are present. The accessory minerals are
sphene and apatite. The most characteristic feature, however, is the
ferruginosity of the colored minerals, which for the pyroxene, amphiboles
and biotites in the shadow granites is 50—60%. This reaches 77—84% in the
granosyenites, just 1 m away. It should be emphasized that the typical
minerals of granosyenites — fayalite and orthopyroxene (eulyte) — are absent
in the shadow granites. The quartzites and calciphyres occurring in the
shadow granite near its contact with granosyenite are also devoid of any
apparent contact effects. The quartzites are composed of 95% xenoblastic,
serrated quartz grains, measuring 2—5 mm, with only up to 5% microcline.
The calciphyres contain garnet and calcite in addition to diopside. The
accessory minerals are apatite and sphene. These rocks are neither feldspathized nor enriched in biotite at their contact with the granosyenites.

The shadow granites are in direct contact with fine- and medium-grained
massive (or slightly gneissic) light-gray granosyenites. The contact is
transitional over 10 m to brownish medium- and coarse-grained granosyenites, deviating toward syenites due to their low quartz content. The
granosyenites in the endomorphic zone are considerably finer-grained than
the other rocks of the massif; they are devoid of large K-feldspar
porphyroblasts and on the whole depleted in quartz. These properties
have some influence on their mineralogical composition; they have preserved more plagioclase than the normal 'giant-grained' granosyenites,
and correspondingly less K-feldspar. Their quartz content is variable,
4—20%, and the total content of colored minerals is somewhat high, although
their variety is typical of the granosyenites in the region. The transition
zone between the fine- and medium-grained granosyenites containing K-
feldspar porphyroblasts (up to 1 cm), and normal 'giant-grained' granosyenites with K-feldspar porphyroblasts of 3—5 cm accounting for about
one half the rocks, consists of medium- and coarse-grained varieties with
a gradually increasing content of large porphyroblasts, and in which fayalite
appears as a stable mineral. The smaller grain size of the rocks and the
absence of large porphyroblasts within the 10-m endomorphic zone of the
Eck-Hörner Massif can be explained by a considerably lower grade of
metasomatic recrystallization in the margins of the massif.

These contact properties yield the following conclusions: 1. The Eck-
Hörner Massif is a typical discordant intrusive body, the primary composition of which was drastically different from its present composition.

2. Crystallization of the present rocks of the massif directly from a melt cannot have occurred, since in this case, the host rocks would have undergone thermal-contact alterations, which have nowhere been observed.
3. The processes which produced the charnockitoid rocks of the Eck-Hörner Massif did not involve the host rocks since the same colored minerals in the host rocks have dissimilar ferruginosities, or the rocks contain different minerals, i. e., garnet in shadow granites, fayalite and orthopyroxene (eulyte) in granosyenites. 4. The large K-feldspar porphyroblasts, and granite and pegmatite veins saturating rocks of the Eck-Hörner Massif do not occur in the host rocks, indicating the absence of alkaline metasomatic recrystallization of the host plagiogneisses and migmatites during widespread recrystallization in the granosyenites of the massif.

Minerals of the charnockitoids

The following rock-forming minerals, of variable compositions, are characteristic of the charnockitoid rocks in the region: olivine, orthopyroxene, clinopyroxene, hornblende, biotite, plagioclase and K-feldspars. Some 42 spectroscopic quantitative analyses were performed on these minerals from very small samples (10—20 mg), making possible the selection of fairly homogeneous fractions. In order to reduce the analytical error (the sum of elements often varied from 96 to 104 wt%) all analytical results were scaled to 100%. These were used to calculate the atomic quantities and the number of cations for the crystallochemical formulas and component compositions. Aside from their inadequate accuracy, spectroscopic analyses suffer from still another disadvantage in not differentiating between ferrous and ferric iron. Therefore, the total iron content in the analyses is stated in terms of the ferrous compound, FeO, which is significantly and ubiquitously predominant in the colored minerals (their contents of Fe_2O_3 are very small). The spectroscopic analyses provide fairly complete information on minerals of variable composition, and are helpful in placing the changes occurring under the influence of metasomatic recrystallization and interactions with melts. They make possible delineation of continuous mineral groups of variable composition in the gabbroid — granitoid series (charnockitoids). These vary regularly from basic to acid rocks, thus providing an insight into the causes and trends of the processes of mineral formation.

Olivines, represented exclusively by fayalite with a ferruginosity of 87—95%, occur in nearly all the charnockitoids, but more commonly in syenites and granosyenites. The presence of fayalites in all charnockitoid varieties suggests similar formation conditions for the entire charnockite series. Naturally, fayalite is more common in granosyenites, formed during the maximum development of charnockitization. Olivines are absent from the oldest anorthosites and the youngest granites crystallizing from melts. The fayalite contents are 1—8%, but most commonly 3%. The mineral is represented by small xenoblastic grains of 0.3—0.8 mm, less commonly up to 1.5 mm. It is everywhere replaced in cracks by iddingsite-like products, and occasionally also by iron hydroxides. It is always associated with other colored minerals and is included in newly formed biotite-amphibole aggregates, which locally replace the fayalite grains along their edges.

Spectroscopic analyses of fayalite from diorite-syenite and granosyenite (Table 111) are fairly similar, but differ significantly from the chemical analysis of typical fayalite from ferrogabbro.* This is largely due to intensive replacement of the fayalite by iddingsite, resulting in the appearance of alkalis and alumina, and a considerable (by 13—14%) increase in the content of silica at the expense of iron. Marked contamination of the fayalites by secondary products prevents determination of the normative composition. However, the magnesium content in the fayalite is low, almost the same as its content in the fayalite of ferrogabbros, which indicates an exceptionally high ferruginosity of this olivine. Its total ferruginosity based on analyses is 93—95%, and based on the refractive index is 89—93%, providing still another confirmation of the reliability of optical methods for determination of the composition of olivines.

TABLE 111. Olivines

Oxide	Specimen 93 — diorite-syenite transitional to syenite		Specimen 574d — 'giant-grained' granosyenite		Table 2, from /16/, olivine from fayalite ferrogabbro (No.18)
	wt%	wt% scaled to 100	wt%	wt% scaled to 100	wt%
SiO_2	38.0	43.2	39.9	44.3	30.15
TiO_2	0.5	0.6	0.3	0.3	0.20
Al_2O_3	2.5	2.8	1.4	1.6	0.07
FeO_{tot}	41.1	46.6	44.3	49.3	65.45
MgO	1.9	2.1	1.3	1.4	1.05
MnO	0.6	0.7	1.2	1.3	1.01
CaO	2.1	2.4	0.8	0.9	2.18
K_2O	0.8	0.9	0.6	0.7	—
Na_2O	0.6	0.7	0.2	0.2	—
Σ	88.1	100.0	90.0	100.0	100.11

f, %: $\dfrac{93 \text{ by chemical analysis,}}{89 \text{ by refractive index}}$ $\dfrac{95}{93}$

The following three factors relating to the presence of fayalite in charnockitoid rocks should be noted: 1) the mineral is not present in all

---

* Here and throughout, analyses for comparisons of the chemical compositions of the minerals are based on the literature /16, 17/.

specimens, even from rocks in which it is widespread, e. g., granosyenites; 2) it is always represented by relict grains, replaced by biotite-amphibole aggregates; 3) it occurs more commonly in paragenesis with hedenbergite (or ferroaugite) and rarely with orthopyroxene (eulyte). The following three varieties can therefore be distinguished among the granosyenites with respect to the composition of their colored minerals: a) fayalite-hedenbergite, b) hedenbergite-orthopyroxene (eulyte) and c) purely biotite-amphibole varieties (most widespread). Association (c) is everywhere superimposed on the other two. From this superimposition and also the presence of fayalite in association with alkaline feldspars, it appears that formation conditions involved extra-high alkalinities and relatively shallow depths, since garnet should be produced in a less alkaline environment and at greater depths /43, 44/. The metasomatic recrystallization of gabbroids under conditions of high alkali mobility occurred at moderate depths which were sufficient for the formation of the biotite-amphibole association. This involved the interaction between gabbroids and partial melts, during which this secondary association develops intensively, gradually replacing olivine and pyroxene.

Orthopyroxenes are typomorphic minerals of the charnokitoid series, occurring in a broad range of rocks from gabbroids to granitoids, in the Humboldt Mountains and Petermann Range. The content and composition of orthopyroxenes vary according to the composition of the rocks. Thus, the content of orthopyroxenes in metamorphosed gabbroids is usually 10—30%, and their ferruginosity 53—64%; it is only in rare fayalite-bearing feldspathized gabbroids that pyroxene relics (1%) have a ferruginosity of 72%. The contents of orthopyroxenes in gabbro-norite-diorites are significantly smaller, 4—20%, while their ferruginosity is higher, 57—70%. The content of orthopyroxenes is still lower in diorite-syenites, 2—12%, while their ferruginosity is still higher, 70—84%. They are rarely found in syenites (ferruginosity, 84%) and in granosyenites (ferruginosity, 81—86%). Injective granitic rocks do not contain orthopyroxene. Orthopyroxene occurs fairly often in anorthosites (1—8%) where its ferruginosity is the same as in the gabbroids. Thus, it may be stated that the content of orthopyroxenes decreases, while their ferruginosities increase, from gabbro-norites toward granosyenites. Furthermore, pyroxene is one of the persistent major colored minerals in gabbroids, but it occurs only sporadically and as a relict mineral in granosyenites. The ferruginosity of orthopyroxene in the gabbroids of the Humboldt Mountains and Petermann Range is considerably higher (53—64%) than in average norites and gabbro-norites, where it is 23—40% /16/. The difference is due to the fairly high grade of metamorphism of the gabbroids, particularly feldspathization and silicification.

The habit of orthopyroxene undergoes a corresponding change. Thus, large (2—4 mm) prismatic orthopyroxene grains (ferrohypersthene) with ragged outlines are preserved in gabbro-norites, in spite of the metamorphism which is indicated by corrosion (by amphibole and biotite). A characteristic feature of these grains is their poikiloblastic texture due to profuse inclusions of quartz, biotite and apatite. In places, they contain exsolution structures, with an abundance of fine linear lamellar clinopyroxene. Recrystallization of prismatic grains produces smaller xenoblastic granules, 0.2—0.4 mm in size. The ferrohypersthene is everywhere partially replaced by amphibole and especially by biotite, starting at the edges of the prismatic grains. In diorite-syenites, orthopyroxene (eulyte) generally occurs as corroded relicts and with a skeletal habit owing to abundant inclusions. The grain size of eulyte varies widely from 0.3 to 1.5 mm. It is closely associated with biotite-amphibole aggregates (by which it is persistently replaced) and also forms aggregates with clino-pyroxene. Eulyte is found in a majority of diorite-syenite specimens, but less commonly in syenites, and then only as small relicts (0.3—0.7 mm) packed with inclusions and embedded in biotite-amphibole aggregates. On the other hand, fayalite occurs much more frequently in syenites than in diorite-syenites, appearing in the former in place of eulyte. Eulyte is rare in granosyenites (as in syenites) where it is replaced by fayalite; it forms small (0.1 to 0.4 mm) corroded skeletal grains. It is replaced by biotite which is particularly abundant along grain boundaries.

Six spectroscopic analyses and one chemical analysis of orthopyroxenes (Table 112) from various charnockitoid rocks indicate a mineral series, the members of which, while obeying certain consistencies, also display some differences due to their origins. The orthopyroxenes fall into three distinct composition groups: 1) in metamorphosed gabbroids, 2) in diorite-syenites (and closely similar syenites) and 3) in granosyenites. Primarily, they differ in their ferruginosities; the first group are characterized by ferrohypersthenes with a ferruginosity of 53—58%, the second — by eulytes with a ferruginosity of 70—72%, and the third — by eulytes, approaching ferrosilites, with a ferruginosity of 87%. The ferruginosity of orthopyroxenes determined from refractive indices is only 1—3% different from the values calculated from the analyses, which is within the analytical accuracy. These three groups correspond to the three stages of the transformation of gabbroids into charnockitoids: first stage — partial recrystallization of the gabbroids accompanied by a relatively limited feldspathization; second stage — complete recrystallization under conditions of alkaline metasomatism with formation of syenitic rocks (from varieties that were transitional to gabbroids); third stage — complete recrystallization of the gabbroids during mixing with partial melts, producing hybrid granosyenites.

Only the contents of the major orthopyroxene component, i. e., ferrosilite, are fairly constant in the metamorphosed gabbroids, 47.4—49.2%, whereas the contents of enstatite and diopside fluctuate considerably, 27.6—38% and 3.2—18.5%, respectively. This is due to the different compositions of the gabbroids which range from anorthosites (with maximum content of diopside) to gabbro-norites (with maximum content of enstatite).

The component compositions of each of the other two rock groups are much more constant, and there are significant differences between the groups: 57.6—63% ferrosilite and 20—22% enstatite in diorite-syenites; 80% ferrosilite and 14% enstatite in granosyenites. The Tschermak molecule, mainly corresponding to the augite component, is fairly constant for the majority of charnockitoid varieties, fluctuating slightly from 3.1—5.1% in the gabbroids to 4.7—5.8% in the diorite-syenites and granosyenites. In general, the variation in the composition of orthopyroxenes is controlled

TABLE 112. Orthopyroxenes

Oxide	Specimen 576 — metamorphosed anorthosite				Specimen 578g — metamorphosed norite				Specimen 544 — metamorphosed norite				Specimen 228 — metamorphosed gabbro-norite-diorite			
	wt%	wt% scaled to 100	atomic quantity of cations	cation numbers	wt%	wt% scaled to 100	atomic quantity of cations	cation numbers	wt%	wt% scaled to 100	atomic quantity of cations	cation numbers	wt%	wt% scaled to 100	atomic quantity of cations	cation numbers
SiO_2	50.5	50.4	839	1.99	49.5	51.1	851	2.04	49.2	49.7	828	1.96	51.0	50.4	839	1.99
TiO_2	0.3	0.3	4	0.01	1.0	1.0	13	0.03	0.4	0.4	5	0.01	0.3	0.3	4	0.01
Al_2O_3	2.3	2.3	46	0.11	3.8	3.9	76	0.18	2.3	2.3	46	0.11	2.0	2.0	40	0.09
FeO tot.	28.6	28.5	396	0.94	25.8	26.5	369	0.89	27.8	28.1	391	0.92	28.8	28.5	396	0.94
MgO	11.8	11.8	293	0.70	11.6	12.0	298	0.72	13.8	13.9	345	0.81	13.0	12.9	320	0.76
MnO	0.6	0.6	8	0.02	0.5	0.5	7		0.5	0.5	7	0.01	0.5	0.5	7	0.01
CaO	5.3	5.3	95	0.23	2.8	2.9	52	0.12	4.2	4.3	77	0.18	4.8	4.7	84	0.20
K_2O	0.6	0.6			1.8	1.9			0.6	0.6			0.1	0.1		
Na_2O	0.2	0.2			0.2	0.2			0.2	0.2						
Σ	100.2	100.0	1681	4.00	97.0	100.0	1666	4.00	99.0	100.0	1699	4.00	101.1	100.0	1690	4.00

Crystallochemical formulas

Specimen 576:
$$(Fe^{tot}_{0.94}Mg_{0.70}Mn_{0.02}Ca_{0.23}Ti_{0.01}Al_{0.10})_2[(Si_{1.99}Al_{0.01})_2O_6]$$

Specimen 578g:
$$(Fe_{0.89}Mg_{0.72}Mn_{0.02}Ca_{0.12}Ti_{0.03}Al_{0.18})_{1.96}[Si_{2.04}O_6]$$

Specimen 544:
$$(Fe_{0.92}Mg_{0.81}Mn_{0.01}Ca_{0.18}Ti_{0.01}Al_{0.07})_{2.00}[(Si_{1.96}Al_{0.04})_2O_6]$$

Specimen 228:
$$(Fe_{0.94}Mg_{0.76}Mn_{0.01}Ca_{0.20}Ti_{0.01}Al_{0.08})[(Si_{1.99}Al_{0.01})_2O_6]$$

Component composition

	Specimen 576 at.%	Specimen 578g at.%	Specimen 544 at.%	Specimen 228 at.%
Tschermak molecule	5.1	9.6	3.1	4.1
	$Ca_{0.05}Al_{0.10}Si_{0.05}O_{0.30}$	$Ca_{0.09}Al_{0.18}Si_{0.09}O_{0.54}$	$Ca_{0.03}Al_{0.07}Si_{0.03}O_{0.18}$	$Ca_{0.04}Al_{0.08}Si_{0.04}O_{0.24}$
Diopside	18.5	3.2	15.3	16.3
	$Ca_{0.18}(Mg.Mn)_{0.18}Si_{0.36}O_{1.08}$	$Ca_{0.03}(Mg.Mn)_{0.03}Si_{0.06}O_{0.18}$	$Ca_{0.15}(Mg.Mn)_{0.15}Si_{0.30}O_{0.90}$	$Ca_{0.16}(Mg.Mn)_{0.16}Si_{0.32}O_{0.96}$
Enstatite	27.6	38.0	34.2	31.1
	$(Mg.Mn)_{0.54}Si_{0.54}O_{1.62}$	$(Mg.Mn)_{0.71}Si_{0.71}O_{2.13}$	$(Mg.Mn)_{0.67}Si_{0.67}O_{2.01}$	$(Mg.Mn)_{0.61}Si_{0.61}O_{1.83}$
Ferrosilite	48.8	49.2	47.4	48.5
	$(Fe.Ti)_{0.95}Si_{0.95}O_{2.85}$	$(Fe.Ti)_{0.92}Si_{0.92}O_{2.76}$	$(Fe.Ti)_{0.93}Si_{0.93}O_{2.79}$	$(Fe.Ti)_{0.95}Si_{0.95}O_{2.85}$
	100.0	100.0	100.0	100.0
f, % { from chemical composition / from refractive index	57 / 58	55 / 58	53 / 53	55 / 57

TABLE 112 (continued)

Oxide	Specimen 36g — diorite-syenite				Specimen 228e — syenite-diorite				Specimen 51 — granosyenite (chemical analysis, collection of 1961)			Table 2 from /16/		
	wt%	wt% scaled to 100	atomic quantity of cations	cation numbers	wt%	wt% scaled to 100	atomic quantity of cations	cation numbers	wt%	wt% scaled to 100	atomic quantity of cations	analysis 14: hypersthene from hybridized norite (wt%)	analysis 17: ferrohypersthene from contaminated norite (wt%)	analysis 19: eulyte from granite (wt%)
SiO_2	56.5	55.7	927	2.26	52.5	54.3	904	2.22	47.45	790	2.00	50.60	50.06	44.52
TiO_2	0.3	0.3	4	0.01	0.4	0.4	5	0.01	0.21	3	0.01	0.19	0.32	1.39
Al_2O_3	1.7	1.7	34	0.08	2.0	2.0	40	0.10	1.07	22	0.06	0.16	1.84	4.74
FeO_{tot}	29.2	28.8	401	0.97	30.6	31.6	440	1.08	45.56	634	1.60	26.68	31.45	39.92
MgO	7.9	7.8	194	0.47	6.9	7.1	176	0.43	3.93	98	0.25	18.96	13.63	6.59
MnO	0.7	0.7	10	0.02	0.8	0.8	11	0.03	0.94	13	0.03	0.31	0.19	0.28
CaO	4.4	4.3	77	0.19	3.0	3.1	55	0.13	1.03	19	0.05	1.65	1.43	1.40
K_2O	0.6	0.6			0.6	0.6						0.07		0.39
Na_2O	0.1	0.1			0.1	0.1						0.60	—	0.19
Σ	101.4	100.0	1647	4.00	96.9	100.0	1631	4.00	100.19	1579	4.00	99.22*	97.92*	99.44*

Specimen 36g: $(Fe_{0.97} Mg_{0.47} Mn_{0.02} Ca_{0.19} Ti_{0.01} Al_{0.08})_{1.74} [Si_{2.26} O_6]$

Specimen 228e: $(Fe_{1.08} Mg_{0.43} Mn_{0.03} Ca_{0.13} Ti_{0.01} Al_{0.10})_{1.78} [Si_{2.22} O_6]$

Specimen 51: $(Fe_{1.60} Mg_{0.25} Mn_{0.02} Ca_{0.05} Al_{0.06} Ti_{0.01})_{2.00} [Si_2 O_6]$

Specimen 36g:
$Ca_{0.04} Al_{0.08} Si_{0.04} O_{0.24}$
$Ca_{0.15} (Mg. Mn)_{0.15} Si_{0.30} O_{0.90}$
$Mg_{0.34} Si_{0.34} O_{1.02}$
$(Fe. Ti)_{0.98} Si_{0.98} O_{2.94}$

Specimen 228e:
$Ca_{0.05} Al_{0.10} Si_{0.05} O_{0.30}$
$Ca_{0.08} (Mg. Mn)_{0.08} Si_{0.16} O_{0.48}$
$Mg_{0.38} Si_{0.38} O_{1.14}$
$(Fe. Ti)_{1.09} Si_{1.09} O_{3.27}$

	Specimen 36g	Specimen 228e	Specimen 51	analysis 14	analysis 17	analysis 19
Tschermak molecule	4.7	5.8	5.3			
Diopside	17.7	9.2				
Enstatite	20.0	22.0	14.7			
Ferrosilite	57.6	63.0	80.0			
	100.0	100.0				
f, % { from chemical composition / from refractive index	67 / 70	71 / 72	87 / 86	44 / —	56 / —	77 / —

Note. Here and throughout, the sum of chemical analyses of minerals from /16/ is given without considering H_2O content; the contents of ferric and ferrous iron are combined as total FeO in order to permit a comparison of chemical and spectroscopic analyses.

by the transformation of the gabbroids into charnockitoids. This is mainly expressed by an increase of ferruginosity, due to an intensified recrystallization of the gabbroids and their more active interaction with the alkaline (mainly potassic) metasomatic solutions or partial melts. Indeed, a comparison of the analyses of seven orthopyroxenes reveals that their most variable components are iron (26.5—45.5%) and magnesium (4—14%), whereas the contents of all the other elements (including SiO_2) vary only within 48—55%. The same consistency is noted for magmatic rocks /16/. Thus, orthopyroxene from a hybridized norite contains 27% iron, and a eulyte from granite — 40% iron, probably on account of the latter's higher alkalinity, irrespective of the formation depth of the rocks. Orthopyroxene becomes increasingly unstable with diminishing depth and is replaced by the biotite-amphibole association. At the same time, the appearance of orthopyroxene of low ferruginosity is quite regular in effusive rocks and associated subvolcanic bodies formed near the surface. However, such near-surface magmatic formations should be excluded from the charnockite formations of different depths, since the characteristic features of the latter are not primarily different orthopyroxene ferruginosities, but the association of orthopyroxene with other minerals such as fayalite or garnet.

Clinopyroxenes are less characteristic of the charnockitoids than orthopyroxenes. Although they persistently occur in these rocks, their contents are considerably lower than those of orthopyroxenes. Thus, their content in metamorphosed gabbro-norites is 1—7%, rising to over 30% only in very rare melanocratic varieties, where orthopyroxene nearly disappears and fayalite appears. The ferruginosity of clinopyroxene in gabbroids is 32—56%, but it reaches 86% in the fayalite-bearing varieties. The content of clinopyroxenes (ferruginosity, 38—63%) in gabbro-norite-diorites is approximately the same as in charnockitoids. The content of clinopyroxenes in diorite-syenites is generally 1—10%, seldom reaching 25—27% (in varieties originally pyroxenites). Their ferruginosity is high and variable, 64—97%. At high ferruginosity, the association includes fayalite but lacks orthopyroxene. However, in syenites, clinopyroxene is comparatively rare (2—3%), and its ferruginosity is 80—90%. It is equally rare in granosyenites (although sometimes its content reaches 5%), and its ferruginosity varies from 77 to 95%; in the latter case, it is associated with fayalite. Both clinopyroxene and fayalite are absent from magmatic granitoids.

Clinopyroxene in feldspathized gabbro-norites and gabbro-norite-diorites is closely associated with orthopyroxene, forming ingrowths in and fringes around the latter. In places, it appears to replace the orthopyroxene. Unlike orthopyroxene, clinopyroxene as a rule does not form large prismatic grains but more commonly occurs as small xenoblastic grains, 0.3—0.8 mm in size. It is intensively replaced by amphibole, and prismatic grains of the latter always contain small relict pyroxene. An exception is encountered in the rare rocks approaching pyroxenites, which retain as much as 40% of clinopyroxenes. These are of two generations, 2—3-mm prismatic grains with profuse inclusions of quartz and biotite, and recrystallized aggregates of small (0.3—0.5 mm) grains in close association with fayalite. In diorite-syenites, syenites and granosyenites, where clinopyroxene occurs sporadically, it is usually represented by strongly corroded skeletal grains measuring 0.2—0.5 mm, closely associated with fayalite and embedded in biotite-amphibole aggregates.

It should be emphasized that the pyroxenes locally retain their original prismatic habit and normal dimensions only in basic varieties of charnockitoids. In subalkaline and acid varieties, which are the closest to charnockites, the pyroxenes were clearly recrystallized, which reduced their grain size; they assume a skeletal habit due to an abundance of various secondary inclusions, and are relict in nature.

The six spectroscopic analyses of clinopyroxenes listed in Table 113 clearly reflect the differences in their composition in relation to the rock in which they occur. In this respect, the analyzed minerals fall into two groups: 1) pyroxenes of metamorphic gabbroids, rocks transformed into gabbro-diorites, and likewise those closer to diorite-syenites; with a ferruginosity of 45—54%, and 2) pyroxenes of diorite-syenites and syenites proper; with a ferruginosity of 77—79% and occasionally 92% where they are associated with fayalite. Unfortunately, an analysis of pyroxenes from granosyenites is not available, but the refractive indices suggest that they might form a third group of clinopyroxenes with maximal ferruginosities. One of the most characteristic features of all analyzed pyroxenes is the predominance of Fe + Mg over Ca, which is considerable in the first group of pyroxenes. This feature indicates their similarity to augites and ferroaugites, instead of to pyroxenes of the salite series. Indeed, a comparison of the chemical compositions of the clinopyroxenes with analogous clinopyroxenes from gabbros, reveals that the former are the closest to augite from ferrogabbro. Thus, the contents of silica are 46—51% in the pyroxenes in comparison to 50.5% in augite from gabbro; the alumina content is 1.4—4.8% and 2.2% in the augite; the FeO_{tot} content is 16.5—18% and 17% in the augite; the CaO content is 14—18% and 16.5% in the augite; the content of MgO is 9.0—11.5% and 12.6% in the augite. Pyroxenes of the second group occupy an intermediate position between ferroaugite and hedenbergite in their chemical composition; the content of silica in these pyroxenes is 47.0—50.5% as compared to just a little over 48% in ferroaugites (also in hedenbergite). On the other hand, the content of alumina is 2—2.7% in the pyroxenes as compared to 1% in ferroaugite and 0.3% in hedenbergite. The respective contents of FeO are 27% and 24.5%, those of MgO are 1.3—3.5% and 1%, and those of CaO are 14.5—19.5% and 19—>21%. Thus, the pyroxenes in question are closer to the augite series than to the salite series; this is a characteristic feature of the gabbroids which gave rise to the charnockitoids. The similarity to augites is especially marked in pyroxenes from basic varieties, whereas the clinopyroxenes from alkaline and subalkaline charnockitoids occupy intermediate positions between the ferroaugites and hedenbergites. However, in general, they are closer to the former. An indirect indication that the pyroxenes belong to the augite series is the presence of as much as 11% of the Tschermak molecule in their component composition, as well as a small amount of the hedenbergite molecule proper. The content of the latter in pyroxenes of the third group does not exceed 7%.

TABLE 113. Clinopyroxenes

Oxide	Specimen 544 — metamorphosed norite				Specimen 228 — metamorphosed gabbro-norite-diorite				Specimen 36g — diorite-syenite				Specimen 93 — diorite-syenite transitional to syenite			
	wt%	wt% scaled to 100	atomic quantity of cations	cation numbers	wt%	wt% scaled to 100	atomic quantity of cations	cation numbers	wt%	wt% scaled to 100	atomic quantity of cations	cation numbers	wt%	wt% scaled to 100	atomic quantity of cations	cation numbers
SiO_2	46.0	45.5	758	1.76	51.0	49.9	828	1.93	49.0	50.4	839	2.01	46.3	46.9	781	1.91
TiO_2	1.2	1.2	15	0.03	0.9	0.9	11	0.03	1.4	1.4	18	0.04	0.8	0.8	10	0.02
Al_2O_3	4.9	4.8	94	0.22	3.5	3.4	66	0.15	4.3	4.4	86	0.21	2.7	2.7	52	0.13
FeO_{tot}	17.4	17.2	239	0.56	16.9	16.4	228	0.53	17.7	18.2	253	0.61	23.8	24.1	335	0.82
MgO	11.8	11.6	288	0.67	11.0	10.7	265	0.62	8.7	8.9	221	0.53	3.9	4.0	99	0.24
MnO	0.3	0.3	4	0.01	0.3	0.3	4	0.01	0.4	0.4	6	0.01	0.4	0.4	6	0.01
CaO	18.2	18.0	321	0.75	18.0	17.5	312	0.73	13.4	13.8	246	0.59	19.6	19.9	355	0.87
K_2O	0.8	0.6			0.6	0.6			2.1	2.1			0.6	0.6		
Na_2O	0.8	0.8			0.5	0.5			0.4	0.4			0.6	0.6		
Σ	101.2	100.0	1719	4.00	102.7	100.0	1714	4.00	97.4	100.0	1669	4.00	98.7	100.0	1638	4.00

Crystallochemical formulas

Specimen 544:
$$(Ca_{0.75}Mg_{0.67}Mn_{0.01}Fe_{0.56}Ti_{0.03})2.02 \ [(Si_{1.76}Al_{0.22})1.98 \ O_6]$$

Specimen 228:
$$(Ca_{0.73}Mg_{0.62}Mn_{0.01}Fe_{0.53}Ti_{0.03}Al_{0.08})2 \ [(Si_{1.93}Al_{0.07})2 \ O_6]$$

Specimen 36g:
$$(Ca_{0.59}Mg_{0.53}Mn_{0.01}Fe_{0.61}Ti_{0.04}Al_{0.21})1.99 \ [Si_{2.01} \ O_6]$$

Specimen 93:
$$(Ca_{0.87}Fe_{0.82}Mg_{0.24}Mn_{0.01}Ti_{0.02}Al_{0.04})2.00 \ [Si_{1.91}Al_{0.09})2.00 \ O_6]$$

Component composition

	Specimen 544		Specimen 228		Specimen 36g		Specimen 93	
Tschermak molecule	—		$Ca_{0.04}Al_{0.08}Si_{0.04}O_{0.24}$	4.1	$Ca_{0.10}Al_{0.21}Si_{0.10}O_{0.60}$	10.7	$Ca_{0.02}Al_{0.04}Si_{0.02}O_{0.12}$	2.0
Diopside	$Ca_{0.68}(Mg,Mn)_{0.68}Si_{1.38}O_{4.08}$	67.3	$Ca_{0.63}(Mg,Mn)_{0.63}Si_{1.26}O_{3.78}$	64.3	$Ca_{0.49}(Mg,Mn)_{0.49}Si_{0.98}O_{2.94}$	52.1	$Ca_{0.25}(Mg,Mn)_{0.25}Si_{0.50}O_{1.50}$	25.3
Hedenbergite	$Ca_{0.07}(Fe,Ti)_{0.07}Si_{0.14}O_{0.42}$	6.9	$Ca_{0.06}(Fe,Ti)_{0.06}Si_{0.12}O_{0.36}$	6.1		34.5	$Ca_{0.60}(Fe,Ti)_{0.60}Si_{1.20}O_{3.60}$	60.6
Ferrosilite	$(Fe,Ti)_{0.52}Si_{0.52}O_{1.56}$	25.8	$(Fe,Ti)_{0.50}Si_{0.50}O_{1.50}$	25.5	$(Fe,Ti)_{0.65}Si_{0.65}O_{1.95}$		$(Fe,Ti)_{0.24}Si_{0.24}O_{0.72}$	12.1
Total		100.0%		100.0%		100.0%		100.0%
f,%, by chemical composition		45		46		54		77
f,%, by refractive index		42		48		64		80

TABLE 113 (continued)

Oxide	Specimen 33v — syenite				Specimen 592 — syenite, transitional to diorite-syenite				Table 17/16/. No. 22 — augite from ferrogabbro	Table 18/16/. No.12 — ferro-augite from ferrogabbro	Table 5/16/. No. 37 — hedenbergite
	wt%	wt% scaled to 100	atomic quantity of cations	cation numbers	wt%	wt% scaled to 100	atomic quantity of cations	cation numbers	wt%	wt%	wt%
SiO_2	52.5	50.5	841	2.06	47.6	47.7	794	1.98	50.58	40.18	48.34
TiO_2	0.4	0.4	5	0.01	0.7	0.7	9	0.02	0.61	0.70	0.08
Al_2O_3	2.2	2.1	42	0.10	2.2	2.2	40	0.10	2.20	1.06	0.30
FeO_{tot}	28.2	27.0	376	0.93	27.2	27.2	378	0.94	17.01	27.54	24.44
MgO	4.2	4.0	99	0.24	1.3	1.3	32	0.08	12.60	3.52	1.06
MnO	0.6	0.6	8	0.02	0.6	0.6	8	0.02	0.28	0.53	3.70
CaO	15.1	14.5	259	0.64	19.5	19.5	348	0.86	16.40	18.90	21.30
K_2O	0.6	0.6							0.03	0.04	0.03
Na_2O	0.3	0.3			0.4	0.4			0.21	0.23	0.14
Σ	104.1	100.0	1630	4.00	99.9	100.0	1609	4.00	100.01	100.70	99.85

Crystallochemical formulas

Specimen 33v:
$$(Ca_{0.64}Fe_{0.93}Mg_{0.24}Mn_{0.02}Ti_{0.01}Al_{0.10})_{1.94}[Si_{2.05}O_6]$$

Specimen 592:
$$(Ca_{0.86}Fe_{0.94}Mg_{0.08}Mn_{0.02}Ti_{0.02}Al_{0.08})_{2.00}[(Si_{1.98}Al_{0.02})_{2.00}O_6]$$

Component composition

	Specimen 33v	Specimen 592
Tschermak molecule	5.3 $Ca_{0.05}Al_{0.10}Si_{0.05}O_{0.30}$	4.1 $Ca_{0.04}Al_{0.08}Si_{0.04}O_{0.24}$
Diopside	27.5 $Ca_{0.26}(Mg,Mn)_{0.26}Si_{0.52}O_{1.56}$	10.2 $Ca_{0.10}(Mg,Mn)_{0.10}Si_{0.20}O_{0.60}$
Hedenbergite	34.9 $Ca_{0.33}(Fe,Ti)_{0.33}Si_{0.66}O_{1.98}$	73.5 $Ca_{0.72}(Fe,Ti)_{0.72}Si_{1.44}O_{4.32}$
Ferrosilite	32.3 $(Fe,Ti)_{0.61}Si_{0.61}O_{1.83}$	12.2 $(Fe,Ti)_{0.24}Si_{0.24}O_{0.72}$
Total	100.0%	100.0%
f, % by chemical composition	79	92
f, % by refractive index	80	97

(Table 17/16/. No. 22: f = 43; Table 18/16/. No.12: f = 81; Table 5/16/. No. 37: f = 93)

Notes. 1. The small sodium content in all analyses was ignored in determinations of the component composition; it probably corresponds to 3—4% aegirine molecule, which cannot be computed because of the absence of differentiation between ferrous and ferric iron in the analyses.

2. Specimen 36g contains an excess of $Mg_{0.05}$ and $Si_{0.05}$ (2.7% enstatite).

Another feature of the clinopyroxenes in granitoids is their high content of alkali. The presence of sodium denotes an admixture of the aegirine molecule (3—4%), whereas the presence of potassium, sometimes as much as 2%, is probably related to biotitization of the pyroxenes. Indeed, biotite persistently develops along the finest cracks, and it is impossible to separate it from fine grains of the pyroxenes. The high content of alkalis in the pyroxenes, averaging >1%, could be an indirect result of their recrystallization under conditions of alkaline metasomatism, to which their high ferruginosity is directly related. The ferruginosity of clinopyroxenes determined by spectroscopic analysis is in the majority of cases in satisfactory agreement with the values determined from the refractive indices; the latter are generally 2—5% higher. However, in certain cases (specimen 36g) the difference amounts to 12%, possibly due to the high content of the aegirine molecule, which increases the refractive index.

Hornblendes are among the most widespread colored minerals in the charnockitoids. All varieties from metamorphosed gabbroids to granosyenites contain hornblende together with biotite. The content of hornblende increases with a decreasing content of pyroxenes (which are replaced by the hornblende). The maximum hornblende content occurs in gabbro-norite-diorites and diorite-syenites; this gradually declines in syenites and granosyenites, which are more leucocratic than the basic charnockitoids. Metamorphosed gabbroids contain 2—5% amphibole, and rarely 20—30% where pyroxenes are nearly absent. The ferruginosity of amphibole is usually 55—68%, but it rises to 73—85% in strongly metamorphosed anorthosites composing blocks within acid charnockitoids and granites. The ferruginosity of coexisting pyroxenes is much lower. Characteristically, amphiboles with ferruginosities of 34—48% occur in anorthosites of lower-grade metamorphism. Thus, the variation in the ferruginosity of amphiboles is fairly large and depends on the degree of recrystallization of the rocks under conditions of alkaline metasomatism, to which the amphiboles react much more strongly than the pyroxenes. Amphibole is the leading mafic in gabbro-norite-diorites and diorite-syenites; the content is fairly stable at 10—20% (seldom more). As a rule, its ferruginosity is fairly high, 70—80% (sometimes higher, especially in diorite-syenites). Amphibole is likewise the leading mafic mineral in syenites and granosyenites, but its content is lower, averaging 5—10%, rarely up to 12—15%. The amphibole in these rocks has the maximum ferruginosity, always >80%, more commonly >90%, and locally even 97—100%. Newly formed granites and granodiorites are an exception. Amphibole occurs only in certain specimens and its content does not exceed 3—5%; most important, its ferruginosity is 20—30% lower than in granosyenites. In these rocks, amphibole is associated only with biotite, never occurring in paragenesis with pyroxene. Amphibole is also found in the same association in granitoid veins.

Thus the ferruginosity of amphiboles also generally gradually increases from metamorphosed gabbroids (averaging 60%) to granosyenites (averaging 90%), although its variation is not so regular as in the pyroxenes. This may be due to the fact that the amphiboles, similar to K-feldspars, formed during metamorphism and recrystallization of the original basic rocks under conditions of alkaline metasomatism. The shape and dimensions of the amphibole grains correspond to this genesis, especially in rocks where their contents are high. Thus, amphibole in metagabbro-norites forms rims around pyroxenes and rarely granules of 0.2—0.5 mm. However, already in strongly metamorphosed anorthosites there are independent aggregates of dark green amphiboles with grain sizes of 1.0—1.5 mm. Such aggregates exhibit maculose and banded forms and are partly developed at the expense of plagioclase, since their content reaches 30% in anorthosites that are practically free of pyroxene but contain garnet — almandine. Poikiloblastic and symplektitic quartz ingrowths are common in such amphiboles. The character of amphibole changes drastically in the diorite-syenites and syenites. Prismatic grains of green hornblende measuring 5—6 mm with the habit of porphyroblasts are fairly common, as are also rims around pyroxenes. The amphibole porphyroblasts sometimes retain small relicts of pyroxene and also contain symplektitic quartz ingrowths. Biotite occurs with hornblende in fine-grained xenoblastic aggregates (0.3—0.5 mm). Amphibole in granosyenites is most commonly represented by anhedral grains, 1—2 mm. The grains are diablastic largely due to small inclusions of quartz and plagioclase apparently trapped by the mineral in the course of its growth. Together with the biotite, they form glomerular or banded aggregates with relict pyroxene and fayalite. Larger, sub-euhedral prismatic grains of amphibole (up to 3—5 mm) are fairly common, but as a rule they are packed with fine inclusions, including apatite. The mineral is distinctly pleochroic in deep green colors (more commonly dark green, less commonly bluish green). Amphibole and biotite are the only colored minerals in the majority of granosyenite specimens. Amphibole in injective magmatic granites and granodiorites occurs exclusively as small and irregular grains (0.5—1.0 mm), dark green in color with brownish flecks. It forms glomero-aggregates in association with biotite. Except for apatite, the amphibole in these rocks is practically free of inclusions. No relict colored minerals have been detected in granitoids.

The composition of amphiboles in the principal varieties of charnockitoids is based on ten spectroscopic analyses and one chemical analysis, and their composition in granodiorites by a single analysis (Table 114). The ferruginosity of amphiboles is 63—92%, i. e., 63—72% in diorite-syenites, 77—83% in syenites and 83—92% in granosyenites. It is less than 70% only in granitoids which are not part of the charnockitoid series. The respective contents of FeO and MgO average 22% and 6% in diorite-syenites, 27% and 4% in syenites, 28% and 2% in granosyenites, and 22% and 5% in injective granitoids. All analyzed amphiboles have high contents of CaO, 9—12%, indicating their similarity to the hastingsite series (hastingsites average 10% CaO, 20% FeO, 7% MgO, while the ferrohastingsites contain 25—30% FeO and 2.5% MgO). Hence, the analyzed amphiboles occupy an intermediate position between hastingsites and ferrohastingsites, while the amphiboles of the syenites and granosyenites closely approach the latter. The amphibole of injective granitoids is closest to hastingsites.

The following two features distinguish the analyzed amphiboles from the hastingsite series: a) high content of alkalis and especially potassium

TABLE 114. Hornblendes

Oxide	Specimen 576 — metamorphosed anorthosite				Specimen 36g — diorite-syenite				Specimen 228e — diorite-syenite				Specimen 24 — diorite-syenite			
	wt%	scaled to 100 wt%	atomic quantity of cations	cation numbers	wt%	scaled to 100 wt%	atomic quantity of cations	cation numbers	wt%	scaled to 100 wt%	atomic quantity of cations	cation numbers	wt%	scaled to 100 wt%	atomic quantity of cations	cation numbers
SiO_2	37.2	39.4	656	6.01	44.6	45.2	753	6.84	42.1	43.4	723	6.64	41.6	42.8	713	6.64
TiO_2	5.5	5.8	73	0.67	3.2	3.2	40	0.36	4.1	4.2	53	0.49	2.9	3.0	38	0.35
Al_2O_3	10.6	11.2	220	2.01	8.3	8.4	164	1.49	9.1	9.4	184	1.69	8.8	9.0	176	1.64
FeO_{tot}	24.7	26.2	364	3.33	20.9	21.2	295	2.68	21.2	21.8	304	2.78	24.0	24.6	342	3.18
MgO	4.0	4.2	104	0.95	7.0	7.1	176	1.60	5.8	6.0	149	1.37	4.9	5.0	124	1.15
MnO	0.2	0.2	3	0.03	0.2	0.2	3	0.03	0.2	0.2	3	0.03	0.3	0.3	4	0.04
Σ			1420	13.00			1431	13.00			1416	13.00			1397	13.00
CaO	8.3	8.8	157	1.44	11.7	11.8	210	1.91	11.5	11.8	210	1.93	11.2	11.5	205	1.91
K_2O	2.4	2.6	56	0.51	1.2	1.2	26	0.24	1.6	1.6	34	0.31	1.9	2.0	42	0.39
Na_2O	1.5	1.6	52	0.47	1.7	1.7	54	0.49	1.6	1.6	52	0.48	1.8	1.8	58	0.54
Σ	94.4	100.0		2.42	98.8	100.0		2.64	97.2	100.0		2.72	97.4	100.0		2.84

Crystallochemical formulas

	Specimen 576	Specimen 36g	Specimen 228e	Specimen 24
	$(Ca_{1.44}Na_{0.47}K_{0.51})_{2.40}$	$(Ca_{1.81}Na_{0.49}K_{0.24})_{2.64}$	$(Ca_{1.93}Na_{0.48}K_{0.31})_{2.72}$	$(Ca_{1.91}K_{0.39}Na_{0.54})_{2.84}$
	$(Mg_{0.35}Mn_{0.03}Fe_{3.33}Ti_{0.67}Al_{0.02})_{5.00}$	$(Fe_{2.68}Mg_{1.60}Mn_{0.03}Ti_{0.36}Al_{0.33})_{5.00}$	$(Fe_{2.78}Mg_{1.37}Mn_{0.03}Ti_{0.48}Al_{0.33})_{5.00}$	$(Fe_{3.18}Mg_{1.15}Mn_{1.04}Ti_{0.35}Al_{0.28})_{5.00}$
	$[(Si_{6.01}Al_{1.99})_8 O_{22}] (OH)_2$	$[(Si_{6.84}Al_{1.16})_8 O_{22}] (OH)_2$	$[(Si_{6.64}Al_{1.36})_8 O_{22}] (OH)_2$	$[(Si_{6.64}Al_{1.36})_8 O_{22}] (OH)_2$
f,%, by chemical composition	78	63	67	73
f, %, by refractive index	80	71	72	71

TABLE 114 (continued)

Oxide	Specimen 93 — diorite-syenite, transitional to syenite				Specimen 33v — syenite				Specimen 44 — syenite				Specimen 44g — syenite				Specimen 31b — granosyenite			
	wt %	wt % scaled to 100	atomic quantity of cations	cation numbers	wt %	wt % scaled to 100	atomic quantity of cations	cation numbers	wt %	wt % scaled to 100	atomic quantity of cations	cation numbers	wt %	wt % scaled to 100	atomic quantity of cations	cation numbers	wt %	wt % scaled to 100	atomic quantity of cations	cation numbers
SiO_2	37.6	43.3	721	6.79	41.7	44.8	746	6.91	40.7	41.2	686	6.39	40.8	42.2	703	6.52	40.5	41.5	691	6.37
TiO_2	2.6	3.0	33	0.31	2.1	2.3	29	0.27	3.1	3.1	39	0.36	2.0	2.1	26	0.24	2.8	2.9	36	0.33
Al_2O_3	5.4	6.2	122	1.15	7.4	7.9	154	1.43	9.5	9.6	188	1.75	9.9	10.2	200	1.86	9.9	10.1	198	1.83
FeO_{tot}	23.6	27.2	378	3.56	24.2	26.0	362	3.35	27.2	27.5	383	3.57	27.0	27.9	388	3.60	28.0	28.7	399	3.68
MgO	4.1	4.7	117	1.10	4.0	4.3	107	1.00	3.8	3.8	94	0.87	3.0	3.1	77	0.72	3.2	3.3	82	0.75
MnO	0.6	0.7	10	0.09	0.3	0.3	4	0.04	0.4	0.4	6	0.06	0.5	0.5	7	0.06	0.3	0.3	4	0.04
Σ			1381	13.00			1402	13.00			1396	13.00			1401	13.00			1410	13.00
CaO	11.0	12.7	227	2.14	10.3	11.1	198	1.83	10.6	10.8	193	1.80	9.5	9.8	175	1.62	9.3	9.5	169	1.56
K_2O	1.0	1.2	26	0.24	1.6	1.7	36	0.33	1.6	1.6	34	0.32	2.6	2.7	58	0.54	2.0	2.1	44	0.41
Na_2O	0.9	1.0	32	0.30	1.5	1.6	52	0.48	2.0	2.0	64	0.50	1.5	1.5	48	0.45	1.6	1.6	52	0.48
Σ	86.8	100.0		2.68	93.1	100.0		2.64	98.9	100.0		2.62	96.8	100.0		2.61	97.6	100.0		2.45

Crystallochemical formulas

	Specimen 93	Specimen 33v	Specimen 44	Specimen 44g	Specimen 31b
	$(Ca_{2.14}K_{0.24}Na_{0.30})_{2.68}$ $(Fe_{3.56}Mg_{1.10}Mn_{0.08}Ti_{0.25})_{5.00}$ $[(Si_{6.79}Al_{1.15}Ti_{0.06})_{8.00}O_{22}](OH)_2$	$(Ca_{1.83}Na_{0.48}K_{0.33})_{2.64}$ $(Fe_{3.35}Mg_{1.00}Mn_{0.04}Ti_{0.27}Al_{0.34})_{5.00}$ $[(Si_{6.91}Al_{1.09})_{8.00}O_{22}](OH)_2$	$(Ca_{1.80}Na_{0.50}K_{0.32})_{2.62}$ $(Mg_{0.87}Mn_{0.06}Fe_{3.57}Ti_{0.36}Al_{0.14})_{5.00}$ $[(Si_{6.39}Al_{1.61})_{8.00}O_{22}](OH)_2$	$(Ca_{1.62}Na_{0.45}K_{0.54})_{2.61}$ $(Mg_{0.22}Mn_{0.06}Fe_{3.60}Ti_{0.24}Al_{0.38})_{5.00}$ $[(Si_{6.52}Al_{1.48})_{8.00}O_{22}](OH)_2$	$(Ca_{1.56}Na_{0.48}K_{0.41})_{2.45}$ $(Mg_{0.75}Mn_{0.04}Fe_{3.68}Ti_{0.33}Al_{0.20})_{5.00}$ $[(Si_{6.37}Al_{1.63})_{8.00}O_{22}](OH)_2$
f, %, by chemical composition	76	77	80	83	83
f, %, by refractive index	80	80	87	89	90

TABLE 114 (continued)

Oxide	Specimen 574d—granosyenite				Specimen 51 — granosyenite (from collection of 1961)			Specimen 562 — granodiorite				Table 43 /16/			
	w t%	wt% scaled to 100	atomic quantity of cations	cation numbers	wt%	atomic quantity of cations	cation numbers	wt%	wt% scaled to 100	atomic quantity of cations	cation numbers	No. 14: ferro-hastingsite from granite, wt%	No. 22: ferro-hastingsite from syenite, wt%	No. 24: ferro-hastingsite from hornblende granite, wt%	No. 15: hastingsite from schist, wt%
SiO_2	42.8	43.3	721	6.89	38.83	647	6.15	43.9	44.0	733	6.76	39.56	38.41	38.77	42.89
TiO_2	2.5	2.5	31	0.30	2.38	30	0.29	1.6	1.6	20	0.18	1.46	1.26	2.56	0.75
Al_2O_3	9.7	9.8	192	1.83	11.77	231	2.20	10.7	10.7	210	1.90	12.18	16.39	10.08	13.95
FeO_{tot}	26.8	27.2	378	3.61	29.04	403	3.78	22.2	22.2	308	2.88	27.28	25.50	30.61	19.46
MgO	1.4	1.4	35	0.33	2.33	58	0.54	5.3	5.3	132	1.22	4.43	2.54	2.53	7.41
MnO	0.3	0.3	4	0.04	0.25	4	0.04	0.4	0.4	6	0.06	0.09	0.15	0.60	0.27
Σ			1361	13.00		1383	13.00			1409	13.00				
CaO	12.3	12.4	221	2.10	10.08	180	1.71	10.7	10.7	191	1.76	9.98	10.52	9.65	9.75
K_2O	1.7	1.7	36	0.34	1.80	38	0.36	3.9	3.9	82	0.75	1.38	1.95	1.18	0.85
Na_2O	1.4	1.4	46	0.44	0.75	24	0.23	1.2	1.2	38	0.35	1.81	2.95	1.61	2.83
Σ	98.9	100.0		2.88	97.33		2.30	99.9	100.0		2.86	99.37	99.67	97.65	99.85

Crystallochemical formulas

$(Ca_{2.10}Na_{0.44}K_{0.34})_{2.88}$	$(Ca_{1.71}Na_{0.23}K_{0.36})_{2.30}$	$(Ca_{1.76}K_{0.75}Na_{0.35})_{2.86}$	
$(Mg_{0.33}Mn_{0.04}Fe_{3.61}Ti_{0.72})_{3.00}$	$(Mg_{0.54}Mn_{0.04}Fe_{3.78}Ti_{0.29}Al_{0.35})_{5.00}$	$(Mg_{1.22}Mn_{0.08}Fe_{2.88}Ti_{0.18}Al_{0.66})_{5.00}$	
$[(Si_{6.89}Al_{1.11})_{8.00}O_{22}](OH)_2$	$[(Si_{6.15}Al_{1.85})_{8.00}O_{22}](OH)_2$	$[(Si_{6.76}Al_{1.24})_{8.00}O_{22}](OH)_2$	

	574d	51	562	No. 14	No. 22	No. 24	No. 15
f , % by chemical composition	92	87	70	86			
f , % by refractive index	91	97	68		94	92	72

(1.5—4.0% K_2O as compared to <1% in hastingsites and 1—2% in ferrohastingsites); b) high content of silica (40—45% SiO_2 as compared to ~43%
in hastingsites and 38—39% in ferrohastingsites). These features are explained by the crystallization conditions of amphiboles which formed during
recrystallization of gabbroids interacting with alkaline metasomatic solutions or partial melts. This is also the cause for the high ferruginosity of
the amphiboles in such rocks as metamorphosed anorthosites and diorite-
syenites. An increase of iron and alkalis (especially potassium) and also
silicon in amphiboles during granitization of schists has been reported by
several investigators from different regions in the world /43/. A notable
feature is the high content of titanium (3—5%) in the amphiboles under
consideration; it is somewhat lower only in granosyenites and granodiorites.
The titanium content is 1.5—2.5% in typical ferrohastingsite and still lower
in hastingsite. This is possibly due to the original composition of the rocks
giving rise to hornblende charnockitoids which, as is known, belong among
the gabbroids. The more basic varieties of charnockitoids have nearly
double the titanium content recorded for the more acid varieties. Because of the high titanium content in the amphiboles, their ferruginosity
determined from refractive indices is somewhat higher (2—8%) than the
ferruginosity computed from the analyses.

Biotite is the most widespread mineral of the charnockitoids, but its
contents vary widely in different rock types. The maximum biotite contents
(5—20%, average of 10%) are found in metamorphosed, feldspathized and
silicified gabbroids. The content is appreciably lower in anorthosites and
gabbro-norites (2—8%), and in diorite-syenites and syenites (2—5%). It is
somewhat higher in granosyenites (3—8%) and especially in injective
granitoids (5—20%, average of 10%). Characteristically, however, some
specimens with up to 20% biotite occur even among the charnockitoid
varieties that commonly have low contents of this mineral. For example,
strongly recrystallized gabbro-anorthosites in which pyroxenes are no longer
present and in which the plagioclase has been deoxidized to intermediate
andesine, contain 20% biotite which has the maximum ferruginosity for
this group of rocks. Some varieties of melanocratic granosyenites devoid
of pyroxenes and fayalite contain as much as 18% biotite with a maximum
ferruginosity similar to that of nearly pure lepidomelane. On the whole,
the ferruginosity of biotites is always higher than that of the coexisting
pyroxenes. This difference is more pronounced in basic and intermediate
than in subalkaline and acid rocks.

Metamorphosed gabbro-norites and anorthosites contain biotite of two
generations, 1) early biotites formed during charnockitization with ferruginosities of 60—80% or higher (15—20% above the ferruginosity of coexisting
pyroxenes) and 2) secondary biotites, formed during subsequent superimposed metamorphism, with ferruginosities of 17—36% (lower than those of
the coexistent pyroxenes — 40—50%). In the latter case, the biotite is represented by fine booklets and linear elongated flakes, 0.5—1.5 mm long, sometimes forming glomero-aggregates. The biotite in syenite-diorites and
syenites forms aggregates of fine flakes together with fayalite and relict
pyroxenes, which are replaced by the biotite. Biotite may be idioblastic

(1—2 mm), often intergrown with quartz. It is nearly always associated with amphibole, which is prevalent in these rocks. There are many varieties practically devoid of biotite but always containing amphibole. The biotite is dark brown in color and strongly pleochroic. Its ferruginosity in diorite-syenites is 66—86%, averaging 76%, and in syenites 78—93%, usually 90%. In granosyenites, biotite almost totally replaces orthopyroxene, which is preserved as sporadic relicts. Certain of the granosyenites contain only hastingsite in addition to the biotite and thus are theoretically not charnock-ites. However, they almost invariably form gradual transitions to eulyte- and fayalite-bearing granosyenites, which also contain secondary biotite and amphibole. The ferruginosity of biotite in these rocks is nearly always high, 80—95%, seldom as low as 73—75%. The biotite is represented by flakes of varying sizes, closely associated with the amphibole. The larger flakes, 1.5—2 mm long, are often packed with inclusions of quartz and accessory minerals, and are thus diablastic. The same flakes contain relict pyroxene and fine intrusions of ore along the cleavage. Biotite is the leading colored mineral in injective granodiorites and granites outside the charnockitoid series, where hornblende occurs only sporadically and in subordinate amounts. The biotite in these rocks is represented by flakes 1—2 mm long, uniformly disseminated throughout the rocks, and less commonly, concentrated in aggregates. The biotite contains abundant inclusions of accessory apatite, zircon, orthite and sphene, not infrequently totaling 20—25 vol.% of the host mineral (diablastic). Symplektitic quartz ingrowths occur in the biotite.

The composition of biotites from different intrusive rocks in the region is characterized by eleven quantitative spectroscopic analyses listed in Table 115. They fall into four groups with respect to the Fe : Mg ratio, with the following ferruginosities: a) 60—66% in metamorphosed anorthosites and norites, b) 60—75% in diorite-syenites, c) 82—85% in syenites and grano-syenites, and d) 71—79% in injective granodiorites and granites. These groups likewise have regular ratios of other elements reflecting the compositional features of the original rocks and their formation processes. The mica of meta-anorthosites is different from the other biotites in its very high contents of alumina (up to 20%) and calcium (>2%), 1.5—2.0 times higher than in biotites from average gabbroids. This is analogous with the composition of meta-anorthosites and indicates that the biotite formed during metamorphism, and not by crystallization from a magma. The contents of these elements in charnockitoid varieties are very close to those in rocks of the gabbro—granite series. A noteworthy feature is the high content of titanium in biotites of nearly all the charnockitoid varieties (4.5—5.5%), found only in normal gabbroids, but not in subalkaline rocks such as the syenites and granosyenites. This is another indication of the development of the syenite and granosyenite from gabbroids during metasomatic re-crystallization. Probably, the high titanium content is related to the high ferruginosity of the biotites, computed from the refractive indices. This is 2—8% higher than the ferruginosity values determined from the analyses, with the exception of biotite from anorthosites having a titanium content lower than in the biotite from granites. Characteristically, the contents of

TABLE 115. Biotites

Oxide	Specimen 546 — metamorphosed anorthosite				Specimen 544 — metamorphosed norite				Specimen 36g — diorite-syenite				Specimen 228e — diorite-syenite			
	wt%	wt% scaled to 100	atomic quantity of cations	cation numbers	wt%	wt% scaled to 100	atomic quantity of cations	cation numbers	wt%	wt% scaled to 100	atomic quantity of cations	cation numbers	wt%	wt% scaled to 100	atomic quantity of cations	cation numbers
SiO_2	39.4	38.0	633	2.78	42.6	40.4	673	3.17	40.6	45.5	758	3.44	40.8	42.5	708	3.30
TiO_2	1.7	1.6	20	0.09	4.8	4.5	56	0.26	3.6	4.0	50	0.23	5.2	5.4	68	0.32
Al_2O_3	20.0	19.2	376	1.65	14.4	13.6	266	1.25	11.4	12.9	252	1.44	11.7	12.2	240	1.12
FeO	25.4	24.4	340	1.49	24.6	23.3	324	1.53	20.4	22.8	318	1.44	23.2	24.2	337	1.57
MgO	9.4	9.0	223	0.98	7.0	6.6	164	0.77	5.9	6.6	164	0.74	5.8	6.0	149	0.69
MnO	0.2	0.2	3	0.01	0.2	0.2	3	0.02	0.1	0.1		0.01	0.1	0.1	1	—
Σ			1595	7.00			1486	7.00			1543	7.00			1503	7.00
CaO	2.3	2.2	39	0.17	0.8	0.8	14	0.07	1.1	1.2	21	0.10	2.0	2.1	38	0.18
K_2O	5.0	4.8	102	0.45	10.7	10.1	214	1.01	5.5	6.2	132	0.60	6.6	6.9	146	0.68
Na_2O	0.6	0.6	20	0.09	0.5	0.5	16	0.08	0.6	0.7	22	0.10	0.6	0.6	20	0.09
Σ	104.0	100.0		0.71	105.6	100.0		1.16	89.2	100.0		0.80	96.0	100.0		0.95

Crystallochemical formulas

$(K_{0.45}Na_{0.09}Ca_{0.17})_{0.71}$ $(Mg_{0.98}Fe_{1.49}Mn_{0.01}Ti_{0.09}$ $Al_{0.43})_{3.00}$ $[(Si_{2.76}Al_{1.22})_{4.00}O_{10}](OH)_2$	$(K_{1.01}Na_{0.08}Ca_{0.07})_{1.16}$ $(Mg_{0.77}Mn_{0.02}Fe_{1.53}Ti_{0.26}$ $Al_{0.42})_{3.00}$ $[(Si_{3.17}Al_{0.83})_{4.00}O_{10}](OH)_2$	$(K_{0.60}Na_{0.10}Ca_{0.10})_{0.80}$ $(Mg_{0.74}Mn_{0.01}Fe_{1.44}Ti_{0.23}$ $Al_{0.58})_{3.00}$ $[(Si_{3.44}Al_{0.56})_{4.00}O_{10}](OH)_2$	$(K_{0.68}Na_{0.09}Ca_{0.18})_{0.95}$ $(Mg_{0.69}Fe_{1.57}Ti_{0.32}Al_{0.42})_{3.00}$ $[(Si_{3.30}Al_{0.70})_{4.00}O_{10}](OH)_2$
f, %, by chemical composition: 60	66	66	70
f, %, by refractive index: 52	64	74	82

TABLE 115 (continued)

Oxide	Specimen 249 — diorite-syenite				Specimen 44 — syenite				Specimen 31b — granosyenite				Specimen 551 — apodiorite			
	wt%	wt% scaled to 100	atomic quantity of cations	cation numbers	wt%	wt% scaled to 100	atomic quantity of cations	cation numbers	wt%	wt% scaled to 100	atomic quantity of cations	cation numbers	wt%	wt% scaled to 100	atomic quantity of cations	cation numbers
SiO_2	44.6	45.3	754	3.53	39.5	41.5	691	3.25	35.7	38.9	648	3.11	38.8	41.2	680	3.14
TiO_2	4.8	4.9	61	0.29	4.8	5.0	63	0.30	4.5	4.9	61	0.29	2.1	2.2	28	0.13
Al_2O_3	10.8	11.0	216	1.01	11.7	12.3	242	1.14	11.9	12.9	252	1.21	13.5	14.3	280	1.28
FeO	23.0	23.4	326	1.53	28.4	29.8	415	1.95	27.6	30.0	417	2.00	26.4	28.1	390	1.79
MgO	5.3	5.4	134	0.63	2.9	3.0	74	0.35	3.0	3.3	82	0.39	5.3	5.6	139	0.64
MnO	0.2	0.2	3	0.01	0.2	0.2	3	0.01	0.1	0.1	1	–	0.3	0.3	4	0.02
Σ	98.4	100.0	1494	7.00	95.4	100.0	1488	7.00	91.9	100.0	1461	7.00	94.3	100.0	1528	7.00
CaO	2.2	2.2	39	0.18	0.5	0.5	9	0.04	1.3	1.4	25	0.12	0.4	0.4	7	0.03
K_2O	6.3	6.4	136	0.64	6.9	7.2	152	0.71	6.5	7.1	150	0.72	7.2	7.6	162	0.74
Na_2O	1.2	1.2	38	0.18	0.5	0.5	16	0.08	1.3	1.4	46	0.22	0.3	0.3	10	0.05
Σ		100.0		1.00		100.0		0.83		100.0		1.06		100.0		0.82

Crystallochemical formulas

Specimen 249	Specimen 44	Specimen 31b	Specimen 551
$(K_{0.64}Na_{0.18}Ca_{0.18})_{1.00}$	$(K_{0.71}Na_{0.08}Ca_{0.04})_{0.83}$	$(K_{0.72}Na_{0.22}Ca_{0.12})_{1.06}$	$(K_{0.74}Na_{0.05}Ca_{0.03})_{0.82}$
$(Fe_{1.53}Mg_{0.63}Mn_{0.01}Ti_{0.29}Al_{0.54})_{3.00}$	$(Mg_{0.35}Mn_{0.01}Fe_{1.95}Ti_{0.30}Al_{0.39})_{3.00}$	$(Mg_{0.39}Fe_{2.00}Ti_{0.29}Al_{0.32})_{3.00}$	$(Mg_{0.64}Mn_{0.02}Fe_{1.79}Ti_{0.13}Al_{0.42})_{3.00}$
$[(Si_{3.53}Al_{0.47})_{4.00}O_{10}](OH)_2$	$[(Si_{3.25}Al_{0.75})_{4.00}O_{10}](OH)_2$	$[(Si_{3.11}Al_{0.89})_{4.00}O_{10}](OH)_2$	$[(Si_{3.14}Al_{0.86})_{4.00}O_{10}](OH)_2$

	Specimen 249	Specimen 44	Specimen 31b	Specimen 551
f, % by chemical composition	71	85	84	74
f, % by refractive indices	77	90	82	—

TABLE 115 (continued)

Oxide	Specimen 562 — granodiorite				Specimen 539 — granite				Table 12 /17/			
									No. 4: biotite from norite	No. 7: biotite from granodiorite	No. 8: biotite from nepheline syenite	No. 14: lepidomelane from granite
	wt%	wt% scaled to 100	atomic quantity of cations	cation numbers	wt%	wt% scaled to 100	atomic quantity of cations	cation numbers	wt%	wt%	wt%	wt%
SiO_2	40.2	40.4	673	3.16	39.1	39.6	659	3.12	37.35	38.30	37.80	37.38
TiO_2	2.0	2.0	25	0.12	2.9	2.9	36	0.17	5.28	3.60	0.62	1.84
Al_2O_3	14.9	15.0	294	1.39	16.8	17.0	334	1.58	15.82	13.99	12.87	11.89
FeO	24.8	25.0	348	1.64	25.4	25.6	356	1.68	19.85	24.22	25.89	33.03
MgO	5.6	5.6	139	0.66	3.7	3.7	92	0.44	10.25	7.96	8.22	2.22
MnO	0.4	0.4	6	0.03	0.2	0.2	3	0.01	0.02	0.09	0.88	0.41
Σ			1485	7.00			1480	7.00				
CaO	0.6	0.6	11	0.05	0.3	0.3	5	0.02	1.30	0.90	—	0.16
K_2O	10.3	10.4	220	1.04	10.1	10.2	214	1.01	8.16	8.31	8.65	8.78
Na_2O	0.6	0.6	20	0.09	0.5	0.5	16	0.08	0.52	0.50	1.53	0.39
Σ	99.4	100.0		1.18	99.0	100.0		1.11	98.55*	97.91*	96.64*	96.30

$(K_{1.04}Na_{0.09}Ca_{0.05})_{1.18}$
$(Mg_{0.66}Mn_{0.03}Fe_{1.64}Ti_{0.12}Al_{0.55})_{3.00}$
$[(Si_{3.16}Al_{0.84})_{4.00}O_{10}](OH)_2$

$(K_{1.01}Na_{0.08}Ca_{0.02})_{1.11}$
$(Mg_{0.44}Mn_{0.01}Fe_{1.68}Ti_{0.17}Al_{0.70})_{3.00}$
$[(Si_{3.12}Al_{0.88})_{4.00}O_{10}](OH)_2$

The total does not include F and H_2O. together amounting to 2—4%.

	562	539	No. 4	No. 7	No. 8	No. 14
f, % by chemical composition	71	79	52	63	64	89
f, % by refractive indices	—	81	—	—	—	—

titanium in the biotites from injective granitoids is slightly over 2%, which is similar to the content of this element in the biotites from acid magmatic rocks. The majority of analyzed biotites are considerably closer to lepido-melane than to normal biotites, reflecting their genesis as secondary min-erals under conditions of metasomatic recrystallization at high potassium potentials. At the same time, attention is attracted by the somewhat high silica content in nearly all analyzed biotites, which is probably due to the presence of symplektitic quartz ingrowths.

Plagioclase is a widespread mineral in charnockitoids and is present, in varying amounts, in all the varieties of this formation. Its composition varies regularly, from An 50—60 in metamorphosed gabbroids to An 25—30 in granosyenites and An 23—30 in magmatic granitoids. The ferruginosity of colored minerals (especially pyroxenes) varies inversely with the An content of plagioclase; commonly from 50—60% in gabbroids to 80—90% in granosyenites. However, these proportions are not strictly regular, since the composition of plagioclase varies over a fairly broad range in the same variety of charnockitoids. Moreover, a single specimen of certain char-nockitoid varieties may exhibit considerable variations in the plagioclase composition, e. g., from labradorite to oligoclase. This is due to the presence of relict basic plagioclase with the recrystallized acid plagioclase. Thus, the An content in single plagioclase grains varies from 37 to 66% in metagabbroids, and from 25 to 40% in gabbro-diorites and diorite-syenites, becoming more stable only in syenites and granosyenites, where it is con-fined to within 23—30% (rarely 35%).

The amount of plagioclase present in different varieties of charnockitoids is even more variable: it forms 50—70% of metagabbroids, 40—50% of gabbro-diorites, 20—40% of diorite-syenites, 5—15% of syenites, and 10—20% (seldom more) of granosyenites. It varies in injective granitoids from 10—20% in granites to 30—40% in granodiorites. Apparently, recrystalliza-tion of gabbroids under conditions of alkaline metasomatism was an irregu-lar process with an intensity depending on the degree of interaction between the original rock and partial melts or alkaline solutions. This explains the lack of a complete correlation between the basicity of plagioclase and the ferruginosity of coexistent pyroxenes, although the general trend of this correlation is still clear.

Plagioclase laths in metagabbroids have preserved their prismatic habits (0.5—5 cm), although somewhat cataclastized. Such laths, locally broken but more often exhibiting irregular polysynthetic twins, in places with diffuse zonation, occur in a comminuted mass of plagioclase grains measur-ing ~ 1 mm. The laths may be distinctly twinned according to the albite or complex twin laws and are labradoritic in composition (An 55—65). The matrix grains were 'dezoned' during recrystallization and are now andesines (An 37—42).

The diorite-syenites have retained appreciable amounts of prismatic plagioclase laths of 3—7 mm. They are porphyroblastic with local diffuse zonation. The bulk of plagioclase has been recrystallized to near euhedral grains of 1—2 mm. The relict plagioclase laths are scarcer in syenites and contain an abundance of myrmekitic quartz ingrowths. The recrystal-lized euhedral plagioclase has been considerably deoxidized (to oligoclase-andesine, An 28—35) in comparison to the relict laths (basic andesine, An 40—45). The superimposed cataclasis resulted in comminution of both the relict laths and the recrystallized aggregates. The plagioclase in granosyenites is almost completely recrystallized, producing euhedral and even prismatic laths, measuring 2—5 mm, with fairly constant compositions corresponding to oligoclase, An 27—28. However, certain sporadic prismatic laths up to 2 cm long with a more basic composition occur locally. These are diffusely zoned andesines; An 40 at the center and An 32 along the edges. At contacts with K-feldspar, plagioclase develops an abundance of myrmekitic ingrowths and is strongly corroded by the K-feldspar. Cataclasis produces fine-grained areas of feldspars with grains up to 1 mm.

Finally, oligoclase in injective granitoids generally forms euhedral grains of 0.5—1 cm, which are somewhat affected by cataclasis. Among these are larger relict zoned plagioclase laths, from An 54 in the central portions to An 12 on the edges. These are broken, corroded and exhibit bent polysynthetic twins. The zonation of such laths was enhanced by interaction with melts from which the granites crystallized. This explains why the edges are represented by albite although the central portions consist of labradorite.

One of the most characteristic features of the plagioclase in charnockit-oids is the abundance of myrmekitic quartz ingrowths and extreme scarcity of antiperthitic ingrowths. The K-feldspar which corrodes and replaces the plagioclase (as indicated by the abundance of myrmekitic ingrowths) contains a profusion of perthitic ingrowths. This further indicates that the original rocks of charnockitoids were gabbroids, the plagioclase of which did not contain antiperthitic inclusions and was not enriched in them during development of the K-feldspar. In contrast, the K-feldspar contains abundant relicts of plagioclase grains and perthite testifying to its later formation.

K-feldspars are among the major rock-forming minerals in alkaline and subalkaline varieties of charnockitoids. They compose 2—3% of gab-broids, 5—10% of gabbrodiorites, then increase appreciably (to 30—40%) in diorite-syenites and especially in syenites where they make up 70—80% of the rocks. The content of K-feldspars (including porphyroblasts) declines somewhat, to 50—60%, in granosyenites, which are the most widespread charnockitoid variety. K-feldspars in the granosyenites largely form porphyroblasts, measuring 2—5 cm. These exhibit the habit of prismatic laths with ragged boundaries. The porphyroblasts are slightly cataclastized. Simple twins are ubiquitous, and microcline crosshatching appears locally. The porphyroblasts often contain inclusions of fused quartz and plagioclase granules, often amounting to 10—15%; the latter contain an abundance of fine microperthitic ingrowths.

In other charnockitoid varieties, particularly in syenites, where K-feldspar is the dominant mineral, it is represented by two generations, euhedral grains of 5—6 mm surrounded by a granoblastic matrix of finer grains measuring 1—2 mm. Simple twins are widespread and microcline crosshatching is less common. As before, the euhedral laths of K-feldspar contain an abundance of poikiloblastic inclusions of quartz and plagioclase.

X-ray diffraction analysis of K-feldspars revealed that the charnockitoids mainly contain orthoclases that are only slightly triclinic (Table 116). High and intermediate microcline occur only sporadically, in contact aureoles of charnockitic intrusions. It appears that orthoclase develops in charnockitoids as a primary mineral, whereas the microcline is produced during cataclasis and recrystallization of the orthoclase in the solid state. The structural properties of K-feldspars are reflected in optic-axial angle which is −59° to −67° for high orthoclase, −72° to −75° for intermediate varieties and -80° for microcline. The majority of specimens examined by X-ray diffraction contain perthitic albite ingrowths (10—20%); only a few specimens contain less than 5% of such ingrowths. The X-ray analysis permits the determination of the composition of the homogeneous phase of orthoclase, which contains 5—15% albitic components. Two quantitative spectroscopic analyses (Table 116) indicate a sodium content of ~4%. Therefore, the computed content of the albite molecule in the K-feldspars is 27—28%. This value apparently reflects the combined contents of the albite components in the analyzed specimens, consisting of isomorphic admixtures of sodium in pure orthoclase and the sodium in perthitic ingrowths.

TABLE 116. K-feldspars

Oxide	Specimen 44				Specimen 592			
	wt%	wt% scaled to 100	atomic quantity of cations	cation numbers	wt%	wt% scaled to 100	atomic quantity of cations	cation numbers
SiO_2	66.1	63.3	1054	2.86	64.3	63.0	1049	2.84
TiO_2	0.1	0.1	1	—	0.1	0.1	1	—
Al_2O_3	18.8	18.0	354	0.98	19.5	19.2	376	1.01
CaO	0.3	0.3	5	0.01	0.4	0.4	7	0.02
K_2O	15.0	14.4	306	0.83	14.0	13.7	298	0.81
Na_2O	4.1	3.9	126	0.34	3.7	3.6	120	0.32
Σ	104.4	100.0	1846	5.00	102.0	100.0	1851	5.00

Crystallochemical formulas

$(K_{0.83}Na_{0.34}Ca_{0.01})_{1.08}Al_{0.96}(Si_{2.86}O_8)$ $(K_{0.81}Na_{0.32}Ca_{0.02})_{1.05}Al_{1.01}(Si_{2.84}O_8)$

Component composition

Anorthite	$Ca_{0.01}Al_{0.02}SiO_{0.02}O_{0.08}$	0.9	$Ca_{0.02}Al_{0.04}Si_{0.04}O_{0.16}$	1.7
Albite	$Na_{0.34}Al_{0.34}Si_{1.02}O_{2.62}$	28.4	$Na_{0.32}Al_{0.32}Si_{0.96}O_{2.56}$	27.8
Orthoclase	$K_{0.83}Al_{0.83}Si_{2.49}O_{6.64}$	70.7	$K_{0.81}Al_{0.81}Si_{2.43}O_{6.48}$	70.5
		100.0		100.0

Note. Scaling to the component composition results in an Al deficit of 0.23% in specimen 44 and 0.16% in specimen 592 and an Si deficit of 0.67% in specimen 44 and 0.59% in specimen 592.

The small admixture of CaO indicates the presence in orthoclase of 1—2% anorthite. A comparison of the albite component in the K-feldspar and in the coexisting plagioclase makes possible the determination of the formation temperature of K-feldspar — 600—610°C; Barth's method /81, 82/. This temperature permits the crystallization of K-feldspar from eutectic melts at the depth of formation of charnockitoid bodies (from gabbroid intrusions interacting with the same melt). These melts are also the source of the metasome in migmatites.

In concluding the description of the rock-forming minerals of charnockitoids, it should be emphasized that the majority of these rocks underwent varying degrees of cataclasis in the solid state, which largely disturbed their crystallographic forms. This interferes with determination of the crystallization sequence of the minerals and their interrelationships. K-feldspar porphyroblasts were the least disturbed (usually only at the edges). They were 'protected' during cataclasis by the matrix which is often comminuted to a considerable extent. The cataclasis especially affected quartz, plagioclase and orthoclase segregations in the matrix. Its effect on the colored minerals was less marked. Quartz usually possesses wavy extinction and is commonly transformed into a mosaic aggregate. The plagioclase laths are cracked and sometimes broken into pieces that have been shifted relative to one another.

Chemical properties of charnockitoids and associated rocks

Of the 46 chemical analyses, 32 refer to charnockitoids and the remainder to associated rocks, i. e., anorthosites, injective granites and granodiorites, vein granites and, finally, xenoliths (Table 117). Most interesting are the analyses of charnockitoids, arbitrarily grouped together for purposes of petrographic description in five varieties which form a nearly continuous series with respect to composition, from metagabbroids to granosyenites. In the petrographic description, the chemical differences between the charnockitoid varieties and magmatic rocks of corresponding designations were described as follows: a) high iron content in colored minerals and high potassium content in feldspars; b) high titanium content in colored minerals and partly in ore minerals; c) low magnesium and calcium contents in colored minerals; d) low content of silica. These deviations reflect the nature of their genesis, i. e., formation from original gabbroids under conditions of intensive recrystallization and interaction with partial melts and alkaline solutions, making for extensive development of metamorphic processes. All deviations of charnockitoids from the corresponding groups of magmatic rocks can be traced in the continuous and gradual variation of the chemical composition of the individual varieties. In this case, too, it is possible to distinguish fairly readily the same five varieties, every one of which is characterized by similar contents of the major rock-forming elements, particularly silica, iron, titanium and potassium. Against the background of considerable variations in the contents of these four elements (Table 118) there are slight fluctuations of Na_2O, from 2.17—2.77%

TABLE 117. Chemical analyses of intrusive rocks from the Humboldt Mountains and Petermann Range

Specimen No.	Rocks	SiO$_2$	TiO$_2$	Al$_2$O$_3$	Fe$_2$O$_3$	FeO	MnO	MgO	CaO	Na$_2$O	K$_2$O	P$_2$O$_5$	CuO	NiO	Loss on ignition
576	Anorthosites of different grades of metamorphism	52.59	1.64	21.53	2.24	4.45	0.07	1.37	8.54	3.94	1.94	1.13			0.37
545		53.48	0.84	25.56	0.80	2.78	0.04	0.98	10.21	4.20	0.91	0.16			0.32
578		54.88	0.60	24.59	1.02	2.31	0.04	0.89	8.93	4.40	1.61	0.47			0.22
577		54.99	1.10	21.80	1.11	3.54	0.07	1.25	7.76	4.13	2.35	0.55			1.30
546		55.08	0.50	26.90	0.27	1.06	traces	0.36	9.70	4.75	0.79	0.15			0.36
586d		57.18	0.22	25.83	0.50	1.08	0.01	0.57	7.86	5.45	1.22	0.10			0.70
578g	Metamorphosed norites and gabbro-norites	43.71	5.68	13.87	3.06	13.90	0.24	4.91	8.37	2.17	0.66	2.21	0.17	0.02	1.16
575d		45.13	4.64	13.96	3.54	11.27	0.21	5.05	8.59	2.48	1.07	2.56	0.35	0.02	1.35
544		47.90	3.92	17.15	1.52	9.59	0.18	3.88	9.54	2.77	0.82	1.63			0.67
36b	Metamorphosed gabbro-norite-diorites	50.95	3.68	13.76	3.17	8.19	0.16	4.19	6.74	2.65	2.53	1.92			1.19
823		51.74	3.55	14.97	1.76	9.08	0.17	3.87	6.85	2.95	2.20	1.27			1.04
228		52.14	3.84	13.97	1.96	9.01	0.14	3.91	6.74	2.88	2.73	1.78			0.90
836		52.22	1.93	15.55	2.48	9.84	0.17	3.32	6.64	2.73	2.85	1.38	0.19	—	0.84
228zh		53.61	3.36	13.81	1.80	9.34	0.15	3.21	6.35	2.82	2.80	1.58			0.95
811		53.72	1.31	16.24	3.00	7.71	0.16	4.79	6.98	3.18	1.96	0.28			1.04
228z		55.15	2.60	13.67	2.73	9.03	0.17	2.55	5.80	3.00	3.29	1.22			0.78
249	Diorite-syenites	54.90	1.80	15.72	2.45	7.36	0.11	2.40	4.82	3.19	4.82	0.69		Fluorine, 0.70%	0.90
807		55.08	1.77	16.14	2.07	7.58	0.14	1.95	4.57	3.86	5.40	0.41			0.78
36g		55.73	2.60	13.24	2.22	8.69	0.14	2.48	5.91	3.05	3.17	2.06			0.68
36v		57.34	2.28	12.66	2.58	8.10	0.14	2.38	5.40	2.81	3.44	1.92			0.74
592a		58.36	1.96	14.46	1.90	7.90	0.13	1.88	5.14	3.18	3.86	0.77			0.33
228e		59.50	1.45	16.69	3.14	4.99	0.10	1.45	4.36	3.40	4.37	0.53			0.59
546v		60.13	0.68	15.62	2.25	4.89	0.14	1.07	5.19	3.50	4.82	0.13			1.37
592	Diorite-syenites transitional to syenites	59.94	0.70	14.75	2.66	7.58	0.16	0.71	4.13	3.16	5.00	0.28			0.82
93		60.44	1.12	14.56	4.98	5.58	0.15	0.75	3.58	3.08	5.24	0.30			0.57

TABLE 117 (continued)

Specimen No.	Rocks	SiO_2	TiO_2	Al_2O_3	Fe_2O_3	FeO	MnO	MgO	CaO	Na_2O	K_2O	P_2O_5	CuO	NiO	Loss on ignition
44	Syenites	60.34	1.18	14.69	2.56	6.59	0.08	1.13	3.79	3.18	5.00	0.44			0.95
44a		61.24	0.72	16.02	2.41	5.19	0.08	1.09	3.29	3.80	4.85	0.36			0.95
44v		61.78	1.10	14.63	2.09	6.20	0.10	1.08	3.18	3.36	5.00	0.36	0.74		1.04
44g		61.29	1.00	14.49	0.96	7.40	0.10	1.06	3.34	3.00	4.79	0.39			1.22
283	Leucocratic syenites	60.70	0.38	18.50	1.66	3.00	0.07	0.80	2.74	3.42	8.28	0.17			0.15
283b		60.84	0.40	18.22	1.59	3.19	0.08	0.92	2.86	3.34	7.72	0.20			0.48
31b	Granosyenites	66.70	0.40	15.69	1.30	2.15	0.03	1.37	1.79	2.90	7.24	0.14			0.10
35a		65.97	0.74	14.17	1.89	5.34	0.12	0.23	2.77	3.24	5.33	0.08			0.14
38a		65.17	0.88	14.54	1.64	4.54	0.07	1.41	2.63	3.00	5.00	0.30			0.53
581		64.74	0.53	15.65	1.98	3.88	0.08	0.71	3.33	3.23	5.30	0.21			0.33
38		65.32	1.04	14.13	2.11	4.74	0.07	1.12	2.62	3.00	5.32	0.30			0.59
57	Plagiogranites	66.23	0.76	13.18	1.60	7.90	0.13	0.80	3.73	2.53	1.47	0.15	0.40		1.36
57d		68.48	0.80	14.61	1.68	4.81	0.06	0.43	3.57	3.00	1.62	0.10	0.07		0.87
551	Granodiorite	61.99	1.92	13.68	1.23	6.75	0.09	1.47	3.91	3.05	4.13	0.69			0.99
586	Granite	61.19	0.40	12.97	1.77	3.03	0.08	0.55	2.35	3.00	5.15	0.12			1.31
587		69.32	0.60	13.91	0.88	2.98	0.03	1.09	2.02	3.00	5.33	0.22			0.45
539		70.12	0.52	14.02	0.87	2.58	0.04	0.89	1.35	2.86	5.85	0.26	0.01	0.01	0.61
57g		70.50	0.44	13.45	1.14	3.73	0.06	0.39	1.89	2.16	5.60	0.11			2.60
31	Vein leucocratic granite	77.25	0.32	10.28	0.76	2.01	traces	0.89	1.17	2.30	4.65	0.07			0.40
57 v	Feldspathized biotite-cordierite plagiogneiss	64.99	1.60	16.40	1.82	7.25	0.05	2.31	0.67	1.06	1.77	0.23			2.15
249a	Shadow granite	69.06	0.80	13.77	1.89	3.66	0.06	1.43	2.51	2.85	3.60	0.18			0.65

Notes. 1. Mineral composition of analyzed specimens is listed in Tables 102—110. 2. Specimens 823, 836 and 811, 807 and 35a were taken from Ravich's collection of 1961, the rest from collections of 1967.

TABLE 117 (continued)

Specimen No.	Σ	H₂O at 105—110°	CO₂	S_tot	a	c	b	s	a'	f'	m'	c'	n	t	φ	Q	a/c
576	99.81	0.09			12.5	9.5	11.2	66.8	—	60.7	22.7	16.6	76.2	2.2	18.7	−0.9	1.3
545	100.28	0.15			11.9	13.2	6.2	68.7	—	59.7	29.3	11.0	87.2	1.1	12.2	+0.4	0.9
578	99.96	0.32			13.3	11.6	5.5	69.6	—	60.2	30.1	9.7	80.6	0.9	16.4	+1.0	1.1
577	99.95	0.11	0,71		13.7	9.1	8.2	69.0	—	57.7	27.9	14.4	72.8	1.5	12.6	+1.5	1.5
546	99.92	0.12	0,24		13.2	3.2	2.9	70.7	26.3	50.0	23.7	—	89.5	0.6	10.5	+1.8	1.0
586d	100.72	0.05	0,04		14.9	1.3	4.3	70.5	40.7	35.6	23.7	—	87.1	0.3	10.2	+0.9	1.4
578g	99.94	0.39	0,50		6.0	6.8	29.6	57.6	—	57.1	29.5	13.4	83.3	8.9	9.3	−3.6	0.9
575d	100.04	0.25	0,26		7.5	6.1	28.4	58.0	—	51.5	31.5	17.1	76.9	7.16	11.1	−5.1	1.2
544	99.94	0.18			7.8	8.4	22.2	61.6	—	50.6	31.4	18.0	83.3	5.8	5.9	−0.8	0.9
36b	99.85	0.06	0,16	0,04	9.9	4.6	22.4	63.1	—	49.5	33.0	17.5	61.4	5.1	12.7	+1.8	2.15
823	99.45	0.17		0,02	10.0	5.4	20.6	64.0	—	51.7	32.7	15.6	67.6	5.0	7.5	+2.6	1.8
228	100.00				10.6	4.2	21.4	63.8	—	49.2	31.6	19.2	61.8	5.2	7.8	+2.2	2.5
836	99.95	0.20		сл.	10.5	5.3	20.0	64.5	—	58.1	27.9	14.0	58.6	2.7	10.9	+3.3	1.9
228zh	99.97				10.0	4.2	20.0	65.3	—	53.9	27.6	18.5	60.0	4.5	7.7	+5.4	2.5
811	100.37				10.0	6.0	21.0	63.0	—	48.2	39.0	12.8	71.2	1.8	12.5	0	1.7
228z	99.99	0.17		0,04	11.5	3.5	19.2	65.8	—	58.3	23.0	18.7	57.8	3.5	12.2	+5.1	3.3
249	99.86	0.30		0,04	14.4	3.6	16.1	65.9	—	59.1	25.7	15.2	50.5	2.5	13.9	−0.6	4.0
807	99.75	0.09			16.7	2.6	15.7	65.0	—	59.6	21.8	18.6	52.1	2.3	11.6	−6.0	6.4
36g	99.97	0.12		0,03	11.5	3.2	18.7	66.6	—	55.7	22.5	21.8	59.0	3.4	10.3	+7.0	3.6
36v	99.79	0.19		0,04	11.2	3.0	17.8	68.0	—	57.0	22.8	20.2	55.6	2.9	12.4	+10.6	3.7
592a	99.87	0.19	0,18		12.8	3.4	15.5	68.3	—	60.2	20.8	19.0	55.9	2.5	10.6	+7.6	3.8
228e	100.57	0.22	0,29		14.3	4.3	11.3	70.1	—	67.7	22.3	10.0	53.9	1.9	23.6	+7.3	3.3
546v	99.79				14.9	3.2	11.9	70.0	—	57.3	15.2	27.5	52.3	0.9	16.4	+7.0	4.66
592	99.89	0.19	0,06		14.3	2.8	13.3	69.6	—	73.9	8.9	17.2	49.0	0.9	17.7	+7.8	5.1
93	100.34	0.25			14.4	2.6	12.9	70.1	—	76.0	10.1	13.9	47.6	1.3	33.2	+8.6	5.5

TABLE 117 (continued)

Speci-men No.	Σ	H₂O at 105–110°	CO₂	S_tot	a	c	b	s	a'	f'	m'	c'	n	t	φ	Q	a/c
44	99.93	0.09		traces	14.5	2.7	12.5	70.3	—	68.6	15.4	16.0	49.5	1.5	17.6	+8.9	5.4
44a	100.00	0.32		0.04	15.6	3.1	10.1	71.2	—	71.1	18.6	10.3	54.0	0.9	20.7	+8.1	5.0
44v	99.92	0.07	0.17		14.7	2.5	11.1	71.7	—	70.2	16.8	13.0	50.5	1.3	16.1	+11.5	5.9
44g	99.78	0.13	0.09	traces	13.8	3.0	11.1	72.1	—	72.9	16.4	10.7	48.5	1.3	7.6	+13.6	4.6
283	99.87	0.26			19.9	2.7	6.7	70.7	—	67.7	20.8	11.5	38.5	0.5	23.0	−1.1	7.4
283b	99.84	0.22			19.0	2.9	6.8	71.3	—	67.0	23.7	9.3	39.7	0.5	20.6	+1.7	6.55
31b	99.81	0.32		traces	16.7	2.1	5.5	75.7	—	56.8	42.0	1.2	38.2	0.4	19.7	+15.9	8.0
35a	100.02				14.6	2.1	8.3	75.0	—	80.5	4.9	14.6	48.2	0.8	19.6	+18.7	7.0
38a	99.71	0.26		traces	13.8	2.8	8.5	74.9	—	67.2	28.0	4.8	47.5	1.0	16.0	+19.4	4.9
581	99.97	0.18	0.15		14.9	3.1	7.6	74.4	—	71.2	15.3	13.5	48.4	0.6	21.6	+15.9	4.8
38	100.36	0.10			14.1	2.3	9.0	74.6	—	70.0	21.0	9.0	46.1	1.2	19.5	+18.7	6.1
57	100.24	0.19	0.36	0.02	7.8	4.6	11.1	76.5	6.2	81.5	12.3	—	72.0	0.9	12.3	+32.8	1.7
57d	100.10	0.19		traces	8.8	4.3	8.9	78.0	22.9	68.7	8.4	—	73.8	0.9	16.8	+34.1	2.0
551	99.90	0.09	0.29		12.8	2.8	11.9	72.5	—	62.7	20.6	16.7	52.7	2.3	8.1	+16.6	4.6
586	99.92	0.18			13.9	1.6	6.5	78.0	—	67.0	14.4	18.6	46.6	0.4	22.7	+26.6	8.7
587	99.83	0.16			14.0	2.2	5.7	78.1	—	63.5	31.8	4.7	46.2	0.7	14.2	+26.0	6.3
539	99.99	0.08			14.6	1.6	5.2	78.6	10.3	61.5	28.2	—	42.2	0.5	15.4	+26.4	9.1
57g	100.07	0.04		traces	12.7	2.3	5.7	79.3	9.4	78.8	11.8	—	37.2	0.4	16.5	+30.9	5.5
31	100.10	0.20		•	11.3	0.9	4.3	83.5	—	56.7	32.8	10.5	42.5	0.3	14.9	+43.5	12.6
57v	100.30	0.18	0.06	0.11	4.5	0.8	25.5	69.2	55.5	30.5	14.0	—	47.2	1.8	5.4	+28.6	5.6
249a	100.46	0.22	0.21		11.2	3.0	8.3	77.5	9.7	61.3	29.0	—	54.8	0.9	19.3	+29.6	3.7

in metagabbroids to 2.90—3.24% in granosyenites, and of Al_2O_3, from 13.87—17.15% in metagabbroids to 14.13—15.69% in granosyenites. The contents of these elements for all other charnockitoid varieties also fall within these limits. Another characteristic feature is that the minimum contents of elements in one variety correspond to their average contents in the neighboring variety; the contents of titanium and iron gradually decline, and the contents of silica and potassium equally gradually increase, from basic to acid rocks.

TABLE 118. Variation ranges for the contents of major chemical elements in charnockitoids

Charnockitoid varieties	Ranges of contents, wt%			
	SiO_2	TiO_2	FeO	K_2O
Metagabbroid	43.71—47.90	3.92—5.68	9.59—13.90	0.66—1.07
Feldspathized gabbro-norite-diorite	50.95—55.15	1.31—3.84	7.71—9.84	1.96—3.29
Diorite-syenite	54.90—60.44	0.70—2.60	4.89—8.69	3.17—5.40
Syenite	60.34—61.78	0.38—1.18	3.00—7.40	4.79—8.28
Granosyenite	64.74—66.70	0.40—1.04	2.15—5.34	5.00—7.24

The comparison leads to the following conclusions: 1) During the formation of charnockitoids, aluminum and especially sodium behaved as inert components, their content varying relatively little from basic to acid rocks, which would be impossible if the rocks had been formed by magmatic differentiation. 2) The very high iron content in all charnockitoid groups indicates: a) its high content in the original basic rocks and b) its high concentration in colored minerals during formation of the most acid charnockitoid varieties. 3) The titanium content in the original basic rock was high; it is diminished in alkaline and in acid charnockitoid varieties, but nevertheless remains fairly high. 4) The content of potassium, which is fairly high in nearly all the charnockitoid varieties, increases markedly in alkaline and acid varieties, by a factor of at least 7—8. This attests to the mobility and very high concentration of potassium in the course of charnockitoid formation, which is nearly impossible under conditions of magmatic differentiation and is possible only under conditions of intensive alkaline metasomatism. 5) The gradual increase in the contents of silica, from 43% in basic to 68% in acid and subalkaline charnockitoid varieties, indicates its considerable influx during charnockitoid formation from partial melts participating in the charnockitization of the basic rocks.

The chemical properties of charnockitoids do not coincide with those of the normal series of magmatic rocks. The former contain Mg-Fe colored minerals, the total ferruginosity of which increases significantly in intermediate and acid varieties, while the content of calcic colored minerals is low, diminishing in intermediate and acid varieties. The charnockitoids are distinguished by high alkalinity with a prevalence of potassium over sodium, the content of which varies little from basic to acid varieties. They are characterized by very high titanium contents, especially in intermediate and basic varieties. In spite of the existence of fairly basic charnockitoid varieties, all of them are silica-saturated and the majority even oversaturated.

Six analyses of anorthosites reveal specific features distinguishing them from the charnockitoid series, although all specimens exhibit clear signs of metamorphism. In the first place, the meta-anorthosites have preserved very high contents of alumina (21.53—26.90%), calcium (7.86—10.21%) and sodium (3.94—5.45%), whereas the content of potassium is low (0.70—1.94%). The same applies to the content of iron in colored minerals (1.06—4.45%). These properties indicate a very low grade of granitization, and therefore, the anorthosites are not transformed into charnockites under conditions applying to gabbro-norite transformation. However, very peculiar fayalite plagiogranites with low contents of alkalis, and especially potassium (1.47—1.62%), discovered in the south of the region, may have originated by re-crystallization of anorthosites involving a heavy influx of silica and a limited influx of alkalis (analyses of specimens 57 and 57d). According to data from five analyses, injective granitoids differ little from magmatic granites and granodiorites, but differ significantly even from acid charnockites in the following respects: low content of titanium and iron in the colored minerals, with consequent absence of eulyte and fayalite, the part of which is played by biotite and partly by hornblende; high content of silica, especially in acid varieties; low content of calcium in plagioclase, so that the latter is, as a rule, represented by oligoclase. The analogous veins of these granites differ still more markedly from acid charnockites. Two analyses of xenoliths in acid and intermediate charnockites reveal that the formation processes of the latter are manifested in the recrystallization of rocks under conditions of alkaline metasomatism which had a relatively small effect on the compo-sition of the xenoliths. This refers to their fairly low content of alkalis, which was not increased on their inclusion in the charnockites. The same applies to all the other elements, which have undergone little change in comparison to ordinary plagiogneisses and their shadow granites, to which the xenoliths belong. The content of silica constitutes an exception, increas-ing appreciably in the xenoliths in comparison to the original rocks. It should be noted, however, that the xenoliths probably occur in the upper portions of intrusions, where charnockitization of gabbroids occurred to only a limited extent.

Physical properties of charnockitoids

The physical properties of charnockitoids and anorthosites were deter-mined for 65 specimens. The porosity was found to be extremely variable as is seen from Table 119; it is lowest in the youngest injective granitoids and in the oldest anorthosites and gabbroids which underwent relatively small alterations. It increases appreciably in markedly recrystallized and metasomatized rocks approaching charnockites proper.

TABLE 119. Mean porosities of charnockitoids and associated rocks

Rocks	Number of specimens	Porosity, %		
		minimum	maximum	mean
Metamorphosed anorthosites . . .	6	0.36	2.15	1.04
Metamorphosed gabbroids	4	0.62	2.89	1.42
Gabbro-norite-diorites	5	1.28	3.52	2.53
Diorite-syenites	9	0.68	4.21	2.15
Syenites	5	1.91	3.53	2.52
Granosyenites	3	1.20	2.65	1.93
Granitoids	5	0.14	1.02	0.51
	37			

TABLE 120. Mean densities of charnockitoids and associated rocks

Rocks	Mean density	Number of specimens	Minimum value	Maximum value
Metamorphosed anorthosites	2.78	17	2.66	2.90
Metamorphosed gabbroids	3.03	4	2.97	3.09
Gabbro-norite-diorites	2.89	10	2.85	2.93
Diorite-syenites	2.81	10	2.78	2.84
Syenites	2.72	8	2.67	2.79
Granosyenites	2.68	11	2.64	2.72
Granites	2.70	5	2.65	2.75
		65		

Data on the mean densities are listed in Table 120. The density of
anorthosites varies widely, averaging 2.66—2.90 g/cm^3. The high variation
of density values indicates that they have a heterogeneous mineral composition. If all other rocks are considered apart from the anorthosites,
distinct differences in densities are observed in spite of the very small
number of specimens for every group. The mean density of metamorphosed
gabbroids varies from 2.97 to 3.09 g/cm^3. The density of the majority
of gabbroid rocks studied in various regions of the world lies within the
same limits. The mean density of gabbros, 2.976 g/cm^3 according to
R. Daly, likewise falls within these limits. The mean density of gabbro-
norite-diorites is 2.85—2.93 g/cm^3. Thus, these rocks 'lie' directly next
to the gabbroids with respect to densities, but are separated from the
gabbroids (without overlapping); the minimum density of gabbroids is
greater than the maximum density of gabbro-norite-diorites. The latter
are evidently enriched in the lighter salic minerals. The density of diorite-
syenites is still lower and they are undoubtedly more leucocratic than the
gabbro-norite-diorites. The mean density of diorite-syenites is 2.78—
2.84 g/cm^3. As in the preceding case, the diorite-syenites differ distinctly,
with respect to density, from the heavier gabbro-norite-diorites. The

minimum density of the latter exceeds the maximum density of the former. The pattern is somewhat less clear for the syenites, granosyenites and granites. All these rocks are lighter than the diorite-syenites, although the boundary is not clearly delimited since the minimum density of diorite-syenites is nearly equal to the maximum density of syenites. The differences between these groups are commensurate with the density measurement error. Possibly, the syenites have a higher density ($2.72 \ g/cm^3$), since the average density of granosyenites is $2.68 \ g/cm^3$. Apparently, these rocks form a single group, characterized by a very definite composition and other properties. On this assumption, the mean density of rocks in this group should be $2.70 \ g/cm^3$, with an RMS error of $\pm 0.05 \ g/cm^3$.

The magnetic susceptibility of the various rocks varies widely. There are both weakly and strongly magnetic specimens in every group of rocks, their magnetic susceptibilities often differing by factors of hundreds and thousands of units. The consistency of these differences is indicated by the density-magnetic susceptibility graph reproduced in Figure 60, where the x-axis is the magnetic susceptibility on a logarithmic scale and the y-axis is the density. The 'zero' coordinates are in the top left corner of the diagram. In this case, heavy rocks are located below, producing the visual impression of gravitational differentiation. All investigated rocks appear in the graph as a cluster of symbols corresponding to the rock groups under consideration. Attention is attracted by the near-linear boundary of the left portion of the cluster. The specimens located near this boundary possess the minimum magnetic susceptibility for the given density. Thus, it follows that the minimum magnetic susceptibility of rocks is higher for higher density. Since the latter depends on the mineralogical composition of rocks, the maximum magnetic susceptibility may be said to be likewise dependent, to a certain extent, on the mineralogical composition. The right-hand boundary of the cluster is less distinct. Nevertheless, it may be assumed to be near-linear, like the left-hand boundary. Furthermore, both these lines in the graph seem to be parallel, the majority of symbols approaching either the right or the left cluster boundary. This confirms the previous assumption that all these rocks fall into two subgroups with respect to their magnetic susceptibility. The most distinctly represented subgroup is that of weakly magnetic rocks, the magnetic susceptibility of which corresponds to the minimum value for the given density. The weakly magnetic subgroup of gabbroids has a magnetic susceptibility of the order of 100 to $200 \cdot 10^{-6}$ CGSM. In the case of gabbro-norite-diorites and diorite-syenites it varies approximately from $40 \cdot 10^{-6}$ to $100 \cdot 10^{-6}$ CGSM units, and from $40 \cdot 10^{-6}$ to $80 \cdot 10^{-6}$ CGSM units in the case of syenites, granosyenites and granitoids. Aside from the weakly magnetic rocks, every group also seems to include a strongly magnetic subgroup, although it is less distinctly delimited. In the case of gabbroids, the rocks of this subgroup have magnetic susceptibilities of $1000 \cdot 10^{-6}$ to $4000 \cdot 10^{-6}$ CGSM. The strongly magnetic gabbro-norite-diorites and diorite-syenites have magnetic susceptibilities of $400 \cdot 10^{-6}$ to $1000 \cdot 10^{-6}$ CGSM units, while the magnetic susceptibility of strongly magnetic syenites, granosyenites and granitoids varies approximately from $200 \cdot 10^{-6}$ to $400 \cdot 10^{-6}$ CGSM units. The fact

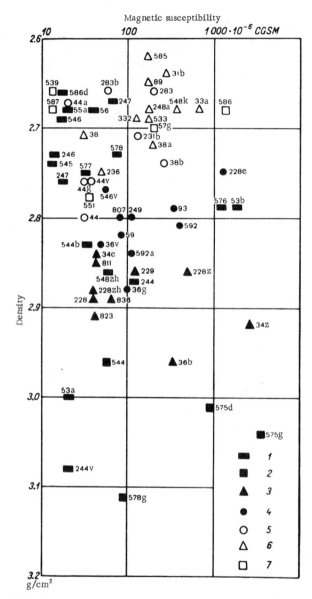

FIGURE 60. Density-magnetic susceptibility graph for intrusive rocks from the Humboldt Mountains and Petermann Range:

1) anorthosites; 2) metagabbroids; 3) gabbro-norite-diorites; 4) diorite-syenites; 5) syenites; 6) granosyenites; 7) granitoids.

that both the weakly magnetic and strongly magnetic subgroups are present in all rocks under consideration, suggests the following assumptions: 1) All these rocks originated simultaneously in an acid environment and then underwent repeated metamorphism in an alkaline environment (also simultaneously), either in their entirety or in certain areas. 2) These alterations occurred more than once during the formation of every rock, whatever the age and genetic sequence; the number of changes of acid and alkaline environments was possibly much larger than the number of rock varieties.

Absolute dating of charnockitoids

To estimate the formation time of charnockitoids, ten radioactive datings for whole rocks were carried out at the Radium Institute of the Academy of Sciences of the USSR under the direction of A. Ya. Krylov. These included samples of nearly all charnockite varieties of the Humboldt Mountains and Petermann Range, as well as one dating of biotite from a pegmatite vein occurring in a diorite-syenite (Table 121). The considerable scatter of the absolute datings, from 360 to 485 million years, does not indicate that the ages of rocks were actually different, since the specimens were sometimes obtained from the same (e. g., specimens 38 and 38a) or from adjacent outcrops. There may be some relationship between the datings and the composition of the different varieties of charnockitoids, the smallest absolute datings (specimens 38, 38a, 41) being obtained for rocks that are richest in K-feldspar porphyroblasts.

TABLE 121. Absolute dating of charnockitoids from the Humboldt Mountains and Petermann Range

Specimen No.	Rocks	K, %	Ar, $cm^3/g \cdot 10^{-5}$	Age, millions of years
93	Weakly feldspathized gabbroid	3.06	6.16	465
44	Biotitized gabbroid	4.40	7.64	400
36	Feldspathized gabbro-diorite	2.45	4.01	390
34	Feldspathized gabbro-diorite	3.14	6.24	460
826*	Quartz-bearing diorite-syenite	3.99	7.93	460
836*	Quartz-bearing diorite-syenite	3.30	6.31	450
38a	Porphyroblastic granosyenite	4.53	6.75	360
38	Porphyroblastic granosyenite	4.65	10.98	400
41	'Giant-grained' porphyroblastic granosyenite	4.96	4.85	390
811i	Pegmatite in gabbro-syenite	5.83	12.30	485
54v	Biotite from pegmatite	7.13	14.70	475

Note. The specimens marked with an asterisk are from Ravich's collection of 1961 /57/.

As is known, absolute dating for whole rocks is generally 10—15% below dating based on mica alone, and therefore, the ages of charnockitoids from the Humboldt Mountains and Petermann Range are close to 500 million years. This is in agreement with the absolute datings of a great majority of intrusive charnockitoids in the crystalline basement of the Antarctic Platform. Such absolute dating can hardly indicate the true formation time of the charnockitoids, which would in this case be Upper Cambrian or even Ordovician. Although such an age cannot be totally precluded because of the limited amount of information available for the crystalline basement of the Antarctic Platform, it would nevertheless be more realistic to relate the formation of charnockitoids to a superimposed stage of regional metamorphism and ultrametamorphism. This probably occurred in the crystalline basement in the first half of the Proterozoic, or certainly in the pre-Riphean. The absolute ages corresponding to the Cambrian may be related to block movements in the rigid crystalline basement affecting the preservation of radioactive argon in the basement rocks.

CHARNOCKITOIDS OF OTHER REGIONS IN EAST ANTARCTICA

After the fairly detailed description of the charnockitoids of the Humboldt Mountains and Petermann Range on Queen Maud Land, this section will provide a brief description of other intrusive charnockitoids occurring in the crystalline basement of the Antarctic Platform. These were discovered and studied, to varying degrees, by Soviet and other geologists over the last 10—12 years. All such intrusions are concentrated in East Antarctica, where crystalline basement blocks of the granulite facies, reworked in the amphibolite facies, have been discovered.

Petrographic and chemical analyses of 52 specimens from different regions in Antarctica made possible the identification of similar charnockitoid rock occurring separately or together (Tables 122 and 124). The charnockitoid intrusives of East Antarctica consist of nearly the same rock types as in the Humboldt Mountains and Petermann Range: Mainly 1) feldspathized gabbroids, 2) feldspathized gabbro-norite-diorites, 3) diorite-syenites, 4) granosyenites, 5) pyroxene granites and plagiogranites /57/. Only pyroxene syenites have not yet been identified, possibly due to the incomplete field investigations. Rocks which closely resemble the syenites occur among the more basic diorite-syenites and the more acid granosyenites, some specimens of which contain 60—65% or more K-feldspar. The arbitrary nature of the demarcation of the different charnockitoid varieties, reflected in significant fluctuations in the rock-forming minerals and chemical compositions, should be emphasized (Tables 123, 125). However, in general, each variety is distinguished by a fairly definite mineral composition. The most important features in this respect are as follows: a) K-feldspar contents, gradually increasing from feldspathized gabbroids (3—5%) to granosyenites (45—59%); b) An content in plagioclase, gradually declining from feldspathized gabbroids (50—70%) to granosyenites

(25—35%); c) quartz content, increasing from feldspathized gabbroids (2—3%) to granosyenites (15—20%) and granites (30—35%); d) content of pyroxenes, gradually declining from feldspathized gabbroids (20—40%) to granosyenites (5—10%) and granites (1—5%); at the same time the ferruginosity of pyroxenes, especially that of the orthopyroxenes, increases from hypersthenes (40—50%) to eulyte (80%), accompanied by the gradual disappearance of clinopyroxene.

In spite of the quantitative fluctuations of the chemical elements in these rocks, there is a distinct trend toward a fairly definite composition of every variety, manifested in the following features: a) gradual increase of silica from 46—52% in feldspathized gabbroids to 65—70% in granosyenites and 73% in granites; b) irregular but steadily declining contents of iron and magnesium in colored minerals, from 8—13% and 5—15%, respectively, in feldspathized gabbroids and to 2—5% and 1%, respectively, in granosyenites; c) steady decline of calcium contents, from 6—10% in feldspathized gabbroids to 2—3% in granosyenites and 1—2% in granites; d) steady and significant increase of potassium content from 0.5—1.5% in feldspathized gabbroids to 5—6% in granosyenites and granites (Tables 124 and 125). An origin by differentiation or nonsimultaneous crystallization is precluded by the frequent occurrence of nearly all varieties within a single charnockitoid intrusion without any clear-cut signs of intrusive relationships. The gradual transitions from one variety to another and the trend of mineral and chemical transformations in coexisting varieties, suggest that they are granitization products of gabbroids which interacted with partial melts and alkaline solutions. Thus, their genesis may be assumed to be similar to that of the charnockitoids in the Humboldt Mountains and Petermann Range.

However, the geological features and composition of numerous charnockitoid intrusions in the crystalline basement of the Antarctic Platform are not uniform and therefore their individual examination will probably elucidate several additional features of their genesis.

Charnockitoids of central Queen Maud Land, which were examined by the authors in 1960—1961, are represented by several intrusions, among which the Lodochnikov Massif stands out by its large size, over 4000 km^2 /58/. The massif is broken by large mountain glaciers and there is thus no assurance that it is an entity. However, unless the massif consists of several bodies, its shape should be that of a huge irregular lens (in plan) stretching N-S over nearly 200 km. Its component rocks are characterized by unoriented massive structures with a prevalence of porphyroblastic textures. The massif is mainly composed of 'giant-grained' porphyroblastic granosyenites (probably forming its central portion) with feldspathized gabbro-norite-diorites and especially diorite-syenites predominating on its flanks (Table 122). This produces the impression of a marginal facies of more basic rocks. However, the porphyroblastic granosyenites in places form direct contacts with migmatites and shadow granitoids, while diorite-syenites occur at considerable distances from contacts with the host rocks. Intrusive contacts with containing migmatites and shadow granites, as well as with less widespread pyroxene schists, amphibolites and calciphyres, were observed in several outcrops.

TABLE 122. Mineralogical composition and characteristics of intrusive charnockitoids in East Antarctica

Specimen No.	Rocks	Sampling site	K-feldspar	plagioclase	quartz	olivine	orthopyroxene	clinopyroxene	amphibole	biotite	garnet	ore mineral	apatite	sphene	zircon	orthite	An content of plagioclase
1133a	Feldspathized norites and gabbro-norites	Mirny area	2	53	—	—	23	14	—	—	—	8	o.s.*	—	—	—	50
1131g		" "	—	67	—	—	22	4	—	1	—	6	—	—	—	—	50—55
1140		Bunger Oasis	12	56	1	—	17	8	—	—	—	3	3	—	—	—	74
752		Mirny area	—	55	—	—	38	2	2	2	—	1	o.s.	—	o.s.	—	—
1138		Bunger Oasis	12	53	—	3	21	5	—	—	—	4	2	—	—	—	60
935		"	4	40	5	—	39	4	—	2	—	5	1	—	—	—	60
446			1	52	5	—	23	12	—	4	—	2	1	—	—	—	—
1145g		Mirny area	4	70	10	—	20	—	1	1	—	3	1	—	—	—	40—45
638		Bunger Oasis	6	62	10	—	13	2	12	3	—	3	1	o.s.	o.s.	—	57
131		Lodochnikov Massif on Queen Maud Land	23	34	—	o.s.	8	o.s.	—	6	—	4	3	o.s.	o.s.	o.s.	31
522a	Quartz-bearing gabbro-norite-diorites	Titov Massif, Queen Maud Land	30	47	15	—	2	•	4	2	—	5	—	—	o.s.	—	35
24k		Bunger Oasis	19	36	15	o.s.	—	—	6	12	—	4	1	—	o.s.	—	33
209		Mount Strathcona, Denman Glacier area	20	47	14	—	7	1	—	2	—	1	o.s.	—	o.s.	—	53
1187			11	59	—	—	7	2	—	6	—	—	—	—	—	—	45
24d		Titov Massif, Queen Maud Land	10	46	10	o.s.	15	10	1	5	—	3	o.s.	—	—	—	33
145		Lodochnikov Massif on Queen Maud Land	15	58	7	—	14	1	4	1	—	—	1	—	—	—	34
615		Bunger Oasis	20	44	18	—	10	1	3	1	—	2	o.s.	—	—	—	41
1202		Reinbolt Hills on the fringe of Amery Ice Shelf	26	45	20	—	4	—	4	1	—	1	1	o.s.	o.s.	—	45—48
371		Bunger Oasis	15	50	10	—	14	6	—	1	—	3	1	—	—	—	40
308		Whisnant Nunatak on the fringe of Amery Ice Shelf	2	78	3	—	5	1	6	4	—	1	—	—	—	—	42
71		Vestfold Oasis	35	31	9	—	—	4	11	4	—	5	1	—	—	—	35
365		Bunger Oasis	15	50	15	—	10	1	2	2	—	4	1	—	—	—	35
5		Enderby Land	20	46	20	—	10	—	—	—	—	3	—	—	—	—	37

Sample	Rock type	Locality															
367	Quartz-bearing diorite-syenites	Bunger Oasis	22	37	22		6		7	2		3	1				
372		"	22	43	18		8	3	1	1		3	1				35
1190		Gillies Is., Denman Glacier area	20	37	20		1		2	18		1	1				38
251		Grearson Oasis	35	25	22		3		8	3		4					37
642v		Lodochnikov Massif on Queen Maud Land	20	52	10	8		5	5			o.s.	o.s.		o.s.		37
179		Grearson Oasis	31	38	14		2	2	8	3		2					37—44
220		Enderby Land	23	45	15		12		1	1		1					33—34
183		Grearson Oasis	30	40	21		1		6	6		1					33—38
1230		Henry Bay area	7	39	27		2		20	6		1					37—44
1229		"	31	34	20		11		6			3					42
43—1b		Mirny area	14	52	19		10		1			o.s.					35—40
132v		Lodochnikov Massif on Queen Maud Land	38	36	7	3			5			1	1				35
786a	Quartz syenite	Enderby Land	65	15	10		7		1			1	1				32—35
1119		Mirny area	28	42	18		8		2			2	o.s.				
865		David Island, Denman Glacier area	56	26	10		o.s.		5			1					25—28
631a		Lodochnikov Massif on Queen Maud Land	60	18	10		4	3	3	2		2					29
1109v	Granosyenites	Mirny area	49	30	12	4	o.s.			4		1					27—33
140		Lodochnikov Massif on Queen Maud Land	50	20	18				2	10		o.s.					28
277		Enderby Land	46	18	20		12			1	2	3	2				
50g		Mirny area	43	20	26	6	o.s.	3		1	2	1	o.s.				
786b		Enderby Land	57	5	20	o.s.	1		18	8		o.s.	·	o.s.		o.s.	32
1109a		Mirny area	30	35	26				2			1	1	·		o.s.	
512		Lodochnikov Massif on Queen Maud Land	34	27	25							1	1	2	1	·	24
1175v	Hypersthene pla- giogranites	Mount Gist, Denman Glacier area		36	39		o.s.			22		1	o.s.				42
1172		As above		34	40					23		1	1				40
62		Vestfold Oasis		63	27		5			2		2	o.s.				35
14		"		61	35		1			1		1	o.s.				35—38
631b	Eulyte granites	Lodochnikov Massif on Queen Maud Land	57	13	25		5			1		o.s.	o.s.	o.s.	o.s.		28
70		Vestfold Oasis	47	10	40		1		1	1		1	·				33—35

TABLE 122 (continued)

Specimen No.	Rocks	Sampling site	olivine n_z	olivine n_x	olivine ferruginosity, at.%	orthopyroxene n_z	orthopyroxene n_x	orthopyroxene ferruginosity, at.%	clinopyroxene n_z	clinopyroxene n_x	clinopyroxene ferruginosity, at.%	amphibole n_z	amphibole n_x	amphibole ferruginosity, at.%	biotite n_z	biotite ferruginosity, at.%
1133a	Feldspathized norites and gabbro–norites	Mirny area				1.728	1.714	51	1.725	1.701	48					
1131g		" "				1.728	1.714	51	1.724	1.700	47					
140		Bunger Oasis				1.698	1.686	27	1.704	1.681	16					
752		Mirny area				1.718	1.703	43								
1133		Bunger Oasis				1.717	1.703	42	1.712	1.688	28					
935																
446																
1145g	Quartz-bearing gabbro–norite-diorites	Mirny area														
638		Bunger Oasis														
131		Lodochnikov Massif on Queen Maud Land				1.757	1.738	74	1.731	1.706	57	1.706	1.682	71	1.677	77
522a		Titov Massif, Queen Maud Land				1.765	1.746	81				1.713	1.685	79	1.682	82
24k		Titov Massif, Queen Maud Land				1.757	1.739	74				1.718	1.692	83	1.693	92
209		Bunger Oasis				1.743	1.725	63								
1187		Mount Strathcona, Denman Glacier area														
24d		Titov Massif, Queen Maud Land				1.757	1.739	74	1.739	1.713	70				1.693	92
145		Lodochnikov Massif, Queen Maud Land				1.757	1.738	74	1.736	1.710	66	1.703	1.680	67	1.677	77
615		Bunger Oasis														
1202		Reinbolt Hills on the fringe of Amery Ice Shelf				1.762	1.742	78				1.708	1.687	73	1.676	76
371		Bunger Oasis				1.745	1.728	65	1.730	1.702	56					
308		Whitsnant Nunatak on the fringe of Amery Ice Shelf														
71		Vestfold Oasis														
365		Bunger Oasis				1.746	1.728	66								
5		Enderby Land													1.675	75

Rock type	Specimen	Locality														
Quartz-bearing diorite-syenites	367	Bunger Oasis				1.748	1.731	68								
	372	"				1.746	1.728	66								
	1190	Gillies Is., Denman Glacier area							1.730	1.706	56	1.702	1.682	66	1.677	77
	251	Grearson Oasis														
	642v	Lodochnikov Massif on Queen Maud Land														
	179	Grearson Oasis				1.738	1.722	60				1.701	1.679	65	1.667	68
	220	Enderby Land				1.746	1.728	66				1.707	1.685	72	1.678	78
	183	Grearson Oasis				1.733	1.717	56								
	1230	Grearson Oasis														
	1229	Henry Bay area				1.764	1.741	80								
	43–1b	Mirny area														
	132v	Lodochnikov Massif on Queen Maud Land	1.862	1.811	93	1.765	1.746	81				1.713	1.686	79	1.691	90
Quartz syenite	786a	Enderby Land														
Granosyenites	1119	Mirny area				1.758	1.740	74				1.710	1.690	75	1.690	89
	865	David Island, Denman Glacier area				1.760	1.741	77				1.718	1.693	83		
	631a	Lodochnikov Massif on Queen Maud Land	1.862	1.812	93	1.767	1.748	83								
	1109v	Mirny area										1.724	1.704	96	1.697	96
	140	Lodochnikov Massif on Queen Maud Land														
	277	Enderby Land										1.701	1.677	65		
	50g	Mirny area														
	786b	Enderby Land							1.748	1.723	85					
	512	Mirny area / Lodochnikov Massif on Queen Maud Land	1.835	1.790	80							1.715	1.696	84		
Hypersthene pla-giogranites	1175v	Mount Gist, Denman Glacier area				1.740	1.721	60								
	1172	As above				1.740	1.721	60								
	62	Vestfold Oasis														
	14	"														
Eulyte granites	613b	Lodochnikov Massif on Queen Maud Land														
	70	Vestfold Oasis														

Note. In specimen 1172, the garnet contains 70% almandine (n = 1.799, sp.gr. 4.06).

* [o.s. = optic sign.]

The contacts are mostly discordant, steep, and usually fairly distinct. Contact effects of charnockitoids on the various migmatized and granitized schists are undetectable. Furthermore, the composition of the granitization products of basic schists is very similar to that of the rocks in the massif, which further impedes the establishment of the contact effects. The biotitization, amphibolization and feldspathization of schists in contact with the charnockitoids can be explained by the initial stage of granitization of these rocks which took place before the appearance of the charnockites.

A characteristic feature of the Lodochnikov Massif is the presence of a comparatively small number of xenoliths and larger remnants (skialithic) of the host rock with undisturbed layering. The xenoliths exhibit a variety of dimensions and shapes, ranging from angular blocks measuring 3—4 m to rounded and lenticular inclusions of 5—10 cm. The skialiths are migmatite layers, tens of meters thick and traceable over hundreds of meters along strike. No distinct contact effects of charnockites on the xenoliths or skialiths were observed; the latter are never fused along their edges and have constant compositions. Large K-feldspar porphyroblasts analogous to those in the charnockites occur only sporadically. The somewhat higher grade of biotitization and amphibolization of the xenoliths may have been attained at the time of their migmatization. Veins are not widespread. Their most characteristic feature is their composition, different from that of the charnockites. However, they are analogous to the granitoids, aplites and pegmatites in the host migmatites. These veins are derivatives of the partial melts which were the major sources of the migmatite metasome. Veins similar to charnockitoids are practically absent. Several smaller massifs have been encountered, mostly east of the Lodochnikov Massif and, characteristically, they occur only in polymetamorphic rocks. Charnockitoid intrusions measuring tens and, less commonly, a few hundreds of square kilometers in area, present a great variety of shapes, but domed forms are the most widespread. They are composed of the same rocks as in the Lodochnikov Massif. However, feldspathized gabbro-diorites and syenite-diorites are almost as widespread as granosyenites. They also include the same intrusions as in the Humboldt Mountains and Petermann Range.

Solov'ev et al. /58/ investigated the charnockitoid intrusions in central Queen Maud Land in 1960—1961, and suggested their magmatic origin. In his opinion, "crystallization of charnockites took place under katazonal conditions (high temperatures and pressures, low activity of water and oxygen), under relatively quiet tectonic conditions, with a prolonged and gradual fall of the melt temperature in an environment of heated host rocks. . . Such conditions did not ensure the rapid separation of volatiles from the melts. The crystallization of the alkaline melt-solution remaining in the pore spaces of the solid phase and producing alkaline metasomatism phenomena was superimposed on the early solid phases." Solov'ev, emphasizing the genetic relationship of the charnockitoids to the gabbro-anorthosite formation, assumes "that the parent melt was close in composition to the granodiorite of quartz-diorite melt and its differentiation took place in a deep-seated magma chamber, mainly before the intrusion and crystallization of solid phases." Solov'ev's notions on the crystallization mechanism of charnockites suffer

TABLE 123. Quantitative fluctuations of rock-forming minerals in charnockitoid varieties of East Antarctica, vol.%

Rock groups	Minerals								An content of plagioclase
	K-feldspar	plagioclase	quartz	olivine	orthopyroxene	clinopyroxene	amphibole	biotite	
Feldspathized gabbro-norites	0—12	40—67 (50—55)	0—5	0—3	17—38 (20—23)	2—14 (4—8)	0—2	0—4 (1—2)	50—74
Feldspathized quartz-bearing gabbro-norite-diorites	4—30 (15—20)	34—70 (45—50)	3—30 (10—15)	o.s.*	2—20 (5—13)	1—10 (1—2)	0—12 (1—6)	1—12 (1—5)	35—53
Quartz-bearing diorite-syenites	14—38 (15—25)	25—52 (30—40)	9—27 (17—22)	0—8	2—12 (3—10)	(0—5)	1—20 (5—8)	1—6 (1—3)	35—40
Granosyenites	28—60 (45—55)	5—42 (20—30)	10—26 (12—20)	0—6	1—8	0—3	2—18 (2—5)	1—8 (2—4)	24—35
Hypersthene plagiogranites	—	34—63	27—40	0	1—5	—	—	1—2	35—42
Eulyte granites	47—55	11—13	25—40	0	1—5	—	—	1—2	28—30

Notes. 1. The extreme values may be distorted in several cases since the mineral contents were largely determined by optical methods and to a lesser extent on the Wentworth stage. 2. The figures in parentheses indicate the most commonly encountered contents.
* [o.s. = optic sign.]

TABLE 124. Chemical analyses of intrusive charnockitoids from East Antarctica

Specimen No.	Rocks	Sampling site	SiO_2	TiO_2	Al_2O_3	Fe_2O_3	FeO	MnO	MgO	CaO	BaO
1133a	Feldspathized norites and gabbro-norites	Mirny area	46.32	4.37	13.60	2.26	12.73	0.24	5.42	9.31	—
1131g		"	47.97	3.66	14.38	1.54	12.65	0.27	5.82	8.42	—
1140		"	48.00	3.68	13.71	1.72	12.06	0.25	4.76	8.61	—
752		Bunger Oasis	49.91	0.70	13.55	0.63	10.50	0.28	14.79	7.23	—
1138		Mirny area	50.75	3.30	14.38	1.83	10.50	0.22	4.77	7.82	—
935		Bunger Oasis	51.18	1.92	11.56	3.37	13.46	0.36	9.10	5.63	—
446		"	51.79	1.16	15.62	1.93	8.42	0.25	7.00	9.79	—
1145g	Feldspathized quartz-bearing gabbro-norite-diorites	Mirny area	53.21	2.80	16.74	1.09	10.53	0.25	1.98	6.18	—
638		Bunger Oasis	54.70	1.24	17.22	2.14	7.59	0.23	5.04	7.29	—
131		Lodochnikov Massif, Queen Maud Land	54.69	2.50	14.21	2.81	9.27	0.16	2.69	5.85	0.26
522a		Titov Massif, Queen Maud Land	55.11	2.69	15.46	1.38	9.38	0.14	2.27	6.56	—
24zh		Bunger Oasis	56.30	2.54	14.96	2.73	8.53	0.03	2.10	5.46	—
209		Bunger Oasis	56.46	2.24	15.03	2.68	8.01	0.25	2.97	5.14	—
1187		Mount Strathcona, Denman Glacier area	57.04	1.62	15.49	1.82	8.55	0.23	3.16	5.88	—
24d		Titov Massif, Queen Maud Land	57.00	2.48	15.30	2.30	8.64	0.14	1.79	4.98	—
145		Lodochnikov Massif, Queen Maud Land	57.36	2.14	15.76	1.29	8.44	0.13	1.68	6.04	—
615		Bunger Oasis	58.27	2.04	15.36	2.71	6.90	0.24	2.35	6.06	—
1202		Reinbolt Hills, fringe of Amery Ice Shelf	58.62	2.18	14.17	1.52	9.07	0.21	1.63	5.26	—
371		Bunger Oasis	59.65	1.80	14.13	2.21	7.98	0.23	2.23	5.67	—
308		Whisnant Nunatak, fringe of Amery Ice Shelf	61.85	0.92	15.41	1.95	6.24	0.15	2.37	5.74	—
71	Quartz-bearing diorite-syenites	Vestfold Oasis	55.57	1.30	15.91	4.42	5.30	0.13	3.18	5.30	—
365		Bunger Oasis	61.19	1.48	14.68	2.21	6.34	0.19	1.75	5.15	—
5		Enderby Land	61.63	1.32	14.42	2.76	5.73	0.13	1.32	4.22	—
367		Bunger Oasis	62.31	1.38	14.10	1.92	6.63	0.20	1.71	4.80	0.27
372		"	62.34	1.40	13.96	1.77	6.58	0.17	1.81	5.18	—
1190		Gillies Is., Denman Glacier area	62.38	1.53	14.88	1.86	5.30	0.12	1.56	3.42	—

Rock type	No.	Locality									
Quartz-bearing diorite-syenites	251	Grearson Oasis	62.83	1.24	13.39	1.89	5.10	0.17	1.80	3.44	—
	642v	Lodochnikov Massif, Queen Maud Land	63.09	0.98	15.3	1.52	7.00	0.13	0.63	4.10	—
	179	Grearson Oasis	63.51	1.39	13.93	2.78	5.29	0.17	1.79	4.01	—
	226	Enderby Land	63.7	1.0	15.09	2.71	4.49	0.09	1.59	3.43	—
	183	Grearson Oasis	63.90	1.40	13.71	2.46	5.48	0.17	1.85	3.91	—
	1230	Henry Bay area	62.94	1.16	14.55	2.89	5.16	0.21	1.40	3.88	—
	1229	" "	63.37	1.12	14.03	2.13	5.84	0.25	1.32	4.44	—
	43-1b	Mirny area	64.34	1.15	14.31	1.08	6.79	0.15	1.37	3.30	—
	132k	Lodochnikov Massif, Queen Maud Land	61.55	1.05	15.28	2.46	6.43	0.14	0.78	3.76	0.20
	786a	Enderby Land	62.13	1.18	14.82	2.49	4.93	0.13	1.02	3.65	0.25
	1119	Mirny area	64.44	0.89	15.11	1.10	5.18	0.09	0.59	3.10	—
	865	David Island, Denman Glacier area	64.69	0.72	14.32	1.38	5.03	0.17	0.88	3.09	—
	631a	Lodochnikov Massif, Queen Maud Land	65.36	0.79	15.39	1.00	4.68	0.06	0.75	3.05	—
Granosyenites	1109v	Mirny area	67.20	0.77	14.35	0.73	4.34	0.08	0.58	1.70	—
	140	Lodochnikov Massif, Queen Maud Land	67.90	0.33	15.24	1.57	2.91	0.03	0.38	2.20	—
	277	Enderby Land	67.91	0.44	14.40	1.88	2.27	0.09	1.17	2.10	0.30
	50g	Mirny area	68.57	0.65	14.17	1.48	3.41	0.15	0.59	2.88	0.17
	786b	Enderby Land	69.19	0.59	13.60	1.70	2.69	0.06	0.50	2.07	—
	1109a	Mirny area	69.52	0.58	14.69	0.80	3.39	0.07	0.46	1.79	—
	512	Lodochnikov Massif, Queen Maud Land	70.93	0.47	12.87	1.43	3.59	0.07	0.17	1.94	—
Hypersthene plagio-granites	1175v	Mount Gist, Denman Glacier area	63.19	1.17	14.53	0.71	9.43	0.44	2.12	2.71	—
	1172	" " "	65.96	0.94	14.29	1.46	5.30	0.26	1.52	3.48	—
	62	Vestfold Oasis	66.09	0.55	16.54	1.84	3.11	0.06	1.38	4.52	—
	14	Vestfold Oasis	70.81	0.30	15.17	0.85	1.95	0.04	1.02	4.85	—
Eulyte granites	631b	Lodochnikov Massif, Queen Maud Land	73.22	0.20	13.59	0.67	1.73	0.04	0.25	1.33	—
	70	Vestfold Oasis	73.32	0.16	13.74	0.98	1.67	0.01	0.45	1.86	—

TABLE 124 (continued)

Specimen No.	Na$_2$O	K$_2$O	P$_2$O$_5$	Loss on ignition	Total	H$_2$O	CO$_2$	S$_{tot}$	a	c	b	s	a'	f'	m'	c'	n	t	φ	Q	a/c
1133a	2.80	0.69	1.90	0.91	100.45	—	—	—	7.4	5.5	29.7	54.4	—	49.0	31.0	20.0	85.0	6.0	6.6	−8.5	1.4
1131g	2.82	0.59	1.53	0.70	100.35	—	—	—	7.2	6.2	27.9	58.7	—	50.0	35.0	15.0	88.0	5.0	4.5	−3.2	1.2
1140	2.93	1.65	1.60	0.86	99.83	0.17	—	—	9.0	4.8	27.4	58.8	—	49	30	21	73	6	5.6	−5.2	1.9
752	0.96	0.25	0.08	1.33	100.21	—	—	—	2.5	7.4	35.3	54.8	—	29.3	67.9	2.8	84.2	1.1	1.5	−2.8	0.3
1138	3.02	1.47	1.42	0.63	100.11	0.22	—	—	8.5	5.3	24.6	61.2	—	49	33	18	76	5	6.3	−0.7	1.7
935	1.63	1.15	0.21	0.89	100.46	—	—	—	5.2	4.9	32.1	57.8	—	48.2	46.5	5.3	66.7	2.7	8.6	+0.3	1.1
446	2.29	0.87	0.16	1.27	100.55	—	—	—	6.8	7.7	22.2	63.3	—	37.4	44.8	17.8	78.8	1.7	6.2	+5.9	0.9
1145g	3.97	1.33	0.57	1.03	99.68	0.24	—	—	11.2	6.2	16.9	65.7	—	70	20	10	82	4	5.9	+2.8	1.8
638	2.27	1.73	0.37	0.45	100.27	—	—	—	7.6	8.1	19.3	65.0	—	49.1	45.5	5.4	66.7	1.6	9.5	+6.7	0.9
131	2.72	3.06	0.94	0.80	99.96	—	—	—	10.8	4.3	19.1	65.8	—	60.2	24.5	15.3	57.2	3.3	12.4	+5.7	2.5
522a	3.07	2.43	1.09	0.33	99.92	—	—	—	10.5	5.4	17.3	66.8	—	61.1	22.7	16.2	65.4	3.6	7.3	+7.2	1.9
24zh	3.05	3.27	0.74	0.86	100.57	—	—	—	11.7	4.4	16.6	67.3	—	64.0	21.8	14.2	58.3	3.3	14.2	+6.8	2.7
209	2.42	2.96	0.66	0.78	100.00	—	—	—	10.0	5.3	16.7	68.0	—	62.6	30.7	6.7	55.0	2.9	14.3	+10.7	1.9
1187	2.64	2.42	0.32	0.87	100.04	—	—	—	9.5	5.8	16.7	67.1	—	59.3	32.1	8.6	63.2	2.1	9.1	+10.6	1.6
24d	3.32	3.15	0.69	0.79	100.58	—	—	—	12.1	4.1	15.4	68.1	—	67.8	20.4	11.8	60.9	3.2	12.7	+7.6	2.75
145	3.15	2.62	1.03	0.36	100.00	—	—	—	11.1	4.6	15.2	68.9	—	64.6	20.1	15.3	64.6	2.7	7.7	+10.3	2.1
615	2.37	3.00	0.75	0.47	100.52	—	—	—	9.8	5.6	15.1	69.4	—	61.0	26.6	12.4	54.3	2.5	15.6	+13.6	1.75
1202	2.49	3.30	0.76	0.81	100.02	0.17	—	0.01	10.4	4.6	16.0	69.9	—	67.0	19.0	14.0	53.0	3.0	8.3	+14.4	2.3
371	2.72	2.82	0.43	0.68	100.55	—	—	—	10.1	4.4	16.0	69.5	—	60.4	23.9	15.7	59.5	2.3	11.9	+14.4	2.3
308	3.00	1.29	0.32	1.08	100.32	—	—	—	8.6	6.3	12.8	72.3	—	61.4	31.5	7.1	77.4	1.1	13.0	+21.1	1.3
71	4.15	3.14	0.91	0.76	99.74	—	—	—	13.3	3.9	17.0	65.2	—	52.8	31.6	15.6	67.0	1.9	22.4	−1.3	3.6
365	2.75	3.49	0.36	0.44	100.02	—	—	—	11.3	4.3	17.0	71.2	—	62.0	22.4	15.6	54.9	1.8	14.6	+15.5	2.6
5	2.71	3.93	0.69	0.76	99.89	0.27	—	—	11.9	3.9	11.5	72.7	—	69.1	19.4	11.5	51.8	1.5	20.2	+17.7	3.1
367	2.72	3.72	0.36	0.33	100.18	—	—	—	11.3	3.7	13.1	71.9	—	62.0	21.9	16.1	53.0	1.7	12.5	+17.0	3.1
372	2.72	3.32	0.37	0.93	100.55	—	—	—	10.8	4.0	13.3	71.9	—	59.2	23.0	17.8	55.7	1.7	11.2	+18.7	2.7
1190	3.38	4.05	0.62	1.06	100.06	—	—	—	13.5	3.3	10.4	72.8	—	65.6	25.8	8.6	56.1	1.8	15.9	+15.3	4.1

Sample					Total																
251	2.81	14.11	0.36	0.99	100.11	—	—	—	12.3	2.3	11.2	73.6	—	60.2	28.0	11.0	50.6	1.4	14.9	+19.7	4.2
642v	3.53	3.79	0.09	0.31	100.47	—	—	—	13.3	3.6	10.5	72.6	—	76.4	10.5	13.1	58.8	1.2	11.8	+15.0	3.7
179	2.86	3.59	0.42	0.40	100.14	traces	—	—	11.4	3.5	10.5	73.2	—	63.2	25.9	10.9	54.8	1.7	19.5	+20.1	3.3
226	2.77	4.00	0.43	0.32	99.59	—	0.18	—	12.0	4.2	9.6	74.2	—	71.0	29.0	0	51.7	1.2	24.6	+20.2	2.9
183	3.46	2.89	0.42	0.52	100.15	—	—	0.43	11.7	3.2	12.7	72.9	—	61.9	25.4	12.7	64.4	1.7	17.7	+19.2	3.7
1230	2.65	3.69	0.37	1.29	100.19	—	—	0.38	11.4	4.2	12.2	72.7	—	71.6	22.6	5.8	52.4	1.4	23.2	+20.4	2.7
1229	2.61	3.68	0.43	1.12	100.34	—	—	0.20	11.1	3.9	11.5	73.7	—	66.4	19.8	13.8	51.9	1.3	15.6	+20.9	2.8
43—1b	3.00	3.88	0.20	0.76	99.83	—	—	—	11.5	3.8	10.2	74.5	—	75	23	2	57		9.2	+22.2	3.0
132k	2.91	4.50	0.32	0.71	100.09	—	—	—	13.2	3.8	10.7	72.3	—	79.9	12.3	7.8	49.5	1.3	20.8	+14.4	3.5
786a	2.74	4.65	0.69	1.08	99.76	—	—	0.25	13.1	3.6	9.8	73.5	—	72.7	18.0	9.3	46.8	1.4	22.5	+17.2	3.5
1119	3.41	5.23	0.30	0.82	100.26	—	—	—	15.1	2.6	8.2	74.1	—	73.1	12.6	14.3	50.0	0.8	11.8	+15.4	5.8
865	3.80	4.80	0.42	0.73	100.03	—	—	—	15.1	1.8	9.4	73.7	—	64.8	15.8	19.4	54.5	0.9	13.0	+15.4	8.4
631a	3.22	5.28	0.22	0.13	99.93	—	—	0.12	14.7	2.9	7.5	74.9	—	71.6	17.4	11.0	48.2		11.0	+17.5	5.1
1109v	3.05	6.55	0.18	0.43	100.06	—	—	—	16.1	1	6.3	76.2	—	76	15	9	41	0.4	9	+18.8	11.5
140	2.98	6.00	0.04	0.28	99.86	—	—	0.40	15.3	2.5	4.8	77.4	—	85.7	12.9	1.4	42.9	0.4	28.6	+21.7	6.1
277	2.87	4.63	0.37	1.19	99.62	—	—	—	13.0	2.6	7.0	77.4	15.7	55.5	28.4	—	48.4	0.8	23.5	+26.2	5.0
50g	2.28	5.11	0.10	0.69	100.08	—	—	0.26	12.4	3.2	6.0	78.4	—	55.9	17.4	4.7	41.2	0.7	20.9	+28.7	3.8
786b	2.55	5.45	0.25	0.97	99.79	—	—	0.27	13.4	2.4	4.9	77.4	—	80.3	15.8	3.9	41.4	0.7	28.9	+28.8	5.6
1109a	3.23	5.93	0.05	0.31	100.25	—	—	0.26	15.5	1.9	4.9	77.7	—	79.5	15.1	5.4	41.4		13.7	+22.5	8.2
512	2.91	5.14	0.08	0.73	100.38	—	—	—	13.5	1.7	5.5	79.3	—	83.1	4.8	12.1	46.5	0.5	21.7	+29.9	8.0
1175v	1.85	2.86	0.43	0.87	100.34	—	—	—	8.1	3.2	17.6	71.1	25.0	54.9	20.1	—	49.2	1.4	3.0	+22.8	2.5
1172	2.31	3.60	0.28	0.79	100.19	—	—	—	10.3	4.2	9.6	75.9	4.3	68.6	27.1	—	49.3	1.1	12.9	+27.0	2.5
62	4.85	0.76	0.14	0.51	100.35	—	—	—	11.8	5.2	7.1	75.9	—	63.5	32.7	3.8	90.7	0.6	21.2	+23.0	2.3
14	3.94	0.63	0.10	0.79	100.45	—	—	—	9.5	5.4	4.8	80.3	—	54.2	34.7	11.1	91.4	0.3	16.7	+36.2	1.8
631b	3.46	5.18	0.09	0.19	99.95	—	—	—	14.5	1.5	2.7	81.1	—	80.0	15.0	5.0	50.5	0.2	20.0	+31.3	6.0
70	3.48	4.08	0.03	0.50	100.29	—	—	—	13.3	2.2	3.2	81.3	—	72.9	22.9	—	56.0	0.2	25.0	+33.8	6.1

Note. The mineralogical composition of analyzed specimens is given in Table 122.

TABLE 125. Quantitative fluctuations of chemical elements in charnockitoid varieties of East Antarctica, wt%

Rock groups	Chemical elements									Number of chemical analyses
	SiO_2	TiO_2	Al_2O_3	Fe_2O_3	FeO	MgO	CaO	Na_2O	K_2O	
Feldspathized gabbro-norites	46.32—51.79	1.16—4.37	11.56—15.62	0.63—2.26	8.42—13.46	4.77—14.79	5.63—9.79	0.96—3.02	0.59—1.65	7
Feldspathized quartz-bearing gabbro-norite-diorites	53.21—61.85	0.92—2.80	14.21—17.22	1.09—2.81	6.24—10.53	1.68—5.04	4.98—7.29	2.27—3.32	1.29—3.30	13
Quartz-bearing diorite-syenites	55.57—65.96	0.94—1.53	13.93—15.91	1.08—4.42	4.93—6.63	0.78—3.18	3.42—5.30	2.31—4.15	2.39—4.65	16
Granosyenites	64.44—70.93	0.33—0.89	12.87—15.39	0.73—1.88	2.27—5.18	0.46—1.17	1.70—3.10	2.55—3.80	4.63—6.55	10
Hypersthene plagio-granites	63.19—70.81	0.30—1.17	14.29—16.54	0.71—1.46	1.95—9.43	1.02—2.12	2.71—4.85	1.85—4.85	0.63—2.86	4
Eulyte granites	73.22—73.32	0.16—0.20	13.59—13.74	0.67—0.98	1.67—1.73	0.45—0.75	1.33—1.86	3.46—3.48	4.08—5.18	2

from several obscurities and contradictions: Thus a) intrusion of charnockites into heated katazonal rocks is in disagreement with the crystallization of amphibole and biotite; b) the nature of the differentiation within
the magma chamber is unknown, and so is the nature of the melts and rocks
formed under the described conditions; c) the idea of residual alkaline melts
in the pores as agents of potassium metasomatism is incompatible with the magmatic differentiation processes as well as with the large scale of the development of K-feldspar porphyroblasts in charnockites (often accounting
for one half of the rock volume); d) it remains unknown which rocks
crystallized directly from a melt and whether they are present in the
composition of the charnockite intrusions in their original form. From
the standpoint of magmatism, it is impossible to explain many characteristic
features of intrusive charnockitoids, as follows: a) similarity between the
mineral composition of charnockitoids and the paragenesis of minerals in
the host migmatites and shadow granites; b) coexistence within a single
exposure of rocks with a variety of compositions (e. g., diorite-syenites,
syenites and granosyenites), lacking intrusive interrelationships and, on
the contrary, showing gradual transitions between one another; c) presence
of xenoliths and sporadic large skialiths of host rocks within the intrusions;
d) absence (or else an insignificant and indistinct manifestation) of contact
effects of charnockitoids on the containing rocks; e) absence of veins similar
to charnockitoids; f) exceptionally high content of metasomatic K-feldspar
porphyroblasts in the most widespread intrusive rocks; g) predominance of
crystalline and corrosion-metasomatic textures in the charnockitoids,
that are especially characteristic in the interrelationships between the
rock-forming minerals.

As yet, the problem of the genesis of the charnockitoid intrusions on
Queen Maud Land cannot be provided with an unambiguous solution, in the
first place because of insufficient data. However, the considerable similarity between the composition of rocks of the Lodochnikov Massif (and the
surrounding bodies) and that of intrusions of the Humboldt Mountains and
Petermann Range, suggests that the latter likewise originated mainly from
gabbroids that were granitized in the course of tectonic-magmatic activization of the crystalline basement. In this respect, it must be emphasized
that no gabbroid intrusions have as yet been discovered on the vast central
part of Queen Maud Land, although such intrusions are generally widespread
in other crystalline basement regions, e. g., Sør Rondane Mountains in
eastern Queen Maud Land, where intrusions of metamorphosed and cataclastized gabbroids occupy at least 20% of an area covering over 10,000 km^2.
However, if the Lodochnikov Massif is regarded as a single intrusive body,
and if its fairly uniform composition over large areas showing clear signs
of the participation of a melt in its formation is taken into account, it is
impossible to preclude the possibility of the rheomorphic genesis of this massif.
This rheomorphic genesis would involve abyssal melts as the principal
agents for the mobilization of a tremendous quantity of mobile solid masses
capable of intrusion, especially during periods of crystalline basement
activization.

Porphyroblastic charnockitoids of Enderby Land
were examined by Soviet geologists in 1963—1966. They are represented
by four diffuse bodies, the largest of which has an area of ~1000 km² in
the Napier Mountains. Other bodies, with areas of 100—300 km², are located
on the eastern margin of the Tange Promontory in the north of Vernadskii
Peninsula (Mount Hurley) and in the Dismal Mountains (the Cyclops Nunataks).
The porphyroblastic charnockites in the Napier Mountains occur in shadow
perthitic charnockites with which they do not form any distinct contact.
The composition of the porphyroblastic charnockites (Table 122) corresponds to quartz syenites and granosyenites. They consist of 60%
K-feldspar porphyroblasts, measuring 10 × 4 cm, the interstices of which
are filled with medium-grained aggregates of andesine, An 32—35, orthoclase,
quartz (10—20%), ferrohypersthene (ferruginosity, 65%), hornblende and
biotite (ferruginosity 65—67%). The colored minerals account for about
7—10 vol.% of the rock. Small cordierite porphyroblasts, as well as lenticular inclusions (80 × 20 cm) of shadow enderbites and amphibolites, occur
in the charnockites. Rocks of the Tange Promontory are similar to charnockites of the Napier Mountains, but differ from the latter in their profusion
of lenticular intrusions of shadow enderbites and charnockites shadow
garnet granites and spinel-sapphirine rocks. In the Tange Promontory
charnockites, andesine, An 37 (45%), predominates over orthoclase (20%);
they contain 15—20% quartz, 11% orthopyroxene (ferruginosity, 66%), 1% clinopyroxene, 4% biotite and 3% ore. The chemical composition (Table 124)
of Enderby Land charnockitoids corresponds to diorite-syenites (with deviations toward syenites) and granosyenites. Their textures are controlled by
abundant randomly oriented feldspar porphyroblasts, imparting a massive
coarse-to 'giant-grained' habit. The porphyroblasts are often diablastic
due to the abundance of small inclusions of plagioclase, quartz and even
hypersthene. The included grains exhibit group extinction, indicating
the metasomatic origin of the porphyroblasts. The matrix is granoblastic with glomeroblastic concentrations of colored minerals. Antiperthitic replacement ingrowths are intensively developed in the plagioclase grains. Hypersthene is replaced by amphibole and biotite, forming
characteristic fringes. Consequently, the porphyroblastic charnockitoids
of Enderby Land may be recognized as metasomatic rocks formed from
shadow charnockites and enderbites by intensive K-feldspar porphyro-
blastosis. The newly formed porphyroblastic charnockitoids retain xenoliths of host rocks as well as undigested relicts of shadow enderbites and
charnockites (Figure 61).

Charnockitoids of Mac-Robertson Land, where they are
known as "Mawson granites," were briefly investigated in 1955—1956 during
a reconnaissance by Australian geologists /90/. They have been studied in
greater detail in the Mawson Station area, where there are two low rock
exposures with areas of 80 × 400 m and 600 × 100 m, entirely composed of
porphyroblastic charnockites. Their compositions correspond to granosyenites and quartz syenites. The exposure on which the station huts are
located is ~50 m, and is composed of porphyroblastic, in places slightly
gneissified, charnockites with an abundance of xenoliths as well as small
veins of aplites and pegmatites.

FIGURE 61. Skialiths of shadow biotite-garnet granitoids (light color) and porphyroblastic charnockites, from the Dismal Mountains on Enderby Land, 30 m high (exposure 226).

The charnockites contain over $\frac{1}{3}$ K-feldspar porphyroblasts, measuring 2—3 cm. In places, the porphyroblasts are linear, parallel to the strike of skialiths. The porphyroblasts are embedded in a medium-grained crystal-line matrix dominated by plagioclase (andesine, An 30—35). The leading colored mineral is highly ferruginous hypersthene; other colored minerals present are secondary garnet, biotite and less commonly hornblende. As much as 10 vol.% of the charnockites is composed of linear xenoliths and skialiths of granitized basic schists, reaching lengths of 10—15 m and widths varying from a few dozen cm to 2 m. Besides the feldspathized schists of basic composition, there are small xenoliths of garnet-biotite gneisses. Other skialiths include a pyroxene-magnetite rock occurring as lenses up to 0.5 m wide and 5 m long. One lens, measuring 5 m along its long axis, consists of quartz with abundant inclusions of sapphirine. Veins of peg-matites and aplites are common in the charnockites. The largest pegmatite vein is 1.5—1.7 m thick and has been traced over nearly 300 m along strike. Other veins are thinner and may be traced over dozens of meters. The charnockites have also been found to contain fine mylonite zones, only

10—15 cm wide. Near the station, there are dozens of small islands consisting mainly of slightly gneissified porphyroblastic charnockites. The interrelationships between the charnockites and the host rocks are obscure,
since schists are absent from a majority of the islands. The charnockites
on offshore islands, like those of the Mawson Station area, contain xenoliths
and skialiths of schists, veins of aplites and pegmatites.

The Australian investigators, who resumed studies of the charnockites in
1965 /132/, have reported that these rocks form 90% of the exposures in the
Mawson Station area over an area of more than 10,000 km². They occur
130 km west of the Mawson Station, where an intrusive body of charnockites
is located in the Howard Bay area, as well as 80 km to the south, where they
were discovered in the Brown Mountains. Porphyroblastic charnockites with
a coarse-grained, sometimes slightly gneissified matrix, predominate at all
these sites. There are also subordinate quantities of equigranular medium-
grained rocks with a higher grade of gneissification. In places there are
intrusive contacts between the charnockites and the host schists and their
migmatites. The charnockites mainly consist of perthitic orthoclase, with
porphyroblasts 1—5 cm long in a matrix resembling equigranular charnockite. At least 30% of the matrix consists of plagioclase, varying in composition from oligoclase-andesine (in rocks with a high content of orthoclase)
to labradorite-bytownite (in rocks devoid of K-feldspar). Up to 15% is
composed of quartz and nearly the same amount of colored minerals. The
latter are dominated by ferruginous hypersthene and also include variable
amounts of biotite; hornblende and garnet are rare. Equigranular charnockites contain more quartz and plagioclase and less colored minerals than the
porphyroblastic charnockites. On the other hand, they have a larger content
of boudinaged skialiths of pyroxene schists, as well as xenoliths of biotite-
garnet gneiss. They also contain more pegmatitic and aplitic veins. In
certain equigranular charnockites, biotite completely replaces hypersthene
and clinopyroxene is replaced by hornblende. Garnet is more common in
such rocks than in the porphyroblastic varieties. The few descriptions of
rocks classified as charnockites by Australian geologists are not sufficient
to determine their detailed composition and origin. However, chemical
analyses from the same sources indicate a considerable heterogeneity in
composition, corresponding to hypersthene quartz diorites, diorite-
syenites, granodiorites, granosyenites and less commonly granites. Reports
of intrusive contacts and the mapped shapes of the charnockite bodies suggest
an intrusive nature, while the abundance of xenoliths, skialiths and other
inclusions, not always corresponding in composition to the host rocks and
always products of the granulite facies, indicates the rheomorphic genesis of
these intrusions.

Charnockitoids on the eastern margin of the Amery
Ice Shelf form isolated flat-topped nunataks. The most typical rocks
were encountered in the Reinbolt Hills and were examined in some detail
by Klimov in 1957 /57/ (mainly in the Jennings Promontory). In this area,
outcrops are composed of fairly uniform coarse-grained charnockitoids,
in places assuming a porphyritic habit due to the presence of K-feldspar porphyroblasts measuring 2—3 cm. In places, the charnockites contain rounded

xenoliths of biotite-amphibole gneiss, locally cross-cut by aplitic veinlets. The mineralogical composition of the Jennings Promontory charnockites (Table 122) corresponds to quartz-bearing diorite-syenites; basic andesine (An 45—48) somewhat predominates over K-feldspar, with 10—15% quartz, up to 5% ferrohypersthene, 4% amphibole and 1% biotite. Their complex texture consists of K-feldspar porphyroblasts embedded in a recrystallized granoblastic quartz-plagioclase aggregate (plagioclase is euhedral relative to quartz and relict hypersthene). The hypersthene is replaced by amphibole and biotite. The chemical composition (Table 124) of these charnockites corresponds to quartz-bearing feldspathized gabbro-norite-diorite. The Whisnant Nunatak charnockitoids examined by Solov'ev in 1965 /57/ are possibly a continuation of the Reinbolt Hills Massif. They are represented by quartz-bearing hypersthene diorites with a very low grade of feldspathization. However, they are highly amphibolized and biotit-ized and are schistose. Their composition is dominated by andesine (An 37—43); the colored minerals are ferrohypersthene, salite, hornblende and biotite, accounting for about 20%, while quartz and K-feldspar make up about 10%. Chemically, they correspond to quartz-bearing gabbro-norite-diorites (Table 124). In this respect, they are similar to charnockitoids of the Reinbolt Hills. Granosyenite outcrops occur still farther north of the Whisnant Nunatak, on Mount Caroline Mikkelsen, and may also constitute a continuation of the Reinbolt Hills intrusions. These granosyenites contain 40% K-feldspar porphyroblasts embedded in a medium- to coarse-grained matrix consisting of plagioclase, An 26—34, orthoclase, quartz (10—20%) and highly ferruginous — 92% — biotite (4—7%). Biotite possibly replaces hypersthene in the same manner as it replaces relict hornblende.

The eastern rim of the Amery Ice Shelf apparently contains a fairly large massif of charnockitoids, with an area of several hundred square kilometers. This consists of a variety of rocks ranging from gabbro-norite-diorite to granosyenite, apparently as in the case of the Humboldt Mountains and Petermann Range or the Bunger Oasis. To date, there are no reliable data on the geological setting of this presumed massif, since a description of how these charnockitoid rocks relate to one another and to the host crystalline basement rocks is yet lacking. The only known data suggest that they occur among migmatized and granitized schists of the granulite facies.

Still another charnockite massif was discovered and very briefly investigated by Australian geologists on the SW margin of the Amery Ice Shelf near Lake Beaver /57/. According to the Australian maps, the massif occupies an area of approximately 900 km^2. No detailed information has been reported on geological structure, except that it is composed of massive and porphyroblastic rocks of the "Mawson granite" type.

Charnockitoids of the Vestfold Oasis occupy an area exceeding 400 km^2. In 1956 the oasis was visited by Voronov and then by Ravich, both of whom gathered a small collection of rocks /57/. Among these samples, hypersthene granitoids appear to be abundant. Similar granitoids are ubiquitous in the Vestfold Oasis, in the form of comparatively small, often sheet-like bodies occurring in migmatized and granitized pyroxene-plagioclase schists. The composition of the granitoids (Table 122) corresponds to medium-grained, weakly gneissic quartz-bearing pyroxene diorite-syenites, hypersthene plagiogranites and eulyte granites. They exhibit a combination of porphyroblastic and granoblastic textures, with replacement phenomena and intergrowths of minerals. The prevailing rock types are hypersthene plagiogranites, containing over 60% andesine (An 35—38) and 30% quartz; they are fairly leucocratic with up to 7—8% colored minerals consisting of hypersthene which is replaced by biotite and less commonly by amphibole. Such rocks are closer to enderbites than to charnockites. Certain bodies are composed of rocks with a diorite-syenite composition, containing nearly equal amounts of andesine (An 35) and K-feldspar, less than 10% quartz and up to 20% colored minerals. The latter are dominated by amphibole and biotite with relict salitic pyroxene. It appears that the two rocks are genetically related; however, one variety is largely feldspathized and the other, largely silicified (quartz). Their common genesis is confirmed by an identical plagioclase composition in both varieties. A very high grade of feldspathization is characteristic of the alaskitic variety, which contains only ~10% andesine (An 35), but nearly 50% K-feldspar, about 40% quartz and less than 2% biotitized eulyte. The chemical compositions of these granitoids (Table 124) fall into the three groups: diorite-syenites, plagiogranites and alaskitic granites, differing from one another mainly in their contents of potassium and silica, whereas their contents of calcium, and especially of sodium, remain fairly constant. These mineralogical and chemical compositions of the Vestfold Oasis charnockitoids indicate their granitization origin, which cannot be more specifically defined because of the inadequate data on the rocks. However, their geological, mineralogical and chemical properties preclude the possibility of a genesis by magmatic differentiation.

Charnockitoids of the Mirny Observatory area, covering ~10 km^2 on some two dozen rocky islands and coastal nunataks, probably form only a part of a larger massif. In 1956/7, Klimov made a detailed investigation of these outcrops /57/ and concluded that the Mirny area contained an exposed uplifted block of the Antarctic Platform crystalline basement composed of the following: granulite facies schists of various degrees of migmatization and granitization; intrusive gabbroids which were injected after regional metamorphism of the surrounding schists but were substantially metamorphosed and partly granitized (charnockitized) during later ultrametamorphism; injective leucodiorites and plagiogranites forming the metasome of agmatized schists and metamorphic gabbroids; rheomorphic charnockites formed after the intrusion of gabbroids during the later ultrametamorphism of the schists. This sequence of formation was proposed by Klimov on the basis of the structural relations of the rocks, although he also mentioned that all varieties formed inclusions in charnockites and had participated in intrusive movements during the formation of the charnockite massif. Thus, their structural relationships are still questionable. Intrusive contacts between the charnockites and the three earlier complexes have not yet been located in the region. However, the following varieties of indirect contacts were observed: —agmatites occurring between the charnockites and host rocks. The paleosome consists of lenses of pyroxene-plagioclase schists and the metasome of a nearly massive hypersthene granite (Morennyi Nunatak); — an intrusive body of charnockitized gabbroids occurs at the contact between the charnockites and migmatized schists (Komsomol'skaya Nunatak); — a wedge of the charnockite massif in the host rocks forms a gradual transition into a zone of net-veined hypersthene plagiogranites (Komsomol'skaya Nunatak); — the injection plagiogranites form a gradual transition to charnockites (Tokarev Island); — numerous agmatite areas occur largely on the periphery of the charnockite massif; the paleosome consists of blocks or fragmented inclusions of pyroxene-plagioclase schists and metamorphosed gabbroids, and the metasome of hypersthene leucodiorite, plagiogranite, or granites. Away from these contact zones, the charnockite massif is composed of homogeneous, mainly coarse-grained hypersthene and fayalite granitoids. These are massive or slightly gneissic with compositions corresponding to granodiorites and granites. These features of the massif suggest that the charnockites originated simultaneously with the metasome of the agmatites, and the charnockitization of the older gabbroids was likewise related to the development of the agmatites. The presence of relatively little-altered dikes (up to 3 m thick) of gabbro-dolerites exhibiting chilled contacts with the agmatite aureole is indicative of intrusive rocks younger in age than the charnockitoids.

A close examination of the composition of the so-called metamorphosed gabbroids and charnockitized gabbroids /57/, which are ascribed to different origins by Klimov, indicates that the former only constitute the initial stage in an overall process resulting in the latter. It should be noted that the orthopyroxene in the metamorphosed gabbro-norites is represented by ferrohypersthene, with a ferruginosity of 53—56% (50—55% in gabbro-dolerites); its metamorphism is manifested firstly by the appearance of biotite (up to 7—8%) and comparatively rare inclusions of quartz and K-feldspar. It is thus clear that the metamorphism of gabbroids is, in fact, the initial stage in their charnockitization. Analyses of the mineral and chemical compositions of the Mirny charnockites (Tables 122, 124) indicate that they are represented mainly by typical eulyte and fayalite granosyenites and therefore only belong to quartz diorite-syenites in rare cases; however, the metamorphosed gabbroids correspond to feldspathized gabbro-norites, and the so-called leucodiorites to feldspathized gabbro-norite-diorites. Unfortunately, Klimov did not report the chemical analyses of the charnockitized gabbroids, but their mineral composition /57/ suggests that they correspond to diorite-syenites according to the terminology presented herein (Klimov's monzonite-diorites and gabbro-monzonites). On the whole, the charnockitoid rocks in the Mirny area are represented by all five varieties, from gabbro-norites to granosyenites. These rocks may be assumed to have originated from an integrated process of charnockitization of gabbroid intrusions: development of a partial melt with a granitic composition which produced the metasome of the agmatites (very widespread in the region); development of charnockitic rocks by the interaction between the metasome material and the basic host rocks, their composition ranging from plagiogranites to leucodiorites.

The entire area containing outcrops on the islands and nunataks in the Mirny area, totaling some 10 km^2, is apparently located on the periphery of a large charnockitoid massif. The central portions of this massif were identified on Adams Island, more than 20 km from Mirny, and probably continue even farther. The containing rocks are apparently limited to exomorphic aureoles of the massif composed of unusual block migmatites and agmatites which form a gradual transition (particularly the metasome) to the rocks of the massif. It must be emphasized that the extensive occurrence of the block migmatites and agmatites in aureoles is largely due to an intensive fracturing of the uplifted block of the crystalline basement within which the Mirny charnockitoid complex is located. This complex structural pattern of the peripheral portions of the Mirny charnockitoid complex (primarily the absence of clear intrusive contacts with the containing rocks) led Klimov to assume rather complex formation mechanics involving a series of rheomorphic processes: "the charnockites are rocks formed by a partial fusion and transition to an intrusive state of previously granitized strata of basic schists" /57; p. 268/. Klimov then emphasized the characteristic structure and compositional features of charnockitoids reflecting specific rheomorphic processes involved in the formation of the Mirny intrusion: a) the major colored minerals in the charnockites (highly ferruginous hypersthene and fayalite) are developed mainly along grain contacts in recrystallized granoblastic aggregates; they are thus not early magmatic but late metamorphic products; b) cataclasis and recrystallization of the early products of magmatic recrystallization (feldspars and quartz) are associated with the metasomatic development of K-feldspar porphyroblasts (the composition of the melt was close to that of plagiogranites); c) the essential metamorphism of the charnockites during their formation precludes the possibility of even a rough estimate of the quantitative ratios of solid components and melts in their initial formation stage; d) the extensive manifestation of cataclasis and recrystallization processes already present in relatively early stages of formation, indicates a limited quantity of melt and, predominantly, a solid state of the material. However, these features of the Mirny complex do not conclusively indicate that the rocks are a product of the interaction of the schists, mobilized during the intrusive movements, with the plagiogranitic melt. The close spatial relationships of the charnockitoids and the highly fractured gabbroids, and the extensive development of agmatites around the massif, indicate that the charnockitoids were products of interaction (in zones of intensive fracturing) between gabbroids and melts, the latter also producing the metasome of the agmatites.

Both genetic assumptions preclude a purely magmatic origin of the Mirny massif. At the same time, the close spatial and genetic relationships between the gabbroids and charnockitoids, and the extensive development of block migmatites and agmatites due to the formation of the charnockitoids fully validate the assumption that the charnockitoids originated from older intrusions of gabbroids in the period of tectonic activization of the crystalline basement accompanied by an extensive development of agmatites. In this case, it is not necessary to assume intrusive movements of abyssally mobilized blocks of basic schists interacting with regenerated plagiogranitic

magma, and the intrusion of this mass into a cavity, formed in an unknown
manner, in the solid crystalline basement. A more plausible assumption is
the formation of the charnockitoid massif at the site of a fractured gabbroid
intrusion during tectonic activization. The latter always involves complex
ultrametamorphic processes (including migmatization and granitization).
In this case, the crystalline basement strata had previously been metamorphosed under granulite facies conditions. The charnockitization of gabbroids
proceeded nonuniformly and under considerably lower pressure than the
formation of the supracrustal basement complex, as indicated by the ubiquitous appearance of fayalite and the amphibole-biotite mineral association
in the charnockitoids.

Charnockitoids in the vicinity of the Denman Glacier and
Shackleton Ice Shelf (nearly 150 km from west to east and over
100 km from north to south) were discovered during a reconnaissance by
Soviet geologists in the 1956/57 season. Dozens of coastal outcrops, nunataks and rocky islands proved to be composed of charnockitoids /57/. They
include unusual hypersthene plagiogranites of Mount Gist and Mount Astronomicheskaya, feldspathized gabbro-norite-diorites of Mount Strathcona, the
Charcot and Delay massifs, the diorite-syenites of Gillies Islands and
hypersthene granosyenites of David Island (Table 122). No information
was obtained on the mode of occurrence of the different types of charnockitoids and their relationships with the containing rocks. However, even a
minimum examination of these rocks in the Denman Glacier area indicates
the presence of nearly the entire range of charnockitoid varieties, from
feldspathized gabbroids to plagiogranites (enderbites) and granosyenites
(charnockites proper).

Mount Gist plagiogranites are represented by porphyroblastic coarse-
grained rocks, containing 15—20% porphyroblasts of basic andesine, An 40—42,
with the addition, in places, of nearly the same quantity of K-feldspar porphyroblasts. In general, such rocks are closer to enderbites than to
charnockites. They average 40% plagioclase, 35% quartz, up to 20% secondary biotite, 3% ferrohypersthene relicts, 2% garnet and about 1% magnetite,
apatite and zircon. Feldspathization enhances the importance of K-feldspar
and diminishes the part played by quartz. The Mount Strathcona granitoids
are represented by medium- and coarse-grained rocks, externally in- .
distinguishable from the charnockitoids of the Mirny area. They exhibit
a combination of magmatic and metamorphic textures, the former represented by prismatic forms of elongated laths of basic andesine, An 45, up
to 2 cm long, and the latter, by complex metablastic K-feldspar segregations
which replace the plagioclase. Their composition corresponds to feldspathized and quartz-bearing gabbro-norite-diorites, since they contain 50% or
more andesine, 10—15% each of K-feldspar and quartz. The colored minerals
(15—20%) are represented by ferrohypersthene (ferruginosity >60%), ferrosilite, and secondary biotite. The charnockitoids of Gillies Islands are
diorite-syenites with varieties transitional to granosyenites. They are
represented by massive, coarse-grained rocks, externally resembling the
Mirny charnockites. The relatively more basic varieties exhibit a relict
gabbro-ophitic texture, gradually transformed into a granoblastic texture

with metasomatic elements (cataclasis, recrystallization and feldspathization). They contain 2—20% quartz, 2—10% K-feldspar, and 27—57% basic andesine, An 46—38. Secondary biotite is the main colored mineral (17—18%), and hornblende occurs sporadically. An important role is played by ferrohypersthene (up to 10%) with a ferruginosity of 55—65%. With reference to the chemical composition, the magnesium, calcium, and particularly iron contents are similar to those in diorites, the potassium content corresponds to the granite series, and the silica content to the syenite series. Such complex combinations of elements are very characteristic of typical Antarctic charnockitoids (see descriptions of rocks in the Bunger Oasis, Humboldt Mountains and Petermann Range, etc.).

The gabbro-norite-diorites of Cape Charcot are represented by massive medium-grained rocks with relict gabbroic textures disturbed by recrystallization processes. Nearly 70% of the rock is made up of elongated prismatic laths of basic andesine, An 45—48, 2—7 mm long and 1—3 mm across. The colored minerals (20%) are largely represented by hypersthene and to a lesser extent by clinopyroxene. They are replaced to a limited extent by biotite and hornblende. Quartz and K-feldspar are sporadic. The gabbronorite-diorites of Delay Point differ from analogous rocks of Cape Charcot. They are coarser-grained and exhibit a significantly higher grade of amphibolization, and especially biotitization. The resulting rocks contain 50% basic andesine, An 48, in the form of prismatic laths, and nearly 20% ferrohypersthene and clinopyroxene. The pyroxenes are replaced by amphibole (3—5%) and biotite (10—15%); the colored minerals total almost 40%. In both locations, the modified gabbroids contain numerous leucogranite and aplite veins, 20—50 cm thick. These are net veins accounting for as much as 10 vol.% of bedrock exposures. The gabbroids are weakly granitized in both locations, but are highly enriched in fissure veins, which are crystallization products of partial melts.

David Island, with an area of several dozen square kilometers, is entirely composed of eulyte granosyenites. They are represented by massive coarse-grained porphyroblastic rocks, containing about 50 vol.% K-feldspar porphyroblasts, 1—3 cm long. Gneissic structures are only characteristic of highly cataclastized granosyenites occurring in comparatively narrow zones. The granosyenites are fairly uniform throughout the island and contain sporadic xenoliths (relicts?) of metamorphosed gabbroids with relict gabbro-ophitic textures. The xenoliths reach 2 × 3 m in size, but generally are up to tens of centimeters long. They locally contain nearly equal amounts of basic andesine, clinopyroxene, and orthopyroxene, the latter two intensively replaced by biotite and amphibole. Characteristically, the orthopyroxene is represented by ferrohypersthene with a ferruginosity not below 57%. The granosyenites themselves contain slightly over 50% K-feldspar, 25% oligoclase, An 25—28, only 10—15% quartz and 10% colored minerals. These include ferrosilite, eulyte (with ferruginosity 73—77%), secondary biotite (less commonly hornblende), as well as accessory ilmenite, orthite and apatite. The David Island granosyenites are very similar to the Mirny charnockites. It must be emphasized that the David Island granosyenites are in close proximity to the gabbro-norite-diorites of the Charcot and Delay massifs, and are probably closely genetically related, as in other regions of East Antarctica. Unfortunately, it was not possible to make direct observations of the relationships between these rocks.

Charnockitoids of the Bunger Oasis are represented by two massifs which were studied by the authors in 1956/57, during the course of geological mapping to a scale of 1:100,000 /57/. The southern massif is exposed on an area of some 15 km^2, and lies within highly migmatized bipyroxene schists. Direct contacts are traceable only in the SW margin of the massif. These contact zones are indistinct and include gradual transition zones. On the whole, however, the contacts are intrusive in nature, trending across the strike of the host rocks. The northern massif is exposed over an area of 30 km^2, most of it concealed under ice and fjord water. Only on its western margin is the massif in contact with the migmatized biotite-garnet plagiogneisses, where it is broken into blocks. The contact is very indistinct because of intense fracture zones. However, it generally appears to be discordant relative to the structures of the host migmatites. The Bunger Oasis massif is composed of two rock groups; gabbroids of various grades of charnockitization (mainly feldspathized), and rocks approaching quartz syenite-diorites to granosyenites in composition. The latter do not include normal or porphyroblastic 'giant-grained' granosyenites. Although there are gradual transitions between these two rock groups, they are respectively concentrated in the marginal and central portions of the massif. Rocks of the first group are especially widespread in the northern massif, composing a strip to the west, several kilometers wide and traceable over 15 km along strike. The charnockitized gabbroids within this strip are intensely fractured and permeated by a network of alaskitic and aplitic veins, 1—6 m thick, accounting for about 8—10 vol.% of the gabbroid exposures.

The charnockitized gabbroids are represented by massive medium-grained rocks with relict panidiomorphogranular (prismatic) textures that are transitional to a gabbro-ophitic texture. These are transformed into heteroblastic textures with metasomatic xenoblastic quartz-orthoclase aggregates due to cataclasis and incomplete recrystallization. The composition of charnockitized gabbroids is variable (Table 122); 35—70% labradorite, An 55—74, 1—10% K-feldspar, 2—10% quartz, 15—40% orthopyroxene (hypersthene of ferruginosity 27—43%), 1—18% clinopyroxene (ferruginosity usually 3—4%), 1—9% secondary biotite, 0—7% secondary amphibole, 1—6% ilmenite, 0.1—1.5% apatite. The chemical composition of the charnockitized gabbroids corresponds to feldspathized gabbro-norites and gabbro-norite-diorites, with high contents of titanium, iron and magnesium and in places also of alkalis, and low contents of calcium and aluminum, in comparison to average gabbros (Table 124).

The higher-grade charnockitization of the gabbroids results in qualitatively different rocks which are tentatively termed ferrohypersthene quartz-bearing syenite-diorites, transitional to granosyenites. Rocks of this type predominate in the Bunger Oasis charnockitic massifs. They are represented by massive medium- and coarse-grained, often porphyritic rocks and exhibit heteroblastic textures with relict prismatic plagioclase laths, up to 1 cm in length. The porphyritic habits of certain varieties is due to

plagioclase phenocrysts and not to K-feldspar as in charnockites of other
regions in East Antarctica. The metasomatic textural elements are due
to poikiloxenoblastic segregations of K-feldspar (up to 0.5 cm) and still
smaller xenoblastic quartz grains. Granoblastic areas developed by the
recrystallization of plagioclase and pyroxene, resulting in smaller grain
sizes and giving rise to glomero-aggregates of colored minerals containing
secondary biotite and amphibole together with the primary pyroxenes. The
resulting rocks combine relict magmatic and superimposed metamorphic
textures which are further complicated by cataclasis. The composition of
such diorite-syenites is extremely variable due to the superimposed
feldspathization and recrystallization (Table 122): 30—60% plagioclase,
An 35—53, 10—40% K-feldspar, 7—25% quartz, 5—20% clinopyroxene (ferruginosity, 44—60%), 1—5% biotite, 2—10% hornblende, 2—6% ore, and 0.5—
1.5% apatite. Their chemical composition corresponds to varieties intermediate between diorite and syenite, since the iron content is characteristic
of diorites (and even higher), but the contents of magnesium and calcium
are low and contents of alkalis are high (Table 124). The diorite-syenites
in places contain small xenoliths or layers of migmatized bipyroxene
schists, the latter traceable 2—20 m along strike. The contacts of such inclusions are diffuse, and their orientation random. It is impossible to differentiate between the alterations in the schists prior to their inclusion in the
gabbroids and those subsequent to the latter's charnockitization. At any rate,
their mineral composition is fairly close to that of the host rock.

The charnockitoid massifs of the Bunger Oasis differ considerably from
many other analogous massifs in East Antarctica (e.g., the intrusions of
Queen Maud Land and the Mirny area) in their more basic composition. They
thus lack the typical granosyenites and, of course, granites. Another
characteristic feature is the absence of fayalite, denoting more abyssal
conditions of formation. All available data indicate that the Bunger Oasis
massifs were initially intrusive gabbroid bodies, cross-cutting the host
rocks, with which at present they form very indistinct contacts. The absence
of clear contacts and traces of contact effects is explained by the simultaneous superimposition of granitization processes on both the gabbroid intrusions and the host schists. This superimposed granitization was related
to tectonic-magmatic activization at a time when the basement schists had
already been metamorphosed under granulite facies conditions. The
effect of basement activization on the schists and the gabbroid intrusions
may only be surmised. In the authors' opinion, the following were the
characteristic events: the basement rocks were fragmented into separate
rocks, cataclastized and metamorphosed; the appearance of partial melts
resulted in interactions with the fractured gabbroids, first causing
feldspathization and then the development of leucocratic veins. The
intensification of the interaction and the appearance of alkaline metasomatic solutions resulted in further reworking of the gabbroids, accompanied by
their recrystallization and transformation into charnockitoids. However,
this charnockitization process did not reach its culmination in the Bunger
Oasis area, since no typical charnockites of acid and of alkaline compositions have been found. The stage of solid-rock mobilization in the

crystalline basement during interaction with melts was not reached. Thus
rheomorphic bodies that would be produced during intrusive movements
were not encountered in the Bunger Oasis.

Charnockitoids of the Windmill Islands and Grearson
Oasis on the Budd Coast were investigated by P. S. Voronov late in 1956.
His collection of 130 specimens was processed by M. G. Ravich, who was
the first to identify charnockitoids in the area. Subsequently, in 1959/60,
the area was studied by Australian geologists, who supplemented the
description of charnockitoids /57/. The latter are very widespread in the
Grearson Oasis, especially in its southern part. They apparently form an
independent massif with an area of at least 20 km^2 in the area of the
Browning Peninsula and Peterson Island. Analogous rocks occur further
north, forming the Odbert and Ardery Islands. Contacts between the massive
charnockitoids and the host granulite facies schists were not observed.
Therefore, there is no information concerning the mode of occurrence of
the massifs. It is important to note, however, that the majority of investigated charnockitoid bodies occur in bipyroxene schists with low migmatization and granitization grades. The charnockitoids are represented by
fairly uniform, slightly cataclastized, medium- and coarse-grained massive
rocks. The texture may be described as porphyrogranoblastic, with a relict
prismatic texture due to euhedral plagioclase laths, up to ~5 mm. However,
the porphyroblasts consist of larger prismatic segregations of K-feldspar,
the content of which does not exceed 10—15%. The composition of the charnockitoids is variable, mainly because of the wide range in the contents of
quartz, 10—30%, and K-feldspar, 25—35%. The plagioclase content varies
correspondingly from 25 to 40%; it is always represented by andesine,
An 35—45. Irrespective of the colored-mineral content, which varies from
10 to 20%, a majority of the varieties contain orthopyroxene, 1—8%, represented by ferrohypersthene with a ferruginosity of 55—60% or higher. The
remainder consist of secondary hornblende and biotite; clinopyroxene
occurs sporadically (Table 122). On the basis of the variable mineral composition, the charnockitoids may be differentiated into varieties approaching
granites, granosyenites and quartz diorites. However, this characterization
is rather formal, in view of the similar chemical compositions of all
varieties, notwithstanding the significant fluctuations of the quartz contents
in thin sections. Indeed, chemical analyses of the three charnockitoid
varieties are indicative of quartz-bearing diorite-syenites; they contain
nearly identical amounts of silica, aluminum, iron, magnesium and calcium,
differing only in the alkali content, which increases in the subalkaline
varieties (Table 124).

Charnockitoids on the Henry Bay Islands are the only outcrops along Sabrina Coast for a stretch of several hundred kilometers. The
islands were visited by L. V. Klimov and D. S. Solov'ev early in 1958, the
former providing separate descriptions for the granitic charnockites of
Chick Island and the porphyroblastic granites of the Henry Islands /57/. These
two varieties are very similar in composition. They are not granitic,
although they usually contain some 20% quartz. This last feature is very
characteristic of the charnockitoids. Unfortunately, the cursory survey of

the islands did not yield any data concerning the mode of occurrence of the charnockitoids and their relationships with the host schists. However, some idea of the host rocks may be obtained from an examination of the composition of xenoliths.

The Chick Island charnockites are massive, coarse-grained rocks, in places assuming a porphyritic habit due to the presence of K-feldspar metablasts, measuring up to 5 cm. Their complex texture combines a granoblastic matrix with K-feldspar porphyroblasts and relicts of plagioclase laths. They contain nearly equal amounts of plagioclase, An 37—46, and K-feldspar, each averaging 30%. Quartz forms up to 20% and colored minerals at least 15%. The latter always include eulyte (2—3%) with a ferruginosity of about 80%; the bulk of these minerals consists of secondary hornblende and biotite, also with high ferruginosities. The chemical composition of these charnockites is equivalent to quartz-bearing syenite-diorites, considerably enriched in quartz (Table 124). Coarse-grained amphibole granitoids form unusual pockets in the charnockites, and contain up to 20% hornblende. In these rocks, amphibole forms large metablasts, with symplektitic ingrowths at the boundary between the metablasts and K-feldspar porphyroblasts. The charnockites often contain xenoliths of metadolerites and of granitized pyroxene gneisses. Their composition differs from that of the charnockites in a significantly higher content of colored minerals, which include eulyte. The xenoliths also contain K-feldspar and a fairly basic andesine, and in places, garnet. The porphyroblastic granites of the Henry Islands differ from the charnockites of Chick Island mainly in the absence of hypersthene. The former have a more pronounced porphyroblastic texture, K-feldspar metablasts measuring 2—3 cm everywhere accounting for 10—15 vol.% of the rocks. The plagioclase of these so-called "granites" (since they often contain 20—25% quartz) is represented by basic andesine, An 37—44, and they locally have a high content (up to 30%) of colored minerals (particularly hornblende). The ratio of plagioclase and K-feldspar is the same as in the Chick Island charnockites. Similar to the latter, the porphyroblastic granites of the Henry Islands contain xenoliths of strongly amphibolized pyroxene-plagioclase schists and amphibolized and biotitized pyroxene plagiogneisses. Characteristically, the plagioclase in the xenoliths is always represented by andesine, An 37—40, irrespective of the rock composition; the pyroxenes are limited to clinopyroxene. Orthopyroxene is absent from both the xenoliths and the host rock.

The chemical composition of the porphyroblastic granites of the Henry Islands is nearly the same as that of the Chick Island charnockites. The former are therefore quartz-bearing diorite-syenites, with an even higher quartz content than in the Chick Island charnockites (Table 124). This is probably related to the granitization of gabbroids, which is reflected not only in their composition, but also by the complex combination of magmatic and superimposed metamorphic features. From this standpoint, the porphyroblastic granitoids may be regarded as a product of a higher-grade granitization (under amphibolite facies conditions) than the granitization which produced the Chick Island charnockitoids. It should be noted that gradual transitions

between the two types occur locally. On the whole, the Henry Bay charnockitoids are similar to the Grearson Oasis charnockitoids, from which
they are separated by many hundreds of kilometers.

The above-described charnockitoid intrusions encountered in eleven
regions of East Antarctica (from 4 to 121° E. long.) probably constitute only
a part of the total number of massifs included in the Antarctic Platform
crystalline basement. Several other known intrusions have not yet been
described, while a great majority are concealed under the ice sheet. The
existence of certain intrusions is doubtful, and they were therefore excluded,
e. g., charnockitoid rocks of Adélie Land, especially those encountered in
the Astrolabe Glacier area on Géologie Archipelago (140° E.long.). According to the French investigator Bellair /84/, the numerous islands in the
archipelago feature two charnockitic varieties. They contain unaltered or
relict hypersthene, the latter being intensively replaced by hydrous minerals,
especially biotite and amphibole. The chemical composition of these rocks
approaches granodiorites on the one hand and granosyenites on the other.
Large relicts of basic rocks (norites), possibly occurring as veins, are
present. Unfortunately, no information has been reported on the modes of
occurrence of these charnockitoids, nor are accurate descriptions of their
textures and mineral compositions available. Therefore, it is impossible
to ascertain whether these rocks are indeed intrusives. From the fragmentary descriptions provided by several non-Soviet investigators working
in East Antarctica, it is difficult to decide if they represent actual charnockitoids.

In general, it appears that the Antarctic Platform crystalline basement is
very rich in charnockitoid intrusions. In several well-exposed areas, these
intrusions occupy at least 10% of the total area, and sometimes even more.

Many archipelagoes and coastal rocky oases are almost entirely composed of charnockitoids, which are much more resistant to weathering than
schists of various grades of granitization and migmatization.

THE COMPOSITION AND GENESIS OF
CHARNOCKITOID MASSIFS

A brief review of the available data on the charnockitoid massifs of East
Antarctica, including the massifs of the Humboldt Mountains and Petermann
Range, Bunger Oasis and Mirny area, permits certain conclusions concerning
the genesis of these rocks. The conclusions are not exhaustive, since far
from all charnockitoid massifs in the Antarctic Platform crystalline basement have been discovered or investigated, and even those already visited
by geologists, have largely been examined on a small scale.

To begin this discussion, the principal features of composition and mode
of occurrence of the charnockitoids and their host rocks are presented
below:

1. Charnockitoid massifs form discordant intrusions, ranging from a few
tens to several thousands of square kilometers, massifs of 50–150 km^2

predominating. They have a variety of forms but are more commonly domed. In many cases, the shape of charnockitoid massifs may have been inherited from the gabbroid intrusions from which they were formed. Hence, many charnockitoid massifs are apointrusive. Major independent gabbroid intrusions are absent from regions that have several charnockitoid massifs, although highly metamorphosed associated basic veins and dikes are present.

2. The charnockitoid massifs can be divided into at least two types with respect to their composition; the type references are the Lodochnikov Massif and the Bunger Oasis massifs. The Lodochnikov type is distinguished by a broad variety of rocks, ranging from feldspathized gabbroids to porphyroblastic granosyenites (and in rare cases, granites). The Bunger Oasis type has a narrower range of rocks, ranging from feldspathized gabbroids to diorite-syenites (rarely, syenites). The first type includes the Lodochnikov Massif, the surrounding smaller massifs (among them the bodies of the Humboldt Mountains and Petermann Range), as well as the massifs of Enderby Land and Mac-Robertson Land, the western fringe of the Amery Ice Shelf, the Mirny and David areas, etc. The second type includes the massifs of the Bunger Oasis, the bodies in the Reinbolt Hills on the eastern fringe of the Amery Ice Shelf, Mount Strathcona and the Gillies Islands on the southern fringe of the Denman Glacier, Grearson Oasis and Windmill Islands and finally the Henry Islands and Chick Island (Henry Bay). The second type appears to have undergone an incomplete uniform granitization reaching only to syenitization, whereas the first type underwent complete and diversified granitization terminating in the formation of K-feldspar porphyroblasts, usually accounting for one half of the volume of acid rocks, and rendering them subalkaline. The range of processes in massifs of the second type is probably limited to metasomatic reworking of the original basic rocks, by interaction with alkaline-siliceous solutions; in the Lodochnikov type, the same original rock, interacting with selective melts, formed a plastic mass capable of intrusive movements, i. e., their genesis is rheomorphic. The rather rare bodies of hypersthene plagiogranites differ markedly from these charnockitoid massifs and are preferably classified with enderbites. As yet, they have been encountered only in the Vestfold Oasis, and on Mount Gist and Mount Astronomicheskaya on the SW margin of the Denman Glacier. Their formation was possibly related to the initial, incomplete stage of granitization of basic intrusive rocks.

3. These different charnockitoids massifs are of different absolute ages, possibly indicating either their formation in separate tectonic-magmatic events in the activization of the crystalline basement, or a repeated rejuvenation of certain charnockitoids formed at an early stage, as indicated by certain geological data. Thus, the hypersthene plagiogranites of the Vestfold Oasis have been dated at 1475 million years; the second type of charnockitoids has been dated at 880—945 million years in the Grearson Oasis and Windmill Islands and 700—755 million years in the Bunger Oasis, Mount Strathcona, the Henry Bay Islands, etc. Finally, charnockitoids of the first type have been dated at 400—490 million years /57/. All these dates were obtained by the K-Ar method for whole rocks. As a rule, the results are 10—15% too low. Thus, the formation of the charnockitoid massifs may

probably be related to four epochs of tectonic-magmatic activization occurring approximately 1500—1600, 1000—1100, 800—900 and 500—600 million
years ago, unless one ascribes these epochs to nonuniform rejuvenation of
the charnockitoids, which, according to geological data, were classified by
the authors as Lower Proterozoic in age.

4. Although not all massifs contain all varieties, the charnockitoid
character remains nearly the same everywhere. It is difficult to detect
significant differences between feldspathized gabbroids, diorite-syenites or
granosyenites from different massifs with respect either to structure or
mineral composition. The same applies to the very slight contact effects
and rare veins which are nearly identical in all charnockitoid massifs irrespective of the rock varieties. This indicates an integral nature of
charnockitoid formation processes, although they may have had different
intensities in different regions, resulting in dissimilar rock varieties. One
of the most characteristic features of the charnockitoid formation in the
crystalline basement is the close spatial relationship between gabbroids and
charnockites, manifested by gradual transitions of feldspathized gabbroids to
rocks with the composition of feldspathized gabbro-norite-diorites, diorite-
syenites (sometimes syenites), to porphyroblastic granosyenites and much
less frequently to granites. The result is a group of rocks linked by gradual
transitions, which is a typical granitization series with subalkaline rather
than acid trends. These transitions are often observed within a single large
outcrop. They are often revealed only in the course of petrographic and
chemical processing of the specimens and are indistinguishable in the field.
However, in some cases, the pronounced difference between extreme compositions in the granitization series, produces an impression of their
mechanical contact, which is enhanced by the color differences. However,
it is impossible to represent this granitization series as a differentiated
rock series produced by crystallization from a magma, because of the
absence of clear contacts between the different varieties, the absence of any
trace of contact effects and the absence of any complex intrusions of concentric or sheet layered character. It is furthermore difficult to determine
the composition of such a magma, since it would not correspond either to
basic melts (mantle) or to eutectic melts (produced within the crust). The
differentiation of a basaltic magma produces the normal series of rocks
from gabbros through diorites and granodiorites to granites, whereas the
charnockitoids are an anomalous rock series with subalkaline and even
alkaline trends, which is characteristic of a granitization series originating
from basic rocks.

5. The minerals of charnockitoids form unusual series, with compositions that vary regularly with an increasing granitization grade of the rock.
Orthopyroxene, which is the major typomorphic femic mineral, varies in composition from hypersthene, with a ferruginosity of 40—50% in feldspathized gabbroids, to ferrosilite, with a ferruginosity of 80—90% in granosyenites. Its content varies correspondingly from 20—30% in the former to 2—3% in the latter,
where it gradually disappears and is superseded by the biotite-amphibole
association. The habit of orthopyroxenes varies appreciably with their increasing ferruginosity and diminishing contents. Thus, metagabbroids

contain relatively large, 2—4-mm, prismatic grains, whereas the diorite-syenites, and especially granosyenites, contain small, 0.1—0.4-mm, corroded, often skeletal, granules of eulyte and ferrosilite. On the whole, these variations are gradual, but there are also irregular changes in the composition of orthopyroxenes, depending on the nonuniform degree of the metasomatic reworking of the rocks.

Plagioclase also developed in a similar manner, its basicity and contents decreasing appreciably from feldspathized gabbroids to granosyenites. Metagabbroids contain 50—70% labradorite, An 50—60, diorite-syenites contain 20—40% andesine, An 30—40, and granosyenites contain 10—20% oligoclase-andesine, An 25—30. Characteristically, plagioclase more acid than oligoclase, An 20, does not occur anywhere in the charnockitoid series. There is a corresponding variation in the habits of plagioclase; metagabbroids retain prismatic laths of 1—2 cm, with broken and bent twins; such laths become scarce in diorite-syenites, where the bulk of plagioclase consists of recrystallized euhedral grains not larger than 1—2 mm; in granosyenites, further recrystallization of plagioclase under conditions of intensive metasomatism results in larger grains measuring 2—5 mm, with a habit approaching that of prismatic laths.

Clinopyroxenes form a series similar to orthopyroxenes, their ferruginosities varying from 40% in metagabbroids to 95% in granosyenites, while their contents are considerably smaller than those of orthopyroxenes. One of the most characteristic features of clinopyroxenes in charnockitoids is the prevalence of Fe + Mg over Ca, indicating their similarity to augites and ferroaugites. These are more characteristic for basic magmatic rocks than for schists which characteristically contain salites and hedenbergites.

Fayalite, with a ferruginosity of 87—95%, usually absent from shadow charnockites, is very characteristic of the massive charnockoids in Antarctica. Significantly, fayalite mainly occurs in granosyenites, where high-ferruginosity orthopyroxene disappears. However, they retain clinopyroxenes of maximum ferruginosities. When fayalite is present in other varieties of charnockitoids (e. g., diorite-syenites), all other colored minerals also have very high ferruginosities. These features indicate a highly alkaline environment in which highly ferruginous colored minerals in the most acid and alkaline charnockitoids are stable. The presence of fayalite also attests to relatively shallow depths of formation, since garnet would have formed (instead of the fayalite) at greater depths, especially in rocks that had been sufficiently saturated in alumina. K-feldspars are the most characteristic salic mineral of the charnockitoids. Their contents vary from 2—3% in metagabbroids to 50—60% in granosyenites. In the latter, they are mainly represented by 2—3-cm porphyroblasts containing 5—30% microperthitic ingrowths. The K-feldspars are generally low triclinic orthoclase, irrespective of the charnockitoid variety. High and intermediate microcline is found only in endomorphic aureoles of charnockite intrusions, as a result of the recrystallization of orthoclase in the solid state. The formation temperature of orthoclase, determined by Barth's method, is 600—610°C; thus crystallization may have occurred from a selective melt or may have resulted from metasomatic recrystallization due to the reaction of alkaline solutions with the basic original rock. Biotite and hornblende are the most widespread colored minerals in the charnockitoids. Although these are secondary, they reflect, to a certain extent, the granitization grade of the rocks. Thus, their ferruginosities generally vary from 50—60% in metagabbroids to 95—100% in syenites and granosyenites, and are always higher than those in the coexisting pyroxenes which they replace. The predominant amphibole in the charnockitoids is therefore close to ferrohastingsite, and the predominant biotite is close to lepidomelane. However, there is no strong correlation between the composition of these secondary minerals and the granitization grade. The amphibole and biotite react more sensitively to metasomatic recrystallization of a rock and high ferruginosities (up to 80—90%) were noted even in metagabbroids as well as in gabbro-norite-diorites. This feature is related to local metasomatic activity resulting in a secondary-mineral composition of a somewhat higher granitization grade than that of the entire rock.

6. The chemical compositions of charnockitoids exhibit the following characteristic features which are indicators with regard to genesis: a) the sodium and aluminum contents in different varieties are nearly constant, in spite of the significant difference in mineral compositions. They were thus inert during the formation of the charnockitoid series, which would have been impossible had these rocks been formed by magmatic differentiation; b) the high content of iron in all the charnockitoid varieties, from basic to acid, in comparison to average magmatic rocks, suggests its high content in the original gabbroids and its concentration in the colored minerals of the resulting granitoids; c) titanium contents are very high in all charnockitoid varieties, particularly in the granosyenites and even more acid varieties where the Ti content is nearly equivalent to that in basic magmatic rocks; d) the potassium content is also high; in the subalkaline and alkaline charnockitoid varieties, it is up to 7—8 times higher than in the basic varieties. This could not result from magmatic differentiation, requiring the participation of intensive alkaline metasomatism; e) according to their chemical composition, the charnockitoids form a continuous rock series which is far closer to a granitization series than to a normal magmatic differentiation series.

7. No significant contact effects have been observed between the charnockitoid massifs and the host schists. The latter exhibit various grades of migmatization and granitization, and contain boudins of calciphyres and intercalations of quartzites. Characteristically, neither the endomorphic zones of massifs nor the host rocks contain large K-feldspar porphyroblasts, although these are very widespread in charnockitoids of a granosyenitic composition. The composition of xenoliths in the charnockitoid massifs has likewise undergone only slight alteration in relation to the massif rocks.

On the whole, processes which produced the charnockitoids did not affect the host rocks. Other processes which were probably responsible for the superimposed metamorphism and ultrametamorphism of the host rocks (mainly repeated migmatization and granitization) occurred almost simultaneously or somewhat earlier. Vein charnockitoids are practically nonexistent. The veins of diverse compositions which are spatially related to the charnockitoid massifs do not contain eulyte, hedenbergite or fayalite. The veins are composed of two groups of rocks — basic and acid. The former are diabases with a high grade of metamorphism, which are the vein analogs of metagabbroids. The latter include a variety of granitoids that are crystallization products of partial melts contaminated by components from nearby rocks. The rocks containing the charnockitoid massifs are always schists showing various grades of migmatization and granitization. In many locations, it is possible to establish that the migmatization and granitization were superimposed, indicating repeated deep metamorphism (e. g., Mirny area, Humboldt Mountains, etc.). The most conspicuous superimposed ultrametamorphism occurred during the Early Proterozoic — based on geological data, or in the Early Cambrian — based on absolute dates. It is mainly manifested in huge agmatite fields (from more ancient layers of migmatites) and relatively small bodies of granites — a crystallization product of partial melts. It also yielded zoned pegmatites and the widespread aplitic granite veins. Characteristically, the superimposed ultrametamorphism occurred in the high-grade amphibolite facies and the rocks contain coexisting nonequilibrium mineral associations of the older granulite and superimposed amphibolite facies.

These data on the mode of occurrence and composition of Antarctic charnockitoids, make possible an estimation of their genesis, and in the first place, the rejection of the hypothesis of magmatic origin by differentiation at depth and in situ. The appearance of the charnockitoid massifs may be related to the Early Proterozoic stage of the tectono-magmatic activization of the crystalline basement. Considering the presence of Riphean low-grade metamorphics in the upper platform, it may be assumed that the main period of superimposed metamorphism and the formation of the charnockite massifs occurred at least in the pre-Riphean. Radioactive dates of crystalline basement rocks (500—600 million years) indicate Late Baikal folding (Ross, in Antarctica), which inverted the Antarctic geosynclines, superseded by mountain building which led to several 'geoblocks,' preserved in the structure of Antarctica to the present day. During the activization period, the rigid crystalline basement of the Antarctic Platform, probably formed already in the Late Archean (similar to the crystalline basements of the other Gondwanian platforms), underwent a substantial tectonic rearrangement under granulite facies conditions, and furthermore various metamorphic and migmatization processes actively affected the previously formed crystalline rocks. The tectonic preparation, manifested firstly in the appearance of an entire series of large and small faults and accompanying zones of the cataclasis and fracturing of rigid rocks, created optimum conditions for extensive solid-state recrystallization processes. It also resulted in plastic masses, low-temperature fusion, mobilization and movement along weakened zones, and finally, concentration of the most mobile metasomatic solutions in these zones. The latter filtered into overlying horizons and interacted with cataclastized masses of the crystalline basement. All these transformations of crystalline basement rocks during tectonic activization reflect different stages of the temporary integral ultrametamorphic process occurring separately or together at different depths. As a result, the following formations were produced in the crystalline basement: 1) huge fields of agmatites with a granitic metasome and a paleosome of older layered migmatites; 2) diffuse sheets of metasomatic shadow granitoids developed from older schists and their migmatites; 3) small scattered bodies of magmatic intrusive granites; 4) charnockitoid massifs of various dimensions and genesis; 5) granitoid and pegmatite veins.

The charnockitoid massifs should be divided into two groups according to their composition and probably also genesis. The first group is mainly composed of diorite-syenite varieties and the second of granosyenite varieties, although varying quantities of all the other varieties occur in the massifs of either group. Massifs of the first group are distinguished by their comparatively small dimensions (tens, rarely a few hundreds of square kilometers) and older radioactive dates, ranging from 500 to 1500 million years, comprising two or three rejuvenation stages of the charnockitoids. Massifs of the second group are characterized by their large dimensions (hundreds and thousands of square kilometers) and constant values of radioactive dates, 450—500 million years, which correspond to the last stage of the tectonic rearrangement of the crystalline basement. This is manifested mainly in the formation and shifting of rigid blocks of metamorphic rocks. Massifs of the first group have a more motley composition and are closer to the original gabbroid rocks, whereas massifs of the second group are composed of 70—80% fairly uniform porphyroblastic granosyenites, differing significantly in composition from the starting rocks. Massifs of the second group are predominant in the Antarctic Platform crystalline basement. Therefore, it may be assumed that massifs of the first group were formed on the sites of original gabbroid intrusions by metasomatic recrystallization in the course of interaction (after previous tectonic preparation) with partial melts and alkaline solutions. The metasomatic recrystallization of gabbroids in the solid state did not completely obliterate the textures and minerals of the parent rock, although the latter's composition was significantly altered, and the newly formed rocks were enriched in K-feldspar and quartz. There was also a considerable increase in the ferruginosity of pyroxenes which were partially replaced by amphibole and biotite. Such charnockitoid massifs are actually apogabbroid rocks inheriting the mode of occurrence of the gabbroids. Massifs of the second group probably had a very complex genesis, having been formed by an interaction of various ultrametamorphic processes, instead of only metasomatic recrystallization (which is the initial stage of ultrametamorphism). Their genesis combines recrystallization of gabbroid intrusions in the solid state and mixing with selective melts, conversion of abyssal portions of the intrusion and their surrounding shadow charnockites to a plastic state and recrystallization of metasomatic K-feldspar porphyroblasts, resulting in the formation of charnockitoids of acid and subalkaline compositions. The melts produced during this complex process combine with the major portion of the original rocks (partially in a plastic state) to yield limited intrusions. The interaction of melts with solid components results in alterations in the composition of the melts during crystallization or re-crystallization. These interactions produce rocks of an anomalous series, i. e., the charnockitoids. Thus basic and acid rocks with deviations toward subalkaline and even alkaline varieties are found. Aside from the salic minerals of granites (K-feldspar and quartz), there are mafic minerals of gabbroids (pyroxenes and olivine), while plagioclase is represented by andesine even in acid varieties. Another anomalous feature is the very high ferruginosity of the mafic minerals, both relict pyroxenes and secondary biotite and amphibole, due to the extraordinarily high alkalinity of the environment in which they were formed. The acid and subalkaline varieties of charnockites consist essentially of highly ferruginous minerals such as fayalite, ferrosilite, hedenbergite, ferrohastingsite and lepidomelane. The third anomalous feature is the existence in these rocks of relict magmatic, metagranoblastic and metasomatic textures as well as the remarkable coexistence in the same massifs of basic (metagabbroids), intermediate (diorite-syenites), alkaline (syenites), subalkaline (granosyenites) and, less frequently, acid (granites) rocks forming the charnockitoid series. This series differs from all other ultrametamorphic granitization series. Finally, the fourth characteristic feature of the charnockitoids is their formation in the upper amphibolite facies. This creates certain difficulties in interpreting the mineral parageneses of these rocks and sometimes leads to incorrect assumptions about their genesis.

Thus, the charnockitoids display nearly all features of metamorphic processes which took place in the Antarctic Precambrian shields and the crystalline basement of the platform, especially during their tectonic activization. Charnockitoid massifs of different geneses may be formed in different stages of the ultrametamorphic processes: 1) apogabbroid, related to metasomatic recrystallization of gabbroids; 2) rheomorphic, related to partial fusion and mobilization of plastic masses capable of intrusive movements. A third possibility is the formation of massive porphyroblastic charnockites from shadow granitoids with a charnockitic trend, when the latter are exposed to the influence of alkaline metasomatic solutions, resulting in abundant K-feldspar porphyroblasts transforming the gneissic and relatively fine-grained shadow charnockites into massive and 'giant-grained' rocks. This genesis of porphyroblastic charnockitoids is probable for the Enderby Land and certain other massifs.

Massive charnockitoids occur in nearly all the crystalline basements of Gondwanian platforms. Apogabbroid intrusions are not confined to Antarctica but also occur in Western Australia. Rheomorphic intrusions of charnockitoids, apparently the most widespread ones in Antarctica, occur extensively in South Africa /99, 113/, Australia /142/ and Brazil /99/. To date, purely magmatic intrusions of charnockites have been identified only in Precambrian shields in the northern hemisphere, e. g., Karelia /53/. Nevertheless their existence may also be assumed in the crystalline basements of Gondwanian platforms, where they are difficult to distinguish from rheomorphic intrusions.

In rounding off the description of charnockitoids we would like to emphasize the controversial nature of the assumptions concerning the formation time based solely on absolute radioactive dates. These fall into four groups, suggesting four epochs of tectonic-magmatic activization. The last, occurring 450—550 million years ago, may be regarded as the most intensive, since over 90% of absolute dates for whole rocks in the crystalline basement fall in this interval /57/. However, certain geological data contradict a formation time related to the Late Baikal tectogenesis 500—550 million years ago. These data include the presence of gently dipping terrigenous-volcanogenic Riphean deposits of low-grade metamorphism in contact with the crystalline basement in western Queen Maud Land. These underwent intensive superimposed metamorphism and ultrametamorphism in the amphibolite facies, rather suggesting a pre-Riphean date for these processes. Furthermore, the presence, in the Prince Charles Mountains, of a jaspilite suite (greenschist facies) indicates an age which should not be less than Middle Proterozoic. The jaspilites occur among crystalline basement strata which underwent intensive superimposed metamorphism in the amphibolite facies, likewise indicating a pre-Middle Proterozoic Age for the metamorphic processes involved in the formation of the polymetamorphic complexes and intrusive charnockites. The great majority of absolute dates can be explained by assuming block movements of the basement resulting in a loss of argon. Furthermore, radiogenic argon is partially lost at depths of 3—5 km and at temperatures of 250—300° /47/. If one takes into account the metamorphism under amphibolite facies conditions, i. e., at temperatures of 550—600°C and at depths exceeding 5 km, one is led to conclude that the ages established are not the true ages, since they are too low.

Chapter VI

GREENSCHIST FACIES

The greenschist facies of metamorphism includes rocks in which ordinary hornblende has been completely replaced by actinolite, while oligoclase and andesine have been replaced by albite. The presence in these rocks of spessartite does not affect the facies. However, the appearance of almandine, kyanite and, rarely, andalusite may indicate the presence of relict amphibolite facies minerals. On the whole, this group of rocks is distinguished by a nearly ubiquitous development of mineral associations of the greenschist facies. The greenschist facies rocks compose two formation types, differing in origin, formation time and position in the crystalline basement: 1) relatively young, probably Middle Proterozoic strata, up to 3 km thick, forming in narrow downwarps in the crystalline basement; and 2) tectonic zones of diaphthorites, with thicknesses ranging from tens of meters to 2 km, mostly formed in the Late Precambrian — Early Paleozoic. These diaphthorites are related to the superimposition of Baikal folding on mobile regions of the rigid crystalline basement. However, the formation of thin tectonic zones of diaphthorites possibly also occurred in later times (mylonites). The appearance of such zones was due to block tectonics which possibly continued until the glaciation of the continent in the Paleogene.

FORMATION OF SCHISTS, QUARTZITES
AND JASPILITES*

The only region in East Antarctica which is known with certainty to contain rocks metamorphosed under greenschist facies conditions is the southern part of the Prince Charles Mountains. This comprises a folded formation of relatively weakly metamorphosed sedimentary rocks with a total thickness of at least 3 km. They form two comparatively narrow (10—20 km) sublatitudinal mountain chains surrounding the Fisher Outlet Glacier The same formation evidently also occurs at the base of the ice filled depression. It should be pointed out that the southern part of the Prince Charles Mountains is more than 500 km from the coast and has been relatively little studied. Only about one quarter of the exposed areas has been subjected to a brief geological investigation by Australian and Soviet expeditions /131/. Therefore, several tectonic, stratigraphic and metamorphic aspects have remained obscure. The strata lie in a narrow downwarp (graben-synclinorium) within Lower Proterozoic (?) metamorphic

* The author of this section is D.S.Solov'ev.

rocks of the amphibolite facies (quartz-staurolite subfacies) of the crystalline basement. The age of sediments filling the downwarp was determined
by the author as Middle Proterozoic, while their folding and regional
metamorphism apparently occurred during a cycle of the Gothian tectogenesis /31/.

The Middle Proterozoic deposits were tentatively differentiated into
two series on the basis of lithological characteristics, differences in the grade of
metamorphism and nature of the folding. The Sodruzhestvo Series consists
of various phyllites, marble-limestone, jaspilite and other rocks, all metamorphosed under conditions of the sericite-chlorite subfacies and occurring
in the Sodruzhestvo Mountains (Mounts Rubin, Ruker, etc.). Other rocks of
less differentiated composition but higher grade of metamorphism (biotite-
chlorite subfacies), consisting mainly of quartz schists and quartzites, form
the northern mountain fringe of the Fisher Glacier (Mounts Rymill, Seddon,
Menzies, etc.). These have been designated as the Menzies Series. Each
series is a few kilometers thick. The Sodruzhestvo Series is apparently
younger than the Menzies Series, and a considerable portion of its section
belongs to the upper Middle Proterozoic (Figure 62). The Sodruzhestvo
Series is distinguished by undisturbed monoclinal folding with beds dipping
south and southwest at angles of 45–75°; the Menzies Series has been
largely crumpled into deep isoclinal folds with ~E—W-trending axial planes.
The thickness of the beds varies from a few meters to 20 m. Fracture
zones cemented by quartz-carbonate veins are a typical feature. Primary
intrusive rocks consist only of sporadic layered orthoamphibolites (Mount
Seddon). According to Australian geologists, the Menzies Series quartzites
are intruded by thick sheets of cataclastized and gneissified two-mica
granites. Similar granites were examined by the author on Mount Patrick,
where they intrude greenschist facies diaphthorites formed from amphibolite facies gneisses. The petrography, petrochemistry and genesis of the
greenschist facies rocks (regional metamorphism) are described according
to data obtained during the author's investigations. They are given a very brief
treatment in the papers published by Australian geologists. The rocks are
described separately for each of the series.

Rocks of the Sodruzhestvo Series were studied in two partial sections,
on the eastern slope of Mt. Rubin and in the central part of Mt. Ruker
(Figure 63). The dominant rocks are quartz-calcite-sericite-chlorite
schists, quartz-carbonate schists, marble-limestone, jaspilites, and chlorite-
sericite quartzites.

Quartz-calcite-sericite-chlorite schists have a granolepidoblastic texture and are finely schistose. The grain size varies from about 0.001 to
0.01 mm. The rocks are composed of subparallel sericite and chlorite (60–80%),
with small irregular grains of quartz (5–15%), plagioclase (5–10%),
magnetite (3–5%) and calcite (1–15%). Some intercalations contain up to
2–3% prismatic epidote packed with inclusions of broken magnetite. X-ray
diffraction analyses of quartz-calcite-sericite-chlorite schists from
Mt. Rubin (specimen 12zh) indicated the presence of hydromica (dioctahedral
muscovite 2M), chlorite and quartz. According to the refractive indices
($n_z \cong n_y = 1.611$–1.616), the pale green chlorite is a ripidolite. The refractive indices are: sericite, $n_z = 1.597$ (muscovite 2M); and epidote,
$n_z = 1.738$, $n_x = 1.716$. The heavy-mineral fraction was found to contain

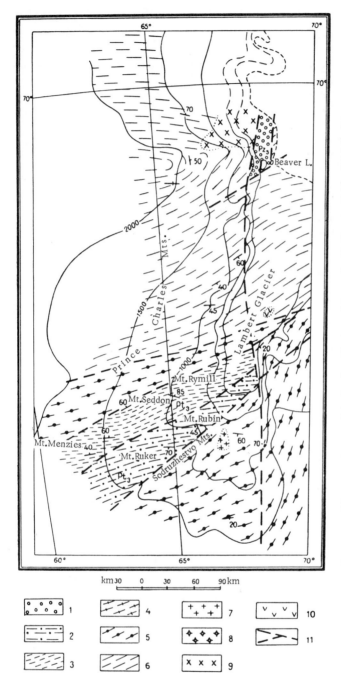

FIGURE 62. Schematic geologic map of the mountains around the Lambert Glacier and Amery Ice Shelf; compiled by D.S.Solov'ev.

1) Amery Series: Upper Paleozoic sandstones, siltstones, clay, carbonaceous shales, and gritstones; 2) Sodruzhestvo Series: Middle Proterozoic quartz-calcite-sericite-chlorite schists, quartz-carbonate schists, marble-limestone, jaspilites, and chlorite-sericite quartzites — upper structural tier of the platform basement; 3) Menzies Series: Middle Proterozoic chlorite-biotite-sericite quartzites, quartz schists, chlorite-biotite-garnet quartzites, quartz-chlorite-epidote-sericite schists, and orthoamphibolites — upper structural tier of the platform basement; 4) Archean biotite granite-gneisses — undetermined structural setting; 5) Archean biotite-garnet and biotite-hornblende plagiogneisses, staurolite-garnet quartzites, amphibolites, and biotite-cummingtonite schists — southern structural facies zone of the lower tier of the platform basement; 6) Archean migmatized and granitized biotite-garnet, garnet-cordierite-sillimanite plagiogneisses and quartzite-gneisses, biotite and biotite-hornblende gneisses, amphibolites, bipyroxene schists and shadow granitoids — northern structural facies zone of the lower tier of the platform basement; 7) biotite granites; 8) biotite granosyenites; 9) ferrohypersthene granites, granosyenites and quartz syenite-diorites (intrusive charnockites); 10) metamorphosed gabbroids; 11) large fault dislocations.

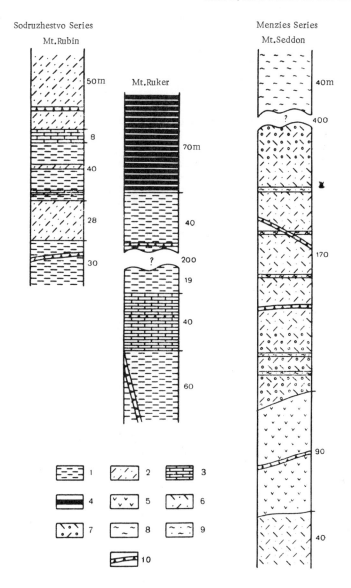

FIGURE 63. Partial profiles of the Sodruzhestvo and Menzies Series:

1) quartz-calcite-sericite-chlorite schists; 2) chlorite-sericite quartzites; 3) marble-limestone and quartz-carbonate schists; 4) jaspilites; 5) orthoamphibolites; 6) chlorite-sericite-biotite quartzites and quartz schists; 7) chlorite-biotite-sericite-garnet quartzites and quartz schists; 8) quartz-sericite-chlorite schists; 9) quartz-chlorite-epidote-sericite schists; 10) breccia zones cemented by quartz.

clinopyroxene ($n_z = 1.723$, $n_x = 1.698$), hornblende ($n_z = 1.673$, $n_x = 1.658$), pink garnet ($n = 1.780$), anatase, chromite, sphene, staurolite, tourmaline, zircon, apatite, rutile, sphalerite, chalcopyrite, and pyrrhotite. The total content of these minerals does not exceed 1—2 vol. % of the rock. With the exception of copper, nickel and iron sulfides and sphene, all are clastic in origin (with indications of transport). Chemical analyses of the quartz-calcite-sericite-chlorite schists were carried out on two samples from Mt. Rubin and Mt. Ruker (Table 126) representing a most widespread variety of schists, composing over two-thirds of the examined sections. The alumina content is moderate for such rocks; the iron content is very high and, in the Mt. Ruker schists, the calcium oxide content is nearly insignificant. The last two features are explained by high magnetite content in the Mt. Ruker schists and the high calcite content in the Mt. Rubin schists. The schists are similar with respect to the contents of the other components. Spectroscopic analyses established the presence of barium, copper, chromium, cobalt, lead, zinc, vanadium , strontium and zirconium in amounts up to ~0.01%.

TABLE 126. Chemical composition of greenschist facies rocks, wt%

Component	Sodruzhestvo Series			Menzies Series	
	specimen 12	specimen 17b	specimen 16	specimen 18	specimen 19b
SiO_2	62.79	40.62	56.67	67.38	77.97
TiO_2	0.60	0.10	0.70	1.00	0.66
Al_2O_3	11.06	2.18	13.58	13.41	9.83
Fe_2O_3	4.50	25.74	3.47	5.02	0.87
Cr_2O_3	0.02	0.06	0.04	0.04	0.07
FeO	1.51	21.96	12.17	2.76	4.26
CaO	4.08	1.69	0.53	0.39	0.50
MgO	3.58	1.77	3.80	2.64	0.91
MnO	0.10	0.20	0.11	0.08	0.08
K_2O	2.48	0.63	2.71	2.28	2.08
Na_2O	1.80	traces	0.97	2.00	1.17
P_2O_5	0.21	0.45	0.21	0.21	0.11
Cl	0.03	0.03	0.07	0.04	0.03
F	0.04	0.01	0.08	traces	0.09
Loss on ignition	7.25	4.92	4.77	2.72	1.18
Total	100.03	100.36	99.88	99.97	99.81
CO_2	5.79	5.25	0.60	0.22	0.18
H_2O (105—110°)	0.42	0.30	0.65	0.51	0.25
H_2O (total)	1.76	0.66	4.30	2.71	1.08

Note. Specimen 12: Mt.Rubin, quartz-calcite-sericite-chlorite schist; specimen 17b: Mt.Ruker, jaspilite; specimen 16: Mt.Ruker, quartz-calcite-sericite chlorite schists; specimen 18: Mt.Seddon, chlorite-biotite-garnet-quartz schist; specimen 19d: Mt.Seddon, quartz-chlorite-sericite schist.

Quartz-carbonate schists (Figure 64) and marble-limestone form several varieties with different quantitative ratios of carbonate (calcite, dolomite, siderite) and silicate (quartz, plagioclase, sericite, chlorite) minerals. Calcite and dolomite make up 85—95 vol. % of the rock in marble-limestone, and 60—70 vol. % in quartz-carbonate schists. The rocks are granoblastic-equigranular and massive or foliated. The carbonate grains vary in size from 0.1 to 0.3 mm and the silicate minerals are < 0.1 mm. The latter

FIGURE 64. Quartz-carbonate schists of granoblastic texture (thin section 12i, × 57, crossed nicols)

form irregular aggregates or are concentrated in fine intercalations or lenticular segregations. They are dominated by quartz. A carbonate of the magnesite-siderite series (n_o = 1.728) is also present. The quartz-carbonate schists are strongly chloritized and are grass-green in color near quartz veins.

The jaspilites are finely banded rocks (Figure 65) composed of alternating quartz-magnetite, magnetite-quartz and lesser magnetite-carbonate bands, 0.1—2.0 cm thick. All bands are rich in magnetite, and some are nearly monomineralic. The quartz-magnetite bands consist of an aggregate of minute (0.03—0.1 mm) magnetite and hematite grains, (35—80%) as well as quartz with admixtures of chlorite and sericite. Essentially quartz bands contain up to 15% magnetite. The magnetite-carbonate bands are composed of calcite (70%), magnetite (20—30%), sericite plus chlorite (up to 10%). The magnetite is subhedral, less commonly anhedral, and is replaced by secondary iron hydroxides. Hematite occurs in thin laminae. Most of the magnetite in the carbonate bands is included in grains of calcite and magnesite-siderite (?). Part of the carbonates in jaspilites is apparently of metasomatic origin and is related to numerous quartz-calcite veinlets. The heavy fraction of jaspilites was found to contain siderite, pyrite, epidote, magnetite, ilmenite, tourmaline, apatite, zircon and rutile; the five are clastic in origin. The combined content of ferrous and ferric iron in the jaspilites is 47.7% (Table 126). The analytical excess of CO_2 relative to CaO confirms the ferromagnesian nature of the carbonate in these rocks. Spectroscopic investigation of the jaspilites revealed the presence of trace amounts of barium, strontium, copper, chromium, nickel, cobalt, molybdenum, gallium and zirconium.

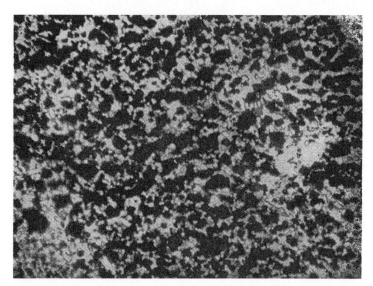

FIGURE 65. Jaspilite (thin section 17b, × 57, crossed nicols)

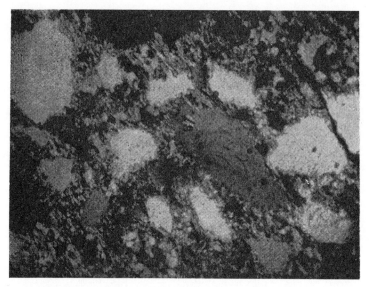

FIGURE 66. Chlorite-sericite quartzites of blastoaleuritic texture (thin section 17g, × 57, crossed nicols)

The chlorite-sericite quartzites (Figure 66) occur mainly in the Mt. Rubin section. They are granoblastic to lepidogranoblastic in texture and massive to schistose. Recrystallized clastic material is represented by quartz (80—85%), measuring 0.03—0.1 mm. Chlorite plus sericite ($\sim$15%) indicate the pelitic nature of the original cement. Magnetite is a minor component (1—2%). These quartzites differ from the quartz-calcite-sericite-chlorite schists in their high content of quartz and the absence of carbonate. The heavy fraction of the quartzites (specimens 121 and 12v) contain pink almandine garnet ($n = 1.780$), brown andradite garnet ($n = 1.800$), green ($n_z = 1.720$, $n_x = 1.696$) and light brown ($n_z = 1.726$, $n_x = 1.702$) clino-pyroxene, hypersthene ($n_z = 1.731$, $n_x = 1.716$), hornblende ($n_z = 1.660$, $n_x = 1.642$), ilmenite, pyrrhotite, magnetite, pyrite, chalcopyrite, sphene, epidote, tour-maline, zircon, rutile, anatase and apatite. The range of clastic heavy minerals in the quartzites is thus considerably broader than that in the schists.

The most widespread rocks in the Menzies Series are micaceous and feldspathic quartzites and quartz schists containing variable amounts of chlorite, muscovite, biotite, magnetite, and less frequently, spessartite garnet (bedding varies from 0.5 to 100 m) /131/. In the Menzies Series section and on Mt. Seddon, it is possible to distinguish three types of meta-sedimentary rocks similar in their general lithological-petrographic properties: 1) chlorite-mica quartzites and quartz schists; 2) chlorite-biotite-garnet quartzites and quartz schists; 3) quartz-chlorite-epidote-sericite schists. Orthoamphibolites have been described as meta-morphosed intrusive rocks.

Chlorite-mica quartzites and quartz schists occur together and exhibit gradual transitions. They vary in their different quantitative ratios of quartz, chlorite, sericite, plagioclase, and biotite, reflecting the changes in composition of the original plagioclase, from silty quartzose sandstones to argil-laceous quartzose siltstones. The rocks are very similar in their external ap-pearance. They are massive to schistose with granoblastic and lepidogranoblast-ic textures. In general, grain sizes do not exceed 0.1 mm. Quartz forms 85% of the quartzites and 60% of the quartz schists. Clastic plagioclase (andesine, An 30—32) — 5—15% and neogenic albite, An 7, are always present. Relatively large clastic quartz and plagioclase grains are recrystallized along their edges where they contain chlorite and sericite. The latter two, together with biotite (totaling 5—7% in quartzites and about 30% in quartz schists) form small irregular parallel flakes. Magnetite (1—3%) is widely disseminated. Thin sections show sporadic clastic grains of zircon and tourmaline and, in addition, the heavy fraction contains almandine garnet, hypersthene, spinel, hornblende, pyrite, ilmenite and apatite.

Chlorite-biotite-garnet quartzites and quartz schists differ from the quartzites and schists of the first group in the presence of late almandine-spessartite garnet and the larger size of the biotite. The rocks are nearly identical with respect to the other characteristics. Garnet is subhedral, 1—2 mm (Figure 67), and the central portions contain inclusions of quartz and plagioclase (?). It makes up 1—2% of quartzites and up to 10% of quartz schists. The chemical composition of the garnet, according to spectro-scopic silicate analysis, is as follows (specimen 19z, wt %): SiO_2, 37.6; TiO_2, 0.2; Al_2O_3, 17.2; Fe_2O_3, 25.2; CaO, 5.9; MgO, 1.4; MnO, 7.8; total,

95.3. The refractive index of the analyzed garnet is, $n = 1.810$ and the lattice constant $a = 11.534 \text{Å}$. The computed component composition (mole %) is pyrope — 6, almandine, andradite and grossular — total 74, spessartite — 20. Biotite forms irregular flakes, 1—2 mm in size. Together with the garnet it forms porphyroblasts. The ferruginosity of the biotite is 55% ($n_y = 1.658$—1.665). The chemical composition of a garnet-bearing quartz schist is given in Table 126 (specimen 19d). A noteworthy feature is the low content of ferric iron (0.83%), due to the presence of biotite in place of magnetite and hematite.

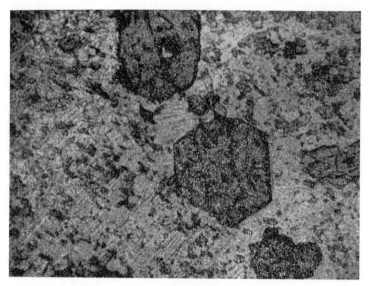

FIGURE 67. Idiomorphic spessartite garnet in Menzies Series quartzites (thin section 19v, × 58, crossed nicols)

Quartz-chlorite-sericite schists are represented by gray and greenish gray, fine-grained layered rocks. Their texture is microlepidogranoblastic, with grain size < 0.1 mm. The schists have high variations in the mineral contents: quartz (10—50%), chlorite (20—40%) and sericite (10—40%). Magnetite (2—5%) is always present, and epidote occurs locally. The heavy minerals consist of tourmaline, clinopyroxene ($n_z = 1.713$, $n_x = 1.6888$), zircon and ilmenite. Chlorite is green and judging from its refractive index (1.618) it is probably a ripidolite. These schists are similar in external appearance, composition and texture to the corresponding schists in the Sodruzhestvo Series, and differ only by the absence of carbonate.

Orthoamphibolites form a sill-like body, 90 m thick, cutting the quartzites and schists of Mt. Seddon at a small angle. They are dark gray, medium-grained rocks, and are schistose to massive. The strike of schistosity is parallel to that in the host rocks. The orthoamphibolite in the central portion of the sill contains 50% hornblende, 40% plagioclase, 4% biotite, 4% magnetite and 2% quartz. The texture is microporphyroblastic. The matrix consists of a fine-grained (0.5 mm and less) granoblastic aggregate of plagioclase, An 23, magnetite, biotite (replacing the hornblende), and apatite. Acicular segregations and prismatic grains (1×3 mm) of hornblende are embedded in this matrix. The hornblende is pleochroic in olive-brown and blue-green tinges. Its optical parameters (n_z = 1.685–1.687, n_x = 1.660–1.664, 2V = 68–73°) indicate common hornblende rich in iron and titanium. The ferruginosity of the biotite is about 47% (n_y = 1.644–1.648). The chemical composition of orthoamphibolite from the center of the sill is presented in Table 126. On the basis of the composition and Zavaritskii's parameters, the rock is close to a silica-undersaturated gabbro-diabase, which apparently represents the original rock. The orthoamphibolite is somewhat different near its contact with the host-rock micaceous quartzites, where it contains 30% hornblende, 25% biotite, 25% plagioclase, 5% quartz, 10% magnetite and 5% garnet. The garnet is pink in color and forms subhedral grains measuring 0.1–0.2 mm. In places, the garnet is rich in plagioclase and quartz inclusions. According to morphological features and refractive index (n = = 1.810), it resembles the spessartite garnet from the surrounding rocks. Other mineral components of endomorphic orthoamphibolite do not differ in their optical and other properties from those in the central portion of the sill. The metamorphism of the original gabbro-diabase resulted in complete recrystallization of primary minerals, accompanied by a replacement of the pyroxenes by hornblende and a deoxidation of the plagioclase.

Large (up to 1.2 m) boulders of meta-conglomerates derived from the Sodruzhestvo and Menzies Series occur at the foot of Mt. Rubin and Mt. Seddon but have not yet been found in situ. They consist of 60–90% well-rounded quartzite pebbles, 1–15 cm in diameter; interstices are filled with quartz schist. The latter contains mainly quartz plus 5–15% spessartite garnet, 20–30% magnetite, 3–10% biotite, 10–15% chlorite and rare ferroactinolite segregations. These indicate metamorphism of the conglomerates under greenschist facies conditions. The metamorphosed conglomerates also belong to the Middle Proterozoic deposits.

Since these data are insufficient for a comprehensive description of the schist-quartzite formation, the conclusions presented herein are tentative. Rocks of both series are predominantly sedimentary in origin. The accumulation of the sediments took place in an aquatic environment; the source rocks were predominantly migmatites and shadow granitoids of the crystalline basement.

A comparison of the sections of the Sodruzhestvo and Menzies Series reveals the following common features: a) the composition of both series is dominated by ferruginous-siliceous and aluminous-siliceous sediments, volcanogenic rocks being rare; b) regional metamorphism, closely related to folding, took place in the epizone and reached the greenschist facies; c) the folds in both series have the same axial plane trends; d) breccia zones are cemented by quartz. However, the series are not stratigraphic equivalents, notwithstanding their considerable similarity. This conclusion stems from the fact that the Menzies Series lacks certain beds which occur in the Sodruzhestvo Series, i.e., jaspilite, marble-limestone and calcareous schist. Rocks of the Menzies Series also exhibit a somewhat higher grade of metamorphism and more intensive folding.

Rocks of the Sodruzhestvo Series may be divided into the following three groups, with respect to the composition of the original sediments and mineral parageneses: 1. Siliceous-argillaceous sediments oversaturated in silica, saturated in aluminum to varying degrees, and partially in calcium and iron; transformed into a variety of phyllites and quartzites. Their characteristic mineral association is quartz + sericite (dioctahedral muscovite 2M) + chlorite (ripidolite) + magnetite + (hematite) + calcite + + epidote. 2. Siliceous-argillaceous-carbonate and carbonate sediments with high concentrations of calcium and magnesium and low contents of silica and alumina; quartz-carbonate schist to marble-limestone, differing from one another in the quantitative ratios of calcite, dolomite, quartz, sericite and chlorite. 3. Siliceous-ferruginous sediments strongly over-saturated in silica and iron, and with very low contents of alumina, calcium and magnesium; jaspilites containing magnetite + hematite + quartz + + sericite + chlorite + magnesite-siderite. The above associations of minerals originated by regional metamorphism of sedimentary rocks of varying compositions, under conditions of the sericite-chlorite subfacies of the greenschist facies.

These data on the Menzies and Sodruzhestvo Series suggest that the metamorphic strata in the southern part of the Prince Charles Mountains differ from formations in geosynclinal zones but, at the same time, are not typical of platform deposits. In the authors' opinion, the accumulation of sediments, metamorphism and development of tectonic forms took place in narrow downwarps within the crystalline basement (on continental-type crust), along a series of major regional, ~E-W, faults. The geological development of such downwarps apparently concluded the stabilization (cratonization) of the crystalline basement of the pre-Riphean Antarctic Plat-form. Judging from paleobotanical investigations and the Middle Proterozoic age of similar quartzite and jaspilite strata on other continents, the earliest downwarping began in the Lower to Middle Proterozoic. Metamorphism and folding were most probably confined to the Lower Riphean (Gothian tectonic complex), i.e., these processes had been completed by the start of deposition of the Vendean sediments in the platform mantle of Queen Maud Land and the Riphean sediments in the Baikal (Ross) fold zone of the Transantarctic Mountains. As yet, no analogous greenschists, with respect to age and structure, have been discovered in other regions of Antarctica. However, according to several properties, they may be correlated with the Nullaginian System (Hammersley Group) in Australia /87/ and the Minas System (Itabira Formation) in South America /31/. On the African continent similar formations occur in the basement complex below the Witwatersrand System.

DIAPHTHORITES

Diaphthoritic schists have been found in many coastal regions of East Antarctica, where they are formed from various rocks of the crystalline basement of the Antarctic Platform, including intrusive gabbroids. However,

they have been more or less satisfactorily studied only in a few locations:
1) Penck Trough (1—2°W) on the western margin of Queen Maud Land;
2) Schirmacher Oasis (11°E) in central Queen Maud Land; 3) the Sør
Rondane Mountains (22—25°E) in eastern Queen Maud Land; 4) Knuckey
Peaks (51°30'E) in eastern Enderby Land; 5) Bunger Oasis (100—102°E)
on Knox Coast; 6) Grearson Oasis (110—111°E) on Budd Coast. In other
regions, the presence of diaphthoritic schist zones, often accompanied by
mylonitic and cataclastic rocks, has been noted. These include the diaphthoresis zones with dikes of metabasites in the Vestfold Oasis (78—79°E)
and in the coastal zone of Adélie Land (140—145°E), where thick greenschist
units, probably diaphthoritic, have been reported /57/.

The largest known zone of diaphthoritic schists occurs in the ∼N—S-
trending Penck Trough. This trough is some 40 km wide and appears to be
an ice-filled graben, with outcops of diaphthorites occurring on the western
spurs of the Neumayer Cliffs, Gburek Peaks and Midbresrabben Hill. Isolated
nearly vertical (80—85°, N and S dipping) beds of diaphthorites exhibit
visible thicknesses ranging from a few hundred meters to a few kilometers
/57/. The diaphthorites are mainly represented by actinolite, less frequently epidote-actinolite and chloride-epidote, schists formed from aphibolites,
garnet-amphibole schists, plagiogneisses, metabasites and calciphyres. The
various migmatites subjected to diaphthoresis were transformed into finely
schistose ultramylonites. In this region, the diaphthorites were formed
from monometamorphic amphibolite facies rocks. Actinolite schists,
colored various shades of green, are of finely schistose structure with a
nematoblastic texture. They consist of elongated prismatic and acicular
grains of actinolite (80%), less commonly tremolite, 1—3 mm long.
Ferruginosity of the actinolite varies from 30 to 45%. The randomly
arranged aggregates of actinolite contain disseminated talc, chlorite,
sphene and ore. The actinolite schists in diopside rocks contain amphibole —
39% ferroactinolite and 61% grammatite. The epidote-actinolite schists
contain quartz (10—20%), and commonly, broken relics of oligoclase,
An 18—21 (15—25%) which are locally albitized. The bulk of the schists consists of microgranular aggregates of epidote (up to 0.1 mm) embedded in an
actinolite matrix. The epidote-chlorite schists contain nearly equal
amounts of chlorite and epidote. Their actinolite content is low (1—3%),
but on the other hand, they often contain much sphene (up to 10—15%) and
late fine-grained calcite. There are some varieties of chlorite schists
with a high content of fine quartz mosaics and with a considerably diminished
content of epidote. In addition to the quartz in the schist matrix, there are also
filiform quartz veinlets which are typically diaphthoritic. An unusual unit of
strongly cataclastized quartzites (about 100 m thick) with kyanite (probably
relict) was encountered on Midbresrabben Hill within diaphthorites of
garnet-amphibole plagiogneisses transformed into actinolite schists containing talc and epidote. These quartzites consist of recrystallized large
(up to 1 cm) poikiloblastic grains of quartz containing prismatic kyanite
grains (n_x = 1.727±0.003), 3—6 mm long, accounting for up to 7—8 vol.% of
the rock. The content of small relict cordierite grains is approximately
the same. Chlorite and talc (15—20%) are fairly abundant.

In the Schirmacher Oasis, the zone of diaphthorites is only 50 m thick. They are formed from bipyroxene schists, migmatites, and shadow granites in polymetamorphic rocks. The bipyroxene schists yield epidote-actinolite schists, and migmatites and shadow granites produce fairly compact, finely banded ultramylonites. The finely comminuted matrix of such mylonites has a high content of sericite; chlorite and epidote form glomero-aggregates which are nonuniformly disseminated in the matrix. Sporadic plagioclase porphyroclasts and rare microcline porphyroclasts are broken, markedly cracked and often embedded in the sericite-epidote aggregates.

Extraordinarily abundant, thick diaphthorite zones, separated by narrow glaciers, extend E—W over close to 100 km in the SW part of the Sør Rondane Mountains. These zones are so closely spaced that reconnaissance produces the impression of an integrated broad belt of diaphthorites containing highly altered bodies of gabbroids and granitoids and, less commonly, isolated blocks of diaphthorized biotite-amphibole plagiogneisses. The rocks have been so highly altered by diaphthoresis that their primary composition is at times difficult to determine. It appears that the unusual amphibolites (with actinolite) were formed from gabbroids, epidote schists with abundant relicts of basic plagioclase — from anorthosites, various greenschists — from amphibole-biotite plagiogneisses and, finally, microschists — from migmatites. The diaphthorized gabbroids have the habit of massive cataclasites, but they are not always schistose. They have a characteristic greenish-gray color, with a slight bluish tinge. Besides the massive and coarsely schistose varieties, so-called "striped diaphthorites" also occur. These are composed of alternating fine bands of different colors. The schistosity and banding strike E—W and dip up to 75° mainly toward the south. The texture of these diaphthorites is cataclastic, with a very complex pattern. Relicts of gabbroic textures are locally preserved in the predominantly nematoblastic matrix. Various amphiboles (50—80%) are the principal minerals. Highly disintegrated plagioclase packed with epidote-chlorite aggregates also occurs. Some varieties contain 5—15% late diaphthoritic quartz. Sphene is the main accessory mineral and apatite is rare. The amphiboles are represented by relict hornblendes with ferruginosities of 46—59%, in broken prismatic grains, measuring 1—2 mm, embedded in acicular-fibrous aggregates of the dominant tremolite-actinolite, with a ferruginosity of 10—25%. Plagioclase also exhibits a dual nature, with relict prismatic laths of labradorite embedded in epidote-zoisite aggregates and scattered granules of albite. Thus, the diaphthoresis of massive gabbroids was incomplete, hence the coexistence of the primary amphibolite facies minerals with the superimposed greenschist facies minerals. Diaphthorized anorthosites are much less common than diaphthorized gabbroids. They are massive in habit with a greenish-brown color. Their texture is blastocataclastic with prismatic-granular relicts. More than half of the rock consists of broken bytownite grains embedded in an epidote-zoisite aggregate. Maculose aggregates of actinolite needles, with ferruginosities varying from 30 to 45%, account for 10—20%. Plagiogneisses gave rise to typical diaphthoritic greenschists, consisting of albite, epidote, and chlorite, in nearly equal quantities, with relict andesine and hornblende, and scattered sericite, quartz and calcite. The latter two minerals are diaphthoritic. Small (up to 1 mm) corroded almandine grains packed with chlorite and quartz inclusions are rare relicts. Diaphthorites resembling schistose ultramylonites were probably formed from migmatites. The matrix consists of minute (0.1—0.2 mm) quartz, albitized plagioclase, chlorite, sericite, and maculose epidote aggregates, which are uniformly linear, even in thin section. These microschists are highly silicified, containing very fine veinlets and fine lenticular segregations of quartz (12—30%).

A zone of diaphthoritic schists, at least 100 m thick, has been found on the Knuckey Peaks. The predominant variety is actinolite schists with relict laths of common hornblende and broken oligoclase grains, probably formed from pyroxene-plagioclase schists. Wherever the latter had been migmatized, the actinolite schists are interbedded with unusual leucocratic microschists, consisting of a very fine-grained comminuted matrix of albite and quartz, with a small admixture of biotite. These schists are in places cut by granite-pegmatite veins, which are also transformed into blasto-mylonites.

Diaphthoritic schists have been noted on Enderby Land, in endomorphic zones of thick (20—50 m) diabase dikes, which are not very widespread (50—60 dikes on an area of 30,000 km^2). Such diaphthoritic zones in dikes are only a few meters thick and are composed of quartz-epidote-actinolite-chlorite schists, with relicts of autometamorphic hornblende and deoxidized plagioclase. Most of the plagioclase has been replaced by epidote, some of which is pseudomorphic. The pyroxenes are almost completely replaced by actinolite aggregates, which contain relict hornblende. It is difficult to decide whether these endomorphic zones in diabase dikes are true diaphthorites related to tectonic faults, or greenschists originated in the final stages of autometamorphic processes.

In the Bunger Oasis, diaphthoritic schists are localized in comparatively narrow, long zones (1—10 km long), with thicknesses not exceeding a few hundred meters. They mainly strike ~E—W, less commonly ~N—S, and are usually located in the largest faults /57/. The diaphthoritic schists are represented by blastase rocks, without any traces of mylonitization. Their genesis is related to the relatively deep-seated diaphthoresis of schists, migmatites and shadow granites. The main feature of the diaphthoresis is the recrystallization of rocks in zones of intensive tectonism, mainly under greenschist facies conditions. The mineral parageneses of the diaphthorites are characterized by actinolite, epidote, grossular, sphene, etc., with relict plagioclase and pyroxene. Biotite-actinolite schists formed from pyroxene schists are the most widespread in the Bunger Oasis; actinolite schists formed from metabasites and phlogopite-tremolite schists from calciphyres are considerably less common. Diaphthorites from high-alumina schists are as rare as the original rocks themselves. Diaphthorites from migmaties are represented by unusual microgneisses, in which the difference between the paleosome and metasome has been obliterated; however, the strongest diaphthoritic alterations occurred in the paleosome. Biotite-actinolite schists are represented by greenish-gray, fine- and medium-grained rocks. Their textures are exclusively nemato-lepidogranoblastic, only slightly disturbed by superimposed cataclasis.

A majority of minerals are xenoblastic, idioblasts being formed only by
amphibole. The grain size is 0.5—2 mm. The composition of these schists
is distinguished by a nonequilibrium association of relict and neogenic minerals;
i. e., 30—40% recrystallized plagioclase, 30—40% amphibole, 15—20% biotite,
10—15% epidote, ore and sporadic garnet. Relict pyroxene is extremely
rare but, characteristically, it preserves the ferruginosity of the starting
schists (35—40%) which remains unaltered in the course of diaphthoresis.
The plagioclase was heterogeneously recrystallized. Thus zoned laths of
labradorite-bytownite and small albite-oligoclase grains are present in a
single specimen. The former are intensively replaced, in places, by
epidote-zoisite aggregates, whereas the latter form the matrix, being stable
in the paragenesis with actinolite and epidote. Amphibole, as a rule, is
represented by actinolite aggregates of elongated prismatic crystals;
tremolite aggregates are more rare. Biotite forms fine idioblasts, greenish-
brown in color; its ferruginosity is low, 30%, which is characteristic of
low-temperature varieties. Grossular garnet grains (n = 1.750, sp. gr. =
= 3.60), measuring up to 1 mm, occur in the biotite-actinolite aggregates. The prevailing accessory minerals are sphene and apatite.
These diaphthoritic schists are often permeated by fine parallel quartz
veinlets, which are sometimes so abundant that the schists assume the
habit of finely layered migmatites. Actinolite schists were probably
formed from ultrametabasites, since they are nearly free of plagioclase.
They contain 70—75% of elongated prismatic and acicular actinolite aggregates. The interstices in the actinolite aggregates are filled with microgranular quartz (up to 10—15%). Fine-grained biotite, accounting for
5—7 vol. % of the rocks, is closely associated with an equal amount of ore,
sphene, and minute apatite crystallites. The clinopyroxene relicts have a
ferruginosity of ~ 30%. Phlogopite-tremolite schists are formed from
calciphyre boudins, retaining the latter's shape. They consist of 85—90%
elongated prismatic (or fibrous) tremolite aggregates, and 10—15% minute
phlogopite flakes. Diopside rocks give rise to maculose scapolite-
phlogopite-tremolite schists. Quartz-biotite-garnet schists are produced
by diaphthoresis of high-alumina sillimanite-cordierite rocks. Locally,
kyanite (6—10%) occurs in place of sillimanite. The kyanite grains exhibit
typical polysynthetic twins, and a relatively high index of refraction
(n_z= 1.730). Garnet, locally constituting 25—30%, probably formed by
diaphthoresis accompanied by stress. Aside from the garnet and kyanite,
these schists contain biotite (40%) and quartz (10—20%). The ordinary
diaphthoritic minerals — chlorite and sericite — appear merely as
small admixtures. These schists constitute the only known occurrence of
diaphthoritic rocks formed under relatively high pressures. The possibility
that kyanite and garnet are relict minerals, cannot be excluded. In that
case the schists bear no relationship to the diaphthorites, but are rocks of progressive regional metamorphism that "found their way" into the diaphthoritic zone. Diaphthoresis of migmatites produced microgneiss consisting of banded actinolite-epidote aggregates containing sphene and brown iron
hydroxides. These are interbedded with very fine-grained quartz-feldspar
aggregates, dominated by albite-oligoclase.

In the Grearson Oasis, diaphthoritic schists occur in rather narrow
near-fault zones. Three types of diaphthoritic schists have been found in
the oasis; actinolite schists, chlorite-sericite-quartz schists and microschists derived from granitoids /57/. The actinolite schists are represented by fine- and medium-grained rocks with a greenish-gray color and
a characteristic nematolepidogranoblastic texture with grain sizes of
0.5—1.5 mm. One half of the rock consists of heavily sericitized relict
plagioclase laths, varying in composition from basic andesine to albite.
Between these, are aggregates of acicular actinolite (veins), biotite, chlorite,
and epidote. A characteristic feature is the presence of relict pyroxene
grains with a ferruginosity that is normal for granulite facies schists and
does not vary during diaphthoresis. Chlorite-sericite-quartz schists are the
most common variety; sericite-epidote-chlorite-quartz schists are less
common. The quartz (30—40%) forms independent intercalations, consisting
of large (5 mm) and small (0.5—1.0 mm) ragged grains often penetrating
into the intercalations of colored minerals. The quartz intercalations
locally contain broken relict plagioclase and microcline. These intercalations alternate with banded aggregates of sericite (25—30%), which are
rimmed with fine-grained biotite (5—10%) and chlorite (5—8%). The biotite
contains fine-grained rutile (sagenite-like) and ore. Concentrations of
apatite occur in sericite aggregates. Another variety of schist consists of
epidote aggregates embedded in a chlorite-sericite-biotite-sphene matrix.
Highly irregular to lenticular intercalations are composed of cataclastized
quartz grains, containing relicts of sericitized plagioclase. Some of the
plagioclase together with the garnet was pseudomorphously replaced by
chlorite, and is included in the sericite-epidote aggregates. Diaphthoresis
of granitoids produced unusual microschists in which banded biotite-
epidote-chlorite aggregates, with abundant inclusions of skeletal ore and
relict pyroxene, alternate with lenticular mosaic intercalations of quartz in
which are embedded broken laths of sericitized plagioclase and microcline.

The examination of individual zones of diaphthoritic schists permits a
description of the overall patterns of diaphthoritic processes for the Antarctic Platform crystalline basement. Firstly, they are consistently related
to disjunctive tectonics and are located within zones of heavily fractured
rocks, both internally and along the margins. These zones vary in width
from a few tens of meters to several kilometers, and are traceable along
the strike over distances varying from a few hundred meters to tens of
kilometers. In places (e. g., in the southwestern part of the Sør Rondane
Mountains) these zones are extremely closely spaced and thus form very
large belts of diaphthorites, stretching over 100 km and more. In general,
diaphthorite zones are more widespread within monometamorphic strata
of the amphibolite facies than among granulite facies strata. This may be
due to the higher level of occurrence in the crystalline basement of the
former. Characteristically, the diaphthoritic schists are represented by
typical blastose rocks, highly recrystallized, so that even traces of the
primary cataclasis have been obliterated. At the same time, notwithstanding
the significant grade of recrystallization and extensive development of
superimposed mineral parageneses of the greenschist facies, diaphthoritic
schists sometimes contain small amounts of relict minerals of the
granulite and amphibolite facies. These include hypersthene, pyrope-
almandine garnet, common hornblende, and kyanite, as well as incompletely

albitized andesine and even labradorite. However, in the majority of cases, diaphthoritic schists are devoid of such relict minerals, and consist of equilibrium associations of greenschist facies minerals.

The most widespread diaphthoritic rocks are actinolite and epidote-actinolite schists; epidote-chlorite and chlorite-sericite schists are somewhat less widespread, while biotite-actinolite and phlogopite-tremolite schists, formed for example from calciphyres, are comparatively rare. Unusual leucocratic microschists, consisting of a microgranular quartz-feldspathic matrix formed from finely layered migmatites and shadow granites, occur in large amounts only very locally. The prevailing structure of the diaphthorites is schistose, less commonly banded, as in ultramylonites. Their texture is most commonly nematogranoblastic with a metablastic development of quartz and albite. The mineral associations of diaphthorites are controlled by the paragenesis of actinolite with epidote, chlorite and albite, and less commonly with biotite and sericite. The ferruginosity of the colored minerals in diaphthorites is lower than that in the parent rocks of the granulite and amphibolite facies. Diaphthoresis is very often accompanied by silicification (and enrichment in metablasts) resulting in mosaic aggregates and very fine veinlets of quartz, with which equally fine veinlets of calcite are locally associated.

The chemical composition of diaphthorites is almost entirely dependent on the composition of parent rocks and, on the whole, is only little different from the latter /57/. Thus, diaphthoresis of metabasites and bipyroxene schists produces rocks that are somewhat enriched in iron, sodium, and especially silica and depleted in magnesian-calcic components. Although the ferruginosity of their colored minerals is low, the content of minerals such as actinolite and epidote is nearly double that in the original rocks. The increase in the sodium content is related to the ubiquitous albitization of plagioclase. Different alterations occur in high-alumina schists, which in the course of diaphthoresis become enriched in calcium and partially in iron, and depleted in silica and alkalis. The diaphthoresis of shadow granites likewise causes enrichment in iron and calcium and a depletion in silica and alkalis. On the whole, diaphthoresis is the opposite of migmatization and granitization, and consequently migmatites and shadow granites are destroyed and the differences between them and basic schists are gradually obliterated.

The texture and mineral and chemical compositions of diaphthoritic schists, as well as their persistent spatial relationship with faults, indicate that their formation proceeded in a manner totally different from the formation of all other regional-metamorphic rocks constituting the crystalline basement; their genesis is evidently related to faults in the rigid crystalline basement. As yet, it is impossible to date the diaphthoritic processes. They probably occurred repeatedly but mainly in the Precambrian, particularly in relation to various stages of tectonic-magmatic activization. However, diaphthoresis is only possible at depths permitting recrystallization and the development of new mineral associations related to hydration and redistribution of elements in the minerals. The tectonic movements resulting in shallow faults were usually accompanied by the formation of zones of cataclasis and mylonites, without any significant alteration in the mineral composition of the original rocks.

Chapter VII

FEATURES OF REGIONAL METAMORPHISM
AND ULTRAMETAMORPHISM

Regional metamorphism and ultrametamorphism of thick volcanogenic and sedimentary formations accumulated in early periods of the Earth's geological history (mainly in the Archean and partly in the Lower Protero-zoic) are among the leading processes in formation of the crystalline basements of the Earth's ancient platforms. Among the latter, it is possible to group the platforms of the southern hemisphere, i.e., the African, South American, Antarctic, Australian and Indian platforms which have similar geological structures. They are therefore considered under the common name of Gondwanian platforms, after the hypothetical supercontinent Gondwana, which possibly contained all these platforms some 200 million years ago /7/. The mantles as well as the crystalline basements of these platforms possess many common structural features, suggesting that Gondwana existed from Archean times. These common features in-clude the following: a) unique composition of the original sedimentary and volcanogenic deposits, at least 20 km thick, with a predominance of magmatic rocks of intermediate and basic compositions; b) characteristics of region-al metamorphism and ultrametamorphism — predominance of high-tempera-ture, medium-pressure metamorphic facies, the importance of migmatites and shadow granites with enderbitic-charnockitic trends, the widespread occurrence of rheomorphic charnockitoid intrusions, and finally, the multi-stage nature of all these processes, resulting in polymetamorphic formations; c) similar complexes of intrusive formations of platform nature perme-ating the crystalline basement after cratonization /56/.

A notable feature is the extensive occurrence of presently exposed crystalline basement metamorphic formations in Gondwanian platforms. These account for 30 to 50% of the platform areas. In ancient platforms of the northern hemisphere, formations of this kind occupy less than 15% of the total area. This feature is probably related to the widespread occurrence of block tectonics in the Gondwanian platforms. The Antarctic Platform, which was the core of Gondwana, exhibits all the characteristic features of that supercontinent, including its crystalline basement.

STRUCTURE OF THE CRYSTALLINE BASEMENT

The crystalline basement of the Antarctic Platform is exposed mainly in coastal block mountain systems stretching, with gaps, along the east coast of Antarctica from 12°W long. to 135°E long., over 8,000 km /57/. This fact was regarded by many investigators as evidence of the monolithic nature of the entire huge region of East Antarctica, considered to be an integral ancient "East Antarctic shield" /12/ fringed by "pericratonic" and geosynclinal systems. Only with respect to the Lambert Glacier area, where block mountains penetrate more than 600 km inland, was the presence of "intracratonic ramifications" of these systems sometimes recognized. Thus, the Antarctic Platform, with an area exceeding 10,000,000 km^2, was regarded as a single region of ancient cratonization existing as a huge subglacial "supershield" partially covered by various horizons (mainly Paleozoic) of the platform mantle. Similarly large crystalline shields are unknown for other Gondwanian platforms. The largest shields, e. g., those in Guiana and Brazil, do not exceed 1,500,000 km^2 each. Therefore, in the authors' opinion, it is more likely that several crystalline shields occur within East Antarctica, separated by platform mantle regions and also by geosynclinal (mostly Late Baikal) fold systems.

The areas containing crystalline basement exposures, surrounded by subglacial areas, that are classified as shields of the Antarctic Platform possess the following characteristics: a) a history of steady, prolonged (relatively mild) uplifts and a high degree of erosion; b) the ubiquitous development of regional metamorphic rocks of the granulite facies, with widespread ultrametagenic charnockites and enderbites; c) the absence of polymetamorphic formations with complex intrusions of apogabbroid charnokitoids; d) the possible presence of rocks with the oldest absolute dates (3,000—3,300 million years), as suggested by the oldest absolute dates of rocks in the crystalline basement of other Gondwanian platforms /73/. At this stage, at least two shields satisfy the above conditions: 1) the Victoria Shield (mostly concealed under ice), comprising the steady, but relatively mild uplift of the central subglacial regions of Victoria Land and extending to exposed seaboards on Adélie Land and Wilkes Land (between 110 and 150°E. long.); 2) the Enderby Shield, comprising nearly the entire subglacial part of Enderby Land and the coastal exposure (between 45 and 65°E. long.). The area of each of these shields is at least 1,000,000 km^2 and possibly considerably larger. There are possibly two other stable geoblocks of the crystalline basement (platforms?) in West Antarctica under the thick ice sheet near the Ross and Filchner ice shelves.

Within the presumed shields and platforms, the consolidation of the crystalline basement was probably completed already in the Upper Archean-Lower Proteozoic, after which it underwent only block rearrangements related to faults. In many other regions of Antarctica, the Upper Archean crystalline basement was subjected to repeated rearrangements during the Proterozoic, which ended in the period of Late Baikal tectogenesis. The most substantial rearrangement of such mobile blocks of the crystalline basement apparently took place in the Lower Proterozoic. It consisted of a drastic reworking of tectonic structures, intrusion of magmatic masses of primarily andesite-basalt and regenerated granitic composition, extensive reworking of the granulite facies rocks under conditions of the high-grade

amphibolite facies, with consequent extensive development of polymetamorphic rocks. All the subsequent rearrangements of such blocks were
terminated in the period of Late Baikal tectogenesis. They were mainly
confined to the development of block tectonics related to faults and to the
intrusion along the latter of limited magmatic masses. The uplifting of
the crystalline basement blocks resulted in a rejuvenation of their rocks
/38/, and therefore the absolute dates usually lie between 450 and 550 million years.

There is also a third type of crystalline basement block, composed exclusively of monometamorphic rocks of the amphibolite facies devoid of
either ultrametagenic or intrusive charnockites. As a rule, such blocks in
coastal mountains alternate with blocks of polymetamorphic rocks, the
latter appearing as median masses within the former. It is assumed that
the blocks of monometamorphic rocks are formations of a younger structural tier of the crystalline basement, which originated in the Lower
Proterozoic simultaneously with the repeated metamorphism of the Upper
Archean mobile blocks. Their location on the same level in the present-
day erosion section may be explained by block tectonics. Blocks of this
type underwent comparatively small uplifts, which attained their maximum
in the period of the Late Baikal tectogenesis; the degree of their erosion is
comparatively limited and they are therefore saturated with hypabyssal
intrusions.

Hence, it is feasible to distinguish the following three types of crystalline
basement regions within the Antarctic Platform: two types of the lower
structural tier, i. e., stabile and mobile, and one type of the upper structural
tier, in which the former two types appear as median masses. The stable
regions are distinguished by the oldest (Upper Archean) cratonization of the
Earth's crust. They underwent steady and prolonged, but relatively mild,
uplift. Intensive differentiated upliftings are utterly precluded in their case;
abyssal faults and block tectonics are relatively limited within their
boundaries. The structure of stable regions is controlled by a combination
of the domes of shadow granitoids and linear fold zones of rocks of a lower
granitization grade. Such regions best correspond to the oldest shields of
Gondwanian platforms /56/. The mobile regions of the lower structural tier
were involved in tectonic movements and metamorphic processes which
formed the upper structural tier of the crystalline basement, and, therefore,
cratonization of the Earth's crust within their boundaries was completed in
the Lower Proterozoic. Their characteristic features are differentiated
uplift (intensive or mild) alternating with subsidence. The structures of
mobile regions are controlled by a combination of large brachy-folds (erstwhile domes) with superimposed smaller linear fold forms, the strike of
which is close to that of the fold systems of the upper structural tier.
Deep-seated faults and block tectonics, as well as a variety of magmatic
and rheomorphic intrusions, are very widespread within these regions.

Blocks of the upper structural tier were possibly formed on the site of
protogeosynclinal downwarps of the lower structural tier; some "juttings"
of the latter are found among the former, their habit being similar to that
of the basement "juttings." The structures of the upper tier blocks are
very complex; these are linear fold systems the axial planes of which have
highly variable strikes. The nature of the structures is similar to that of

the fold systems originating on the site of geosynclines. Rocks of the upper tier of the crystalline basement originated at smaller depths and at lower metamorphic temperatures than the lower tier rocks, and are therefore devoid of ultrametagenic and intrusive charnockites; the grade of granitiza- tion is somewhat low, and therefore migmatites predominate markedly over shadow granites; plagiogneisses have been preserved, having undergone only regional metamorphism. Formation of the upper structural tier by consolidation of the Lower Proterozoic protogeosynclinal systems on the Archean foundation, completed the cratonization of the crystalline basement of the Antarctic Platform. The upper structural tier can be included in the crystalline basement by virtue of the similarity of its constituent sedimen- tary-volcanogenic formations to the oldest starting formations of the lower structural tier, and also because the former cannot be regarded as typical geosynclinal deposits (the start of their formation marked the first phase in the disintegration of the Antarctic craton, which began not later than the Upper Proterozoic, when it also reached its culmination). Moreover, the Late Proterozoic decratonization may be presumed to have inherited the natural pattern of the upper crystalline tier, which therefore predetermined the nature of decratonization at its very inception.

The last echo of cratonization was the formation of Middle Proterozoic greenschist and quartzite-jaspilite strata, accumulated in residual downwarps of the upper structural tier of the crystalline basement, in structures of the trough type. In structural setting and formational composition, they are transitional between the upper tier of the crystalline basement and the basal Riphean complexes of its mantle. The structures of greenschist strata are characterized by isoclinal and simple linear fold complexes, similar to the fold systems of intraformational downwarps.

In view of the above data, the notion of the "East Antarctic Shield" as the integral structure of the Antarctic Platform crystalline basement must be discarded. The crystalline basement is found to possess a much more complex structure, consisting of at least two tiers, the lower of which con- sists of stable and mobile regions; the latter appear as the median masses in the upper tier structures which are fairly similar to fold formations of the geosynclinal complex. An integral shield, subsequently transformed into the crystalline basement of the Antarctic Platform, possibly existed in the Archean as a part of the overall structure of the hypothetical Gondwanian continent. Its further development in the course of the Lower Proterozoic led to the formation of a very complex pattern combining three types of structural complexes, the later ones being superimposed on the earlier ones. The cratonization of the crystalline basement was mainly completed in the Lower Proterozoic. Subsequent thereto, and until the completion of the Baikal tectogenesis, the rigid crystalline basement was subjected to "splits" (producing mobile blocks), developed unequally in the three structural regions. It was only after the completion of the Baikal tectogenesis that the crystalline basement acquired the tectonic structure found in its present erosion section of exposed bedrock and inferred from geophysical and neotec- tonic data obtained from below the thick ice cover. These specific structural features of the crystalline basement of Antarctica probably predetermined its outlines on its separation as an independent continent at a considerably later time when the platform regions of Gondwana were broken into the separate continents of the southern hemisphere.

ORIGINAL ROCKS OF THE CRYSTALLINE BASEMENT

The composition of the original rocks of the entire Antarctic crystalline basement is nearly the same, irrespective of the structural setting of the three regions, although the quantitative ratios vary somewhat. The original rocks fall into the following three distinct classes: 1) basic (and to a small extent ultrabasic) magmatic rocks, that are the parent rocks of calcareous-magnesian and magnesian schists, their migmatites and certain varieties of shadow granites; magmatic rocks of intermediate composition that are parent rocks for enderbites and the majority of ultrametagenic charnockites; 2) pelitic and, to a considerably lesser extent, psammitic sediments that are parent rocks for aluminous schists, their migmatites and shadow granites, as well as quartzites; 3) carbonate sediments, that are parent rocks for marbles and calciphyres. An analysis of the thicknesses of dozens of profiles of metamorphic suites and series reveals that rocks of the first class account for 60—65% of the crystalline basement of the Antarctic Platform (not more than 1—2% hyperbasites), rocks of the second class account for 25—30% (2—3% quartzites), and those of the third class account for 5—10%. These ratios vary in the rocks of the upper structural tier of the crystalline basement, where the content of original terrigenous sediment is nearly doubled, approaching the content of the original volcanics. The increase in the quantity of sedimentary-terrigenous rocks is mainly due to psammitic deposits of diverse compositions, and therefore the upper structural tier of the crystalline basement contains fairly large quantities of quartz-feldspar metamorphic rocks predominating not only over quartzites, but also over aluminous schists. Rocks of the quartzite-jaspilite formation are an isolated phenomenon, with very local development; to date, they have been found only in the graben-synclinorium in the Prince Charles Mountains. They were formed from rather rare ferruginous-siliceous sediments.

In chemical composition, the pyroxene-plagioclase (calcareous-magnesian) schists are, on the whole, very close to the average composition of diabases and basalts, with deviations toward olivine basalts. All dissimilarities between schists and basic magmatic rocks are related to amphibolization, biotitization and feldspathization of the former, under conditions of low-grade granitization. The most general dissimilarities between schists and basic magmatic rocks (high calcium and low iron contents, as compared to a constant content of magnesium in colored minerals and a partial deanorthitization of plagioclase) indicate a higher pressure and a lower temperature of metamorphism of the granulite facies in comparison to the crystallization conditions of the basic magmatic rocks. Amphibolization produces only slight alterations in the composition of schists; these include an increase in potassium, sodium, titanium and iron, and a decrease in magnesium and calcium. Biotitization of schists is accompanied by a rise in the potassium content and some decrease in ferrous iron and calcium. The most pronounced change in the composition of schists is caused by feldspathization, which appreciably raises the content of potassium and partially of silica and ferric iron, and lowers the content of ferrous iron, magnesium and calcium. In other words, the overall chemical trend of alteration processes in the pyroxene-plagioclase schists, relative to the parent basic magmatic rocks, lies within low grades of granitization.

However, calcareous-magnesian schists of a low granitization grade are less common than highly granitized varieties which were transformed into ultrametagenic charnockitoids. The bulk of the latter, especially enderbites, was probably formed from more acid rocks corresponding to the composition of intermediate plagiogneisses, the original rocks for which could be andesites. A comparison of andesite and enderbite reveals that the former contains more potassium and ferromagnesian components, as well as calcium in plagioclases, while the latter is richer in silica and sodium and is also locally oversaturated in alumina — alumina-oversaturated andesites are much less common. Considering the chemical mechanism involved in granitization, enderbites may be regarded as metamorphic analogs of andesites. In attempting to visualize the consecutive stages in the metamorphism of andesites, it is clear that they must become enriched in silica in the greenschist stage, depleted in potassium in the amphibolite stage, and enriched in sodium and depleted in calcium in the granulite stage, with the corresponding liberation of alumina from plagioclase and its incorporation in the colored minerals.

The various pyroxene (magnesian) schists (commonly without olivine) are fairly close to ultrabasic magmatic rocks in chemical composition, but differ from the latter (peridotites and pyroxenites) in their low content of silica, magnesium and calcium and high content of aluminum and ferrous iron. This is primarily due to their metamorphism under granulite facies conditions. The fairly high potassium content of schists is due to biotitization. Other alterations are uncharacteristic for these rocks, since they virtually do not lend themselves to granitization.

The chemical composition of little-altered aluminous schists can be roughly established, with rare exceptions. Since they are oversaturated in alumina and silicon, aluminous schists lend themselves most readily to migmatization and granitization and are the principal source of partial melts. Therefore, they are nearly always found to be granitized. However, in very rare cases, sillimanite-garnet schists, occurring as intercalations in bipyroxene-plagioclase schists, are "protected" against granitization. In this case, they are very similar to terrigenous pelitic deposits, differing from the latter in their high content of alumina relative to that of all the other elements. The high Si:Al ratio (> 3) is espeically notable. The chemical composition (ratios of elements) of sillimanite-garnet schist is not comparable with that of any magmatic rock, and it is undoubtedly the result of metamorphism of terrigenous sediments.

The quartzites clearly owe their origin to psammitic deposits. Characteristically, the quartzites never consist of quartz alone, and in this respect they may be divided into aluminous and feldspathic types. The aluminous quartzites fall into six varieties: spinel-sillimanite, sillimanite, sillimanite-garnet, sillimanite-hypersthene, hypersthene-cordierite and garnet quartzites, containing, in addition to quartz, up to 15—40% admixtures of other minerals. The feldspathic quartzites are more homogeneous and contain 5–15% feldspar. The mineral associations of the quartzites are indicative of the granulite facies. However, their parent rocks were psammites with an admixture primarily of argillaceous and partly of calcareous material.

Marbles and their calciphyres were probably sedimentary-chemogenic deposits, dominated by dolomites and less commonly limestones. Their mode of occurrence, i. e., stratified layers with thicknesses ranging from a few meters to tens of meters traceable over 1–2 km along strike, clearly indicates their origin by sedimentation. Characteristically, marbles and calciphyres are practically unknown in the oldest deposits of the Enderby shield (the Napier structural-facies zone), whereas in all the other zones dominated by granulite facies rocks, and especially in zones of amphibolite facies rocks of the upper structural tier of the crystalline basement, the carbonate deposits become increasingly important.

This composition of the original Archean (and largely also Lower Proterozoic) deposits denotes formation conditions which were not repeated in other, younger epochs. Indeed, the association of metavolcanics with quartzites, high-alumina schists and marbles is unusual for the younger geosynclinal deposits. The significant predominance of volcanics (basic and intermediate compositions) over terrigenous and chemogenic sedimentary deposits indicates a high permeability of the Earth's crust to subcrustal magmatic masses in the Archean, and its low degree of mechanical disintegration. The presence of rocks high in alumina, carbonates and iron is probably due to profound chemical, mostly subaqueous, decomposition of basic volcanics, and not to their mechanical destruction.

In the Earth's history, the Archean Era was probably an epoch of accumulation of basic and intermediate volcanics, their disintegration in an aquatic environment, precipitation of specific chemogenic sediments from solutions, and the mixing of magmatic products with these sediments and terrigenous deposits. This formational composition of Archean deposits precludes a sharp differentiation of the upper horizons of the Earth's crust into the disintegration, ablation and accumulation regions (geosynclines) characteristic of younger epochs. The Earth's crust in the Archean abounded in faults due to the movement of deep masses, and these faults served as penetration paths for magma, often in the form of subaqueous eruptions, since an aqueous envelope existed on the surface of the Earth's crust even in the early stages of its development. This is revealed, in the first place, by the composition of certain sedimentary deposits of chemogenic nature.

METAMORPHIC FACIES

The major processes in the formation of the crystalline basement of the Antarctic Platform are related to regional metamorphism and ultrametamorphism of specific sedimentary-volcanogenic strata accumulated over hundreds of millions of years during the Earth's earliest epochs (combined thickness of at least 20 km). Facies determinations of these strata are

based on studies of equilibrium mineral associations. Therefore, the
identification of stable associations provided the basis for facies analysis,
which established the presence in the Antarctic Platform crystalline basement of all three facies of regional metamorphism, i. e., granulite (most
widespread), amphibolite and greenschist (least widespread), with a prevalence of polymetamorphic rocks formed by mineral associations of the
granulite and superimposed amphibolite facies. Rocks of the epidote-
amphibolite facies only occur to a very limited extent and mostly in
diaphthoritic formations. This broad range of development of regional-
metamorphic processes is one of the most characteristic features of the
crystalline basement of Gondwanian platforms.

Another characteristic feature of the metamorphic facies of the crystalline basement of the Antarctic and probably also other Gondwanian platforms,
is the considerable predominance of regional metamorphic facies of
medium pressures, whereas high-pressure facies occur only locally and to
a very limited extent. The latter include the garnet-clinopyroxene (with
amphibole) subfacies of the granulite facies, producing granulites in a
narrow zone in central Enderby Land and in the syncline core in the Humboldt Mountains; and the staurolite-kyanite subfacies of the amphibolite
facies, in the southern structural-facies zone of the Lambert Glacier.

The third characteristic feature of the crystalline basement of the Antarctic Platform is the very extensive manifestation of migmatization and
granitization, which began under granulite facies conditions but were usually
completed under high-grade amphibolite facies conditions. Therefore it
is sometimes difficult to distinguish between the mineral associations of
these two metamorphic facies on the basis of granitization products.

Granulite facies

The granulite facies may be divided into the following three subfacies:
1) pyroxene-granulite, the highest-temperature subfacies; 2) hornblende-
granulite, medium-pressure subfacies; and 3) the hornblende-garnet-
clinopyroxene, high-pressure subfacies. The polymetamorphic rocks contain relics of all three subfacies, but mostly of the latter two. Before we
embark on a description of the granulite subfacies, it should be emphasized
that the crystalline basement rocks may be divided into the following three
large groups according to their behavior toward granitization processes:
a) those lending themselves to granitization only with difficulty or scarcely
at all, including marbles and calciphyres, quartzites and magnesian schists;
b) those readily lending themselves to granitization, including aluminous
schists and allied terrigenous rocks, transformed into migmatites and
shadow granites; c) rocks occupying an intermediate position between
groups (a) and (b), the so-called calcareous-magnesian schists, which are
granitized and transformed into the charnockite series under certain
tectonic conditions, while in all other cases the pyroxene-plagioclase rocks
are preserved with only a relatively low grade of granitization, manifested
by biotitization and feldspathization. The residual (ultimate) granitization

phenomena include the formation of secondary hydrous minerals which are produced in significant quantities depending on the composition of the rocks. The presence of secondary minerals seriously impedes the identification of stable associations, especially for the differentiation of the three granulite subfacies.

The pyroxene-granulite subfacies is extremely widespread in the central part of the Enderby shield, where it occupies an area of at least 30,000 km^2, being concentrated in the so-called Napier structural-facies zone.   As yet, it has not been discovered in other regions of the Antarctic Platform, although its presence within the subglacial Victoria shield is very probable.   The most stable parageneses of this subfacies are as follows: a) $plag_{40-80}$ + hyp_{25-55} + $clpy_{30-45}$ + (qz +Kfs), characteristic of the pyroxene-plagioclase schists of various grades of feldspathization; b) $plag_{30-50}$ + hyp_{40-55} + $clpy_{30-40}$ + qz + (Kfs), characteristic of enderbites; c) $plag_{25-35}$ + Kfs (perthite) + qz + hyp_{40-70} + ($clpy_{40-50}$), characteristic of perthitic charnockites; d) $plag_{20-30}$ + Kfs (perthite) + qz + gar_{60-70} + (sill), characteristic of perthitic shadow granites.

The following two temperature stages are distinctly discernible in the pyroxene-granulite subfacies: I — enderbites with t = 1,100—1200°C; II — perthitic charnockites with t = 900—1000°C.

The major rocks in this subfacies are enderbites and perthitic charnockites.   Enderbites are produced mainly by the granitization of rocks of andesitic composition, which probably went through the stage of plagiogneisses in the course of metamorphism, although the plagiogneisses were not preserved under granulite facies conditions.   The more melanocratic varieties of enderbites were possibly formed from basalts that went through the stage of bipyroxene schists, sporadic relicts of which have been preserved in enderbites.   The enderbites themselves sometimes appear as the metasome or paleosome of these schists.   In the latter case, the metasome consists of perthitic charnockites.   The latter are likewise often formed in the course of further granitization of enderbites.   The classical enderbites consist of 60—70% antiperthitic plagioclase, 10—20% quartz and 5—15% hypersthene.   In addition, they may contain clinopyroxene and/or hornblende (0.5—4.0%), as well as perthitic orthoclase (1—5%); biotite is a sporadic accessory.   The composition of plagioclase varies from oligoclase (An 26—28) to andesine (An 40—45); it often has a diffuse zonal structure and contains 10—20% antiperthitic orthoclase ingrowths.   The hypersthene has the lowest ferruginosity (36—57%) found for this mineral in all granitized rocks of the crystalline basement.   The enderbites display a significant predominance of sodium over potassium (factor of 3—4) and a slight predominance of iron over magnesium.   Enderbitization consists of a loss of ferrous iron, magnesium and calcium and an influx of sodium.   The process is accompanied by a redistribution of silicon and aluminum by bimetasomatism, giving rise to melanocratic and leucocratic varieties, the former occurring as relicts within the latter.   Perthitic charnockites, spatially and genetically closely related to enderbites, display significant fluctuations in the contents of the rock-forming minerals: 30—80% perthite, 10—40% quartz, 1—10% plagioclase, 1—20% orthopyroxene; clinopyroxene and secondary biotite (instead of hornblende as in enderbites) are sporadic.   The

K-feldspar in these charnockites contains 40—60% perthitic plagioclase ingrowths, their composition fluctuating between An 23 and An 36, corresponding to the composition of independent plagioclase grains in the rocks. Orthopyroxene is significantly more ferruginous (47—76%) than in enderbites. On the whole, the charnockites differ from enderbites in their high alkalinity (the contents of potassium and sodium are nearly equal), a low content of highly ferruginous colored minerals, and a somewhat lower basicity of the plagioclase. All these features indicate that the perthitic charnockites are products of further granitization of enderbites, accompanied by an influx of potassium, the removal of cations from the colored minerals, and a partial loss of sodium. It must be emphasized that the perthitic charnockites are a specific variety of this group of rocks, produced together with enderbites under conditions of the highest-temperature granulite subfacies. The lower-temperature granulite subfacies yield bifeldspar charnockites (with rare enderbites), which predominate in the crystalline basement of the Antarctic Platform.

Rocks of the pyroxene-granulite subfacies comprise the majority of aluminous quartzites and bimetasomatic rocks, produced at the contact of perthitic charnockites and quartzites with pyroxene rocks and their migmatites. The aluminous quartzites are transformed primarily into sillimanite-hypersthene, hypersthene-cordierite, cordierite and partially spinel-sillimanite quartzites. The pyroxenes in such rocks have low ferruginosities — 15—35%. A somewhat higher ferruginosity is found in the cordierites — 20—40%. The antiperthitic plagioclase admixture is an andesine (An 35—37), and the K-feldspar, a microclinized perthite. These quartzites lend themselves to granitization only with difficulty, although they are products of the highest-temperature granulite subfacies. Bimetasomatic high-alumina rocks, encountered on Enderby Land only in the Napier zone of maximum metamorphism, are even more interesting. They include sillimanite-hypersthene-cordierite, hypersthene-cordierite, spinel-hypersthene-garnet-cordierite and garnet-hypersthene-cordierite rocks. Their composition is dominated by the minerals listed in their designations, although they often also contain significant amounts of quartz and K-feldspar, and occasionally also biotite. The ferruginosity of the minerals is comparatively low, averaging 20—30% for orthopyroxenes and 16—30% for cordierite. The hypersthene characteristically contains 7—11% alumina. Remarkably, the ferruginosity of the minerals in relatively large blocks of bimetasomatic rocks varies appreciably, from a minimum at the center to a maximum in the margin. The ferruginosity of coexisting hypersthene, cordierite and biotite is nearly the same. The charnockites are enriched in mafic and depleted in salic elements in the contact zone; the reverse occurs in the pyroxene rocks. These bimetasomatic rocks indicate a broad range of regional granitization of granulite facies rocks. Granitization starts with the formation of enderbites, continues during the formation of perthitic charnockites, and is completed by the formation of charnockites proper (bifeldspar charnockites). During bimetasomatism the exchange of elements between the solution-melt and the rock undergoing granitization reaches its maximum in areas where rocks of contrasting compositions are in contact with one another.

The hornblende-granulite subfacies is characterized by an ultrametagenic charnockite series, represented by an intricate complex of migmatites and shadow granitoids containing relics of the original pyroxene schists. This series comprises the majority of the crystalline basement regions, including the Rayner structural-facies zone on Enderby Land (surrounding the Napier zone), the central part of Queen Maud Land, Mac-Robertson Land, the northern structural-facies zone of the Lambert Glacier and, finally, the numerous rocky oases and nunataks on the seaboard of East Antarctica (between 70 and 145°E. long.). The most stable parageneses of the hornblende-granulite subfacies are as follows: a) $plag_{40-60} + hyp_{30-55} + clpy_{30-40} + biot_{30-60} + horn_{40-50} + (qz + Kfs)$, characteristic of biotitized and feldspathized pyroxene-plagioclase schists; b) $plag_{25-45} + hyp_{40-60} + biot_{40-60} + qz + (Kfs + clpy_{35-40})$, characteristic of biotite enderbites; c) $plag_{25-45} + Kfs + qz + hyp_{55-75} + biot_{55-70}$, characteristic of bifeldspar charnockites; d) $plag_{20-30} + Kfs + qz + gar_{60-70} + biot_{60-80} + (sill + cord)$, characteristic of the very widespread shadow granites. The following two temperature equilibrium stages may be distinguished for the hornblende-granulite subfacies: I — corresponding to the formation temperature of biotite enderbites (900—1000°); II — corresponding to the formation temperature of bifeldspar charnockites (700—800°C). The similarity of the parageneses of the subfacies in question to those produced by superimposition of the amphibolite facies on the pyroxene-granulite subfacies suggests the following three developmental types of the hornblende-granulite subfacies: a) the Rayner zone of Enderby Land, where relics of the pyroxene-granulite subfacies occur in some areas in the form of perthitic charnockites; b) all other regions of the granulite facies, in the crystalline basement, where these relics are absent (the regions that are the most characteristic in this respect include the Bunger Oasis, Mac-Robertson Land, Princess Elizabeth Land, etc.); c) the central part of Queen Maud Land, Grearson Oasis, Molodezhnaya Station area, etc., where amphibolite facies parageneses are superimposed on rocks of the hornblende-granulite subfacies, producing typical polymetamorphic rocks.

The same original volcanics for the series of enderbite-perthitic charnockites were probably also the parent rocks for the bifeldspar charnockite series and their migmatites. However, the enderbite-perthitic charnockite series was formed under conditions of the highest-temperature pyroxene-granulite subfacies, but the bifeldspar charnockites and their migmatites are the products of the hornblende-granulite subfacies. A distinction should probably be drawn between the original rocks of migmatites and bifeldspar charnockites, which belong to shadow granite formations. In the case of the former (more precisely, their paleosome), it is preferable to regard basic volcanics (basalts) as the parent rocks, whereas intermediate volcanics (andesites) are more likely in the latter case. Bipyroxene-plagioclase schists which were not digested by granitization locally alternate with coarsely layered migmatites and are closest to basic volcanics in composition. The paleosomes of coarsely layered migmatites are unusual garnet-pyroxene rocks, containing 30—35% colored minerals. Their metasomes are leucocratic shadow granites and alaskitic granites. The migmatites are persistently interbedded with bifeldspar charnockites (in the same exposures), providing still further evidence of the different starting compositions of the two rocks, since their formation conditions were naturally identical. In the process of migmatization, the pyroxene-plagioclase schists, which had previously undergone extensive tectonic preparation, interacted with partial melts (arriving from outside and which subsequently formed the metasome). The schists themselves were transformed into the paleosome of migmatites, having undergone the following alterations: a) enrichment in quartz and K-feldspar replacing the basic plagioclase; b) decrease in the basicity of plagioclase from labradorite to andesine and the appearance of abundant antiperthitic ingrowths (up to 30 vol.% of the host mineral); c) an increase in the ferruginosity of the pyroxenes, averaging 15—20% (in relation to the basic schists), and a decrease in their content by a factor of 2 or more; d) the appearance of neogenic garnet with a ferruginosity of 60—80% (the higher the ferruginosity of hypersthene, the higher that of the garnet); e) the appearance of appreciable amounts of biotite, its ferruginosity being always somewhat higher than that of orthopyroxene. These alterations of the paleosome may be related to the metasomatic recrystallization of basic schists during the formation of the metasome from partial melts. The formation of garnet is a more complex problem. In the authors' opinion, it is related to reactive interrelationships between plagioclase and hypersthene, accompanied by loss of calcium and a redistribution of alumina. There is also the possibility that the garnet is of bimetasomatic genesis, having formed at the contact of a paleosome and metasome of contrasting compositions. It should be noted that the contact of these two migmatite constituents is often marked by a garnet fringe.

Bifeldspar charnockites, when formed from metavolcanics of intermediate composition, probably pass through the stage of plagiogneisses, and possibly also of migmatites; their alteration followed a trend similar to that in migmatites, but was much more intensive. It can be described as follows: a) the charnockites become greatly enriched in K-feldspars — metasomatic replacement of plagioclase; b) the basicity of plagioclase decreases to acid andesine and even oligoclase, but stops at An 20; c) the ferruginosity of orthopyroxene increases to 70—75% (seldom more) and its content becomes minimal; d) the charnockites persistently contain biotite of a maximum ferruginosity, and sporadically garnet with a ferruginosity up to 70—75%. For an elucidation of certain aspects of the genesis of bifeldspar charnockites, it is useful to compare their composition with that of perthitic charnockites. The former differ from the latter in a considerable predominance of potassium over sodium (by a factor of 2 or more), whereas their total alkalinity is nearly the same and the content of mafic components in the colored minerals is higher. They are thus more melanocratic and contain such minerals as biotite, which is virtually absent from perthitic charnockites. Hence, it is obvious that the bifeldspar charnockites contain hydrous as well as nonhydrous colored minerals and are distinguished by a higher activity of potassium. The mesoperthitic charnockites are formed under drier conditions and at lower potassium activity. This also indicates a lower temperature and pressure during the formation of bifeldspar charnockites in comparison to enderbites and perthitic charnockites.

Formation of the former is probably completed under conditions of high-grade amphibolite facies. The similarity between the chemical composition of charnockites and that of crustal magmatic granitoids (from quartz diorites to alaskites) is one of the manifestations of their subsequent genetic relationships, since the former may apparently be regarded as the parent rocks of the latter, which formed in younger epochs during periods of tectonic-magmatic activization of the crystalline basement. On the other hand, the formation of ultrametagenic charnockites from the original volcanics (products of subcrustal magmas) during the formation of the crystalline basement is completely in accord with the historical development of the Earth's crust.

Characteristically, the Southern Indian charnockites (Madras type area), which are the standard reference for this formation /128/, are analogous to ultrametagenic bifeldspar charnockites with respect to mode of occurrence, texture and composition /57/. Therefore the term "charnockite proper" should be applied to shadow bifeldspar granites with the following characteristics: a) granoblastic and metasomatic corrosion textures and relict shadow structures; b) paragenesis of alkaline feldspars with highly ferruginous pyroxenes, especially ferrohypersthenes (occasionally with eulytes), and sporadically with garnet; c) presence of secondary biotite and, less commonly, hornblende; d) occurrence within migmatized and granitized granulite facies rocks in crystalline basements of ancient platforms. Ultrametagenic charnockites are widespread in the shields and crystalline basements of the Gondwanian platforms. The largest areas of such rocks are known from the crystalline basement of the Antarctic Platform /57/. In Southern India, besides the classical Pallavaram province, charnockites are widespread in Mahabalipuram, Ootakamund, Kerala and other areas /128/, as well as on Ceylon /125/. Ultrametagenic charnockites are widespread in the Central Sahara /96/, in the southern west Nile, Uganda /99/, South Africa /113/ and, finally, in the shields and crystalline basement of the Australian Platform.

In addition to the ultrametagenic charnockite series, the subfacies under consideration includes a fairly widespread ultrametagenic granite series, formed from sedimentary-terrigenous rocks, primarily aluminous schists. The latter occur only to an insignificant extent among rocks of the pyroxene-granulite subfacies. In particular, they include perthitic shadow granites in the form of small concordant sheet bodies and shadow granites as the metasome of coarsely layered migmatites, the paleosome of which is charnockitic. Aluminous schists and closely related sedimentary-terrigenous deposits, which are oversaturated in alumina and silica, readily lend themselves to migmatization and granitization. Therefore, nongranitized rocks are practically absent among them; they are largely migmatized or transformed into shadow granites. At the same time, the aluminous sedimentary-terrigenous deposits, in the course of their regional metamorphism, become the chief source of partial melts, largely interacting with the regionally metamorphosed volcanics, producing migmatites and shadow granites of the charnockitic variety.

As in the case of the differentiation of the charnockite series into enderbites and charnockites, the ultrametagenic granite series can likewise be divided into shadow plagiogranites and the metasome of migmatites (of corresponding composition) on the one hand, and bifeldspar shadow granites and the corresponding metasome, on the other. This subdivision was pre-determined by the original composition of the sedimentary-terrigenous rocks. However, an important role in the development of shadow granites of different compositions is also played by the different stages in the granitiza-tion process, with sodium and potassium metasomatism, respectively, pre-dominating in the earlier and later stages. Shadow plagiogranites differ from bifeldspar shadow granites in their significantly lower content of potassium and higher contents of mafic components in the colored minerals. The contents of silicon, aluminum and sodium are approximately the same in both granite varieties. Plagiogranites often serve as the paleosome for shadow bifeldspar granite migmatites, suggesting the possible origin of the latter from the former after further granitization. There is an equal likelihood that they originated directly from partial melts of various com-positions. This origin of shadow granitoids would be in agreement with their interlayering in the same exposure. Characteristically, these rocks differ from shadow charnockites only in their slight oversaturation in alumina. In general, varieties of calcareous-magnesian and aluminous schists of high-grade granitization gradually become more similar to each other in composition, losing almost all signs of their original composition, and making it extremely difficult to decide on the nature of the rocks from which they were formed.

Ultrametamorphics of the granite series are represented mostly by finely layered migmatites with a gradual transition to shadow granites. The former are distinguished by a fine alternation of the paleosome and meta-some, which occur in nearly equal quantities. However, the shadow granites have retained only 10—20% of their parent rock in the form of intermittent, very fine layers or in intricately shaped schlieren. The mineral associa-tions produced by migmatization and granitization of sedimentary-terri-genous deposits (probably after previous transformation of the latter into various gneisses and schists) are distinguished by the following character-istics: a) increasing feldspathization, with replacement of plagioclase by microcline; b) gradual decrease in the basicity of plagioclase from andesine (An 35) to oligoclase (An 20); c) gradual decrease of cordierite and silli-manite and their ultimate disappearance; d) gradual increase in the total ferruginosity of garnets (the content of the almandine molecule increasing from 50—60% in migmatites to 65—70% in shadow granites) and of biotite (from 55—70% in the paleosome of migmatites to 75—90% in the schlieren of shadow granites), along with a decrease in their total contents. The ultra-metamorphic reworking of the original terrigenous deposits produces a granitization series from biotite-garnet plagiogneisses, cordierite-silli-manite and garnet-sillimanite schists to shadow garnet-biotite granites; the intermediate members of the series are represented by layered mig-matites with gradually diminishing content of paleosome. The formation of this series probably begins under granulite facies conditions, but is com-pleted in the amphibolite facies, with the appearance of hydrous minerals.

Under conditions of the hornblende-granulite subfacies, carbonate deposits produce marbles and calciphyres, as well as diopside rocks. Although they often occur within migmatites and shadow granites, they remain practically ungranitized. Calcareous sediments are recrystallized and transformed into fairly pure marbles, while the more widespread dolomitic sediments produce mostly diopside calciphyres or forsterite marbles containing spinels, humite and sparsely disseminated corundum. Diopside rocks, sometimes also spinel-bearing, develop at contacts of calciphyres with migmatites and shadow granites. The ferruginosity of all colored minerals in carbonate rocks is the lowest. Thus, the content of the fayalite component in forsterite does not usually rise above 10%, although it occasionally reaches 23% when, along with the forsterite, there is garnet consisting of 60% almandine, 25% grossular and 15% pyrope. The ferruginosity of spinel is 0—4%, rarely 15%. The diopside averages 9—15% (and rarely up to 20%) of the hedenbergite molecule. It is sometimes associated with amphibole replacing diopside, represented by a low-iron pargasite. Secondary phlogopite has a ferruginosity of 3—4%. The diopside rocks have a less complicated composition than the calciphyres. Usually, they consist entirely of diopside with a ferruginosity of 3—12%. The ferruginosity of diopside in diopside-plagioclase varieties increases to 14—33%, while the An content in the plagioclase varies from 60 to 90%. The ferruginosity of diopside remains the same in the scapolite-diopside varieties; the scapolite is represented by meionite, containing not more than 30% of the marialite molecule. The low ferruginosity of all colored minerals in calciphyres results from their exceedingly low grade of granitization. However, it is reflected in the paragenesis of forsterite (or clinohumite) and spinel which are replaced by diopside and phlogopite. In general, the rocks contain an association of the four minerals, although with a distinct superimposed development of diopside and phlogopite. Other alterations of calciphyres occur at their contact with shadow granites, migmatite metasomes, and granite veins. This consists in the development of bimetasomatic diopside, diopside-plagioclase and diopside-scapolite rocks, from both calciphyres and granitoids. Thin layers of calciphyres are often entirely replaced by diopside rocks.

In concluding the description of the characteristics of the hornblende-granulite subfacies, it should be emphasized that a great majority of quartzites, i. e., the most widespread sillimanite-garnet and garnet varieties, are formed under the metamorphic conditions of this subfacies, whereas the highest-temperature cordierite- and hypersthene-bearing quartzites are formed under conditions of the pyroxene-granulite subfacies.

The hornblende-garnet-clinopyroxene-granulite subfacies, which produces granulites, differs from the foregoing subfacies only in the higher pressure under which it was formed; the metamorphic temperatures are the same. It is manifested locally in zones with intensively developed stress. These zones are primarily related to deep-seated faults and are located in consolidated areas of the crystalline basement, since the effect of stress is the strongest on fairly rigid masses. The granulites are paratectonic rocks, originating mainly from shadow granitoids and their migmatites of the charnockitic variety. However, certain units of simple biotite-garnet compositions may have been formed from previously granitized aluminous schists interbedded with granitized calcareous-magnesian schists, producing ultrametagenic charnockites and then granulites. The latter correspond to the classical type of Saxon granulites. The stable parageneses of the hornblende-clinopyroxene-garnet-granulite subfacies are as follows: a) $plag_{35-50}$ + $clpy_{50-55}$ + gar_{75-80} + (qz +Kfs), characteristic of garnet-pyroxene-plagioclase schists; b) $plag_{20-30}$ + $clpy_{50-75}$ + gar_{75-85} + + $horn_{60-80}$ + (hyp_{50-70} +$biot_{60-80}$), characteristic of granulites; c) $plag_{20-30}$ + + Kfs + qz + gar_{70-80} + ($biot_{50-60}$ +$horn_{60-70}$), characteristic of specific shadow granites. The formation conditions of the granulites — $t = 600-800°C$ and $P = 9.9-13$ kbar — are especially characteristic of the subfacies in question.

The following two large granulite areas are the only ones yet discovered within the crystalline basement: 1) Enderby Land, on the eastern boundary of the Napier and Rayner structural zones; and 2) in the core of the syncline, which is the main structure of the Humboldt Mountains, where the granulite formation reaches a thickness of 4 km (forming almost the entire Schüssel Suite) and has been traced over dozens of kilometers along strike. In both formations, the granulites contain sheets of metabasites and beds of calciphyres and quartzites, which likewise underwent a partial granulation. The Enderby Land granulites possess the typical parageneses of the hornblende-clinopyroxene-garnet subfacies, probably superimposed on the parageneses of the hornblende-granulite subfacies. The granulites in the Humboldt Mountains possess a mineral association containing relict minerals of the granulite facies together with neogenic minerals of the amphibolite facies, and thus are typical of polymetamorphic rocks. It is difficult to determine the degree of participation of the superimposed amphibolite facies in the transformation of erstwhile ultrametagenic bifeldspar charnockites into granulites. At any rate, granulites can also be produced under conditions of the granulite facies alone. However, the superimposition of the later amphibolite facies metamorphism not only invests the granulites with specific textural features, but also produces unstable mineral associations, this being characteristic of classical granulites of the Saxon type, which, consequently, are also polymetamorphic rocks.

Granulites of the crystalline basement are typical paratectonites, combining granoblastic and granulitic textures, the latter replacing the former partially or entirely. The great majority of granulites are close to granites in composition, while their mineral parageneses are the closest to ultrametagenic charnockites, from which they mainly formed. The foremost characteristic feature of the mineral parageneses of granulites is the association of highly ferruginous clinopyroxene (ferruginosity, 50—75%) and garnet (ferruginosity, 75—85%). Aside from the predominant almandine molecule (averaging 50—60%), the garnet also has a high content of grossular (averaging 15—25%) as well as pyrope (likewise 15—25%). The content of orthopyroxene is considerably smaller than that of clinopyroxene. The former occurs sporadically, with a ferruginosity of up to 70%. Among the salic minerals (the contents of which fluctuate widely) triclinized perthitic orthoclase predominates to varying degrees over oligoclase (An 20—30). The quartz content is extremely variable (10—40%), related to the superimposition of the amphibolite facies. Biotite is the leading colored mineral (50—60%), often occurring together with hornblende.

Amphibolite facies

Rocks of the amphibolite facies occur widely in the crystalline basement, although they are less abundant than the granulite facies rocks. They form separate block mountain systems, alternating with or surrounding similar mountain systems composed of granulite facies rocks. Direct (nontectonic) contacts between rocks of these two metamorphic facies have not been observed. Rocks of the amphibolite facies were identified only comparatively recently, and have therefore been less studied than the granulite facies rocks, although they are no less complex than the latter. At this stage, the amphibolite facies may be subdivided into the sillmanite-almandine and staurolite-kyanite subfacies. The former (the highest-temperature subfacies of the amphibolite facies) was formed under medium pressure, while the latter, lower-temperature subfacies is characterized by high pressure. A great majority of the amphibolite facies regions are composed of rocks of the sillimanite-almandine subfacies. This includes the western part and "outskirts" of Queen Maud Land, certain blocks within the Humboldt Mountains and Petermann Range, Sør Rondane and Yamato Mountains, Prince Olav Coast, etc. Primary rocks of the staurolite-kyanite subfacies have been found by the authors only in the southern structural zone of the Lambert Glacier area.

Rocks of the sillimanite-almandine subfacies have been best studied in the Humboldt Mountains and Petermann Range — a formation at least 6—7 km thick, designated the Insel Series. This series is composed mainly of migmatites or biotite-amphibole and biotite plagiogneisses with subordinate shadow granites. Boudinaged ortho-amphibolites and layers of calciphyres and quartzites account for up to 5%. Nearly the same volume is occupied by layers and crosscutting veins of granitoids. A very characteristic feature is the absence of apointrusive and rheomorphic charnockitoids, in place of which occur intrusions of metagabbroids and various microcline granitoids (mainly with biotite or with biotite and amphibole). Rocks of this subfacies are dominated by products of the regional metamorphism and granitization of volcanics, probably of a more acid composition than those of the granulite facies. Sillimanite (fibrolite)-garnet plagiogneisses and schists, their migmatites and shadow granites (products of the regional metamorphism and granitization of sedimentary-terrigenous deposits) are somewhat less common.

The mineral associations of ortho-amphibolites (resistant to granitization) are the closest to the mineral parageneses of the subfacies in question. However, there are the following two characteristic extreme parageneses: a) those without microcline and quartz, i. e., $horn_{24-34}$ + $biot_{29-33}$ + $plag_{62-89}$ + + $(clpy_{18-26})$, with colored minerals of a relatively low ferruginosity; and b) those with microcline and quartz, i. e., $horn_{40-54}$ + $biot_{35-47}$ + $plag_{40-65}$ + +qz+$micr$+$(clpy_{30-36})$, of a somewhat higher ferruginosity. The paleosome of migmatites is distinguished by a still more ferruginous association of minerals — $horn_{44-68}$ + $biot_{52-62}$ + $plag_{26-33}$ + qz, while the association with the maximum ferruginosity is found in shadow granites — $horn_{69-84}$ + + $biot_{56-80}$ + $plag_{20-30}$ +$micr$ +qz +gar_{79-92}. The result is an unusual series of amphibolite facies rocks, ranging from amphibolites to biotite-amphibole shadow granites; relatively low-iron clinopyroxene is stable in the former, but is completely replaced by highly ferruginous garnet in the latter. The ferruginosities of the other colored minerals increase gradually (double, on the average) in the shadow granite in comparison to the amphibolites, and this is accompanied by a considerable decrease in the basicity of plagioclase and the appearance of significant amounts of microcline which replaces the plagioclase. In other words, there is a classical granitization series of the amphibolite facies, differing markedly from the granitization series of the granulite facies (charnockitic trend). However, both series probably originated from volcanics of similar compositions. A decisive part in the granitization of rocks under amphibolite facies conditions is played by partial melts. These develop during recrystallization when considerable quantities of aqueous solutions are liberated, resulting in the prevalence of hydrous colored minerals in the amphibolite facies parageneses. The partial melts play an equally important part in vein formation. Metamorphic strata consisting of monomineralic rocks of the amphibolite facies or of polymetamorphic formations with superimposed amphibolite facies are very rich in veins of various granitoids. For example, the monometamorphic rocks of the pyroxene-granulite facies in the Napier zone contain very rare veins, and then only of plagiogranitic composition, while the alaskitic and pegmatitic veins, characteristic of amphibolite facies products, are totally absent. Another characteristic feature of amphibolite facies strata and polymetamorphic formations is the extensive occurrence of agmatites, which are very rarely present in the granulite facies. The migmatites and shadow granites of the sillimanite-almandine subfacies, containing high-alumina minerals, are identified primarily by the composition of their garnet, which always has a high content of almandine (70—80%) and a low content of pyrope (7—15%). The garnet of analogous granulite facies rocks averages 50—60% almandine (rarely up to 70%) and 30—40% pyrope. The sillimanite is usually represented by the fibrolite variety. The biotite, although of high ferruginosity, falls short of lepidomelane, as in the granulite facies.

The metamorphic facies are most distinctly identified by the mineral associations of carbonate rocks. The granulite facies calciphyres are characterized by the mineral paragenesis of carbonates with forsterite, humite and spinel, and their bimetasomatic diopside rocks are distinguished by a low ferruginosity of clinopyroxenes (averaging 10—20%) and the presence of pargasite. Analogous amphibolite facies rocks have carbonate in paragenesis with clinopyroxenes of the salite series, in which ferruginosity does not drop below 40% (often reaching 55—60%), and they are accompanied by hornblende (ferruginosity, 50—60%) and grossular. Amphibole (of the tremolite-actinolite series) and clinozoisite, which are already minerals of the epidote-amphibolite facies, also occur. Quartzites of the amphibolite facies are of uniform composition. Besides a small admixture of almandine and biotite, they usually contain significant amounts of oligoclase. Even sillimanite is very rare in these quartzites; cordierite and hypersthene are invariably absent.

Rocks of the staurolite-kyanite subfacies can be differentiated from other subfacies of the amphibolite facies by their low-grade granitization, with a consequent prevalence of plagiogneiss, quartzite and amphibolite. This feature is due not only to the original rock composition, but also to the relatively low temperature of the subfacies. The high pressures do not favor either the formation of partial melts or the development of metasomatic granitization processes. Primary formations of this subfacies have been identified only in the southern structural zone of the Lambert Glacier area. In several other regions, mineral parageneses of this subfacies are superimposed on mineral associations of the higher-temperature sillimanite-almandine subfacies. Among the primary rocks of this subfacies, amphibolites (particularly those containing cummingtonite) are well preserved, as are thin intercalations of staurolite-garnet-biotite quartz-ites, alternating with biotite-hornblende plagiogneisses. This very unusu-al formation, about 1 km thick, is utterly devoid of migmatites and shadow granites and has very scant vein formations, but includes a body of appreci-ably gneissified biotite-microcline granites. The cummingtonite amphi-bolites are of a remarkably uniform composition, consisting of 90% cum-mingtonite of comparatively low ferruginosity (23%), and 10% biotite of high ferruginosity (40%). The quartzites contain over 90% quartz, the remaining 10% consisting of staurolite, garnet (ferruginosity, 87%) and biotite (ferru-ginosity, 50%), with an insignificant admixture of plagioclase (An 30). The plagiogneisses consist of oligoclase (An 25) and quartz, with only 15—20% hornblende (ferruginosity, 65%) and biotite (ferruginosity, 59%).

Much more widespread are mineral associations of this subfacies super-imposed on a paragenesis of the higher-temperature sillimanite-almandine subfacies. Thus, within the biotite-garnet plagiogneisses of Prince Olav Coast, one finds boudinaged intercalations of amphibolites (up to 10 m thick) containing, besides common hornblende, amphibole of the anthophyllite-gedrite or cummingtonite-grunerite series. The latter are still more common as the paleosome of migmatites from biotite-amphibolite plagio-gneisses and in melanocratic amphibole-biotite schlieren in shadow granites in the Insel Series of the Humboldt Mountains. In these cases, the total ferruginosity of cummingtonite, and especially of grunerite, is always higher than that of the coexisting hornblende and biotite. Such associations are hardly stable, especially in the presence of plagioclase and biotite. The association becomes completely stable with the disappearance of common hornblende, but it is superimposed by the still lower-temperature, high-pressure association of kyanite and staurolite with muscovite. The appearance of amphiboles of the cummingtonite-grunerite series is apparent-ly due to the specific conditions of the ferromagnesian metasomatism related to migmatization and granitization of the containing rocks. Conse-quently, the parageneses under consideration occur in dark layers of melanocratic plagiogneisses and still more often as relics in shadow granites. Even more characteristic, however, is the superimposition (in regional metamorphism) of the staurolite-kyanite subfacies on high-alumina schists and plagiogneisses formed under conditions of the sillimanite-almandine subfacies. This is distinct in certain zones of Prince Olav Coast and on the flanks of the Penck Trough on Queen Maud Land. In this case, the rocks contain two coexisting mineral associations: 1) the early association of biotite with sillimanite, cordierite or garnet; and 2) the later association of fibrolite, kyanite, staurolite and muscovite. The early association is gradually but completely replaced by the later.

Polymetamorphic formations

Polymetamorphic rocks are widespread in the crystalline basement of the Antarctic Platform, occurring in the so-called mobile regions. In contrast to Enderby Land, which is a classical example of a stable region (shield), Queen Maud Land (especially its central part — the Humboldt Mountains and Petermann Range) is an equally classical example of a mobile region composed of polymetamorphic rocks. Characteristically, there are large blocks of monometamorphic rocks of the amphibolite facies on the fringes of the mobile regions. The polymetamorphic rocks were formed from rocks of the oldest granulite facies, on which a later stage of regional metamorphism of the amphibolite facies was superimposed. This is perceived fairly distinctly from the presence of mineral associations of both facies, the majority of which are unstable. An important impediment to the identification of polymetamorphic rocks is the fact that granitization of any rocks under granulite facies conditions is completed under the conditions of the high-grade amphibolite facies. Therefore, when a new stage of amphibolite facies metamorphism with accompanying granitization is superimposed, it is difficult to differentiate between the mineral associations of the primary and superimposed processes. Thus a polymetamorphic origin is best determined in rocks that are resistant to granitization, on the basis of unstable mineral associations, e. g., in marbles and calciphyres. Nevertheless, the chemical composition of minerals of polymetamorphic rocks is usually transitional between that of minerals in separately existing monometamorphic rocks of the granulite and amphibolite facies, which is also helpful in the identification of polymetamorphic formations.

Before we embark on a description of the mineral associations that are the principal criterion for the identification of polymetamorphic rocks, the following characteristic features (in comparison to monometamorphic rocks of any metamorphic facies) should be noted: a) polymetamorphic formations are highly veined, the veins being mainly the products of the crystallization of partial melts in fissures (later stage of metamorphism); b) the extensive occurrence of agmatites, usually with layered migmatites and shadow granitoids (earlier stage of metamorphism represented by the paleosome); c) superimposition of the highest-temperature subfacies of the amphibolite facies on the lowest-temperature subfacies of the granulite facies, i. e., superimposition of the sillimanite-almandine subfacies on the hornblende-granulite subfacies; d) extensive occurrence of superimposed metasomatic recrystallization (in the solid state) of early metamorphic formations and interactions with partial melts, especially during the formation of polymetamorphic shadow granitoids; e) diversity of textures due to a combination of primary homeoblastic and secondary heteroblastic forms, produced during the recrystallization and superimposition of corrosion-metasomatic elements on granulite facies rocks (under amphibolite facies conditions).

The mineral associations of polymetamorphic rocks formed from volcanics are characterized by a combination of two parageneses; 1) the early paragenesis of orthopyroxene and clinopyroxene with basic (partially intermediate) plagioclase; and 2) the late paragenesis of hornblende with garnet and biotite and intermediate (partially acid) plagioclase. Significant amounts of K-feldspar and quartz appear in migmatized and granitized rocks, but it is impossible to determine the metamorphic facies to which these minerals belong. Moreover, quartz probably was present in both parageneses even before the onset of granitization. Facies differentiation of the mineral parageneses of polymetamorphic rocks formed from aluminous sedimentary-terrigenous deposits appears impossible, since almost identical mineral associations are characteristic of both metamorphic facies (and especially of their boundary subfacies). However, the composition of garnet is different in the granulite and amphibolite facies, especially with respect to the pyrope-almandine ratio — garnets of polymetamorphic rocks occupy an intermediate position.

Orthopyroxenes, which are typical of the granulite facies, remain as relict minerals in polymetamorphic rocks, but they acquire the following characteristic features: a) their ferruginosity, as a rule not below 40% in the paleosome of migmatites, rises to 70% in ultrametagenic charnockites; b) they are gradually replaced by biotite (in a highly alkaline environment) or garnet (in the presence of low alkalinity) due to the interactions of the pyroxene with plagioclase, and hence their forms are skeletal; c) they are completely replaced by biotite and/or garnet when the ferruginosity exceeds 70%; d) a moderate content of aluminum (within 1—4%), whereas high-alumina hypersthenes (Al_2O_3 content in the rocks, 9—12%) are produced only under granulite facies conditions (e. g., during bimetasomatism); e) a high calcium content in comparison to granulite facies pyroxenes.

Clinopyroxenes are represented by two mineral groups, salitic and augitic. Salitic pyroxenes are equally present in carbonate rocks of both the granulite and amphibolite facies, whereas the augitic series is characteristic only of the granulite facies. The ferruginosity of diopsides in granulite facies calciphyres is 5—15%, sometimes reaching 20—25% in diopsidic rocks; it is 40—50%, occasionally reaching 60%, in the amphibolite facies. Calciphyres of polymetamorphic genesis fairly often contain two generations of clinopyroxenes, with ferruginosities (in the same specimen) of 13—20% and 37—46%; the first-generation clinopyroxene is unstable and is replaced by that of the second generation. A characteristic feature of the augites of polymetamorphic rocks is their high ferruginosity (not below 32—37% in the paleosome of migmatites and up to 60—75% in shadow granites of the charnockitic series); hypersthenes follow the same trend. When ferruginosities of both pyroxenes are similar, they both become unstable and are replaced by biotite and/or garnet. A comparison of the chemical composition of the augites of these polymetamorphic rocks with that of augites from metamorphic rocks in other regions indicates that the former occupy an intermediate position between the clinopyroxenes of bipyroxene schists and amphibolites, with respect to the contents of the majority of elements.

Hornblende is present in rocks of all metamorphic facies, and it is therefore rather difficult to establish its characteristic features for polymetamorphic rocks.   However, an analysis of the composition of common hornblende in granulites of the Humboldt Mountains, which are undoubtedly polymetamorphic rocks, reveals several characteristics distinguishing it from
other hornblende, including common hornblende of the amphibolite facies.
These characteristics include a maximum ferruginosity (up to 80%), high
contents of titanium (4—5%) and alkalis (3.5—4.5%), and low contents of
calcium and silica (3—4% each).   Thus, hornblende associated with pyroxenes
in polymetamorphic rocks is clearly distinctive only in varities of
high-grade granitization.   Assuming hornblende to be equally widespread in
rocks of the granulite and amphibolite facies (considering, of course, the
different compositions), in the polymetamorphic rocks it occupies an intermediate position in regard to its chemical composition.

Garnets react rather sensitively to their conditions of formation.   The
reaction manifests itself primarily in the pyrope-almandine ratio, which
gradually decreases from the granulite to the amphibolite facies.   This
clearly involves an increase in the total ferruginosity of the mineral.
Garnets of any polymetamorphic rocks occupy an intermediate position —
those in the paleosome of polymetamorphic rocks are closer to granulite
facies garnets (average ferruginosity, 65—70%), while those of shadow charnockites (average ferruginosity, 75—80%) are closer to the amphibolite
facies garnets (ferruginosity, 80—90%).

On the whole, polymetamorphic rocks exhibit a higher grade of granitization than do granulite facies rocks, and a greater variety of types of
migmatites than do the amphibolite facies rocks.   The mineral parageneses
of both metamorphic facies become increasingly similar, especially in the
polymetamorphic shadow granitoids.   This similarity is manifest mainly
in an increased ferruginosity of coexisting minerals, but only to a certain
limit, beyond which the granulite facies minerals become unstable and are
completely replaced by amphibolite facies minerals of maximum
ferruginosity.   Therefore, polymetamorphic rocks are easiest to recognize
when they do not lend themselves to granitization and when they contain
coexisting nonequilibrium associations of minerals of the two facies of
metamorphism.   The emphasis given by the authors to the study of
polymetamorphic rocks is due to their importance both in deciphering the
metamorphic processes which produced the crystalline basement of the Antarctic Platform and in reconstructing the geological history of the formation
of the crystalline basement.   Polymetamorphic rocks give vivid evidence
of the drastic tectonic and metamorphic rearrangement of the oldest,
mobile crystalline basement regions.   There were protrusions of the foundation on which the later basement tier was formed, while the oldest mobile
regions assumed the position of median masses.   The stable regions have
preserved, in the form of shields, the oldest formations of the lower structural tier of the crystalline basement, belonging to granulite facies
formations.

Apointrusive and rheomorphic charnockitoids

Massive, most commonly porphyroblastic charnockitoids of an intrusive nature (often inherited) may likewise be classified, in the majority of cases, as a special formation of polymetamorphic rocks. They underwent several formative stages, from the original magmatic stage (formation of basic and possibly also intermediate rocks) to the final ultrametamorphic stage (formation of the charnockitoid series). As a rule, their genesis was the outcome of the combined effects of magmatic and metamorphic processes, similar to the formation of many other rocks in the crystalline basement of the Antarctic Platform. The only distinctive feature is that the so-called charnockitoid intrusions are exclusively confined to the crystalline basement (more precisely, its lower structural tier) and were usually formed under the same conditions as polymetamorphic rocks. They therefore are constituents of the crystalline basement itself. Many aspects of the genesis of massive charnockitoids remain to be clarified, but a painstaking analysis of their composition, mode of occurrence and relationships with the containing metamorphic rocks clearly indicates their unusual conditions of formation (differing from those of the magmatic and regionally metamorphic rocks.

Massive charnockitoids form independent rock bodies measuring a few tens to several hundreds of square kilometers. There are a few areas of several thousand square kilometers, but these may prove to be composed of several bodies lying close to one another, since they are large blocks divided by mountain glaciers. Significantly, gabbroid intrusions are absent from regions with charnockitoid massifs. The intrusions are intensively metamorphosed and occur only in strata of the upper tier of the amphibolite facies. The charnockitoid massifs should be divided into at least two types with respect to composition: type I (predominant) — a wide range of rocks, from feldspathized gabbroids to 'giant-grained' porphyroblastic granosyenites (rarely granites); and type II — a narrower range of rocks, from feldspathized gabbroids to diorite-syenites (rarely syenites) of comparatively small dimensions. Although different massifs vary in the range of rocks, the rock textures and compositions are identical in all crystalline basement massifs. It should be emphasized that the charnockitoid varieties have no textural and, especially, compositional equivalents among normal magmatic rocks. Furthermore, their varied designations are largely artificial, since they are often compound terms made up of the designations of two bordering intrusive rocks to which they are closest in composition. All charnockitoid varieties within a single massif are spatially related and form gradual transitions to one another, though in a definite sequence, from feldspathized gabbroids and dioritic rocks to diorite-syenites and sometimes syenites, porphyroblastic granosyenites and, rarely, granites. Only the terminal varieties of the series locally form (especially in the largest massifs) large accumulations of homogeneous composition, e. g., the porphyroblastic granosyenites forming isolated massifs, measuring tens and hundreds of square kilometers. However, in similarity to other charnockitoid varieties, these too do not form distinct contacts, but exhibit gradual transitions to the bordering varieties. The result is a complex typical of a granitization series developed from basic rocks toward a subalkaline trend. However, typical alkaline syenites are the ultimate product of the series in many cases.

All charnockitoid varieties (irrespective of composition) display the same range of minerals, although in different quantitative ratios. However, the composition of every colored mineral, and in the first place its ferruginosity, and the basicity of plagioclase vary in relation to the rock composition, thereby also producing a granitization series of minerals. Orthopyroxene, the principal typomorphic mineral of the charnockitoids, varies in composition from hypersthene (ferruginosity, 40—50%) in feldspathized gabbroids to ferrosilite (ferruginosity, 80—90%) in granosyenites. Its ferruginosity is intermediate in rocks of intermediate composition. At the same time, there is a corresponding variation in the content of this mineral, from 20—30% in gabbroids to 2—3% in granosyenites. Clinopyroxenes show a similar behavior, their ferruginosity varying from 37—40% in gabbroids to 90—95% in granosyenites, which is usually 7—10% below that of orthopyroxenes. The ferruginosities of both pyroxenes are the same only in highly ferruginous varieties. In the case of clinopyroxene the ferruginosity reaches higher values since orthopyroxene becomes unstable at ferruginosities above 85—90% and is replaced by fayalite. Plagioclases likewise undergo changes, their basicity and content decreasing in parallel with increasing ferruginosity of the pyroxenes. Thus, feldspathized gabbroids contain 50—70% labradorite (An 50—60), diorite-syenites contain 25—40% andesine (An 30—40), and granosyenites contain 10—20% oligoclase (An 25—30). Oligoclase in charnockitoids is never more acid than An 20. Fayalite is characteristic only of massive charnockitoids, occurring mainly in granosyemites and syenites, where orthopyroxenes reach their maximum ferruginosity and become unstable, Characteristically, the ferruginosity of fayalite is never below 87%, often rising to 95—100%. The absence of fayalite from the host shadow granitoids (with the charnockite association of minerals) is thus explained, since the latter's ferruginosity (including orthopyroxene) is always 10—15% lower than that in the massive charnockites. K-feldspar, together with quartz, is the most typical salic mineral of charnockitoids. Contents of K-feldspar vary from 2—5% in metagabbroids to 50—60% in granosyenites (the content of quartz does not rise above 20—25%). In the granosyenites, K-feldspar forms porphyroblasts measuring 2—5 cm and containing 5—30% perthite ingrowths. It is mainly represented by slightly triclinic orthoclase, but intermediate or even high microcline occurs in granosyenites. Its formation temperature was determined by Barth's method as 600—610°C, indicative either of crystallization from a partial melt or of formation by metasomatic recrystallization under the influence of alkaline solutions on the basic parent rock. Hornblende and biotite are the most widespread colored minerals, and predominate in the more acid charnockitoids. Their ferruginosities vary from 50—60% in metagabbroids to 95—100% in syenites and granosyenites, being always somewhat higher than the ferruginosity of the pyroxenes they replaced. Therefore the prevailing varieties of amphiboles in charnockitoids are close to ferrohastingsite, while the biotites are close to lepidomelane. They are coarser-grained than the pyroxene relics (often skeletal) embedded among them. The secondary nature of these minerals relative to the pyroxenes is beyond doubt and they probably formed simultaneously with the crystallization of K-feldspar, which intensively replaces the plagioclase.

The chemical properties of charnockitoids permit several conclusions concerning their origin. The very insignificant variation in the contents of sodium and aluminum in the different varieties indicates the inert behavior of these elements during the formation of charnockitoids. The content of potassium varies markedly, increasing seven-to-eight fold in the ultimate varieties of these series (syenites and granosyenites) in comparison to the initial varieties (feldspathized gabbroids). This points to a very mobile behavior of potassium, which is characteristic of meta-somatic processes arising from the interaction between gabbroids and a partial melt. An indirect indication of the basic composition of parent rocks is provided by the excessively high titanium content of the charnocki-toids which, even in syenites and granosyenites, does not fall below its con-tent in the average magmatic gabbros.

In concluding this description of the characteristic features of massive charnockitoids, it should be emphasized that no visible contact effects were observed either on the host migmatized and granitized schists or on the included calciphyres and quartzites. Furthermore, the mineral associations of host polymetamorphic rocks are somewhat similar to those of the massive charnockitoids. However, the colored minerals in the host rocks exhibit a somewhat low ferruginosity, even if these are close to charnockites in composition (fayalite is absent). Another feature is the lack of garnet in massive charnockitoids in contrast to the situation in the migmatite and shadow granite host rocks where this mineral is widespread. In the authors' opinion, these features are interrelated and are due to a very high environ-mental alkalinity during the formation of the massive charnockitoids. Thus their colored minerals have maximum ferruginosities, fayalite appears, and biotite (close to lepidomelane) takes the place of garnet. This biotite is the only colored mineral in a majority of porphyroblastic granosyenites. A relatively low environmental alkalinity during the formation of the host polymetamorphic rocks had the opposite effect: garnet is widespread and biotite subordinate; the ferruginosities of the colored minerals are, as a rule, 10—20% lower than those in the massive charnockites; ferrohyper-sthene and even eulyte are never replaced by fayalite.

The data on massive charnockitoids make possible an approach to the problem of their genesis. Although the possibility of a magmatic genesis of charnockitoids by differentiation at depth or in situ is discarded, it should be noted that normal magmatic charnockites may occur in the crystalline basement of the Antarctic Platform. Such massifs would contain rocks of fairly uniform composition, colored minerals of low ferruginosity (in com-parison to the rheomorphic and metasomatic charnockites) and magmatic textures.

The formation of charnockitoid massifs described herein is related to the Early Proterozoic stage of tectonic-ultrametamorphic activization of the crystalline basement. This tectonism was first manifested in a rearrange-ment of the structures of the previously rigid Upper Archean crystalline basement. Consequently, the rocks were subjected to intensive fracturing and recrystallization in the solid state and were extensively converted to fairly plastic masses, including the fusion of components with low melting points. This resulted in favorable conditions for an extensive development of ultrametamorphic processes, including the formation of partial melts and their interaction with the tectonically prepared oldest magmatic rocks of the crystalline basement, the mobilization of the plastic masses and their slow intrusion over relatively short distances, and the formation of anatectic melts capable of active intrusion over considerable distances into overlying horizons of the Earth's crust. These processes produced a variety of ultrametamorphic rocks: a) a series of granite veins, related agmatites and other repeatedly migmatized beds; b) sheets of shadow granitoids of polymetamorphic origin, combining the mineral parageneses of the primary granulite and superimposed amphibolite facies; c) charnockitoid massifs of rheomorphic and metasomatic genesis and rarely of magmatic genesis; d) small bodies of magmatic granitoids, crystallization products of a partial melt altered by interaction with the host rocks. Metasomatic processes related to alkaline solutions (abundantly produced by the interaction of melts with hydrous host rocks and remaining for a protracted period in the mobile state) were superimposed on all the newly formed rock bodies.

The genesis of charnockitoid massifs was complex and apparently proceeded in the following three ways: I. Metasomatic recrystallization of tectonically prepared gabbroid intrusions, interacting with partial melts and highly alkaline solutions. In spite of the high grade of reworking of the original rocks, numerous relicts are preserved. These are enriched in K-feldspar and thereby transformed into dioritic and syenitic rocks, in which the ferruginosity of pyroxenes gradually increases, fayalite appears and the secondary minerals (hornblende and biotite) gradually replace the primary minerals. The result is a typical nonequilibrium mineral association, which is characteristic of the polymetamorphic rocks. From this standpoint, such charnockitoid massifs are actually apogabbroid rocks which inherited the mode of occurrence of the gabbroids. II. Formation of rheomorphic intrusions of charnockitoids distinguished by a significant prevalence of prophyroblastic charnockites proper (granosyenites) over all other varieties. The genesis of these intrusions is very complex, combining: a) recrystallization of gabbroids and their mixing with melts, b) conversion to a plastic state of the gabbroids' host rocks and, probably, of the deepest portions of the gabbroid intrusions themselves, c) partial fusion of the low-melting host rocks, d) mobilization of the parent rocks mixed with the melts and their intrusion. The considerable quantity of melts formed in the course of such complex processes combines with an equal or greater quantity of the solid original rock, including relicts of gabbroids, skialiths of basic rocks, refractory minerals (mainly pyroxenes), etc. The interaction of melts with solid components during rather limited movement leads to a modification of the composition of both components. Further alterations are induced by alkaline metasomatism. The essence of the interaction is the development of an anomalous (as compared to a normal intrusive series) rock series, the charnockitoids. These anomalous rocks — feldspathized gabbroids (approaching monzonites), diorite-syenites, syenites and granosyenites — form gradual transitions to one another and alternate irregularly within the same massif. The anomalous composition of these rocks is characterized by the coexistence of granitic salic minerals (orthoclase, acid plagioclase and quartz) with gabbroic mafic minerals (pyroxenes and olivine). The latter exhibit a considerable increase in ferruginosity. Thus olivine in rheomorphic charnockites is represented by fayalite, orthopyroxene by eulyte, clinopyroxene by hedenbergite, amphibole by ferrohastingsite, and biotite by lepidomelane. Rheomorphic charnockitoids are also polymetamorphic rocks, since the cooling of partial melts and rheomorphic masses liberates water, which, at falling temperatures, results in the appearance of mineral associations of the amphibolite facies which are superimposed on the granulite facies. III. Formation of magmatic intrusions which are apparently products of anatectic melts, the crystalliza- tion of which starts at considerable depths, producing high-temperature mineral associations (plagioclase, pyroxenes and orthoclase of an early generation), and ends at medium depths with the formation of a medium- temperature association (orthoclase-quartz-amphibole-biotite). Unlike the situation in the rheomorphic intrusions, the mafic minerals of magmatic charnockites have a moderate ferruginosity, averaging 50—60%. Such magmatic charnockites are typical platform intrusions and are therefore confined to stable regions of the crystalline basement, whereas the meta- somatic and rheomorphic charnockitoid massifs are located in the mobile regions.

Since the term charnockite proper is used for ultrametagenic rocks of the shadow granitoid type, it may be useful to designate their intrusive analogs. This is based on their composition and on their typomorphic colored minerals (e. g., eulyte granosyenites, ferrohypersthene syenite- diorite, etc.). However, it is desirable to reserve the designation "charnockite (or charnockitoid) formation" for the unusual rock series under consideration in order to emphasize its distinctive nature, differing from that of other intrusive series of magmatic origin.

Greenschist facies

Primary rocks of the greenschist facies are presently limited to the quartzite-jaspilite formation (3 km thick) occurring in the southern part of the Lambert Glacier. This was probably formed in a comparatively narrow downwarp in the crystalline basement. The formation is only tentatively included in the crystalline basement; however, its pre-Riphean age, based on analogy with similar formations in other Gondwanian plat- forms /31, 87/, leads one to presume a basement origin, since Riphean deposits form the upper part of the platform /59/. In this respect, it should be noted that this formation is uniformly regionally metamorphosed and crumpled into complex isoclinal and simpler linear folds. The original rocks were terrigenous and chemogenic sediments, apparently without volcanics. Regional metamorphism under greenschist facies condi- tions produced schists of two subfacies: biotite-chlorite schists — biot + chl + gar (spessartite) + magn + qz ± ep ± alb; sericite-chlorite schists — chl + ser + qz + calc + ep ± hem. Also included are chlorite-sericite quartzites, marmorized limestones and jaspilites with a visible thickness exceeding 70 m.

Secondary rocks of the greenschist facies include diaphthorites related to faults, resulting in narrow zones (from tens and hundreds of meters to a few kilometers) of schists formed from various crystalline basement rocks, including massive charnockitoids. The most widespread diaphthorites are actinolite and epidote-actinolite schists; epidote-chlorite and chlorite-sericite schists are somewhat less widespread. Relatively rare varieties include biotite-actinolite schists and also phlogopite-tremolite schists formed from calciphyres. In places, the diaphthoritic schists have preserved a very small amount of relict minerals, including hypersthene, pyrope-almandine garnet, hornblende, kyanite and even incompletely albitized labradorite. However, a great majority of the diaphthoritic schists are represented by completely recrystallized rocks with an equilibrium mineral association of the greenschist facies. The mineral associations of diaphthorites are controlled by the paragenesis of actinolite with epidote, chlorite, albite and quartz, and, less commonly, with biotite and sericite. The ferruginosity of colored minerals of the diaphthorites is significantly lower than that of minerals in the parent rocks. Diaphthoresis is often accompanied by a superimposed silicification of the schists, and the appearance of minute calcite veinlets, and occasionally, aplite veinlets.

The chemical modifications of diaphthoritic rocks are minor and nonuniform, depending on the composition of the parent rocks. Some redistribution of elements takes place: basic schists and their derivatives are somewhat enriched in alkalis and silica and slightly depleted in magnesian-calcic components; however, aluminous schists and their derivatives are enriched in ferromagnesian components and depleted in alkalis and silica. Diaphthoresis could only take place at depths required for recrystallization of rocks and the formation of the new mineral association without participation of any external factors, such as contact metamorphism. They are considered to be of Precambrian age, formed largely during the Baikal folding, when the rigid crystalline basement underwent block rearrangement. The latter resulted in a rejuvenation of absolute dates of the basement rocks. Faulting certainly continued in the Phanerozoic, but, as a rule, the faults produced zones of cataclasis and mylonites without recrystallization.

PROFILE OF THE EARTH'S CRUST
IN THE CRYSTALLINE BASEMENT

A profile of the Earth's crust in the mobile region of the crystalline basement was based on the results of deep seismic soundings in the region of Novolazarevskaya Station, located 100 km north of the Humboldt Mountains. It was constructed from 16 deep seismic soundings over a sublatitudinal linear profile (azimuth, 102°) 425 km long. They were carried out for the first time in Antarctica by the Geological-Geophysical Division of the 14th Soviet Antarctic Expedition led by D. S. Solov'ev and A. L. Kogan. The profile for the examined regions was prepared by Kogan (Figure 68). The results of seismic sounding permit the determination of the crustal thickness, the degree of stratification, the mode of occurrence of seismic boundaries, and the position of deep-seated fault zones in the investigated region.

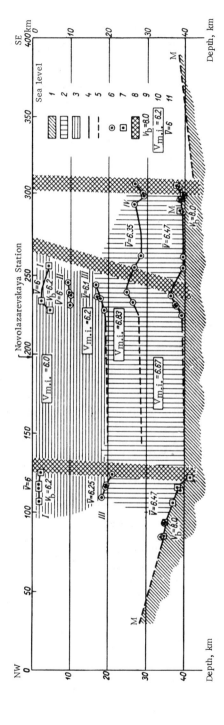

FIGURE 68. Profile of Earth's crust for the Antarctic Platform crystalline basement (Queen Maud Land), prepared by A. L. Kogan, 1970:

1) mantle; 2) granulite-basite layer; 3) charnockite layer; 4) seismic boundaries; 5) interpolation of seismic boundaries from gravimetric data; 6) depth, from reflected waves; 7) depth, from refracted waves; 8) fault zones; 9) boundary velocities, km/sec; 10) mean-interval velocities, km/sec; 11) mean velocities from the surface, km/sec.

The Earth's crust within the profile consists of several large blocks, averaging 100 km. Its thickness is 40 km in the central blocks and 2—4 km less in fault zones. Four intracrustal boundaries were traced, the principal ones lying at depths of 17—20 km, representing an interface between the two principal layers. The upper layer is characterized by elastic wave velocities of 6.0—6.2 km/sec. It averages 20 km in thickness. The density of its constituent rocks is 2.90—2.95 g/cm^3. The lower layer is characterized by markedly higher layer velocities (6.67—6.83 km/sec) and the density of its constituent rocks is 2.04—3.07 g/cm^3. The mantle lies at depths of 37—40 km and has a density of at least 3.3 g/cm^3. The Moho has a boundary velocity of 7.9—8.0 km/sec. It is uplifted at angles of up to 11° in fault regions physically represented by fracture zones without magmatic injections; it is near horizontal in other parts of the central block. Other fault zones are filled with intrusive bodies of basic composition penetrating into the crust. The width of the fault zones is fairly constant (10—20 km).

The profile of the Antarctic Platform crystalline basement (Figure 68) is very similar to the crust profiles of the Baltic Shield /36/, which are also some 40 km thick. Two features of the crystalline basement of the Antarctic Platform are important: the velocity of elastic waves in the lower layer is somewhat lower than that in the standard basaltic layer, while their velocity in the upper layer is higher than that in the standard granitic layer (5.5 to 6 km/sec). This suggests that the upper layer of the Earth's crust in the region of the Novolazarevskaya Station is composed of charnockitic rocks and their migmatites, and therefore, the layer should be termed "charnockitic." It is of interest to note that its thickness coincides with that of the metamorphic strata of the crystalline basement assumed by the present authors. Thus the upper layer may be regarded as the crystalline basement proper. The lower layer is closer to metabasite and bipyroxene schist than to standard basalts, with respect to density and velocity of elastic waves, and should preferably be termed granulite-basite layer, reflecting the metamorphism of basic rocks under granulite facies conditions. The true granitic layer (together with strata of sedimentary origin) probably occurs as the uppermost layer in erstwhile geosynclines. These were subsequently transformed into the folded mountain regions, where the Earth's crust is up to 60 km thick, as has been established, for instance, for the Pamir-Altai fold zone /36/. There are indirect data indicating that the Earth's crustal thickness in the Transantarctic Mountains region likewise reaches 55 km /85/, and its upper layer is probably granitic.

An excellent confirmation of the block structure of the mountain systems in the Antarctic Platform crystalline basement is provided by long-lived deep-seated faults penetrating to the mantle, as distinctly revealed by deep seismic sounding. Characteristically, many faults are typical diaphthoresis zones, while others served as the paths for intrusion of magmatic masses. An interesting datum is the size of blocks between the faults, established from seismic soundings, which varies between 50 and 150 km. Similar dimensions of blocks are usually established by geological mapping of exposed areas. This constancy of block dimensions for the majority of crystalline basement regions suggests a strictly defined fault system. The cause for this consistency remains to be revealed by future investigators.

ABSOLUTE DATING OF CRYSTALLINE
BASEMENT ROCKS

At present, over 300 absolute dates have been obtained for rocks of the
crystalline basement of the Antarctic Platform; over 200 of these datings
were performed in the USSR. The great majority of determinations were by
the K-Ar whole rock method. Only a few dozens mineral age-determinations
by the K-Ar method were made (mainly on mica). Lead and strontium
methods were also applied. Since several dozen papers and summarizing
reviews have been published on the absolute dating of rocks in Antarctica
/38/, there is no need to provide tables of results. This discussion is
therefore limited to a differentiation of age groups.

A description of the age groups should be preceded by several remarks
concerning the reliability of different dating methods, and an elucidation of
certain general consistencies, in this respect, for Antarctica. The reli-
abilities of the methods for absolute dating of rocks may be evaluated in the
following manner: a) the most reliable data are obtained with variations
of the lead method, by which losses of radioactive elements are less probable and there is a possibility of control using four variants in the computation of different isotope ratios (unfortunately, less than ten such determinations are available for the crystalline basement rocks); b) the strontium
method in its isochronous variations (for whole rocks) is close to the lead
method in accuracy, but as yet it has not been applied to Antarctic rocks;
c) the strontium method on micas yields results that are not much more
accurate than those obtained with the argon method on the same minerals;
d) the argon method yields the most reliable values for amphiboles and
pyroxenes. Determinations on whole rocks, especially acid ones, usually
yield absolute datings that are 15–30% low.

The following factors must be borne in mind when interpreting the absolute dates for crystalline basement rocks: a) all radioactive dating
methods yield true formation time only for those rocks (or minerals) which
have not undergone metamorphism throughout the period of their existence;
b) metamorphic processes (primary and superimposed) alter the ratios of
primary radioactive elements and their decay products, and consequently
absolute dates for metamorphic rocks show the time of their last alteration;
c) besides metamorphism proper, loss of decay products of radioactive
elements is also caused by the so-called "cryptometamorphic" phenomena,
including dynamic stress, heating of rocks, and hydrochemical influences;
furthermore, these phenomena may have no effect on the texture and composition of rocks and minerals and therefore will not be detected by petrographic analysis. Such cryptometamorphism includes phenomena related
to block tectonics, when individual large rock blocks ascend from depths
while others descend, leading to a loss of radioactive elements and therefore
to low absolute dates.

At present, it is possible to distinguish six age groups of varying reli-
abilities and occurrence. The first group (1,800–2,000 million years) has
been established from isolated determinations by the argon method on
metabasites from the Vestfold Oasis and one determination by the lead
method /3/ on a chevkinite from Enderby Land. Such dates are very rare –

confined to about 1% of the total determinations for crystalline basement rocks. However, these dates cannot be regarded as representative for the oldest rocks in the crystalline basement, which were classified by the authors as Upper Archean (from geological data), The dates obtained probably reflect the time of intrusion of the fairly widespread metabasite dikes into the rigid crystalline basement. The second group (1,500—1,560 million years) was determined by all methods (from isolated measurements on Adélie Land, in the Vestfold Oasis and on Enderby Land) for different rocks (including also a radioactive mineral). These dates are as rare as those for the first group and it is impossible to relate them to any geological events in the crystalline basement; it may only be assumed that the radioactive minerals were formed by a vein series developed within the rigid crystalline basement. The third group (1,000—1,300 million years) extends over a broad range of time and is established from more than twenty determinations by all methods (mainly by the argon whole rock method). It includes rocks in the Bunger and Grearson oases, other small crystalline basement exposures, and the Transantarctic Mountains, the foundations of which are regarded by the authors as Riphean fold structures. This age group lies close to the Proterozoic-Riphean boundary and may be related to an activation stage of the crystalline basement. The fourth (820—900 million years) and fifth groups (600—800 million years) were also established from many determinations, almost entirely by the argon whole rock method. These groups are probably the least reliable, although they are considered as representative of rocks less than 1,000 million years in age. It is not yet possible to relate these absolute dates to any definite geological event. The sixth group (440—570 million years), the most widespread in the crystalline basement rocks, has been established by all the methods, in over 200 determinations (mainly by the argon whole rock method).

Rocks of this age occur in many regions of the crystalline basement but are especially widespread in Queen Maud Land, the block mountain systems of which stretch (intermittently) latitudinally over nearly 2,500 km. These absolute dates coincide with the Late Baikal (Ross) tectonic-magmatic cycle, which formed the fold mountain systems of the Transantarctic Mountains. It appears that the rigid crystalline basement reacted to the tectonic movements, which formed the great majority of fold systems in Antarctica, by folding and a shifting of blocks along faults. The extensive block tectonics is a characteristic feature of the block mountains of Antarctica. Phenomena related to block tectonics, probably of a cryptometamorphic nature, caused a significant rejuvenation of the crystalline basement rocks. It should be emphasized that rocks of the sixth group are widespread on Gondwanian continents, but are comparatively rare on continents of the northern hemisphere.

The currently available absolute dates for rocks of the crystalline basement contribute little to the interpretation of its geological history. They relate to secondary phenomena superimposed during the Middle and Upper Proterozoic (Riphean), i. e., in the later epochs of the existence of the crystalline basement as a rigid craton. However, absolute dating of rocks is an important tool which should not be neglected in investigations of the geological history of the crystalline basement. Dating by the argon method

for whole rocks should be discarded in the future, and replaced by the isochronous variety of the strontium method.   The number of datings by the lead
method should be increased by a factor of several tens.   On the other hand,
more thorough studies should be made of the geological history of the
formation of the crystalline basement.   It will then be possible to discover
older rocks marking the major stages in the formation of the rigid basement and, moreover, thus making possible a reliable geological interpretation of phenomena which came about in younger epochs.

MINERAL RESOURCES

No special studies were made of the mineral resources of the crystalline
basement.   Ore manifestations were noted incidentally along with the geological
studies.   However, only a few territories (amounting to some 2% of the more
or less exposed areas) were investigated on medium and large scales.   It is
thus natural that very few such manifestations were discovered.   Therefore, their
scarcity by no means proves a lack of mineral resources, especially in view
of the abundance of mineral resources in crystalline basements of other
Gondwanian platforms.

Within the crystalline basement of the Antarctic Platform, there are
considerable iron-ore manifestations and indications of deposits of phlogopite,
muscovite, graphite, rock crystal and topaz, as well as insignificant (as yet)
mineralization of molybdenum and rare and trace elements (tantalum,
niobium, cerium, lanthanum, etc.), related to young platform intrusions
(among them nepheline syenites).

Three types of iron ores were noted: a) magnetite schists of metamorphic
genesis; b) metasomatic ores related to contact processes and bimetasomatism; and c) deposits of jaspilites, which are the most important type.
The last-mentioned ores are known in the upper reaches of the Lambert
Glacier (southern part of the Prince Charles Mountain) within schists
of the greenschist facies.   Jaspilite beds on Mount Ruker have a
visible thickness of at least 70 m.   The jaspilites are finely banded rocks
composed of alternating quartz-magnetite and magnetite-quartz intercalations, 0.1—2 cm thick, with a subordinate amount of magnetite-carbonate
layers.   The total iron content is 47.7%.   The jaspilites contain admixtures
of copper, chromium, nickel, cobalt, gallium and zirconium.   Unfortunately,
we were only able to spend a few hours at the jaspilite exposures.   However, on the basis of areal observations, their strike could be traced over
a distance of more than 100 km.   Their economic value is beyond doubt,
particularly since the known deposit is probably not the only one in
existence.   Magnetite mineralization located in aluminous schists is widespread on Enderby Land in the Condon Series, near its boundary with the
underlying — metavolcanitic — Raggatt Series.   The zone of mineralization
stretches over nearly 150 km.   The magnetite content in the rocks is
25—30%, and this is doubled in rocks that are saturated with fine monomineralic magnetite veinlets.   The mineralization zone has not been
investigated in any detail, although the magnetite accumulation appears to be

very promising. Bimetasomatic garnet-magnetite lodes have been found in the central part of Queen Maud Land (Hedden-Berg, etc.) and at various points on Enderby Land. They are 0.5—2.0 m thick and are traceable over tens of meters along strike. Although the dimensions of magnetite lode deposits are smaller than those of the two foregoing types of mineralization, the magnetite lodes have very high iron contents.

Phlogopite accumulations of commercial interest have been encountered at several points on Enderby Land (Nye Mountains, etc.) and on Queen Maud Land (Humboldt Mountains). The phlogopite is most often concentrated in boudinaged layers of diopside rocks, several meters thick, traced over hundreds of meters along strike. Phlogopite pockets attain the size of 40—60 cm, and some individual crystals measure 5—10 cm across. The phlogopite content of the diopside rocks is 2—4%. This kind of phlogopitization is promising, since most of the known phlogopite deposits in the world are of this type.

Muscovite accumulations occur in pegmatite veins that have been discovered in the aluminous Condon Series on Enderby Land and the Prince Olav Coast, as well as in the Humboldt Mountains on Queen Maud Land. The veins reach a thickness of 2—3 m, and are traceable over tens and hundreds of meters along strike. The muscovite crystals often reach a size of $10 \times 10 \times 5$ cm. The veins contain several percent of the mica.

The pegmatite veins, usually of high-grade greisenization, also contain beryl crystals up to 7—8 cm long, in addition to the muscovite. The beryl usually forms pockets, 15—30 cm across, consisting of green, translucent crystals. There are approximately two or three beryl-bearing pockets per 10 m^2 of pegmatite vein.

Rock crystal has been found at more than ten locations in the Humboldt Mountains and the peaks fringing them to the south and west. Unusual quartz-feldspar veins ("block pegmatites"), 1—3 m thick, have been traced over tens of meters along strike. Their "bulges" contain rock crystal, 0.3—0.7 m long, occurring in cavities. Talus at the base of mountains (e. g., Mount Titov) contains at least 4—5% rock crystal fragments. At several other sites the disintegration of pegmatite veins has produced placers containing fragments and small crystals of rock crystal. The rock crystal is smoky and violet in color and largely translucent.

Graphite was found at several localities in central Queen Maud Land. Large flakes measuring 2—3 cm have been discovered in pegmatite veins. Finely disseminated graphite (up to 10%) is known to occur in marble layers.

These "incidental" finds of mineral resources suggest that the crystalline basement of the Antarctic Platform is promising with respect to iron ore deposits and valuable nonmetal resources such as phlogopite, muscovite, rock crystal and graphite. The potential mineral resources of the crystalline basement of the Antarctic Platform are certainly not limited to these finds, since this basement is similar to the basements of other Gondwanian platforms, which contain deposits of iron, radioactive ore, gold, diamonds, copper and nickel, that are the richest in the world.

FURTHER STUDIES OF THE CRYSTALLINE BASEMENT

The crystalline basement is the principal and dominant geological formation in East Antarctica. Except for the Transantarctic Mountains, which divide the continent into two unequal parts (large eastern and small western sections), the coastal block mountains along nearly the entire perimeter of East Antarctica expose metamorphic and intrusive rocks of the crystalline basement, with an abundant and diversified vein series. Therefore, the Soviet geologists, working mostly in East Antarctica where a widespread network of Soviet stations has been established, have always paid considerable attention to the geological-petrological aspects of the crystalline basement. The principal effort has been devoted to reconnaissance and small-scale studies. More detailed investigations have encompassed only 2–3% of the exposed crystalline basement areas, primarily because of the limited size of Soviet Antarctic geological expeditions. Obviously, this work could not yield more than preliminary, tentative data on the geological structure and composition of the crystalline basement rocks. Therefore, the tasks to be tackled in future are extensive and varied.

In the first place, there is a need to determine the stratigraphic relationship and correlations of the different structural-facies zones of the crystalline basement. Sporadic attempts in this direction carried out in the Humboldt Mountains and on Enderby Land yielded promising results. However, similar work must be done in dozens of other regions and it must be based principally on medium- to large-scale surveys. An important element in stratigraphic studies of metamorphic formations is the absolute dating of rocks, which until now was done mostly by the argon whole rock method, often yielding insufficiently accurate data which are difficult to interpret. Therefore, the extensive application of the isochronous variety of the strontium method and especially of the lead method with radioactive minerals is another important task in future stratigraphic studies of the basement.

The consistencies of mineral development in all facies of regional metamorphism presented herein justify more profound studies of the mineral parageneses and the compilation of a genetic classification for metamorphic rocks at different levels in the Earth's crust. Nonequilibrium associations of polymetamorphic rocks merit special attention; thus an elucidation of their geneses and place in the series of mineral parageneses should be attempted. In studies of the metamorphic facies, special attential should be paid to mineral associations and formation conditions of amphibolite facies rocks, which are no less widespread than the granulite facies rocks. To date, the amphibolite facies has been inadequately studied, since its presence was noted only a few years ago.

Studies of ultrametamorphic formations, extremely widespread in the crystalline basement, must be continued. From this standpoint, attention should be paid to the intrusive and apointrusive charnockitoids, reflecting a variety of elements of ultrametamorphic processes, beginning with magmatic and ending with metasomatic. Studies of the modes of occurrence of charnockitoid massifs, their interrelationships with the host rocks and with one another, and the equilibrium and, especially, the nonequilibrium mineral associations (investigations of which are still in their initial stage) must be continued in order to make possible a better understanding of their genesis.

There is a need for comparative studies of the geological-structural and petrological features of the crystalline basement of the Antarctic Platform and of the basements of other Gondwanian platforms. The preliminary data suggest that the basements of all these platforms have much in common. Finally, there is the need for more detailed reconnaissance of mineral resources, particularly the determination of metallogenic provinces.

All these tasks call for detailed geological and geophysical investigations. The importance of geophysical surveys in Antarctica can scarcely be over-emphasized, since over 95% of the continent is utterly devoid of bedrock exposures, while 70—90% of the remaining area is covered by glaciers. In this respect, Antarctica may be compared to an ocean with numerous offshore islands. Ocean bottoms are covered by a water column of 1—6 km or more, while Antarctica carries an ice cover averaging 2.5—3.0 km in thickness. Therefore, small-scale areal gravimetric and magnetic surveys, along with deep seismic sounding profiles, are as necessary in Antarctica as regular geological mapping is on other continents.

BIBLIOGRAPHY

1. Azhgirei, G.D. Structural Geology. — Moscow State University, 1956. (Russian)
2. Atherton, M.P. The Composition of Garnets in Regional-Metamorphosed Rocks. — In: Controls of Metamorphism. Edited by Pitcher, Wallaces, S. and W. Glenys Flinn. New York, Wiley, 1965.
3. Atrashenok, L.Ya., G.V.Avdzeiko, L.V.Klimov, A.Ya.Krylov, and Yu.I.Silin. Comparative Data on the Absolute Age of Antarctica Rocks (Lead and Argon Methods). — In: Vorposy datirovkii drevneishikh (katarkheiskikh) geologicheskikh obrazovanii i osnovnykh porod. Moscow, "Nauka," 1967. (Russian)
4. Boyd, F.R. and J.L.England. The Rhombic Enstatite — Clinoenstatite Inversion. — Carnegie Inst. Washington Year Book, 64:117—120. 1965.
5. Boyd, F.R. and J.L.England. Effect of Pressure on Phase Relations in the System $MgO-Al_2O_3-SiO_2$. — Carnegie Inst. Washington. Year Book, 62:121—4. 1963.
6. Borneman—Starynkevich, I.D. Handbook on Calculation of Mineral Formulas. — Moscow, "Nauka," 1964.
7. Wegener, A. Origin of Continents and Oceans. — Dover, 1965.
8. Velikoslavinskii, D.A. Effect of the Composition of Country Rocks and Specific Properties of Metamorphism on the Composition of Pyralspite Garnets. — In: Regional'nyi metamorfizm dokembriiskikh formatsii SSSR. Moscow—Leningrad, "Nauka," 1965. (Russian)
9. Velikoslavinskii, D.A. Chemical Composition of Biotites as an Index of Intensity and Type of Regional Metamorphism. — In: "Geologiya dokembriya." Leningrad, "Nauka," 1968. (Russian)
10. Velikoslavinskii, D.A., Yu.M.Sokolov, and V.A.Glebovitskii. Zonation of Progressive Regional Metamorphism and Metallogenic Specialization of Metamorphic Zones. — In: "Geologiya dokembriya." Leningrad, "Nauka," 1968. (Russian)
11. Winkler, H.G. Petrogenesis of Metamorphic Rocks. 2nd ed. — Springer Verlag, 1967.
12. Voronov, P.S. On the Structure of Antarctica. — In: Sbornik statei po geologii Antarktiki, No.2, 1960. (Trudy Sci. Res. Inst. Arctic Geology), (Russian)
13. Voronov, P.S. Tectonics and Neotectonics of Antarctica. — In: Antarktika. Moscow, "Nauka," 1964. (Russian)
14. Grigor'ev, D.P. Principles of Constitution of Minerals. — Moscow, Gosgeoltekhizdat, 1962. (Russian)
15. Deer, William, A. et al. Introduction to the Rock Forming Minerals. Vol.1. — New York, Wiley, 1965.
16. Deer, William, A. et al. Introduction to the Rock Forming Minerals. Vol.2. — New York, Wiley, 1966.
17. Deer, William, A. et al. Introduction to the Rock Forming Minerals. Vol.3. — New York, Wiley, 1966.
18. Deer, William, A. et al. Introduction to the Rock Forming Minerals, Vol.4. — New York, Wiley, 1966.
19. Deer, William, A. et al. Introduction to the Rock Forming Minerals, Vol.5. — New York, Wiley, 1966.
20. Dobretsov, N.L., V.V.Reverdatto, V.S.Sobolev, N.V.Sobolev, and V.V.Khlestov. Facies of Metamorphism. Vol.1. Edited by Sobolev, V.S. — Moscow, "Nedra," 1970. (Russian)
21. Drugova, G.M., L.V.Klimov, M.D.Krylova, D.A.Mikhailov, N.G.Sudovikov, and Z.G.Ushakova. Geology of the Precambrian of the Aldan Mining Region. — Trudy Labor. Geol. Dokembr. AN SSSR, No.8, Leningrad, 1959. (Russian)
22. Drugova, G.M. and V.A.Glebovitskii. Some Patterns of Changes in the Composition of Garnet, Biotite and Hornblende with Regional Metamorphism. — In: Regional'nyi metamorfizm dokembriiskikh formatsii SSSR. Moscow—Leningrad, "Nauka," 1965. (Russian)
23. Zavaritskii, A.N. Conversion of Chemical Analyses of Igneous Rocks. — Leningrad, Ob"edn. nauch.-tekh. izd. Narod. Komiss. Tyazh. Prom. SSSR, 1933. (Russian)
24. Zavaritskii, A.N. On Pegmatites as an Intermediate Formation between Igneous Rocks and Ore Veins. — In: Osnovnye problemy v uchenii o magmotogennykh rudnykh mestorozhdeniyakh. Moscow, AN SSSR, 1955. (Russian)

25. Znachko-Yavorskii, G.A. Main Features of the Relief of Central Enderby Land. — Inf. Byull. Sov. Antarkt. Eksped., No.48, 1964. (Russian)

26. Kadenskii, A.A. Geology and Petrology of the Southern Part of Anabar Shield. — Moscow-Leningrad, AN SSSR, 1961. (Russian)

27. Kamenev, E.N. Geological Structure of the East of Enderby Land. — Leningrad, Gidrometeoizdat, 1969. (Trudy Soviet Antarct. Exped., Vol.50). (Russian)

28. Kamanev, E.N., L.V. Klimov, and O.G. Shulyatin. Geological Structure of Enderby Land and Prince Olav Coast. — In: Antarktika, Moscow, 1965. (Russian)

29. Kitsul, V.I. Chemical Composition and Physical Properties of Garnets from Metamorphic Rocks of the "Iengr" Series and "Ungrinsk" Complex of the Aldan Shield. — Moscow, "Nauka," 1966. (Russian)

30. Klimov, L.V. Geological Investigations in the Region of Prince Olav Coast. — Inf. Byull. Sov. Antarkt. Eksped., No.51, 1965. (Russian)

31. Kolotukhina, S.E. Main Characteristics of the Development of the South American Continent. — Izv. AN SSSR, geol. ser., No.8, 1968. (Russian)

32. Korzhinskii, D.S. Synopsis of Metasomatic Processes. — In: Osnovnye problemy v uchenii o magmato-gennykh rudnykh mestorozhdeniyakh. Moscow, AN SSSR, 1955. (Russian)

33. Korzhinskii, D.S. Physicochemical Basis of the Analysis of the Paragenesis of Minerals. — Moscow, AN SSSR, 1957. (Russian)

34. Korzhinskii, D.S. The Role of Alkalinity in the Formation of Charnockite Gneisses. Trudy Vost.— Sib. Geol. Inst., No.5, 1961. (Russian)

35. Korikovskii, S.P. Metamorphism, Granitization and Postmagmatic Processes in the Precambrian "Udokano-Stanovaya" Zone. — Moscow, "Nauka," 1967. (Russian)

36. Kosminskaya, I.P. Method of Deep Seismic Sounding of the Earth's Crust and Upper Mantle. — Moscow, "Nauka,", 1968. (Russian)

37. Krishnan, M.S. The Precambrian Stratigraphy of India. — 21st Int. Geol. Congr. rep. 29, p. 95—107. Copenhagen, 1960.

38. Krylov, A.Ya. and M.G.Ravich. Absolute Age of Rocks of the Antarctic Platform. — In: Absolyutnyi vozrast geologicheskikh formatsii. Moscow, "Nauka," 1964. (Russian)

39. Lebedev, V.I. and Yu.V. Nagaitsev. Granites and Garnets of the Northeastern Ladoga Area. — Mineralogiya i Geokhimiya, No.11, 1967. (Russian)

40. Lebedev, V.I. and Yu.V. Nagaitsev. Contribution to the Method of Determining the Garnet Composition according to the Index of Refraction and Contents of FeO, Fe_2O_3 and MnO. — Mineralogiya i Geokhimiya, No.2, 1967. (Russian)

41. Lutst, B.G. Petrology of Granulite Facies of the Anabar Massif. — Moscow, "Nauka," 1964. (Russian)

42. Marakushev, A.A. Eclogitic Schists in Precambrian Metamorphic Complexes and their Formation Conditions. — Geologiya i Geofizika, No.1, 1962. (Russian)

43. Marakushev, A.A. Problems of Mineral Facies of Metamorphic and Metasomatic Rocks. — Moscow, "Nauka," 1965. (Russian)

44. Marakushev, A.A., I.A. Tararin, and B.L. Zalishchak. Mineral Facies of Acid-Alkaline Low-Calcium Granitoids. — In: Mineral'nye fatsii granitoidov i ikh rudonosnost'. Moscow, "Nauka," 1966. (Russian)

45. Marfunin, A.S. Feldspars—Phase Relations, Optical Properties and Geological Distribution. — Moscow, AN SSSR, 1962. (Russian)

46. Muratov, M.V. Precambrian Geosynclinal Fold Systems and Some Features of their Development. — Geotektonika, No.2, 1970. (Russian)

47. Murbat, S. Isotope Relation in Metamorphic Rocks. — In: Controls of Metamorphism. Edited by Pitcher, Wallaces, S. and W. Glenys Flinn. New York, Wiley, 1965.

48. Pavlovskii, E.V. On the Position of Anorthosites in Tectonic-Magmatic Process. — In: Vulkanizm i tektogenez. Moscow, "Nauka," 1968. (Russian)

49. Pavlovskii, E.V. and M.S. Markov. Some General Problems of Geotectonics. — In: Struktura dokembriya i svyaz' magmatizma s tektonikoi. Moscow, AN SSSR, 1963. (Russian)

50. Perchuk, L.L. Biotite-Garnet Geothermometer. — Doklady AN SSSR, Vol.177, No.2, 1967. (Russian)

51. Perchuk, L.L. Principles of the Effect of Temperature and Pressure on the Equilibria of Natural Ferro-magnesian Minerals. — Izv. AN SSSR, geol. ser., No.12, 1968. (Russian)

52. Perchuk, L.L. Paragenesis of Orthopyroxene with Garnets in Metamorphic Rocks. — In: Ocherki fiziko-khimicheskoi petrologii, Vol.1. Moscow, "Nauka," 1969. (Russian)

53. Pushkarev, Yu.D. and K.A.Shchurkin. Characteristics (Features) of the Structure of the Zone of Contact between the Belomorides and the Karelides. — In: Deformatsiya i struktura dokembriiskikh tolshch. Moscow, "Nauka," 1967. (Russian)

54. Rabkin, M.I. Geology and Petrology of the Anabar Crystalline Shield. — Moscow, Gosgeoltekhizdat, 1959. (Russian)

55. Ravich, M.G. Enderbites of the Central "Pobuzh'e."— Sovetskaya Geologiya, No.9, 1967. (Russian)

56. Ravich, M.G. Regional Metamorphism and Ultrametamorphism of Crystalline Basement of the Antarctic and Other Gondwana Platforms. — In: Geologiya dokembriya. Leningrad, "Nauka," 1968. (Russian)

57. Ravich, M.G., L.V.Klimov, and D.S.Solov'ev. Precambrian of East Antarctica. — Moscow, "Nedra," 1965. (Russian)

58. Ravich, M.G. and D.S.Solov'ev. Geology and Petrology of the Central Part of the Mountains of Queen Maud Land. — Trudy Sci. Res. Inst. of Arctic Geology (NIIGA), Vol.141, 1966. (Russian)

59. Ravich, M.G. and G.E.Grikurov. Principal Features of Antarctic Tectonics. — Sovetskaya Geologiya, No.1, 1970. (Russian)

60. Skinner, B.J. and F.R.Boyd. Aluminous Enstatites. — Carnegie Inst. Washington. Year Book, 63:163—165. 1964.

61. Smolin, P.P. Contribution to the Petrogenetic Significance of Polymorphism of $MgSiO_3$ and Related Mineralogical Aspects. — Izv. AN SSSR, geol. ser., No.11, 1968. (Russian)

62. Sobolev, N.V. Paragenetic Types of Garnets. — Moscow, "Nauka," 1964. (Russian)

63. Sikolov, Yu.M. Relationship of Mica-Bearing Pegmatitic Veins of "Mamsk" Region to Regional Metamorphism. — In: Nekotorye voprosy geologii Agiatskoi chasti SSSR. Leningrad, AN SSSR, 1959. (Russian)

64. Sokolov, Yu.M. and V.M.Taevskii. Metallogenic Provinces of Metamorphogenic Mica-Bearing Pegmatites. — In: Regional'nyi metamorfizm i metamorfogennoe rudoobrazovanie. Leningrad, "Nauka," 1970. (Russian)

65. Solov'ev, S.P. Chemical Properties of Magmatic Rocks and Some Problems of Petro-chemistry. — Leningrad, "Nauka," 1970. (Russian)

66., Solov'ev, D.S., E.N.Kamenov, and M.G.Ravich. Geological Investigations in 1965—1966. — Inf. Byull. Soviet Antarctic Exped., No.62, 1967. (Russian)

67. Reference Book on Petrography of Sedimentary Rocks, Vol.2. — Leningrad, Gostoptekhizdat, 1958. (Russian)

68. Sudovikov, N.G. Regional Metamorphism and Some Problems of Petrology. — Leningrad State Univ., 1964. (Russian)

69. Sudovikov, N.G. Rapakivi and Late Orogenic Intrusions. — Moscow—Leningrad, "Nauka," 1967. (Russian)

70. Sudovikov, N.G., V.A.Glebovitskii, G.M.Drugova, M.D.Krylova, A.N.Neelov, and I.S.Sedova. Geology and Petrology of the Southern Fringe of the Aldan Shield.—Leningrad, "Nauka," 1965. (Russian)

71. Turner, Francis J. and J.Verhoogen. Igneous and Metamorphic Petrology. 2nd ed.—McGraw—Hill, 1960.

72. Treger, V.E. Tables for Optical Determination of Rock-Forming Minerals. — Moscow, Gosgeoltekhizdat, 1958. (Russian)

73. Tugarinov, A.I. and G.V.Voitkevich. Precambrian Geochronology of Continents. — Moscow, "Nedra," 1966. (Russian)

74. Haun, R.A. Pyroxenes of Metamorphic Rocks. — In: Controls of Metamorphism. — Edited by Pitcher, Wallaces, S. and W. Glenys Flinn. New York, Wiley, 1965.

75. Chetverikov, S.D. Handbook on Petrochemical Conversion of Chemical Analyses of Rocks and Deter-mination of their Types. — Moscow, Gosgeoltekhizdat, 1956. (Russian)

76. Shemyakin, V.M. On the Connection between the Composition and Refraction of Orthopyroxenes. — Zapiski Vses. Mineral. Obshch., Part 97, No.1, Ser.2, 1968. (Russian)

77. Shulyatin, O.G., E.N.Kamenev, and S.F.Dukhanin. Geological Investigations in Central Enderby Land in February and March of 1963. — Inf. Byull. Soviet Antarctic Exped., No.46, 1964. (Russian)

78. Yanshin, A.L. Problems of Median Masses. — Byull. Moscow Obshch. Isp. Prir., Vol.70, geol. ser., Vol.40, No.6, 1965. (Russian)

79. A t l a s, L. The Polymorphism of $MgSiO_3$ and Solid State Equilibria in the System $MgSiO_3$–$CaMgSi_2O_6$. – J. Geol., Vol.60 (1952), 125.

80. A u t e n b o e r, T. van, and W.L o y. The Geology of the Sør-Rondane Antarctica. – Data Report. Central Part of the Range, 1966. (Brusselles Centre National de Recherches Polaires de Belgique)

81. B a r t h, T.F.W. The Feldspar Geologic Thermometers. – Neues Jb. Miner. Abh., Vol.82, 1951.

82. B a r t h, T.F.W. Zonal Structure in Feldspars of Crystalline Schists. – 3rd Reunion Intern. Realtiv. á étaf solide, sec.3. Madrid, 1956.

83. B a r t h, T.F.W. Principles of Classification and Norm Calculations of Metamorphic Rocks. – J. Geol., Vol.67, No.2, 1959.

84. B e l l a i r, M.P.I. Sur les formations anciennes de l'archipel de Pointe-Géologie (Terre Adèlie). II. Pétrographie du socle cristallin de la Terre Adèlie. Extraits. – C. r. hébd. Séanc. Acad. Sci., 15–24 Mai, 1961.

85. B e n t l e y, C.B. Crystal Geophysics in Antarctica. – Geo Times, Vol.11, No.4, 1966.

86. B o y d, F.R. and Y.L. E n g l a n d. Minerals of the Mantle: Aluminous Enstatite. – Rep. Dir. Geophys. Lab. Carnegie Instn., Vol.59, No.49, 1960.

87. B r o w n, D.A., K.S.W. C a m p b e l l, and K.A.W. C r o c k. The Geological Evolution of Australia and New Zealand. – New York, Pergamon, 1968.

88. B r u y n z e e l, D. A Petrographic Study of the Waterfall Gorge Profile at Insizwa. – Annale Univ. Stellenbosch, 1957.

89. B u d d i n g t o n, A.F. Chemical Petrology of Some Metamorphosed Adirondack Gabbroic, Syenitic and Quartz Syenitic Rocks. – Am. J. Sci., 1952.

90. C r o h n, P.W.A. Contribution to the Geology and Glaciology of the Western Part of Australian Antarctic Territory. – Bull. Bur. Miner. Resour. Geol. Geophys., Dept. Nat. Develop., 52, 1959,

91. E s k o l a, P. Orijarvi Re-interpreted. – Bull. Commn. géol. Finl., No.150, 1950.

92. E s k o l a, P. On the Granulites of Lapland. – Am. J. Sci., Pt.1, 1952.

93. F o s h a g, W.F. The Shallowater Meteorite: a New Aubrite. – Am. Miner., Vol.25, 1940.

94. F r i e d m a n, G.M. Petrology of the Mamesagamesing Lake Norite Mass, Ontario, Canada. – Am. J. Sci., Vol.253, 1955.

95. F r i e d m a n, G.M. Structure and Petrology of the Caribou Lake Intrusive Body, Ontario, Canada. – Bull. Geol. Soc. Am., Vol.68, 1957.

96. G i r a u d, P. Les roches à caractère Charnockitique de la série d'un Ouzzal en Ahaggar (Sahara Central). Essai de nomenclature des séries Charnockitiques. – In: Reports XXII Sess. 1.G. C., Pt.XIII. New Delhi, 1964.

97. H e n r i q u e s, A. The Influence of Cations on the Optical Properties of Orthopyroxenes. – Ark. Kemi Miner. Geol., Vol.2, 1958.

98. H e n r y, N.F.M. Lamellar Structure of Orthopyroxenes. – Mineral Mag., Vol.26, 1954.

99. H e p w o r t h, J.V. The Charnockites of Southern West Nile, Uganda, and their Paragenesis. – In: Reports XXIII Sess. I.G.C. Pt.XIII. New Delhi, 1964.

100. H e s s, H.H. Pyroxenes of Common Mafic Magmas, Pt.2. – Am. Miner., Vol.26, 1941.

101. H e s s, H.H. Chemical Composition and Optical Properties of Common Clinopyroxenes. – Am. Miner., Vol.34, 1949.

102. H e s s, H.H. Orthopyroxenes of the Bushveld Type, Ion Substitutions and Changes in Unit Cell Dimensions. – Am. J. Sci., 1952.

103. H e s s, H.H. Stillwater Igneous Complex, Montana. – Mem. Geol. Soc. Am., p.60, 1960.

104. H o l l a n d, T.N. The Charnockite Series, a Group of Archean, Hypersthenic Rocks in Penninsular India. – Mem. Geol. Surv. India, Vol .28, Pt.2, 1900.

105. H o r i, F. Effects of Constituent Cations on the Optical Properties of Clinopyroxenes. – Scient. Pap. Coll. Gen. Educ. Tokyo, Vol.4, 1954.

106. H o w i e, R.A. and A.P. S u b r a m a n i a m. The Paragenesis of Garnet in Charnockite, Enderbite, and Related Granulites. – Mineral Mag., Vol.31, No.238, 1957.

107. J u c k e s, L.M. The Geology of Northeastern Heimefrontfjella, Dronning Maud Land. – Brit. Antarct. Surv. Sci. Rep., No.65, 1970.

108. K e n n e d y, G.C. Charts for Correlation of Optical Properties with Chemical Composition of Some Common Rock-Forming Minerals. – Am. Miner., Vol.32, 1947.

109. K i z a k i, K. Tectonics and Petrography of the East Ongul Island Lützow-Holm. Buct Antarctika. —
      IARE 1956–1962. Scient. Rep. geol. ser. C., No.2, 1964.
110. K i z a k i, K. Geology and Petrography of the Yamato Sanmyaku, East Antarctica. — Scient. Rep geol.;
      ser. C., No.3, 1965.
111. K r e t z, R. Distribution of Magnesium and Iron between Orthopyroxene and Calcic Pyroxene in Natural
      Mineral Assemblages. — J. Geol., Vol.71, No.6, 1963.
112. K u n o, H. Study of Orthopyroxenes from Volcanic Rocks. — Am. Miner., Vol.39, 1954.
113. M c I v e r, I.R. and T.W. G e v e r r s. Charnockites and Associated Hypersthene -bearing Rocks in
      Southern Natal, South Africa.. — In: Reports XXII sess. I.G.C., Pt.XIII. New Delhi, 1964.
114. M c L e o d, I.R. An Outline of Geology of the Seefor from Longitude 45° to 80° E, Antarctica. — In:
      Antarctic Geology. Amsterdam, 1964.
115. M u i r, I.D. The Clinopyroxenes of the Skaergaard Intrusion. Eastern Greenland. — Mineral Mag., Vol.30,
      1951.
116. M u i r, I.D. and C.E. T i l l e y. The Compositions of Coexisting Pyroxenes in Metamorphic
      Assemblages. — Geol. Mag., Vol.95, 1958.
117. P a r r a s, K. On the Charnockites in the Light of a Highly Metamorphic Rock Complex in Southwestern
      Finland. — Bull. Commn, géol. Finl., No.181, 1958.
118. P o l d e r v a a r t, A. The Relationship of Orthopyroxene to Pigeonite. — Mineral Mag., Vol.28, 1947.
119. P o l d e r v a a r t, A. Correlation of Physical Properties and Chemical Composition in the Plagioclase,
      Olivine and Orthopyroxene Series. — Am. Miner., Vol. 35, 1950.
120. P o l d e r v a a r t, A. and H.H. H e s s. Pyroxenes in the Crystallization of Basaltic Magma. — J. Geol.,
      Vol.59, 1951.
121. R a m b e r g, H. and G. D e V o r e. The Distribution of Fe^{++} and Mg^{++} in Coexisting Olivines and
      Pyroxenes. — J. Geol., Vol.59, 1951.
122. R i e c k e r, R.E. and T.P. R o o n e y. Deformation and Polymorphism of Enstatite under Shear Stress. —
      Bull. Geol. Soc. Am., Vol.78, No.8, 1967.
123. S a x e n a, S.K. Chemical Study of Phase Equilibria in Charnockites. Varberg, Sweden. — Am. Miner.,
      Vol.53, Nos.9–10. 1968.
124. S c h a i r e r, J.F. and F.R. B o y d. Pyroxenes: The Join $MgSiO_3$–$CaMgSi_2O_6$. — Ann. Rep. Dir. Geophys.
      Lab. Carnegie Instn., 1957.
125. S e a r l e, D.L. Metamorphic History of Ceylon and the Origin of the Charnockite Series. — In:
      Reports XXII Sess. I.G.C. Pt.XIII. New Delhi, 1964.
126. S e n, S.K. Potassium Content of Natural Plagioclases and the Origin of Antiperthites. — J. Geol., Vol.67,
      1959.
127. S m i t h, J.V. Magnesium Pyroxenes at High Temperature: Inversions in Clinoenstatite. — Nature,
      Vol.222, No.5190, 1969.
128. S u b r a m a n i a m, A. Charnockites of the Type Area Near Madras. — Am. J. Sci., Vol.257, No.5, 1959.
129. T h o m s o n, J.W. Petrography of Some Basement Complex Rocks from Tottanfjella, Dronning Maud
      Land. — Brit. Antarct. Surv. Bull., No.17, 1968.
130. T i l l e y, C.E. Enderbite, a New Member of the Charnockite Series. — Geol. Mag., Vol.73, No.7, 1936.
131. T r a i l, D.S. Schists and Granite in the Southern Prince Charles Mountains. — In: Antarctic Geology.
      Amsterdam, 1964.
132. T r a i l, D.S., J.R. M c L e o d, P.Y. C o c k, and G.R. W a l l s. Geological Investigations by the Australian
      National Antarctic Research Expeditions, 1965. Rept., No.118, 1967.
133. T u r n e r, F.Y., H. H e a r d, and D.T. G r i g g s. Experimental Deformation of Enstatite and Accompanying
      Inversion to Clinoenstatite. — Intern. Geol. Congress. Pt.XVIII. Copenhagen, 1960.
134. T u t t l e, O.F. Optical Studies on Alkali Feldspars. — Am. J. Sci., 1952.
135. W a a r d, D. de. A Proposed Subdivision of the Granulite Facies. — Am. J. Sci., Vol.263, 1965.
136. W a a r d, D. de. On Water–Vapor Pressure in Zones of Regional Metamorphism and the Nature of the
      Hornblende-Granulite Facies. — Koninkl. Nederl. Acad. Wetenschappen, Geology Proceedings,
      Ser. B, Vol.69, No.4, 1966.
137. W a t z n a u e r, A. Der Begriff "Granulit." — Monatsberichte, Vol.10, No.12, 1968.
138. W e g m a n n, S.E. Über Diapirismus (besonders im Grundgebirge). — Bull. Commn. géol. Finl., No.92,
      1930.
139. W e g m a n n, S.E. Zur Deutung der Migmatite. — Geol. Rundschau, Vol.26, Nos.1–2, 1935.

140. White, A.J. Clinopyroxenes from Eclogites and Basic Granulites. — Am. Miner., Vol. 49, No.4, 1964.

141. Wilson, A.F. Co-existing Pyroxenes: Some Causes of Variation and Anomalies in the Optically Derived Compositional Tie-Lines, with Particular Reference to Charnockitic Rocks. — Geol. Mag., Vol.97, 1960.

142. Wilson, A.F. The Petrological Features and Structural Setting of Australian Granulites and Charnockites. — In: Rept. XXII Sess. I.G.C. Pt.XIII. New Delhi, 1964.

APPENDIX

Zavaritskii's Numerical Characteristics

Zavaritskii's numerical characteristics are parameters which can be calculated from the chemical analysis of a rock. They reflect the quantitative molar relations between the rock constituents.

Zavaritskii's mathematical scheme for the calculation of his parameters is based on a standard procedure. The resulting values can be recalculated so as to give the source data (weight percent). The mathematics involved is relatively simple, and the parameters obtained clearly reflect the most important chemical characteristics of the analyzed magmatic rock.

The numerical characteristics allow for the clarification of the following properties of rocks:

1) the ratio of salic to femic constituents as reflected by the chemical differences between the aluminosilicates and "simple" silicates (olivines, pyroxenes, etc.);

2) the relative saturation of the rock with respect to silica;

3) the general composition of the feldspars, i.e., the ratio of alkali-aluminosilicates to calcium-aluminosilicates;

4) the compositional relations within the alkali-aluminosilicates and "simple" silicates.

In order to express quantitatively these diagnostic properties, Zavaritskii makes use of two groups of values, namely:

i) Principal numerical characteristics, used for expressing the first three mentioned properties;

ii) Complementary numerical characteristics, used for expressing the fourth-mentioned property.

As already stated, these parameters are based on molar ratios, i.e., the chemical weight percentages are divided by the respective molecular weights, prior to any further calculation. In order to simplify subsequent calculations the number of constituents taken into consideration is reduced by adding MnO to FeO and TiO_2 to SiO_2. Iron is calculated as the bivalent ion. Hydrogen (as water) is not taken into account (the primary water content of the rock generally changes radically during secondary processes). Oxygen is eliminated from the calculation since its amount is dependent on the number of metal atoms and their valence. The remaining constituents are therefore Si, Al, Fe, Mg, Ca, Na and K.

The principal numerical characteristics consist of the following values — a, c, b and s; by definition $a + b + c + s = 100$.

These parameters have the following significance:

a is the relative number of the alkali-metal atoms bound to aluminum in the aluminosilicate mineral lattices.

c is the relative number of calcium atoms bound with aluminum in the aluminosilicates. Rocks deficient in alumina, relative to alkali-metals, will contain sodium ferrisilicates instead of the "normal" calcium aluminosilicates.

b is the relative number of all remaining metal atoms (excluding silicon and titanium) which constitute the "simple" silicates and are not included in the aluminosilicates.

s is the relative number of silicon atoms (including titanium).

This group of parameters is obtained from the chemical analysis by the following procedure:

1) weight percentages, as stated in the chemical analysis, are converted to molar proportions using suitable tables;

2) the values of silica and titania are added to give the value S;

3) the alkalis are summed: if $(K_2O + Na_2O) < Al_2O_3$, this sum is multiplied by two to give the value A;

4) if $(K_2O + Na_2O) > Al_2O_3$, alumina (multiplied by two) will be the limiting value of A. The alkali excess over alumina $[(K_2O + Na_2O) - Al_2O_3]$ multiplied by two (Na_2O') is then calculated to obtain $\bar{C}$;

5) if CaO exceeds the alumina excess with respect to alkalis $[CaO > Al_2O_3 - (K_2O + Na_2O)]$, the difference is defined as the value C;

6) if there is an excess of alumina over calcium plus alkalis $[Al_2O_3 > CaO + Na_2O + K_2O]$, C will equal CaO. The alumina excess is then multiplied by two and is added to the value B;

7) the molar proportion of Fe_2O_3, multiplied by two, is added to that of FeO (+ MnO) in order to obtain FeO'. When dealing with rocks oversaturated in alkalis, the value $\bar{C}$ should be subtracted from FeO' (for each sodium atom in excess of alumina one iron atom should be reserved in order to form sodium ferrisilicates);

8) in the rare case when $\bar{C} >$ FeO' (there is not sufficient iron to combine with the excess sodium for the formation of ferrisilicates), the difference $(\bar{C} - FeO')$ is defined as Na';

9) the difference (CaO $-$ C) is calculated to give the excess of calcium, i.e., CaO';

10) the parameter B is obtained by the summation of FeO + MgO + CaO'. Al_2O_3' (multiplied by two) and Na' are added to B if they are present;

11) the values A, C, B and S (or A, $\bar{C}$, B and S) thus obtained are recalculated to percentages of their sum to give the principal numerical characteristics a, c, b and s (or a, $\bar{c}$, b and s) respectively.

The complementary numerical characteristics consist of the following eight parameters: f', m' and c' which reflect the role played by iron, magnesium and calcium, respectively, in "simple" silicate minerals; n is a measure of the relative amount of sodium molecule in the alkali aluminosilicates. The amount of titanium in the rock is represented by the parameter t, while the relative importance of ferric iron included in the "simple" silicates is expressed by the parameter φ. Rocks rich in alumina yield the value a' instead of c', which reflects the surplus of alumina left after combination with all the calcium atoms in the aluminosilicates. This alumina excess is included, as already explained, in group B. When $\bar{C} >$ FeO', the complementary numerical characteristic n' is obtained, which reflect the relative amount of sodium left over in B after combining the maximum possible amount of sodium in aluminosilicates and ferrisilicates.

Using Zavaritskii's numerical characteristics a magmatic rock may be related to one of the following four types:

i) rocks with a normal composition — the principal numerical characteristics are a, c, b and s and the complementary parameters are f', m', and c' and n, t and φ;

ii) rocks oversaturated in alumina — the principal parameters are a, $\bar{c}$, b and s and the complementary parameters are a', f' and m' and n, t and φ;

iii) rocks slightly oversaturated with respect to alkalis — the principal parameters are a, $\bar{c}$, b and s and the complementary parameters are f', m' and c' and n, t and φ;

iv) rocks markedly oversaturated with respect to alkalis — the principal parameters are a, $\bar{c}$, b and s and the complementary parameters are n', m' and c' and n t and φ.

The degree of saturation with respect to silica is represented by the parameter Q, i.e., the relative number of silicon atoms. If the value of Q is positive, it indicates the possible occurrence of free silica (as quartz) in the rock. Rocks composed of silica-saturated minerals, but lacking free silica, will give Q values approximating zero, while undersaturated rocks will yield negative values of Q. The Q values are readily obtained from principal numerical characteristics (according to the ratio of silicon to metal atoms in the rock-forming silicates) as follows:

1) $Q = s - (3a + 2c + b)$ — for normal rocks;

2) $Q = s - (3a + 2\bar{c} + b)$ — for rocks containing sodium ferrisilicate.

The relation between Zavaritskii's parameters and the commonly used Niggli values is here provided.

In the case of normal rocks, $a:c:b:s = 2\,alk : [al - alk] : [fm + c - (al - alk)] : si$.

In the case of rocks oversaturated with respect to alkalis, $a:\bar{c}:b:s = 2al:2[alk-al]:[fm + c-2(alk-al)]:si$.

In the case of rocks oversaturated with respect to alumina, $a:c:b:s = 2\,alk:c:[fm + 2(al-alk) - 2c]:si$.

The complementary numerical characteristics may be expressed in Niggli values as follows:

normal rocks — $f' : m': c' = fm(1-mg):fm.mg: [c-(al-alk)]$;

rocks oversaturated with respect to alumina — $a':f': m' = [(al-alk)-c]: fm(1-mg):fm.mg$;

rocks oversaturated with respect to alkalis — $f':m':c' = [fm- 2(alk-al)](1-mg):[fm- 2(alk-al)]mg:c$.

SUBJECT INDEX

Date Due
